THE WOMAN THAT I AM

The Literature and Culture of Contemporary Women of Color

THE WOMAN THAT I AM

The Literature
and Culture of
Contemporary
Women of Color

D. Soyini Madison
The University of North Carolina
at Chapel Hill

St. Martin's Press • New York

Senior editor: Karen J. Allanson
Development editor: Melissa Cook Candela
Managing editor: Patricia Mansfield-Phelan
Project editor: Suzanne Holt / Erica Appel
Production supervisor: Alan Fischer
Art director: Sheree Goodman
Text design: Carla Weise / Levavi & Levavi
Cover art: E. H. Sorrells-Adewale

For information, write:
St. Martin's Press, Inc.
175 Fifth Avenue
New York, NY 10010

ISBN: 0-312-07956-7 (paperback)
        0-312-10012-4 (hardcover)

Library of Congress Cataloging-in-Publication Data

The Woman that I am : the literature and culture of contemporary women of color /
    edited by D. Soyini Madison.
        p.   cm.
    ISBN 0-312-10012-4 (hc)
    ISBN 0-312-07956-7 (pbk)
    1. American literature—Women authors.   2. Ethnic groups—United
States—Literary collections.   3. Women—United States—Literary
collections.   4. American literature—20th century.   5. Ethnic
groups—United States.   6. Women—United States.   I. Madison, D.
Soyini.
PS508.W7W576   1993
810.9'9287'08996—dc20   92-62775
                                                                                      CIP

Acknowledgments and copyrights can be found at the back of the book on pages 703–709, which constitute an extension of the copyright page.

To Mejai and Torkwase

In loving ourselves for who we are—American women of color—we can make a vision for the future where we are free to fulfill our human potential. This new framework will not support repression, hatred, exploitation and isolation, but will be a human and beautiful framework, created in a community, bonded not by color, sex or class, but by love and the common goal for the liberation of mind, heart, and spirit.

Merle Woo
from "Letter to Ma"

THE WOMAN THAT I AM IS A COLLECTION OF POETRY, SHORT STORIES, plays, cultural narratives, and critical perspectives by contemporary American women of color—women who are writing about their lives and their experiences right now. During my years of research, teaching, and community activism focused on women of color, I have collected writing that seems to open up the worlds of these women most successfully to my students and to express what Gloria Anzaldúa calls "a consciousness of the Borderlands." I offer this collection now to other instructors, to students, to general readers, and to all women, with an invitation to share the poignancy and the power of these pieces and to experience some of the pivotal moments that shape these women's lives.

A Wide Range of Selections

Four ethnicities are represented in this book: Native American, African American, Latina American, and Asian American. I have attempted to gather into one volume many favorite pieces, such as Alice Walker's "In Search of Our Mothers' Gardens" and Leslie Marmon Silko's "Storyteller," with a great deal of material that is rarely available in an anthology. Many of the selections included here are classics in the making. Angela Jackson's *Shango Diaspora: An African-American Myth of Womanhood and Love*, for example, has been performed across the United States, and now it will, I hope, find the attention it deserves in the classroom: the play appears in print in its entirety here for the first time.

The selections included in this collection are drawn from a variety of single-authored prose and fiction works, as well as anthologies, journals, pamphlets, magazines, and whatever else I found that seemed fruitful. Achieving a balance of voices and viewpoints was my objective in planning this text, but only the reader can judge my success in opening this anthology to multiple perspectives (for any editor claiming to relinquish completely his or her own affinities for the sake of diversity is surely unaware of the subjective power of the unconscious).

Apparatus That Provides Context

Because I recognize that many students will be encountering this material for the first time, I have included an introduction that provides background on women's roles in the literary history of each of the four cultures represented in the text. You will also find brief biographical notes on each author, conveniently gathered at the back of the book. A special introductory head-note to the Cultural Narratives and Critical Perspectives sections (page 433) suggests to students the wide array of forms through which contemporary women of color express their thoughts about their cultural positions and their art.

A Flexible Organization with Alternate Approaches

Three tables of contents will, I hope, offer both the teacher and the student flexibility in using this book. The primary table of contents is arranged by genre to help place those selections that may be familiar in a basic context. I also felt that generic organization would offer more freedom for readers to use their own creative instincts (and their own ideologies) to initiate dialogues among the various voices represented here.

Of course, organizing these writings by genre is not without its problems: one of the most essential features of almost all the selections included in this anthology is that they challenge traditional categories, crossing boundaries in search of new forms and new subjects. Criticism shades into autobiography and prose slips into the music of poetry in these selections, so my generic classifications are as open to classroom exploration and challenge as the content of the pieces. I hope the two alternate tables of contents—one by theme and one by ethnicity—open the floor to just such considerations.

I have taught my course in the literature and culture of women of color from the standpoint of genre, theme, and culture. Each method has its advantages and disadvantages, but I usually teach by theme. I see the pivotal experiences of women of color manifested in four themes that comprise the first alternate table of contents:

- Crossing Thresholds: Growing from Girlhood to Womanhood
- Shades of Intimacy: Love and Sexuality
- Confrontations: Race, Class, and Social Justice
- Being a Woman: Feminism, Family, and Women's Traditions

These themes seem to express best the turning points—the obligatory crossroads—in the lives of contemporary women of color, and the selections articulate and reflect them from a number of perspectives.

Whether you choose to approach the readings by genre, theme, or culture, it is my hope that the women in this book inspire you to read more of their work and to explore the writing of women of color not included in these pages. Although there are more than one hundred writers representing a range of ideological and expressive traditions in this anthology, many other voices are not included. One book cannot encompass the magnitude of these cultures.

Acknowledgments

I am happy to acknowledge and give a heartfelt "thank you" to several individuals who have contributed in various ways to this work:

To James Samuel Madison, my father, who was my idol and my anchor, and who taught me how to love words.

To Harry Amana for your kindness, intelligence, and sensitivity and for being a wonderful critic, friend, and motivator as I struggled to make deadlines.

To Dexter Fisher and Gloria Anzaldúa for your important works, for your brilliance, and for starting it all.

To Dwight Conquergood for your genius and inspiration, and for always being there with just the right words to get me back on track when work and life get too complicated.

To Beverly W. Long, V. William Balthrop, and Sue E. Estroff for taking time out from your busy schedules to give me valuable feedback.

To the faculty and staff in the Department of Communication Studies at the University of North Carolina at Chapel Hill for being such great colleagues.

To Robert P. Lowman, Chair, University Research Council at the University of North Carolina for helping to fund this project.

To Ruel Tyson and the Arts and Humanities Institute for your encouragement and support.

To Randall "Randy" T. Hill, Rosa Perelmuter, Leticia Zervas-Gaytan, and Fred Gardaphe for your helpful comments.

To Judith Hamara, Margo Crawford, and Linda Kerr Norflett for your friendship; you helped keep me sane during this process.

To Michelle Violanti, Deborah Austin, Valaya Tanarugsachock, Heidi Hamilton, Laura Montenez, Debbie Morrison, Michelle Nawar, and especially Sabrina Evans for all your time and hard work at the copy machine, on the phone, at the computer, and running back and forth between the library and my office with stacks of books, journals and information. Although it seemed like you were doing the drudge work, it was invaluable to me. You gave me the time and freedom to read, read, read, and ponder each selection included in this book. Without your assistance, this book would not have been possible.

To Paul Montenez and Laura Montenez for your invaluable help with translations.

To Laynie Brown, former associate editor at St. Martin's Press, for your suggestions and encouragement.

To Melissa Cook Candela, associate editor at St. Martin's Press, for your patience, efficiency, helpful suggestions, and sincere belief in this project.

To Cheryl Besenjak for your patience and persistence in securing permissions.

To Suzanne Holt, Erica Appel, and Denise Quirk at St. Martin's for guiding this project through production.

To those colleagues across the country who offered helpful comments that were essential in shaping this book: Nancy Clasby (University of Miami), Pamela Collins (State University of New York at Cobleskill), Dwight Conquergood (Northwestern University), Elizabeth Fox-Genovese (Emory University), Beverly Guy-Sheftall (Spelman College), Judith Hamera (California State University at Los Angeles), Ines Hernandez (University of California at Davis), Kathleen Hickok (Iowa State University), Deepika Karle (Bowling Green State University), Linda Kerr Norflett (North Carolina Central University), Patricia Palmerton (Hamline University), Jewell Rhodes (California State University at Northridge), Maya Sonenberg (Oregon State University), Mary S. Strine (University of Utah), and Pat Washington (State University of New York at Binghamton).

To my son, Mejai, and my daughter, Torkwase, for never letting me forget what is most important.

To Jonie Lee Madison, Ernestine Cole Wilson, and Sonja Hanes Stone, who will forever live in my heart and whose spirits guide me through each day.

CONTENTS

Short Stories 157

Drama 293

CONTENTS BY THEME

Crossing Thresholds: Growing from Girlhood to Womanhood

Shades of Intimacy: Love and Sexuality

Being a Woman: Feminism, Family, and Women's Traditions

CONTENTS BY ETHNICITY

Native American Writers

African American Writers

Latina American Writers

Asian American Writers

THE WOMAN THAT I AM

The Literature and Culture of Contemporary Women of Color

Introduction

I REMEMBER MY MOTHER STANDING, IN "COLORED WOMAN" STYLE, HER arms akimbo and her head tilted to the side, speaking quietly but forcefully in a tone that could scare a bull. She would willfully declare: "Being the woman that I am I will make a way out of no way." These were *mother's* words, but they are also the words and the will of *all* women of color who assert who they are, who create sound out of silence, and who build worlds out of remnants.

The Woman That I Am is a proclamation of the "I" in each individual woman's identity, but it is also a testament to the collective power of women of color. It is a tribute to "woman talk"—to the human need to be heard, listened to, and understood. "The woman that I am" represents both unity and diversity, and it echoes the West African saying, "I am because We are and We are because I am." The individual and the collective are mutually dependent on both their sameness and their difference.

My hope is that this anthology serves as a kind of celebration of what is different and what is the same about us American women of color. I also hope that it contributes to the work of scholars, activists, artists, and progressive thinkers who believe in the rich diversity of human expression. As women of color, we represent ourselves multifariously, our standpoints variously radical, moderate, and conservative. Our diversity reflects the complexity of living with and struggling against the forces of racism and sexism, classism and xenophobia, and homophobia. The differences among us women of color in the United States make problematic any attempt to place us comfortably under one rubric. Each ethnicity descends from a history that has its own unique traditions, worldviews, and ways of naming its past and present; as Shirley Geok-Lin Lim observes of Asian cultures in the introduction to *The Forbidden Stitch*, "We do not share a common history, a common original culture or language, not even a common physique or color" (Lim, Tsutakawa, and Donnelly 10).

The languages, the immigration histories, and the geopolitics of the original homelands of Asian American women are broadly divergent. The differences confronting Native American, Latina American, and African American women within our own cultures are also striking: differences in class, education, religion, economics, family structure, region, and sexual orientation may at first appear to divide us more than our shared racial identity unites us. Consequently, in certain instances, one may feel race is less a factor in determining identity than how one thinks and behaves in the world. Is race more a matter of social construction than genetics? How do we responsibly take into account differences both across racial lines and within races as we read and examine the literature and culture of women of color?

1

These questions and the discussion of difference emphasize that when we refer to women of color, we must understand them not as a homogenous group but as one governed by a dynamic of difference. But a focus on difference can only take us so far; women of color also share deeply rooted commonalities. As women of color the Native, Latina, African, and Asian in us has positioned us as "Other," as a "minority" sometimes ambiguously inside and sometimes threateningly outside dominant society. This reality constantly confronts us shaping our worldview and identity. We are "colored" women, and the "coloredness" of our skin is ingrained in our consciousness. As Anna Julia Cooper, a nineteenth-century African American writer, educator, and intellectual, said, "When and where I enter . . . my race enters with me."

All people of color have had to carve out, invent, and imagine new expressive forms—forms that evolve from our particular historical struggles and victories as we negotiate our place in the United States. These new creative forms are generated by the collective will of a people to name and arm themselves against hostile and insensitive forces. We are constantly operating within two symbol systems, within two cultures. The American part of being Native American, Latina American, African American and Asian American signifies that our "colored" history and ancestry is connected to an American history and ancestry. The "colored" part and the American part sometimes harmoniously coexist, but at times they battle in the interior domains of our psyches and in the public spaces of our cities and neighborhoods. We are betwixt and between the American dream—receiving, resisting, and revisioning who we are and what we think.

Therefore, if I were to identify the main theme of this book or sketch its central perspective, I would have to admit that for better or worse the selections included here work against establishing a unified subject or viewpoint. This does not mean these readings were chosen helter-skelter, rather they strive to represent the diverse subjects and forms through which the writers express what it means to be a woman and to be of color in contemporary American society.

These writers are part of a triumphant tradition, and each piece in this collection represents a victory in a long struggle to speak out and be heard. The histories of each of the cultures included in this book—Native American, African American, Latina American, and Asian American—are enormously rich and complex, and I cannot do justice to them here. However, I offer a sketch of the key aspects of the history of women's roles (particularly as expressed in their writing) in these cultures to give readers new to these pieces a sense of the context from which they grow.

The overview of each culture has a different emphasis and focus relative to that culture's particular experience in North America: the Native American section discusses belief systems passed down through narrative despite the disruption of relocation; the African American section discusses slavery and resistance movements and the effect of institutionalized racism on the culture and literature of African American women; the Latina section discusses the history of conquest and the patriarchal mythic traditions that permeate the work of Latina writers; the Asian American section discusses immigration experiences and how the experiences and the resulting sense of alienation affects Asian women. I chose these varying themes to reflect and emphasize the unique histories of each group; however, the themes share a common thread in highlighting the cultural and historical contributions of specific women. Therefore, all these sections cite the literary pioneers and early fighters for social justice whose works and visions influence contemporary writers.

Native Americans

Fire by Joy Harjo

> a woman can't survive
> by her own breath
>   alone
> she must know
> the voices of mountains
> she must recognize
> the foreverness of blue sky
> she must flow
> with the elusive
> bodies
> of night wind women
> who will take her into
> her own self
> look at me
> i am not a separate woman
> i am a continuance
> of blue sky
> i am the throat
> of the sandia mountains
> a night wind woman
> who burns
> with every breath
> she takes

Joy Harjo's poem reflects the fortitude and defiance of generations of Indian women—"night wind women" who know the inseparability of woman, land, and sky. As Native Americans and as women, they know that this continuum and all it encompasses is life; it is breath. The inseparability of the land and its people, violently made separate by time and "progress," is the call of the woman "who burns with every breath."

    Leslie Marmon Silko says that "storytelling for Indians is like a natural resource" (qtd. in Fisher 118). It was and is through the story that history is unveiled and passed on from the hearts and minds of one generation to the next: that moral codes, values, and ethics are understood; that the practical survival lessons of everyday life are taught; and that cultural pride, dignity, and identity are instilled. The Native American writer Linda Hogan suggests, "The stories we hold secret are stories of our growth as women, our transformations, the waking moments of realization that change the direction of our lives. They are sacred stories."(Bruchac, Hogan, and McDaniel ix). Examples of these stories may be found in such early recorded life histories of Indian women as *The Autobiography of Foxwoman* (Truman Michelson, 1918), *Waheenee: An Indian Girl's Story* (Gilbert Wilson, 1921); and *The Autobiography of a Papago Woman* (Ruth Underhill, 1936). Ella Deloria's collection, *Dakota Texts* (1932), is now considered a classic. Deloria, a Yanton Sioux, recounted womens' experiences from a Native American ethnographic perspective, an exception to the usual practice of the "outsider" recording the stories and culture of Native American people. All these collections of stories began to uncover the many facets of women's experiences, breaking the "squaw" stereotype and presenting the more complex realities in the lives of Native American women.

For Native American people, oral culture serves to preserve traditions that were threatened by encroachment by European settlers three centuries ago and subsequently by policies of the U.S. government and, as Leslie Marmon Silko says, to "keep us alive." It is the spoken word and reverence for tradition that are the seeds for the Native American literary and cultural movement of the 1960s and 1970s. A brief history of Native relocation due to white settlement and several nineteenth- and early twentieth-century Native American women who prefigured this modern movement deserve mention.

During the early days of European settlement, Natives and settlers generally maintained amicable relations. This period was short lived, however, as whites claimed the right to greater portions of land, and as a result, fierce fighting between Natives and whites ensued. But the violence and destruction over land took a turn when American independence was won in the last part of the eighteenth century. The new government formed treaties with certain tribes to establish order and coexistence. These treaties were understood as legally binding, but as time passed and more settlers arrived, the treaties were broken, and the promises and agreements on which they were built disintegrated into a shameful history of destruction.

To free more land for settlers, Congress passed the Indian Removal Act in 1830, which ordered almost all eastern tribes to be moved west of the Mississippi River. The West was then proclaimed as "Indian Territory" since it was believed that the land was of little value and was inhabited by only a few settlers.

In 1849, when gold was discovered in California, an influx of settlers and adventurers traveled westward. Because of this mass migration, most of the lands promised the Indians were confiscated. Gold brought the need for further development and the building of railroads. Federal legislation, including the 1887 General Allotment Act, which divided tribal lands and distributed them to individuals, led to the demise and further removal of more Indians for the benefit of white settlers. The permanent homeland for Indians, Indian Territory, proved to be another broken promise. The Indians fought to keep what was promised them, but they were finally defeated.

Paula Gunn Allen describes the effects of white settlement and mercantile interests on Native peoples and the land:

> With loss of population on the Native side and enormous increase on the Western side, our land holdings, rights to self-governance, water, hunting, fishing, and religious rights were abrogated, and our most precious mainstay, the community of being with all our relatives, was severely curtailed. Not only were Native peoples held prisoner in forts, camps, and on reservations, not only were they forbidden to practice their religions or prevented from doing so by having their mobility restricted (most groups practice many religious ceremonies in places outside of the village or camp, sometimes great distances away), but the life forms and the land itself were altered beyond recognition, and in the course of white settlement from 1850 to 1950 all but destroyed (16).

Yet, the history of the American Indian is also a history of resistance, survival, and courageous women like Sarah Winnemucca Hopkins, Wa Wa Calachaw Bonita Nunez, E. Pauline Johnson, Ella Deloria, and Zitkala-Sӑ, among others.

In 1883, Sarah Winnemucca Hopkins, a Piute, wrote *Life Among the Piutes*, an account of the Indian wars and the broken treaties that nearly devastated her people. Hopkins's determination to make public the struggle of her tribe resulted in legislation favorable to the Piute cause. Another advocate for her people was Humishuma (Cristal Galler), an Okanogan, who in 1916 published *Myths and Legends of The Sioux*, one of the first publications to illuminate with respect and authenticity the indigenous culture and oral traditions of Native Americans. In 1927 Humishuma—who was also called Mourning Dove—wrote what some have considered the first American Indian novel by a woman, *Cogewea, The Half Blood*. The novel depicts the trials of a "half-breed" Indian woman and stresses the importance of preserving traditions. Humishuma was one of the first writers to celebrate and affirm the richness of Native culture by weaving rich descriptions of its customs and traditions into her story.

In 1901, Zitkala-Sӑ, a Dakota Sioux, compiled a collection of stories and trickster tales from her childhood, entitled *Old Indian Legends*. In 1921, she published *American Indian Stories*, which was based on her experiences at an Anglo boarding school. The book describes the pain and alienation she felt as an Indian surrounded by Anglo-American language and customs.

These women writers were among the first to provide a look at Native cultures in all their varied struggles and achievements. Although most were subjected to the criticism and patronizing attitudes of white sponsors and publishers, these women were steadfast in protecting the integrity of their stories. Whereas these Native accounts may seem to some modern readers contrived or of little literary merit, their historical value is immeasurable, particularly, as literary scholar Dexter Fisher argues, for their "insights into the conflicts surrounding the transition to reservation life" (8).

On both the literary and political fronts, these early Indian women were making their marks. In 1911, the Society of American Indians (SAI) was established to redress injustices and make the U.S. federal government accountable for a history of broken promises to Native Americans. Post-reservation Indians organized to defend their legal rights and the right of self-determination for Indians across North America. Zitkala-Sä, committed to the struggle for justice for Native peoples, was named the secretary treasurer of the SAI. She traveled the country calling for fairness in the settlements of tribal land claims, for reforms regarding the way in which the Bureau of Indian Affairs (BIA) was managed, and for employment of Indians within the BIA. In 1926, she founded the National Council of American Indians and she was a central figure in organizing the General Federation of Women's Clubs to join in the council's investigations of government abuses. It was through the efforts of pan-Indian organizations and progressive thinkers that the Indian Reorganization Act of 1934 officially ended the 1887 General Allotment Act policy and reinstituted tribal ownership of reservations.

And even after this victory, Zitkala-Sä continued to speak out against injustices to Indians; she served as president of the Council until her death in 1938.

Native people continued their fight to regain lands and rights, to proclaim the truths of their history, and to move toward greater economic, cultural, and political power. Across the United States, Native Americans have organized on many fronts—through the activism of the Red Power Movement, the American Indian Movement (AIM), and various pan-Indian organizations, as well as through community empowerment inspired by pow wows among Indian populations throughout urban and rural America. Linda Hogan states: "We have survived and in that survival is our life, strength, our spirituality. And we are telling about it . . . " (Bruchac, Hogan, and McDaniel xiv).

African Americans

Ancestors: In Praise of the Imperishable
by Sandra Jackson-Opoku

> Much more than just one woman,
>   there are endless spirits
>   roaming inside me
>   River Mothers
>   moving, and
>   memory much
>   older
>   I
>   And
>   who but we

fall heir to such
memory, such dream?

River Mothers moving,
History wrapped around my tongue

There are spirits, stirring inside me

Sandra Jackson-Opoku's poem calls forth the "imperishable" power of the ancestors who live on eternally through the generations. To know and speak history is to preserve the motion of the ancestors, a rhythm essential to the life force. African American people begin their story by paying homage to the "stirring inside." These spirits must be named, or else it will be impossible to begin the story. The naming begins in Africa in such well-developed and prosperous West African kingdoms as Ghana, Mali, Songhay, and Guinea. However, history intervened and, as a result, the reverence for and significance of naming spirits that was so much a part of West African tradition was to change, manifesting itself in different forms and practices with the onslaught of European colonization and the slave trade. Nonetheless, black people traded as slaves to America carried memories of their ancestors and the power of naming spirits with them across the ocean and across time. Despite the cruel abuses and dehumanizing restrictions slavery placed on black people, the power of naming endured and slaves constructed forms of expression—spirituals, work songs, sermons, oral poetry, slave narratives, tales, and riddles, among others—to keep alive their knowledge, creativity, and resourcefulness, and to reflect powerfully the material conditions of and philosophical viewpoints developed within slave culture. As in many cultures, oral traditions within the world of the slave served as catalysts for written expression.

Two slave women, Linda Brent and Elizabeth Keckley, were among the first to write autobiographies capturing the interior life and struggle of women and slaves in nineteenth-century America. Linda Brent's narrative, *Incidents in the Life of a Slave Girl* (1860), reflected her relentless will to give voice to her experiences under continuing threat and restraint. Elizabeth Keckley's *Behind The Scenes, or Thirty Years a Slave and Four Years in the White House* (1868) describes her experiences as Mary Todd Lincoln's dressmaker and provides a fascinating perspective on the Lincoln years.

However, even before Brent and Keckley, black women had begun building a literary tradition. It was the slave girl Lucy Terry who in 1746 wrote "Bars Flight," which is considered the first published poem written by an African American. Phillis Wheatley, a slave born in Africa and purchased by the Wheatley family of Boston, was, in 1773, the first to publish a book of poetry and to win minor acclaim as a poet. The work of many free black women appeared in antislavery journals and contributed to the emerging African American literary tradition. Charlotte Forten was the first to keep and publish journalistic accounts of racism and slavery by recording, from 1854 to 1864, specific injustices she experienced as a student in Massachusetts and, later, as a teacher in South Carolina.

Francis Ellen Watkins Harper was a free black and an activist for women's rights and racial equality. Harper traveled throughout the country lecturing for women's rights and the abolition of slavery, and she also wrote four volumes of poetry, including *Sketches of Southern Life* (1872), and the first novel written by an African American woman, *Iola Leroy: or Shadows Uplifted* (1892).

These early nineteenth-century writers, endowed with the eloquence and commitment to voice their people's struggle, were supported by two other extraordinary women, Mary Church Terrell and Ida B. Wells. These two women were leaders within the Black Women's Club Movement, and they were at the forefront of the antilynching campaign; they also campaigned for racial equality and women's rights. Both women were born into families of ex-slaves. Ida B. Wells, who lost her parents as a teenager, became a teacher to support her five brothers and sisters and to "help the race." Later, while still a young woman, she started a newspaper that was to become one of this country's strongest weapons against lynching and other racist activities. Wells traveled across the United States and in Europe to deliver her antilynching message; in her autobiography (1895) she wrote:

> Not all or nearly all of the murders done by white men, during the past thirty years in the South, have come to light, but the statistics as gathered and preserved by white men, and which have not been questioned, show that during these years more than ten thousand Negroes have been killed in cold blood without the formality of judicial trial and legal execution (qtd. in Lerner 199).

Mary Church Terrell graduated from Oberlin College and later studied abroad. She used her education throughout her adult life to teach and help lead African Americans toward liberation. Terrell has been called "the driving force that molded the Black Women's Club Movement into a powerful political group" (Davis 135). In 1904 she wrote:

> Before 1904 was three months old, thirty-one negroes had been lynched. Of this number, fifteen were murdered within one week in Arkansas, and one was shot to death in Springfield, Ohio, by a mob composed of men who did not take the trouble to wear masks. Hanging, shooting, and burning black men, women and children in the United States have become so common that such occurrences create but little sensation and evoke but slight comment now (qtd. in Lerner 207).

Terrell and Wells profoundly changed the course of history, particularly in the manner in which they compelled most Americans—many for the first time—to listen to the social and political demands of African American women. The public and the courts were influenced by their speeches, activism, and writing. As forerunners of contemporary writers, these women were among the very first to lay the foundation and fight the battles in order for the voices of black women to be heard.

At age sixty-three Wells traveled to Arkansas to investigate and plan a strategy against those involved in a brutal mob attack on African American sharecroppers. Just before her death, she led a black women's demonstration against racist policies at a Chicago establishment. Terrell, also active until her death, marched in a Washington D.C. picket line at the age of ninety. African Americans whose contributions helped shape the identity of their race during the periods of slavery, Reconstruction, and post-Reconstruction, also flourished during the period known as the Harlem Renaissance. During the 1920s, in New York City's Harlem, black artists, writers, and scholars represented in their writing what it meant to be a person of African descent in America and in the world. Although African American women during this period did not receive as much support and recognition as African American men, the intellectual and creative impact of women like Georgia Douglass Johnson, Nella Larsen, Jessie Fauset, Alice Dunbar Nelson, Ann Spencer, Amy-Jacques Garvey, and Gwendolyn Bennett are indisputable.

The legacy of the writers of the Harlem Renaissance and their literary forebears was inherited and given a new and unique power by modern writer Zora Neale Hurston. Novelist, journalist, folklorist, and critic, Hurston is one of the most prolific African American writers; she wrote in many genres ranging from novels to autobiography. Alice Walker's remembrance of Hurston captures the magnitude of her contribution: "The intellectual and spiritual foremother of generations of black women writers, Hurston believed in the beauty of black expressions and traditions and in the psychological wholeness of black life" (1).

It is the work of Zora Neale Hurston and the early pioneers of African American activism and literature whose thoughts, deeds, and words were the first to break through the walls of silence and lies. Although this brief sketch only points to a few of the historical contributions of African American women, American history is ripe with so many others: Civil Rights workers, such as Fannie Lou Hammer, Charlotta Bass, and Ella Baker; freedom fighters from the Black Power era, such as Angela Davis, Shirley Chisholm, and Kathleen Cleaver; from their various perspectives, these women helped transform history. There are also the "ordinary" black women whose names will never make it into the history books, but whose extraordinary works and spirits changed many, many lives. These are the women who form the bridge by which contemporary black women writers may cross with gratitude, with pride, and with purpose. As Mary McLeod Bethune once said, "[The African American woman] has been quick to seize every opportunity which presented itself to come more and more into the open and strive directly for the uplift of the race and nation. In that direction, her achievements have been amazing . . . " (Bethone 580).

Latina Americans

Hermano by Angela de Hoyos

> I was born too late
> in a land
> that no longer belongs to me
> (so it says, right here in this Texas History)

(The land belongs) to a pilgrim
arrived here only yesterday
whose racist tongue says to me: I hate
Meskins. You're a Meskin. Why don't you
go back to where you came from?
Yes, amigo . . . ! Why don't I? Why don't I
resurrect the Pinta, the Niña and the Santa Maria

and you can scare up your little 'Flor de Mayo'
so we can all sail back
to where we came from: the motherland womb.

I was born too late
or perhaps I was born too soon:
It is not yet my time;
this is not yet my home.

I must wait for the conquering barbarian
to learn the Spanish word for love:
HERMANO

In "Hermano," the history of the dispossession of the Latino people is force-fully expressed. All people feel passion for the land where their history begins and where their ancestors built the foundations of their culture, and that passion leaps into a fire of resentment and resistance when their land—and their very identities—is claimed by de Hoyos's "conquering barbarian." The telling of history will always be subjective, and de Hoyos depicts the classic confrontation between the conquered and the conqueror. The myths and stereotypes that grow out of "subjective" history are themes prevalent in much Latina literature.

The indigenous cultures of Latinos are native to the southwestern United States and Mexico, and extend to the southern end of South America. The histories of these cultures are punctuated by aggression and colonization by such countries as Spain, Portugal, and France. During the long period of conquest, Europeans brought with them laws and customs from ancient Rome, or "Latina," and it is for this reason that the lands from Mexico to South America are referred to as Latin America. Over time, the customs of the indigenous people (Olmec, Aztec, Maya, Toltec, Inca) began in turn to transform these new laws, and the result was the emergence of the *mestizo*, or "mixed blood," culture. I use the term *Latina* to refer to women of Latin American descent because it symbolizes the ethnic diversity of these populations and the cultural resistance and inventiveness of the Indian people. *Hispanic* alludes to Spain as the conqueror and, as recent critics have argued, "distorts the origin and roots of these populations, preventing and excusing the dominant culture from understanding, respecting, and taking into account all the complexities of culture other than its own" (Ortega and Sternbach 7).

Hernando Cortés is said to be the major force in the conquest of Mexico.

Cortés sailed from Cuba in 1519 with eleven ships and about 650 Spanish soldiers. Defeating large numbers of Indians along the coast, he and his men settled in Veracruz, the first Spanish settlement that is now Mexico. The history of Cortés and the conquest are often equated with the history of the Indian woman who was his aide and lover; she is known by the names Malinche, Malintzin, and Marina.

Norma Alarcón, a Chicana feminist and critic, provides an engaging interpretation of Malinche's historical context. Alarcón describes Malinche as a native woman who was sold into slavery by her parents to enhance her brother's inheritance. She was eventually given to Cortés when he arrived in Mexico to be of "service" to him in whatever his demands might be. Malinche became Cortés's interpreter, guide, strategist, nurse, and lover. She was with him as his advisor, cohort, and companion throughout his conquest. She bore him a son, but Cortés later married a Spanish noblewoman. After his marriage, he gave Malinche some land and arranged for her to marry one of his lieutenants (182-85).

The patriarchal view of Malinche has been one where her name was and still is synonymous with betrayal and treachery—a vile traitor responsible for the downfall of her people and the invasion by Spain. Alarcón, like many other postcolonial critics, is calling for a revisionist analysis that topples traditional patriarchal interpretations that have taken "facts" of history and constructed them in ways that are harmful to women (182). Alarcón contends that, as Malinche has been the literal and symbolic figure blamed for the exploitation of the Indians, as the curse leading the race to victimization, this patriarchal view is oblivious to her condition as a slave: "life in bondage was of no account, and continues to be of no account" (182). The people of Mexico continue to be under the dominion of European colonial rule well into the nineteenth century. Even after Mexico attained its independence, the government tended to be repressive.

Under the dictatorship of Porfiro Diaz from about 1876 to 1911, Mexican women—especially the poor and illiterate—were severely oppressed. Most women worked in factories or slaved as farmworkers, domestic servants, seamstresses, and prostitutes: Shirlene Soto, a recent critic describes the lives of Latinas during the period this way:

> When women worked in the tobacco fields, miscarriages were frequent due to the noxious effects tobacco has on pregnancies. Infant mortality was high because of the poor health of the mother and sometimes because of the pulmonary diseases children contracted when they began strenuous work at a young age. Yanqui Indian women were often forcibly transported to the tobacco plantations and assigned as sexual partners to the male workers, many of whom were Asian. Male workers who were married were forced to share attractive wives with planters or bosses. Other women were requisitely placed in mixed dormitories at the end of the work day and had to fend for themselves (qtd. in Hernandez 16).

One woman, Sara Estela Ramirez, set out to expose these conditions. A Texas-Mexican feminist, journalist, labor leader, teacher, and revolutionary, she was instrumental in the Mexican resistance movement against Diaz's dictatorship. She was an active member of the Mexican Liberal party, and she started her own newspaper and collaborated with other women journalists and activists in the name of freedom for women and for the Mexican people. As Ramirez and her sisters in the struggle—Elisa Acuna y Rosetti, Delores Jimenez y Muro, and Aurora Colin—worked to unseat oppression, they endured retaliation: their presses were confiscated and destroyed and they suffered harassment and imprisonment (Hernandez 17). Nonetheless, they remained steadfast in their efforts to bring about radical change because they believed the liberation of women and the liberation of Mexico were inseparable. Sara Estela Ramirez was only twenty-nine when she died, but throughout her short life she worked tirelessly under the conviction that women must be primary agents in achieving change.

The life of a real Latina, as the struggle of Sara Estela Ramirez dramatizes, sharply contrasts the ideal Latina image represented by two central mythological figures in Latin culture—the Virgin of Guadalupe and La Llorona.

The Virgin of Guadalupe is the descendent of Tonantzin, Indian Earth Mother and the Aztec goddess of fertility, feminine energy, and the generative powers of the universe. Tonantzin was believed to be the indigenous brown goddess and true essence of woman as mother, protector, nurturer. But the symbolic meaning of Tonantzin was embellished, reflecting the history of the mixed heritage from an Indian mother and a Spanish father. When the Spanish introduced the cult of the Virgin into Mexico, Tonantzin was then identified with Guadalupe. The Virgin of Guadalupe is revered as mother of the *mestizo* race and, unlike Malinche "the betrayer," she is loyal to her people, the essence of virtue, self-sacrifice, and humility.

Like the Virgin of Guadalupe, the origins of La Llorona (the "weeping woman") are both Spanish and Indian. La Llorona is said to have been a native woman who, upon discovering her husband's infidelity, murdered their children and was condemned to an eternity of sorrow and weeping. According to legend, she continues to wander through the night crying out for her children.

These historical and mythological representations of Latinas reflect the impact of European culture and religion in embellishing and concretizing certain patriarchal beliefs that were already in place within the indigenous culture.

The Latina identity is complex and ambiguous, embodying within it roles from the mythological Virgin of Guadalupe and La Llorona to the history of the slave Malinche. These representations symbolize the extremes of purity, guilt, and betrayal that both Latin and European traditions have ascribed to womanhood; they help us understand the concept of "machismo"—the male authority and phallocentric constructions of identity and behavior imposed on Latinas. But today Latinas are building on their heritage and casting new light on the notions of machismo and what it means to be *mestiza*. They are retelling the stories of Malinche, the Virgin of Guadalupe, and La Llorona, illuminating the complexity and contradictions within them and creating a space in which contemporary Latinas can live and write with dignity. Chicana writer and cultural critic Gloria Anzaldúa writes: "I am an act of kneading, of uniting and joining that not only has produced both a creature of darkness and a creature of light, but also a creature that questions the definitions of light and dark and gives them new meanings" (380).

Asian Americans

Second Nature by Diana Chang

How do I feel?
Fine wrist to small feet?
I cough Chinese.

To me, it occurs that Cézanne
Is not a Sung painter

(My condition is no less gratuitous than this remark)

The old China muses through me.
I am foreign to the new.
I sleep upon dead years.

Sometimes I dream in Chinese
I dream my father's dreams

I wake, grown up
And someone else.

I am the thin edge I sit on.
I begin to gray—white and black and in between.
My hair is America.

New England moonlight in me.

I attend what is Chinese
In everyone.

We are in the air.

I shuttle passportless within myself,
My eyes slant around both hemispheres,
Gaze through walls

And long still to be
Accustomed,
At home here,

Strange to say.

Diana Chang's poem evokes the sense of foreignness and alienation most Asian American women—and most women of color—experience in haunting the "thin edge" between two cultures as they make a place for themselves in the United States. But generalizing about Asian American women is problematic because Asian cultures constitute such a great diversity of ethnicities. Shirley Geok-Lin Lim writes: "If the women's movement has discovered difference to be a liberating rather than an oppressive principle, through which new visions, new understanding and new orders of society can be generated, the experiences of being an Asian American woman is an exemplar of living in difference" (Lim, Tsutakawa, and Donnelly 10).

Pakistani, Filipino, Hawaiian, Japanese, Indian, Korean, Hmong, Chinese, and Vietnamese populations are all Asian cultures, each with its own unique history. Nonetheless, I have chosen to risk oversimplifying the heterogeneity of these cultures in this overview in order to provide the new reader of these texts with at least a minimal background that may serve as a starting point for understanding and appreciating the victories and struggles from which these voices emerged.

In the 1970s politics and war caused many refugees from Vietnam, Laos, and Cambodia to emigrate to this country. When she arrived in the United States, Ba Tam, a Vietnamese woman, said, "I was happy! It is just like heaven! Because people live here in freedom" (qtd. in Freeman 425). But soon she began to feel the experience of loss for her native culture, and in her story (recorded less than a month after her arrival), she expresses her alienation and disillusionment:

> In Vietnam, in a village, from one end to another, everybody knows each other. Even in the city where I lived, we knew each other and visited one another. If I was sick, my friends visited me, and I did the same for them. I would see my friends at the market. When I think of that, I miss not having people I know nearby. It's very sad. Over here I live at home, and I cannot go anywhere. In Vietnam, if I felt sad, I'd go to visit my friends, my fellow "sisters" . . . I am very sad and I have nowhere to go (qtd. in Freeman 426).

Ba Tam's narrative is reminiscent of the loneliness, fear, and sense of displacement that thousands of Asian immigrants experienced more than a century before.

The first Asians arrived in the United States in the 1840s with hardly a woman among them. Thousands of immigrant men—Chinese, Filipino, Japanese, Indian, and Korean—traveled the Pacific to work in the mines, plantations, railroads, and fields of Hawaii and the West Coast. Asian women were scarce because of emigration restrictions in their homelands and because the call for labor directed its appeals to men.

As Asian men began flooding the labor market, particularly in California, racial discrimination began to rise and state and federal laws were passed to limit immigration—first from China and then, by 1924, from all of Asia. These exclusionary quota laws were not lifted until 1965.

During World War II, institutionalized discrimination against Japanese immigrants and Japanese Americans reached a new height. The Japanese overseas were the enemy, and the distinction from Japanese Americans proved difficult to make. The demand that Japanese Americans be placed in internment camps inland from the West Coast was implemented in 1942 when fears of a Japanese threat to security were heard in various sectors of society. The general argument was that the Japanese were an unknown people, and although they might be loyal and true Americans, there were those who could be a threat.

Families were taken from their homes and told they could only keep what they could carry. Special trains took them to assembly centers, where they discovered they would be living in unsanitary conditions, in stockyards, race tracks, and fairgrounds.

Jeanne Wakatsuki Houston tells of her internment in Manzanar Camp, in Owens Valley, California, the first permanent camp to open:

> As the months at Manzanar turned to years, it became a world unto itself, with its own logic and familiar ways. In time, staying there seemed far simpler than moving once again to another, unknown place. It was if the war were forgotten, our reason for being there forgotten. The present, the little bit of busywork you had right in front of you, became the most urgent thing. In such a narrowed world, in order to survive, you learn to contain your rage and your despair, and you try to re-create, as well you can, your normality, some sense of things continuing. The fact that America had accused us, or excluded us, or imprisoned us, or whatever it might be called, did not change the kind of world we wanted. Most of us were born in this country; we had no other models (85).

For many Asian women, traditional philosophy greatly influenced their fate at home and in North America. In the case of Chinese women, nineteenth-century Confucian ideology governed Chinese culture, and one of the principles of Confucianism emphasizes feudal loyalty and filial piety. Women were expected by duty and custom to remain at home while men ventured out to seek adventure and riches. Some of the first women to arrive in the United States did not emigrate of their own accord.

The relative absence of women, the prevalent economic hardships, and the frequent brutality that was sanctioned in the nineteenth century against women of color is emblematized in the infamous history of Chinese prostitution. Historian Judy Yung writes:

> The demand for Chinese prostitutes in California was primarily due to the shortage of Chinese women and the prohibitions against relations between white women and Chinese men, both of which made it nearly impossible for Chinese men to marry and raise families. Captives of an organized trade, most of these women were kidnapped, lured or purchased by procurers in China, brought to America by importers, and sold to brothel owners who paid Chinese highbinder [professional killers], policemen, and immigration officials to protect the business. Most prostitutes did not have the individual or collective means to resist their fate. Refusing to work only brought on beatings and other physical tortures. At best, a prostitute

might hope to be redeemed by a wealthy client. For some, suicide, madness, or violent death proved to be the only way out of misery (18).

Yung tells of one Chinese woman who tried to run away and then nearly froze to death in the Nevada Hills; when she was finally found, her feet were frozen and had to be amputated. She later went on a hunger strike to protest her prostitution.

Some women did manage to escape enslavement. Polly Bemis, born in poverty in northern China, was sold to bandits for two bags of seed and shipped to America as a slave. A Chinese saloon keeper in an Idaho mining camp bought her in an auction, and he later sold her in a poker game to Charles Bemis, who became her husband. Subsequently, she devoted her life to nursing and serving others, and she is remembered by those who tell her story and by the naming of Polly Bemis Creek on the land that became her permanent home.

Prostitution was in decline by 1880, but challenges remained for Chinese and other Asian women caught up in the interlocking oppressions of race, economic class, and gender. Many held low-paying jobs, either bringing work into their homes or working outside it. They tended livestock, did laundry and cooking, and took in boarders; in fishing villages, they often helped haul in the catch and dry it (Yung 24).

During the early twentieth century, many Japanese women came to America as "picture brides" whose marriages were arranged by their parents with a man they had never met. The wedding ceremonies were performed in Japan with only the bride and her family present; the woman would then journey to America—usually to the Pacific coast or Hawaii—to meet her husband for the first time. "Picture brides" were acceptable in Japanese culture because marriage was less a joining of individuals than a banding together of families. But when the Issei (as these first-generation women were called) arrived in the United States, they had to adjust to a new way of life.

From the time of their arrival in America to the present, Asian women have worked their way into every stratum of American life, as laborers, intellectuals, scientists, artists, and activists. Their literary heritage is impressive and varied. One of the first writers to depict Chinese American life through her short stories and autobiographical reflections was Sui Sin Far; she published a collection of short stories, *Mrs. Spring Fragrance* (1921), under the name of Edith Eaton. In 1950, Jade Snow Wong published *Fifth Chinese Daughter*, an autobiographical novel describing a young girl's experience of her dual Chinese and American heritage. In *Nisei Daughter* (1953), Monica Sone depicts the effects of the World War II internment camps on Japanese Americans (Nisei refers to second-generation Japanese Americans), and in *Frontiers of Love* (1956), Diana Chang delves into what Dexter Fisher calls the "internal psychological conflicts of being Eurasian" that Sui Sin Far had addressed more than thirty years earlier (Fisher 436).

Over time, Asian women in the United States began to dismantle the myth of the docile, submissive Oriental and to challenge the stereotype that Asian Americans are the "model minority." They are creating new identities for themselves that are more empowering. "Muliebrity" is a contemporary comment on such women; it is a glimpse of an "ordinary" woman who remakes profoundly on her own terms what appears to be the smallest piece of the world.

Muliebrity by Sujata Bhatt

> I have thought so much about the girl
> who gathered cow dung in a wide, round basket
> along the main road passing by our house
> and the Radhavallabh temple in Maninagar.
> I have thought so much about the way she
> moved her hands and her waist
> and the smell of cow dung and road-dust and wet canna lilies,
> the smell of monkey breath and freshly washed clothes
> and the dust from crows' wings which smells different—
> and again the smell of cow dung as the girl scoops
> it up, all these smells surrounding me separately
> and simultaneously—I have thought so much
> but have been unwilling to use her for a metaphor,
> for a nice image—but most of all unwilling
> to forget her or to explain to anyone the greatness
> and the power glistening through her cheekbones
> each time she found a particularly promising
> mound of dung—

This poem by Sujata Bhatt, who was born in India and immigrated to the United States in 1968, is a tribute to the grace and fortitude of women who defy and transform history. It speaks to the human spirit that creates something beautiful from even the tightest and most restricted of spaces, and it speaks to the outsider as an alchemist and a welder who can transform margins into potential sites of resistance where new empowering experiences begin. "Muliebrity" is a kind of praise song sung especially for the woman of color who has worked, lived, and known the worst up close. It is for the woman who has survived despite the worst, all the while transforming "dung" into "power glistening through her cheekbones" as she goes.

Works Cited

Alarcón, Norma. "Chicana's Feminist Literature: A Revision through Mallintzin or Malintzin: Putting Flesh Back on the Object." *This Bridge Called My Back: Writings by Radical Women of Color.* Cherríe Moraga and Gloria Anzaldúa. Latham: Kitchen Table, 1973.

Allen, Paula Gunn. *Spider Woman's Granddaughters: Traditional Tales and Contemporary Writing by Native American Women.* New York: Fawcett Columbine, 1989.

Anzaldúa, Gloria, ed. *Making Face, Making Soul: Creative and Critical Perspectives by Women of Color.* New York: Women of Color Press, 1990.

Bethune, Mary McLeod. "A Century of Progress of Negro Women." In *Black Women in White America: A Documentary History,* ed. Gerda Lerner. New York: Vintage, 1973.

Bruchac, Carol, Linda Hogan, and Judith McDaniel, eds. *The Stories We Hold Secret: Tales of Women's Spiritual Development.* Greenfield Center, NY: Greenfield Review, 1986.

Davis, Angela Y. *Women, Race, and Class.* New York: Vintage, 1983.

Fisher, Dexter, ed. *The Third Woman: Minority Women Writers of the United States.* New York: Houghton, 1980.

Freeman, James M. *Hearts of Sorrow: Vietnamese American Lives.* Stanford UP, 1989.

Hernandez, Inés. "Sara Estela Ramirez: Sembradora." *Women Writers.* 6.1, pp. 13–26 (Spring 1989).

Houston, Jeanne Wakatsuki, and James D. Houston. *Farewell to Manzanar.* Boston: Houghton, 1973.

Lerner, Gerda, ed. *Black Women in White America: A Documentary History.* New York: Vintage, 1973.

Lim, Shirley Geok-Lin, Mayumi Tsutakawa, and Margarita Donnelly, eds. *The Forbidden Stitch: An Asian-American Women's Anthology.* Corvallis, OR: Calyx Books, 1989.

Ortega, Eliana, and Sternbach, Nancy Saporta. "At the Threshold of the Unnamed." *Breaking Boundaries: Latina Writing and Critical Readings.* Amherst: U of Massachusetts P, 1989.

Walker, Alice, ed. *I Love Myself When I Am Laughing: A Zora Neale Hurston Reader.* New York: Feminist, 1979.

Yung, Judy. *Chinese Women of America: A Pictorial History.* Seattle: U of Washington P, 1986.

Poetry is the way we help give name to the nameless so it can be thought. The farthest horizons of our hopes and fears are cobbled by our poems, carved from the rock experiences of our daily lives.

AUDRE LORDE

"Poetry Is Not a Luxury,"
Sister/Outsider: Essays and Speeches

POETRY

The Beirut-Hell Express*

Etel Adnan

. . . but there are different treatises
always taken again as a heritage
in which, like tired continents, great
figures closed into their insanity have sunk . . .

—Malek Alloula, "*Villes,*" *Algiers '68*

The human race is going to the cemetery
in great upheavals

two horses reciting MAO

my uneasiness
to be heroic

> bread and roses
> flowers and flames

Gamal Abdel Nasser's[1] death is
lived in the universe of
JAZZ Mingus's[2] bass
shocks with no return
what to do with wonder if not
some pain in the head one California
night   the road   and black
trees against which are rubbing
their faces   two men   in waiting? . . .

---

* Although this poem was written five years before the Lebanese Civil War (1975), it serves as a prophesy of the war, a war that continues on to this day.

[1] Gamal Abdel Nasser (1918–1970) led the revolt that overthrew King Furuk in 1915 and established Egypt as a republic. When Syria and Egypt formed the United Arab Republic in 1958, Nasser became president. He fought in the Arab War against Israel in 1948–1949. Nasser's book, *Egypt's Liberation: The Philosophy of Revolution* (1955) was a call to unite all Arabs under Egyptian leadership.

[2] Charles "Charlie" Mingus (b.1922) is a popular Jazz musician who plays bass and piano and is a composer. Born in Nogales, Arizona, Mingus published a biography, *Beneath The Underground*, in 1971. His better known works include: "Revelation," "Black Saint and Sinister Lady," and "Thrice Upon a Theme."

taxi drivers urinate standing
on the Damascus-Beirut-Damascus
        road
        inglorious itinerary
        I inhabit the tiniest country
        in an expanding universe

        I love the women who are veiled
        like my aunt used to be
        and those who go naked
        at the American crossroads where
        drugs are growing: they are
        crabs lying on the back of
        starfish in the sea

        I love the men who cover their
        head and show but one eye
        not the blind one but the one
        which looks inside.
        From two thousand years of History I
        keep but JAZZ
        because it is Black. I banished
        colors and dried up the sea
        here you only eat sand . . .
                        we all are torturers
                        one shadowless morning
                        one morning!
        Don't you know that I live
        in San Rafael with San Quentin[1] for neighbor
        a nightmare on which the sun
        sets in tears
                        the Bay at its feet and
                        the moon . . . it's always she
                        rising above the hair
                        of a woman four times suicidal
                        and an island a single one
                        Angel Island[2] uninhabited

[1] San Quentin State Prison on a small peninsula in San Francisco Bay.
[2] Angel Island is the largest island in San Francisco Bay. From 1863 to 1946 it was a U.S. base
    and was for a long time the site of a quarantine and immigration station. During World
    War II it served as an internment camp.

and in the Prison
George Jackson[3] and Sirhan Sirhan[4]
                    a cold nail
                    enters the skin
20,000 dead in Amman
20,000 shining nails around the head
of the King
20,000 ghosts   heavy weights   stinking
            the air   crime   the autumn of the criminal.

The flag of prophecy floats on
                    the ships
Fire!   let the hurricane enter
the holes   and like a boiling river
carry away the angels stricken with fear
on the summits of the Sannine![5]
move on   people full of slime
let your lemonades go to the sea
let your casino crumble
let your race horses carry their owners
to those undergrounds where Babylon
used to cook its poisons

liberation like a spring still
under the ground   is growing what
seems to be hands open at the level
of the soil   there is no grass on this earth.

My father was Ouranos[6]
and my mother Queen Zenobia[7]

---

[3] George Jackson was killed in August 1971 in what some believed was an unsuccessful escape attempt from San Quentin prison. A controversial figure, regarded both as a murderer and a freedom fighter, Jackson spoke out against social injustice and developed a friendship with Angela Davis, which received a great deal of attention.

[4] In 1969, during the campaign for the Democratic nomination for president in California, Sirhan Bishara Sirhan, a Jordanian-born Arab, assassinated Attorney General Robert F. Kennedy and was convicted and given the death penalty. In 1972 the sentence was changed to life imprisonment after the California Supreme Court declared the state's death penalty unconstitutional.

[5] Mount Sannine (Sannin): A snow-capped Lebanese mountain.

[6] Ouranos, the planet Uranus, is the Arab pronunciation. In Greek mythology Uranus is the sky personified as a god.

[7] Queen Zenobia, Nabatean queen of Palmyra, Syria, from the third century, who also ruled over Egypt and Anatolia defying the Roman empire. After a long and difficult siege of the Roman city, she was captured in 272 A.D., but killed herself with a poison ring rather than submit to captivity. Most Arabs view Zenobia as a heroine who defied foreign conquest.

I am the initial Fish
rejected on the beach
but determined to live.

Do you know   imbeciles   that Rimbaud[8]
was among us a century ago
from Beirut to Aden-Arabia
and that Fouad Gabriel Naffah the poet
I repeat Fouad Gabriel Naffah
is among us
crucified by your thickness
burned with nitrogen
yes people of Beirut go on
snoring let nitrate burn
these pine-tree forests where
you throw your garbage   your paper towels
the country is the dumpsite
for the foreign merchandise
that everyone refuses

Tammouz's country[9] is an
open sore
his degenerate descendants
have their shoes shined
by the hands of a herd of beggars
                you borrowed your masks
                from the pigs and the cows
there have been three earthquakes
in the Third century
destroying three times Beirut
and a fourth one is coming!

the world is being born
the people are coming
the people are coming
        the eagle has carried the message
            to the tribe
        the camel has carried the message
            to the tribe
        the shark has carried the message
            to the tribe

[8] Rimbaud, a nineteenth-century French poet.
[9] Tammouz, an ancient Mesopotamian god of fertility who was wounded by a wild boar. It is
  believed that his blood restores life to vegetation (spring) and causes the Nahr Ibrahim
  River to flow red. Tammouz's love is Ishtar, who brought him back from the dead. It is
  said that Babylonian women sacrificed their virginity at Ishtar's temple in celebration of
  Tammouz's restoration.

from everywhere in the world they are
      coming.
The Revolution is coming . . .

In New York I say the hell with America
In Moscow I say the hell with Stalin
In Rabat[10] I say the hell with Hassan II[11]

      hello the beggar
      hello to the fedai
      hello to Mohammad the visionary
      hello to the prisoner

In the evening when darkness moves
      as slow as mud
I watch the prostitutes
      it is forbidden that women
      think
I watch our servants
      it is forbidden that women go
      to sleep
I watch our brides
      going to bed alone
      it is forbidden that women
      lie as gazelles
on the infinite fields of the Arabian plains

On the fields
      on the Arabian plains
      on the face of the desert
      on the streets of our
      bitch-in-heat cities
      there are only
      the maimed
            and governments with no end
            crime barks higher than
                  hyenas
            BABYLON BABYLON
        I announce your resurrections
            and your death.
We shall go from the Resistance
to the psychic conquest

      and then to prophecy

[10] Rabat, a city in Tunisia.
[11] Hassan II, born in Rabat, became king of Morocco in 1961. He succeeded his father, King
    Muhammad V. Hassan wrote Morocco's first constitution, adopted in 1962.

and from the prophecy to the divine
the divine is the people-who-suffer

Comrade Dostoevsky[12]
is in Beirut   he stays
at the Orient-Prince Hotel, he
eats at the Horseshoe cafe
he swims—you're not kidding—
at the St. George he yawns
—imagine that!—at the A.U.B.[13]
and for his redemption he counts
the typographical errors of the
daily an-Nahar
Comrade Dostoevsky
enjoys but the Koran
understands but compassion

Comrade Dostoevsky
is arrested by the Security Service
and he laughs   laughs   and his laughter
is broadcast on the radios of
the whole world
                    I caught it on channel 14
                    in California

O how I would like to break the sky
and provoke the lightning
bring down the deluge on this
        town!
Calmly we have prostituted
even the plants   Vulture-faced
sorrow is crying
while the boat refuses to leave

In the middle of History
In the heart of the hexagon
at the leverage point of the
building
at the meeting spot
of honor

                lives and dies
                Gamal Abdel Nassar

[12] Fyodor Dostoevsky (1821–1881), Russian philosopher, novelist, and short story writer.
[13] A.U.B.: American University of Beirut, Lebanon.

and his grave witnesses its
first miracle

I am going to talk to you
about the moslem saints: and the naked
girls lying by our dead . . .

It is in Jabal Amman[14]
that you should look for resurrection
it is in the Wahdat Camp[15]
that you should look for spring
it is on the bones of Abou Sliman[16]
that you should write koranic
                verses

City more unreal than the wind
although pregnant with the sins of
            the world
it is in your belly that foreigners
exercise the alchemy of treason

                    I love the October breeze
                    the red skies which foretell
                    the coming wars
                    above the sea
                    acetylene lamps light
                    the fishermen and the
                    boats . . .

Hamra Street: our nerves shrink at this name
            blood becomes white   the pedestrian
            becomes a ghost   the Lebanese pound
            exudes a stench

            and I fall on my knees
            in front of the children we sell
            for the pleasure of some night
            for the afternoon pleasure or
            the four in the morning one   sadism
            costs so little in Beirut

---

[14] Jabal Amman, meaning the mountain (Jabal) of the capitol (Amman is the capitol of Jordan).
[15] Wahdat Camp, a major Palestinian refugee camp in Amman, Jordan, understood as a strong-
    hold for guerrillas in the 1970 clashes between Palestinian forces and "Black September,"
    the Jordanian army.
[16] Abou Sliman, *Abou* meaning father, was a name given to symbolize political activism and
    those fighting for the liberation of Palestine.

City! how many crimes in your bars   how
much alcohol in the fountains of the old houses
what a monetary orgy in the call of the
muezzin!

city more famous than hell
passenger of all passages
eldest daughter of all trade
                object of our nocturnal love
                you have intoxicated us with
                your irremediable purity.

The tempest has   come
the trumpet has sounded JAZZ is
manifested   delirium has advanced   the hour
the hour   the hour   has stopped   we
are naked   destiny is there in front
Gilgamesh[17] has eaten his secret plant

people of Beirut   covered with numbers
swimming in butter   numbed
with evil thoughts

remember September the 18th![18]

a motorized angel has crossed the sky

                break your mirrors
                look toward Mount Sannine
                look at the sun which is emerging
                        new

bring out your swords
cut open the Arabian gut
                from side to side
                let freedom explode!

I have spontaneous funerary orations
for the metals: no sulfur
or manganese   but potassium

---

[17] Gilgamesh, a legendary Babylonian king who is the hero of the Gilgamesh Epic, predating
the Old Testament, where Gilgamesh faces a series of trials and tests much like Noah and
the flood in Genesis.

[18] September 18, the date that the Sabra and Shatila Massacre, an attack on two refugee camps
by Phalongist militiamen, was made public.

chloride in the water for the donkeys
and mortuary chalk on the
houses

traitors the painters: they plunge
                              in buckets of acid
traitors the poets: they speak of roses
                              when the city is an
                              asphalt garden
traitors the officials: they have as umbilical
                              cords the telephone lines
                              that link them to Washington
                              Vladivostok
traitors the priests: there is a business shuttle
                              in the schools and consciences
                              covered with vermin
let liberation liberate!

City!

                    you are at the foot of the
                              pink mountain and each one of us
                              is a legend

One out of two bums is covered with lice
what a velvet on his tender skin   a live
hair   young men coming out of the Empire
Cinema with swollen lips   masturbation in
the dark   atavistic hunger installed in
the belly   the smell of the film becoming
woman   the big desert of love is going
to cover them in the grave already made
they only know how to love their mother . . .

I know streets where the police
rape anything going on two feet

                    the sons of the rich
                    go by them in speedy cars
                    glassy eyed   cold
                    stone
I would like to announce the fabulous
acceleration of the planets and the
dynamics of catastrophe: sons of Canaanites[19]

[19] Canaanites, the inhabitants of Canaan before its conquest by the Hebrews.

you are dying for the very last time
Take a train, my friend, the train
for Amman
> "it is the only place on earth
> which proposes to us an occult
> life and proposes it at the surface
> of life"

it is Antonin Artaud[20] who is saying it

Our fate is the one
of the Red Indian: the oiliferous
hordes are going to destroy the very
banks they built as numerous as chimneys

we have mornings with no memories

I predict a tidal wave
    dried up well
    anthill   a southern wart
    is gnawing
at the land formerly said   of the Ancestor

We have perspired   at noon   an
icy sweat   we have seen thieves
met on the sidewalk an astronaut wearing
a wig   our housewives have skins which
are burned   nitroglycerine bags put in the
frontal lobe of their lovers explode under
the fatuous laughter of the enemy

> Beirut is a witch-city
> which acts on the world
> as an ill omen

What to do with innocence if not
a parade   like a face tumor
one night with a strong light
in California   the road and the beach
the black trees against which
Ahmad-the-Violence and Khalil-Debauchery
rub their phallus because they are
scared   scared   scared   of the Express
train which is carrying away their
double   at fast speed

[20] Antonin Artaud, a French theorist (1896–1948), born in Marseilles, France.

a speed
of death
in the dry
ravines
of the city
which is burned
with American phosphorus

It has been a million years
since the Hashemites[21] left
Mecca in the belly of the first
dinosaur to finish up in this
massacre!

    It has been a million years
    since Amman-Ugliness
    has been condemned on the throne
    of the Apocalypse of the Oil.

I took a long walk on Beirut's Corniche
with Al-Ghazali as a companion

    I took olive oil in the Greek
    churches and anointed him
    Prince of the City

Comrade al-Ghazali
stays at the Metropol
eats at Barmaki's   chats with
his Lebanese friends of the
theatre at Wimpy's   and receives
his mail care of Interpol[22]
His own letters are sent by
a traveling whale

    they play the flute in the
    popular quarters of the city
    in order to quiet down the anger
    of the citizens . . .

[21] Hashemites, members of the royal dynasty of the Kingdom of Jordan and the former Kingdom
of Iraq and understood to be descendants of Mohammed.
[22] Interpol, the International Criminal Police Commission, whose purpose is to assist police
in member nations with international crime investigations.

The god Shamash[23] has come back
in Irbid[24]
in Zarka[25]
In Ur[26] and in
Basrah[27]

the dead are coming back in order to fight again
because the living are cowards!

> people of Beirut
> in bikinis   in slips
> covered with feathers if
> need be
> take the first Express

> (take your vertebrae and squeeze out
> colonialism like pus)

so that there be
air

so that there be
water

so that there be
earth

so that there be
fire

> take the Beirut——Hell Express
> take the Express
> it is more than too late
> the train is whistling stamping spitting
> the Beirut——Hell Express.

[1991]

---

[23] Shamash, the sun god in Babylonian and Assyrian mythology.

[24] Irbid, a town in northern Jordan, forty miles north of Amman.

[25] Zarka, located in lower Egypt on the Domietta branch of the Nile and northeast of Mansura.

[26] Ur, the ancient city of Sumer, located in southern Mesopotamia. An important city of Sumerian culture and identified in the Bible as the home of Abraham.

[27] Basrah, an Iraqi port city located in extreme southeastern Iraq, at the headwaters of the Persian Gulf.

Ai (Pelorhankhe Ogawa)

1

Yesterday, the man who calls himself "Our Father"
made me crawl on smashed Coke bottles.
Today, I sleep. I think I sleep,
till someone beats on the door, with what?—
sticks, pans—but I don't move.
I'm used to it.
Still, when Our Father rushes into the room
and drags me out, I feel the old fear.
In the interrogation room,
he knocks me to the floor,
then sits on the side of his desk,
his arms folded, that sad look on his face
I know so well. He shakes his head slowly,
stops, and smiles.
"I've got something special today," he says,
"for a fucking whore of a terrorist bitch."
I want to say nothing,
knowing how denial angers him,
but I can't stop myself.
I'm not a terrorist, I say.
"That's not what I heard," he replies, standing up.
"Aren't you the friend of a friend of a friend
of a terrorist son of a bitch
who was heard two years ago to say
that someone ought to do something
about this government?"
I don't answer.
Already, I've begun to admit that it must be true.
"I lack just one thing," he says, "the name."
"I know you think you're innocent,
but you aren't.
Everyone is guilty."
He slaps me, then pushes one side of my face
toward the green glass.

2

I've been stung by a swarm of bees.
I'm eight. I'm running for the pond
on my uncle Oscar's farm.
Oscar, I cry. Our Father sighs deeply,
lifts me up, and sets me down in a chair.
"This Oscar," he says, handing me a notebook and pen,
"where can I find him?"
I don't hesitate, as I take the pen
and set it down
on the clean, blank paper.

3

Our Father lets me off
a block from my apartment.
He keeps the motor running,
but comes and leans
against the car beside me.
I try to guess the month. March, April? I say.
He tells me it's September,
to just take a look at the sky.
Then he tells me he was a prisoner once too.
I stare at his face,
the dry, sallow skin,
the long scar running from temple to chin.
"Oh this," he touches the scar gently,
"I got this playing soccer.
No, the real scars don't show.
You should know that.
You need time, though, to sort it all out.
I'm still a young man,
but sometimes I feel as old as the Bible.
But this is a celebration."
He takes a bottle of wine from the car
and we drink, while the stars glitter above us.
Done, he tosses the bottle into the street.
"Freedom," he says, "freedom is something you earn.
The others don't understand that, but we do."

[1986]

Suicid/ing(ed) Indian Women

Paula Gunn Allen

I. Kyukuh

broken, a
tremble like
windowpane in gusted
wind I envision you
Kyukuh
on the southern shore writing
stepping slowly in the circle
as traditional in your view
as Wolverine in any metropolis
but your shaken
voice, is it a small wind
we carry in our genes?
A fear of disappearance?
An utterance that hovers
at the edges of the lips,
forever to-be-said?
The stories around Laguna say
that She, Iyetiko, left the people
longtimeago. There was a drought.
She gave them some toys for gambling,
you know, but the men gambled everything,
no matter how their wives pleaded, or
even their aunts, and hid in the kivas so the women
couldn't nag, and they wouldn't even do the necessary
dancing. So Iyetiko got angry and went away. That's
what the story says, and maybe it's so.
Maybe She knew that we could do without her presence
in the flesh, and She left the perfect ear of corn
behind to remind them that she was near, to honor
women, the woman in the earth, and in themselves,
but they call themselves her name, they call themselves
Mother, so maybe they sent her away and made up the rest.

II. Laguna

small woman huddled on the couch
soft light and shadows try to comfort you
Laguna would-be-suicide
why do you cling
to the vanished lakebed?

Even the water has left
the village.
You hardly speak
except to say confusion fills your mind
how can you escape the ties of brutaldrunken father
gossipy sisters/aunts scolding uncles/brothers
who want you to buy and cook their food
you eat little yourself you say
why must you in your beauty and strength
huddle helpless on the edge of the couch
laugh mocking your own helpless pain
why are things so terrible at Laguna that you
can't see another world around you like the lamps
soft and comforting around this room?

III. Navajo

earthwoman
as authentic as any whiteman
could wish you
marry out and
unhappy you beautiful/strong/brown
and your flowing black hair
Navajo maiden you can't
understand why your squawman sits in a chair
orders you and your young sisters about
you knew the reservation was no place to be
you giggle about the agonies of your past
the men your mother married
it will not be like that for you,
and you know
it must unless you get away
but how divide yourself
from your flesh? Division
does not come easy to a woman,
it is against the tribe
laws which only women honor
nor do you understand that
so you perch uneasily
on the edge of the reservation
and make joking fantasies
do for real

IV. Shipapu

Beautiful corn woman
lost all those centuries ago

stolen as your children
for generations have been
and it is not right
that this should be
but the law is such.
They abandoned you,
defied the women,
gambled and lost.
And you left them.
They don't tell how they
put women out of the center
except your emblem,
but death and destruction
have followed them,
the people lost the beautiful
first home, KUSHKUTRET
to the raging gods of war
and wander homeless now
beside the dead lake.
They have taken your name.

[1982]

Our Grandmothers

Maya Angelou

She lay, skin down on the moist dirt,
the canebrake rustling
with the whispers of leaves, and
loud longing of hounds and
the ransack of hunters crackling the near branches.

She muttered, lifting her head a nod toward freedom,
I shall not, I shall not be moved.

She gathered her babies,
their tears slick as oil on black faces,
their young eyes canvassing mornings of madness.
Momma, is Master going to sell you
from us tomorrow?

Yes.
Unless you keep walking more
and talking less.
Yes.
Unless the keeper of our lives
releases me from all commandments.
Yes.
And your lives,
never mine to live,
will be executed upon the killing floor of innocents.
Unless you match my heart and words,
saying with me,

I shall not be moved.

In Virginia tobacco fields,
leaning into the curve
on Steinway
pianos, along Arkansas roads,
in the red hills of Georgia,
into the palms of her chained hands, she
cried against calamity,
You have tried to destroy me
and though I perish daily,

I shall not be moved.

Her universe, often
summarized into one black body
falling finally from the tree to her feet,
made her cry each time in a new voice.
All my past hastens to defeat,
and strangers claim the glory of my love,
Iniquity has bound me to his bed,

yet, I must not be moved.

She heard the names,
swirling ribbons in the wind of history:
nigger, nigger bitch, heifer,
mammy, property, creature, ape, baboon,
whore, hot tail, thing, it.
She said, But my description cannot
fit your tongue, for
I have a certain way of being in this world,
and I shall not, I shall not be moved.

No angel stretched protecting wings
above the heads of her children,
fluttering and urging the winds of reason
into the confusion of their lives.
They sprouted like young weeds,
but she could not shield their growth
from the grinding blades of ignorance, nor
shape them into symbolic topiaries.
She sent them away,
underground, overland, in coaches and
shoeless.
When you learn, teach.
When you get, give.
As for me,

I shall not be moved.

She stood in midocean, seeking dry land.
She searched God's face.
Assured,
she placed her fire of service
on the altar, and though
clothed in the finery of faith,
when she appeared at the temple door,
no sign welcomed
Black Grandmother. Enter here.

Into the crashing sound,
into wickedness, she cried,
No one, no, nor no one million
ones dare deny me God. I go forth
alone, and stand as ten thousand.

The Divine upon my right
impels me to pull forever
at the latch on Freedom's gate.

The Holy Spirit upon my left leads my
feet without ceasing into the camp of the
righteous and into the tents of the free.

These momma faces, lemon-yellow, plum-purple,
honey-brown, have grimaced and twisted
down a pyramid of years.
She is Sheba and Sojourner,
  Harriet and Zora,
  Mary Bethune and Angela,
  Annie to Zenobia.

She stands
before the abortion clinic,
confounded by the lack of choices.
In the Welfare line,
reduced to the pity of handouts.
Ordained in the pulpit, shielded
by the mysteries.
In the operating room,
husbanding life.
In the choir loft,
holding God in her throat.
On lonely street corners,
hawking her body.
In the classroom, loving the
children to understanding.

Centered on the world's stage,
she sings to her loves and beloveds,
to her foes and detractors:
However I am perceived and deceived,
however my ignorance and conceits,
lay aside your fears that I will be undone,

for I shall not be moved.

[1990]

I Want to Renegade

S. Brandi Barnes

I wanna break laws—
    binding us,
    touch your hands/wet your lips
I wanna renegade
    wanna stroke your body/sweet oil your skin
    wrap you in my kinte kloth;[1]

[1] Kinte Kloth, a woven cloth indigenous to certain parts of subsaharan Africa, usually in bright
colors and geometric patterns.

I wanna renegade
  ride wild/hide out
  wanna kidnap you
    borrow and not return
    put your smile across my back;
I wanna tease your taunting me,
    saddle up to you b . . a . . b . . b . . y
  stick'em up/rob the bank;
I wanna sunrise with you
  and snuggle midnight velvet
  wanna tickle your ear
  wanna fire with you
wanna slide under and over,
wanna feel and thrill you
from top to toe you;
wanna make your skin scream
wanna chill your spine
pour grapes on your body and
spoon you honey . . . spoon you;
I wanna steal and bandit your body
with a slow dance;
keep you til dust,
break the law/be a fugitive,
I want to renegade
  hide you/outlaw on you b . . a . . b . . b . . y
they'll move me from
  10 Most Wanted—to MOST WANTED;
They'll try to find me/flush me out
  try to take me/take me alive;
to put me in the pokey—b . . a . . b . . b . . y
lock me up,
throw keys away,
I'll be forever wanted
the -way-I-want- you!

[1987]

My Womb

Esmeralda Bernal

my womb
a public domain
erotica a doormat
trampled on by
birthright

my womb a
legislated periphery
no longer mine
but public space

my womb
a palestinian front
fighting for
the right to be
a private space

[1986]

Farolita

Mei-Mei Berssenbrugge

Take a strip of white paper, turn
the top of the strip in your right hand so
it faces the floor, then glue the ends together
If you go along on the outside, it seems
I am not connected to you. I'm trying
to think now if it has to be white paper
Can it show some light through?

It seems I go out on it without any door, into
blue hatchings by yellow grass on snow. This time

of year the air is blue, or inside a shadow. How did she
get through the wall? He was standing at the door waiting
for her. She stands in the field at dusk wearing a black cowboy
hat. She's afraid she becomes something bad at night. She
dreams of killing him, then thinks it is a story she read
She dreams what is going to happen to him. The blue is a false trail
She knows that it is an emanation of the real cloth
The blue mountain is light through fouled air. The blue
air is left after sucking the light

They told her there was a morada[1] across from her house
just a little up from the Kents. She never wanted to go
there. In a magazine its long Christ held flowers
and an ax. Toward town, in low sun, she sees light
in flapping laundry. It was just movement at first. She has
heard the processions walk by. At first you think their
singing is a moan in the wind. He too makes a ritual
out of holding her breasts to cold glass. She thinks someone is
stealing her black cigarettes. She considers its madonna
a kind of barker, or an emanation of scored flesh. The
yellow grass has nevertheless been trampled by cows
and turns to mud, though nothing was green there, before
A white cloth tears off in the wind and flattens itself
against a fence, holding shadows the way black plastic holds
little hands of water in its folds on the field

I am talking about the color white. Please don't try to make
me think I have not murdered you in my dream. He is taking
her to a dinner party across the road. An artist tells
her about a film he conceived, that is all one color, the
color inside a shadow. She tries not to assume this is
because he is going blind. She loves him. He is a capitalist
Sparks shot out the chimney and streaked outside the glass
wall like an opened lens on their cigarettes in the dark. One
log burning heated the vast room. The whole wall was hot
to touch. She folded each napkin so its white bird flew off
to the left. Each fish leapt off white on the Japanese
plates. Her host's sculptures had undergone amputations
They'd been hung by their wrists from a beam, but were
all smooth now. She drank some vodka and ice. The ice
which had been refrozen, held little bubbles in the act
of rising that were half light. She realized it was
time to go attach herself, at home

---

[1] Morada, a dark woman or a dark-skinned woman.

Trying to tell me it is every color, that is their way
of drawing you in. Keep your eye on the leaf dangling
from a bare branch. It is dead, but is moving and
seems to have candlelight on it, though when white
chrysanthemums arrived, she couldn't help accepting
She told her mother they were from George. Her mother
told all the neighbors. They wanted her to marry
She thought she was pregnant. She wondered if paper were
suitable for its clothes, so she pretended to make patterns
for the clothes, but they *were* the clothes

White light from her fingers, I think it is
electricity leaking from the wall, but it washes back
from hitting the wall. I demeaned myself in front of a
blind man, because I'm afraid of myself at night. If
he lights my cigarette when I complain how it goes out, the
flame goes out. I am afraid I might drop my bag and
secretly scoop the used matches up. It ricochets from a
box canyon. It doesn't recognize her as it strikes, so
she is visible, too. The whole valley becomes a white
bowl. The phosphorus wedge of a police car over-
exposes outlines of her friends. They'd been passing
a bottle of Merseault inside the pick-up. They told her
not to sit there like a wooden doll answering his personal
questions. She grew confused. She tried to draw in her cape
She walked a little away and rolled over on the snow
Her foot became a horse's head in the fire

The Eurasian at the party would not speak to her. Little lights
inside paper sacks cast willow flames on the snow
the little lights that line paths
of the courtyard. You have to assume each is the same, so
the maze recedes and is not a vertical map of varying sacks
on a blank wall, since it is dark, oh
Mei-mei, you've walked in that garden before. I'm sick of
these dry gardens. Everyone tells me I should get angry at him
The nun's voice quavered behind a screen. There was a shadow
voice to hers of another one singing quietly and
a little off. I prefer to think it was the light back
How can he dream of tying me to his bed, in a blizzard
with snow to my thigh? He tells me I am flirting
with the void. I am not Chinese. I invite him to step
out to the garden for plum blossoms. They would be
very beautiful, now. Their petals would

blanket the snow like snow on sand
but it is morning

Open the door
Light falls like a collar point on the blond floor boards
She crosses this point, and light falls on her
and it falls on her as she goes out
but it is different light

[1983]

For Mama
(and her mamas, too)

Nora Brooks Blakely

Red/gold souls dance through our minds
Whirling up thoughts of Other who is still here.
Memories make lives livable again.
Memories call learnings and giggles galore,
Yes—and flashes of hot pink pain and stopsoul sorrows, too,

but

she lives
and chuckles and "pshaws" and "coo's" away—
As long as we light love candles of thought and times-when,
As long as our regrettings are syncopated sadnesses with a happy beat,
As long as you are of she
And all are in me
We'll laugh and straighten
And root ourselves in the here.

[1979]

To Grandmother's House We Go

Nora Brooks Blakely

It's not there now, although it is
Light cranes its head around corners
  and gingerly reaches in through walls
  where holes crowd each other like
      hungry sharks.
I used to sit here
  curled in comfort in the living room
  or
  erect in the straight-backed air
     of the dining room.
Here,
Until I was eight
  were games with grandfather
  who gave me soft wool blanket days
of open-doored love
and laughter paths.

Here,
Until she was ninety
  was grandmother
  with her attentive, listening ears,
  stern standards,
  sudden chuckles,
  and her cancellations of the crude.

But, here
  and now
  the walls gape,
  Tears of tar are frozen
    on the downstreak.
Night sits inside and defeats the sun.

Flames have snatched my memories
    for a late night snack.
There are no hills or woods
    over or through that lead here,
No streets to point to what isn't there.

  Except the thought trails
    and back roads smiles
    that will always go
    to grandmother's house.

[1984]

for all my Grandmothers

Beth Brant

A hairnet covered her head.
a net
encasing the silver strands.
A cage confining the wildness.
No thread escaped.

(once, your hair coursed down your back
streaming behind
as you ran through the woods.
Catching on branches,
the crackling filaments
gathered leaves.
Burrs attached themselves.
A redbird plucked a shiny thread
for her nest,
shed a feather that glided
into the black cloud and
became a part of you.
You sang as you ran.
Your moccasins
skimmed the earth.
Heh ho oh heh heh)

Prematurely taken
from the woodland.
Giving birth
to children that grew
in a world that is white.
Prematurely
you put your hair up and
covered it
with a net.
Prematurely grey
they called it.

Hair Binding.

Damming the flow.

With no words, quietly
the hair fell out
formed webs on your dresser

on your pillow
in your brush.
These tangled strands
pushed to the back of a drawer
wait for me.
To untangle
To comb through
To weave together the split fibers
and make a material
Strong enough
to encompass our lives.

[1989]

The Lovers of the Poor

Gwendolyn Brooks

    arrive. The ladies from the Ladies' Betterment
  League
Arrive in the afternoon, the late light slanting
In diluted gold bars across the boulevard brag
Of proud, seamed faces with mercy and murder hinting
Here, there, interrupting, all deep and debonair,
The pink paint on the innocence of fear;
Walk in a gingerly manner up the hall.
Cutting with knives served by their softest care,
Served by their love, so barbarously fair.
Whose mothers taught: You'd better not be cruel!
You had better not throw stones upon the wrens!
Herein they kiss and coddle and assault
Anew and dearly in the innocence
With which they baffle nature. Who are full,
Sleek, tender-clad, fit, fiftyish, a-glow, all
Sweetly abortive, hinting at fat fruit,
Judge it high time that fiftyish fingers felt
Beneath the lovelier planes of enterprise.
To resurrect. To moisten with milky chill.
To be a random hitching post or plush.
To be, for wet eyes, random and handy hem.
    Their guild is giving money to the poor.
The worthy poor. The very very worthy

And beautiful poor. Perhaps just not too swarthy?
Perhaps just not too dirty nor too dim
Nor—passionate. In truth, what they could wish
Is—something less than derelict or dull.
Not staunch enough to stab, though, gaze for gaze!
God shield them sharply from the beggar-bold!
The noxious needy ones whose battle's bald
Nonetheless for being voiceless, hits one down.

　　　But it's all so bad! and entirely too much for them.
The stench; the urine, cabbage, and dead beans,
Dead porridges of assorted dusty grains,
The old smoke, *heavy* diapers, and, they're told,
Something called chitterlings.[1] The darkness. Drawn
Darkness, or dirty light. The soil that stirs
The soil that looks the soil of centuries.
And for that matter the *general* oldness. Old
Wood. Old marble. Old tile. Old old old.
Not homekind Oldness! Not Lake Forest, Glencoe.
Nothing is sturdy, nothing is majestic,
There is no quiet drama, no rubbed glaze, no
Unkillable infirmity of such
A tasteful turn as lately they have left,
Glencoe, Lake Forest, and to which their cars
Must presently restore them. When they're done
Will dullards and distortions of this fistic[2]
Patience of the poor and put-upon.

　　　They've never seen such a make-do-ness as
Newspaper rugs before! In this, this "flat,"
Their hostess is gathering up the oozed, the rich
Rugs of the morning (tattered! the bespattered . . .),
Readies to spread clean rugs for afternoon.
Here is a scene for you. The Ladies look,
In horror, behind a substantial citizeness
Whose trains clank out across her swollen heart.
Who, arms akimbo, almost fills a door.
All tumbling children, quilts dragged to the floor
And tortured thereover, potato peelings, soft-
Eyed kitten, hunched-up, haggard, to-be-hurt.

　　　Their League is allotting largesse to the Lost.
But to put their clean, their pretty money, to put
Their money collected from delicate rose-fingers
Tipped with their hundred flawless rose-nails seems . . .

---

[1] Chitterlings, a fried food dish made from the small intestine of pigs.
[2] Fistic, done with or having to do with the fists.

They own Spode,[3] Lowestoft,[4] candelabra,
Mantels, and hostess gowns, and sunburst clocks,
Turtle soup, Chippendale,[5] red satin "hangings,"
Aubussons[6] and Hattie Carnegie.[7] They Winter
In Palm Beach; cross the Water in June; attend,
When suitable, the nice Art Institute;
Buy the right books in the best bindings; saunter
On Michigan, Easter mornings, in sun or wind.
Oh Squalor! This sick four-story hulk, this fibre
With fissures everywhere! Why, what are bringings
Of loathe-love largesse? What shall peril hungers
So old old, what shall flatter the desolate?
Tin can, blocked fire escape and chitterling
And swaggering seeking youth and the puzzled wreckage
Of the middle passage, and urine and stale shames
And, again, the porridges of the underslung
And children children children. Heavens! That
Was a rat, surely, off there, in the shadows? Long
And long-tailed? Gray? The Ladies from the Ladies'
Betterment League agree it will be better
To achieve the outer air that rights and steadies
To hie to a house that does not holler, to ring
Bells elsetime, better presently to cater
To no more Possibilities, to get
Away. Perhaps the money can be posted.
Perhaps they two may choose another Slum!
Some serious sooty half-unhappy home!—
Where loathe-love likelier may be invested.
　　Keeping their scented bodies in the center
Of the hall as they walk down the hysterical hall,
They allow their lovely skirts to graze no wall,
Are off at what they manage of a canter,
And, resuming all the clues of what they were,
Try to avoid inhaling the laden air.

[1944]

---

[3] Spode, ceramic ware, such as bone china, made by Josiah Spode (1754–1825), one of the most acclaimed potters in Staffordshire, England.
[4] Lowestoft, a delicately colored blue and white china produced in England during the second half of the eighteenth century.
[5] Chippendale, an eighteenth-century style of English furniture designed by Thomas Chippendale, and known for its graceful outline and detailed ornamentation.
[6] Abusson, from France, a woven rug similar to tapestry.
[7] Hattie Carnegie, born Henrietta Koningeiser in Vienna around 1886, was a wealthy fashion designer. The "Carnegie look" meant women should never indulge in extremes and should dress to please men.

Ana Castillo

the antihero
always gets the woman
not in the end
an anticlimax instead
in the end
spits on her
stretched out body
a spasmodic carpet
yearning still
washes himself

doesn't know why
it is that way searching
not finding finding
not wanting wanting more
or nothing
in the end the key is
to leave her yearning lest
she discover that is all

[1983]

Poem For The Young White Man Who Asked Me How I, An Intelligent, Well-Read Person, Could Believe In The War Between Races

Lorna Dee Cervantes

In my land there are no distinctions.
The barbed wire politics of oppression
have been torn down long ago. The only reminder
of past battles, lost or won, is a slight
rutting in the fertile fields.

In my land
people write poems about love,
full of nothing but contented childlike syllables.
Everyone reads Russian short stories and weeps.
There are no boundaries.
There is no hunger, no
complicated famine or greed.

I am not a revolutionary.
I don't even like political poems.
Do you think I can believe in a war between races?
I can deny it. I can forget about it
when I'm safe,
living on my own continent of harmony
and home, but I am not
there.

I believe in revolution
because everywhere the crosses are burning,
sharp-shooting goose-steppers round every corner,
there are snipers in the schools . . .
(I know you don't believe this.
You think this is nothing
but faddish exaggeration. But they
are not shooting at you.)

I'm marked by the color of my skin.
The bullets are discrete and designed to kill slowly.
They are aiming at my children.
These are facts.
Let me show you my wounds: my stumbling mind, my
"excuse me" tongue, and this
nagging preoccupation
with the feeling of not being good enough.

These bullets bury deeper than logic.

Outside my door
there is a real enemy
who hates me.

I am a poet
who yearns to dance on rooftops,
to whisper delicate lines about joy
and the blessings of human understanding.
I try. I go to my land, my tower of words and
bolt the door, but the typewriter doesn't fade out
the sounds of blasting and muffled outrage.
My own days bring me slaps on the face.
Every day I am deluged with reminders
that this is not
my land

and this is my land

I do not believe in the war between races

but in this country
there is war.

[1981]

africans sleeping in the park at night
Eileen Cherry

"sistuh"
they asked me if i wanted to
lie on the grass and drink stout
and feel the warm fire in my belly
the heartbeat in my head
the dragon's breath pouring out of my nostrils.

they asked. "sistuh" if i wanted to dance
in the velvet shadows
wallow in cool leaves under a thousand
diamond eyes. hear my own cry over the lake's
burn herbs and musky scents.

they asked me if i savored the taste of rest. "sistuh"
i said yes
i use
some strong trusting brews that bring
the thickness of sleep that
release me to know—
my breath is inseparable
from the wind.

[1984]

We Are Americans Now,
We Live in the Tundra
Marilyn (Mei Ling) Chin

Today in hazy San Francisco, I face seaward
Toward China, a giant begonia—

Pink, fragrant, bitten
By verdigris[1] and insects. I sing her

---

[1] Verdigris, a green or greenish blue poisonous pigment formed by the action of acetic acid on copper.

A blues song; even a Chinese girl gets the blues,
Her reticence is black and blue.

Let's sing about the extinct
Bengal tigers, about giant Pandas—

"Ling Ling loves Xing Xing . . . yet,
We will not mate. We are

Not impotent, we are important.
We blame the environment, we blame the zoo!"

What shall we plant for the future?
Bamboo, sasagrass, coconut palms? No!

Legumes, wheat, maize, old swines
To milk the new.

We are Americans now, we live in the tundra
Of the logical, a sea of cities, a wood of cars.

Farewell my ancestors:
Hirsute Taoists, failed scholars, farewell

My wetnurse who feared and loathed the Catholics,
Who called out:

> Now that the half-men have occupied Canton
> Hide your daughters, lock your doors!

[1989]

I Make the Fire

Chrystos

as the sun rises   gold to gold
smoky britches in the sky
boogie down wood   snap & pop
Across my shoulder falls
shadow of Eagle

as I go to the wood shed
Tiny green feathers of new growth fir
curl & dance under my feet
Heavy winds last night
In my arms a sweet smell of cedar
debris from the shake mill
I'm a woman who carries kindling
& her past
as she prays

[1991]

Those Tears

Chrystos

of a white woman who came to the group for Women of Color
only
her grief cut us into guilt while we clutched the straw
of this tiny square inch we have which we need
so desperately when we need so much more
We talked her into leaving
which took 10 minutes of our precious 60
Those legion white Lesbians whose feelings are hurt
because we have a Lesbians of Color Potluck
once a month for 2 hours
without them
Those tears of the straight woman
because we kicked out her boyfriend at the Lesbians only
poetry reading where no microphone was provided
& the room was much too small for all of us
shouting that we were imperialists
though I had spent 8 minutes trying to explain
to her that an oppressed people
cannot oppress their oppressor
She ignored me
charged into the room weeping & storming
taking up 9 minutes of our precious tiny square inch
Ah those tears

which could be jails, graves, rapists, thieves, thugs
those tears which are so puffed up with inappropriate grief
Those women who are used to having their tears work
rage at us
when they don't
We are not real Feminists they say
We do not love women
I yell back with a wet face
Where are our jobs?   Our apartments?
Our voices in parliament or congress?
Where is our safety from beatings, from murder?
You cannot even respect us to allow us
60 uninterrupted minutes for ourselves
Your tears are chains
Feminism is the right of each woman
to claim her own life her own time
her own uninterrupted 60 hours
                        60 days
                        60 years
No matter how sensitive you are
if you are white
you are
No matter how sensitive you are
if you are a man
you are
We who are not allowed to speak have the right
to define our terms our turf
These facts are not debatable
Give us our inch
& we'll hand you a hanky

[1991]

what the mirror said

Lucille Clifton

listen,
you a wonder.
you a city
of a woman.

you got a geography
of your own.
listen,
somebody need a map
to understand you.
somebody need directions
to move around you.
listen,
woman,
you not a noplace
anonymous
girl;
mister with his hands on you
he got his hands on
some
damn
body!

[1980]

Una Mujer Loca*

Judith Ortiz Cofer

When she closes her eyes,
the world empties from her head
like oil through a funnel.
Under the clear blue canopy
of her fantasy, she invents
new sounds for a tongue
all her own, and colors
so pure she must spend hours
holding on to each hue.
So far has she gone
into herself,

* *Una Mujer Loca*, a crazy woman. Loca, also meaning fantastic or terrific.

that the taunting voices
from the outside calling
her *Loca, Loca*
reach her as bright beams
of light lining the road
to the kingdom where
she is the sole ruler.

[1986]

What the Gypsy Said to Her Children
Judith Ortiz Cofer

We are like the dead,
invisible to those who do not
want to see,
and our only protection against
the killing silence of their eyes is color:
the crimson of our tents pitched
like a scream
in the fields of our foes,
the amber of our fires
where we gather to lift our voices
in the purple lament of our songs.
And beyond the scope of their senses
where all colors blend into one,
we will build our cities of light,
we will carve them
out of the granite of their hatred.
with our own brown hands.

[1988]

Lucha Corpi

I. Marina Mother

They made her of the softest clay
and dried her under the rays of the tropical sun.
With the blood of a tender lamb
her name was written by the elders
on the bark of that tree
as old as they.

Steeped in tradition, mystic
and mute she was sold—
from hand to hand, night to night,
denied and desecrated, waiting for the dawn
and for the owl's song
that would never come;
her womb sacked of its fruit,
her soul thinned to a handful of dust.

You no longer loved her, the elders denied her,
and the child who cried out to her "mamá!"
grew up and called her "whore."

II. Marina Virgin

Of her own accord, before the altar
of the crucified god she knelt.
Because she loved you, she only saw
the bleeding man, and loved in him
her secret and mourning memory of you.

* Doña Marina, known also as Malinaali Tepenal, Malintzin, or La Malinche, was an Aztec
  noblewoman presented to Hernan Cortés, when he landed in Veracruz, Mexico, in 1519.
  She served throughout Cortés' conquest as his interpreter, diplomat, nurse, comrade-at-
  arms, and lover. Marina bore Cortés a son, but despite their long companionship, he
  eventually married a European woman of noble rank. To compensate, Cortés married
  Marina to one of his lieutenants and presented her with a gift of land. Marina has become
  an ambivalent figure because she is both idolized as a mother-goddess and reviled as a
  traitor. Her Indian name, *Malinche*, is synonymous in Mexico with treachery and betrayal
  and her vindication is the subject of this poem.

She washed away her sins
with holy water, covered her body
with a long, thick cloth
so no one would know
her brown skin had been damned.

Once, you stopped to wonder
where her soul was hidden,
not knowing she had planted it
in the entrails of that earth
her hands had cultivated—
the moist, black earth of your life.

III. The Devil's Daughter

When she died, lightning struck in the north,
and on the new stone altar the incense burned
all night long. Her mystic pulsing
silenced, the ancient idol
shattered, her name
devoured by the wind in one deep growl
(her name so like the salt depths of the sea)—
little remained. Only a half-germinated seed.

IV. She (Marina Distant)

She. A flower perhaps, a pool of fresh water . . .
a tropical night,
or a sorrowful child, enclosed
in a prison of the softest clay:
mourning shadow of an ancestral memory,
crossing the bridge at daybreak,
her hands full of earth and sun.

[1976]

Lucha Corpi

A flavor of vanilla drifts
on the Sunday air.

Melancholy of an orange,
clinging still,
brilliant, seductive
past the promise of its blooming.

Guadalupe was bathing in the river
that Sunday, late,

a promise of milk in her breasts,
vanilla scent in her hair
cinnamon flavor in her eyes,
cocoa-flower between her legs

and in her mouth a daze
of sugarcane.

He came upon her there
surrounded by water
in a flood of evening light.

And on the instant cut the flower
wrung blood from the milk

dashed vanilla on the silence
of the river bank
drained the burning liquid
of her lips

and then he was gone,
leaving behind him a trail of shadow
drooping at the water's edge.

Her mother found her there, and at the sight
took a handful of salt from her pouch
to throw over her shoulder.

A few days later, her father
accepted the gift of a fine mare.

And Guadalupe . . . Guadalupe hung her life
from the orange tree in the garden,
and stayed there quietly,
her eyes open to the river.

An orange clings to the branch
the promise lost of its blooming.

Ancestral longing
seizes the mind.

A scent of vanilla drifts
on the evening air.

Translated by Catherine Rodriguez-Nieto.

[1978]

In the Morning

Jayne Cortez

Disguised in my mouth as a swampland
nailed to my teeth like a rising sun
you come out in the middle of fish-scales
you bleed into gourds wrapped with red ants
you syncopate the air with lungs like screams from yazoo[1]
like X rated tongues
and nickel plated fingers of a raw ghost man
you touch brown nipples to knives
and somewhere stripped like a whirlwind
stripped for the shrine room
you sing to me through the side face of a black rooster

In the morning in the morning in the morning
all over my door like a rooster
in the morning in the morning in the morning

[1] Yazoo, the Yazoo River in Mississippi, which flows into the Mississippi River.

And studded in my kidneys like perforated hiccups
inflamed in my ribs like three hoops of thunder through a screw
a star-bent-bolt of quivering colons
you breathe into veiled rays and scented ice holes
you fire the space like the flair of embalmed pigeons
and palpitate with the worms and venom and wailing flanks
and somewhere inside this fever
inside my patinaed pubic and camouflaged slit
stooped forward on fangs
in rear of your face
you shake to me in the full crown of a black rooster

In the morning in the morning in the morning

Masquerading in my horn like a river
eclipsed to these infantries of dentures of diving spears
you enter broken mirrors through fragmented pipe spit
you pull into a shadow ring of magic jelly
you wear the sacrificial blood of nightfall
you lift the ceiling with my tropical slush dance
you slide and tremble with the reputation of an earthquake
and when i kick through walls
to shine like silver
when i shine like brass through crust in a compound
when i shine shine shine
you wail to me in the drum call of a black rooster

In the morning in the morning in the morning
gonna kill me a rooster
in the morning
early in the morning
way down in the morning
before the sun passes by
in the morning in the morning in the morning

In the morning
when the deep sea goes through a dogs bite
and you spit on tip of your long knife

In the morning in the morning
when peroxide falls on a bed of broken glass
and the sun rises like a polyester ball of menses
in the morning
gonna firedance in the petro
in the morning
turn loose the blues in the funky jungle
in the morning

I said when you see the morning coming like
a two-headed twister
let it blow let it blow
in the morning in the morning
all swollen up like an ocean in the morning
early in the morning
before the cream dries in the bushes
in the morning
when you hear the rooster cry
cry rooster cry
in the morning in the morning in my evilness of this morning

I said
disguised in my mouth as a swampland
nailed to my teeth like a rising sun
you come out in the middle of fish-scales
you bleed into gourds wrapped with red ants
you syncopate the air with lungs like screams from yazoo
like X rated tongues
and nickel plated fingers of a raw ghost man
you touch brown nipples into knives
and somewhere stripped like a whirlwind
stripped for the shrine room
you sing to me through the side face of a black rooster

In the morning in the morning in the morning

[1981]

Reunion

Thadious M. Davis

(for Frances)
Girls together we think
eyeing each other's womanhood
your two sturdy-legged sons
their fingers dimpled touch
smear soothe your house or heart
my matched pair of Siamese
their eyes cool survey
guard guide my study or mood

Girls together once in the city that care forgot
during hot evenings elongated summers
the two of us in the sweat of days
growing through ankle socks knee-highs
ribbons and headbands

Girls together sharing pleasures that girls will
we fix our hair with Dixie Peach[1]
eye-buy flats at Maison Blanche
giggle at CYO socials
we slow drag to Aaron Neville[2]
and smell of Avon

Girls together riding the St. Charles car
round the belt just for adventure
we stand arm-in-arm against the turn-off
lingering on neutral grounds to talk secret-talk
we phone in the dark and whisper
things that girls dream

Girls together storing valuable in snaps and diaries
we read about worlds outside the South
learn to kiss behind hibiscus
to feast on oyster loaves   cherry cokes
we discover differences
in boys and books

Growing together
we measure distance like rings on palm trees
move up   out
spread frond-like in casual directions apart
at home or away in college and marriage
but with every growth we remember how
we laid by a stock of coal
to warm cold spells ahead
(those sharp seasons that come damp and certain
in exotic New Orleans and tropical girlhood)

Now in our separate grown-woman-space we light
together our chunks of coal against chills
we hear our voices clairvoyant
Girls together   in warmth
we see into ourselves the love
we know into our nights the bond

[1981]

---

[1] Dixie Peach, a thick hair oil and conditioner for Black hair.
[2] Aaron Neville, a studio musician and vocalist from New Orleans, Louisiana, who rose to
    fame during the late 1960s as a keyboard player.

Adolescence—I

Rita Dove

In water-heavy nights behind grandmother's porch
We knelt in the tickling grasses and whispered:
Linda's face hung before us, pale as a pecan,
And it grew wise as she said:
    "A boy's lips are soft,
    As soft as baby's skin."
The air closed over her words.
A firefly whirred near my ear, and in the distance
I could hear streetlamps ping
Into miniature suns
Against a feathery sky.

[1989]

Adolescence—II

Rita Dove

Although it is night, I sit in the bathroom, waiting.
Sweat prickles behind my knees, the baby-breasts are alert.
Venetian blinds slice up the moon; the tiles quiver in pale strips.

Then they come, the three seal men with eyes as round
As dinner plates and eyelashes like sharpened tines.
They bring the scent of licorice. One sits in the washbowl,

One on the bathtub edge; one leans against the door.
"Can you feel it yet?" they whisper.
I don't know what to say, again. They chuckle,

Patting their sleek bodies with their hands.
"Well, maybe next time." And they rise,
Glittering like pools of ink under moonlight,

And vanish. I clutch at the ragged holes
They leave behind, here at the edge of darkness.
Night rests like a ball of fur on my tongue.

[1989]

Rita Dove

With Dad gone, Mom and I worked
The dusky rows of tomatoes.
As they glowed orange in sunlight
And rotted in shadow, I too
Grew orange and softer, swelling out
Starched cotton slips.

The texture of twilight made me think of
Lengths of Dotted Swiss. In my room
I wrapped scarred knees in dresses
That once went to big-band dances;
I baptized my earlobes with rosewater.
Along the window-sill, the lipstick stubs
Glittered in their steel shells.

Looking out at the rows of clay
And chicken manure, I dreamed how it would happen:
He would meet me by the blue spruce,
A carnation over his heart, saying,
"I have come for you, Madam;
I have loved you in my dreams."
At his touch, the scabs would fall away.
Over his shoulder, I see my father coming toward us:
He carries his tears in a bowl,
And blood hangs in the pine-soaked air.

[1989]

Dear John Wayne

Louise Erdrich

August and the drive-in picture is packed.
We lounge on the hood of the Pontiac
surrounded by the slow-burning spirals they sell
at the window, to vanquish the hordes of mosquitoes.
Nothing works. They break through the smoke-screen for blood.

Always the look-out spots the Indians first,
spread north to south, barring progress.
The Sioux, or Cheyenne, or some bunch
in spectacular columns, arranged like SAC[1] missiles,
their feathers bristling in the meaningful sunset.

The drum breaks. There will be no parlance.
Only the arrows whining, a death-cloud of nerves
swarming down on the settlers
who die beautifully, tumbling like dust weeds
into the history that brought us all here
together: this wide screen beneath the sign of the bear.

The sky fills, acres of blue squint and eye
that the crowd cheers. His face moves over us,
a thick cloud of vengeance, pitted
like the land that was once flesh. Each rut,
each scar makes a promise: *It is
not over, this fight, not as long as you resist.*

Everything we see belongs to us.
A few laughing Indians fall over the hood
slipping in the hot spilled butter.
The eye sees a lot, John, but the heart is so blind.
How will you know what you own?
He smiles, a horizon of teeth
the credits reel over, and then the white fields
again blowing in the true-to-life dark.
The dark films over everything.
We get into the car
scratching our mosquito bites, speechless and small
as people are when the movie is done.
We are back in ourselves.

How can we help but keep hearing his voice,
the flip side of the sound-track, still playing:
*Come on, boys, we've got them
where we want them, drunk, running.
They will give us what we want, what we need:
The heart is a strange wood inside of everything
we see, burning, doubling, splitting out of its skin.*

[1988]

[1] SAC missiles, Strategic Air Command missiles.

I Am a Black Woman

Mari Evans

I am a black woman
the music of my song
some sweet arpeggio[1] of tears
is written in a minor key
and I
can be heard humming in the night
Can be heard
        humming
in the night

I saw my mate leap screaming to the sea
and I/with these hands/cupped the lifebreath
from my issue in the canebreak
I lost Nat's swinging body in a rain of tears
and heard my son scream all the way from Anzio[2]
for Peace he never knew. . . . I
learned Da Nang[3] and Pork Chop Hill[4]
in anguish
Now my nostrils know the gas
and these trigger tire/d fingers
seek the softness in my warrior's beard

      I
      am a black woman
      tall as a cypress
      strong
      beyond all definition still
      defying place
      and time

---

[1] Arpeggio, notes of a chord sounding in rapid succession instead of together.

[2] Anzio, province of southern central Italy, a port of the Tyrrhenian Sea. In January 1944, allied troops landed here to draw German troops from Cassino and allow a break through to Rome.

[3] Da Nang, South Vietnam's second largest city and site of the northernmost major air base. In 1965 the landing of the Ninth Marine Expeditionary Brigade at Da Nang marked the first significant introduction to United States ground forces.

[4] Pork Chop Hill, a widely publicized battle scene in the Korean War.

and circumstance
  assailed
    impervious
      indestructible
Look
  on me and be
renewed

[1983]

Adulthood

Nikki Giovanni

(for claudia)
i usta wonder who i'd be

when i was a little girl in indianapolis
sitting on doctors porches with post-dawn pre-debs
(wondering would my aunt drag me to church sunday)
i was meaningless
and i wondered if life
would give me a chance to mean

i found a new life in the withdrawal from all things
not like my image

when i was a teen-ager i usta sit
on front steps conversing
the gym teachers son with embryonic eyes
about the essential essence of the universe
(and other bullshit stuff)
recognizing the basic powerlessness of me

but then i went to college where i learned
that just because everything i was was unreal
i could be real and not just real through withdrawal
into emotional crosshairs or colored bourgeoisie intellectual pretensions
but from involvement with things approaching reality
i could possibly have a life

so catatonic emotions and time wasting sex games
were replaced with functioning commitments to logic and
necessity and the gray area was slowly darkened into
a black thing
for a while progress was being made along with a certain degree
of happiness cause i wrote a book and found a love
and organized a theatre and even gave some lectures on
Black history
and began to believe all good people could get
together and win without bloodshed
then
hammarskjold was killed
and lumumba was killed
and diem was killed
and kennedy was killed
and malcolm was killed
and evers was killed
and schwerner, chaney and goodman were killed
and liuzzo was killed
and stokely fled the country
and le roi was arrested
and rap was arrested
and pollard, thompson and cooper were killed
and king was killed
and kennedy was killed
and i sometimes wonder why i didn't become a debutante
sitting on porches, going to church all the time, wondering
is my eye make-up on straight
or a withdrawn discoursing on the stars and moon
instead of a for real Black person who must now feel
and inflict
pain

[1978]

The Second Time

Rebecca Gonzales

The second time to love
we avoid absolutes,
as the marsh refuses
to be either land or water;

we walk cautiously
along frayed banks,
like herons
on hinged legs;

we push measured roots,
as the marsh grass does,
squeezing deep to find water,
shallow not to drink too much,

we are careful
to breathe in unison
to distinguish us
from the predators;

we grow the curious strength
of tender rice sprouts
growing green
out of the water;

and every now and then
we sun our frailties
in the frank view of alligators
just to feel vulnerable again.

[1981]

When I Cut My Hair

Rayna Green

when I cut my hair
at thirty-five
Grandma said she'd forgive me
for cutting it
without her permission

but I cried out everytime
I touched my head

years from then
and Grandma dead
it came back to me last night when
you said you wanted it all

your rich body grounding me safe
the touch of your hair
took me out
I saw pigeon feathers
red wool
and fur

and it wrapped me
with the startled past
so sudden
your hair falling all around us

I touched center
and forgave myself

[1984]

Motown/Smokey Robinson

Jessica Hagedorn

hey girl, how long you been here?
did you come with yr daddy in 1959 on a second-class boat
cryin' all the while cuz you didn't want to leave the barrio
the girls back there who wore their hair loose
lotsa orange lipstick and movies on sundays
quiapo market[1] in the morning, yr grandma chewin' red tobacco
roast pig? . . . yeah, and it tasted good . . .
hey girl, did you haveta live in stockton with yr daddy
and talk to old farmers who emigrated in 1941?
did yr daddy promise you to a fifty-eight-year-old bachelor
who stank of cigars . . . and did you
run away to san francisco / go to poly high / rat your hair /
hang around woolworth's / chinatown at three in the morning
go to the cow palace and catch SMOKEY ROBINSON
cry and scream at his gold jacket
Dance every friday night in the mission / go steady with ruben?
(yr daddy can't stand it cuz he's a spik)

---

[1] Quiapo market, a fishing village market in Chile where grain, vegetables, and livestock are
   sold.

and the sailors you dreamed of in manila with yellow hair
did they take you to the beach to ride the ferris wheel?
Life's never been so fine!
you and carmen harmonize "be my baby" by the ronettes
and 1965 you get laid at a party / carmen's house
and you get pregnant and ruben marries you
and you give up harmonizing . . .
hey girl, you sleep without dreams
and remember the barrios and how it's all the same:
manila / the mission / chinatown / east l.a. / harlem / fillmore st.
and you're gettin' kinda fat and smokey robinson's gettin' old

> *ooh baby baby baby*
> *ooh baby baby*
> *ooh . . .*

but he still looks good!!!

> *i love you*
> *i need you*
> *i need you*
> *i want you*
> *ooh ooh*
> *baby baby*
> *ooh*

[1983]

Spider Dream

Elaine Hall

I woke this morning and sunlight
    scalded my face
I went into the kitchen to make tea
    saw a spider drinking from the tap
(I say sunlight scalded my face, but
    my window faces west)

The spider's egg-sac was full
I went to bed and slept awhile

My left leg hurt in my sleep and
      when I woke again, I saw
      an open sore running the length
      of an old scar
(I had injured that leg on a tin can
      when I was five)

In this open scar gleamed the eggs
      Mother-Spider had buried in me
Spiders, new life, hatching
      running out in all directions
To find water
      or forgiveness
      or
      a way to be?

[1984]

I Give You Back

Joy Harjo

I release you, my beautiful and terrible
fear. I release you. You were my beloved
and hated twin, but now, I don't know you
as myself. I release you with all the
pain I would know at the death of
my daughters.

You are not my blood anymore.

I give you back to the white soldiers
who burned down my home, beheaded my children,
raped and sodomized my brothers and sisters.
I give you back to those who stole the
food from our plates when we were starving.

I release you, fear, because you hold
these scenes in front of me and I was born
with eyes that can never close.

I release you, fear, so you can no longer
keep me naked and frozen in the winter,
or smothered under blankets in the summer.

I release you
I release you
I release you
I release you

I am not afraid to be angry.
I am not afraid to rejoice.
I am not afraid to be black.
I am not afraid to be white.
I am not afraid to be hungry.
I am not afraid to be full.
I am not afraid to be hated.
I am not afraid to be loved.

to be loved, to be loved, fear.

Oh, you have choked me, but I gave you the leash.
You have gutted me but I gave you the knife.
You have devoured me, but I laid myself across the fire.
You held my mother down and raped her,
                 but I gave you the heated thing.

I take myself back, fear.
You are not my shadow any longer.
I won't hold you in my hands.
You can't live in my eyes, my ears, my voice
my belly, or in my heart my heart
my heart   my heart

But come here, fear
I am alive and you are so afraid
                       of dying.

[1983]

The History of Fire

Linda Hogan

My mother is a fire beneath stone.
My father, lava.

My grandmother is a match,
my sister straw.

Grandfather is kindling like trees of the world.
My brothers are gunpowder,

and I am smoke with gray hair,
ash with black fingers and palms.

I am wind for the fire.

My dear one is a jar of burned bones
I have saved.

This is where our living goes
and still we breathe,

and even the dry grass
with sun and lightning above it

has no choice but to grow
and then lie down

with no other end in sight.

Air is between these words,
fanning the flame.

[1988]

The Lost Girls

Linda Hogan

I don't remember when
the girl of myself turned her back
and walked away, that girl
whose thin arms
once held this body
and refused to work too hard
or listen in school, said the hell then
and turned,
that dark child,
that laughter and weeper
without shame, who turned
and skipped away.

And that other one
gone from me
and me
not even starting to knot
in vein or joint,
that curving girl
I loved to love with,
who danced away
the leather of red high heels
and thin legs, dancing like stopping
would mean the end of the world
and it does.

We go on
or we don't,
knowing about our inner women
and when they left us
like we were bad mothers or lovers
who wronged ourselves.

Some days it seems
one of them is watching, a shadow
at the edge of woods
with loose hair
clear down the back
and arms with dark moles
crossed before the dress I made
with my two red hands.

You there, girl, take my calloused hand.
I'm going to laugh and weep tonight,
quit all my jobs and I mean it this time,
do you believe me? I'm going to
put on those dancing shoes
and move till I can't stand
it anymore,
then touch myself clear down
to the sole of each sweet foot. That's all
the words I need,
not poems, not that talking mother
I was with milk and stories
peeking in at night,
but that lover of the moon
dancing outside when no one looks,
all right, then, even when they do,
and kissing each leaf of trees and squash,
and loving all the girls and women
I have always been.

[1988]

What I Said as a Child

Angela Jackson

What I said as a child I say
as a woman:
>   There is romance in common
>   movement
>   of sound and sand.
>   Religion of a
>   kind is
>   true, affirmed.

>   Ours is the worn water and ripe fire, leaves
>   that burn alongside the road
>   into
>   smoke
>   thick as Nigerian oil. A cover
>   for
>   magic and skill

We balanced a house of extended families
               atop our heads.
The music drifted down
               around our faces.
Wind crossed our cheeks
               in scarifications.
Spirits feathered around our waists
and fell to our knees:
a dance
of prayers that I said as a child
I say again:

We walked in the air of the ancestors, hot, and tight
like
the space between two breasts. A crossing
of tongues
in the middle of an African night

The future is a quiet bed, a spread
               of hunger, and fallenwish
       is mystery to divine:
a drug technique
               hidden in a man's hands.
We sit on the edge of our own echo, and craft.

What I said as a child I say as a woman:

We are from a house of balance and control.
The road ahead is burning smoke and oils.
What comes after is an act of will.

[1987]

In Her Solitude:
The Inca Divining Spider (Ana)

Angela Jackson

It is dark in the pot
where he keeps me. The Inca priest
with gold rings on his golden wrist.

El Dorado. I smell the clay and the sweat
from the human hands that made
my bowl of solitude.
Where I wait in darkness,
captive, humming.

The priest, his hand trembles when he
lets in sun to look at me.
He squints
at the way I sit.
When I sprawl, legs spread,
extravagantly, loitering
in my pot—it's a good sign
and his teeth glint a smile.
When I sit
with even one leg folded
under me
like the woman that I am
with a bad attitude—he trembles
from smile to fingers—
tremors. I am a Bad
Omen.

He seals me in again
and prays and prays
for my legs to
open.

[1984]

I Done Got So Thirsty That My
Mouth Waters at the Thought of Rain

Patricia Jones

i done got so thirsty that my mouth waters
at the thought of rain
let it come down on into me/ like this pain
let it just intensify my eyes
let the will slip away in an avalanche of tears
all choked up
all choked up

all choked up
been dancing on a dream too long
& found myself lost in this desert/ no
lovers tonight/ not a one
no rain for days
got too much sun/ burning through my heart
every bone/ muscle/ corpuscle
aches
aches
aches
been running through these streets
looking for a coolness/ a coolness
been running through these streets
looking for your face/ your face/ that
soft smile/ long gone/ cross that barrier
past tense
songs rolling on the tongues of angels
i don't hear them/ off at a distance/ six
men beat up on one/ bottle breaks/ blue lights
flashing/ get the cops/ GET THE COPS/ a
screaming/ through the dancing music
. a quick mambo baby 'fore i goes
yeah
& the tight lips of the drunken women
they walk past the windows/ broken/ like
the windows/ oh these women/ bellies so swollen
tongues don't move 'cept to curse/ oh these
women broken/ like glass gouged into the
face of the pendejito[1] who was in the wrong
place on the wrong saturday night
come on
come on
come on
come on rain/ come on water/ down this dry
throat/ got no time for dying like this/ in
the sun/ give me some greenery/ some fertility
tell me bout female forms & what happens to
them when they are abandoned
all you get is sticks & mud/ drying

i been thirsty so long that my mouth feels
like parchment/ got words written cross it/ dead
stories bout dead feelings/ dried up/ dead
i been this thirsty so long that my hands are

[1] Pendejito, meaning punk or hoodlum.

crusts of brown bread flaking out into the
fields eaten by dying men/ no sustenance
no dreams/ dancing

i been thirsty been dry been drinking in the
sun/ no moisture/ not a drop of blood saliva
all of it taken out of me removed/ the removal
of fingers/ the loss of touch/ what is velvet &
how am i to know your lips/ the whore's short skirt
reveals soft flabby knees that bulge with fat wishes
loss of taste/ what makes me come/ nothing/ i just
do it/ for the money/ for the time passing/ no man's
hands can ever move me/ again/ my voice is the dryest
wind/ hard sound/ diamonds on the sidewalk/ what is in her
hair/ that scent/ god only knows/ what ever did he do
this for/ why are you looking at the other way/ what happened
here/ just this desert dry sand falling falling on the
orphan and the whore/ some want light in the darkness
candles have turned my soul to ashes/ what kinds of
movements/ slow/ slow/ slow i've been so thirsty/ so truly
in need of liquids/ water/ wine/ whiskey/ leche con dulces
dulces/ sweet water on my tongue/ need to move these female
forms round over this dry ground/ need to get down eighth
avenue without seeing broken women pass by/ as bottles break
cross the pendejo's throat & the cops come
too late

i've been thirsty so long my mouth dreams
at the thought of water dancing
dancing in the blood of women dripping
on the sidewalk like flooded houses
wasted of time and touch

[1981]

War and Memory

June Jordan

(Dedicated to Jane Creighton)

I

Daddy at the stove or sink. Large
knife nearby or artfully
suspended by his clean hand handsome
even in its menace
slamming the silverware drawer
open and shut/the spoons
suddenly loud as the yelling
at my mother
no (she would say) no
Granville no
about: would he
be late/had she
hidden away the Chinese laundry shirts
again/did she think
it right that he (a man in his own house)
should serve himself a cup of tea a plate
of food/perhaps she thought that he
should cook the cabbage and the pot roast
for himself
as well?
It sure did seem she wanted him to lose
his job because she could not find
the keys
he could not find
and no (she would attempt to disagree)
no Granville no
but was he
trying to destroy her with his mouth
"My mouth?!" my Daddy hunkered down
incredulous and burly now
with anger, "What you mean, 'My mouth'?! You, woman!
  Who
you talk to in that way?
I am master of this castle!" Here
he'd gesture with a kitchen fork
around the sagging clutter
laugh and choke the rage tears
watering his eyes: "You no to speak to me

like that: You hear?
You damn Black woman!"
And my mother
backing up or hunching smaller
than frail bones should easily allow
began to munch on saltine
crackers
let the flat crumbs scatter on her full lips
and the oilcloth
on the table

"You answer me!" he'd scream, at last:
"I speak to you. You answer me!"
And she might struggle then
to swallow
or to mumble finally out loud:
"And who are you supposed to be? The Queen
of England? Or the King?"
And he
berserk with fury lifted
chair or frying pan
and I'd attack
in her defense: "No
Daddy! No!" rushing for his knees
and begging, "Please
don't, Daddy, please!"
He'd come down hard: My head
break into daylight pain
or rip me spinning crookedly across the floor.
I'd match him fast
for madness
lineage in wild display
age six
my pigtails long enough to hang me
from the ceiling
I would race about for weaponry
another chair a knife
a flowered glass
the radio
"You stop it, Daddy! Stop it!":
brandishing my arsenal
my mother
silently
beside the point.
He'd seize me or he'd duck the glass
"You devil child!
You damn Black devil child!"

"And what are you supposed to be?"
My mother might inquire
from the doorway:
"White? Are you supposed to be a white man
Granville?"
"Not white, but right!" And I would have to bite and kick
or race away
sometimes out the house and racing
still for blocks
my daddy chasing
after me

II

Daddy at the table reading
all about the Fiji Islanders or childhood
in Brazil
his favorite National Geographic research
into life beyond our
neighborhood
my mother looking into
the refrigerator
"Momma!" I cried, after staring at the front page
photo of The Daily News.
"What's this a picture of?"
It was Black and White,
But nothing else. No people
and no houses anywhere. My mother
came and took a look above my shoulder.
"It's about the Jews": she said.
"The Jews?"
"It's not! It's more about those Nazis!" Daddy
interjected.
"No, Granville, no!
It's about the Jews. In the war going on,"
my mother amplified, "the German soldiers
take away the Jewish families and they make
them march through snow until they die!"

"What kind of an ignorant
woman are you?" Daddy shouted out, "It's
not the snow. It's Nazi camps: the concentration
camps!"
"The camps?" I asked them, eagerly: "The Nazis?"
I was quite confused, "But in this picture,
Daddy, I can't see nobody."
"*Any*body," he corrected me: "You can't see

anybody!" "Yes, but what," I persevered, "what is this a
picture of?"
"That's the trail of blood left by the Jewish girls
and women on the snow because the Germans
make them march so long."
"Does the snow make feet bleed, Momma?
Where does the bleeding come from?"

My mother told me I should put away
the papers and not continue to upset myself
about these things I could not understand
and I remember
wondering if my family was a war
going on
and if
there would soon be blood
someplace in the house
and where
the blood of my family would come from

III

The Spanish Civil War:
I think I read about that one.

IV

Joan DeFreitas/2 doors up
she latched onto a soldier
fat cat bulging at the belt
and he didn't look like Hollywood
said he should
so I couldn't picture him defending
me or anyone
but then I couldn't picture war or North
Korea
at that time

V

There was tv
There were buses down to Washington, D.C.
You could go and meet your friends
from everywhere.
It was very exciting.
The tear gas burned like crazy.
The President kept lying to us.

Crowd counts at the rallies.
Body counts on the news.
Ketchup on the steps of universities.
Blood on the bandages around the head of the Vietnamese
women shot between the eyes.
Big guys.

Aerial spray missions.
Little people
Shot at close range
"Hell no! We won't go!"
"Hell no! We won't go!"
Make love
Kill anything that moves.
Kent State.[1]
American artillery unlimited at Jackson State[2]
Who raised these devil children?
Who invented these Americans with pony
tails and Afros and tee shirts and statistical
arguments against the mining of the harbors
of a country far away?

And I remember turning from the footage of the tat-tat-tat-
tat-tat-tat
helicopters
and I wondered how democracy would travel from the graves
at Kent State
to the hidden trenches
of Hanoi

VI

Plump during The War on Poverty
I remember making pretty good
money (6 bucks an hour)

[1] In 1970 student protests at Kent State University, over the U.S. invasion of Cambodia, led authorities to bring in the National Guard. The protest escalated and guardsmen shot thirteen students; four of the students were killed—of the thirteen students hit, the majority of them had no connection with the disturbance. They had only been passing to their next class.

[2] In 1970 a student protest was organized at Jackson State University, a traditionally black college in Jackson, Mississippi. The students were protesting for social justice, for Black studies in the curriculum, and against the invasion of Cambodia. During the protest, police killed two students. Many were outraged because, although the Kent State deaths were a tragedy and were nationally and internationally condemned, hardly any public or media attention was given to the two black students killed that same year at Jackson State.

as a city planner and my former
husband married my best
friend and I was never positive
about the next month's rent but
once I left my son sitting
on his lunchbox in the early rain
waiting for a day-care pickup and I went
to redesign low-income housing for the Lower
East Side of Manhattan and three hours after that
I got a phone call from my neighbors
that the pickup never came
that Christopher was waiting
on the sidewalk
in his yellow slicker
on his lunchbox
in the rain.

VII

I used to sometimes call the government
to tell them how my parents
ate real butter or stole sugar
from The Victory Rations
we received

I sometimes called the Operator
asking for Police
to beat my father up for beating me
so bad
but no one listened to
a tattletale
like me:

I think I felt relieved
because the government didn't send a rescue
face or voice to my imagination
and I hated
the police
but what else could you do?

Peace never meant a thing to me.

I wanted everyone to mold
the plastic bag for margerine
save stamps
plant carrots
and

(imitating Joe "Brown Bomber" Louis)
fight hard
fight fair
And from the freedom days
that blazed outside my mind
I fell in love
I fell in love with Black men White
men Black
women White women
and I
dared myself to say The Palestinians
and I
worried about unilateral words like Lesbian or Nationalist
and I
tried to speak Spanish when I travelled to Managua
and I
dreamed about The Fourteenth Amendment
and I
defied the hatred of the hateful everywhere
as best I could
I mean
I took long nightly walks to emulate the Chinese
    Revolutionaries
and I
always wore one sweater less than absolutely necessary to
    keep warm

and I wrote everything I knew how to write against apartheid
and I
thought I was a warrior growing up
and I
buried my father with all of the ceremony all of the music
    I could piece together
and I
lust for justice
and I
make that quest arthritic/pigeon-toed/however
and I
invent the mother of the courage I require not to quit

[1989]

Alison Kim

I like crack-seed
After I married
I no like.
I like only sewing.
Too busy for eat anything.

Uncle Allen two years older than Uncle Albert
and Uncle Albert one year older than your mother
Your mother two years older than Aunty Alma
Aunty Alma one year older than Tom
and Tom one year older than Boy
and Boy two years older than Uncle Bung Choy

Seven kids I have
I raise them all my own
My husband no give me money
I sew all my kids' clothes
And I try to sell to the neighbors
I sell one dress for one dollar.

I like crack-seed
After married
I no like.
I like only sewing.
Too busy for eat anything.

[1989]

Into Such Assembly

Myung Mi Kim

1.

Can you read and write English? Yes __. No __.
Write down the following sentences in English as I dictate them.
 There is a dog in the road.
 It is raining.
Do you renounce allegiance to any other country but this?
Now tell me, who is the president of the United States?
You will all stand now. Raise your right hands.

Cable car rides over swan-flecked ponds
Red lacquer chests in our slateblue house
Chrysanthemums trailing bloom after bloom
Ivory, russet, pale yellow petals crushed
Between fingers, that green smell, if jade would smell
So-Sah's thatched roofs shading miso hung to dry—
Sweet potatoes grow on the rock-choked side of the mountain
The other, the pine wet green side of the mountain
Hides a lush clearing where we picnic and sing:
 Sung-Bul-Sah, geep eun bahm ae[1]

Neither, neither

Who is mother tongue, who is father country?

2.

Do they have trees in Korea? Do the children eat out of garbage cans?

We had a Dalmation
We rode the train on weekends from Seoul to So-Sah[2] where we grew grapes

We ate on the patio surrounded by dahlias

Over there, ass is cheap—those girls live to make you happy

Over there, we had a slateblue house with a flat roof where
I made many snowmen, over there

---

[1] *Sung Bul Sah* is the name of the Buddhist temple; *geep eun bahm ae* means late at night or
 midnight. The whole phrase refers to a passage from a Korean folk song: "late at night at
 the temple."
[2] So-Sah is a town between Seoul and Inchon.

No, "th", "th", put your tongue against the roof of your mouth,
lean slightly against the back of the top teeth, then bring your
bottom teeth up to barely touch your tongue and breathe out, and
you should feel the tongue vibrating, "th", "th", look in the mirror,
that's better

And with distance traveled, as part of it

How often when it rains here does it rain there?

One gives over to a language and then

What is given, given over?

3.

This rain eats into most anything

    And when we had been scattered over the face of the earth
    We could not speak to one another

The creek rises, the rain-fed current rises

    Color given up, sap given up
    Weeds branches groves what they make as one

This rain gouging already gouged valleys
And they fill, fill, flow over

    What gives way losing gulch, mesa, peak, state, nation

Land, ocean dissolving
The continent and the peninsula, the peninsula and continent
Of one piece sweeping

One table laden with one crumb
Every mouthful off a spoon whole

Each drop strewn into such assembly

[1989]

On Writing Asian-American Poetry

Geraldine Kudaka

Takamura Kotaro°
speaks
of fireplaces
ancient magpie homes
where
Chieko° lived

    my mixed up
    poems
    are hybrid races:
    an american birth

Takahashi Mutsuo°
knows
of minos, pungent sex,
male tongues,
and sturdy legs

    under a terrible
    sunrise
    my grandparents
    came to america

Shiraishi Kazuko°
swirls cocks
and shadows
into statuesque carvings

    we ate rice
    and langendorf bread
    plates of
    padded bras, blondes,
    John Wayne, pigs n tofu

shinkansen° trains rush by
transporting kimono bodies
in suits and ties

    we said the pledge
    of allegiance
    and learned english
    as a 2nd language

A Japanese poet

*The wife of Kotaro in the Japanese film
Portrait of Chieko*

A Japanese poet

A Japanese poet

high-speed trains

outside new york
there is a
blizzard blazing

i invited you over
& fed you tea
behind coy hands you
snickered

> *Ne chotto suifu-san*
> *Umi kara agatta bakari no°*

"Hello, sailor boy / In from the sea!"
(Asakawa Maki's translation of an
excerpt from Langston Hughes's "Port
Town.")

you took my poems
you took my soul
your hands rusty hangers
aborting my child

> we learned racism
> & believed
> blondes had more fun

you became the judge
and i condemned
your lily white suburbs
and i ghetto splattered

> *my tempura-kim chi° menu*
> *spilled on tatami mat*
> my black hair black eyes
> scan your proper stance

names of food dishes

Asakawa Maki°
jazz priestess of
japaaan
wails Langston Hughes

Japanese jazz singer

> *Ne chotto suifu-san*
> *Umi kara agatta bakari no*

in america
did the vastness
of camps
feed
myopic vision?

i s h o u l d a t o l d y o u

last nite
i shoulda told you
you're not my friend
anymore

i shoulda said
something like/   are you
one of them
eternal children
them momma cooks n cleans
them turn out
saccharin sweet

i shoulda told you
'bout ladies & them
wouldbesaxmen
who can't understand
a word of poetry

i could catch
myself
hanging rumours
out to dry,
trying to objectify
bass clefs
& syncopated sounds

& 'stead of going
crazy,
i'd pick up a stethoscope &
in fine print
the by-lines glare
Everybody's Got a Melody

his receiver works
intermittently
& is sooo cooool
wrapped up in tapedeck
spools
& spinnin' on
six feet down

someone shoulda told you
when a man
does what he loves best,
he's never angry or
bitter or phony or cruel

& sometimes
even Viva Ricado
goes off
the brink
'cause it's hard to be cool
& contented
every day of the week

&, oh yeah,
i didn't tell you
three hours
before
i was cookin' his food
& feelin' kinda blue

i can't be bottling up
like good vintage wine

& feelin' kinda blue
i started to cry
& his screaming words
slammed thru the air
& it was cold cold
                cold

i shoulda told you
i can sing the blues

[1980]

Wonder Woman

Genny Lim

Sometimes I see reflections on bits of glass on sidewalks
I catch the glimmer of empty bottles floating out to sea
Sometimes I stretch my arms way above my head and wonder if
There are women along the Mekong[1] doing the same

[1] *Mekong*—The largest stream on the Indochinese Peninsula. It flows southeastward from Tibet
and forms part of the boundary between Thailand and Laos.

Sometimes I stare longingly at women who I will never know
Generous, laughing women with wrinkled cheeks and white teeth
Dragging along chubby, rosy-cheeked babies on fat, wobbly legs
Sometimes I stare at Chinese grandmothers
Getting on the 30 Stockton with shopping bags
Japanese women tourists in European hats
Middle-aged mothers with laundry carts
Young wives holding hands with their husbands
Lesbian women holding hands in coffee-houses
Smiling debutantes with bouquets of yellow daffodils
Silver-haired matrons with silver rhinestoned poodles
Painted prostitutes posing along MacArthur Boulevard
Giddy teenage girls snapping gum in fast cars
Widows clutching bibles, crucifixes

I look at them and wonder if
They are a part of me
I look in their eyes and wonder if
They share my dreams

I wonder if the woman in mink is content
If the stockbroker's wife is afraid of growing old
If the professor's wife is an alcoholic
If the woman in prison is me

There are copper-tanned women in Hyannis Port[2] playing tennis
Women who eat with finger bowls
There are women in factories punching time clocks
Women tired every waking hour of the day
I wonder why there are women born with silver spoons
   in their mouths
Women who have never known a day of hunger
Women who have never changed their own bed linen
And I wonder why there are women who must work
Women who must clean other women's houses
Women who must shell shrimps for pennies a day
Women who must sew other women's clothes
Who must cook
Who must die
In childbirth
In dreams

Why must woman stand divided?
Building the walls that tear them down?

[2] Hyannis Port, Massachusetts, a summer resort, located on the southern part of Cape Cod.

Jill-of-all-trades
Lover, mother, housewife, friend, breadwinner
Heart and spade
A woman is a ritual
A house that must accommodate
A house that must endure
Generation after generation
Of wind and torment, of fire and rain
A house with echoing rooms
Closets with hidden cries
Walls with stretchmarks
Windows with eyes

Short, tall, skinny, fat
Pregnant, married, white, yellow, black, brown, red
Professional, working-class, aristocrat
Women cooking over coals in sampans
Women shining tiffany spoons in glass houses
Women stretching their arms way above the clouds
In Samarkand, in San Francisco
Along the Mekong

[1981]

Children Are Color-blind

Genny Lim

I never painted myself yellow
the way I colored the sun when I was five.
The way I colored whitefolks with the "flesh" crayola.
Yellow pages adults thumbed through for restaurants,
taxis, airlines, plumbers . . .
The color of summer squash, corn, eggyolk, innocence and tapioca.

My children knew before they were taught.
They envisioned rainbows emblazoned over alleyways;
Clouds floating over hilltops like a freedom shroud.
With hands clasped, time dragged them along and they followed.

Wind-flushed cheeks persimmon,
eyes dilated like dark pearls staring out the backseat windows,
they speed through childhood like greyhounds
into the knot of night, hills fanning out,
an ocean ending at an underpass,
a horizon blunted by lorries, skyscrapers,
vision blurring at the brink of poverty.

Dani, my three-year-old, recites the alphabet from
billboards flashing by like pages of a cartoon flipbook,
where above, carpetbaggers patrol the freeways like
Olympic gods hustling their hi-tech neon gospel,
looking down from the fast lane,
dropping Kool dreams, booze dreams, fancy car dreams,
fast foods dreams, sex dreams and no-tomorrow dreams
like eight balls into your easy psychic pocket.

"Only girls with black hair, black eyes can join!"
My eight-year-old was chided at school for excluding a blonde
from her circle. "Only girls with black hair, black eyes
can join!" taunted the little Asian girls, black hair,
black eyes flashing, mirroring, mimicking what they heard
as the message of the medium, the message of the world-at-large:
 "Apartheid, segregation, self-determination!
 Segregation, apartheid, revolution!"
Like a contrapuntal[1] hymn, like a curse that refrains in
a melody trapped.

Sometimes at night I touch the children when they're sleeping
and the coolness of my fingers sends shivers through them that
is a foreshadowing, a guilt imparted.

Dani doesn't paint herself yellow
the way I colored the sun.
The way she dances in its light as I watch from the shadow.
No, she says green is her favorite color.
"It's the color of life!"

[1989]

---

[1] Contrapuntal, marked by counterpoint.

I Am the Weaver

Abbey Lincoln (Aminata Moseka)

I am the weaver.
I knit and sew and twine and braid and
plait and twist and turn and
zig zag and compose and
create and make things be . . .
See, makin' it is the magic word for me,
I am the weaver . . . and knead
and press and paste and mass and
make dough and bread.

I am a kneader of a mud wall construction . . .
and bring into being, into form by shaping
and putting parts and ingredients together,
and build, construct, fabricate, fashion,
devise and formulate
ways of doing things,
and cause and bring about and produce
and prepare for use.

I am the weaver and make the beds in which people lie.

I establish
and make a rule
that only members could attend
to get and acquire
and make money . . .
and do and perform
or make a quick movement.

I am the weaver
and succeed in becoming the lover of tricks,
and take with a card and name the trump and
shuffle the cards
in a game . . .
to get a score.
I am the weaver.

To cause something to be
I start to do something.
To go, to proceed, to tend, extend,
to point, to behave in a particular manner,

and make bold,
make steady,
make ready and
make fast.

I increase in depth and volume
and rise and accumulate
as does the tide,
the sea,
water in a ship.

I am widely and variously used
in idiomatic phrases
many of which use the key word—make—
faces,
make fun make
eyes,
make good and make sure.

I am the weaver,
the act and process of making,
the way in which something appears,
is made,
style,
build, construction, type, sort, brand,
the disposition, character
and nature,
the weaver,
the maker.

[1983]

The Woman Thing

Audre Lorde

The hunters are back
from beating the winter's face
in search of a challenge or task
in search of food
making fresh tracks
for their children's hunger

they do not watch the sun
they cannot wear its heat
for a sign of triumph
or freedom.

The hunters are treading heavily
homeward through snow
marked by their own bloody footprints.
Emptyhanded the hunters return
snow-maddened
sustained by their rages.

In the night after food they will seek
young girls for their amusement.
Now the hunters are coming
and the unbaked girls
flee from their angers.

All this day I have craved
food for my child's hunger
emptyhanded
the hunters come shouting
injustice drips from their mouths
like stale snow
melted in sunlight.

The woman thing
my mother taught me
bakes off its covering of snow
like a rising Blackening sun.

[1964]

Offspring

Naomi Long Madgett

I tried to tell her:
    This way the twig is bent.
    Born of my trunk and strengthened by my roots,
    you must stretch newgrown branches
    closer to the sun
    than I can reach.

I wanted to say:
>Extend my self to that far atmosphere
>only my dreams allow.

But the twig broke,
and yesterday I saw her
walking down an unfamiliar street,
>feet confident,
>face slanted upward toward a threatening sky,
and
>she was smiling
>and she was
>her very free
>her very individual
>unpliable
>own.

[1972]

Generations of Women

Janice Mirikitani

I.

>She rests,
rocking to ritual,
the same sun fades
the same blue dress
covering her knees
turned inward
from weariness.
The day is like the work
she shoulders,
sacks of meal, corn, barley.
But her sorrow wears
like steady rain.
She buried him yesterday.
Incense still gathered
in her knuckles knotted
from the rubbings
the massage with nameless

oils, on his swollen gouted feet,
his steel girded back
muscled from carrying calves,
turning brutal rock,
building fields of promises,
gardens alive with camellias,
peaches, clover.

Time has sucked my body.
He is buried
in his one black suit
we kept in mothballs
for that day.
I want to lay next to him
in my goldthreaded wedding
kimono, grandly purple
with white cranes in flight,
drape my bones with
wisteria.
I want to shed the century
of incense resting in my pores
like sweat or dirt.
I want to fly with the birds
in this eternal silk,
heading sunward
for warm matings.
I want this soil
that wraps him
to sleep in the smell
of my work.

    Obachan
walked to the store
wearing respectable
shoes, leather
hard like a wall
against her sole.
She carefully fingered her coins
in the pocket of her thinning
blue dress,
saved for sugar, salt and yellow onions.
The clerk's single syllable spit
out a white wall—
JAP.
She turned to the door
with shopping bag empty as the sound
of her feet in

respectable shoes.
There are no tears
for moments as these.

II.

Her body speaks,
arms long,
thin as a mantis.

> *I am afraid*
> *to leave this room*
> *of myself, imprisoned*
> *by walls of cloth.*
> *Only the man clocks*
> *my moments*
> *as he fingers the*
> *corners of my fabric,*
> *empty buttonholes,*
> *my muslin,*
> *sandy as a desert.*
> *I wait.*
> *I wait for his presence,*
> *my flesh like*
> *sheets drying in the wind.*
> *I wait,*
> *weaving chains of flowers*
> *to scent my hands,*
> *color my skin,*
> *mourn my loss.*
> *I wait*
> *for him to open*
> *the bloom*
> *hidden in the folds*
> *of flannel.*
> *I do not remember*
> *being beautiful or proud.*

Some losses
can't be counted:
departures to desert camps
and barracks,
men leaving to separate
camps or wars
and finally to houses
walled white full with women
in silk dresses,

wilted flowers and rhinestones
around their necks,
fast drinking, quick joking
women with red lipstick
sleek
and slippery as satin.
Her thin arms
chained by wringing
and worry
and barbed wire
slashing her youth,
her neck bowed to history
and past pain that haunts
her like a slain woman-child.

I watched as they
let her die—seventh sister
born like a blue fish into
that dry orange day.
No more women, they prayed,
a son. A son to carry on the name.

Some losses can't be counted:
abandonments left her
frightened, hungry,
made her count the grains
of rice,
wrinkles in her cheek,
pieces of rock in the desert
sand, shadows of guardtower
soldiers, mornings without
waking men,
the syllables of her name.
Some imprisonments are permanent:
white walls encaged her
with a single syllable:
JAP.
Her lips puckered
from humiliations
that made her feel like mildewed cloth,
smelling with neglect.
Her body a room
helpless to the exit of men.
The day he left her for the
red-lipped woman,
she, damp, wringing,
stood between desert camps

and bedrooms,
brooding for unburied female infants,
her thin arms dripping chains
of flowers
weighted with tears.

III.

    Two generations
spit me out
like phlegm,
uncooked rice
one syllable words,
a woman foetus.

[1987]

Loving from Vietnam to Zimbabwe

Janice Mirikitani

Here, in this crimson
room,
with silk skimming our skin,
I shape into thought
these strange burnings
starting in my fingertips
as they lick your nipples,
hairs standing to the touch.

        You are marching in
        the delta
        the river water
        at your boots
        sucking through the leather.
        Sand has caked your color yellow.

Your chest moves
to the rhythm of my heart,
warm skin singing.

You plod, weighted by
days of marching
nights of terror
holding this patch of ground
shaped like a crotch.

My teeth on your
shoulder
hungry to enter your flesh
as you call me strange names.

Water/water
sinking sand.
They are coming
as you raise the blade
of your bayonet,
clean it with
your sweat.

My mouth driven
to your thighs
the sweet inside
just below the swinging
songs of your life.

Deeper into
the Mekong,[1]
The grass has eyes
the wind has flesh
and you feel the trigger
pressed back for release.

Your thighs tremble
your long fingers like marsh grass
in my hair
as I reach down
onto Mt. Inyangani.[2]

You have seen them
hanging in the trees
after american troops
had finished.

[1] See footnote on page 98, *Wonder Woman* by Genny Lim.
[2] Mt. Inyangani, located in southern Zimbabwe and extending south along the Mozambique
    border.

Slanted eyes bugging,
crooked necks,
genitals swinging from
their mouths.

Sweat from your neck
I think they are tears
as I move
into the grassy plain
of your chest.

You never saw them alive
but knew they looked like me
And you got sick a lot
wondering what color
their blood.

As I hold
your skin between my
teeth
I can feel the blood
pulsing
on my tongue
springing like the
beginning
of Zambezi River.[3]

You turned in your rage
knowing how they have used you.
Not the invisible ones
whose soil you were sent to seize
but those behind you,
pushing you,
pulling
        pulling
your trigger.

And I massage
your back
large/black like the shadowed
belly of a leaf
as you in
your stillness
hold me
like a bird.

[3] Zambezi River, one of Africa's great rivers in south central and southeast Africa.

They stripped you.
Held you down
in the sand
took the bayonet off your gun
and began to slice . . .
lopped off your head
and expected you to die.

I, in the heavy
hot air
between us,
in the crimson room
that begins to blur
feel you enter
my harbor/kiss
the lips of my soul.
Call me my Strange Names

My Lai[4]
Bach Mai[5]
Haiphong[6]

Loving in this world
is the sliver splinting
edge
is the dare
in the teeth of the tiger
the pain of jungle rot
the horror of flesh unsealed
the madness of surviving.

[1980]

[4] My Lai, the most publicized massacre of the Vietnam War, 1968. Unarmed civilians, mostly women and children, were killed in the village of My Lai.
[5] Bach Mai, a southern suburb of Hanoi, North Vietnam. It was part of the U.S.-imposed bombing raids on the Hanoi and Haiphong areas.
[6] Haiphong, a main port city of North Vietnam.

Cherríe Moraga

I am a welder.
Not an alchemist.
I am interested in the blend
of common elements to make
a common thing.

No magic here.
Only the heat of my desire to fuse
what I already know
exists. Is possible.

We plead to each other,
we all come from the same rock
we all come from the same rock
ignoring the fact that we bend
at different temperatures
that each of us is malleable
up to a point.

Yes, fusion *is* possible
but only if things get hot enough—
all else is temporary adhesion,
patching up.

It is the intimacy of steel melting
into steel, the fire of our individual
passion to take hold of ourselves
that makes sculpture of our lives,
builds buildings.

And I am not talking about skyscrapers,
merely structures that can support us
without fear
of trembling.

For too long a time
the heat of my heavy hands
has been smoldering
in the pockets of other
people's business—
they need oxygen to make fire.

I am now
coming up for air.
Yes, I *am*
picking up the torch.

I am the welder.
I understand the capacity of heat
to change the shape of things.
I am suited to work
within the realm of sparks
out of control.

I am the welder.
I am taking the power
into my own hands.

[1981]

My Father and the Figtree

Naomi Shihab Nye

For other fruits my father was indifferent.
He'd point at the cherry trees and say,
"See those? I wish they were figs."
In the evenings he sat by my bed
weaving folktales like vivid little scarves.
They always involved a figtree.
Even when it didn't fit, he'd stick it in.
Once Joha was walking down the road and he saw a figtree.
Or, he tied his camel to a figtree and went to sleep.
Or, later when they caught and arrested him,
his pockets were full of figs.

At age six I ate a dried fig and shrugged.
"That's not what I'm talking about!" he said,
"I'm talking about a fig straight from the earth—
gift of Allah!—on a branch so heavy it touches the ground.
I'm talking about picking the largest fattest sweetest fig
in the world and putting it in my mouth."
(Here he'd stop and close his eyes.)

Years passed, we lived in many houses, none had figtrees.
We had lima beans, zucchini, parsley, beets.
"Plant one!" my mother said, but my father never did.
He tended garden half-heartedly, forgot to water,
let the okra get too big.
"What a dreamer he is. Look how many things he starts
and doesn't finish."

The last time he moved, I got a phone call.
My father, in Arabic, chanting a song I'd never heard.
"What's that?" I said.
"Wait till you see!"
He took me out back to the new yard.
There, in the middle of Dallas, Texas,
a tree with the largest, fattest, sweetest figs in the world.
"It's a figtree song!" he said,
plucking his fruits like ripe tokens,
emblems, assurance
of a world that was always his own.

[1978]

Where Will You Be?

Pat Parker

Boots are being polished
Trumpeters clean their horns
Chains and locks forged
The crusade has begun.

Once again flags of Christ
are unfurled in the dawn
and cries of soul saviors
sing apocalyptic on air waves.

Citizens, good citizens all
parade into voting booths
and in self-righteous sanctity
X away our right to life.

I do not believe as some
that the vote is an end,
I fear even more
It is just a beginning.

So I must make assessment
Look to you and ask:
Where will you be
when they come?

They will not come
a mob rolling
through the streets,
but quickly and quietly
move into our homes
and remove the evil,
the queerness,
the faggotry,
the perverseness
from their midst.
They will not come
clothed in brown,
and swastikas, or
bearing chests heavy with
gleaming crosses.
The time and need
for ruses are over.
They will come
in business suits
to buy your homes
and bring bodies to
fill your jobs.
They will come in robes
to rehabilitate
and white coats
to subjugate
and where will you be
when they come?

Where will we *all* be
when they come?
And they will come—

they will come
because we are
defined as opposite—
perverse
and we are perverse.

Every time we watched
a queer hassled in the
streets and said nothing—
It was an act of perversion.

Everytime we lied about
the boyfriend or girlfriend
at coffee break—
It was an act of perversion.

Everytime we heard,
"I don't mind gays
but why must they
be blatant?" and said nothing—
It was an act of perversion.

Everytime we let a lesbian mother
lose her child and did not fill
the courtrooms—
It was an act of perversion.

Everytime we let straights
make out in our bars while
we couldn't touch because
of laws—
It was an act of perversion.

Everytime we put on the proper
clothes to go to a family
wedding and left our lovers
at home—
It was an act of perversion.

Everytime we heard
"Who I go to bed with
is my personal choice—
It's personal not political"
and said nothing—
It was an act of perversion.

Everytime we let straight relatives
bury our dead and push our
lovers away—
It was an act of perversion.

And they will come.
They will come for

the perverts
& it won't matter
if you're
> homosexual, not a faggot
> lesbian, not a dyke
> gay, not queer

It won't matter
if you
> own your business
> have a good job
> or are on S.S.I.[1]

It won't matter
if you're
> Black
> Chicano
> Native American
> Asian
> or White

It won't matter
if you're from
> New York
> or Los Angeles
> Galveston
> or Sioux Falls

It won't matter
if you're
> Butch, or Fem
> Not into roles
> Monogamous
> Non Monogamous

It won't matter
If you're
> Catholic
> Baptist
> Atheist
> Jewish
> or M.C.C.[2]

They will come
They will come
to the cities
and to the land
to your front rooms

---

[1] S.S.I., Supplemental Security Income.
[2] M.C.C., Mennonite Central Committee.

and in *your* closets.
They will come for
the perverts
and where will
you be
When they come?

[1978]

First Stop/City of Senses

Carmen M. Pursifull

I learned to fly
and left behind
a scene of desolation.

I've swooped over heads
astounding people of the city
spread feathers for crowds
which oohed at hues luxuriant
trilled flamenco rhythms
for the pretty Puerto Ricans.

> Eventually
> exhibiting my wings
> began to bore me.

I wandered through the sky
amidst the neon-speckled spires
and mountain high penthouses
sheltered me with perches
affording me a seat to view
a scene to feed the senses.

My eyes were fed a world of knees
hiked high upon a shoulder
of nests with burrowed faces
and of throats with swollen features
with howls that cut the evening
their cries bouncing off the buildings.

I tried to emulate
the acts of man
while on the wing

falling on my feathers
much to my humiliation.
I learned some forms of mating
must be done recumbent
        so to speak
then tried to hike my feathers
on an acquiescent pigeon

        to no avail.

I knew to practice these positions
I would have to clip my wings
come down to earth
and try my hand at being
a citizen of senses
in a metamorphosed frame.

It wasn't long before I was adept
my appetites appeased
running through the senses of the city.

        That too grew dull
        and jaded to a point
        of constant yawn.

I traded in my almost disappearing wings
withdrawing to the borough of restraint.
It was a barren place.
No movie houses prodding eyes
with images of life.
No entertaining feats
to distract the meditative.
No theatre to interact
our necessary egos
just me and the neverending landscape
of my barren inner self.

        Confronted
        so to speak
        with emptiness

I found that I could visualize a tree
a rosebush climbing on a trellis

the house I once would own.
A faceless gent of moderate means
was leaning on a fence
and unknown redbirds filled the air
with ringing songs of spring
their presence known
because I actually heard them.
My palette rioted the scene
with rampant blooms
and once again my senses were alive
but with a different flair.
This was an earth which I had visualized.

The seasons quickly spun before my eyes
as if to speed a picture to my brain
to help me understand
the many uses of the senses.

[1986]

Good-bye, My Loved One

Diana Rivera

1.

Imagine
a house tucked with souls.
One springs out in the flight of the flycatcher.
Imagine
a dense, dark night
early December,
plunging into
the unknown.

In this unrelenting black denseness,
I long for the candles I saw in a daydream,
huge thick candles with huge thick flames
lining and lighting the dark highway,
hundreds of candles on both sides,
when I was at peace.

Now in this darkness
I come across a few lights, a blue
hue there, a small pink window afar.
Not the holy lights of denial and sacrifice,
and grateful deeds, but the lights,
the tiny, little bulbs of passion,
compressed, all inside small spheres.
They come and go,
travel, vanish,
reappear,
they want to fly loose in owned-splendor, to sparkle
in the tingly neons of happiness.

The memories of the good pour back
into this tiny goblet which is heart,
that which the mind forgets
when the road is rocky—
Passion
has broken from its jar in an explosion of
comets and stars,
and at last the new moon, the floating fingernail
swings back across seeking the unlit stars,
and then my hand forgets
its trembling.

Oh, sorrow, splintering heart!
a dim, but steady glimmer
copulates and breaks in half
to become
a constellation of blue-lit lamplights
spreading far into my steady night.

And I am breaking,
a leaf, ripped in half, the thin
middle vein dangling,
not held
to much but the remaining
small end of the stem, winds blowing in shafts.
And then, it's raining.

The filling well
drowns and grows
when lamplights float
against my eyes.

Pain travels through my veins
and into my eyes,

and the attempt at clearer vision
throbs alive in this dance of night,

and I am glad,
and so my death keeps growing,
dispersing like brown puddles under summer skies,
splitting open my red pomegranate,
a band of black hair over the horizon line—
to visions, farther and inviolate.

2.

And so, tonight, the moon is cut in half,
little neon lights keep chasing my torn eyes,
bouncing, tumbling, flowing into waves,
haloes, flickering like birds,
vanishing, appearing
golden,
indigo

tender and lunatic
following
every sharp and pebbled curve ahead.

3.

Oh, long, lingering moon sigh

dragon eyes of headlights,
confinement,
seeing,
breaking into the night,

you know when your heart is hollow,
stitched-up,
you know when it echoes no longer.

[1989]

Marina Rivera

Abandoning us
they toss jests
of nine lives,
they guess we trap mice
feast on small grey birds
mistify widows and
drink their wine
plot with witches
rub their oiled thighs
in the glare of fires.
Perhaps we could.
But they tie
the sacks double
throw us toward
the darkest surge
of swift rivers.
We are let to
fall from cars
stranded at junctions
have tried to hide
our bodies tasted
by coyote, rat, fly
the same as they,
our eyes green grapes
then spots of jam
sampled by ants.
Truth is our bodies
make a smudge of blood
a furred clump

on the freeway
just as dead
as the next mongrel.
The only difference
is we last longer
long enough to
have our hunger squared
long enough to breed
see the kits born blind
scabs for lids.
No call for it
a prejudice for claws
the angle of our chins
our hauteur of the leash
the fish on our breath
that we licked our
own slick backs
instead of their hands
that we mocked their gates
vaulted their fences?
If anything
our eyes are the reason.
Though hungry
we have the eyes
of successful politicians
a combination of
righteous cunning
the looks of gods denied.

[1976]

Poem for Some Black Women

Carolyn M. Rodgers

i am lonely.
all the people i know
i know too well

there was comfort in that
at first but now
we know each others miseries
   too well.
we are
   lonely women, who spend time waiting for
   occasional flings

we live with fear.
we are lonely.
we are talented, dedicated, well read
   BLACK, COMMITTED,

we are lonely.

we understand the world problems
Black women's problems with Black men
   but all
we really understand is
   lonely.

when we laugh,
we are so happy to laugh
we cry when we laugh
   we are lonely.
we are busy people
always doing things
fearing getting trapped in rooms
loud with empty . . .
               yet
knowing the music of silence/hating it/hoarding it
loving it/treasuring it,
   it often birthing our creativity
             we are lonely

being soft and being hard
supporting our selves, earning our own bread
soft/hard/hard/soft/
knowing that need must not show
                    will frighten away
knowing that we must
walk back-wards nonchalantly on our tip-toesssss
    into
happiness,
    if only for stingy moments

we know too much
we learn to understand everything,
to make too much sense out
of the world,
of pain
                    of lonely . . .

we buy clothes, we take trips,
we wish, we pray, we meditate, we curse, we crave, we coo, we caw,

            we need ourselves sick, we need, we need,
we lonely we grow tired of tears we grow tired of fear
we grow tired but must al-ways be soft and not too serious . . .

            not too smart not too bitchy not too sapphire
            not too dumb not too not too not too
a little less a little more

            add here detract there

            .lonely.

[1981]

Wendy Rose

Tell me it was just a dream,
my husband, a clever trick
made by some tin-faced village god
or ghost-coyote pretending
to frighten me with his claim
that our marriage is made
of malice and money. Oh tell me again
how you admire my hands, how
my jasmine tea is rich and strong,
my singing sweet, my eyes so dark
you would lose yourself swimming,
man into flesh, as you mapped the pond
you would own. That was not all.
The room grew cold
as if to joke with these
warm days; the curtains blew out
and fell back against
the moon-painted sill.
I rose from my bed like a spirit
and, not a spirit at all, floated
slowly to my great glass oval
to see myself reflected
as the burnished bronze woman,
skin smooth and tender,
I know myself to be in the dark
above the confusion
of French perfumes and
I was there in the mirror
and I was not.

---

* Julia Pastrana, 1832–1860, was a singer and dancer billed in the circus as "The Ugliest Woman in the World" or "Lion Lady." She was a Mexican Indian, born with a deformed bone structure of the face and hair growing from her entire body. Her manager, in an attempt to maintain control over her professional life, married her. She believed in him and was heard to say on the morning of her wedding, "I know he loves me for my own sake." When she gave birth to her son, she saw that he had inherited her own deformities plus some lethal gene that killed him at the age of six hours. In less than a week, Julia also died. Her husband, unwilling to abandon his financial investment, had Julia and her infant son stuffed and mounted in a wood and glass case. As recently as 1975 they were exhibited at locations in the United States and Europe.

I had become hard
as the temple stones of Otomi,[1]
hair grown over my ancient face
like black moss, gray
as jungle fog soaking green
the tallest tree tops.
I was frail as
the breaking dry branches
of my winter wand canyons
standing so still as if
to stand forever. Oh
such a small room—
no bigger than my elbows outstretched
and just as tall as my head.
A small room from which
to sing open the doors
with my cold graceful mouth,
my rigid lips, silences
dead as yesterday, cruel as what
the children say, cold
as the coins that glitter
in your pink fist.
And another terrifying magic
in the cold of that tall box: in my arms
or standing next to me
on a tall table by my right shoulder
a tiny doll that
looked like me . . . oh my husband
tell me again
this is only a dream
I wake from warm
and today is still today,
summer sun and quick rain;
tell me, husband, how you love me
for my self one more time.
It scares me so
to be with child
lioness
with cub.

[1984]

---

[1] Otomi, originally from the central Mexican highlands, the most numerous among the surviving speakers of the Otomangean linguistic family and number more than three thousand.

Wendy Rose

Hand by hand
bone by bone
dancing on the ladder
like mosquitoes
climbing
foot by foot
heel hanging in space
impressions of spruce
cut into our flesh
hand by hand
thumbs wrapped
in daylight
we   emerge
we   emerge
like wind
like dust
we travel a life time
each moment climbing
we handle time
like something
fragile
we fulfill
what we say
in the songs
we name
the landscape
of our skin
the map on the backs
of our hands
bone by bone
one people
bleeding
leading on
to a trail
our ancestors knew

what we do
at night
in the scent
of spruce
and clay
we   emerge
we   emerge
Anasazi[1] throats
Anasazi feet
at the top
of the world
in the taste
of daylight
a sound
of birth
a whirl
of blood
a spin
of song

[1984]

---

* Sipapu, the entrance to the underworld and the place of emergence. It is part of the belief
    that the earth always existed and the human race emerged from an opening called Sipapu.
[1] The Anasazi were ancient cliffdwellers and ancestors of the Hopi people.

Sonia Sanchez

Past

Come into Black geography
you, seated like Manzu's[1] cardinal,
come up through tongues
multiplying memories
and to avoid descent
among wounds
cruising like ships,
climb into these sockets
golden with brine.

because i was born
musician to two
black braids, i
cut a blue
song for america.
and you, cushioned
by middleclass springs
saw ghettos
that stretched
voices into dust
turned corners
where people walked
on their faces.
i sang unbending
songs and gathered gods.

1. Woman

Come ride my birth, earth mother
tell me how i have become, became
this woman with razor blades between
her teeth.

[1] Giacomo Manzu, an Italian sculptor who created the figure of the seated cardinal.

      sing me my history O earth mother
about tongues multiplying memories
about breaths contained in straw.
pull me from the throat of mankind
where worms eat, O earth mother.
come to this Black woman. you.
rider of earth pilgrimages.
tell me how i have held five bodies
in one large cocktail of love
and still have the thirst of the beginning sip.
tell me. tellLLLLLL me. earth mother
for i want to rediscover me. the secret of me
the river of me. the morning ease of me.
i want my body to carry my words like aqueducts.
i want to make the world my diary
and speak rivers.

rise up earth mother
out of rope-strung-trees
dancing a windless dance
come phantom mother
dance me a breakfast of births
let your mouth spill me forth
so i creak with your mornings.
come old mother, light up my mind
with a story bright as the sun.

2. Earth Mother

(low singing is heard)

old/	Bells. bells. bells.
woman's/	let the bells ring.
voice/	BELLS. BELLS. BELLS.
	ring the bells to announce
	this your earth mother.
	for the day is turning
	in my thighs And you are born
	BLACK GIRL.

      come, i am calling to you.
      this old earth mother of the elaborate dreams
      come. come nearer. girl. NEARER.
      i can almost see your face now.
      COME CLOSER.

Low/
laugh/
yes. there you are. i have stuffed
your whole history in my mouth
i. your earth mother
was that hungry once. for knowledge.
come closer. ah little Black girl
i see you.
i can see you coming
towards me little girl
running from seven to thirty-five
in one day.
i can see you coming
girl made of black braids
i can see you coming
in the arena of youth
girl shaking your butt to double dutch days
i can see you coming
girl racing dawns
i can see you coming
girl made of black rain
i can see you coming.

3. young/black/girl

Fivetenfifteentwenty
twentyfivethirtythirtyfiveforty
fortyfivefiftyfiftyfivesixty
sixtyfiveseventy
seventyfiveeighty
eightyfiveninety
ninetyfiveonehundredreadyornothere i come
REAdyornothereicome!
one
two
three. i see you.
              and you. and YOU. AND YOU.

AND YOU U U U U U U—step/mother.
woman of my father's youth
who stands at a mirror
elaborate with smells
all shiny like my new copper penny.
telling me through a parade of smiles
you are to be my new mother. and your painted lips
outlined against time become time
and i look on time and hear you
who threw me in angry afternoon closets
til i slipped beneath the cracks

like light. and time stopped.
and i turned into myself
a young girl breathing in crusts
and listened to those calling me.

to/   no matter what they do
be/   they won't find me
chanted/ no matter what they say
          i won't come out.

          i have hidden myself behind black braids
          and stutters and cannot be seen.

to/   no matter what they do
be/   they won't find me
chanted/ no matter what they say
          i won't come out

          i listen to words asking
          what did she say?
          why can't she talk normal talk?
          there's something wrong with that one!
          she got the demon inside of her or something!
          strange one!!
          too quiet!!!

to/   no matter what they say
be/   they won't find me
chanted/ no matter what they say
          i won't come out . . .

Coming out from alabama
to the island city of corner store jews
patting bigbuttedblack women in tune
        to girlie can I help ya?
        girlie what you want today?
        a good sale on pork today.
        girlie.
            girlie.
                girlie.

coming out from alabama
to the island city of perpetual adolescence
where i drink my young breasts
and stay thirsty

always hungry for more than the
georgewashingtonhighschoolhuntercollegedays
of america.
       remember parties
       where we'd grindddddDDDD
       and grindddddDDDDD
       but not too close
       cuz if you gave it up
       everybody would know. and tell.
       and grindddding was enough. the closeness
       of bodies in project basement
       recreation rooms was enough
       to satisfy the platter's sounds
       spinning you into body after body
       then walking across the room
       where young girls watched each other
       like black vultures
       pretending nothing had happened
       leaving young brothers in conditions
       they satisfied with out of the
       neighborhood girls . . .

Coming out from alabama
into smells i could not smell
into nites that corner lights
lit dimly.

i walked into young
womanhood. Could not hear
my footsteps in the streets
could not hear the rhythm of
young Black womanhood.

[1978]

Defining the Grateful Gesture

Yvonne Sapia

According to our mother,
when she was a child
what was placed before her
for dinner was not a feast,
but she would eat it
to gain back the strength
taken from her by long hot days
of working in her mother's house
and helping her father make
candy in the family kitchen.
No idle passenger
Traveling through life was she.

And that's why she resolved
to tell stories about
the appreciation for satisfied hunger.
When we would sit down
for our evening meal
of arroz con pollo[1]
or frijoles negros con plátanos[2]
she would expect us
to be reverent to the sources
of our undeserved nourishment
and to strike a thankful pose
before each lift of the fork
or swirl of the spoon.

For the dishes she prepared,
we were ungrateful,
she would say, and repeat
her archetypal tale about the Pérez
brothers who stumbled over themselves
with health in her girlhood town
of Ponce,[3] looking like ripe mangoes,
their cheeks rosed despite poverty.

---

[1] Arroz con pollo, meaning rice with chicken.
[2] Frijoles negros con plátanos, meaning black beans with (fried) plantains.
[3] Ponce, several towns and cities named after Juan Ponce de León (1460–1521), governor of
    Puerto Rico and Spanish explorer.

My mother would then tell us about the day
she saw Mrs. Pérez searching
the neighborhood garbage,
picking out with a missionary's care
the edible potato peels, the plantain skins,
the shafts of old celery to take
home to her muchachos
who required more food
than she could afford.

Although my brothers and I
never quite mastered the ritual
of obedience our mother craved,
and as supplicants failed
to feed her with our worthiness,
we'd sit like solemn loaves of bread,
sighing over the white plates
with a sense of realization, or relief,
guilty about possessing appetite.

[1986]

five

Ntozake Shange

her dreams came true & passed
all dreams do
                        n she waz jus a yng thing
wit nothin left   to sleep on/ a
tomorrow imagined
jus come & gone/
                        the hornplayer o.d.'d
                        the dancer waz gay.
her earrings
loopin her shoulders
irregular waz commonplace

                    she dreamt a woman waz a tree
                    asymmetrical danglin

like she waz
always livin dreams
makin somethin into nothin but a vision
& she loved these things
her plants the rockin-chair
any street in san francisco when the fog came in
how the sun picked her up each mornin
she woke in heat
to not a thing she knew
not a dream she cd maneuver
not a glimpse of what she had in store for herself
she had known dream too intimately
for the relationship to continue/
she waz whatta dream waz

nothin made into somethin
breath & blood become a vision
dream dressed up in crepe/ went out on the town
she went on in her life like she tried
not to/ imagine

her dreams had passed
as all dreams do
couched round her eyes

[1972]

Metamorphosis

Carol P. Snow

I think I am a dancer,
    a singer of songs,
    a story-teller.

I fly and swim,
    walk on four legs,
    slide through the grass on my belly.

I breathe through gills,
    through hollow fragile bone,
    shake feathers into place on my wings.

I roll in the dust,
    smooth my fur with raspy tongue,
    startle at unexpected sounds.

I walk upright,
    two-legged, a woman,
    warm and soft, strong and vulnerable.

I walk in silence,
    with laughter, with spoken word,
    with solitary tears, with open heart.

[1989]

Keep a Dime

Debra Swallow

Broken Treaties, FBI, What civil rights?!
Trials, Convictions, Appeals, Courtrooms, Truckstops,
    Holiday Inns
Endless highways, two bottles of No-Doze
Phone call, phone bills, another pack
    of Marlboro Reds,
Sleeping bags, legal pads,
    (gotta write tomorrow's press release)
Organizing rallies, slide shows,
Speaking forums, pow wows, feasts,
    giveaways, wars.
Another pot of coffee—make it to go
    please,
Only 80 more miles, who brought the
    banners, signs, flags, literature,
    posters, pins?
Mailing lists, donations please, we have
    a struggle to continue.
Gas money, postage, air fare, cab fare,
    printing bills.
Gotta score a tipi, a coleman lamp and batteries
    for the $200 portable stereo.

Teach the children and their parents the
      1868 treaty and Leonard Peltier,[1] the IRA-BIA[2]
      and summer's 49's.
Make a bustle and a roach and
      don't forget the deerhide guncase.
Spend your money on the movement
But keep a dime for the phone,
      it's worth a lawyer you know.
Women's work is never done.

[1984]

Suburban Indian Pride

Tahnahga

I remember

    Mom

On that blistering day
as the heat waves rose
from the black tarred highway
on our way back from the
Seminole Reservation
a full day of basketball
running and playing
you worried about me getting
ringworm in my barefeet
those days that Judy Jumper
and I shared as kids

Remember that day

    Mom

[1] Leonard Peltier, born around 1944, an Indian leader accused of murder; however, many feel
    he was framed.
[2] IRA-BIA, Indian Reorganization Act-Bureau of Indian Affairs.

We saw the movie "Billy Jack"
It seemed half the Seminole Nation
was there
Judy Jumper and I saying
"Right on"—with fist in the air
"Those yellow belly white suckers
got what they deserved"
that day of awakening for Judy Jumper
and me

Remember what you said

Mom

That day as we drove
to our white suburban home
fifty miles from the Reservation

"Be proud that you are
Indian, but be careful
who you tell."

[1989]

Giving Back

Tahnahga

It is time,
before the spring equinox to give back this lodge
a time of rebirth
a time to remember what was given by the ancient ones . . .
remembering old wisdom, given through prayer and song . . .

Now i stand before you,
your bones bleached as white as grandmother moon.
in your nakedness, i remember your beauty.
a young sapling peeled to expose your inner bark
bending to form this lodge of woman's womb
the beauty as you stood, a sacred place to come together . . .

Now i must take your frail bones,
return them to mother earth

these bones of time,
battered by changing seasons,
battered by a people who forgot the beauty of your lodge . . .
this sacredness for which you were built,
can we fully understand the depth of your soul.

Standing here,
watching as the flames dance over your body,
this giving back

I remember,
the sacredness; which we came together
as the smoke swirled above the cool summer wind
a sacred fire, where tobacco offerings have been layed
for a blessing within this lodge.
This body made from willow who gave herself for
the ongoing of the people.

I remember,
what you said dear sister,
the willow who gives her life is symbolic of our mothers womb . . .
from within we are reborn, purified to receive this gift of light,
power of all generations . . .
within this darkness, our prayers are heard;
beating hearts come as one.
the Grandfathers hear our prayers,
an eagle calls,
as we felt his wings against our face, this healing power;
we sang as we watched the coming of Blue Flame Woman.
she dances, she swirls, she flies, for a moment we too are free.
free from our humanness, together we dance,
Blue Flame Woman has touched us all.

I will remember,
always dear sister, the warmth and protection as we raised
the flap of your womb,
crawling on hands and knees, to greet the night sky
of rebirth,
this breath of life steam and wonder do we share.

[1989]

Mary Tallmountain

(for my Grandmother)
I see you sitting
Implanted by roots
Coiled deep from your thighs.
Roots, flesh red, centuries pale.
Hairsprings wound tight
Through fertile earthscapes
Where each layer feeds the next
Into depths immutable.

Though you must rise, must
Move large and slow
When it is time, O my
Gnarled mother-vine, ancient
As vanished ages,
Your spirit remains
Nourished,
Nourishing me.

I see your figure wrapped in skins
Curved into a mound of earth
Holding your rich dark roots.
Matmiya,
I see you sitting.

[1984]

My Mother Sews Blouses

Gina Valdés

My mother sews blouses
for a dollar a piece.
They must be working on
black cloth again, I see

her fingers sliding on
her eyelids.

Six months ago she went
to the old oculist, the
one who "knows all about
eyes," who turned her
eyelids inside out and
scraped them with a tiny
knife to get the black
lint out.

Her eyes were bright and
clear for a few months.
She's blinking now,
talking about night
school.

[1986]

In the Summer after
"Issue Year" Winter (1873)

Roberta Hill Whiteman

I scratch earth around timpsila
on this hill while below me,
hanging in still air, a hawk
searches the creekbed for my brothers.
Squat leaves, I'll braid your roots
into such long ropes, they'll cover
the rump of my stallion.
Withered flower, feed us now
buffalo rot in the waist high-grass.

Hear my sisters laugh?
They dream of feasts, of warriors
to owl dance with them
when this war is over. They don't see
our children eating treebark, cornstalks,

these roots. Their eyes gleam
in shallow cheeks. The wagon people
do not think relationship is wealth.

Sisters, last night the wind
returned my prayer, allowing me to hear
Dog Soldiers singing at Ash Hollow.
I threw away my blanket
stained with lies.
Above the wings of my tipi,
I heard the old woman in Maka Sica
sigh for us. Then I knew
the distance of High Back Bone's death—
fire from another world away. Even they
may never stop its motion.

Yesterday at noon, I heard
my Cheyenne sister moan as she waded
through deep snow before soldiers
cut up her corpse to sell
as souvenirs. Are my brothers
here? Ghosts bring all my joy.
I walk this good road between rock
and sky. They dare not threaten with death
one already dead.

[1984]

Author's note: I based the incidents in the poem on Batiste Good's Winter Count, which marks
the years for the Brule Lakota between 1700–1880. One of the incidents mentioned is the
1856 capture of Little Thunder and Batiste Good and one hundred and thirty Lakota at
Ash Hollow. The U.S. policy was to imprison Indian people, steal their horses and weapons,
arrest or kill the chiefs in order to force them into signing agreements which allowed for
railroad construction, improvement of the Bozeman Trail, and the establishment of military
posts. The Dog Soldiers are one of the Warrior Societies that vowed to stake themselves
to the ground and fight to the death defending their people. Reference is also made to
Chivington's bloody spree at Sand Creek in 1864.

   Another incident mentioned is the death of High Back Bone, a chief who was shot at
long range by Crows and Shoshones around 1870–1871. Shooting from a great distance
was contrary to plains warfare because a "brave" warrior touched his enemy with a coupe
stick instead of firing from a safe distance. During the years mentioned in the poem,
the Lakota and their allies, the Arapahoe and the Cheyenne, confronted white diseases,
decreasing buffalo herds, starvation, and the further reduction of their lands by treaty
agreements, which were then broken and resulted in battles with white soldiers. "Issue
Year" refers to blankets and goods given to the Lakotas in 1873–74. Incidentally, after the
first "Issue Year" of 1858–1859, a smallpox epidemic is listed two years after, and in the
year following 1873, another epidemic marks the year–"Measles and Sickness Used Up the
People Winter."

Roberta Hill Whiteman

These are notes to lightning in my bedroom.
A star forged from linen thread and patches.
Purple, yellow, red like diamond suckers, children

of the star gleam on sweaty nights. The quilt unfolds
against sheets, moving, warm clouds of Chinook.
It covers my cuts, my red birch clusters under pine.

Under it your mouth begins a legend,
and wide as the plain, I hope Wisconsin marshes
promise your caress. The candle locks

us in forest smells, your cheek tattered
by shadow. Sweetened by wings, my mothlike heart
flies nightly among geraniums.

We know of land that looks lonely,
but isn't, of beef with hides of velveteen,
of sorrow, an eddy in blood.

Star quilt, sewn from dawn light by fingers
of flint, take away those touches
meant for noisier skins,

anoint us with grass and twilight air,
so we may embrace, two bitter roots
pushing back into the dust.

[1989]

from "The Iconography of Childhood"

Sherley Anne Williams

ii

These are tales told in darkness
in the quiet at the ends
of the day's heat, surprised in
the shadowed rooms of houses
drowsing in the evening sun.

In this one there is music
and three women; some child is
messing with the victrola.
Before Miss Irma can speak
Ray Charles[1] does of "The Nighttime"
and *Awww* it Is the fabled

music *yo'alls* seldom given
air play in those Valley towns
heard mostly in the juke-joints
we'd been told About; and so
longed for in those first years in
the Valley it had come to

seem almost illicit to
us. But the women pay us
no mind. We settle in the
wonder of the music and
their softly lit faces listening
at the songs of our grown.

iii

Summer mornings we
rose early to go
and rob the trees
bringing home the
blossoms we were told

---

[1] Ray Charles, a singer, pianist, songwriter, bandleader, and record company executive, has
had to overcome racial prejudice and blindness.

were like a white girl's
skin. And we believed
this as though we'd
never seen a white
girl except in
movies and magazines.

We handled the
flowers roughly
sticking them in oily
braids or behind
dirty ears laughing
as we preened ourselves;
savoring the brown
of the magnolias'
aging as though our color
had rubbed off
on the petals' creamy
flesh transforming some
white girl's face into
ornaments for our
rough unruly heads.

v

The buildings of the
Projects were arrayed
like barracks in
uniform rows we
called regulation
ugly, the World in
less than one square block.
What dreams our people
had dreamed there seemed to
us just like the Valley
so much heat and dust.

Home training was
measured by the day's
light in scolds and
ironing cords; we
slipped away from chores
and errands from
orders to stay in
call to tarry in
the streets: gon learn what
downhome didn't teach.

And
Sundown didn't hold us
long. Yet even then
some grown-up sat still
and shadowed waiting
for us as the sky
above the Valley
                    dimmed.

vi

Showfare cost a lot
but we ran the
movies every chance
we got, mostly grade
B musicals that
became the language
of our dreams. Baby
Lois sang in the
rain for the hell of
it; Helen was a
vamp. Ruise was the
blood-red rose of
Texas, her skin as
smooth and dark as a
bud with just a hint
of red.

Sweating and
slightly shamefaced, we
danced our own routines
seeing our futures
in gestures from some
half remembered films.
We danced crystal
sidewalks thrilled in the
arms of neighborhood
boys and beheld our
selves as we could be
beyond the Projects:
the nine and ten year
old stars of stage and
screen and black men's hearts.

[1983]

When I Was Growing Up

Nellie Wong

I know now that once I longed to be white.
How? you ask.
Let me tell you the ways.

when I was growing up, people told me
I was dark and I believed my own darkness
in the mirror, in my soul, my own narrow vision

when I was growing up, my sisters
with fair skin got praised
for their beauty, and in the dark
I fell further, crushed between high walls

when I was growing up, I read magazines
and saw movies, blonde movie stars, white skin,
sensuous lips and to be elevated, to become
a woman, a desirable woman, I began to wear
imaginary pale skin

when I was growing up, I was proud
of my English, my grammar, my spelling
fitting into the group of smart children
smart Chinese children, fitting in,
belonging, getting in line

when I was growing up and went to high school,
I discovered the rich white girls, a few yellow girls,
their imported cotton dresses, their cashmere sweaters,
their curly hair and I thought that I too should have
what these lucky girls had

when I was growing up, I hungered
for American food, American styles,
coded: white and even to me, a child
born of Chinese parents, being Chinese
was feeling foreign, was limiting,
was unAmerican

when I was growing up and a white man wanted
to take me out, I thought I was special,

an exotic gardenia, anxious to fit
the stereotype of an oriental chick

      when I was growing up, I felt ashamed
      of some yellow men, their small bones,
      their frail bodies, their spitting
      on the streets, their coughing,
      their lying in sunless rooms,
      shooting themselves in the arms

when I was growing up, people would ask
if I were Filipino, Polynesian, Portuguese.
They named all colors except white, the shell
of my soul, but not my dark, rough skin

      when I was growing up, I felt
      dirty. I thought that god
      made white people clean
      and no matter how much I bathed,
      I could not change, I could not shed
      my skin in the gray water

      when I was growing up, I swore
      I would run away to purple mountains,
      houses by the sea with nothing over
      my head, with space to breathe,
      uncongested with yellow people in an area
      called Chinatown, in an area I later learned
      was a ghetto, one of many hearts
      of Asian America

I know now that once I longed to be white
How many more ways? you ask.
Haven't I told you enough?

                        [1981]

For an Asian Woman Who Says My Poetry Gives Her a Stomachache

Nellie Wong

You would rather scream out your anger in a workshop
and then you would find peace
and you ask if I find peace
by becoming more angry in my poetry

You turn to my sister-poet and say she's found peace
because her style is soft
and mine shouts

I jokingly say that I do find peace
when I sleep for at least 6 hours
but I give you my one true answer:

Peace does not exist
not while a woman is being raped
a child is being abused
a lesbian is being beaten
a man is denied work because of his race

and if I could document my life in snapshots
I would take hours to describe the pains
of being a girl and a young woman
who thought beauty
was being white
        useless
        a mother
        a wife

seen only in the eyes of the racist beholder
wrapped in the arms of the capitalist media
starved in the binds of patriarchal culture

and how I screamed in silence for years
beating myself down, delirious in my victimization
preferring the cotton-spun candy I thought was life

and now in my hours of awakening
as my hair turns white
my anger moves, a storm into the sunlight
where women and men fight alongside each other
in the battles against degradation, poverty, manipulation, fear
where anger is pure as the love I have for freedom
where desire is the catalyst for action
where the possibilities are rice and flowers and children
growing strong everywhere

[1989]

The Handbook of Sex
of the Plain Girl

Marian Yee

She calls herself the plain girl, but I
am plainer. Nothing is homelier
than the floor of my breasts; this house
of bones. Everything I know of sex
is large-breasted, blue-eyed, and blonde.

    I am woman learned in these ways—
    lie still, I will teach you.
    I have pulled back the quilts,
    swept clean the pillows, softened
    the lamp. I will unfasten my robe,
    set my hair free. Quietly
    let me smooth your skin into peace.
    This is how you please a man.

I ran away from the first boy who said I
was beautiful. What do I know
of pleasing a man? Mother will not answer
my questions, and these pictures she gives me—
do men and women really do this?

    Come into my red—let white
    iron burn, reshape and find its form
    in heat. My Master,
    my Emperor. I am yours tonight.

On the page, she crouches to receive him
as a glove enfolds the hand.
But this man beside me—who is he?
He calls my plainness beauty, and I,
who have little enough to give, will find
this reason enough to give
everything.

Men know nothing of sex—ask a man
what sex is and he will show you
his penis—we have much to teach:
my Master, my child, let me teach you
about your lips, your thighs,
your cheeks, the bones
of your hip.

But what can you teach about the pain
of his entrance, and later, the ache
of his departure? You, who taught
the Emperor to live forever,
teach me what to do with love.

[1989]

There is no agony like bearing an

untold story inside you.

ZORA NEALE HURSTON

Dust Tracks on a Road

SHORT STORIES

Deep Purple

Paula Gunn Allen

IT WAS LATE. THE MEETING HAD GONE ON FOREVER. LEELA HAD TO BE up by six to make it to work. She was tired and stoned on the sensamilla[1] she and Karen had smoked on their short, shivering walk home from the meeting.

The thunder and lightning that had played intermittently on the southern horizon all evening continued their display. Occasional bursts of sheet lightning illuminated the room briefly, while the flashes of thunder serpents marked their jagged trail through the dark ground with a distant crack. There was no rain expected. Only the gods conversing with one another, female to male, in noisy, ebullient exchange.

As from a far distance Leela could hear anger echoing. Her anger, that should have had her gut in tangles, her face muscles tight. But if tangled or tight she didn't feel it, floating as she was far from immediacies. She gazed at her face in the mirror, dim-lit from light in the hall. She hadn't turned the bathroom light on, fearing its shattering brightness.

"Man, what a trip!" she thought. Then corrected herself quickly, "I mean, gee, what a trip. No, not gee," she giggled silently, "gee is probably short for Jesus, and we want no hint of patriarchalism in this house. In this mirror. In this head. Both the one on the body and the one the body and head are standing in. You shouldn't even be living here!" she scolded herself.

The anger burst through her haze: "Goddammit, Karen Powers, I hate you for getting me into this! You tick me off, sweetie, you and your perfect politics. Damn you!" She seethed in a low mumble.

"I hate being used! Why oh why do I go to these damned meetings? Why do I love that damn woman? What do we have in common, anyway?" Feeling calmer, she squeezed toothpaste onto her purple toothbrush with exaggerated care. "The color purple? Purple prose, maybe. But, color? Naw. Too many of us don't have any, don't want any, and are sure as hell pretending we'd like to be close to some, like you, Karen dear, my one and only love."

She treasured the brush, felt triumphant in having found one in exactly that shade of deep purple. She had thought of it as a symbol of community, of belonging, of true love and commitment. For a second she recognized that the community she sought was made of the same stuff as the toothbrush.

She found an old tune in the litter of her mind. *When the deep purple falls over sleepy garden walls.* She felt with a rush the feelings the song had long evoked, the longing, the sense of love, of closeness, the heat of a New

[1] marijuana

Mexico July day giving way to the purple shadows of a cool, sky-brilliant night, the memory of rain falling in purple sheets from the bellies of great thunderheads. She was filled with a feeling of loss, of despair, as a sudden flash of lightning illuminated the great gulf between how she wanted her world to be and how it was. "Yeah," she taunted the thunder serpents, "and it's not July, either. It's October and winter's a-comin' in. So you can stop with the fireworks, gang. You're out of time!"

Her thoughts drifted to the adobe-walled yard, the adobe house where she and her lover, Karen, had spent the evening. She was almost numb to the despair hovering in the shadowy spaces of the bathroom, her reflection in the mirror rebounding over the flat planes of her dark face, making it somehow darker.

"Let's see. There must have been thirty or thirty-five mostly standard American brand dykes and a smattering of deviants, which included me twice: two fatties—me and Isabel; five coloreds—me, Isabel, Gilda, Dorothy, and Trini; and a couple of leather dykes—Trini and the blond woman whose name I forgot to get.

"Of course Trini would show up. She smelled blood probably. Drank herself silly. I was just as glad she was there in her slick d.a.[2] hair style, her leather vest, heavy metal studded wrist band, her lined and scarred face. We're so few, and watching Julia and her gang get uptight as Trini got more and more blasted was a trip. Back in that loop again. The thing about sensamilla is that it gets you into the weirdest loops."

Leela had felt a warm sympathy with Trini, a tough-talking Chicana bull-dyke, and had wished that she, Leela, could be as bold and brazen as Trini, as direct with people and clear about her real position in the world of the mostly middle-class suburban-bred lesbians she hung out with. Trini seemed to know exactly what the white women Leela hung out with thought of her. Even Leela, so good at not noticing whatever might make her too uncomfortable, had noticed their patronizing friendliness, their self-conscious political carefulness masking the contempt that flickered in and out of their lips like snake tongues. Leela was reminded of the snake she had seen the week before. It had been strange, seeing a rattler this late in the year. She had been walking down the path toward her mother's apartment when she spotted a small snake slithering across it. She stopped, and so did the snake. She had said, "Hi, snake," and the creature had curled itself gracefully into a figure-eight then raised its head and flickered its tongue at her. She had wondered if it was trying to taste or sense her. She thought it might coil all the way into a spiral and strike at her, but it didn't. They had stood silently regarding one another for a time, until Leela took a small step forward. At that, the snake had fled into the bushes where it disappeared. "Bye," Leela had said as it disappeared.

In her present marijuana clarity, Leela wondered if her friends' contempt for men and maleness masked their contempt of women like Trini.

---

[2] *duck's arse*: a male hairstyle popular in the 1950s.

"For sure," she thought, "Trini makes me feel weird too. Scared. Ashamed. Of what, I wonder? Of looking like that? Of being seen like that? Of harboring a secret lech for her style, her bull-dyke type? A lech? Isn't *leche* the Spanish word for milk? *Leche* mama, milky mama, *leche* baby."

She wondered what Trini had in mind when she came to the meeting—something she'd only done once or twice before. Leela had the idea that Antonia Gracia and Imelda Chavez, the women Beau had thrown out, were buddies of Trini's.

The thunder serpents and sheet lightning played the role of chorus and commentator throughout the meeting at Kay and Julia's house, a few blocks from Leela's. There, brokers who denied they had any power planned an assault on the livelihood of a real, live, black bulldagger. In spite of the thunders' impressive efforts, nothing had been resolved.

Kay, the president of the lesbian feminist organization Leela and Karen belonged to, Kay's lover, Julia, and their cohorts had been determined in pursuing their argument. As nearly as Leela could tell, those intent on confronting what they termed Beau's racism in making a couple of *cholas*[3] leave the bar didn't seem to notice that Beau was black.

Two of the black women there, Dorothy and Gilda, had tried to head off this organized attack on a black sister, and in the end Leela had doggedly sided with them. She had remained outwardly tactful, inwardly unsettled by the color lines suddenly drawn by a group she had thought of as her friends.

But the Organization's officers had stood unmoved by the colored women's detailing of Beau's contributions to the community. As far as Leela could see, the officers had a cause, and were swept up by the heady feeling of importance and power that went with it.

"They've got to have noticed that Big Beau is deep, dark gloriously black as the sky at midnight. Could that be what caused their attack?" she wondered.

"Or maybe what really gets them is that Bodacious Beauregarde Baptiste the Bad Black Bulldagger from New Orleans has the bad taste to own a jumping women's bar uptown. Maybe they're torqued that she wields so much power in our little woman's world."

Uneasy with her reflections, Leela wriggled uncomfortably in her place in a far corner of the crowded living room where shadows partially veiled her. Her thoughts were making her even more uneasy. She didn't like her suspicions, but the situation had brought them to a head.

From the way Trini stared coldly at Kay as she talked, from the way Isabel Mendoza seemed to almost disappear into her chair, from the way Dorothy and Gilda glanced at each other, Leela judged that her discomfort was shared by the other women of color at the meeting.

Kay, a slender, carefully groomed woman with luxurious light brown hair

[3] Mexican term for female gang members. It is also used to connote a close relationship between women in the same way that "homegirls" does. The term can also refer to Mexicans with strong Indian features.

and intense-eyes, had written up a formal grievance statement accusing Beau of racism, exploitation of women, and lack of concern for the women's community. She wanted Beau to admit to the charges leveled against her and to publicly apologize to the women she'd thrown out of the bar. If Beau failed to meet those demands, Kay said in her clear, well-modulated voice, the Organization for Women and Lesbians would stage a girlcott of Beau's bar, La Coatlique, which the women usually called the Snake Den.

Leela noticed that most of the women at the meeting didn't really agree to Kay's decisions. They simply said nothing, making it seem that they agreed with whoever had the floor. Leela knew they had come to the meeting mainly for something to do, that they would attend a few meetings over the year, attend the parties, and make some connections.

Leela's partner Karen and her closest friends, Jennie and Meg, had not been among the silent. But they had done little to clarify the situation. They were what they referred to as "the red diaper contingent," and their chosen mission in life was to promote class consciousness and get certain points into the minds of whomever was handy. While she felt deeply bonded with Karen, Leela never understood what the points were.

As she did at every meeting, Karen had taken up her cause. Leela had not listened. Gazing around the crowded room, she noticed the heavy stillness that had blanketed it as Karen spoke. It seemed everyone had abandoned their bodies, leaving only breathing corpses in their place. She noticed lovers who moments before had been leaning close and cuddling each other shifting their positions until they were turned away from one another, no longer touching, no longer linked.

Their faces, which earlier had been at least attentive, went slack and blank, as though the life had gone out of them. Even their posture was lifeless, sort of slumped and heavy. They reminded her of corpses she had loaded into her ambulance, of people suffering from massive strokes. She realized that she had seen the same thing happen a number of times in the five or six years she had known Karen, and wondered why she hadn't paid attention to it before now.

A burst of lightning closely followed by a crack of thunder interrupted Karen's monologue, and Kay used the lull to reclaim the floor. She stood for a moment, slim and compelling, and in a voice just loud enough to command attention, over the chorus of "oh's" and exclamations of "that was close!" she read from her typed statement.

"It is essential that we as lesbian feminists oppose patriarchy in all of its forms. That includes calling our sisters to account when they employ patriarchal methods in businesses that cater only to women."

She continued, shifting her weight so that her usually militaristic bearing more closely reflected her prep-school breeding. "As lesbians we commit ourselves to the dignity of women, and that means to the respectful and loving treatment of women in our enterprises, organizations, and relationships."

A few women murmured agreement, and Kay continued reading. "Our commitment to building a woman's community is both spiritual and political, and that includes watching over our economic base, and in accordance with that view it's crystal clear that our business must rest on the basic principles of feminist vision.

"Though she may not have done so maliciously, Beau Baptiste has betrayed those principles which we are committed to, and we ask that she issue a formal apology to the women she has barred from Coatlique, open her books and employee policies to public scrutiny, join with representatives of the women's community, including members of this Organization, to draw up policies concerning customers' rights and responsibilities, and agree to abide by the Association of Feminist Business Women's Resolution on Fair Business Practices."

She looked up from her papers, "Of course we'll supply her with a copy of them, in case she's mislaid the one we sent her last year after they were drawn up."

Another loud clap of thunder erupted, almost drowning Dorothy's loud protest: "You've gotta be kidding!" She stood abruptly. "What is this, the Feminist First Reich?"

"No," Gilda said, irony thick in her voice, "it's the New Women's Plantation. And what's going to become of Beau if she says no, Missy?" she challenged Kay.

Kay cleared her throat and replied in her coolest tone, "As I said earlier, we'll call for a community-wide girlcott of the Coatlique, the Snake's Den."

A number of women murmured their agreement. Some, who had been looking distressed with Dorothy and Gilda's protests, were beginning to shift about, as though preparing to get up and go in search of more relaxing entertainment. Gilda and Dorothy clearly were not among the content, but before one of them could say anything, Karen's buddy Meg cut in.

"It'd be better, Kay, if you included something about the structure of the Organization. I think we ought to stipulate that Beau reorganize the Snake's Den as a collective. I mean," Meg's voice took on a more pronounced twang, "as long as we're saying Beau should follow sound feminist business practices, we ought to make it really clear how a feminist enterprise operates."

"Right on!" Julia belted as she untangled herself from the cushion she was curled on and stood, her lanky presence seeming to tower over the seated women. She paused for a moment, her eyes wandering over the faces of the women sitting and lying around the room, then said, "I mean, why should we just make a dent in what's basically a colonial situation? Thing is, we need to nip reverse racism in the bud, and make certain the community moves in a positive direction."

A loud crash of thunder greeted her words. The lamps in the room flickered a few times then steadied.

Falling abruptly silent, as though her power had been turned off, Julia caught Kay's impatient stare, and blinked rapidly, as though she'd suddenly awakened from a light doze. Someone responded to her point but she seemed not to hear. Instead she ducked her head and collapsed slowly to her cushion, eerily resembling an inner tube that had suddenly sprung a leak. Leela knew Julia and Karen had spent the afternoon together. Given Julia's proclivity for taking on the opinions and attitudes of the strongest personality she'd been most recently influenced by, Leela was not surprised at her outburst or sudden deflation. "She's a sort of psychological chameleon," Leela thought. "Takes on the protective coloration of her surroundings."

Karen said, "I think we should give Meg's proposal careful consideration before we decide on a final draft. That means we need to take a long look at Kay's proposal. Anyone seriously against a couple of weeks' delay?" Pausing for the barest fraction of a breath to glance around the mostly silent room, she continued, "If we're agreed, let's appoint a smaller committee to get together after this meeting and work on it. Maybe Meg, Isabel, Julia, Dorothy, and of course Kay, and," she paused again looking quickly around the room, "how about you, Leela?" she asked.

"Uh," Leela began, "say what? I feel like I didn't hear the lonesome whistle blow!" Her face felt flushed. She didn't like being pulled out of the shadows, or being forced to take sides. She folded her arms tightly across her chest and drew a shaky breath, glancing at Dorothy, Gilda, and Trini. The reassurance she sought didn't seem forthcoming.

"Uh, well, I guess one color's same as another, right?" she grinned, lifting her hair out of her eyes. She glanced uncomfortably at Isabel, wanting to ask her if she was willing to be roped into Karen's ploy.

She took a breath. "Okay, I'll do it. But, if I'm gonna be on the committee, I'm gonna talk to Beau first. Maybe Isabel will talk to Imelda and Tonia. I don't really know what's happening, except for some gossip I heard and then what Kay said."

She was surprised when her offer was met by a loud chorus of agreement. One young stranger, her platinum hair framing her face in aggressive spikes, suddenly erupted into life.

"I've never been to one of these meetings before, and after what I've heard tonight I might never come to another one, but for what it's worth, that's the only plan I've heard yet that makes any sense," she said.

"I think that Leela—that's your name, right?" she asked, continuing when Leela nodded, "that Leela should not only talk to Beau but she oughtta report back to us at next month's meeting. And someone else oughtta talk to the other women, maybe get them to come and tell us what went down. Then, after we get some real information, maybe we'll decide to drop it. Which is what we probably oughtta do anyway. But let's take this one step at a time, gang."

Her voice had gotten louder as she spoke, and her pale, delicate features had turned red, whether from nervousness or fervor, but Leela warmed to the big woman who looked somehow fragile.

Everyone quickly agreed, Trini offering to join Leela to talk to Beau about the complaints. "Me and *mi carnal*[4] Beau need a good rap, joo know?" Trini said in an exaggerated Mexican accent.

At that, the group dissolved into small groups of talking, laughing women.

---

[4] A male expression connoting close friendship and suggesting a literal or figurative blood tie.

Relief flashed brightly through the room; raised voices rumbled into sharp laughter and exclamations of greeting as the women rose and began to move toward the kitchen for drinks or smokes and crowded around the dining room table for food.

Relieved to be out of the spotlight, Leela moved through the crowd to the kitchen, hoping for a sip of wine and maybe some weed. She figured somebody would be out there with a joint going by now. She was right.

She spotted the punk dyke who had spoken up earlier slouching against the refrigerator. The woman's costume included five earrings in one ear, smooth black leather pants, a heavy metal-studded belt, and a wristband on one arm. The other arm sported an intricate tattoo that climbed it and disappeared beneath the white thin cloth of her T-shirt. She was a large woman, tall as Leela and broad-shouldered. Leela pushed through the tiny room to her side. Sure enough, she had a joint in her hand.

As Leela took her place next to the woman their hands reached out automatically, one offering, the other taking, the socially sanctified weed. They stood companionably for a moment, and then the woman said, "You know that blond woman, the one in the radical chic blazer standing by the door?" She nodded in the direction of one of Karen's friends.

"Yeah," Leela said. "Megan. We call her Meg."

"Well," said her stoned companion, "I used to work with her. She ruined the gig for all of us, and I quit."

"Yeah?" Leela said, not as interested in the woman's story as in her stash. "Where was that?"

"At one of the big law firms downtown. I was working as a proofreader, you know, going over the documents checking 'em for mistakes. It was a cool job. We gals took care of each other, did as little as possible, got paid for it. Got paid pretty good, matter of fact. Came in late, left early, you know, just sort of messed around. It was a cool scene. The dudes we worked for were cool, acted like they didn't give a shit as long as we got the stuff to 'em in a steady stream.

"Anyways, that broad comes to work there and next thing you know she's trying to organize us, get us in some union, yammering about the dignity of the poor workers, the rights of the poor workers, the health of the poor workers. She kept sending off memos, agitating for phones, different lighting, better ventilation, you know, the whole nine yards.

"Next thing she's got the boys all riled, and they start clocking what time we come in, leave, take a shit, you know. Hassling us. About the time she was getting up a full head of steam around unionizing, I split. Wasn't worth working there anymore. No way."

The woman offered the roach to Leela. It was tightly held by a heavy paperclip, one of the extra large ones. "Some of my bootlegged treasure from that scene," the woman said, nodding at the clip. Leela declined the last toke.

The woman snorted in derision. "Working class, my ass. That woman never took a working class in her life, you know what I mean?"

Leela nodded. She knew what the woman meant.

Kay made her way through the crush to where Leela was standing. "Leela," she said, "I want to thank you for your offer to mediate this issue. It was a stroke of genius, offering to talk to Beau." She smiled warmly and placed her well-manicured hand on Leela's arm, drawing Leela toward her. "It's so pleasing to know that women of color are getting involved in issues that are important to the larger women's community."

Leela regarded her blankly. She never knew what to make of Kay. She felt wary, almost cold whenever she talked to her, but she also felt reassured, even comforted by the woman's seeming warmth and confidence. In her confusion she usually reacted with friendliness, as she did now.

She put her arm around Kay's waist and smiled down at her. "Not to worry, Kay old girl," she said. "Beau's surely gonna see that you don't mean any harm by all this," she waved vaguely in the direction of the papers Kay was holding, "and only have the best interests of our community at heart." She took the papers from Kay and leafed through them.

"Those are for you," Kay said, her voice tinged with confusing warmth. "You can take them and show them to Beauregarde, so she'll know what's being said. I don't want to seem underhanded," she added, gazing guilelessly into Leela's eyes.

"Tell her to call me if she wants to know any more about this. I'd be happy to chat with her and get her side of the story.

"You know, I tried to reach her," she confided, dropping her voice and leaning closer to Leela. "I called her a couple of weeks ago, right after those women called me about what Beau had done."

Kay sighed softly, holding Leela's gaze steadily for a moment. Looking away she raised her voice. "Apparently she didn't care to discuss it. She never returned my call." Her tone was carefully pitched to carry through the noise of the room. When Leela looked around she saw a number of women looking at them.

"You should know," Kay continued crisply, "that Imelda and Tonia were very upset. They said they hadn't been able to sleep or eat for days. Imelda took me aside and said she'd come home from work one day and found Tonia lying there unconscious. Evidently she'd taken a massive dose of tranquilizers in an attempt at suicide. Understandably, Imelda was frantic with worry, and convinced Tonia, after getting her cleaned out and more or less coherent again, to come and talk to us. She said it was the only way she could get Tonia to agree not to do anything so drastic again."

Leela stared at Kay, momentarily speechless. "Wow," she said finally, running a hand through her hair. "You sure about that? I have the idea that Tonia's a heavy user. Maybe she o.d.'d. One of the drivers at work told me he took her to the hospital on an overdose last year." Taking a small breath, Leela ploughed on, her neck flushing with warmth.

"I think Beau's okay. Really. I mean, a sister's a sister, eh? and she's had some pretty tough times herself from what I hear. I mean, Beau's older of course, and maybe she's not as political as some of us, but she's a good head. A woman named Allie works with my mom, and she's old friends with Beau. She's told me a lot about Beau's past. Besides, Beau's been real good to lots of us. I can't believe she'd try and kill someone, or not give a shit if she knew somebody had o.d.'d."

"Well," said Kay, drawing closer to Leela, "we can't know for certain until someone talks to her."

Leela drew imperceptibly away, impatient with the sparring, suddenly desperate to break free. In spite of the usually calming marijuana, she could feel her fear turning to anger, her sense of comfort turning to a powerful conviction that Kay was the enemy and she, Leela, was betraying someone or something unutterably precious.

"Well, maybe Beau won't agree that there's a problem, or maybe she won't feel responsible for Tonia's overdose since she's had the rules posted clearly for years now. Tonia and Imelda must have known they were breaking them and would be thrown out," she said, her heartbeat sounding painfully loud in her ears.

"On the other hand, I think it's some kind of betrayal when women trash a woman-owned business." She eyed Kay briefly to measure the effect of her words. "Especially one owned by a woman of color."

"Let's not think of it that way," the white woman said. "Even people of color can be backward in their politics. Look at the ones in the present administration! Trying to say affirmative action isn't necessary anymore, that comparable worth is a farce . . . I'm sure you don't agree with that, do you?"

Leela felt her stomach contract painfully. "Of course not, Kay," she replied, forcing her mouth into a grin. "I just think it'd be a good idea to get Beau's side of the argument before we go riding in like the cavalry to the slaughter."

Kay's eyes went distant and cold. "I'm sure you're right," she said. Her perfunctory smile did not warm the rest of her face. "I have faith in you, Leela," she said levelly. Withdrawing from Leela's arm, she moved away, disappearing quickly into the other room.

"Whew," the spike-haired woman said, glancing at Leela. "You sure got her riled!"

"Yeah, well, I guess I shouldn't have rubbed her fur the wrong way," Leela shrugged. Her stomach felt like an ant's nest, with all the creatures stinging her at once.

Her companion patted Leela's back. "Let's salute the girls who got free," she said, grinning, and turned sideways so Leela could see her tattoo, flexing her muscles so the snake on her arm sprang to life.

As she did so, the uncurtained window behind her lit suddenly with three successive flashes of brilliant blue light. It returned to blackness for a moment, then Leela saw four thunder serpents hurl themselves jaggedly groundward. The furious shock of sound that followed seemed to crack the pane. Someone screamed, then everyone laughed.

"What a weird night," Leela said.

"Yeah," the blond stranger said, nodding. "Awesome."

Leela contemplated her companion's tattoo. "Where'd you get that?" she asked suddenly.

"Actually," the dyke began, "in San Diego. Pretty boss, huh?"

"Yeah. Wish I had the courage to get one. How much did it cost?"

"Don't remember," the dyke said. "I was stoned. Probably a couple hundred, maybe more. A girl can't spend too much on her beauty, you know. You thinkin' 'bout getting one?"

"I dunno," Leela said vaguely. "Maybe. Maybe someday."

The gods were all around. And it seemed that last night they were aiming to be heard. Leela dressed in the predawn darkness, then turned on the kitchen light. Sitting at the kitchen table, she sipped herbal tea and munched rice cakes, her eyes nearly shut against the glare of the artificial light.

She was still caught in the rhythm of the dreams that had gripped her. The chime of the electronic alarm had scarcely turned her awareness dayward. She was barely awake enough to pull on her light blue uniform and tie her shoes.

Now, slumped over the table, she rolled a joint, her first of the day.

Flashes of her dream tumbled on her mind screen. Something about snakes falling through the midnight sky. Snakes that were starfires hurtling through the atmosphere to land far out on the western mesas in terrifying explosions. Snake egg fireballs, dozens of them, erupting all along the western horizon above Albuquerque. The total silence, the brilliant, blinding light.

In the dream she had been out on the west mesa at Volcano Cliffs, high above the western rim of the city. She had found a circle of stones on the southern edge of the southernmost cliff, and in it somebody had dropped a rubber floor mat from a car. Leaning down to get a closer look, she had seen a design in the black rubber. It was a jagged bolt of lightning surrounded by a circle. It was then that the firesnake bolts had plummeted from the sky and dropped their explosive eggs all along the slope behind her.

After that, she remembered trying to get home, to her mother's. Running in total, frightful silence. Running, but her feet not touching the ground. Running, not flying, but then riding in some sort of airborne vehicle. Not a helicopter, not a plane. Something like a car, like a science fiction hovercar.

Someone was sitting beside her, the pilot or driver. They were talking but she didn't see his face. He told her to look below as they crossed the Rio Grande, heading northeast. The cottonwood trees of the bosque along the river turned into snakes, thousands of them, their black and gold bodies sliding over and under one another in a sea of orderly, almost beautiful motion. Oddly, she hadn't been afraid.

"Look up there," he commanded, pointing to the Sandias that rose stark and sheer above the writhing city. She followed his pointing finger and gasped. High above the eastern peaks she saw a giant white cloud mushrooming. It was filled with light. Light so bright it seemed she could see the bones of the great peaks below outlined in it.

As she watched in utter stillness the vast mushroom cloud took on the form of a giant woman, perfectly contained in the brilliance, perfectly, blindingly white.

The car she was in began to sink toward the valley floor as a thick, purplish mist surrounded it. The last thing she remembered seeing was her guide's right hand. It was pale and square, burnished with a light scatter of gold-red hairs. On his middle finger he wore a large ring, set with a round onyx stone engraved with a lightning bolt.

Recovering her wits, Leela sighed deeply and finished the last of her cold tea. "Sure wish I knew what was going on," she sighed again. "If this was the old times, or if Maggie had been a traditional, I could have gone to the medicine woman or someone and talked about this. As it is, I guess I better get to work."

She got up, picked up her warm jacket, and slinging it over her shoulder clicked off the light and shut the kitchen door.

"Rats," she swore as she started down the walk to her car. "Forgot to brush my teeth."

[1989]

A Girl's Story

Toni Cade Bambara

SHE WAS AFRAID TO LOOK AT HERSELF JUST YET. BY THE TIME I COUNT TO twenty, she decided, if the bleeding hasn't stopped . . . she went blank. She hoisted her hips higher toward the wall. Already her footprints were visible. Sweat prints on the wall, though she was shivering. She swung her feet away from the map she'd made with Dada Bibi, the map of Africa done in clay and acrylics. The bright colors of Mozambique distracted her for a moment. She pictured herself in one of the wraps Dada Bibi had made for them to dance in. Pictured herself in Africa talking another language in that warm, rich way Dada Bibi and the brother who tutored the little kids did. Peaceful, friendly, sharing.

Rae Ann swept through her head again for other possible remedies to her situation. For a nosebleed, you put your head way back and stuffed tissue up your nostrils. Once she'd seen her brother Horace plaster his whole set of keys on the back of the neck. The time he had the fight with Joe Lee and his nose bled. Well, she'd tried ice cubes on the neck, on the stomach, on the thighs. Had stuffed herself with tissue. Had put her hips atop a pile of sofa cushions. And still she was bleeding. And what was she going to do about M'Dear's towels? No one would miss the panties and skirt she'd bundled up in the bottom of the garbage. But she couldn't just disappear a towel, certainly not two. M'Dear always counted up the stacks of laundry before the Saturday put-away.

Rae Ann thought about Dada Bibi over at the Center. If the shiny-faced woman were here now with her, it wouldn't be so bad. She'd know exactly what to do. She would sit in the chair and examine Rae Ann's schoolbooks. Would talk calmly. Would help her. Would tell her there was nothing to worry about, that she was a good girl and was not being punished. Would give an explanation and make things right. But between the house and the Center she could bleed to death.

Between her bed and the toilet she'd already left many a trail. Had already ragged the green sponge a piece, scrubbing up after herself. If Horace came home, she could maybe ask him to run over to the Center. Cept he'd want to know what for. Besides, he didn't go round the Center any more since they jumped on his case so bad about joining the army. He didn't want to hear no more shit about the Vietnamese were his brothers and sisters, were fighting the same enemy as Black folks and was he crazy, stupid or what. And he surely wouldn't want to have to walk all the long way back alone with Dada Bibi in her long skirt and turban, trying to make conversation and getting all tongue-tied sliding around the cussin he always did, and everybody checking them out walking as they were toward his house and all. But maybe if she told him it was an emergency and cried hard, he wouldn't ask her nothing, would just go.

Yesterday Dada Bibi had hugged her hello and didn't even fuss where you been little sister and why ain't you been coming round, don't you want to know about your heritage, ain't you got no pride? Dada Bibi never said none of them things ever. She just hugged you and helped you do whatever it was you thought you came to do at the Center. Rae Ann had come to cut a dress for graduation. She'd be going to intermediate in the fall, and that was a big thing. And maybe she had come to hear about the African queens. Yesterday as they sewed, Dada Bibi told them about some African queen in the old days who kept putting off marriage cause she had to be a soldier and get the Europeans out the land and stop the slaving.

She liked the part where Dada Bibi would have the dude come over to propose umpteen times. Rae Ann could just see him knocking real polite on the screen door and everything. Not like Horace do, or like Pee Wee neither, the boy she was halfway liking but really couldn't say she respected any. They just stood on the corner and hollered for their women, who had better show up quick or later for their ass.

Dada Bibi would have the dude say, "Well, darling, another harvest has past and I now have twenty acres to work and have started building on the new house and the cattle have multiplied. When can we marry?" And then Dada Bibi would have the sister say, "My husband-to-be, there are enemies in the land, crushing our people, our traditions underfoot. We must raise an army and throw them out." And then the dude would go sell a cow or something and help organize the folks on the block to get guns and all. And the sister would get the blacksmith to make her this bad armor stuff. Course Gretchen got to interrupt the story to say the sister chumping the dude, taking his money to have her some boss jewelry made and what a fool he was. But the girls tell her to hush so they can hear the rest. Dada Bibi maintaining it's important to deal with how Gretchen seeing things go down. But no one really wants to give Gretchen's view a play.

Anyway, after many knocks on the screen door and raising of armies and battles, the two of them are old-timers. Then the sister finally says, "My husband-to-be, there is peace in the land now. The children are learning, the folks are working, the elders are happy, our people prosper. Let us get married on the new moon." Gretchen got to spoil it all saying what old folks like that need to get married for, too old to get down anyway. And Dada Bibi try to get the girls to talk that over. But they just tell Gretchen to shut her big mouth and stop hogging all the straight pins. Rae Ann liked to retell the stories to the kids on the block. She always included Gretchen's remarks and everybody's response, since they seemed, in her mind, so much a part of the story.

Rae Ann's legs were tiring. Her left foot was stinging, going to sleep. Her back hurt. And her throat was sore with tension. She looked up at the map and wondered if Dada Bibi had seen the whole trouble coming. When Rae Ann had stayed behind to clean up the sewing scraps, the woman had asked her if there was anything she wanted to talk about now she was getting to be such a young woman. And Rae Ann had hugged her arms across her chest and said, "No, ma'am," cause she figured she might have to hear one of them one-way talks like M'Dear do about not letting boys feel on your tits. But when she got ready to leave, Dada Bibi hugged her like she always did, even to the girls who squirmed out of her reach and would rather not even wave hello and goodbye, just come in and split at their leisure.

"My sister," she had said into her ear, gently releasing her with none of the embarrassed shove her relatives seemed to always punctuate their embraces with. "You're becoming a woman and that's no private thing. It concerns us all who love you. Let's talk sometimes?"

Rae Ann liked the way she always made it a question. Not like the teachers, who just flat-out told you you were going to talk, or rather they were going to talk at you. And not like M'Dear or Aunt Candy, who always just jumped right in talking without even a let's this or could we that.

Maybe Dada Bibi had seen something in her face, in her eyes. Or maybe there had been a telltale spot on the back of her jeans as early as yesterday. Rae Ann twisted her head around toward the pile of clothes on the back of her chair. Upside down her jeans were spotless. Well, then, she reasoned methodically, how did Dada Bibi know? But then who said she had known anything? "That ole plain-face bitch don't know nuthin" was Horace's word to the wise. But just the same, he hung around the bus stop on Tuesday nights, acting blasé like he didn't know Dada Bibi had Tuesday night classes at the college. Not that anybody would speak on this. Joe Lee had cracked and had his ass whipped for his trouble.

Rae Ann was smelling herself and not liking it. She'd already counted three sets of twenties, which meant it was time to move. She rejected the notion of a bath. The last bath had only made it worse. Fore she could even get one foot good out the water, red spots were sliding off the side of the tub onto the tile. She exhaled deeply and tried to make a list in her head. New tissue, tight pants to hold it all in place, the last of the ice tray still in the sink on her twat. She closed her eyes and moaned. Her list was all out of order. She tried again. Check floors and tub. Put towels in bottom of garbage. Put garbage out. Scrape carrots and make salad. Secrete a roll of tissue in her closet for later. Get to the Center. She opened her eyes. What would she say?

Rae Ann pulled her legs down and swung off the bed. She checked to see that the newspaper was still in place before drawing the covers up. She stood and parted the flaps of her bathrobe. Last time she had moved too quickly and the oozing had started, a blob of syrupy brown slipping down the inside of her leg and she afraid to touch it, to stop it, just stood there like a simpleton till it reached her ankle, and then she fled into the bathroom too late. She was looking into the toilet as the water swirled away the first wad of tissue. What if the toilet stuffed up, backed up on the next flush? She could imagine M'Dear bellowing the roof down as the river of red overran the rim and spilled over onto the tiles, flooding the bathroom, splashing past the threshold and onto the hall linoleum.

"Get out the bathroom, willya damn it!"

She jumped and banged an elbow on the sink. She hadn't heard Horace come into the house. He usually announced his arrivals by singing, stamping, and doing a bump-de-bump against the furniture. Had thought she was all alone with her terror. Hadn't even locked the door and here she was with her pants down and the last clump of tissue shredding, sticky red.

"Come on now. I gotta shower fore M'Dear get home."

She was trapped. If she unhooked the roll of toilet paper to take into her room, he'd see that. And M'Dear would be in any minute and would come into her room to set her bags down and get her slippers. If she hid in the closet and squatted down behind the bundles of mothballed blankets . . .

"Hey," Horace was bamming on the door. "You okay?"

Something in her brother's voice startled her. Before she could stop herself she was brimming over and shivering hard.

"Rae Ann?" he called through the door. "Rachel?"

"Don't come in!" she screamed. "Don't come in."

The doorknob was being held in position, she could see that. It had stopped turning. And it seemed to her that he was holding his breath on his side of the door just like she was holding hers on hers.

"Hey," he whispered "you okay?" When she didn't answer, he let go of the knob. She watched it move back into place and then heard him walk away. She sat there hugging herself, trying to ease the chattering of her teeth. She leaned over to yank her washcloth off the hook. And then the smell gripped her. That smell was in everything. In her bed, her clothes, her breath. The smell of death. A dry, rank graveyard smell. The smell of her mother's sickroom years ago, so long ago all the memory that had survived was the smell and the off-yellow color from the lamp, a color she'd never ever seen again anywhere. A brown stain was smack in the middle of the washcloth. She flung it into the basin and ran the water.

"She in there crying."

Rae Ann's heart stopped. M'Dear was in the kitchen. Just behind the medicine cabinet, just behind the wall, they were talking about her. She jumped up and ran to the door.

"Don't be locking that door," the voice boomed through the wall. "We hear you in there."

"And we know what you been doin too," her brother's voice rang out. She wondered what happened to that something that was in his voice just minutes ago. Where had that brother gone to so quick? Maybe cause he was scared he sounded so nice. That time when Furman and his gang were after Pee Wee he had sounded like that. Up on the roof, scrunched between the pigeon coop and the chimney, Pee Wee revealed a voice Rae Ann had never known he had. Told her she was a nice girl and shouldn't mess around with guys like him, would have to be careful. Not at all the voice bragging on the handball court, Pee Wee mounting his motorbike, Pee Wee in the schoolyard smoking. Why did it take scarifying to bring out the voice?

"Horace just scared I may die in here and he won't be able to take his damn shower," she mumbled into the washcloth, gagging on the smell. She was too afraid to think anything else.

"You best get in here, Madame," The voice came at her through the mirror. Madame. She was freezing again. Madame never meant anything good. Madame, you best cut a switch. Madame, there's a letter here from school. Madame, where's the receipt from the telephone bill. Madame, do you think you too grown to mind.

Rae Ann swished around some mouthwash and rewrapped her bathrobe tight. She knew she was waddling, the minute she saw the way they looked at her, but she couldn't get herself together. Horace turned back to a plate in the icebox he was eating from. M'Dear was leaning up against the sink, her hat still on her head, the shopping bags leaning against her legs, her shoes not even unlaced.

"You had somebody in here?"

"No, ma'am."

"Ask her how come she in her bathrobe."

"You hush," the old woman warned, and Horace disappeared behind the icebox door.

"What you been doin?"

"Nothin."

"Don't tell me nothin when I'm trying to find out somethin. Miz Gladys run all the way up to the bus stop to tell me she seen you comin home from school way before three o'clock."

Rae Ann heard the pause, felt the pause on top of her head, weighing it down into her shoulders. She shrugged. She didn't know how to fill it and lift it.

"You play hookey from school today? Went somewhere with somebody?"

"No, ma'am."

M'Dear breathing in and out, the huffin-puffin getting wheezy. It was clear Rae Ann had better say something, cause there wouldn't be too many more questions, just a heavier pausing swelling, swelling to crush her.

"You cold or somethin?" A question that came out finally and lifted her from her knees. She didn't know why she was so grateful to hear it. She hadn't expected it. Was nodding yes while her mouth said no and smiling and fixing to cry all at the same time.

"Tears don't tell me a damn thing, Rachel Ann."

"Tears say a whole lot to me," Horace was telling the toaster, singing it lest the woman get on him again for butting in.

"I sure wish you'd go somewhere," Rae Ann said over her shoulder. It might be easier to talk with just her grandmother. Though she was still a blank as to what she could possibly say to take the hardness out of her grandmother's face. M'Dear's eyes shot from the boy to the girl to the boy then back again, her head swiveling, her eyes flashing, like she was on the trail of something and there was danger sure for somebody.

"M'Dear, I'm bleeding," she heard herself say, huddling smaller into her bathrobe, feeling an oozing on the inside of her leg.

The old woman's face looked red-hot and strangled, and for a minute the girl thought she was going to be slapped.

"Whatcha been doin?" she hissed through clenched teeth. Rae Ann backed up as a whole bunch of questions and accusations tumbled out of the woman's mouth ramming into her. "You been to the barbershop, haven't you? Let that filthy man go up inside you with a clothes hanger. You going to be your mama all over again. Why didn't you come to me? Who's the boy? Tell me his name quick. And you better not lie."

M'Dear had snatched up her pocketbook, not waiting on an answer in the meantime, and was heading out the door, waving Horace to come on. He burned his fingers pulling out the toast, eager for the adventure.

"I didn't do anything," Rae Ann screamed, racing to the door before it closed against the back of her brother. "I didn't do anything, I swear to God," her throat raspy, failing her, the words barely pushed out and audible.

"Oooooh," she heard echoing in the tiled hallway, the word hollow and cool, bouncing off the walls as the old woman shoved past the boy back into the kitchen. "Oh, my goodness," she said through her hands. And then Rae Ann felt the hands on her shoulders moist from the mouth coming right through the terry cloth. The hands giving slight pull, pat, tug but not a clear embrace. "Oh, Rachel Ann," the woman whispered, steering her gently down the hall. "Girl, why didn't you say so?" she said, helping her into bed.

Rae Ann bent her knees and eased herself down onto the newspapers. She watched the woman back out of the room, her hands smoothing her waistband, as though she were leaving the dishes to make a call or leaning up from the dough on the breadboard to shout across the air shaft to Miz Gladys. Smoothing the bulk that bunched up over the waistband, nervous.

"Be right back, sugar," still backing out the room. And Rae Ann glad she'd moved her sneakers out the doorway. That'd be all she needed, M'Dear falling over some sneakers.

"Hush your ugly mouth, cause you don't know what you talkin about," she heard in the kitchen just before the front door slammed. Was she going to get a doctor? Maybe she'd gone for Dada Bibi? That wasn't likely. I ain't studyin them folks over there, M'Dear and Miz Gladys like to say, sucking their teeth at the letters, flyers, posters, numerous papers that came into the block, the building, the house, explaining what the Center was about.

"I ain't nobody's African," Miz Gladys had said. "One hundred percent American and proud of it." And M'Dear had jerked her head in agreement, trashing the latest flyer Rae Ann had slipped onto the table.

Rae Ann had tried to push all they said up against other things in her head. Being American and being proud and they weren't the same in her head. When Dada Bibi talked about Harriet Tubman and them, she felt proud. She felt it in her neck and in her spine. When the brother who ran the program for the little kids talked about powerful white Americans robbing Africa and bombing Vietnam and doing ugly all over the world, causing hard times for Black folks and other colored people, she was glad not to be American. And when she watched the films about Africans fighting white folks so that hospitals and schools could be built for the kids, and the books about Fanny Lew somebody and Malcolm fighting for freedom, and the posters about the kids, kids littler than her even, studying and growing vegetables and all and the print saying how even kids were freedom fighters—she was proud not to be American. What she heard in school she pushed up against what was in her head. Then she started looking, just looking in the teacher's bloodshot eyes, looking at M'Dear's fat, looking at Dada Bibi's shiny skin, to decide just how she was going to arrange things in her head. It was simpler to watch than to listen.

"Ma Dear gone for the ambulance?" Horace in the doorway grinning, biting at the toast. "Old Freeny botch up the job? Next time I can take you to this nurse who—"

"Go to hell, nigger."

"Okay, okay," he said, closing his eyes and raising his hands like he wouldn't dream of pressing the magic number on nobody, would gladly take his pot of gold elsewhere. "But when that dead baby drops down and rips you open, don't yell for me to save ya. You'll bleed to death first."

Her sneaker missed his head by a fraction of an inch. And she sang real loud the Guinea-Bissau marching song the brother at the Center had taught her, to drown out his laughing. Her song ended as the door slammed. She eased into the mattress, not realizing she'd been tensed up and inches off the newspaper. Her body was sore with the clutching. She wanted to sleep, her eyes dry and stinging. She'd been afraid that if she blinked too long, she'd never open them again in life.

"To die for the people." Somebody in one of the films had said that. It had seemed okay to her at first. She tried to picture Pee Wee willing to die for the people. But all the pictures that came into her head about Pee Wee dying were mostly about Pee Wee and not the people. She tried to picture Horace standing up against the cops in the name of the kids, protecting Pee Wee maybe, or the other boys the pigs liked to beat up on. But it didn't exactly fit. She dreamed up another dude altogether. He looked a little like the brother in the film, only he was different cause he was hers. And he was blowing up police stations and running through the alleyways back of the projects, and she hiding him in her closet, sneaking him food from the kitchen. Was helping him load his guns to shoot the big businessmen with. And she was seeing him dragging through the streets, one leg shot off. And the President's special cops bending in the street to squeeze off the final bullet in his back. And she'd be holding his head in her lap, the blood trickling out of the side of his mouth, just like in the movies. But the pictures were no fun after a while.

So when Dada Bibi was rewinding, just looking at them, one at a time, but not pressing any discussion, Rae Ann'd said, "I want to live for the people." And Gretchen had said, "Right on." Wasn't nothin hip about dying. Then they started talking about what they could do with their lives to help Black people, to free Black people. And Gretchen said she didn't know if she'd feel like going to school long enough to teach, and she knew for sure she didn't feel like going back to the country so she couldn't see herself feeding nobody directly.

"Shit. I'm just here and ain't nobody gonna run no lame shit on me. Specially them teachers up at the school. Shit. That's the best I can do for the people, give them teachers hell. Shit," she added again, just to make clear no one had better ask her anything else about what she was prepared to do for her people.

"That's cool," said Dada Bibi, surprising them all. "Giving the teachers some static means you gotta hit them books, eat well, get plenty rest to keep the mind alert. Can't hit them with no lame shit, right?" She nodding to Gretchen.

"That's right," Gretchen said, her ass off her shoulders and her whole self trapped.

Rae Ann sniffled back a tear. She wasn't convinced she was really dying, but there was something righteous in the pain that came with thinking it. Something was wrong. She was being punished, that she knew. But she probably wasn't going to really die. She looked hard at the posters by the window, the wood carving she'd made for Kwanza on her desk, the map on the wall, the picture of Jesus on the closet she shared with her grandmother. She wasn't sure just who to make the promise to. So she simply addressed it to them all. If I can get through this time, she promised, I'm going to do something good. It left her dissatisfied, cold. To die for the people left her scared, mad, it wasn't fair. To live for the people left her confused, faintly inadequate. Was she up to it? And what?

"Here you go," M'Dear was saying, pitching the bag onto her bed. "Dinner be on in a minute."

What's wrong with me, she thought, M'Dear fraid to come in the room and get her slippers, fraid to come near me. What have I done? She up-ended the bag and set everything out neatly. A plan. She had to think methodically and stop all this crying and confusion. I will read everything two times. Then I'll know what to do. She allowed herself a moist blink. She would find out what she had done and take her whipping. Then everything would be like before. M'Dear would come into the room again and set awhile talking while she changed her shoes. Dada Bibi would hug her again. But then Dada Bibi would hug her no matter what. She even hugged the dirty kids from Mason Street. And drank behind them too without even rinsing the cup. Either Dada Bibi had a powerful health to combat germs, she thought, ripping open the packages, or the woman was crazy.

[1977]

Never Marry a Mexican

Sandra Cisneros

NEVER MARRY A MEXICAN, MY MA SAID ONCE AND ALWAYS. SHE SAID THIS because of my father. She said this though she was Mexican too. But she was born here in the U.S., and he was born there, and it's *not* the same, you know.

I'll *never* marry. Not any man. I've known men too intimately. I've witnessed their infidelities, and I've helped them to it. Unzipped and unhooked and agreed to clandestine maneuvers. I've been accomplice, committed premeditated crimes. I'm guilty of having caused deliberate pain to other women. I'm vindictive and cruel, and I'm capable of anything.

I admit, there was a time when all I wanted was to belong to a man. To wear that gold band on my left hand and be worn on his arm like an expensive jewel brilliant in the light of day. Not the sneaking around I did in different bars that all looked the same, red carpets with a black grillwork design, flocked wallpaper, wooden wagon-wheel light fixtures with hurricane lampshades a sick amber color like the drinking glasses you get for free at gas stations.

Dark bars, dark restaurants then. And if not—my apartment, with his toothbrush firmly planted in the toothbrush holder like a flag on the North Pole. The bed so big because he never stayed the whole night. Of course not.

Borrowed. That's how I've had my men. Just the cream skimmed off the top. Just the sweetest part of the fruit, without the bitter skin that daily living with a spouse can rend. They've come to me when they wanted the sweet meat then.

So, no. I've never married and never will. Not because I couldn't, but because I'm too romantic for marriage. Marriage has failed me, you could say. Not a man exists who hasn't disappointed me, whom I could trust to love the way I've loved. It's because I believe too much in marriage that I don't. Better to not marry than live a lie.

Mexican men, forget it. For a long time the men clearing off the tables or chopping meat behind the butcher counter or driving the bus I rode to school every day, those weren't men. Not men I considered as potential lovers. Mexican, Puerto Rican, Cuban, Chilean, Colombian, Panamanian, Salvadorean, Bolivian, Honduran, Argentine, Dominican, Venezuelan, Guatemalan, Ecuadorean, Nicaraguan, Peruvian, Costa Rican, Paraguayan, Uruguayan, I don't care. I never saw them. My mother did this to me.

I guess she did it to spare me and Ximena the pain she went through. Having married a Mexican man at seventeen. Having had to put up with all the grief a Mexican family can put on a girl because she was from *el otro lado*, the other side, and my father had married down by marrying her. If he had married a white woman from *el otro lado*, that would've been different. That would've been marrying up, even if the white girl was poor. But what could be more ridiculous than a Mexican girl who couldn't even speak Spanish, who didn't know enough to set a separate plate for each course at dinner, nor how to fold cloth napkins, nor how to set the silverware.

In my ma's house the plates were always stacked in the center of the table, the knives and forks and spoons standing in a jar, help yourself. All the dishes chipped or cracked and nothing matched. And no tablecloth, ever. And newspapers set on the table whenever my grandpa sliced watermelons, and how embarrassed she would be when her boyfriend, my father, would come over and there were newspapers all over the kitchen floor and table. And my grandpa, big hardworking Mexican man, saying Come, come and eat, and slicing a big wedge of those dark green watermelons, a big slice, he wasn't stingy with food. Never, even during the Depression. Come, come and eat, to whoever came knocking on the back door. Hobos sitting at the dinner table and the children staring and staring. Because my grandfather always made sure they never went without. Flour and rice, by the barrel and by the sack. Potatoes. Big bags of pinto beans. And watermelons, bought three or four at a time, rolled under his bed and brought out when you least expected. My grandpa had survived three wars, one Mexican, two American, and he knew what living without meant. He knew.

My father, on the other hand, did not. True, when he first came to this country he had worked shelling clams, washing dishes, planting hedges, sat on the back of the bus in Little Rock and had the bus driver shout, You—sit up here, and my father had shrugged sheepishly and said, No speak English.

But he was no economic refugee, no immigrant fleeing a war. My father ran away from home because he was afraid of facing his father after his first-year grades at the university proved he'd spent more time fooling around than studying. He left behind a house in Mexico City that was neither poor nor rich, but thought itself better than both. A boy who would get off a bus when he saw a girl he knew board if he didn't have the money to pay her fare. That was the world my father left behind.

I imagine my father in his *fanfarrón* clothes, because that's what he was, a *fanfarrón*. That's what my mother thought the moment she turned around to the voice that was asking her to dance. A big show-off, she'd say years later. Nothing but a big show-off. But she never said why she married him. My father in his shark-blue suits with the starched handkerchief in the breast pocket, his felt fedora, his tweed topcoat with the big shoulders, and heavy British wing tips with the pin-hole design on the heel and toe. Clothes that cost a lot. Expensive. That's what my father's things said. *Calidad.* Quality.

My father must've found the U.S. Mexicans very strange, so foreign from what he knew at home in Mexico City where the servant served watermelon on a plate with silverware and a cloth napkin, or mangos with their own special prongs. Not like this, eating with your legs wide open in the yard, or in the kitchen hunkered over newspapers. *Come, come and eat.* No, never like this.

How I make my living depends. Sometimes I work as a translator. Sometimes I get paid by the word and sometimes by the hour, depending on the job. I do this in the day, and at night I paint. I'd do anything in the day just so I can keep on painting.

I work as a substitute teacher, too, for the San Antonio Independent School District. And that's worse than translating those travel brochures with their tiny print, believe me. I can't stand kids. Not any age. But it pays the rent.

Any way you look at it, what I do to make a living is a form of prostitution. People say, "A painter? How nice," and want to invite me to their parties, have me decorate the lawn like an exotic orchid for hire. But do they buy art?

I'm amphibious. I'm a person who doesn't belong to any class. The rich like to have me around because they envy my creativity; they know they can't buy *that*. The poor don't mind if I live in their neighborhood because they know I'm poor like they are, even if my education and the way I dress keeps us worlds apart. I don't belong to any class. Not to the poor, whose neighborhood I share. Not to the rich, who come to my exhibitions and buy my work. Not to the middle class from which my sister Ximena and I fled.

When I was young, when I first left home and rented that apartment with my sister and her kids right after her husband left, I thought it would be glamorous to be an artist. I wanted to be like Frida[1] or Tina.[2] I was ready to suffer with my camera and my paint brushes in that awful apartment we rented for $150 each because it had high ceilings and those wonderful glass skylights that convinced us we had to have it. Never mind there was no sink

---

[1] Frida Kahlo (1907–1954) was a Mexican artist whose work is characterized by vibrant colors, striking self-portraits, and surrealist images that depict women's pain and suffering.

[2] Tina Modotti (1896–1942), an Italian-born Hollywood actress and photographer renowned for her beauty and political notoriety, was a staunch supporter of the poor and oppressed. Her photographs highlight images of ordinary people, objects, and events.

in the bathroom, and a tub that looked like a sarcophagus, and floorboards that didn't meet, and a hallway to scare away the dead. But fourteen-foot ceilings was enough for us to write a check for the deposit right then and there. We thought it all romantic. You know the place, the one on Zarzamora on top of the barber shop with the Casasola prints of the Mexican Revolution. Neon BIRRIA TEPATITLÁN sign round the corner, two goats knocking their heads together, and all those Mexican bakeries, Las Brisas for *huevos rancheros* and *carnitas*[3] and *barbacoa* on Sundays, and fresh fruit milk shakes, and mango *paletas*,[4] and more signs in Spanish than in English. We thought it was great, great. The barrio looked cute in the daytime, like Sesame Street. Kids hopscotching on the sidewalk, blessed little boogers. And hardware stores that still sold ostrich-feather dusters, and whole families marching out of Our Lady of Guadalupe Church on Sundays, girls in their swirly-whirly dresses and patent-leather shoes, boys in their dress Stacys and shiny shirts.

But nights, that was nothing like what we knew up on the north side. Pistols going off like the wild, wild West, and me and Ximena and the kids huddled in one bed with the lights off listening to it all, saying, Go to sleep, babies, its just firecrackers. But we knew better. Ximena would say, Clemencia, maybe we should go home. And I'd say, Shit! Because she knew as well as I did there was no home to go home to. Not with our mother. Not with that man she married. After Daddy died, it was like we didn't matter. Like Ma was so busy feeling sorry for herself, I don't know. I'm not like Ximena. I still haven't worked it out after all this time, even though our mother's dead now. My half brothers living in that house that should've been ours, me and Ximena's. But that's—how do say it?—water under the damn? I can't ever get the sayings right even though I was born in this country. We didn't say shit like that in our house.

Once Daddy was gone, it was like my ma didn't exist, like if she died, too. I used to have a little finch, twisted one of its tiny red legs between the bars of the cage once, who knows how. The leg just dried up and fell off. My bird lived a long time without it, just a little red stump of a leg. He was fine, really. My mother's memory is like that, like if something already dead dried up and fell off, and I stopped missing where she used to be. Like if I never had a mother. And I'm not ashamed to say it either. When she married that white man, and he and his boys moved into my father's house, it was as if she stopped being my mother. Like I never even had one.

Ma always sick and too busy worrying about her own life, she would've sold us to the Devil if she could. "Because I married so young, *mi'ja*,"[5] she'd

<hr>

[3] *huevos rancheros*: eggs scrambled with onions, tomatoes, and green chiles; *carnitas*: small chunks of meat (usually beef) prepared and served on a skewer.

[4] *paletas*: ice cream or candy on a stick, such as a popsicle or lollipop.

[5] An abbreviation of *mi hija*, or *my daughter*. A term of endearment used by women addressing other women in the same peer group or who are younger and less wise in the ways of the world.

say. "Because your father, he was so much older than me, and I never had a chance to be young. Honey, try to understand . . ." Then I'd stop listening.

That man she met at work, Owen Lambert, the foreman at the photo-finishing plant, who she was seeing even while my father was sick. Even then. That's what I can't forgive.

When my father was coughing up blood and phlegm in the hospital, half his face frozen, and his tongue so fat he couldn't talk, he looked so small with all those tubes and plastic sacks dangling around him. But what I remember most is the smell, like death was already sitting on his chest. And I remember the doctor scraping the phlegm out of my father's mouth with a white washcloth, and my daddy gagging and I wanted to yell, Stop, you stop that, he's my daddy. Goddamn you. Make him live. Daddy, don't. Not yet, not yet, not yet. And how I couldn't hold myself up, I couldn't hold myself up. Like if they'd beaten me, or pulled my insides out through my nostrils, like if they'd stuffed me with cinnamon and cloves, and I just stood there dry-eyed next to Ximena and my mother, Ximena between us because I wouldn't let her stand next to me. Everyone repeating over and over the Ave Marías and Padre Nuestros. The priest sprinkling holy water, *mundo sin fin, amén.*[6]

Drew, remember when you used to call me your Malinalli?[7] It was a joke, a private game between us, because you looked like a Cortez with that beard of yours. My skin dark against yours. Beautiful, you said. You said I was beautiful, and when you said it, Drew, I was.

My Malinalli, Malinche,[8] my courtesan, you said, and yanked my head back by the braid. Calling me that name in between little gulps of breath and the raw kisses you gave, laughing from that black beard of yours.

Before daybreak, you'd be gone, same as always, before I even knew it. And it was as if I'd imagined you, only the teeth marks on my belly and nipples proving me wrong.

Your skin pale, but your hair blacker than a pirate's. Malinalli, you called me, remember? *Mi doradita.*[9] I liked when you spoke to me in my language. I could love myself and think myself worth loving.

Your son. Does he know how much I had to do with his birth? I was the one who convinced you to let him be born. Did you tell him, while his mother lay on her back laboring his birth, I lay in his mother's bed making love to you.

You're nothing without me. I created you from spit and red dust. And I can snuff you between my finger and thumb if I want to. Blow you to kingdom come. You're just a smudge of paint I chose to birth on canvas. And when I made you over, you were no longer a part of her, you were all

---

[6] World without end, amen.
[7] Whore, prostitute.
[8] Same meaning as *Malinalli*.
[9] Literally, *my little golden one*, a term of endearment referring to one who is golden brown in complexion.

mine. The landscape of your body taut as a drum. The heart beneath that hide thrumming and thrumming. Not an inch did I give back.

I paint and repaint you the way I see fit, even now. After all these years. Did you know that? Little fool. You think I went hobbling along with my life, whimpering and whining like some twangy country-and-western when you went back to her. But I've been waiting. Making the world look at you from my eyes. And if that's not power, what is?

Nights I light all the candles in the house, the ones to La Virgen de Guadalupe,[10] the ones to El Niño Fidencio, Don Pedrito Jaramillo, Santo Niño de Atocha, Nuestra Señora de San Juan de los Lagos,[11] and especially, Santa Lucía, with her beautiful eyes on a plate.[12]

Your eyes are beautiful, you said. You said they were the darkest eyes you'd ever seen and kissed each one as if they were capable of miracles. And after you left, I wanted to scoop them out with a spoon, place them on a plate under these blue blue skies, food for the blackbirds.

The boy, your son. The one with the face of that redheaded woman who is your wife. The boy red-freckled like fish food floating on the skin of water. That boy.

I've been waiting patient as a spider all these years, since I was nineteen and he was just an idea hovering in his mother's head, and I'm the one that gave him permission and made it happen, see.

Because your father wanted to leave your mother and live with me. Your mother whining for a child, at least *that*. And he kept saying, Later, we'll see, later. But all along it was me he wanted to be with, it was me, he said.

I want to tell you this evenings when you come to see me. When you're full of talk about what kind of clothes you're going to buy, and what you used to be like when you started high school and what you're like now that you're almost finished. And how everyone knows you as a rocker, and your band, and your new red guitar that you just got because your mother gave you a choice, a guitar or a car, but you don't need a car, do you, because I drive you everywhere. You could be my son if you weren't so light-skinned.

This happened. A long time ago. Before you were born. When you were a moth inside your mother's heart, I was your father's student, yes, just like you're mine now. And your father painted and painted me, because he said, I was his *doradita*, all golden and sun-baked, and that's the kind of woman he likes best, the ones brown as river sand, yes. And he took me under his wing and in his bed, this man, this teacher, your father. I was honored that he'd done me the favor. I was that young.

All I know is I was sleeping with your father the night you were born. In the same bed where you were conceived. I was sleeping with your father and didn't give a damn about that woman, your mother. If she was a brown

[10] A patroness of Mexican and Indian peoples, the Virgin of Guadalupe provides comfort in sickness and protection against evil, particularly war.

[11] Various prominent figures in Mexican religious belief and folklore.

[12] Santa Lucía is a Roman Catholic saint and the protectress against disease of the eyes. She is thought to have been blinded in later life.

woman like me, I might've had a harder time living with myself, but since she's not, I don't care. I was there first, always. I've always been there, in the mirror, under his skin, in the blood, before you were born. And he's been here in my heart before I even knew him. Understand? He's always been here. Always. Dissolving like a hibiscus flower, exploding like a rope into dust. I don't care what's right anymore. I don't care about his wife. She's not *my* sister.

And it's not the last time I've slept with a man the night his wife is birthing a baby. Why do I do that, I wonder? Sleep with a man when his wife is giving life, being suckled by a thing with its eyes still shut. Why do that? It's always given me a bit of crazy joy to be able to kill those women like that, without their knowing it. To know I've had their husbands when they were anchored in blue hospital rooms, their guts yanked inside out, the baby sucking their breasts while their husband sucked mine. All this while their ass stitches were still hurting.

Once, drunk on margaritas, I telephoned your father at four in the morning, woke the bitch up. Hello, she chirped. I want to talk to Drew. Just a moment, she said in her most polite drawing-room English. Just a moment. I laughed about that for weeks. What a stupid ass to pass the phone over to the lug asleep beside her. Excuse me, honey, it's for you. When Drew mumbled hello I was laughing so hard I could hardly talk. Drew? That dumb bitch of a wife of yours, I said, and that's all I could manage. That stupid stupid stupid. No Mexican woman would react like that. Excuse me, honey. It cracked me up.

He's got the same kind of skin, the boy. All the blue veins pale and clear just like his mama. Skin like roses in December. Pretty boy. Little clone. Little cells split into you and you and you. Tell me, baby, which part of you is your mother. I try to imagine her lips, her jaw, her long long legs that wrapped themselves around this father who took me to his bed.

This happened. I'm asleep. Or pretend to be. You're watching me, Drew. I feel your weight when you sit on the corner of the bed, dressed and ready to go, but now you're just watching me sleep. Nothing. Not a word. Not a kiss. Just sitting. You're taking me in, under inspection. What do you think already?

I haven't stopped dreaming you. Did you know that? Do you think it's strange? I never tell, though. I keep it to myself like I do all the thoughts I think of you.

After all these years.

I don't want you looking at me. I don't want you taking me in while I'm asleep. I'll open my eyes and frighten you away.

There. What did I tell you? *Drew? What is it?* Nothing. I'd knew you'd say that.

Let's not talk. We're no good at it. With you I'm useless with words. As if somehow I had to learn to speak all over again, as if the words I needed haven't been invented yet. We're cowards. Come back to bed. At least there I feel I have you for a little. For a moment. For a catch of the breath. You let go. You ache and tug. You rip my skin.

You're almost not a man without your clothes. How do I explain it? You're so much a child in my bed. Nothing but a big boy who needs to be held. I won't let anyone hurt you. My pirate. My slender boy of a man.

After all these years.

I didn't imagine it, did I? A Ganges, an eye of the storm. For a little. When we forgot ourselves, you tugged me, I leapt inside you and split you like an apple. Opened for the other to look and not give back. Something wrenched itself loose. Your body doesn't lie. It's not silent like you.

You're nude as a pearl. You've lost your train of smoke. You're tender as rain. If I'd put you in my mouth you'd dissolve like snow.

You were ashamed to be so naked. Pulled back. But I saw you for what you are, when you opened yourself for me. When you were careless and let yourself through. I caught that catch of the breath. I'm not crazy.

When you slept, you tugged me toward you. You sought me in the dark. I didn't sleep. Every cell, every follicle, every nerve, alert. Watching you sigh and roll and turn and hug me closer to you. I didn't sleep. I was taking *you* in that time.

Your mother? Only once. Years after your father and I stopped seeing each other. At an art exhibition. A show on the photographs of Eugène Atget.[13] Those images, I could look at them for hours. I'd taken a group of students with me.

It was your father I saw first. And in that instant I felt as if everyone in the room, all the sepia-toned photographs, my students, the men in business suits, the high-heeled women, the security guards, everyone, could see me for what I was. I had to scurry out, lead my kids to another gallery, but some things destiny has cut out for you.

He caught up with us in the coat-check area, arm in arm with a redheaded Barbie doll in a fur coat. One of those scary Dallas types, hair yanked into a ponytail, big shiny face like the women behind the cosmetic counters at Neiman's. That's what I remember. She must've been with him all along, only I swear I never saw her until that second.

You could tell from a slight hesitancy, only slight because he's too suave to hesitate, that he was nervous. Then he's walking toward me, and I didn't know what to do, just stood there dazed like those animals crossing the road at night when the headlights stun them.

And I don't know why, but all of a sudden I looked at my shoes and felt ashamed at how old they looked. And he comes up to me, my love, your father, in that way of his with that grin that makes me want to beat him, makes me want to make love to him, and he says in the most sincere voice you ever heard, "Ah, Clemencia! *This* is Megan." No introduction could've been meaner. *This* is Megan. Just like that.

[13] A twentieth-century French commercial photographer whose career spanned 30 years.

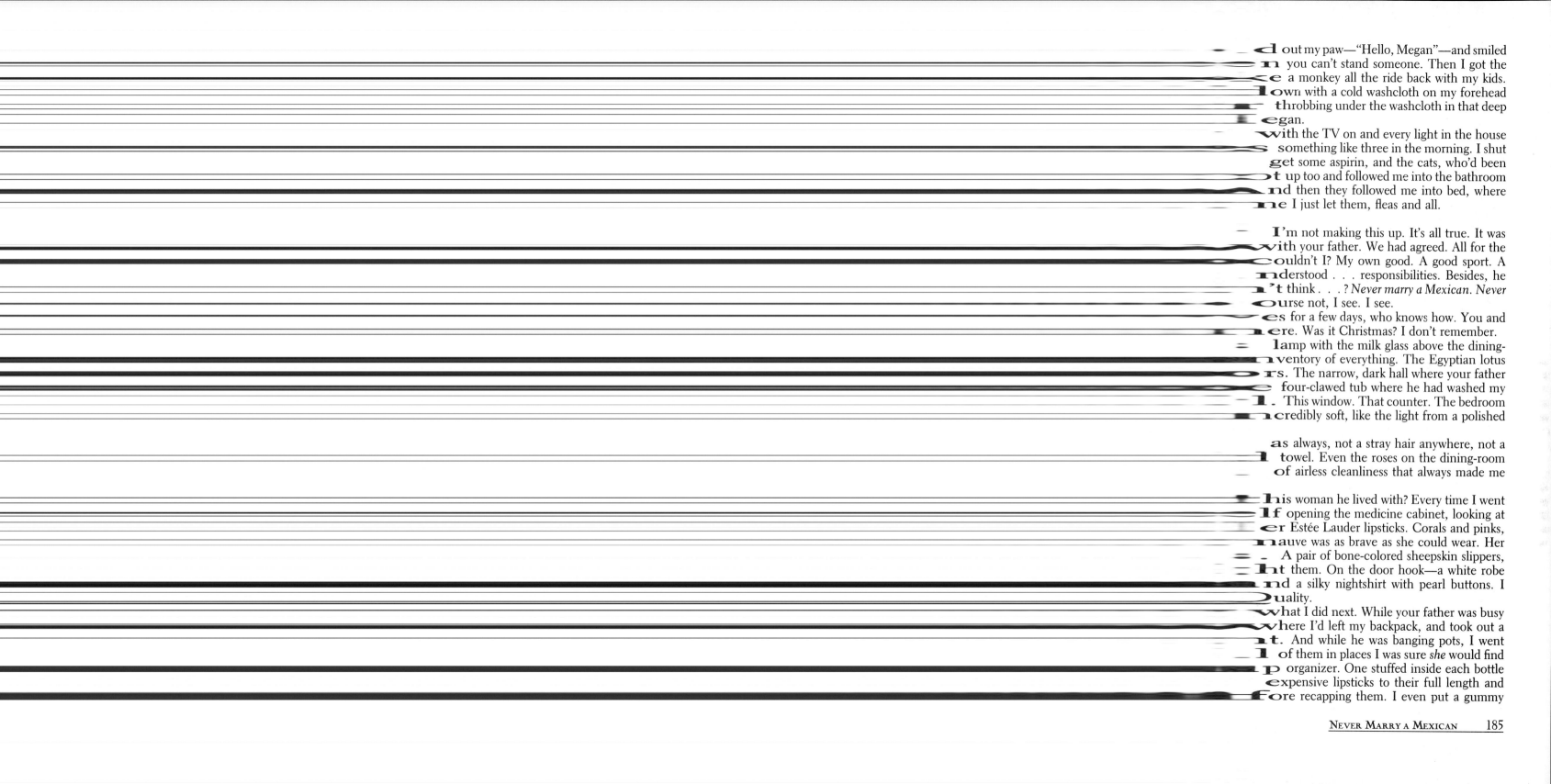

d out my paw—"Hello, Megan"—and smiled
n you can't stand someone. Then I got the
e a monkey all the ride back with my kids.
lown with a cold washcloth on my forehead
throbbing under the washcloth in that deep
egan.
with the TV on and every light in the house
s something like three in the morning. I shut
get some aspirin, and the cats, who'd been
t up too and followed me into the bathroom
nd then they followed me into bed, where
ne I just let them, fleas and all.

I'm not making this up. It's all true. It was
vith your father. We had agreed. All for the
ouldn't I? My own good. A good sport. A
nderstood . . . responsibilities. Besides, he
n't think . . . ? *Never marry a Mexican. Never*
ourse not, I see. I see.
es for a few days, who knows how. You and
ere. Was it Christmas? I don't remember.
lamp with the milk glass above the dining-
nventory of everything. The Egyptian lotus
rs. The narrow, dark hall where your father
e four-clawed tub where he had washed my
l. This window. That counter. The bedroom
ncredibly soft, like the light from a polished

as always, not a stray hair anywhere, not a
l towel. Even the roses on the dining-room
of airless cleanliness that always made me

his woman he lived with? Every time I went
If opening the medicine cabinet, looking at
er Estée Lauder lipsticks. Corals and pinks,
mauve was as brave as she could wear. Her
A pair of bone-colored sheepskin slippers,
ht them. On the door hook—a white robe
nd a silky nightshirt with pearl buttons. I
Quality.
What I did next. While your father was busy
where I'd left my backpack, and took out a
at. And while he was banging pots, I went
l of them in places I was sure *she* would find
p organizer. One stuffed inside each bottle
expensive lipsticks to their full length and
fore recapping them. I even put a gummy

bear in her diaphragm case in the very center of th
moon.

Why bother? Drew could take the blame. Or he
cleaning woman's Mexican voodoo. I knew that, too
a strange satisfaction wandering about the house leavi
she would look.

And just as Drew was shouting, "Dinner!" I saw i
those wooden babushka dolls Drew had brought her f
I know. He'd bought one just like it for me.

I just did what I did, uncapped the doll inside a d
I got to the very center, the tiniest baby inside all
replaced with a gummy bear. And then I put the d
found them, one inside the other, inside the other
which I put inside my pocket. All through dinner I
pocket of my jean jacket. When I touched it, it mad

On the way home, on the bridge over the *arroyo*[14]
I stopped the car, switched on the emergency blinkers
the wooden toy into that muddy creek where winos p
Barbie doll's toy stewing there in that muck. It gave m
before and since.

Then I drove home and slept like the dead.

These mornings, I fix coffee for me, milk for th
woman, and I can't see a trace of my lover in this b
him by immaculate conception.

I sleep with this boy, their son. To make the boy l
his father. To make him want me, hunger, twist in
swallowed glass. I put him in my mouth. Here, little
Boy with hard thighs and just a bit of down and a sm
his father's, and that back like a valentine. Come her
to *mamita*.[17] Here's a bit of toast.

I can tell from the way he looks at me, I have him
sparrow. I have the patience of eternity. Come to m
bird. I don't move. I don't startle him. I let him nibbl
his belly. Stroke him. Before I snap my teeth.

What is it inside me that makes me so crazy at 2
on alcohol in my blood when there isn't any. It's somet l
that poisons the blood and tips me when the night sw
whole sky were leaning against my brain.

And if I killed someone on a night like this? An
instead, I'd be guilty of getting in the line of crossfir

[14] Stream or brook.
[15] Heart.
[16] *My little loved one.* Can have familial, romantic, or sexual co
[17] A diminutive form of *mama*, meaning *mother.*

woman like me, I might've had a harder time living with myself, but since she's not, I don't care. I was there first, always. I've always been there, in the mirror, under his skin, in the blood, before you were born. And he's been here in my heart before I even knew him. Understand? He's always been here. Always. Dissolving like a hibiscus flower, exploding like a rope into dust. I don't care what's right anymore. I don't care about his wife. She's not *my* sister.

And it's not the last time I've slept with a man the night his wife is birthing a baby. Why do I do that, I wonder? Sleep with a man when his wife is giving life, being suckled by a thing with its eyes still shut. Why do that? It's always given me a bit of crazy joy to be able to kill those women like that, without their knowing it. To know I've had their husbands when they were anchored in blue hospital rooms, their guts yanked inside out, the baby sucking their breasts while their husband sucked mine. All this while their ass stitches were still hurting.

Once, drunk on margaritas, I telephoned your father at four in the morning, woke the bitch up. Hello, she chirped. I want to talk to Drew. Just a moment, she said in her most polite drawing-room English. Just a moment. I laughed about that for weeks. What a stupid ass to pass the phone over to the lug asleep beside her. Excuse me, honey, it's for you. When Drew mumbled hello I was laughing so hard I could hardly talk. Drew? That dumb bitch of a wife of yours, I said, and that's all I could manage. That stupid stupid stupid. No Mexican woman would react like that. Excuse me, honey. It cracked me up.

He's got the same kind of skin, the boy. All the blue veins pale and clear just like his mama. Skin like roses in December. Pretty boy. Little clone. Little cells split into you and you and you. Tell me, baby, which part of you is your mother. I try to imagine her lips, her jaw, her long long legs that wrapped themselves around this father who took me to his bed.

This happened. I'm asleep. Or pretend to be. You're watching me, Drew. I feel your weight when you sit on the corner of the bed, dressed and ready to go, but now you're just watching me sleep. Nothing. Not a word. Not a kiss. Just sitting. You're taking me in, under inspection. What do you think already?

I haven't stopped dreaming you. Did you know that? Do you think it's strange? I never tell, though. I keep it to myself like I do all the thoughts I think of you.

After all these years.

I don't want you looking at me. I don't want you taking me in while I'm asleep. I'll open my eyes and frighten you away.

There. What did I tell you? *Drew? What is it?* Nothing. I'd knew you'd say that.

Let's not talk. We're no good at it. With you I'm useless with words. As if somehow I had to learn to speak all over again, as if the words I needed haven't been invented yet. We're cowards. Come back to bed. At least there I feel I have you for a little. For a moment. For a catch of the breath. You let go. You ache and tug. You rip my skin.

You're almost not a man without your clothes. How do I explain it? You're so much a child in my bed. Nothing but a big boy who needs to be held. I won't let anyone hurt you. My pirate. My slender boy of a man.

After all these years.

I didn't imagine it, did I? A Ganges, an eye of the storm. For a little. When we forgot ourselves, you tugged me, I leapt inside you and split you like an apple. Opened for the other to look and not give back. Something wrenched itself loose. Your body doesn't lie. It's not silent like you.

You're nude as a pearl. You've lost your train of smoke. You're tender as rain. If I'd put you in my mouth you'd dissolve like snow.

You were ashamed to be so naked. Pulled back. But I saw you for what you are, when you opened yourself for me. When you were careless and let yourself through. I caught that catch of the breath. I'm not crazy.

When you slept, you tugged me toward you. You sought me in the dark. I didn't sleep. Every cell, every follicle, every nerve, alert. Watching you sigh and roll and turn and hug me closer to you. I didn't sleep. I was taking *you* in that time.

Your mother? Only once. Years after your father and I stopped seeing each other. At an art exhibition. A show on the photographs of Eugène Atget.[13] Those images, I could look at them for hours. I'd taken a group of students with me.

It was your father I saw first. And in that instant I felt as if everyone in the room, all the sepia-toned photographs, my students, the men in business suits, the high-heeled women, the security guards, everyone, could see me for what I was. I had to scurry out, lead my kids to another gallery, but some things destiny has cut out for you.

He caught up with us in the coat-check area, arm in arm with a redheaded Barbie doll in a fur coat. One of those scary Dallas types, hair yanked into a ponytail, big shiny face like the women behind the cosmetic counters at Neiman's. That's what I remember. She must've been with him all along, only I swear I never saw her until that second.

You could tell from a slight hesitancy, only slight because he's too suave to hesitate, that he was nervous. Then he's walking toward me, and I didn't know what to do, just stood there dazed like those animals crossing the road at night when the headlights stun them.

And I don't know why, but all of a sudden I looked at my shoes and felt ashamed at how old they looked. And he comes up to me, my love, your father, in that way of his with that grin that makes me want to beat him, makes me want to make love to him, and he says in the most sincere voice you ever heard, "Ah, Clemencia! *This* is Megan." No introduction could've been meaner. *This* is Megan. Just like that.

[13] A twentieth-century French commercial photographer whose career spanned 30 years.

I grinned like an idiot and held out my paw—"Hello, Megan"—and smiled too much the way you do when you can't stand someone. Then I got the hell out of there, chattering like a monkey all the ride back with my kids. When I got home I had to lie down with a cold washcloth on my forehead and the TV on. All I could hear throbbing under the washcloth in that deep part behind my eyes: *This* is Megan.

And that's how I fell asleep, with the TV on and every light in the house burning. When I woke up it was something like three in the morning. I shut the lights and TV and went to get some aspirin, and the cats, who'd been asleep with me on the couch, got up too and followed me into the bathroom as if they knew what's what. And then they followed me into bed, where they aren't allowed, but this time I just let them, fleas and all.

This happened, too. I swear I'm not making this up. It's all true. It was the last time I was going to be with your father. We had agreed. All for the best. Surely I could see that, couldn't I? My own good. A good sport. A young girl like me. Hadn't I understood . . . responsibilities. Besides, he could *never* marry *me*. You didn't think . . . ? *Never marry a Mexican. Never marry a Mexican* . . . No, of course not, I see. I see.

We had the house to ourselves for a few days, who knows how. You and your mother had gone somewhere. Was it Christmas? I don't remember.

I remember the leaded-glass lamp with the milk glass above the dining-room table. I made a mental inventory of everything. The Egyptian lotus design on the hinges of the doors. The narrow, dark hall where your father and I had made love once. The four-clawed tub where he had washed my hair and rinsed it with a tin bowl. This window. That counter. The bedroom with its light in the morning, incredibly soft, like the light from a polished dime.

The house was immaculate, as always, not a stray hair anywhere, not a flake of dandruff or a crumpled towel. Even the roses on the dining-room table held their breath. A kind of airless cleanliness that always made me want to sneeze.

Why was I so curious about this woman he lived with? Every time I went to the bathroom, I found myself opening the medicine cabinet, looking at all the things that were hers. Her Estée Lauder lipsticks. Corals and pinks, of course. Her nail polishes—mauve was as brave as she could wear. Her cotton balls and blond hairpins. A pair of bone-colored sheepskin slippers, as clean as the day she'd bought them. On the door hook—a white robe with a MADE IN ITALY label, and a silky nightshirt with pearl buttons. I touched the fabrics. *Calidad.* Quality.

I don't know how to explain what I did next. While your father was busy in the kitchen, I went over to where I'd left my backpack, and took out a bag of gummy bears I'd bought. And while he was banging pots, I went around the house and left a trail of them in places I was sure *she* would find them. One in her lucite makeup organizer. One stuffed inside each bottle of nail polish. I untwisted the expensive lipsticks to their full length and smushed a bear on the top before recapping them. I even put a gummy bear in her diaphragm case in the very center of that luminescent rubber moon.

Why bother? Drew could take the blame. Or he could say it was the cleaning woman's Mexican voodoo. I knew that, too. It didn't matter. I got a strange satisfaction wandering about the house leaving them in places only she would look.

And just as Drew was shouting, "Dinner!" I saw it on the desk. One of those wooden babushka dolls Drew had brought her from his trip to Russia. I know. He'd bought one just like it for me.

I just did what I did, uncapped the doll inside a doll inside a doll, until I got to the very center, the tiniest baby inside all the others, and this I replaced with a gummy bear. And then I put the dolls back, just like I'd found them, one inside the other, inside the other. Except for the baby, which I put inside my pocket. All through dinner I kept reaching in the pocket of my jean jacket. When I touched it, it made me feel good.

On the way home, on the bridge over the *arroyo*[14] on Guadalupe Street, I stopped the car, switched on the emergency blinkers, got out, and dropped the wooden toy into that muddy creek where winos piss and rats swim. The Barbie doll's toy stewing there in that muck. It gave me a feeling like nothing before and since.

Then I drove home and slept like the dead.

These mornings, I fix coffee for me, milk for the boy. I think of that woman, and I can't see a trace of my lover in this boy, as if she conceived him by immaculate conception.

I sleep with this boy, their son. To make the boy love me the way I love his father. To make him want me, hunger, twist in his sleep, as if he'd swallowed glass. I put him in my mouth. Here, little piece of my *corazón*.[15] Boy with hard thighs and just a bit of down and a small hard downy ass like his father's, and that back like a valentine. Come here, *mi cariñito*.[16] Come to *mamita*.[17] Here's a bit of toast.

I can tell from the way he looks at me, I have him in my power. Come, sparrow. I have the patience of eternity. Come to *mamita*. My stupid little bird. I don't move. I don't startle him. I let him nibble. All, all for you. Rub his belly. Stroke him. Before I snap my teeth.

What is it inside me that makes me so crazy at 2 A.M.? I can't blame it on alcohol in my blood when there isn't any. It's something worse. Something that poisons the blood and tips me when the night swells and I feel as if the whole sky were leaning against my brain.

And if I killed someone on a night like this? And if it was *me* I killed instead, I'd be guilty of getting in the line of crossfire, innocent bystander,

---

[14] Stream or brook.

[15] Heart.

[16] *My little loved one.* Can have familial, romantic, or sexual connotations.

[17] A diminutive form of *mama*, meaning *mother.*

isn't it a shame. I'd be walking with my head full of images and my back to the guilty. Suicide? I couldn't say. I didn't see it.

Except it's not me who I want to kill. When the gravity of the planets is just right, it all tilts and upsets the visible balance. And that's when it wants to out from my eyes. That's when I get on the telephone, dangerous as a terrorist. There's nothing to do but let it come.

So. What do you think? Are you convinced now I'm as crazy as a tulip or a taxi? As vagrant as a cloud?

Sometimes the sky is so big and I feel so little at night. That's the problem with being a cloud. The sky is so terribly big. Why is it worse at night, when I have such an urge to communicate and no language with which to form the words? Only colors. Pictures. And you know what I have to say isn't always pleasant.

Oh, love, there. I've gone and done it. What good is it? Good or bad, I've done what I had to do and needed to. And you've answered the phone, and startled me away like a bird. And now you're probably swearing under your breath and going back to sleep, with that wife beside you, warm, radiating her own heat, alive under the flannel and down and smelling a bit like milk and hand cream, and that smell familiar and dear to you, oh.

Human beings pass me on the street, and I want to reach out and strum them as if they were guitars. Sometimes all humanity strikes me as lovely. I just want to reach out and stroke someone, and say There, there, it's all right, honey. There, there, there.

[1991]

American Horse

Louise Erdrich

THE WOMAN SLEEPING ON THE COT IN THE WOODSHED WAS ALBERTINE American Horse. The name was left over from her mother's short marriage. The boy was the son of the man she had loved and let go. Buddy was on the cot, too, sitting on the edge because he'd been awake three hours watching out for his mother and besides, she took up the whole cot. Her feet hung over the edge, limp and brown as two trout. Her long arms reached out and slapped at things she saw in her dreams.

Buddy had been knocked awake out of hiding in a washing machine while herds of policemen with dogs searched through a large building with many tiny rooms. When the arm came down, Buddy screamed because it had a blue cuff and sharp silver buttons. "Tss," his mother mumbled, half awake, "wasn't nothing." But Buddy sat up after her breathing went deep again, and he watched.

There was something coming and he knew it.

It was coming from very far off but he had a picture of it in his mind. It was a large thing made of metal with many barbed hooks, points, and drag chains on it, something like a giant potato peeler that rolled out of the sky, scraping clouds down with it and jabbing or crushing everything that lay in its path on the ground.

Buddy watched his mother. If he woke her up, she would know what to do about the thing, but he thought he'd wait until he saw it for sure before he shook her. She was pretty, sleeping, and he liked knowing he could look at her as long and close up as he wanted. He took a strand of her hair and held it in his hands as if it was the rein to a delicate beast. She was strong enough and could pull him along like the horse their name was.

Buddy had his mother's and his grandmother's name because his father had been a big mistake.

"They're all mistakes, even your father. But *you* are the best thing that ever happened to me."

That was what she said when he asked.

Even Kadie, the boyfriend crippled from being in a car wreck, was not as good a thing that had happened to his mother as Buddy was. "He was a medium-size mistake," she said. "He's hurt and I shouldn't even say that, but it's the truth." At the moment, Buddy knew that being the best thing in his mother's life, he was also the reason they were hiding from the cops.

He wanted to touch the satin roses sewed on her pink tee-shirt, but he knew he shouldn't do that even in her sleep. If she woke up and found him touching the roses, she would say, "Quit that, Buddy." Sometimes she told him to stop hugging her like a gorilla. She never said that in the mean voice she used when he oppressed her, but when she said that he loosened up anyway.

There were times he felt like hugging her so hard and in such a special way that she would say to him, "Let's get married." There were also times he closed his eyes and wished that she would die, only a few times, but still it haunted him that his wish might come true. He and Uncle Lawrence would be left alone. Buddy wasn't worried, though, about his mother getting married to somebody else. She had said to her friend, Madonna, "All men suck," when she thought Buddy wasn't listening. He had made an uncertain sound, and when they heard him they took him in their arms.

"Except for you, Buddy," his mother said. "All except for you and maybe Uncle Lawrence, although he's pushing it."

"The cops suck the worst though," Buddy whispered to his mother's sleeping face, "because they're after us." He felt tired again, slumped down, and put his legs beneath the blanket. He closed his eyes and got the feeling that the cot was lifting up beneath him, that it was arching its canvas back and then traveling, traveling very fast and in the wrong direction for when he looked up he saw the three of them were advancing to meet the great metal thing with hooks and barbs and all sorts of sharp equipment to catch their bodies and draw their blood. He heard its insides as it rushed toward them, purring softly like a powerful motor and then they were right in its shadow. He pulled the reins as hard as he could and the beast reared, lifting him. His mother clapped her hand across his mouth.

"Okay," she said. "Lay low. They're outside and they're gonna hunt."

She touched his shoulder and Buddy leaned over with her to look through a crack in the boards.

They were out there all right, Albertine saw them. Two officers and that social worker woman, Vicki Koob. There had been no whistle, no dream, no voice to warn her that they were coming. There was only the crunching sound of cinders in the yard, the engine purring, the dust sifting off their car in a fine light brownish cloud and settling around them.

The three people came to a halt in their husk of metal—the car emblazoned with the North Dakota State Highway Patrol emblem which is the glowing profile of the Sioux policeman, Red Tomahawk, the one who killed Sitting Bull. Albertine gave Buddy the blanket and told him that he might have to wrap it around him and hide underneath the cot.

"We're gonna wait and see what they do." She took him in her lap and hunched her arms around him. "Don't you worry," she whispered against his ear. "Lawrence knows how to fool them."

Buddy didn't want to look at the car and the people. He felt his mother's heart beating beneath his ear so fast it seemed to push the satin roses in and out. He put his face to them carefully and breathed the deep, soft powdery woman smell of her. That smell was also in her little face cream bottles, in her brushes, and around the washbowl after she used it. The satin felt so unbearably smooth against his cheek that he had to press closer. She didn't push him away, like he expected, but hugged him still tighter until he felt as close as he had ever been to back inside her again where she said he came from. Within the smells of her things, her soft skin and the satin of her roses, he closed his eyes then, and took his breaths softly and quickly with her heart.

They were out there, but they didn't dare get out of the car yet because of Lawrence's big, ragged dogs. Three of these dogs had loped up the dirt driveway with the car. They were rangy, alert, and bounced up and down on their cushioned paws like wolves. They didn't waste their energy barking, but positioned themselves quietly, one at either car door and the third in front of the bellied-out screen door to Uncle Lawrence's house. It was six in the morning but the wind was up already, blowing dust, ruffling their short moth-eaten coats. The big brown one on Vicki Koob's side had unusual black and white markings, stripes almost, like a hyena and he grinned at her, tongue out and teeth showing.

"Shoo!" Miss Koob opened her door with a quick jerk.

The brown dog sidestepped the door and jumped before her, tiptoeing.

Its dirty white muzzle curled and its eyes crossed suddenly as if it was zeroing its cross-hair sights in on the exact place it would bite her. She ducked back and slammed the door.

"It's mean," she told Officer Brackett. He was printing out some type of form. The other officer, Harmony, a slow man, had not yet reacted to the car's halt. He had been sitting quietly in the back seat, but now he rolled down his window and with no change in expression unsnapped his holster and drew his pistol out and pointed it at the dog on his side. The dog smacked down on its belly, wiggled under the car and was out and around the back of the house before Harmony drew his gun back. The other dogs vanished with him. From wherever they had disappeared to they began to yap and howl, and the door to the low shoebox-style house fell open.

"Heya, what's going on?"

Uncle Lawrence put his head out the door and opened wide the one eye he had in working order. The eye bulged impossibly wider in outrage when he saw the police car. But the eyes of the two officers and Miss Vicki Koob were wide open too because they had never seen Uncle Lawrence in his sleeping getup or, indeed, witnessed anything like it. For his ribs, which were cracked from a bad fall and still mending, Uncle Lawrence wore a thick white corset laced up the front with a striped sneakers lace. His glass eye and his set of dentures were still out for the night so his face puckered here and there, around its absences and scars, like a damaged but fierce little cake. Although he had a few gray streaks now, Uncle Lawrence's hair was still thick, and because he wore a special contraption of elastic straps around his head every night, two oiled waves always crested on either side of his middle part. All of this would have been sufficient to astonish, even without the most striking part of his outfit—the smoking jacket. It was made of black satin and hung open around his corset, dragging a tasseled belt. Gold thread dragons struggled up the lapels and blasted their furry red breath around his neck. As Lawrence walked down the steps, he put his arms up in surrender and the gold tassels in the inner seams of his sleeves dropped into view.

"My heavens, what a sight." Vicki Koob was impressed.

"A character," apologized Officer Harmony.

As a tribal police officer who could be counted on to help out the State Patrol, Harmony thought he always had to explain about Indians or get twice as tough to show he did not favor them. He was slow-moving and shy but two jumps ahead of other people all the same, and now, as he watched Uncle Lawrence's splendid approach, he gazed speculatively at the torn and bulging pocket of the smoking jacket. Harmony had been inside Uncle Lawrence's house before and knew that above his draped orange-crate shelf of war medals a blue-black German luger was hung carefully in a net of flat-headed nails and fishing line. Thinking of this deadly exhibition, he got out of the car and shambled toward Lawrence with a dreamy little smile of welcome on his face. But when he searched Lawrence, he found that the bulging pocket held only the lonesome-looking dentures from Lawrence's empty jaw. They were still dripping denture polish.

"I had been cleaning them when you arrived," Uncle Lawrence explained with acid dignity.

He took the toothbrush from his other pocket and aimed it like a rifle.

"Quit that, you old idiot." Harmony tossed the toothbrush away. "For once you ain't done nothing. We came for your nephew."

Lawrence looked at Harmony with a faint air of puzzlement.

"Ma Frere, listen," threatened Harmony amiably, "those two white people in the car came to get him for the welfare. They got papers on your nephew that give them the right to take him."

"Papers?" Uncle Lawrence puffed out his deeply pitted cheeks. "Let me see them papers."

The two of them walked over to Vicki's side of the car and she pulled a copy of the court order from her purse. Lawrence put his teeth back in and adjusted them with busy workings of his jaw.

"Just a minute," he reached into his breast pocket as he bent close to Miss Vicki Koob. "I can't read these without I have in my eye."

He took the eye from his breast pocket delicately, and as he popped it into his face the social worker's mouth fell open in a consternated O.

"What is this," she cried in a little voice.

Uncle Lawrence looked at her mildly. The white glass of the eye was cold as lard. The black iris was strangely charged and menacing.

"He's nuts," Brackett huffed along the side of Vicki's neck. "Never mind him."

Vicki's hair had sweated down her nape in tiny corkscrews and some of the hairs were so long and dangly now that they disappeared into the zippered back of her dress. Brackett noticed this as he spoke into her ear. His face grew red and the backs of his hands prickled. He slid under the steering wheel and got out of the car. He walked around the hood to stand with Leo Harmony.

"We could take you in too," said Brackett roughly. Lawrence eyed the officers in what was taken as defiance. "If you don't cooperate, we'll get out the handcuffs," they warned.

One of Lawrence's arms was stiff and would not move until he'd rubbed it with witch hazel in the morning. His other arm worked fine though, and he stuck it out in front of Brackett.

"Get them handcuffs," he urged them. "Put me in a welfare home."

Brackett snapped one side of the handcuffs on Lawrence's good arm and the other to the handle of the police car.

"That's to hold you," he said. "We're wasting our time. Harmony, you search that little shed over by the tall grass and Miss Koob and myself will search the house."

"My rights is violated!" Lawrence shrieked suddenly. They ignored him. He tugged at the handcuff and thought of the good heavy file he kept in his tool box and the German luger oiled and ready but never loaded, because of Buddy, over his shelf. He should have used it on these bad ones, even Harmony in his bigtime white man job. He wouldn't last long in that job anyway before somebody gave him what for.

"It's a damn scheme," said Uncle Lawrence, rattling his chains against the car. He looked over at the shed and thought maybe Albertine and Buddy had sneaked away before the car pulled into the yard. But he sagged, seeing Albertine move like a shadow within the boards. "Oh, it's all a damn scheme," he muttered again.

"I want to find that boy and salvage him," Vicki Koob explained to Officer Brackett as they walked into the house. "Look at his family life—the old man crazy as a bedbug, the mother intoxicated somewhere."

Bracket nodded, energetic, eager. He was a short hopeful redhead who failed consistently to win the hearts of women. Vicki Koob intrigued him. Now, as he watched, she pulled a tiny pen out of an ornamental clip on her blouse. It was attached to a retractable line that would suck the pen back, like a child eating one strand of spaghetti. Something about the pen on its line excited Brackett to the point of discomfort. His hand shook as he opened the screendoor and stepped in, beckoning Miss Koob to follow.

They could see the house was empty at first glance. It was only one rectangular room with whitewashed walls and a little gas stove in the middle. They had already come through the cooking lean-to with the other stove and washstand and rusty old refrigerator. That refrigerator had nothing in it but some wrinkled potatoes and a package of turkey necks. Vicki Koob noted that in her perfect-bound notebook. The beds along the walls of the big room were covered with quilts that Albertine's mother, Sophie, had made from bits of old wool coats and pants that the Sisters sold in bundles at the mission. There was no one hiding beneath the beds. No one was under the little aluminum dinette table covered with a green oilcloth, or the soft brown wood chairs tucked up to it. One wall of the big room was filled with neatly stacked crates of things—old tools and springs and small half-dismantled appliances. Five or six television sets were stacked against the wall. Their control panels spewed colored wires and at least one was cracked all the way across. Only the topmost set, with coat-hanger antenna angled sensitively to catch the bounding signals around Little Shell, looked like it could possibly work.

Not one thing escaped Vicki Koob's trained and cataloguing gaze. She made note of the cupboard that held only commodity flour and coffee. The unsanitary tin oil drum beneath the kitchen window, full of empty surplus pork cans and beer bottles, caught her eye as did Uncle Lawrence's physical and mental deteriorations. She quickly described these "benchmarks of alcoholic dependency within the extended family of Woodrow (Buddy) American Horse" as she walked around the room with the little notebook open, pushed against her belly to steady it. Although Vicki had been there before, Albertine's presence had always made it difficult for her to take notes.

"Twice the maximum allowable space between door and threshold," she wrote now. "Probably no insulation. 2–3 inch cracks in walls inadequately sealed with whitewashed mud." She made a mental note but could see no point in describing Lawrence's stuffed reclining chair that only reclined, the shadeless lamp with its plastic orchid in the bubble glass base, or the three-dimensional picture of Jesus that Lawrence had once demonstrated to her. When plugged in, lights rolled behind the water the Lord stood on so that he seemed to be strolling although he never actually went forward, of course, but only pushed the glowing waves behind him forever like a poor tame rat in a treadmill.

Brackett cleared his throat with a nervous rasp and touched Vicki's shoulder.

"What are you writing?"

She moved away and continued to scribble as if thoroughly absorbed in her work. "Officer Brackett displays an undue amount of interest in my person," she wrote. "Perhaps?"

He snatched playfully at the book, but she hugged it to her chest and moved off smiling. More curls had fallen, wetted to the base of her neck. Looking out the window, she sighed long and loud.

"All night on brush rollers for this. What a joke."

Brackett shoved his hands in his pockets. His mouth opened slightly, then shut with a small throttled cluck.

When Albertine saw Harmony ambling across the yard with his big brown thumbs in his belt, his placid smile, and his tiny black eyes moving back and forth, she put Buddy under the cot. Harmony stopped at the shed and stood quietly. He spread his arms wide to show her he hadn't drawn his big police gun.

"Ma Cousin," he said in the Michif dialect that people used if they were relatives or sometimes if they needed gas or a couple of dollars, "why don't you come out here and stop this foolishness?"

"I ain't your cousin," Albertine said. Anger boiled up in her suddenly. "I ain't related to no pigs."

She bit her lip and watched him through the cracks, circling, a big tan punching dummy with his boots full of sand so he never stayed down once he fell. He was empty inside, all stale air. But he knew how to get to her so much better than a white cop could. And now he was circling because he wasn't sure she didn't have a weapon, maybe a knife or the German luger that was the only thing that her father, Albert American Horse, had left his wife and daughter besides his name. Harmony knew that Albertine was a tall strong woman who took two big men to subdue when she didn't want to go in the drunk tank. She had hard hips, broad shoulders, and stood tall like her Sioux father, the American Horse who was killed threshing in Belle Prairie.

"I feel bad to have to do this," Harmony said to Albertine. "But for godsakes, let's nobody get hurt. Come on out with the boy why don't you. I know you got him in there."

Albertine did not give herself away this time. She let him wonder. Slowly and quietly she pulled her belt through its loops and wrapped it around and around her hand until only the big oval buckle with turquoise chunks shaped into a butterfly stuck out over her knuckles. Harmony was talking but she wasn't listening to what he said. She was listening to the pitch of his voice, the tone of it that would tighten or tremble at a certain moment when he decided to rush the shed. He kept talking slowly and reasonably, flexing the dialect from time to time, even mentioning her father.

"He was a damn good man. I don't care what they say, Albertine, I knew him."

Albertine looked at the stone butterfly that spread its wings across her fist. The wings looked light and cool, not heavy. It almost looked like it was ready to fly. Harmony wanted to get to Albertine through her father but she would not think about American Horse. She concentrated on the sky-blue stone.

Yet the shape of the stone, the color, betrayed her.

She saw her father suddenly, bending at the grille of their old grey car. She was small then. The memory came from so long ago it seemed like a dream—narrowly focused, snapshot clear. He was bending by the grille in the sun. It was hot summer. Wings of sweat, dark blue, spread across the back of his work shirt. He always wore soft blue shirts, the color of shade cloudier than this stone. His stiff hair had grown out of its short haircut and flopped over his forehead. When he stood up and turned away from the car, Albertine saw that he had a butterfly.

"It's dead," he told her. "Broke its wings and died on the grille."

She must have been five, maybe six, wearing one of the boy's tee-shirts Mama bleached in hilex-water. American Horse took the butterfly, a black and yellow one, and rubbed it on Albertine's collarbone and chest and arms until the color and the powder of it were blended into her skin.

"For grace," he said.

And Albertine had felt a strange lightening in her arms, in her chest, when he did this and said, "For grace." The way he said it, grace meant everything the butterfly was. The sharp delicate wings. The way it floated over grass. The way its wings seemed to breathe fanning in the sun. The wisdom of the way it blended into flowers or changed into a leaf. In herself she felt the same kind of possibilities and closed her eyes almost in shock or pain, she felt so light and powerful at that moment.

Then her father had caught her and thrown her high into the air. She could not remember landing in his arms or landing at all. She only remembered the sun filling her eyes and the world tipping crazily behind her, out of sight.

"He was a damn good man," Harmony said again.

Albertine heard his starched uniform gathering before his boots hit the ground. Once, twice, three times. It took him four solid jumps to get right where she wanted him. She kicked the plank door open when he reached for the handle and the corner caught him on the jaw. He faltered, and Albertine hit him flat on the chin with the butterfly. She hit him so hard the shock of it went up her arm like a string pulled taut. Her fist opened, numb, and she let the belt unloop before she closed her hand on the tip end of it and sent the stone butterfly swooping out in a wide circle around her as if it was on the end of a leash. Harmony reeled backward as she walked toward him swinging the belt. She expected him to fall but he just stumbled. And then he took the gun from his hip.

Albertine let the belt go limp. She and Harmony stood within feet of each other, breathing. Each heard the human sound of air going in and out of the other person's lungs. Each read the face of the other as if deciphering letters carved into softly eroding veins of stone. Albertine saw the pattern of tiny arteries that age, drink, and hard living had blown to the surface of the man's face. She saw the spoked wheels of his iris and the arteries like tangled threads that sewed him up. She saw the living net of springs and tissue that held him together, and trapped him. She saw the random, intimate plan of his person.

She took a quick shallow breath and her face went strange and tight. She saw the black veins in the wings of the butterfly, roads burnt into a map, and then she was located somewhere in the net of veins and sinew that was the tragic complexity of the world so she did not see Officer Brackett and Vicki Koob rushing toward her, but felt them instead like flies caught in the same web, rocking it.

"Albertine!" Vicki Koob had stopped in the grass. Her voice was shrill and tight. "It's better this way, Albertine. We're going to help you."

Albertine straightened, threw her shoulders back. Her father's hand was on her chest and shoulders lightening her wonderfully. Then on wings of her father's hands, on dead butterfly wings, Albertine lifted into the air and flew toward the others. The light powerful feeling swept her up the way she had floated higher, seeing the grass below. It was her father throwing her up into the air and out of danger. Her arms opened for bullets but no bullets came. Harmony did not shoot. Instead, he raised his fist and brought it down hard on her head.

Albertine did not fall immediately, but stood in his arms a moment. Perhaps she gazed still farther back behind the covering of his face. Perhaps she was completely stunned and did not think as she sagged and fell. Her face rolled forward and hair covered her features, so it was impossible for Harmony to see with just what particular expression she gazed into the head-splitting wheel of light, or blackness, that overcame her.

Harmony turned the vehicle onto the gravel road that led back to town. He had convinced the other two that Albertine was more trouble than she was worth, and so they left her behind, and Lawrence too. He stood swearing in his cinder driveway as the car rolled out of sight. Buddy sat between the social worker and Officer Brackett. Vicki tried to hold Buddy fast and keep her arm down at the same time, for the words she'd screamed at Albertine had broken the seal of antiperspirant beneath her arms. She was sweating now as though she'd stored an ocean up inside of her. Sweat rolled down her back in a shallow river and pooled at her waist and between her breasts. A thin sheen of water came out on her forearms, her face. Vicki gave an irritated moan but Brackett seemed not to take notice, or take offense at least. Air-conditioned breezes were sweeping over the seat anyway, and very soon they would be comfortable. She smiled at Brackett over Buddy's head. The man grinned back. Buddy stirred. Vicki remembered the emergency chocolate bar she kept in her purse, fished it out, and offered it to Buddy. He did not react, so she closed his fingers over the package and peeled the paper off one end.

The car accelerated. Buddy felt the road and wheels pummeling each other and the rush of the heavy motor purring in high gear. Buddy knew that what he'd seen in his mind that morning, the thing coming out of the sky with barbs and chains, had hooked him. Somehow he was caught and held in the sour tin smell of the pale woman's armpit. Somehow he was pinned between their pounds of breathless flesh. He looked at the chocolate in his hand. He was squeezing the bar so hard that a thin brown trickle had melted down his arm. Automatically, he put the bar in his mouth.

As he bit down he saw his mother very clearly, just as she had been when she carried him from the shed. She was stretched flat on the ground, on her stomach, and her arms were curled around her head as if in sleep. One leg was drawn up and it looked for all the world like she was running full tilt into the ground, as though she had been trying to pass into the earth, to bury herself, but at the last moment something had stopped her.

There was no blood on Albertine, but Buddy tasted blood now at the sight of her, for he bit down hard and cut his own lip. He ate the chocolate, every bit of it, tasting his mother's blood. And when he had the chocolate down inside him and all licked off his hands, he opened his mouth to say thank you to the woman, as his mother had taught him. But instead of a thank you coming out he was astonished to hear a great rattling scream, and then another, rip out of him like pieces of his own body and whirl onto the sharp things all around him.

[1989]

Recuerdo

Guadalupe Valdés Fallis

IT WAS NOON. IT WAS DUSTY. AND THE SUN, BLINDING IN ITS BRIGHTNESS, shone unmercifully on the narrow dirty street.

It was empty. And to Rosa, walking slowly past the bars and the shops and the curio stands, it seemed as if they all were peering out at her, curiously watching what she did.

She walked on . . . toward the river, toward the narrow, muddy strip of land that was the dry Rio Grande; and she wished suddenly that it were night and that the tourists had come across, making the street noisy and gay and full of life.

But it was noon. And there were no happy or laughing Americanos; no eager girls painted and perfumed and waiting for customers; no blaring horns or booming bongos . . . only here and there a hungry dog, a crippled beggar, or a drunk, thirsty and broke from the night before.

She was almost there. She could see the narrow door and the splintered wooden steps. And instinctively she stopped. Afraid suddenly, feeling the hollow emptiness again, and the tightness when she swallowed.

And yet, it was not as if she did not know why he had wanted her to come, why he had sent for her. It was not as though she were a child. Her reflection in a smudged and dirty window told her that she was no longer even a girl.

And still, it was not as if she were old, she told herself, it was only that her body was rounded and full, and her eyes in the dark smooth face were hard and knowing, mirroring the pain and the disappointment and the tears of thirty-five years . . .

She walked to the narrow door slowly, and up the stairs . . . thumping softly on the creaking swollen wood. At the top, across a dingy hallway, she knocked softly at a door. It was ajar, and Rosa could see the worn chairs and the torn linoleum and the paper-littered desk. But she did not go in. Not until the man came to the door and looked out at her impatiently.

He saw her feet first and the tattered sandals. Then her dress clean but faded, a best dress obviously, because it was not patched. Finally, after what seemed to Rosa an eternity, he looked at her face, at her dark black hair knotted neatly on top of her head; and at last, into her eyes.

"Come in, Rosa," he said slowly, "I am glad that you could come."

"Buenas tardes[1] Don Lorenzo," Rosa said meekly, looking up uneasily at the bulky smelly man. "I am sorry I am late."

"Yes," he said mockingly; and turning, he walked back into the small and dirty room.

Rosa followed him, studying him, while he could not see her, seeing the wrinkled trousers, the sweat stained shirt, and the overgrown greasy hair on the back of his pudgy neck.

He turned suddenly, his beady eyes surveying his domain smugly; then deliberately, he walked to the window and straightened the sign that said:

DIVORCES . . . LORENZO PEREZ SAUZA . . . ATTORNEY AT LAW

It was not as important as the neon blinking sign, of course, but sometimes people came from the side street, and it was good to be prepared.

"Well, Rosa," he said, looking at her again, "and where is Maruca?"

"She is sick, señor."

"Sick?"

---

[1] Good afternoon.

"Yes, she has had headaches and she is not well . . . she . . ."

"Has she seen a doctor, Rosa?" The question was mocking again.

"No . . . she . . . it will pass, señor. . . . It's only that now . . . I do not think that she should come to work."

"Oh?" He was looking out of the window distractedly, ignoring her.

"I am sorry, I should have come before," she continued meekly . . .

"Maruca is very pretty, Rosa," Don Lorenzo said suddenly.

"Thank you, señor, you are very kind." She was calmer now . . .

"She will make a man very happy, someday," he continued.

"Yes."

"Do you think she will marry soon then?" he asked her, watching her closely.

"No," she hesitated, "that is, I don't know, she . . . there isn't anyone yet."

"Ah!" It was said quietly but somehow triumphantly . . .

And Rosa waited, wondering what he wanted, sensing something and suddenly suspicious.

"Do you think she likes me, Rosa," he asked her deliberately, baiting her.

And she remembered Maruca's face, tear-stained, embarrassed telling her: "I can't go back, Mama. He does not want me to help in his work. He touches me, Mother . . . and smiles. And today, he put his large sweaty hand on my breast, and held it, smiling, like a cow. Ugly!"

"Why, yes, Don Lorenzo," she lied quickly. "She thinks you are very nice." Her heart was racing now, hoping and yet not daring to—

"I am much of a man, Rosa," he went on slowly, "and the girl is pretty. . . . I would take care of her . . . if she let me."

"Take care of her?" Rosa was praying now, her fingers crossed behind her back.

"Yes, take care of her," he repeated. "I would be good to her, you would have money. And then, perhaps, if there is a child . . . she would need a house . . . "

"A house." Rosa repeated dully. A house for Maruca. That it might be. That it might be, really, was unbelievable. To think of the security, of the happy future frightened her suddenly, and she could only stare at the fat man, her eyes round and very black.

"Think about it, Rosita," he said smiling benevolently . . . "You know me . . ." And Rosa looked at him angrily, remembering, and suddenly feeling very much like being sick.

The walk home was long; and in the heat Rosa grew tired. She wished that she might come to a tree, so that she could sit in the shade and think. But the hills were bare and dry, and there were no trees. There were only shacks surrounded by hungry crying children.

And Rosa thought about her own, about the little ones. The ones that still depended on her even for something to eat. And she felt it again, the strange despair of wanting to cry out: "Don't, don't depend on me! I can hardly depend on myself."

But they had no one else; and until they could beg or steal a piece of bread and a bowl of beans, they would turn to her, only to her, not ever to Pablo.

And it wasn't because he was drunk and lazy, or even because only the last two children belonged to him. He was kind enough to all of them. It was, though, as if they sensed that he was only temporary.

And still it was not that Pablo was bad. He was better actually than the others. He did not beat her when he drank, or steal food from the children. He was not even too demanding. And it gave them a man, after all, a man to protect them. . . . It was enough, really.

True, he had begun to look at Maruca, and it bothered Rosa. But perhaps it WAS really time for Maruca to leave. For the little ones, particularly. Because men are men, she said to herself, and if there is a temptation . . .

But she was not fooling anyone, and when at last she saw the tin and cardboard shack against the side of the hill, with its cluttered front and screaming children, she wanted to turn back.

Maruca saw her first.

"There's Mama," she told the others triumphantly, and at once they took up the shout: "Mama! Mama! Mama!"

The other girl, standing with Maruca, turned to leave as Rosa came closer.

"Buenas tardes," she said uncomfortably, sensing the dislike and wanting to hurry away.

"What did Petra want?" Rosa asked Maruca angrily, even before Petra was out of earshot.

"Mama, por favor, she'll hear you."

"I told you I did not want her in this house."

"We were only talking, Mama. She was telling me about her friends."

"Her friends!" Rosa cut in sharply, "as if we did not know that she goes with the first American that looks at her. Always by the river that one, with one soldier and another, her friends indeed!"

"But she says she has fun, Mama, and they take her to dance and buy her pretty things."

"Yes, yes, and tomorrow, they will give her a baby. . . . And where is the fun then . . . eh? She is in the streets . . . no?"

Rosa was shaking with anger. "Is that what you want? Do you?"

"No, Mama," Maruca said meekly, "I was just listening to her talk."

"Well, remember it," Rosa snapped furiously, but then seeing Maruca's face, she stopped suddenly. "There, there, it's alright," she said softly. "We will talk about it later."

And Rosa watched her, then, herding the children into the house gently, gracefully; slim and small, angular still, with something perhaps a little dolt-ish in the way she held herself, impatient, and yet distrusting, not quite daring to go forward.

And she thought of Don Lorenzo, and for a moment, she wished that he were not so fat, or so ugly, and especially, so sweaty.

But it was an irrecoverable chance! Old men with money did not often come into their world, and never to stay.

To Rosa, they had been merely far away gods at whose houses she had worked as a maid or as a cook; faultless beings who were to be obeyed without question; powerful creatures who had commanded her to come when they needed variety or adventure . . .

But only that.

She had never been clever enough, or even pretty enough to make it be more.

But Maruca! Maruca could have the world.

No need for her to marry a poor young bum who could not even get a job. No need for her to have ten children all hungry and crying. No need for her to dread, even, that the bum might leave her. No need at all.

[1980]

Making Do

Linda Hogan

ROBERTA JAMES BECAME ONE OF THE SILENT PEOPLE IN SEEKER COUNTY when her daughter, Harriet, died at six years of age.

Harriet died of what they used to call consumption.

After the funeral, Grandmother Addie went to stay with Roberta in her grief, as she had done over the years with her children and grandchildren. Addie, in fact, had stayed with Roberta during the time of her pregnancy with Harriet, back when the fifteen-year-old girl wore her boyfriend's black satin jacket that had a map of Korea on the back. And she'd visited further back than that, back to the days when Roberta wore white full skirts and white blouses and the sun came in the door, and she lay there in that hot sun like it was ironed flat against the floor, and she felt good with clean hair and skin and singing a little song to herself. There were oak trees outside. She was waiting. Roberta was waiting there for something that would take her away. But the farthest she got was just outside her skin, that black jacket against her with its map of Korea.

Addie never told Roberta a word of what she knew about divided countries and people who wear them on their backs, but later Roberta knew that her grandmother had seen way down the road what was coming, and warned her in little ways. When she brushed Roberta's dark hair, she told her, "You were born to a different life, Bobbie."

After the funeral, Roberta's mother offered comfort in her own way. "Life goes on," Neva said, but she herself had long belonged to that society of quiet Indian women in Seeker, although no one would have guessed this of the woman who wore Peach Promise lipstick, smiled generously, and kissed the bathroom mirror, leaving a message for Roberta that said, "See you in the a.m. Love."

Grandma Addie tended Angela, Roberta's younger daughter. She fed the baby Angela spoonsful of meal, honey, and milk and held her day and night while Roberta went about the routines of her life. The chores healed her a little; perking coffee and cleaning her mother's lipstick off the mirror. She swept away traces of Harriet with the splintered broom, picking up threads from the girl's dress, black hair from her head, wiping away her footprints.

Occasionally Neva stopped in, clasped her daughter's thin cold hands between her warm ones, and offered advice. "That's why you ought to get married," she said. She wrapped Roberta's shoulders in a large gray sweater. "Then you'd have some man to help when things are down and out. Like Ted here. Well, anyway, Honey," she said at eye level to Roberta, "you sure drew a good card when Harriet was born. Didn't she, Ted?"

"Sure sugar, an ace."

But when Roberta wasn't looking, Neva shook her head slowly and looked down at the floor, and thought their lives were all hopeless.

Roberta didn't get married like her mother suggested. She did take some comfort on those long nights by loving Tom Wilkins. Each night she put pieces of cedar inside his Red Wing boots, to keep him close, and neatly placed them beneath her bed. She knew how to care for herself with this man, keeping him close in almost the same space Harriet had abandoned. She wept slightly at night after he held her and he said, "There now. There now," and patted her on the back.

He brought her favorite Windmill cookies with him from town and he sang late at night so that the ghost of Harriet could move on more easily, like he eventually moved on when Roberta stopped placing cedar in his boots.

"Why didn't that Wilkins boy come back?" Grandma asked. "Choctaw, wasn't he?"

Roberta shrugged as if she hadn't left his boots empty of cedar. "He was prettier than me." She pushed her straggly hair back from her face to show Grandma what she meant.

A month later, Roberta was relieved when the company summoned Tom Wilkins to Louisiana to work on a new oil field and she didn't have to run into him at the store any longer.

Roberta's next child, a son she named Wilkins after the father, died at birth, strangled on his own cord. Roberta had already worn a dark shawl throughout this pregnancy. She looked at his small roughbox and said, "He died of life and I know how that can happen."

She held on to her grandmother's hand.

Grandma Addie and Neva talked about Roberta. "A woman can only hold so much hurt," Grandma said.

"And don't think I don't know it," said Neva.

Roberta surfaced from her withdrawal a half year later, in the spring of

1974, when Angela looked at her like a little grandmother and said, "Mother, I know it is hard, but it's time for me to leave you" and immediately became feverish. Roberta bathed her with alcohol and made blessing-root tea, which she dropped into little Angela's rose-petal mouth with an eye dropper. She prayed fervently to God or Jesus, she had never really understood which was which, and to all the stones and trees and gods of the sky and inner earth that she knew well, and to the animal spirits, and she carried her little Angel to the hospital in the middle of praying, to that house made of brick and window and cinders where dying bodies were kept alive, carried the girl with soft child skin in a small quilt decorated with girls in poke bonnets, and thought how funny it was to wrap a dying child in such sweetness as those red-cheeked girls in the calico bonnets. She blamed herself for ignoring Angela in her own time of grief. Four days later Angela died, wearing a little corn necklace Roberta made, a wristlet of glass beads, and covered with that quilt.

"She even told Roberta she was about to die," Neva told Ted. "Just like an old woman, huh, Bert?"

Roberta went on with her silence through this third death, telling herself over and over what had happened, for the truth was so bad she could not believe it. The inner voice of the throat spoke and repeated the words of loss and Roberta listened hard. "My Angel. My Harriet. All my life gone and broken while I am so young. I'm too young for all this loss."

She dreamed of her backbone and even that was broken in pieces. She dreamed of her house in four pieces. She was broken like the country of Korea or the land of the tribe.

They were all broken, Roberta's thin-skinned father broken by the war. He and Neva raised two boys whose parents had "gone off" as they say of those who come under the control of genie spirits from whiskey bottles, and those boys were certainly broken. And Neva herself had once been a keeper of the gates; she was broken.

In earlier days she read people by their faces and bodies. She was a keeper of gates, opening and closing ways for people to pass through life. "This one has been eating too much grain," she'd say, or "That one was born too rich for her own good and is spoiled. That one is broken in the will to live by this and that." She was a keeper of the family gates as well. She closed doors on those she disliked, if they were dishonest, say, or mean, or small. There was no room for smallness in her life, but she opened the doors wide for those who moved her slightly, in any way, with stirrings of love or pity. She had lusty respect for belligerence, political rebellion, and for vandalism against automobiles or businesses or bosses, and those vandals were among those permitted inside her walls.

And now she was broken, by her own losses and her loneliness.

Roberta cried against Addie's old warm shoulder and Grandma Addie stayed on, moving in all her things, cartons of canning jars, a blue-painted porcelain horse, her dark dresses and aprons, pictures of her grandchildren and great-grandchildren, rose-scented candles of the virgin of Guadalupe,[1] even though she was never a Catholic, and the antlers of the deer.

Roberta ignored her cousins from the churches of the brethren of this and that when they came to comfort her in their ways, telling her that all things were meant to be and that the Lord gives and takes.

Uncle James was older and so he said nothing, and she sat with him, those silent ones together.

Roberta's mother left messages on the bathroom mirror. "There is a time for everything in heaven."

With Grandma there to watch over Neva and the house, Roberta decided one day to pack her dishes, blankets, and clothes into the old Chevy she had bought from Ted, and she drove away from the little square tombstones named Angela, Wilkins, and Harriet, though it nearly broke her heart to leave them. She drove away from all those trying to comfort her with what comforted them. The sorrow in her was like a well too deep for young ground; the sides caved in with anger, but Roberta planned still to return for Grandma Addie. She stopped once, in the flat, neutral land of Goodland, Kansas, and telephoned back.

"You sure you don't want to come with me? It's kind of pretty out this way, Grandma," she lied. She smelled truck exhaust from the phone booth and she watched the long, red-faced boys walking past, those young men who had eaten so much cattle they began to look like them.

"Just go and get settled. I'll be out to visit as soon as you get the first load of laundry hung on the line."

Roberta felt her grandma smile. She hung up the phone and headed back to the overloaded, dusty white car.

She headed for Denver, but wound up just west of there, in a mountain town called The Tropics. Its name was like a politician's vocabulary, a lie. In truth, The Tropics was arid. It was a mine town, uranium most recently. Dust devils whirled sand off the mountains. Even after the heaviest of rains, the water seeped back into the ground, between stones, and the earth was parched again. Still, *Tropics* conjured up visions of tall grasses in outlying savannas, dark rivers, mists, and deep green forests of ferns and trees and water-filled vines. Sometimes it seemed like they were there.

Roberta told herself it was God's acres, that it was fate she had missed the Denver turn-offs from the freeway, that here she could forgive and forget her losses and get on with living. She rented a cabin, got a part-time job working down at the Tropics Grocery where she sold single items to customers who didn't want to travel to town. She sold a bag of flour to one, a can of dog food to another, candy to schoolchildren in the afternoon. She sold boxed doughnuts and cigarettes to work crews in the mornings and 3.2 beer to the same crews after five. She dusted and stacked the buckling

---

[1] A Roman Catholic patroness of Mexican and Indian peoples who provides comfort in sickness and protection against evil.

shelves, and she had time to whittle little birds, as her Uncle James had done. She whittled them and thought of them as toys for the spirits of her children and put them in the windows so the kids would be sure and see them. "This one's for Harriet," she'd tell no one in particular.

When she didn't work she spent her time in bed, completely still and staring straight at the ceiling. They used to say if a person is motionless, their soul will run away from the body, and Roberta counted on that. They say that once a soul decides to leave, it can't be recalled. Roberta lay in that room with its blue walls and blue-flowered blanket. She lay there with her hair pulled back from her round forehead. She held the sunbonnet quilt in her hands and didn't move.

To her disappointment, she remained alive. Every night she prayed to die and join her kids, but every morning she was still living, breathing. Some mornings she pulled at her flesh just to be certain, she was so amazed and despairing to be still alive.

Her soul refused to leave. It had a mind of its own. So Roberta got up and began a restless walking. There were nights in The Tropics that she haunted the dirt roads like a large-shouldered, thin-hipped ghost, like a tough girl with her shoulders held high to protect her broken heart. Roberta Diane James with her dark hair that had been worn thin from the hours she spent lying down trying to send her soul away. Roberta, with her eyes the color of dark river water after a storm when the gold stirs up in it. The left eye still held the trace of a wink in it, despite the thinness of skin stretched over her forehead, the smell of Ivory soap on her as she tried over and over to wash the grief from her flesh.

2

When I first heard how bad things were going for Roberta, I thought about going home, but I heard my other voices tell me it wasn't time. "There is a season for all things," Mom used to say, and I knew Mom would be telling Roberta just that, in her own words, and that Roberta would be fuming inside as I had done with Mom's fifty-cent sayings.

I knew this much: Roberta would need to hold on to her grief and her pain.

Us Chickasaws have lost so much we hold on to everything. Even our muscles hold on to their aches. We love our lovers long after they are gone, better than when they were present.

When we were girls, Roberta and I saved the tops of Coke bottlecaps and covered them with purple cloth like grapes. We made clusters of grapes sitting out there on the porch, or on tire swings in the heat, and we sewed the grapes together. We made do. We drank tea from pickle jars. We used potato water to starch our clothes. We even used our skinny dark legs as paper for tic-tac-toe. Now the girls turn bleach containers into hats, cutting them in fours and crocheting them together.

Our Aunt Bell is famous for holding on and making do. There's a nail in her kitchen for plastic six-pack rings, a box for old jars, a shelf or box for everything, including all the black and white shoes she's worn out as a grown woman. Don't think those boxes or nails mean she's neat, either. She's not. She has hundreds of dusty salt and pepper shakers people gave her, and stacks of old magazines and papers, years of yellowed history all contained in her crowded rooms, and I love her for it, for holding on that way. I have spent hours of my younger life looking at those shakers and reading those papers. Her own children tell her it is a miracle the viruses of science aren't growing to maturity in there.

We save ourselves from loss in whatever ways we can, collecting things, going out to Danceland, getting drunk, reading westerns or finding new loves, but the other side of all this salvation is that we deny the truth. When some man from town steals our land, we say, "Oh, he wouldn't do that. Jimmy Slade is a good old boy. I knew his folks. I used to work for the Slades during the Depression." Never mind that the Slades were not the hungry ones back then.

Some of us southern Indians used to have ranches and cattle. They were all lost piece by piece, or sold to pay for taxes on some land that was also lost. Now and then someone comes around and tells us we should develop our land like we once did. Or they tell us just to go out in the world. We nod and smile at them.

Now and then some of us young people make a tidal wave in the ocean of our history, an anxiety attack in the heart monitor of our race. We get angry and scream out. We get in the news. We strip ourselves bare in the colleges that recruited us as their minority quota and we run out into the snowstorm naked and we get talked about for years as the crazy Indian that did this or that, the one that drove to the gas station and went on straight to Canada, the girl who took out the garbage and never turned and went back. We made do.

I knew some people from up north. You could always tell they were from up north because my friend's daughter had a wall-eye with a hook tattooed on her forearm. Once we went to a pow-wow together and some of the women of the People wore jingle dresses, with what looked like bells. "What are those?" I asked my friend.

They were snuff can lids. Those women of the forests and woodlands, so much making do just like us, like when we use silver salt cans in our dances instead of turtle-shell rattles. We make music of those saltshakers, though now and then some outsider decides we have no culture because we use store-bought shakers and they are not traditional at all.

I defy them: Salt is the substance of our blood, sweat, our secretions, our semen. It is the ocean of ourselves.

Once I saw a railroad engineer's hat in a museum. It was fully beaded. I thought it was a new style like the beaded tennis shoes or the new beaded truckers' hats. But it was made in the late 1800s when the Lakota were forbidden to make traditional items. The mothers took to beading whatever was available, hats of the engineers of death. They covered colony cotton with their art.

We make art out of our loss.

That's why when I heard Roberta was in Colorado and was carving wooden birds, I figured it made sense. Besides, we come from a long line of whittlers and table carvers, people who work with wood, including the Mexican great-grandfather who made santos[2] and a wooden mask that was banned by the priests. Its presence got him excommunicated.

Uncle James carves chains out of trees. We laugh and say it sounds like something *they* would do.

Roberta was carving wooden birds, crows, mourning doves, and even a scissortail or two. She sent some of the birds back home to have Aunt Bell put them on the graves of her little ones.

I think she was trying to carve the souls of her children into the birds. She was making do.

[1989]

From *Black Is* a *Woman's Color*
bell hooks

GOOD HAIR—THAT'S THE EXPRESSION. WE ALL KNOW IT, BEGIN TO HEAR IT when we are small children. When we are sitting between the legs of mothers and sisters getting our hair combed. Good hair is hair that is not kinky, hair that does not feel like balls of steel wool, hair that does not take hours to comb, hair that does not need tons of grease to untangle, hair that is long. Real good hair is straight hair, hair like white folks' hair. Yet no one says so. No one says your hair is so nice, so beautiful because it is like white folks' hair. We pretend that the standards we measure our beauty by are our own invention—that it is questions of time and money that lead us to make distinctions between good hair and bad hair. I know from birth that I am lucky, lucky to have hair at all for I was bald for two years, then lucky finally to have thin almost straight hair, hair that does not need to be hot combed.

We are six girls who live in a house together. We have different textures of hair, short, long, thin, thick. We do not appreciate these differences. We do not celebrate the variety that is ourselves. We do not run our fingers through each other's dry hair after it is washed. We sit in the kitchen and wait our turn for the hot comb, wait to sit in the chair by the stove smelling grease, feeling the heat warm our scalp like a sticky hot summer sun.

For each of us, getting our hair pressed is an important ritual. It is not a sign of our longing to be white. It is not a sign of our quest to be beautiful.

[2] saints.

We are girls. It is a sign of our desire to be women. It is a gesture that says we are approaching womanhood. It is a rite of passage. Before we reach the appropriate age we wear braids and plaits that are symbols of our innocence, our youth, our childhood. Then we are comforted by the parting hands that comb and braid, comforted by the intimacy and bliss. There is a deeper intimacy in the kitchen on Saturday when hair is pressed, when fish is fried, when sodas are passed around, when soul music drifts over the talk. We are women together. This is our ritual and our time. It is a time without men. It is a time when we work to meet each other's needs, to make each other beautiful in whatever way we can. It is a time of laughter and mellow talk. Sometimes it is an occasion for tears and sorrow. Mama is angry, sick of it all, pulling the hair too tight, using too much grease, burning one ear and then the next.

At first I cannot participate in the ritual. I have good hair that does not need pressing. Without the hot comb I remain a child, one of the uninitiated. I plead, I beg, I cry for my turn. They tell me once you start you will be sorry. You will wish you had never straightened your hair. They do not understand that it is not the straightening I seek but the chance to belong, to be one in this world of women. It is finally my turn. I am happy. Happy even though my thin hair straightened looks like black thread, has no body, stands in the air like ends of barbed wire; happy even though the sweet smell of unpressed hair is gone forever. Secretly I had hoped that the hot comb would transform me, turn the thin good hair into thick nappy hair, the kind of hair I like and long for, the kind you can do anything with, wear in all kinds of styles. I am bitterly disappointed in the new look.

A senior in high school, I want to wear a natural, an afro. I want never to get my hair pressed again. It is no longer a rite of passage, a chance to be intimate in the world of women. The intimacy masks betrayal. Together we change ourselves. The closeness, an embrace before parting, a gesture of farewell to love and one another.

Jazz, she learns from her father, is the black man's music, the working man, the poor man, the man on the street. Different from the blues because it does not simply lament, moan, express sorrow; it expresses everything. She listens to a record he is playing, to a record that is being played on the radio. It is the music of John Coltrane.[1] Her father says this is a musician who understands all the black man is longing for, that he takes this longing and blows it out of his saxophone. Like the alchemist, he turns lead into gold. To listen, her father tells her, is to feel understood. She listens, wanting this jazz not to be beyond her, wanting it to address the melancholy parts of her soul. To her, black people make the most passionate music. She knows that there is no such thing as natural rhythm. She knows it is the

---

[1] An American jazz saxophonist and composer (1926–1967), whose style greatly influenced a generation of future saxophone players. Coltrane was one of the most influential post-bebop performers and a controversial jazz avant-garde figure.

intensity of feeling, the constant knowing that death is real and a possibility that makes the music what it is. She knows that it is the transformation of suffering and sorrow into sound that bears witness to the black past. In her dreams she has seen the alchemist turning lead into gold.

On communion Sundays they sing without musical accompaniment. They keep alive the old ways, the call and response. They sing slow and hold each note as if it is caught in the trap of time and struggling to be free. Like the bread and the wine, they do it this way so as not to forget what the past has been. She listens to the strength in the voices of elderly women as they call out. She sings in the choir. She loves the singing. She looks forward to choir practice on Wednesday night. It is the only weekday night that they are away from home. They sit in the basement of the church singing. They sing "hush children, hush children, somebody's calling my name, oh my lord, oh my lordy, what shall I do."

At home her mama listens to music. On Friday nights she sits in her corner on the couch, smoking one cigarette, drinking one can of beer, playing records, staring sadly into the smoke as Brooke Benton[2] sings "you don't miss your water till your well runs dry." Saturday morning they clean house and listen to music. They listen to the soul music on the radio. It is the only time they can hear a whole program with black music. Every other day is country and western or rock 'n roll. In between vacuuming, dusting, and sweeping they listen to the latest songs and show each other the latest dances. She likes to dance, but they make fun of her. She cannot slow dance. She does not know how to follow the lead. She gives up dancing, spends her time listening to the music.

She likes to hear the music of Louis Armstrong. She likes to see the pleasure he brings to her father's face. They watch him on the Ed Sullivan show, making funny faces, singing in his deep voice. It is the trumpet sound that they are waiting for. When he pulls the handkerchief from his pocket to wipe away the dripping sweat she is reminded of the right hand men of God weeping into thin squares of cotton. She imagines tears mingled with Satchmo's[3] sweat, that they are tears of gratitude, that he too is giving thanks for finding in his horn yet another sweet stretching sound he did not know was there.

She wants to express herself—to speak her mind. To them it is just talking back. Each time she opens her mouth she risks punishment. They punish her so often she begins to feel they are persecuting her. When she learns the word *scapegoat* in vocabulary lesson, she is sure it accurately describes her lot in life. Her wilderness, unlike the one the goat is led into, is a wilderness of spirit. They abandon her there to get on with the fun things of life. She lies in her bed upstairs after being punished yet again. She can

---

[2] A rhythm and blues artist and balladeer, Benton (1931–1988) was known for his smooth, rich, smoky vocal sound. He was the first black singer to establish himself as an album artist.

[3] Satchmo, otherwise known as Louis Armstrong (c. 1898–1971), was an American jazz trumpeter and singer, and was one of the all-time jazz greats.

hear the sound of their laughter, their talk. No one hears her crying. Even though she is young, she comes to understand the meaning of exile and loss. They say that she is really not a young girl but an old woman born again into a young girl's body. They do not know how to speak the old woman's language so they are afraid of her. She might be a witch. They have given her a large thick paperback of original fairy tales. On page after page, an old woman is eating children, thinking some wicked deed, performing evil magic. She is not surprised that they fear the old woman inside her. She understands that the old women in the fairy tales do evil because they are misunderstood. She is a lover of old women. She does not mind at all when they look at her and say she must be ninety, look at the way she walks. No! They say she must be at least a hundred. Only a hundred-year-old woman could walk so slow.

Their world is the only world there is. To be exiled from it is to be without life. She cries because she is in mourning. They will not let her wear the color black. It is not a color for girls. To them she already looks too old. She would just look like a damn fool in a black dress. Black is a woman's color.

She finds another world in books. Escaping into the world of novels is one way she learns to enjoy life. However, novels only ease the pain momentarily as she holds the book in hand, as she reads. It is poetry that changes everything. When she discovers the Romantics it is like losing a part of herself and recovering it. She reads them night and day, all the time. She memorizes poems. She recites them while ironing or washing dishes. Reading Emily Dickinson she senses that the spirit can grow in the solitary life. She reads Edna St. Vincent Millay's "Renascence," and she feels with the lines the suppression of spirit, the spiritual death, and the longing to live again. She reads Whitman, Wordsworth, Coleridge. Whitman shows her that language, like the human spirit, need not be trapped in conventional form or traditions. For school she recites "O Captain, My Captain." She would rather recite from *Song of Myself*, but they do not read it in school. They do not read it because it would be hard to understand. She cannot understand why everyone hates to read poetry. She cannot understand their moans and groans. She wishes they did not have to recite poems in school. She cannot bear to hear the frightened voices stumbling through lines as if they are a wilderness and a trap. At home she has an audience. They will turn off the television set and listen to her latest favorite.

She writes her own poetry in secret. She does not want to explain. Her poems are about love and never about death. She is always thinking about death and never about love. She knows that they will think it better to discover secret poems about love. She knows they never speak of death. The punishments continue. She eases her pain in poetry, using it to make the poems live, using the poems to keep on living.

They have never heard their mama and daddy fussing or fighting. They have heard him be harsh, complain that the house should be cleaner, that he should not have to come home from work to a house that is not cleaned just right. They know he gets mad. When he gets mad about the house he begins to clean it himself to show that he can do better. Although he never cooks, he knows how. He would not be able to judge her cooking if he did not cook himself. They are afraid of him when he is mad. They go upstairs to get out of his way. He does not come upstairs. Taking care of children is not a man's work. It does not concern him. He is not even interested—that is, unless something goes wrong. Then he can show her that she is not very good at parenting. They know she is a good mama, "the best." Even though they fear him they are not moved by his opinions. She tries to remember a time when she felt loved by him. She remembers it as being the time when she was a baby girl, a small girl. She remembers him taking her places, taking her to the world inhabited by black men, the barber shop, the pool hall. He took his affections away from her abruptly. She never understood why, only that they went and did not come back. She remembered trying to do whatever she could to bring them back, only they never came. Growing up she stopped trying. He mainly ignored her. She mainly tried to stay out of his way. In her own way she grew to hate wanting his love and not being able to get it. She hated that part of herself that kept wanting his love or even just his approval long after she could see that he was never, never going to give it.

Out of nowhere he comes home from work angry. He reaches the porch yelling and screaming at the woman inside. Yelling that she is his wife and that he can do with her what he wants. They do not understand what is happening. He is pushing, hitting, telling her to shut up. She is pleading, crying. He does not want to hear, to listen. They catch his angry words in their hands like lightning bugs. They store them in a jar to sort them out later. Words about other men, about phone calls, about how he had told her. They do not know what he has told her. They have never heard them in an angry discussion, an argument.

She thinks of all the nights she lies awake in her bed hearing the woman's voice, her mother's voice, hearing his voice. She wonders if it is then that he is telling her the messages he refers to now. Yelling, screaming, hitting, they stare at the red blood that trickles through the crying mouth. They cannot believe that this pleading, crying woman, this woman who does not fight back, is the same person they know. The person they know is strong, gets things done, is a woman of ways and means, a woman of action. They do not know her still, paralyzed, waiting for the next blow, pleading. They do not know her afraid. Even if she does not hit back they want her to run, to run and to not stop running. She wants her to hit him with the table light, the ash tray near her hand. She does not want to see her like this, not fighting back. He notices them long enough to tell them to get out, go upstairs. She refuses to move. She cannot move. She cannot leave her alone. When he says "What are you staring at, do you want some too," she is afraid enough to move, but she does not take her orders from him. She asks the woman if it is right to leave her alone. The woman nods her head yes. She still stands still. It is his movement in her direction that sends her up the stairs. She cannot believe they are not taking a stand, that they go to sleep. She cannot bear their betrayal. When he is not looking she creeps down the steps. She wants the woman to know that she is not alone. She wants to bear witness.

All that she does not understand about marriage, about men and women, is explained to her one night. In her dark place on the stairs she is seeing over and over again the still body of the woman pleading, crying, the moving body of the man angry, yelling. She sees that the man has a gun. She hears him tell the woman that he will kill her. She sits in her place on the stair and demands to know of herself if she is able to come to the rescue, if she is willing to fight, if she is ready to die. Her body shakes with the answers. She is fighting back the tears. When he leaves the room she comes to ask the woman if she is all right, if there is anything she can do. The woman's voice is full of tenderness and hurt. She is now in her role as mother. She tells her daughter to go upstairs and go to sleep, that everything will be all right. The daughter does not believe her. Her eyes are pleading. She does not want to be told to go. She hovers in the shadows. When he returns he tells her that he has told her to get her ass upstairs. She does not look at him. He turns to the woman, tells her to leave, tells her to take the daughter with her.

The woman does not protest. She moves like a robot, hurriedly throwing things into suitcases, boxes. She says nothing to the man. He is still screaming, muttering. When she tried to say to him he was wrong, so wrong, he is more angry, threatening. All the neat drawers are emptied out on the bed, all the precious belongings that can be carried, stuffed, are to be taken. There is sorrow in every gesture, sorrow and pain. It is so thick she feels that she could gather it up in her hands. It is like a dust collecting on everything. She is seeing that the man owns everything, that the woman has only her clothes, her shoes, and other personal belongings. She is seeing that the woman can be told to go, can be sent away in the silent, long hours of the night. She is hearing in her head the man's threats to kill. She can feel the cool metal against her cheek. She can hear the click, the blast. She can see her body falling. No, it is not her body, it is the body of love. It is the death of love she is witnessing. If love were alive she believes it would stop everything. It would steady the man's voice, it would calm his rage. It would take the woman's hand, caress her cheek and with a clean handkerchief wipe her eyes. The gun is pointed at love. He lays it on the table. He wants her to finish her packing and go.

She is again in her role as mother. She tells the daughter that she does not have to flee in the middle of the night, that it is not her fight. The daughter is silent. She is staring into the woman's eyes. She is looking for the bright lights, the care and adoration she has shown the man. The eyes are dark with grief, swollen. She feels that a fire inside the woman is dying out, that she is cold. She is sure the woman will freeze to death if she goes out into the night alone. She takes her hand. She wants to go with her. Yet she hopes there will be no going. She hopes that when the mother's brother comes he will be strong enough to take love's body, and give it mouth to mouth the life it has lost. She hopes he will talk to the man, guide him. She cannot believe the calm way he lifts suitcase, box, sack, carries it to the car without question. She cannot bear the silent agreement that the man is right, that he has done what men are able to do. She cannot take the bits and pieces of her mother's heart and put them together again.

I am always fighting with mama. Everything has come between us. She no longer stands between me and all that would hurt me. She is hurting me. This is my dream of her—that she will stand between me and all that hurts me, that she will protect me at all cost. It is only a dream. In some way I understand that it has to do with marriage, that to be the wife to the husband she must be willing to sacrifice even her daughters for his good. For the mother it is not simple. She is always torn. She works hard to fulfill his needs, our needs. When they are not the same she must maneuver, manipulate, choose. She has chosen. She has decided in his favor. She is a religious woman. She has been told that a man should obey God, that a woman should obey man, that children should obey their fathers and mothers, particularly their mothers. I will not obey.

She says that she punishes me for my own good. I do not know what it is I have done this time. I know that she is ready with her switches, that I am to stand still while she lashes out again and again. In my mind there is the memory of a woman sitting still while she is being hit, punished. In my mind I am remembering how much I want that woman to fight back. Before I can think clearly, my hands reach out, grab the switches, are raised as if to hit her back. For a moment she is stunned, unbelieving. She is shocked. She tells me that I must never ever as long as I live raise my hand against my mother. I tell her I do not have a mother. She is even more shocked; she is enraged. She lashes out again. This time I am still. This time I cry. I see the hurt in her eyes when I say "I do not have a mother." I am ready to be punished because I did not want to hurt. I am ashamed. I am torn. I do not want to stand still and be punished but I do not want to hurt her. It is better to hurt than to cause her pain. She warns me that she will tell him when he comes home, that I may be punished again. I cannot understand her acts of betrayal. I cannot understand that she must be against me to be for him. He and I are strangers. Deep in the night we parted from one another, knowing that nothing would ever be the same. He did not say goodbye. I did not look him in the face. Now we avoid one another. He speaks to me through her.

Although they act as if everything between them is the same, that life is as it was, it is only a game. They are only pretending. There is no pain in the pretense. All pain is hidden. Secrets find a way out in sleep. They say to the mother she cries in her sleep, calls out. In her sleep is the place of remembering. It is the place where there is no pretense. She is dreaming always the same dream. A movie is showing. It is a tragic story of jealousy and lost love. It is called "A Crime of Passion." In the movie a man has killed his wife and daughter. He has killed his wife because he believes she has lovers. He has killed the daughter because she witnesses the death of the wife. At his job he is calm and quiet, a hardworking man, a family man. Neighbors come to testify that the dead woman was young and restless, that the daughter was wild and rebellious. Everyone sympathizes with the man. His story is so sad that they begin to weep. All their handkerchiefs are clean and white. They are like flags waving. They are a signal of peace, of surrender. They are a gesture to the man that he can go on with life.

[1988]

At the Bottom of the River

Jamaica Kincaid

THIS, THEN, IS THE TERRAIN. THE STEEPEST MOUNTAINS, THICKLY COVERED, where huge, sharp rocks might pose the greatest danger and where only the bravest, surest, most deeply arched of human feet will venture, where a large stream might flow, and, flowing perilously, having only a deep ambition to see itself mighty and powerful, bends and curves and dips in many directions, making a welcome and easy path for each idle rill and babbling brook, each trickle of rain fallen on land that lies sloping; and that stream, at last swelled to a great, fast, flowing body of water, falls over a ledge with a roar, a loudness that is more than the opposite of complete silence, then rushes over dry, flat land in imperfect curves—curves as if made by a small boy playfully dragging a toy behind him—then hugs closely to the paths made, ruthlessly conquering the flat plain, the steep ridge, the grassy bed; all day, all day, a stream might flow so, and then it winds its way to a gorge in the earth, a basin of measurable depth and breadth, and so collects itself in a pool: now comes the gloaming, for day will end, and the stream, its flow stilled and gathered up, so that trees growing firmly on its banks, their barks white, their trunks bent, their branches covered with leaves and reaching up, up, are reflected in the depths, awaits the eye, the hand, the foot that shall then give all this a meaning.

But what shall that be? For now here is a man who lives in a world bereft of its very nature. He lies on his bed as if alone in a small room, waiting and waiting and waiting. For what does he wait? He is not yet complete, so he cannot conceive of what it is he waits for. He cannot conceive of the fields of wheat, their kernels ripe and almost bursting, and how happy the sight will make someone. He cannot conceive of the union of opposites, or, for that matter, their very existence. He cannot conceive of flocks of birds in migratory flight, or that night will follow day and season follow season in a seemingly endless cycle, and the beauty and the pleasure and the purpose that might come from all this. He cannot conceive of the wind that ravages the coastline, casting asunder men and cargo, temporarily interrupting the smooth flow of commerce. He cannot conceive of the individual who, on looking up from some dreary, everyday task, is struck just then by the completeness of the above and the below and his own spirit resting in between; or how that same individual, suddenly rounding a corner, catches his own reflection, transparent and suspended in a pane of glass, and so smiles to himself with shy admiration. He cannot conceive of the woman and the child at play—an image so often regarded as a symbol of human contentment; or how calamity will attract the cold and disinterested gaze of children. He cannot conceive of a Sunday: the peal of church bells, the sound of seraphic voices in harmony, the closeness of congregation, the soothing words of praise and the much longed for presence of an unearthly glory. He cannot conceive of how emotions, varying in color and intensity, will rapidly heighten, reach an unbearable pitch, then finally explode in the silence of the evening air. He cannot conceive of the chance invention that changes again and again and forever the great turbulence that is human history. Not for him can thought crash over thought in random and violent succession, leaving his brain suffused in contradiction. He sits in nothing, this man: not in a full space, not in emptiness, not in darkness, not in light or glimmer of. He sits in nothing, in nothing, in nothing.

Look! A man steps out of bed, a good half hour after his wife, and washes himself. He sits down on a chair and at a table that he made with his own hands (the tips of his fingers are stained a thin chocolate brown from nicotine). His wife places before him a bowl of porridge, some cheese, some bread that has been buttered, two boiled eggs, a large cup of tea. He eats. The goats, the sheep, the cows are driven to pasture. A dog barks. His child now enters the room. Walking over, she bends to kiss his hand, which is resting on his knee, and he, waiting for her head to come up, kisses her on the forehead with lips he has purposely moistened. "Sir, it is wet," she says. And he laughs at her as she dries her forehead with the back of her hand. Now, clasping his wife to him, he bids her goodbye, opens the door, and stops. For what does he stop? What does he see? He sees before him himself, standing in sawdust, measuring a hole, just dug, in the ground, putting decorative grooves in a bannister, erecting columns, carving the head of a cherub over a door, lighting a cigarette, pursing his lips, holding newly planed wood at an angle and looking at it with one eye closed; standing with both hands in his pockets, the thumbs out, and rocking back and forth on his heels, he surveys a small accomplishment—a last nail driven in just so. Crossing and recrossing the threshold, he watches the sun, a violent red, set on the horizon, he hears the birds fly home, he sees the insects dancing in the last warmth of the day's light, he hears himself sing out loud:

Now the day is over,
Night is drawing nigh;
Shadows of the evening
Steal across the sky.

All this he sees (and hears). And who is this man, really? So solitary, his eyes sometimes aglow, his heart beating at an abnormal rate with a joy he cannot identify or explain. What is the virtue in him? And then again, what can it matter? For tomorrow the oak will be felled, the trestle will break, the cow's hooves will be made into glue.

But so he stands, forever, crossing and recrossing the threshold, his head lifted up, held aloft and stiff with vanity; then his eyes shift and he sees and he sees, and he is weighed down. First lifted up, then weighed down—always he is so. Shall he seek comfort now? And in what? He seeks out the living fossils. There is the shell of the pearly nautilus lying amidst colored chalk and powdered ink and India rubber in an old tin can, in memory of a day spent blissfully at the sea. The flatworm is now a parasite. Reflect. There is the earth, its surface apparently stilled, its atmosphere hospitable. And yet here stand pile upon pile of rocks of an enormous size, riven and worn down from the pressure of the great seas, now receded. And here the large veins of gold, the bubbling sulfurous fountains, the mountains covered with hot lava; at the bottom of some caves lies the black dust, and below that rich clay sediment, and trapped between the layers are filaments of winged beasts and remnants of invertebrates. "And where shall I be?" asks this man. Then he says, "My body, my soul." But quickly he averts his eyes and feels himself now, hands pressed tightly against his chest. He is standing on the threshold once again, and looking up, he sees his wife holding out toward him his brown felt hat (he had forgotten it); his child crossing the street, joining the throng of children on their way to school, a mixture of broken sentences, mispronounced words, laughter, budding malice, and energy abundant. He looks at the house he has built with his own hands, the books he has read standing on shelves, the fruit-bearing trees that he nursed from seedlings, the larder filled with food that he has provided. He shifts the weight of his body from one foot to the other, in uncertainty but also weighing, weighing . . . He imagines that in one hand he holds emptiness and yearning and in the other desire fulfilled. He thinks of tenderness and love and faith and hope and, yes, goodness. He contemplates the beauty in the common thing: the sun rising up out of the huge, shimmering expanse of water that is the sea; it rises up each day as if made anew, as if for the first time. "Sing again. Sing now," he says in his heart, for he feels the cool breeze at the back of his neck. But again and again he feels the futility in all that. For stretching out before him is a silence so dreadful, a vastness, its length and breadth and depth immeasurable. Nothing.

The branches were dead; a fly hung dead on the branches, its fragile body fluttering in the wind as if it were remnants of a beautiful gown; a beetle had fed on the body of the fly but now lay dead, too. Death on death on death. Dead lay everything. The ground stretching out from the river no longer a verdant pasture but parched and cracked with tiny fissures running up and down and into each other; and, seen from high above, the fissures presented beauty: not a pleasure to the eye but beauty all the same; still, dead, dead it was. Dead lay everything that had lived and dead also lay everything that would live. All had had or would have its season. And what should it matter that its season lasted five billion years or five minutes? There it is now, dead, vanished into darkness, banished from life. First living briefly, then dead in eternity. How vainly I struggle against this. Toil, toil, night and day. Here a house is built. Here a monument is erected to commemorate something called a good deed, or even in remembrance of a woman with exceptional qualities, and all that she loved and all that she did. Here are some children, and immeasurable is the love and special attention lavished on them. Vanished now is the house. Vanished now is the monument. Silent now are the children. I recall the house, I recall the monument, I summon up the children from the eternity of darkness, and sometimes, briefly, they appear, though always slightly shrouded, always as if they had emerged from mounds of ashes, chipped, tarnished, in fragments, or large parts missing: the ribbons, for instance, gone from the children's hair. These children whom I loved best—better than the monument, better than the house—once were so beautiful that they were thought unearthly. Dead is the past. Dead shall the future be. And what stands before my eyes, as soon as I turn my back, dead is that, too. Shall I shed tears? Sorrow is bound to death. Grief is bound to death. Each moment is not as fragile and fleeting as I once thought. Each moment is hard and lasting and so holds much that I must mourn for. And so what a bitter thing to say to me: that life is the intrusion, that to embrace a thing as beauty is the intrusion, that to believe a thing true and therefore undeniable, that is the intrusion; and, yes, false are all appearances. What a bitter thing to say to me, I who for time uncountable have always seen myself as newly born, filled with a truth and a beauty that could not be denied, living in a world of light that I called eternal, a world that can know no end. I now know regret. And that, too, is bound to death. And what do I regret? Surely not that I stand in the knowledge of the presence of death. For knowledge is a good thing; you have said that. What I regret is that in the face of death and all that it is and all that it shall be I stand powerless, that in the face of death my will, to which everything I have ever known bends, stands as if it were nothing more than a string caught in the early-morning wind.

Now! There lived a small creature, and it lived as both male and female inside a mound that it made on the ground, its body wholly covered with short fur, broadly striped, in the colors field-yellow and field-blue. It hunted a honeybee once, and when the bee, in bee anger and fright, stung the creature on the corner of the mouth, the pain was so unbearably delicious that never did this creature hunt a honeybee again. It walked over and over the wide space that surrounded the mound in which it lived. As it walked over and over the wide ground that surrounded the mound in which it lived, it watched its own feet sink into the grass and heard the ever so slight sound the grass made as it gave way to the pressure, and as it saw and heard, it felt a pleasure unbearably delicious, and, each time, the pleasure unbearably delicious was new to this creature. It lived so, banking up each unbearably delicious pleasure in deep, dark memory unspeakable, hoping to perhaps one day throw the memories into a dungeon, or burn them on an ancient pyre, or banish them to land barren, but now it kept them in this way. Then all its unbearably delicious pleasure it kept free, each thing taken, time in, time out, as if it were new, just born. It lived so in a length of time that may be measured to be no less than the blink of an eye, or no more than one hundred millenniums. This creature lived inside and outside its mound, remembering and forgetting, pain and pleasure so equally balanced, each assigned to what it judged a natural conclusion, yet one day it did vanish, leaving no sign of its existence, except for a small spot, which glowed faintly in the darkness that surrounded it. I divined this, and how natural to me that has become. I divined this, and it is not a specter but something that stood here. I show it to you. I yearn to build a monument to it, something of dust, since I now know—and so soon, so soon—what dust really is.

"Death is natural," you said to me, in such a flat, matter-of-fact way, and then you laughed—a laugh so piercing that I felt my eardrums shred, I felt myself mocked. Yet I can see that a tree is natural, that the sea is natural, that the twitter of a twittering bird is natural to a twittering bird. I can see with my own eyes the tree; it stands with limbs spread wide and laden with ripe fruit, its roots planted firmly in the rich soil, and that seems natural to me. I can see with my own eyes the sea, now with a neap tide, its surface smooth and calm; then in the next moment comes a breeze, soft, and small ripples turn into wavelets conquering wavelets, and that seems natural to me again. And the twittering bird twitters away, and that bears a special irritation, though not the irritation of the sting of the evening fly, and that special irritation is mostly ignored, and what could be more natural than that? But death bears no relation to the tree, the sea, the twittering bird. How much more like the earth spinning on its invisible axis death is, and so I might want to reach out with my hand and make the earth stand still, as if it were a bicycle standing on its handlebars upside down, the wheels spun in passing by a pair of idle hands, then stilled in passing by yet another pair of idle hands. Inevitable to life is death and not inevitable to death is life. Inevitable. How the word weighs on my tongue. I glean this: a worm winds its way between furrow and furrow in a garden, its miserable form shuddering, dreading the sharp open beak of any common bird winging its way overhead; the bird, then taking to the open air, spreads its wings in majestic flight, and how noble and triumphant is this bird in flight; but look now, there comes a boy on horseback, his body taut and eager, his hand holding bow and arrow, his aim pointed and definite, and in this way is the bird made dead. The worm, the bird, the boy. And what of the boy? His ends are numberless. I glean again the death in life.

Is life, then, a violent burst of light, like flint struck sharply in the dark? If so, I must continually strive to exist between the day and the day. I see myself as I was as a child. How much I was loved and how much I loved. No small turn of my head, no wrinkle on my brow, no parting of my lips is lost to me. How much I loved myself and how much I was loved by my mother. My mother made up elaborate tales of the origins of ordinary food, just so that I would eat it. My mother sat on some stone steps, her voluminous skirt draped in folds and falling down between her parted legs, and I, playing some distance away, glanced over my shoulder and saw her face—a face that was to me of such wondrous beauty: the lips like a moon in its first and last quarter, a nose with a bony bridge and wide nostrils that flared out and trembled visibly in excitement, ears the lobes of which were large and soft and silk-like; and what pleasure it gave me to press them between my thumb and forefinger. How I worshipped this beauty, and in my childish heart I would always say to it, "Yes, yes, yes." And, glancing over my shoulder, yet again I would silently send to her words of love and adoration, and I would receive from her, in turn and in silence, words of love and adoration. Once, I stood on a platform with three dozen girls, arranged in rows of twelve, all wearing identical white linen dresses with corded sashes of green tied around the waist, all with faces the color of stones found lying on the beach of volcanic islands, singing with the utmost earnestness, in as nearly perfect a harmony as could be managed, minds blank of interpretation:

In our deep vaulted cell
The charm we'll prepare
Too dreadful a practice
For this open air.

Time and time again, I am filled up with all that I thought life might be—glorious moment upon glorious moment of contentment and joy and love running into each other and forming an extraordinary chain: a hymn sung in rounds. Oh, the fields in which I have walked and gazed and gazed at the small cuplike flowers, in wanton hues of red and gold and blue, swaying in the day breeze, and from which I had no trouble tearing myself away, since their end was unknown to me.

I walked to the mouth of the river, and it was then still in the old place near the lime-tree grove. The water was clear and still. I looked in, and at the bottom of the river I could see a house, and it was a house of only one room, with an A-shaped roof. The house was made of rough, heavy planks of unpainted wood, and the roof was of galvanized iron and was painted red. The house had four windows on each of its four sides, and one door. Though the door and the windows were all open, I could not see anything inside and I had no desire to see what was inside. All around the house was a wide stretch of green—green grass freshly mowed a uniform length. The green, green grass of uniform length extended from the house for a distance I could not measure or know just from looking at it. Beyond the green, green grass were lots of pebbles, and they were a white-gray, as if they had been in water for many years and then placed in the sun to dry. They, too, were of a uniform size, and as they lay together they seemed to form a direct contrast to the grass. Then, at the line where the grass ended and the pebbles began, there were flowers: yellow and blue irises, red poppies, daffodils, marigolds. They grew as if wild, intertwined, as if no hand had ever offered guidance or restraint. There were no other living things in the water—no birds, no vertebrates or invertebrates, no fragile insects—and even though the water flowed in the natural way of a river, none of the things that I could see at the bottom moved. The grass, in little wisps, didn't bend slightly; the petals of the flowers didn't tremble. Everything was so true, though—that is, true to itself—and I had no doubt that the things I saw were themselves and not resemblances or representatives. The grass was the grass, and it was the grass without qualification. The green of the grass was green, and I knew it to be so and not partially green, or a kind of green, but green, and the green from which all other greens might come. And it was so with everything else that lay so still at the bottom of the river. It all lay there not like a picture but like a true thing and a different kind of true thing: one that I had never known before. Then I noticed something new: it was the way everything lit up. It was as if the sun shone not from where I stood but from a place way beyond and beneath the ground of the grass and the pebbles. How strange the light was, how it filled up everything, and yet nothing cast a shadow. I looked and looked at what was before me in wonderment and curiosity. What should this mean to me? And what should I do on knowing its meaning? A woman now appeared at the one door. She wore no clothes. Her hair was long and so very black, and it stood out in a straight line away from her head, as if she had commanded it to be that way. I could not see her face. I could see her feet, and I saw that her insteps were high, as if she had been used to climbing high mountains. Her skin was the color of brown clay, and she looked like a statue, liquid and gleaming, just before it is to be put in a kiln. She walked toward the place where the grass ended and the pebbles began. Perhaps it was a great distance, it took such a long time, and yet she never tired. When she got to the place where the green grass ended and the pebbles began, she stopped, then raised her right hand to her forehead, as if to guard her eyes against a far-off glare. She stood on tiptoe, her body swaying from side to side, and she looked at something that was far, far away from where she stood. I got down on my knees and I looked, too. It was a long time before I could see what it was that she saw.

I saw a world in which the sun and the moon shone at the same time. They appeared in a way I had never seen before: the sun was The Sun, a creation of Benevolence and Purpose and not a star among many stars, with a predictable cycle and a predictable end; the moon, too, was The Moon, and it was the creation of Beauty and Purpose and not a body subject to a theory of planetary evolution. The sun and the moon shone uniformly onto everything. Together, they made up the light, and the light fell on everything, and everything seemed transparent, as if the light went through each thing, so that nothing could be hidden. The light shone and shone and fell and fell, but there were no shadows. In this world, on this terrain, there was no day and there was no night. And there were no seasons, and so no storms or cold from which to take shelter. And in this world were many things blessed with unquestionable truth and purpose and beauty. There were steep mountains, there were valleys, there were seas, there were plains of grass, there were deserts, there were rivers, there were forests, there were vertebrates and invertebrates, there were mammals, there were reptiles, there were creatures of the dry land and the water, and there were birds. And they lived in this world not yet divided, not yet examined, not yet numbered, and not yet dead. I looked at this world as it revealed itself to me—how new, how new—and I longed to go there.

I stood above the land and the sea and looked back up at myself as I stood on the bank of the mouth of the river. I saw that my face was round in shape, that my irises took up almost all the space in my eyes, and that my eyes were brown, with yellow-colored and black-colored flecks; that my mouth was large and closed; that my nose, too, was large and my nostrils broken circles; my arms were long, my hands large, the veins pushing up against my skin; my legs were long, and, judging from the shape of them, I was used to running long distances. I saw that my hair grew out long from my head and in a disorderly way, as if I were a strange tree, with many branches. I saw my skin, and it was red. It was the red of flames when a fire is properly fed, the red of flames when a fire burns alone in a darkened place, and not the red of flames when a fire is burning in a cozy room. I saw myself clearly, as if I were looking through a pane of glass.

I stood above the land and the sea, and I felt that I was not myself as I had once known myself to be: I was not made up of flesh and blood and muscles and bones and tissue and cells and vital organs but was made up of my will, and over my will I had complete dominion. I entered the sea then. The sea was without color, and it was without anything that I had known before. It was still, having no currents. It was as warm as freshly spilled blood, and I moved through it as if I had always done so, as if it were a perfectly natural element to me. I moved through deep caverns, but they were without darkness and sudden shifts and turns. I stepped over great ridges and huge bulges of stones, I stooped down and touched the deepest bottom; I stretched myself out and covered end to end a vast crystal plane. Nothing lived here. No plant grew here, no huge sharp-toothed creature with an ancestral memory of hunter and prey searching furiously for food, no sudden shift of wind to disturb the water. How good this water was. How good that I should know no fear. I sat on the edge of a basin. I felt myself swing my feet back and forth in a carefree manner, as if I were a child who had just spent the whole day head bent over sums but now sat in a garden filled with flowers in bloom colored vermillion and gold, the sounds of birds chirping, goats bleating, home from the pasture, the smell of vanilla from the kitchen, which should surely mean pudding with dinner, eyes darting here and there but resting on nothing in particular, a mind conscious of nothing—not happiness, not contentment, and not the memory of night, which soon would come.

I stood up on the edge of the basin and felt myself move. But what self? For I had no feet, or hands, or head, or heart. It was as if those things—my feet, my hands, my head, my heart—having once been there, were now stripped away, as if I had been dipped again and again, over and over, in a large vat filled with some precious elements and were now reduced to something I yet had no name for. I had no name for the thing I had become, so new was it to me, except that I did not exist in pain or pleasure, east or west or north or south, or up or down, or past or present or future, or real or not real. I stood as if I were a prism, many-sided and transparent, refracting and reflecting light as it reached me, light that never could be destroyed. And how beautiful I became. Yet this beauty was not in the way of an ancient city seen after many centuries in ruins, or a woman who has just brushed her hair, or a man who searches for a treasure, or a child who cries immediately on being born, or an apple just picked standing alone on a gleaming white plate, or tiny beads of water left over from a sudden downpour of rain, perhaps—hanging delicately from the bare limbs of trees—or the sound the hummingbird makes with its wings as it propels itself through the earthly air.

Yet what was that light in which I stood? How singly there will the heart desire and pursue the small glowing thing resting in the distance, surrounded by darkness; how, then, if on conquering the distance the heart embraces the small glowing thing until heart and glowing thing are indistinguishable and in this way the darkness is made less? For now a door might suddenly be pushed open and the morning light might rush in, revealing to me creation and a force whose nature is implacable, unmindful of any of the individual needs of existence, and without knowledge of future or past. I might then come to believe in a being whose impartiality I cannot now or ever fully understand and accept. I ask, When shall I, too, be extinguished, so that I cannot be recognized even from my bones? I covet the rocks and the mountains their silence. And so, emerging from my pit, the one I sealed up securely, the one to which I have consigned all my deeds that I care not to reveal—emerging from this pit, I step into a room and I see that the lamp is lit. In the light of the lamp, I see some books, I see a chair, I see a table, I see a pen; I see a bowl of ripe fruit, a bottle of milk, a flute made of wood, the clothes that I will wear. And as I see these things in the light of the lamp, all perishable and transient, how bound up I know I am to all that is human endeavor, to all that is past and to all that shall be, to all that shall be lost and leave no trace. I claim these things then—mine—and now feel myself grow solid and complete, my name filling up my mouth.

[1983]

Preciousness

Clarice Lispector

EARLY IN THE MORNING IT WAS ALWAYS THE SAME THING RENEWED: TO awaken. A thing that was slow, extended, vast. Vastly, she opened her eyes. She was fifteen years old and she was not pretty. But inside her thinness existed the almost majestic vastness in which she stirred, as in a meditation. And within the mist there was something precious. Which did not extend itself, did not compromise itself nor contaminate itself. Which was intense like a jewel. Herself.

She awakened before the others, since to go to school she would have to catch a bus and a train and this would take her an hour. This would also give her an hour. Of daydreams as acute as a crime. The morning breeze violating the window and her face until her lips became hard and icy cold. Then she was smiling. As if smiling in itself were an objective. All this would happen if she were fortunate enough to "avoid having anyone look at her."

When she got up in the morning—the moment of vastness having passed in which everything unfolded—she hastily dressed, persuaded herself that she had no time to take a bath, and her family, still asleep, would never guess how few she took. Under the burning lamp in the dining room she swallowed her coffee which the maid, scratching herself in the gloom of the kitchen, had reheated. She scarcely touched the bread which the butter failed to soften. With her mouth fresh from fasting, her books under her arm, she finally opened the door and passed quickly from the stale warmth of the house into the cold fruition of the morning. Where she no longer felt any need to hurry. She had to cross a long deserted road before reaching the avenue, from the end of which a bus would emerge swaying in the morning haze, with its headlights still lit. In the June breeze, the mysterious act, authoritarian and perfect, was to raise one's arm—and already from afar the trembling bus began to become distorted, obeying the arrogance of her body, representative of a supreme power; from afar the bus started to become uncertain and slow, slow and advancing, every moment more concrete—until it pulled up before her, belching heat and smoke, smoke and heat. Then she got on, as serious as a missionary, because of the workers on the bus who "might say something to her." Those men who were no longer just boys. But she was also afraid of boys, and afraid of the youngest ones too. Afraid they would "say something to her," would look her up and down. In the seriousness of her closed lips there was a great plea: that they should respect her. More than this. As if she had made some vow, she was obliged to be venerated and while, deep inside, her heart beat with fear, she too venerated herself, she, the custodian of a rhythm. If they watched her, she became rigid and sad.

What spared her was that men did not notice her. Although something inside her, as her sixteen years gradually approached in heat and smoke—something might be intensely surprised—and this might surprise some men. As if someone had touched her on the shoulder. A shadow perhaps. On the ground the enormous shadow of a girl without a man, an uncertain element capable of being crystallized which formed part of the monotonous geometry of the great public ceremonies. As if they had touched her on the shoulder. They watched her yet did not see her. She cast a greater shadow than the reality that existed. In the bus the workmen were silent with their lunch boxes on their laps, sleep still hovering on their faces.

She felt ashamed at not trusting them, tired as they were. But until she could forget them, she felt uneasy. The fact is that they "knew." And since she knew too, hence her disquiet. Her father also knew. An old man begging alms knew. Wealth distributed, and silence.

Later, with the gait of a soldier, she crossed—unscathed—the Largo da Lapa, where day had broken. At this point the battle was almost won. On the tram she chose an empty seat, if at all possible, or, if she was lucky, she sat down beside some reassuring woman with a bundle of clothes on her lap, for example—and that was the first truce. Once at school, she would still have to confront the long corridor where her fellow pupils would be standing in conversation, and where the heels of her shoes made a noise that her tense legs were unable to suppress as if she were vainly trying to silence the beating of a heart—those shoes with their own dance rhythm. A vague silence emerged among the boys who perhaps sensed, beneath her pretence, that she was one of the prudes. She passed between the aisles of her fellow pupils growing in stature, and they did not know what to think or say. The noise made by her shoes was ugly. She gave away her own secret with her wooden heels. If the corridor should last a little longer, as if she had forgotten her destiny, she would run with her hands over her ears. She only possessed sturdy shoes. As if they were still the same ones they had solemnly put on her at birth. She crossed the corridor, which seemed as interminable as the silence in a trench and in her expression there was something so ferocious—and proud too because of her shadow—that no one said a word to her. Prohibitive, she forbade them to think.

Until at last she reached the classroom. Where suddenly everything became unimportant and more rapid and light, where her face revealed some freckles, her hair fell over her eyes, and where she was treated like a boy. Where she was intelligent. The astute profession. She appeared to have studied at home. Her curiosity instructed her more than the answers she was given. She divined—feeling in her mouth the bitter taste of heroic pains—she divined the fascinated repulsion her thinking head created in her companions who, once more, did not know what to say about her. Each time more, the great deceiver became more intelligent. She had learned to think. The necessary sacrifice: in this way "no one dared."

At times, while the teacher was speaking, she, intense, nebulous, drew symmetrical lines on her exercise book. If a line, which had to be at the same time both strong and delicate, went outside the imaginary circle where it belonged, everything would collapse: she became self-absorbed and remote, guided by the avidity of her ideal. Sometimes, instead of lines, she drew stars, stars, stars, so many and so high that she came out of this task of foretelling exhausted, lifting her drowsy head.

The return journey home was so full of hunger that impatience and hatred gnawed at her heart. Returning home it seemed another city: in the Largo da Lapa hundreds of people reflected by her hunger seemed to have forgotten, and if they remembered they would bare their teeth. The sun outlined each man with black charcoal. Her own shadow was a black post. At this hour, in which greater caution had to be exercised, she was protected by the kind of ugliness which her hunger accentuated, her features darkened by the adrenaline that darkened the flesh of animals of prey. In the empty house, with the whole family out and about their business, she shouted at the maid who did not even answer. She ate like a centaur. Her face close to her plate, her hair almost in her food.

"Skinny, but you can eat all right," the quick-witted maid was saying.

"Go to blazes," she shouted at her sullenly.

In the empty house, alone with the maid, she no longer walked like a soldier, she no longer needed to exercise caution. But she missed the battle of the streets: the melancholy of freedom, with the horizon still so very remote. She had surrendered to the horizon. But the nostalgia of the present. The lesson of patience, the vow to wait. From which perhaps she might never know how to free herself. The afternoon transforming itself into something interminable and until they all might return home to dinner and she might become to her relief a daughter, there was this heat, her book opened and then closed, an intuition, this heat: she sat down with her head between her hands, feeling desperate. When she was ten, she remembered, a little boy who loved her had thrown a dead rat at her. "Dirty thing!" she had screamed, white with indignation. It had been an experience. She had never told anyone. With her head between her hands, seated. She said fifteen times, "I am well, I am well, I am well," then she realized that she had barely paid attention to the score. Adding to the total, she said once more: "I am well, sixteen." And now she was no longer at the mercy of anyone. Desperate because well and free, she was no longer at anyone's mercy. She had lost her faith. She went to converse with the maid, the ancient priestess. They recognized each other. The two of them barefooted in the kitchen, the smoke rising from the stove. She had lost her faith, but on the border of grace, she sought in the maid only what the latter had already lost, not what she had gained. She pretended to be distracted and, conversing, she avoided conversation. "She imagines that at my age I must know more than I do, in fact, and she is capable of teaching me something," she thought, her head between her hands, defending her ignorance with her body. There were elements missing, but she did not want them from someone who had already forgotten them. The great wait was part of it. And inside that vastness—scheming.

All this, certainly. Prolonged, exhausted, the exasperation. But on the following morning, as an ostrich slowly uncurls its head, she awoke. She awoke to the same intact mystery, and opening her eyes she was the princess of that intact mystery.

As if the factory horn had already whistled, she dressed hastily and downed her coffee in one gulp. She opened the front door. And then she no longer hurried. The great immolation of the streets. Sly, alert, the wife of an apache. A part of the primitive rhythm of a ritual.

It was an even colder and darker morning than the previous ones, and she shivered in her jersey. The white mist left the end of the road invisible. Everything seemed to be enveloped in cotton-wool, one could not even hear the noise of the buses passing along the avenue. She went on walking along the uncertain path of the road. The houses slept behind closed doors. The gardens were hard with frost. In the dark air, not in the sky, but in the middle of the road, there was a star: a great star of ice which had not yet disappeared, hovering uncertainly in the air, humid and formless. Surprised in its delay, it grew round in its hesitation. She looked at the nearby star. She walked alone in the bombarded city.

No, she was not alone. Her eyes glowering with disbelief, at the far end of her street, within the mist, she spied two men. Two youths coming toward her. She looked around her as if she might have mistaken the road or the city. But she had mistaken the minutes; she had left the house before the star and the two men had time to disappear. Her heart contracted with fear.

Her first impulse, confronted with her error, was to retrace her steps and go back into the house until they had passed. "They are going to look at me, I know, there is no one else for them to stare at and they are going to stare at me!" But how could she turn back and escape, if she had been born for difficulties. If her entire slow preparation was to have the unknown outcome to which she, through her devotion, had to adhere, how could she retreat, and then never more forget the shame of having waited in misery behind a door?

And perhaps there might not even be danger. They would not have the courage to say anything because she would pass with a firm gait, her mouth set, moving in her Spanish rhythm.

On heroic legs, she went on walking. As she approached, they also approached—and then they all approached and the road became shorter and shorter. The shoes of the two youths mingled with the noise of her own shoes and it was awful to listen to. It was insistent to listen to. Either their shoes were hollow or the ground was hollow. The stones on the ground gave warning. Everything was hollow and she was listening, powerless to prevent it, the silence of the enclosure communicating with the other streets in the district, and she saw, powerless to prevent it, that the doors had become more securely locked. Even the star had disappeared. In the new pallor of darkness, the road surrendered to the three of them. She was walking and listening to the men, since she could not see them and since she had to know them. She could hear them and surprised herself with her own courage. It was the gift. And the great vocation for a destiny. She advanced, suffering as she obeyed. If she could succeed in thinking about something else, she would not hear their shoes. Nor what they might be saying. Nor the silence in which their paths would cross.

With brusque rigidity she looked at them. When she least expected it, carrying the vow of secrecy, she saw them rapidly. Were they smiling? No, they were serious.

She should not have seen. Because, by seeing, she for an instant was in danger of becoming an individual, and they also. That was what she seemed to have been warned about: so long as she could preserve a world of classical harmony, so long as she remained impersonal, she would be the daughter of the gods, and assisted by that which must be accomplished. But, having seen that which eyes, upon seeing, diminish, she had put herself in danger of being "herself"—a thing tradition did not protect.

For an instant she hesitated completely, lost for a direction to take. But it was too late to retreat. It would not be too late only if she ran; but to run would mean going completely astray, and losing the rhythm that still sustained her, the rhythm that was her only talisman—given to her on the edge of the world where it was for her being alone—on the edge of the world where all memories had been obliterated, and as an incomprehensible reminder, the blind talisman had remained as the rhythm for her destiny to copy, executing it for the consummation of the whole world. Not her own. If she were to run, that order would be altered. And she would never be pardoned her greatest error: haste. And even when one escapes they run behind one, these are things one knows.

Rigid, like a catechist, without altering for a second the slowness with which she advanced, she continued to advance.

"They are going to look at me, I know!" But she tried, through the instinct of a previous life, not to betray her fear. She divined what fear was unleashing. It was to be rapid and painless. Only for a fraction of a second would their paths cross, rapid, instantaneous, because of the advantage in her favor of her being mobile and of them coming in the opposite direction, which would allow the instant to be reduced to the necessary essential—to the collapse of the first of the seven mysteries, so secret that only one knowledge of them remained: the number seven.

"Don't let them say anything, only let them think, I don't mind them thinking."

It would be rapid, and a second after the encounter she would say, in astonishment, striding through other and yet other streets, "It almost didn't hurt." But what in fact followed had no explanation.

What followed were four awkward hands, four awkward hands that did not know what they wanted, four mistaken hands of someone without a vocation, four hands that touched her so unexpectedly that she did the best thing that she could have done in the world of movement: she became paralyzed. They, whose premeditated part was merely that of passing alongside the darkness of her fear, and then the first of the seven mysteries would collapse; they, who would represent but the horizon of a single approaching step, had failed to understand their function and, with the individuality of those who experience fear, they had attacked. It had lasted less than a fraction of a second in that tranquil street. Within a fraction of a second, they touched her as if all seven mysteries belonged to them. Which she preserved in their entirety and became the more a larva and felt seven more years behind.

She did not look at them because her face was turned with serenity toward the void.

But on account of the haste with which they wounded her, she realized that they were more frightened than she was. So terrified that they were no longer there. They were running.

"They were afraid that she might call out for help and that the doors of the houses might open one by one," she reasoned. They did not know that one does not call out for help.

She remained standing, listening in a tranquil frenzy to the sound of their shoes in flight. The pavement was hollow or their shoes were hollow or she herself was hollow. In the hollow sound of their shoes she listened attentively to the fear of both youths. The sound beat clearly on the paving stones as if they were beating incessantly on a door and she were waiting for them to stop. So clear on the bareness of the stone that the tapping of their steps did not seem to grow any more distant: it was there at her feet like a dance of victory. Standing, she had nowhere to sustain herself unless by her hearing.

The sonority did not diminish, their departure was transmitted to her by a scurry of heels ever more precise. Those heels no longer echoed on the pavement, they resounded in the air like castanets,[1] becoming ever more delicate. Then she perceived that for some time now she had heard no further sound. And, carried back by the wind, the silence and an empty road.

Until this moment, she had kept quiet, standing in the middle of the pavement. Then, as if there were several phases of the same immobility, she remained still. A moment later she sighed. And in a new phase she kept still.

She then slowly retreated back toward a wall, hunched up, moving very slowly, as if she had a broken arm, until she was leaning against the wall, where she remained inscribed. And there she remained quite still.

"Not to move is what matters," she thought from afar, "not to move." After a time, she would probably have said to herself, "Now, move your legs a little, very slowly," after which, she sighed and remained quiet, watching. It was still dark.

Then the day broke. Slowly she retrieved her books scattered on the ground. Further ahead lay her open exercise book. When she bent over to pick it up, she saw the large round handwriting which until this morning had been hers.

Then she left. Without knowing how she had filled in the time, unless with steps and more steps, she arrived at the school more than two hours late. Since she had thought about nothing, she did not realize how the time had slipped by. From the presence of the Latin master she discovered with polite surprise that in class they had already starfed on the third hour.

"What happened to you?" whispered the girl with the satchel at her side. "Why?"

"Your face is white. Are you feeling unwell?"

"No," she said so clearly that several pupils looked at her. She got up and said in a loud voice, "Excuse me!"

She went to the lavatory. Where, before the great silence of the tiles, she

[1] An instrument made of two concave pieces of wood held in the hand and clicked together, popularized by Spanish Flamenco dancers who play them while dancing.

cried out in a high shrill voice, "I am all alone in the world! No one will ever help me, no one will ever love me! I am all alone in the world!"

She was standing there, also missing the third class, on the long lavatory bench in front of several wash basins.

"It doesn't matter, I'll copy the notes later, I'll borrow someone's notes and copy them later at home—I am all alone in the world!"

She interrupted herself, beating her clenched fists several times on the bench.

The noise of four shoes suddenly began like a fine and rapid downpour of rain. A blind noise, nothing was reflected on the shiny bricks. Only the clearness of each shoe which never became entangled even once with another shoe. Like nuts falling. It was only a question of waiting as one waits for them to stop knocking on the door. Then they stopped.

When she went to set her hair in front of the mirror, she looked so ugly.

She possessed so little, and they had touched her.

She was so ugly and precious.

Her face was pale, her features grown refined. Her hands, still stained with ink from the previous day, moistening her hair.

"I must take more care of myself," she thought. She did not know how to. The truth is that each time she knew even less how to. The expression of her nose was that of a snout peeping through a hedge.

She went back to the bench and sat down quietly, with her snout.

"A person is nothing. No," she retorted in weak protest, "don't say that," she thought with kindness and melancholy. "A person is something," she said in kindness.

But, during dinner, life assumed an urgent and hysterical meaning.

"I need some new shoes! Mine make a lot of noise, a woman can't walk on wooden heels, it attracts too much attention! No one gives me anything! No one gives me anything!" And she was so feverish and breathless that no one had the courage to tell her that she would not get them. They only said, "You are not a woman and all shoe heels are made of wood."

Until, just as a person grows fat, she ceased, without knowing through which process, to be precious. There is an obscure law which decrees that the egg be protected until the chicken is born, a bird of fire. And she got her new shoes.

[1960]

Two Deserts

Valerie Matsumoto

EMIKO OYAMA THOUGHT THE IMPERIAL VALLEY OF CALIFORNIA WAS THE loneliest place she had ever seen. It was just like the Topaz Relocation Camp, she told her husband Kiyo, but without the barbed wire fence and crowded barracks. Miles of bleached desert punctuated sparsely by creosote bush and abandoned debris faced her from almost every window in their small house. Only the living room had a view of the dirt road which ended in front of their home, and across it, a row of squat faded houses where other farmers' families lived. They waved to her and Kiyo in passing, and Jenny played with the Garcia children, but Emiko's Spanish and their English were too limited for more than casual greetings.

Emiko felt a tug of anticipation on the day the moving van pulled up at the Ishikawas' place across the road—the house which in her mind had become inextricably linked with friendship. She had felt its emptiness as her own when Sats, Yuki and their three children gave up farming and departed for a life which came to her in delicious fragments in Yuki's hastily scrawled letters. Yuki, who made the best sushi rice in the world and had given her the recipe; who could draw shy Kiyo into happy banter. Yuki, whose loud warm laugh made the desert seem less drab, less engulfing.

She had been thinking about Yuki that morning as she weeded the yard and vegetable plot in preparation for planting. Sats and Yuki had advised her to plant marigolds around the vegetables to draw away nematodes, and she liked the idea of a bold orange border. Emiko liked bright colors, especially the flaming scarlet of the bougainvillea which rose above the front door where Kiki their cat lay sunning himself. There was a proud look in the amber eyes, for Kiki the hunter had slain three scorpions and laid them in a row on the porch, their backs crushed and deadly stingers limp, winning extravagant praise from Jenny and Emiko. The scorpions still lay there, at Jenny's insistence, awaiting Kiyo's return that evening. Emiko shuddered every time she entered the house, glancing at the curved stingers and thinking of Jenny's sandaled feet.

Emiko had finished weeding the front border and was about to go inside to escape the heat when she saw the new neighbor woman plodding across the sand toward her. A cotton shift could not conceal her thinness, nor a straw hat her tousled gray curls. Her eyes were fragile lilac glass above the wide smile.

"Hello, I'm Mattie Barnes. I just thought I'd come over and introduce myself while Roy is finishing up with the movers. Your bougainvillea caught my eye first thing and I thought, 'Those are some folks who know what will grow in the desert.' I hope you'll give me some advice about what to plant in my yard once we get settled in."

They talked about adjusting to desert life and Emiko learned that Mattie's husband Roy had recently retired. "We decided to move here because the doctor said it would be better for my lungs," Mattie explained, wiping her brow.

"Would you like a glass of lemonade?" Emiko offered. "Or maybe later, after you've finished moving—"

"Oh, I'd love something cold," Mattie said, adding vaguely, "Roy will take care of everything—he's more particular about those things than I am."

Emiko preceded Mattie into the house, hoping that Jenny was not lying on the cool linoleum, stripped to her underwear. As she crossed the threshold Mattie gave a shriek and stopped abruptly, eyeing the scorpions lined up neatly on the porch.

"What on earth are those things doing here?" ·

"Our cat killed them," Emiko said, feeling too foolish to admit her pride in Kiki's prowess. "Jenny wants me to leave them to show her father when he comes home from the field."

"Awful creatures," Mattie shuddered. "Roy can't stand them, but then, he can't abide insects. He said to me this morning, 'Of all the places we could have moved to, we had to choose the buggiest.'"

There was no buggier place than the Imperial Valley, Emiko agreed, especially in the summer. In the evening the air was thick with mosquitoes, gnats and moths. The cicadas buzzed in deafening chorus from every tree. They danced in frenzied legions around the porch light and did kamikaze dives into the bath water. All of them came in dusty gray hordes, as though the desert had sapped the color from them, but not their energy. Late at night, long after Kiyo had fallen into exhausted sleep, Emiko would lie awake, perspiring, listening to the tinny scrabble of insects trapped between the window glass and screen.

". . . but I like the desert," Mattie was saying, dreamily clinking the ice cubes in her glass. "It's so open and peaceful. As long as I can have a garden, I'll be happy."

Within a few weeks after their arrival, the Barneses had settled into a routine: Roy making daily trips to the local store and the Roadside Cafe; Mattie tending her garden and walking to church once a week with Emiko and Jenny. By the end of June Mattie had been enlisted with Emiko to make crêpe paper flowers for a church bazaar.

"My, your flowers turned out beautifully," Mattie exclaimed one morning, looking wistfully at the cardboard box filled with pink, yellow, scarlet and lavender blossoms set on wire stems. "They'll make lovely corsages." She sighed. "I seem to be all thumbs—my flowers hardly look like flowers. I don't know how you do it. You Japanese are just very artistic people."

Emiko smiled and shook her head with a polite disclaimer, but the bright blur of flowers suddenly dissolved into another mass of paper blooms, carrying her more than a decade into the past. She was a teenager in a flannel shirt and denim pants with rolled cuffs, seated on a cot in a cramped barrack room helping her mother fashion flowers from paper. Her own hands had been clumsy at first, striving to imitate her mother's precise fingers which gave each fragile petal lifelike curves, the look of artless grace. The only flowers in Topaz when elderly Mr. Wakasa was shot by a guard were those that bloomed from the fingertips of *Issei* and *Nisei*[1] women, working late into the night to complete the exquisite wreaths for his funeral. Each flower a silent voice crying with color; each flower a tear.

"I did a little flower-making as a teenager," Emiko said.

"Will you come over and show me how?" Mattie asked. "I'm too embarrassed to take these awful things, and I've still got lots of crêpe paper spread all over the kitchen."

"Sure," Emiko nodded. "I'll help you get started and you'll be a whiz in no time. It isn't too hard; it just takes patience."

Mattie smiled, a slight wheeze in her voice when she said, "I've got plenty of that, too."

They were seated at the Barnes' small table surrounded by bright masses of petals like fallen butterflies, their fingers sticky with florist's tape, when Roy returned from shopping. When he saw Emiko he straightened and pulled his belt up over his paunch.

"A sight for sore eyes!" he boomed, giving her a broad wink. "What mischief are you ladies up to?"

"Emi's teaching me how to make flowers," Mattie explained, holding up a wobbly rose.

"Always flowers! I tell you," he leaned over Emiko's chair and said in a mock conspiratorial voice, "all my wife thinks about is flowers. I keep telling her there are other things in life. Gardening is for old folks."

"And what's wrong with that?" Mattie protested, waving her flower at him. "We *are* old folks."

"Speak for yourself," he winked at Emiko again. "What's so great about gardens, anyway?"

"I hold with the poem that says you're closest to God's heart in a garden," said Mattie.

"Well, I'm not ready to get that close to God's heart yet." There was defiance in Roy's voice. "What do you think about that, Emi?"

"I like working in the yard before it gets too hot," she said carefully. Her words felt tight and deliberate, like the unfurled petals on the yellow rose in her hands. "I don't have Mattie's talent with real flowers, though—aside from the bougainvillea and Jenny's petunias, nothing ever seems to bloom. The soil is too dry and saline for the things I used to grow. Now I've got my hopes pinned on the vegetable garden."

"Vegetables—hmph!" Roy snorted, stomping off to read the paper.

"Oh, that Roy is just like a boy sometimes," Mattie said. "I tell you, don't ever let your husband retire or you'll find him underfoot all day long."

"Doesn't Roy have any hobbies?" Emiko thought of her father and his books, his Japanese brush painting, his meetings.

---

[1] Issei are immigrant Japanese living in the United States; Nisei are second-generation Japanese.

"He used to play golf," Mattie said, "but there's no golf course here. He says this town is one giant sand trap."

"There have been times when I felt that way, too," Emiko admitted lightly.

"Well, don't let Roy hear you say that or you'll never get him off the topic," Mattie chuckled. "The fact is, Roy doesn't much know how to be by himself. I've had forty years to learn, and I've gotten to like it. And I suppose maybe he will too."

Her voice trailed off, and Emiko suddenly realized that Mattie didn't much care whether he did or not.

One day while Emiko was engrossed in pinning a dress pattern for Jenny she suddenly heard a tapping on the screen, like the scrabbling of a large beetle. She half-turned and felt a jolt of alarm at the sight of a grinning gargoyle hunched before the glass, hands splayed open on either side of his face, the caricature of a boy peering covetously into a toy store.

"Hey there! I caught you day-dreaming!" he chortled. "Looks to me like you need some company to wake you up."

"I'm not day-dreaming; I'm trying to figure out how to make a two-and-a-half yard dress out of two yards," she said. "Jenny is growing so fast, I can hardly keep up with her."

Roy walked into the house unbidden, confident of a welcome, and drew a chair up to the table. He fingered the bright cotton print spread over the table and gazed at Emiko, his head cocked to one side.

"You must get pretty lonesome here by yourself all day. No wonder you're sitting here dreaming."

"No," she said, her fingers moving the pattern pieces. "There's so much to do I don't have time to be lonesome. Besides, Jenny is here, and Kiyo comes home for lunch."

"But still—cooped up with a kiddie all day . . ." Roy shook his head. He chose to disregard Kiyo, who had no place in his imagined scenarios, and was hard at work miles away.

Emiko delicately edged the cotton fabric away from Roy's damp, restless fingers. I'll be darned if I offer him something to drink, she thought as he mopped his brow and cast an impatient glance at the kitchen. "I haven't seen Mattie outside this week. How is she feeling?"

"Oh, 'bout the same, 'bout the same," he said, his irritation subsiding into brave resignation. "She has her good days and her bad days. The doctor told her to stay in bed for awhile and take it easy."

"It must be hard on Mattie, having to stay indoors," Emiko said, thinking of her peering out through the pale curtains at the wilting zinnias and the new weeds in the back yard.

"I suppose so—usually you can't tear Mattie away from her garden." Roy shook his head. "Mattie and me are real different. Now, I like people—I've always been the sociable type—but Mattie! All she cares about are plants."

"Well, Kiyo and I have different interests," Emiko said, "but it works out well that way. Maybe you could learn a few things from Mattie about plants."

Even as the suggestion passed her lips, she regretted it. Roy viewed the garden as the site of onerous labor. To Mattie, it was the true world of the heart, with no room for ungentle or impatient hands. It was a place of deeply sown hopes, lovingly nurtured, and its colors were the colors of unspoken dreams.

"Plants!" Roy threw up his hands. "Give me people any time. I always liked people and had a knack for working with them—that's how I moved up in the business."

"Why don't you look into some of the clubs here?" Emiko tried again. "The Elks always need people with experience and time . . ."

"Sweetheart, I'm going to spend my time the way I want. I'm finished with work—it's time to enjoy life! Besides, how much fun can I have with a bunch of old geezers? That's not for me, Emily, my dear." She stiffened as he repeated the name, savoring the syllables. "Emily . . . Emily . . . Yes, I like the sound of that—Emily."

"My name is Emiko," she said quietly, her eyes as hard as agate. "I was named after my grandmother." That unfaltering voice had spoken the same words in first, second, third, fourth, fifth and sixth grades. All the grammar school teachers had sought to change her name, to make her into an Emily: "Emily is so much easier to pronounce, dear, and it's a nice American name." She was such a well-mannered child, the teachers were always amazed at her stubbornness on this one point. Sometimes she was tempted to relent, to give in, but something inside her resisted. "My name is Emiko," she would insist politely. I am an American named Emiko. I was named for my grandmother who was beautiful and loved to swim. When she emerged from the sea, her long black hair would glitter white with salt. I never met her, but she was beautiful and she would laugh when she rose from the waves. "My name is Emiko, Emi for short."

"But Emily is such a pretty name," Roy protested. "It fits you."

"It's not my name," she said, swallowing a hard knot of anger. "I don't like to be called Emily!"

"Temper, temper!" He shook his finger at her, gleeful at having provoked her.

"Well, I guess I'll be in a better temper when I can get some work done," she said, folding up the cloth with tense, deliberate hands. She raised her voice. "Jenny! Let's go out and water the vegetable garden now."

If Jenny thought this a strange task in the heat of the afternoon, it did not show in her face when she skipped out of her room, swinging her straw hat. It still sported a flimsy, rainbow-hued scarf which had been the subject of much pleading in an El Centro dime store. At that moment, Emiko found it an oddly reassuring sight. She smiled and felt her composure return.

"Tell Mattie to let me know if there's anything I can do to help," she told Roy, as he unwillingly followed them out of the house and trudged away across the sand. After they went back inside, Emiko locked the door behind them for the first time. When Kiyo returned home, his face taut with fatigue, she told him it was because of the hoboes who came around.

Emiko went to see Mattie less and less frequently, preferring instead to call her on the phone, even though they lived so close. Roy, however, continued to drop by despite Emiko's aloofness. His unseemly yearning tugged at her with undignified hands, but what he craved most was beyond her power to give. She took to darning and mending in the bedroom with the curtains drawn, ignoring his insistent knock; she tried to do her gardening in the evening after dinner when her husband was home, though it was hard to weed in the dusk. She was beginning to feel caged, pent up, restless. Jenny and Kiyo trod quietly, puzzled by her edginess, but their solicitude only made her feel worse.

Finally, one morning Emiko decided to weed the vegetables, sprouting new and tender. Surely the mid-morning heat would discourage any interference. Although the perspiration soon trickled down her face, she began to enjoy the weeding, pulled into the satisfying rhythm of the work. She was so engrossed that she did not notice when Roy Barnes unlatched the gate and stepped into the yard, a determined twinkle in his faded eye.

"Howdy, Emi! I saw you working away out here by your lonesome and thought maybe you could use some help."

"Thanks, but I'm doing all right," she said, wrenching a clump of puncture vine from the soil and laying it in the weed box carefully to avoid scattering the sharp stickers. Jenny was close by, digging at her petunias and marigolds, ignoring Mr. Barnes, who had no place in the colorful jungle she was imagining.

"If I had a pretty little wife, I sure wouldn't let her burn up out here, no sir," his voice nudged at her as she squatted on the border of the vegetable plot. If Mattie looked out of the window she would see only a pleasant tableau: Roy nodding in neighborly fashion as Emiko pointed out young rows of zucchini and yellow squash, watermelon, cantaloupe, eggplant and tomatoes. Mattie would not see the strain on Emiko's face, turned away from Roy, when he leaned over and mumbled, "Say, you know what I like best in this garden?"

Emiko grabbed the handle of the shovel and stood up before he could tell her, moving away from him to pluck a weed. "I know Mattie likes cantaloupe," she said. "So do I. Kiyo prefers Crenshaws, but I couldn't find any seeds this year. What do you and Mattie have in your garden?"

"Just grass," he said, undeterred. "Mattie's always fussing over her flowers—you know what she's like," he chuckled indulgently, "but I'd rather spend my time doing other things than slaving in the yard."

Emiko hacked away at the stubborn clumps of grass roots and the persistent runners with myriad finer roots, thread-thin but tough as wire. She worked with desperate energy, flustered, her gloved hands sweating on the shovel handle, forehead damp. She was groping for the language to make him understand, to make him leave her in peace, but he was bent on not understanding, not seeing, not leaving until he got what he wanted.

"You know what, Emi?" He moistened his dry lips, beginning to grin reminiscently. "You remind me of somebody I met in Tokyo. Have you ever been to Tokyo?"

"No," she said, digging hard. "Never."

"You'd like it, it's a wonderful place, so clean and neat, and the people so friendly. When I was in Tokyo, I met up with the cutest *geisha*[2] girl you ever saw—just like a little doll. She'd never seen anybody with blue eyes before, and couldn't get over it." He chuckled. "I couldn't think who you reminded me of at first, and then it just hit me that you are the spitting image of her."

"Did Mattie like Tokyo too?" Emiko said, continuing to spade vigorously as his eyes slid over her, imagining a doll in exotic robes.

"She didn't go—it was a business trip," he said impatiently. Then his voice relaxed into a drawl, heavy with insinuation. "After all, I like to do some things on my own." He was moving closer again.

Then she saw it. Emiko had just turned over a rock, and as she raised the shovel, it darted from its refuge, pincers up, the deadly tail curved menacingly over the carapaced back. It moved a little to the left and then the right, beginning the poison dance. Emiko glanced to see where Jenny was and saw Roy jump back hastily; the scorpion, startled by his movement, scuttled sideways toward Jenny, lying on her stomach, still dreaming of her jungle.

The blood pounded in Emiko's head. She brought down the shovel hard with one quick breath, all her rage shooting down the thick handle into the heavy crushing iron. She wielded the shovel like a *samurai*[3] in battle, swinging it down with all her force, battering her enemy to dust. Once had been enough but she struck again and again, until her anger was spent and she leaned on the rough handle, breathing hard.

"Mommy! What did you do?" Jenny had scrambled to Emiko's side, fear in her eyes, gazing at the unrecognizable fragments in the dirt.

"I killed a scorpion," Emiko said. She scornfully tossed the remains into the weed box, and wiped her brow on her arm, like a farmer, or a warrior. "I don't like to kill anything," she said aloud, "but sometimes you have to."

Roy Barnes recoiled from the pitiless knowledge in her eyes. He saw her clearly now but it was too late. His mouth opened and closed but the gush of words had gone dry. He seemed to age before her eyes, like Urashima-taro who opened the precious box of youth and was instantly wrinkled and broken by the unleashed tides of years.

"You'll have to leave now, Mr. Barnes. I'm going in to fix lunch." Emiko's smile was as quiet as unsheathed steel. "Tell Mattie I hope she's feeling better."

She watched him pick his way across the dirt, avoiding the puncture vine and rusted tin cans, looking as gray as the rags that bleached beneath the fierce sun. Jenny stared past him and the small houses of their neighborhood to the desert sand beyond, glittering like an ocean with shards of glass and mica.

---

[2] A Japanese young woman educated in the cultural, literary, and performing arts to serve as a companion for Japanese men.

[3] A member of an elite warrior class in feudal Japan.

"Do you think we might ever find gold?" she asked.

They gazed together over the desert, full of unknown perils and ancient secrets, the dust of dreams and battles.

"Maybe." Emiko stood tall, shading her eyes from the deceptive shimmer. "Maybe."

[1986]

A Wife's Story

Bharati Mukherjee

IMRE SAYS FORGET IT, BUT I'M GOING TO WRITE DAVID MAMET.[1] SO PATELS are hard to sell real estate to. You buy them a beer, whisper Glengarry Glen Ross, and they smell swamp instead of sun and surf. They work hard, eat cheap, live ten to a room, stash their savings under futons in Queens, and before you know it they own half of Hoboken. You say, where's the sweet gullibility that made this nation great?

Polish jokes, Patel[2] jokes: that's not why I want to write Mamet.

Seen their women?

Everybody laughs. Imre laughs. The dozing fat man with the Barnes & Noble sack between his legs, the woman next to him, the usher, everybody. The theater isn't so dark that they can't see me. In my red silk sari I'm conspicuous. Plump, gold paisleys sparkle on my chest.

The actor is just warming up. *Seen their women?* He plays a salesman, he's had a bad day and now he's in a Chinese restaurant trying to loosen up. His face is pink. His wool-blend slacks are creased at the crotch. We bought our tickets at half-price, we're sitting in the front row, but at the edge, and we see things we shouldn't be seeing. At least I do, or think I do. Spittle, actors goosing each other, little winks, streaks of makeup.

Maybe they're improvising dialogue too. Maybe Mamet's provided them with insult kits, Thursdays for Chinese, Wednesdays for Hispanics, today for Indians. Maybe they get together before curtain time, see an Indian woman settling in the front row off to the side, and say to each other: "Hey, forget Friday. Let's get *her* today. See if she cries. See if she walks out." Maybe, like the salesmen they play, they have a little bet on.

Maybe I shouldn't feel betrayed.

[1] A contemporary American dramatist, screenplay writer, and film director whose plays confront the psychological and ethical issues confronting modern urban society.
[2] Surname common to the Bujharati sect, the state of Bujharat in the western part of India.

Their women, he goes again. *They look like they've just been fucked by a dead cat.*

The fat man hoots so hard he nudges my elbow off our shared armrest.

"Imre. I'm going home." But Imre's hunched so far forward he doesn't hear. English isn't his best language. A refugee from Budapest, he has to listen hard. "I didn't pay eighteen dollars to be insulted."

I don't hate Mamet. It's the tyranny of the American dream that scares me. First, you don't exist. Then you're invisible. Then you're funny. Then you're disgusting. Insult, my American friends will tell me, is a kind of acceptance. No instant dignity here. A play like this, back home, would cause riots. Communal, racist, and antisocial. The actors wouldn't make it off stage. This play, and all these awful feelings, would be safely locked up.

I long, at times, for clear-cut answers. Offer me instant dignity, today, and I'll take it.

"What?" Imre moves toward me without taking his eyes off the actor. "Come again?"

Tears come. I want to stand, scream, make an awful scene. I long for ugly, nasty rage.

The actor is ranting, flinging spittle. *Give me a chance. I'm not finished, I can get back on the board. I tell that asshole, give me a real lead. And what does that asshole give me? Patels. Nothing but Patels.*

This time Imre works an arm around my shoulders. "Panna, what is Patel? Why are you taking it all so personally?"

I shrink from his touch, but I don't walk out. Expensive girls' schools in Lausanne and Bombay have trained me to behave well. My manners are exquisite, my feelings are delicate, my gestures refined, my moods undetectable. They have seen me through riots, uprootings, separation, my son's death.

"I'm not taking it personally."

The fat man looks at us. The woman looks too, and shushes.

I stare back at the two of them. Then I stare, mean and cool, at the man's elbow. Under the bright blue polyester Hawaiian shirt sleeve, the elbow looks soft and runny. "Excuse me," I say. My voice has the effortless meanness of well-bred displaced Third World women, though my rhetoric has been learned elsewhere. "You're exploiting my space."

Startled, the man snatches his arm away from me. He cradles it against his breast. By the time he's ready with comebacks, I've turned my back on him. I've probably ruined the first act for him. I know I've ruined it for Imre.

It's not my fault; it's the *situation*. Old colonies wear down. Patels—the new pioneers—have to be suspicious. Idi Amin's lesson is permanent. AT&T wires move good advice from continent to continent. Keep all assets liquid. Get into 7-11s, get out of condos and motels. I know how both sides feel, that's the trouble. The Patel sniffing out scams, the sad salesmen on the stage: postcolonialism has made me their referee. It's hate I long for; simple, brutish, partisan hate.

After the show Imre and I make our way toward Broadway. Sometimes he holds my hand; it doesn't mean anything more than that crazies and drunks are crouched in doorways. Imre's been here over two years, but he's stayed very old-world, very courtly, openly protective of women. I met him in a seminar on special ed. last semester. His wife is a nurse somewhere in the Hungarian countryside. There are two sons, and miles of petitions for their emigration. My husband manages a mill two hundred miles north of Bombay. There are no children.

"You make things tough on yourself," Imre says. He assumed Patel was a Jewish name or maybe Hispanic; everything makes equal sense to him. He found the play tasteless, he worried about the effect of vulgar language on my sensitive ears. "You have to let go a bit." And as though to show me how to let go, he breaks away from me, bounds ahead with his head ducked tight, then dances on amazingly jerky legs. He's a Magyar, he often tells me, and deep down, he's an Asian too. I catch glimpses of it, knife-blade Attila cheekbones, despite the blondish hair. In his faded jeans and leather jacket, he's a rock video star. I watch MTV for hours in the apartment when Charity's working the evening shift at Macy's. I listen to WPLJ on Charity's earphones. Why should I be ashamed? Television in India is so uplifting.

Imre stops as suddenly as he'd started. People walk around us. The summer sidewalk is full of theatergoers in seersucker suits; Imre's year-round jacket is out of place. European. Cops in twos and threes huddle, lightly tap their thighs with night sticks and smile at me with benevolence. I want to wink at them, get us all in trouble, tell them the crazy dancing man is from the Warsaw Pact. I'm too shy to break into dance on Broadway. So I hug Imre instead.

The hug takes him by surprise. He wants me to let go, but he doesn't really expect me to let go. He staggers, though I weigh no more than 104 pounds, and with him, I pitch forward slightly. Then he catches me, and we walk arm in arm to the bus stop. My husband would never dance or hug a woman on Broadway. Nor would my brothers. They aren't stuffy people, but they went to Anglican boarding schools and they have a well-developed sense of what's silly.

"Imre." I squeeze his big, rough hand. "I'm sorry I ruined the evening for you."

"You did nothing of the kind." He sounds tired. "Let's not wait for the bus. Let's splurge and take a cab instead."

Imre always has unexpected funds. The Network, he calls it, Class of '56.

In the back of the cab, without even trying, I feel light, almost free. Memories of Indian destitutes mix with the hordes of New York street people, and they float free, like astronauts, inside my head. I've made it. I'm making something of my life. I've left home, my husband, to get a Ph.D. in special ed. I have a multiple-entry visa and a small scholarship for two years. After that, we'll see. My mother was beaten by her mother-in-law, my grandmother, when she'd registered for French lessons at the Alliance

Française. My grandmother, the eldest daughter of a rich zamindar,[3] was illiterate.

Imre and the cabdriver talk away in Russian. I keep my eyes closed. That way I can feel the floaters better. I'll write Mamet tonight. I feel strong, reckless. Maybe I'll write Steven Spielberg too; tell him that Indians don't eat monkey brains.

We've made it. Patels must have made it. Mamet, Spielberg: they're not condescending to us. Maybe they're a little bit afraid.

Charity Chin, my roommate, is sitting on the floor drinking Chablis out of a plastic wineglass. She is five foot six, three inches taller than me, but weighs a kilo and a half less than I do. She is a "hands" model. Orientals are supposed to have a monopoly in the hands-modelling business, she says. She had her eyes fixed eight or nine months ago and out of gratitude sleeps with her plastic surgeon every third Wednesday.

"Oh, good," Charity says. "I'm glad you're back early. I need to talk."

She's been writing checks. MCI, Con Ed, Bonwit Teller. Envelopes, already stamped and sealed, form a pyramid between her shapely, knee-socked legs. The checkbook's cover is brown plastic, grained to look like cowhide. Each time Charity flips back the cover, white geese fly over sky-colored checks. She makes good money, but she's extravagant. The difference adds up to this shared, rent-controlled Chelsea one-bedroom.

"All right. Talk."

When I first moved in, she was seeing an analyst. Now she sees a nutritionist.

"Eric called. From Oregon."

"What did he want?"

"He wants me to pay half the rent on his loft for last spring. He asked me to move back, remember? He *begged* me."

Eric is Charity's estranged husband.

"What does your nutritionist say?" Eric now wears a red jumpsuit and tills the soil in Rajneeshpuram.

"You think Phil's a creep too, don't you? What else can he be when creeps are all I attract?"

Phil is a flutist with thinning hair. He's very touchy on the subject of *flautists* versus *flutists*. He's touchy on every subject, from music to books to foods to clothes. He teaches at a small college upstate, and Charity bought a used blue Datsun ("Nissan," Phil insists) last month so she could spend weekends with him. She returns every Sunday night, exhausted and exasperated. Phil and I don't have much to say to each other—he's the only musician I know; the men in my family are lawyers, engineers, or in business—but I like him. Around me, he loosens up. When he visits, he bakes us loaves of pumpernickel bread. He waxes our kitchen floor. Like many men in this country, he seems to me a displaced child, or even a woman, looking for

[3] An Indian landholder, or member of the landed aristocracy.

something that passed him by, or for something that he can never have. If he thinks I'm not looking, he sneaks his hands under Charity's sweater, but there isn't too much there. Here, she's a model with high ambitions. In India, she'd be a flat-chested old maid.

I'm shy in front of the lovers. A darkness comes over me when I see them horsing around.

"It isn't the money," Charity says. Oh? I think. "He says he still loves me. Then he turns around and asks me for five hundred."

What's so strange about that, I want to ask. She still loves Eric, and Eric, red jump suit and all, is smart enough to know it. Love is a commodity, hoarded like any other. Mamet knows. But I say, "I'm not the person to ask about love." Charity knows that mine was a traditional Hindu marriage. My parents, with the help of a marriage broker, who was my mother's cousin, picked out a groom. All I had to do was get to know his taste in food.

It'll be a long evening, I'm afraid. Charity likes to confess. I unpleat my silk sari—it no longer looks too showy—wrap it in muslin cloth and put it away in a dresser drawer. Saris are hard to have laundered in Manhattan, though there's a good man in Jackson Heights. My next step will be to brew us a pot of chrysanthemum tea. It's a very special tea from the mainland. Charity's uncle gave it to us. I like him. He's a humpbacked, awkward, terrified man. He runs a gift store on Mott Street, and though he doesn't speak much English, he seems to have done well. Once upon a time he worked for the railways in Chengdu, Szechwan Province, and during the Wuchang Uprising, he was shot at. When I'm down, when I'm lonely for my husband, when I think of our son, or when I need to be held, I think of Charity's uncle. If I hadn't left home, I'd never have heard of the Wuchang Uprising. I've broadened my horizons.

Very late that night my husband calls me from Ahmadabad, a town of textile mills north of Bombay. My husband is a vice president at Lakshmi Cotton Mills. Lakshmi is the goddess of wealth, but LCM (Priv.), Ltd., is doing poorly. Lockouts, strikes, rock-throwings. My husband lives on digitalis, which he calls the food for our *yuga*[4] of discontent.

"We had a bad mishap at the mill today." Then he says nothing for seconds.

The operator comes on. "Do you have the right party, sir? We're trying to reach Mrs. Butt."

"Bhatt," I insist. "*B* for Bombay, *H* for Haryana, *A* for Ahmadabad, double *T* for Tamil Nadu." It's a litany. "This is she."

"One of our lorries was firebombed today. Resulting in three deaths. The driver, old Karamchand, and his two children."

I know how my husband's eyes look this minute, how the eye rims sag and the yellow corneas shine and bulge with pain. He is not an emotional man—the Ahmadabad Institute of Management has trained him to cut

[4] A Hindu cosmological term meaning age or period of mankind. Each period is progressively shorter than the last, reflecting the decline in moral and physical states of existence.

losses, to look on the bright side of economic catastrophes—but tonight he's feeling low. I try to remember a driver named Karamchand, but can't. That part of my life is over, the way *trucks* have replaced *lorries* in my vocabulary, the way Charity Chin and her lurid love life have replaced inherited notions of marital duty. Tomorrow he'll come out of it. Soon he'll be eating again. He'll sleep like a baby. He's been trained to believe in turnovers. Every morning he rubs his scalp with cantharidine oil so his hair will grow back again.

"It could be your car next." Affection, love. Who can tell the difference in a traditional marriage in which a wife still doesn't call her husband by his first name?

"No. They know I'm a flunky, just like them. Well paid, maybe. No need for undue anxiety, please."

Then his voice breaks. He says he needs me, he misses me, he wants me to come to him damp from my evening shower, smelling of sandalwood soap, my braid decorated with jasmines.

"I need you too."

"Not to worry, please," he says. "I am coming in a fortnight's time. I have already made arrangements."

Outside my window, fire trucks whine, up Eighth Avenue. I wonder if he can hear them, what he thinks of a life like mine, led amid disorder.

"I am thinking it'll be like a honeymoon. More or less."

When I was in college, waiting to be married, I imagined honeymoons were only for the more fashionable girls, the girls who came from slightly racy families, smoked Sobranies in the dorm lavatories and put up posters of Kabir Bedi, who was supposed to have made it as a big star in the West. My husband wants us to go to Niagara. I'm not to worry about foreign exchange. He's arranged for extra dollars through the Gujarati Network, with a cousin in San Jose. And he's bought four hundred more on the black market. "Tell me you need me. Panna, please tell me again."

I change out of the cotton pants and shirt I've been wearing all day and put on a sari to meet my husband at JFK. I don't forget the jewelry; the marriage necklace of *mangalsutra*, gold drop earrings, heavy gold bangles. I don't wear them every day. In this borough of vice and greed, who knows when, or whom, desire will overwhelm.

My husband spots me in the crowd and waves. He has lost weight, and changed his glasses. The arm, uplifted in a cheery wave, is bony, frail, almost opalescent.

In the Carey Coach, we hold hands. He strokes my fingers one by one. "How come you aren't wearing my mother's ring?"

"Because muggers know about Indian women," I say. They know with us it's 24-karat. His mother's ring is showy, in ghastly taste anywhere but India: a blood-red Burma ruby set in a gold frame of floral sprays. My mother-in-law got her guru to bless the ring before I left for the States.

He looks disconcerted. He's used to a different role. He's the knowing, suspicious one in the family. He seems to be sulking, and finally he comes out with it. "You've said nothing about my new glasses." I compliment him on the glasses, how chic and Western-executive they make him look. But I can't help the other things, necessities until he learns the ropes. I handle the money, buy the tickets. I don't know if this makes me unhappy.

Charity drives her Nissan upstate, so for two weeks we are to have the apartment to ourselves. This is more privacy than we ever had in India. No parents, no servants, to keep us modest. We play at housekeeping. Imre has lent us a hibachi, and I grill saffron chicken breasts. My husband marvels at the size of the Perdue hens. "They're big like peacocks, no? These Americans, they're really something!" He tries out pizzas, burgers, McNuggets. He chews. He explores. He judges. He loves it all, fears nothing, feels at home in the summer odors, the clutter of Manhattan streets. Since he thinks that the American palate is bland, he carries a bottle of red peppers in his pocket. I wheel a shopping cart down the aisles of the neighborhood Grand Union, and he follows, swiftly, greedily. He picks up hair rinses and high-protein diet powders. There's so much I already take for granted.

One night, Imre stops by. He wants us to go with him to a movie. In his work shirt and red leather tie, he looks arty or strung out. It's only been a week, but I feel as though I am really seeing him for the first time. The yellow hair worn very short at the sides, the wide, narrow lips. He's a good-looking man, but self-conscious, almost arrogant. He's picked the movie we should see. He always tells me what to see, what to read. He buys the *Voice*. He's a natural avant-gardist. For tonight he's chosen *Numéro Deux*.

"Is it a musical?" my husband asks. The Radio City Music Hall is on his list of sights to see. He's read up on the history of the Rockettes. He doesn't catch Imre's sympathetic wink.

Guilt, shame, loyalty. I long to be ungracious, not ingratiate myself with both men.

That night my husband calculates in rupees the money we've wasted on Godard. "That refugee fellow, Nagy, must have a screw loose in his head. I paid very steep price for dollars on the black market."

Some afternoons we go shopping. Back home we hated shopping, but now it is a lovers' project. My husband's shopping list startles me. I feel I am just getting to know him. Maybe, like Imre, freed from the dignities of old-world culture, he too could get drunk and squirt Cheez Whiz on a guest. I watch him dart into stores in his gleaming leather shoes. Jockey shorts on sale in outdoor bins on Broadway entrance him. White tube socks with different bands of color delight him. He looks for microcassettes, for anything small and electronic and smuggleable. He needs a garment bag. He calls it a "wardrobe," and I have to translate.

"All of New York is having sales, no?"

My heart speeds watching him this happy. It's the third week in August, almost the end of summer, and the city smells ripe, it cannot bear more heat, more money, more energy.

"This is so smashing! The prices are so excellent!" Recklessly, my prudent husband signs away traveller's checks. How he intends to smuggle it all back

I don't dare ask. With a microwave, he calculates, we could get rid of our cook.

This has to be love, I think. Charity, Eric, Phil: they may be experts on sex. My husband doesn't chase me around the sofa, but he pushes me down on Charity's battered cushions, and the man who has never entered the kitchen of our Ahmadabad house now comes toward me with a dish tub of steamy water to massage away the pavement heat.

Ten days into his vacation my husband checks out brochures for sight-seeing tours. Shortline, Grayline, Crossroads: his new vinyl briefcase is full of schedules and pamphlets. While I make pancakes out of a mix, he comparison-shops. Tour number one costs $10.95 and will give us the World Trade Center, Chinatown, and the United Nations. Tour number three would take us both uptown *and* downtown for $14.95, but my husband is absolutely sure he doesn't want to see Harlem. We settle for tour number four: Downtown and the Dame. It's offered by a new tour company with a small, dirty office at Eighth and Forty-eighth.

The sidewalk outside the office is colorful with tourists. My husband sends me in to buy the tickets because he has come to feel Americans don't understand his accent.

The dark man, Lebanese probably, behind the counter comes on too friendly. "Come on, doll, make my day!" He won't say which tour is his. "Number four? Honey, no! Look, you've wrecked me! Say you'll change your mind." He takes two twenties and gives back change. He holds the tickets, forcing me to pull. He leans closer. "I'm off after lunch."

My husband must have been watching me from the sidewalk. "What was the chap saying?" he demands. "I told you not to wear pants. He thinks you are Puerto Rican. He thinks he can treat you with disrespect."

The bus is crowded and we have to sit across the aisle from each other. The tour guide begins his patter on Forty-sixth. He looks like an actor, his hair bleached and blow-dried. Up close he must look middle-aged, but from where I sit his skin is smooth and his cheeks faintly red.

"Welcome to the Big Apple, folks." The guide uses a microphone. "Big Apple. That's what we native Manhattan degenerates call our city. Today we have guests from fifteen foreign countries and six states from this U.S. of A. That makes the Tourist Bureau real happy. And let me assure you that while we may be the richest city in the richest country in the world, it's okay to tip your charming and talented attendant." He laughs. Then he swings his hip out into the aisle and sings a song.

"And it's mighty fancy on old Delancey Street, you know. . . ."

My husband looks irritable. The guide is, as expected, a good singer. "The bloody man should be giving us histories of buildings we are passing, no?" I pat his hand, the mood passes. He cranes his neck. Our window seats have both gone to Japanese. It's the tour of his life. Next to this, the quick business trips to Manchester and Glasgow pale.

"And tell me what street compares to Mott Street, in July. . . ."

The guide wants applause. He manages a derisive laugh from the Americans up front. He's working the aisles now. "I coulda been somebody, right? I coulda been a star!" Two or three of us smile, those of us who recognize the parody. He catches my smile. The sun is on his harsh, bleached hair. "Right, your highness? Look, we gotta maharani with us! Couldn't I have been a star?"

"Right!" I say, my voice coming out a squeal. I've been trained to adapt; what else can I say?

We drive through traffic past landmark office buildings and churches. The guide flips his hands. "Art deco," he keeps saying. I hear him confide to one of the Americans: "Beats me. I went to a cheap guide's school." My husband wants to know more about this Art Deco, but the guide sings another song.

"We made a foolish choice," my husband grumbles. "We are sitting in the bus only. We're not going into famous buildings." He scrutinizes the pamphlets in his jacket pocket. I think, at least it's air-conditioned in here. I could sit here in the cool shadows of the city forever.

Only five of us appear to have opted for the "Downtown and the Dame" tour. The others will ride back uptown past the United Nations after we've been dropped off at the pier for the ferry to the Statue of Liberty.

An elderly European pulls a camera out of his wife's designer tote bag. He takes pictures of the boats in the harbor, the Japanese in kimonos eating popcorn, scavenging pigeons, me. Then, pushing his wife ahead of him, he climbs back on the bus and waves to us. For a second I feel terribly lost. I wish we were on the bus going back to the apartment. I know I'll not be able to describe any of this to Charity, or to Imre. I'm too proud to admit I went on a guided tour.

The view of the city from the Circle Line ferry is seductive, unreal. The skyline wavers out of reach, but never quite vanishes. The summer sun pushes through fluffy clouds and dapples the glass of office towers. My husband looks thrilled, even more than he had on the shopping trips down Broadway. Tourists and dreamers, we have spent our life's savings to see this skyline, this statue.

"Quick, take a picture of me!" my husband yells as he moves toward a gap of railings. A Japanese matron has given up her position in order to change film. "Before the Twin Towers disappear!"

I focus, I wait for a large Oriental family to walk out of my range. My husband holds his pose tight against the railing. He wants to look relaxed, an international businessman at home in all the financial markets.

A bearded man slides across the bench toward me. "Like this," he says and helps me get my husband in focus. "You want me to take the photo for you?" His name, he says, is Goran. He is Goran from Yugoslavia, as though that were enough for tracking him down. Imre from Hungary. Panna from India. He pulls the old Leica out of my hand, signaling the Orientals to beat it, and clicks away. "I'm a photographer," he says. He could have been a camera thief. That's what my husband would have assumed. Somehow, I trusted. "Get you a beer?" he asks.

"I don't. Drink, I mean. Thank you very much." I say those last words very loud, for everyone's benefit. The odd bottles of Soave with Imre don't count.

"Too bad." Goran gives back the camera.

"Take one more!" my husband shouts from the railing. "Just to be sure!"

The island itself disappoints. The Lady has brutal scaffolding holding her in. The museum is closed. The snack bar is dirty and expensive. My husband reads out the prices to me. He orders two french fries and two Cokes. We sit at picnic tables and wait for the ferry to take us back.

"What was that hippie chap saying?"

As if I could say. A day-care center has brought its kids, at least forty of them, to the island for the day. The kids, all wearing name tags, run around us. I can't help noticing how many are Indian. Even a Patel, probably a Bhatt if I looked hard enough. They toss hamburger bits at pigeons. They kick styrofoam cups. The pigeons are slow, greedy, persistent. I have to shoo one off the table top. I don't think my husband thinks about our son.

"What hippie?"

"The one on the boat. With the beard and the hair."

My husband doesn't look at me. He shakes out his paper napkin and tries to protect his french fries from pigeon feathers.

"Oh, him. He said he was from Dubrovnik." It isn't true, but I don't want trouble.

"What did he say about Dubrovnik?"

I know enough about Dubrovnik to get by. Imre's told me about it. And about Mostar and Zagreb. In Mostar white Muslims sing the call to prayer. I would like to see that before I die: white Muslims. Whole peoples have moved before me; they've adapted. The night Imre told me about Mostar was also the night I saw my first snow in Manhattan. We'd walked down to Chelsea from Columbia. We'd walked and talked and I hadn't felt tired at all.

"You're too innocent," my husband says. He reaches for my hand. "Panna," he cries with pain in his voice, and I am brought back from perfect, floating memories of snow, "I've come to take you back. I have seen how men watch you."

"What?"

"Come back, now. I have tickets. We have all the things we will ever need. I can't live without you."

A little girl with wiry braids kicks a bottle cap at his shoes. The pigeons wheel and scuttle around us. My husband covers his fries with spread-out fingers. "No kicking," he tells the girl. Her name, Beulah, is printed in green ink on a heart-shaped name tag. He forces a smile, and Beulah smiles back. Then she starts to flap her arms. She flaps, she hops. The pigeons go crazy for fries and scraps.

"Special ed. course is two years," I remind him. "I can't go back."

My husband picks up our trays and throws them into the garbage before I can stop him. He's carried disposability a little too far. "We've been taken," he says, moving toward the dock, though the ferry will not arrive for another twenty minutes. "The ferry costs only two dollars round-trip per person. We should have chosen tour number one for $10.95 instead of tour number four for $14.95."

With my Lebanese friend, I think. "But this way we don't have to worry about cabs. The bus will pick us up at the pier and take us back to midtown. Then we can walk home."

"New York is full of cheats and whatnot. Just like Bombay." He is not accusing me of infidelity. I feel dread all the same.

That night, after we've gone to bed, the phone rings. My husband listens, then hands the phone to me. "What is this woman saying?" He turns on the pink Macy's lamp by the bed. "I am not understanding these Negro people's accents."

The operator repeats the message. It's a cable from one of the directors of Lakshmi Cotton Mills. "Massive violent labor confrontation anticipated. Stop. Return posthaste. Stop. Cable flight details. Signed Kantilal Shah."

"It's not your factory," I say. "You're supposed to be on vacation."

"So, you are worrying about me? Yes? You reject my heartfelt wishes but you worry about me?" He pulls me close, slips the straps of my nightdress off my shoulder. "Wait a minute."

I wait, unclothed, for my husband to come back to me. The water is running in the bathroom. In the ten days he has been here he has learned American rites: deodorants, fragrances. Tomorrow morning he'll call Air India; tomorrow evening he'll be on his way back to Bombay. Tonight I should make up to him for my years away, the gutted trucks, the degree I'll never use in India. I want to pretend with him that nothing has changed.

In the mirror that hangs on the bathroom door, I watch my naked body turn, the breasts, the thighs glow. The body's beauty amazes. I stand here shameless, in ways he has never seen me. I am free, afloat, watching somebody else.

[1988]

Paths upon Water

Tahira Naqvi

THERE HAD BEEN LITTLE WARNING, ACTUALLY NONE AT ALL TO PREPARE her for her first encounter with the sea. At breakfast that morning, her son Raza said, "Ama,[1] we're going to the seaside today. Jamil and Hameeda are

[1] Mother.

coming with us." She had been turning a *paratha*[2] in the frying pan, an onerous task since she had always fried *parathas* on a flat pan with open sides, and as the familiar aroma of dough cooking in butter filled the air around her, she smiled happily and thought, I've only been here a week and already he wants to show me the sea.

Sakina Bano had never seen the sea. Having lived practically all her life in a town which was a good thousand miles from the nearest shoreline, her experience of the sea was limited to what she had chanced to observe in pictures. One picture, in which greenish-blue waves heaved toward a gray sky, she could recollect clearly; it was from a calendar Raza brought home the year he started college in Lahore. The calendar had hung on a wall of her room for many years only to be removed when the interior of the house was whitewashed for her daughter's wedding, and in the ensuing confusion it was misplaced and never found. The nail on which the calendar hung had stayed in the wall since the painter, too lazy to bother with detailed preparation, had simply painted around the nail and over it; whenever Sakina Bano happened to glance at the forgotten nail she remembered the picture. Also distinct in her memory was a scene from a silly Urdu film she had seen with her cousin's wife Zohra and her nieces Zenab and Amina during a rare visit to Lahore several years ago. For some reason she hadn't been able to put it out of her mind. On a brown and white beach, the actor Waheed Murad, now dead but then affectedly handsome, and boyish, pursued the actress Zeba, who skipped awkwardly before him—it isn't at all proper for a woman to be skipping in a public place. Small foam-crested waves lapped up to her, making her *shalwar*[3] stick to her skinny legs, exposing the outline of her thin calves. Why, it was just as bad as baring her legs, for what cover could the wet, gossamer-like fabric of the *shalwar* provide?

The two frolicked by an expanse of water that extended to the horizon and which, even though it was only in a film, had seemed to Sakina Bano frightening in its immensity.

"Will Jamal and his wife have lunch here?" she asked, depositing the dark, glistening *paratha* gently on Raza's plate. She would have to take out a packet of meat from the freezer if she was to give them lunch, she told herself while she poured tea in her son's cup.

"No, I don't think so. I think we'll leave before lunch. We can stop somewhere along the way and have a bite to eat."

"They'll have tea then." She was glad Raza had remembered to pick up a cake at the store the night before (she didn't know why he called it a pound cake), and she would make some rice *kheer*.[4]

If she had anything to do with it, she would avoid long trips and spend most of her time in Raza's apartment cooking his meals and watching him

[2] A soft, flat bread similar to pita bread or Mexican tortillas.
[3] Indian attire worn by younger women and girls consisting of a calf-length skirt and baggy silk or cotton trousers gathered at the ankles. Also known as *kamiz* or *qamis*.
[4] A sweet dessert made with rice, sugar, and milk.

eat. The apartment pleased her. The most she would want to do would be to go out on the lawn once in a while and examine her surroundings.

Bordering each window on the outside were narrow white shutters; these had reminded her of the stiffened icing on a cake served at her niece Amina's birthday once. And on the face of the building the white paint seemed impervious to the effects of the elements. Discolorations or cracks were visible, and she had indeed craned her neck until it hurt while she scrutinized it.

The apartment building was set against a lawn edged with freshly green, sculptured bushes, evenly thick with grass that looked more like a thick carpet than just grass. Located in a quiet section of town, the apartments overlooked a dark, thickly wooded area, a park, Raza had told her. Although tired and groggy on the evening of her arrival from Pakistan, she had not failed to take note of the surroundings into which she found herself. Her first thought was, 'Where is everybody?' while to her son she said, "How nice everything is."

Looking out the window of his sitting room the next morning, she was gladdened at the thought of her son's good fortune. The morning sky was clear like a pale blue, unwrinkled *dupatta*[5] that has been strung out on a line to dry. Everything looked clean, so clean. Was it not as if an unseen hand had polished the sidewalks and swept the road? They now glistened like new metal. 'Where do people throw their trash?' she wondered when she went down to the lawn again, this time with Raza, and gazed out at the shiny road, the rows and rows of neat houses hedged in by such neat white wooden fences. In hasty answer to her own query, she told herself not to be foolish; this was *Amreeka*. Here trash was in its proper place, hidden from view and no doubt disposed of in an appropriate manner. No blackened banana peels redolent with the odor of neglect here, or rotting orange skins, or worse, excrement and refuse to pollute the surroundings and endanger human habitation.

She had sighed in contentment. Happiness descended upon her tangibly like a heavy blanket affording warmth on a chilly morning. Once again, she thanked her Maker. Was He not good to her son?

"Is the sea far from here?" she asked casually, brushing imaginary crumbs from the edges of her plate. Raza must never feel she didn't value his eagerness to show off his new environment. This was his new world after all. If he wanted to take her to the seaside, then seaside it would be. Certainly she was not about to be fussy and upset him.

"No, *Ama*, not too far. An hour-and-a-half's drive, that's all. Do you feel well?" His eyes crinkled in concern as he put aside the newspaper he had been reading to look at her.

She impatiently waved a hand in the air, secretly pleased at his solicitude. "Yes, yes, I'm fine son. Just a little cough, that's all. Now finish your tea and I'll make you another cup." She knew how much he liked tea. Before

[5] A piece of cloth worn by Indian women, usually made of silk, and draped across the neck and shoulders or worn over the head.

she came, he must have had to make it for himself. Such a chore for a man if he must make his own tea.

The subject of the sea didn't come up again until Jamil and his new bride arrived. Jamil, an old college friend of Raza's, angular like him, affable and solicitous, was no stranger to Sakina Bano. But she was meeting his wife Hameeda for the first time. Like herself, the girl was also a newcomer to this country.

"*Khalaji*,[6] the sea's so pretty here, the beaches are so-o-o-o large, nothing like the beaches in Karachi," Hameeda informed Sakina Bano over tea, her young, shrill voice rising and falling excitedly, her lips, dark and fleshy with lipstick, wide open in a little girl's grin. There's wanderlust in her eyes already, Sakina Bano mused, trying to guess her age. Twenty-one or twenty-two. She thought of the girl in Sialkot she and her daughter had been considering for Raza. Was there really a resemblance? Perhaps it was only the youth.

"Well child, for me it will be all the same. I've never been to Karachi. Here, have another slice of cake, you too Jamil, and try the *kheer*."

For some reason Sakina Bano couldn't fathom, sitting next to the young girl whose excitement at the prospect of a visit to the seaside was as undisguised as a child's preoccupation with a new toy, she was suddenly reminded of the actress Zeba. The image of waves lapping on her legs and swishing about her nearly bare calves rose in Sakina Bano's mind again. Like the arrival of an unexpected visitor, a strange question crossed her mind: were Hameeda's legs also skinny like Zeba's?

Drowned in the clamor for the *kheer* which had proven to be a great hit and had been consumed with such rapidity she wished she had made more, the question lost itself.

"*Khalaji*, you must tell Hameeda how you make this," Jamil was saying, and Hameeda hastily interjected, "I think you used a lot of milk."

"Have more," Sakina Bano said.

Tea didn't last long. Within an hour they were on their way to the sea, all of them in Raza's car. Jamil sat in the front with his friend, and Sakina Bano and Hameeda sat in the back, an unfortunate arrangement, Sakina Bano discovered after they had driven for what seemed to her like an hour. It wasn't Hameeda's persistent prattle that vexed her, she realized, it was her perfume. So pungent she could feel it wafting into her nostrils, it irritated the insides of her nose, and then traveled down her throat like the sour after-taste of an overripe orange. But her discomfort was short-lived; soon she became drowsy and idled into sleep.

To be sure she had heard stories of people who swam in the ocean. She wasn't so foolish as to presume that swimming was undertaken fully clothed. After all, many times as a child she had seen young boys and men from her

---

[6] A formal term used to address an elder member of a family. The ending -*ji* connotes extreme respect.

village swim, dressed in nothing but loincloths as they jumped into the muddy waters of the canal that irrigated their fields. But what was this?

As soon as Raza parked the car in a large, compound-like area fenced in by tall walls of wire mesh, and when her dizziness subsided, Sakina Bano glanced out of the window on her left. Her attention was snagged by what she thought was a naked woman. Certain that she was still a little dazed from the long drive, her vision subsequently befogged, Sakina Bano thought nothing of what she had seen. Then the naked figure moved closer. Disbelief gave way to the sudden, awful realization that the figure was indeed real and if not altogether naked, very nearly so.

A thin strip of colored cloth shaped like a flimsy brassiere loosely held the woman's breasts, or rather a part of her breasts; and below, beneath the level of her belly button, no, even lower than that, Sakina Bano observed in horror, was something that reminded her of the loincloths the men and youths in her village wore when they swam or worked on a construction site in the summer.

The girl was pretty, such fine features, hair that shone like a handful of gold thread, and she was young too, not much older than Hameeda perhaps. But the paleness of her skin was marred by irregular red blotches that seemed in dire need of a cooling balm. No one with such redness should be without a covering in the sun, Sakina Bano offered in silent rebuke.

The woman opened the door of her car, which was parked alongside Raza's, and as she leaned over to retrieve something from the interior of her car, Sakina Bano gasped. When the young female lowered her body, her breasts were not only nearly all bared, but stood in imminent danger of spilling out of their meager coverage. O God! Is there no shame here? Sakina Bano's cheeks burned. Hastily she glanced away. In the very next instant she stole a glimpse at her son from the corners of her eyes, anxiously wondering if he too were experiencing something of what she was going through; no, she noted with a mixture of surprise and relief, he and Jamil were taking things out from the trunk of their car. They did not show any signs of discomfort. Did she see a fleeting look of curiosity on Hameeda's face? There was something else, too, she couldn't quite decipher.

Relieved that her male companions were oblivious to the disturbing view of the woman's breasts, Sakina Bano sighed sadly. She shook her head, adjusted her white, chiffon *dupatta* over her head, and slowly eased her person out of her son's car.

The taste of the sea was upon her lips in an instant. Mingled with an occasional but strong whiff of Hameeda's perfume, the smell of fish filled her nostrils and quickly settled in her nose as if to stay there forever.

Milling around were countless groups of scantily clad people, men, women, and children, coming and going in all directions. Is all of *Amreeka* here? she asked herself uneasily. Feeling guilty for having judged Zeba's contrived imprudence on film a little too harshly, she tightened her *dupatta* about her and wondered why her son had chosen to bring her to this place. Did he not know his mother? She was an old woman, and the mother of a son, but she would not surrender to anger or derision and make her son uncomfortable. His poise and confidence were hers too, were they not? Certainly he had brought her to the sea for a purpose. She must not appear ungrateful or intolerant.

While Raza and Jamil walked on casually and without any show of awkwardness, laughing and talking as though they might be in their sitting room rather than a place crowded with people in a state of disconcerting undress, she and Hameeda followed closely behind. Her head swam as she turned her eyes from the glare of the sun and attempted to examine the perturbing nakedness around her.

Sakina Bano's memories of nakedness were short and limited, extending to the time when she bathed her younger brother and sister under the water pump in the courtyard of her father's house, followed by the period in which she bathed her own three children until they were old enough to do it themselves. Of her own nakedness she carried an incomplete image; she had always bathed sitting down, on a low wooden stool.

Once, and that too shortly before his stroke, she came upon her husband getting out of his *dhoti*[7] in their bedroom. Standing absently near the foot of his bed as if waiting for something or someone, the *dhoti* a crumpled heap about his ankles, he lifted his face to look at her blankly when she entered, but made no attempt to move or cover himself. Not only did she have to hand him his pajamas, she also had to assist him as he struggled to pull up first one leg and then the other. A week later he suffered a stroke, in another week he was gone. It had been nearly ten years since he died. But for some reason the image of a naked disoriented man in the middle of a room clung to her mind like permanent discolorations on a well-worn copper pot.

And there was the unforgettable sharp and unsullied picture of her mother's body laid out on a rectangular slab of cracked, yellowed wood for a pre-burial bath, her skin, ash-brown, laced with a thousand wrinkles, soft, like wet, rained-on mud.

But nothing could have prepared her for this. Nakedness, like all things in nature, has a purpose, she firmly told herself as the four of them trudged toward the water.

The July sun on this day was not as hot as the July sun in Sialkot, but a certain oily humidity had begun to attach itself to her face and hands. Lifting a corner of her white *dupatta*, she wiped her face with it. Poor Hameeda, no doubt she too longed to divest herself of the *shalwar* and *qamis* she was wearing and don a swimming suit so she could join the rest of the women on the beach, be more like them. But could she swim?

They continued onward, and after some initial plodding through hot, moist sand, Sakina Bano became sure-footed; instead of having to drag her feet through the weighty volume of over-heated sand, she was now able to tread over it with relative ease. They were receiving stares already, a few vaguely curious, others unguardedly inquisitive.

---

[7] A traditional loincloth resembling baggy knee-length trousers worn by Hindu men of southern Asia.

Where the bodies ended she saw the ocean began, stetching to the horizon in the distance. The picture she had carried in her head of the boyish actor Waheed Murad running after Zeba on a sandy Karachi beach quickly diminished and faded away. The immensity of the sea on film was reduced to a mere blue splash of color, its place usurped by a vastness she could scarce hold within the frame of her vision; a window opened in her head, she drew in the wonder of the sea as it touched the hem of the heavens and, despite the heat, Sakina Bano shivered involuntarily. God's touch is upon the world, she silently whispered to herself.

Again and again, as she had made preparations for the journey across what she liked to refer to as the 'seven seas,' she had been told *Amreeka* was so large that many Pakistans could fit into it. The very idea of Pakistan fitting into anything else was cause for bewilderment, and the analogy left her at once befuddled and awed. But had she expected this?

The bodies sprawled before her on the sand and exposed to the sun's unyielding rays seemed unmindful of what the ocean might have to say about God's touch upon the world. Assuming supine positions, flat either on their backs or their bellies, the people on the beach reminded Sakina Bano of whole red chilies spread on a rag discolored from overuse, and left in the sun to dry and crackle. As sweat began to form in tiny droplets across her forehead and around her mouth, the unhappy thought presented itself to her that she was among people who had indeed lost their sanity.

In summer, one's first thought is to put as much distance as possible between oneself and the sun. Every effort is made to stay indoors; curtains are drawn and jalousies unfurled in order to shut out the fire the sun exudes. In the uneasy silence of a torrid June or July afternoon, even stray dogs seek shade under a tree or behind a bush, curling up into fitful slumber as the sun beats its fervid path across the sky.

Sakina Bano couldn't understand why these men and women wished to scorch their bodies, and why, if they were here by the shore of an ocean which seemed to reach up to God, they didn't at least gaze wide-eyed at the wonder which lay at their feet. Why did they choose instead to shut their eyes and merely wallow in the heat. Their skins had rebelled, the red and darkly-pink blotches spoke for themselves. Perhaps this is a ritual they must, of necessity, follow, she mused. Perhaps they yearn to be brown as we yearn to be white.

She felt an ache insidiously putter behind her eyes. The sun always gave her a headache, even in winter, the only season when sunshine evoked pleasing sensations, when one could look forward to its briskness, its sharp touch. The heat from the sand under the *dari*[8] on which she and Hameeda now sat seeped through the coarse fabric after a while and hugged her thighs; as people in varying shades of pink, white and red skin ran or walked past them, particles of sand flew in the air and landed on her clothes, her hands, her face. Soon she felt sand in her mouth, scraping between her teeth like the remains of *chalia*, heavy on her tongue.

[8] Handwoven carpet or mat, usually made of synthetic material.

Ignoring the sand in her mouth and the hot-water-bottle effect of the sand beneath her thighs, Sakina Bano shifted her attention first toward a woman on her left, and then to the man on her right whose stomach fell broadly in loose folds (like dough left out overnight); he lay supine and still, his face shielded by a straw hat. Puzzled by the glitter on their nakedness, she peered closely and with intense concentration—she had to observe if she were to learn anything. The truth came to her like a flash of sudden light in a dark room: both the man and the woman had smeared their bodies with some kind of oil! Just then she remembered the oversized cucumbers she had encountered on her first trip to the Stop and Shop; shiny and slippery, one fell from her hands as she handled them, and she exclaimed in disbelief, "They've been greased!" How amused Raza had been at her reaction.

It's really very simple, Sakina Bano finally decided, sighing again, these people wish to be fried in the sun. But why? Not wishing to appear ignorant, she kept her mouth shut, although if she had addressed the query to Hameeda, she was sure she would not have received a satisfactory reply. The girl was a newcomer like herself. In addition, she was too young to know the answers to questions which warranted profound thought preceded by profound scrutiny. She didn't look very comfortable either; perhaps the heat was getting to her, too.

Raza and Jamil, both in swimming trunks, appeared totally at ease as they ran to the water and back, occasionally wading in a wave that gently slapped the beach and sometimes disappearing altogether for a second or two under a high wave. Then Sakina Bano couldn't tell where they were. They certainly seemed to be having a good time.

She and Hameeda must be the only women on the beach fully clothed, she reflected, quite a ridiculous sight if one were being viewed from the vantage point of those who were stretched out on the sand. And while Sakina Bano grappled with this disturbing thought, she saw the other woman approaching.

Attired in a *sari*[9] and accompanied by a short, dark man (who had to be her son for he undoubtedly had her nose and her forehead) and an equally short, dark woman, both of whom wore swimming suits (the girl's as brief as that of the woman Sakina Bano had seen earlier in the parking lot), she looked no older than herself. Clutching the front folds of her *sari* as if afraid a sudden wind from the ocean might pull them out unfurling the *sari*, leaving her exposed, she tread upon the sand with a fiercely precarious step, looking only ahead, her eyes shielded with one small, flat palm.

This is how I must appear to the others, Sakina Bano ruminated. Suddenly, she felt a great sadness clutching at her chest and rising into her throat like a sigh as she watched the woman in the *sari* begin to make herself

---

[9] Also spelled *saree*, this is the traditional principal outer garment worn by women on the Indian subcontinent. Made of brightly colored silk or cotton fabric, this long piece of cloth is folded and tucked in at the waist to form a long skirt, with the free end draped over the shoulder or worn over the head as a hood.

comfortable on a large, multi-colored towel thrown on the sand by her son and his wife; those two hurriedly dashed off in the direction of the water. Why are they in such haste? Sakina Bano wondered.

Her knees drawn up, one arm tensely wrapped around them, the woman appeared to be watching her son and her daughter-in-law. But could Sakina Bano really be sure? The woman's hand against her forehead concealed her eyes. As she continued to observe the woman's slight figure around which the green and orange cotton *sari* had been carelessly draped, she wondered what part of India she might be from. Perhaps the south, which meant she spoke no Hindi, which also meant a conversation would not be at all possible.

Sakina Bano's attention returned to Hameeda who had not said a word all this time. Like a break-through during muddled thought, it suddenly occurred to Sakina Bano that there was a distinct possibility Hameeda would be swimming if it weren't for her. In deference to her older companion she was probably foregoing the chance to swim. Will Raza's wife also wear a scant swimming suit and bare her body in the presence of strange men? The question disturbed her; she tried to shrug it aside. But it wouldn't go away. Stubbornly it returned, not alone this time but accompanied by the picture of a young woman who vaguely resembled the actress Zeba and who was clothed, partially, in a swimming suit much like the ones Sakina Bano saw about her. Running behind her was a man, not Waheed Murad, but alas, her own son, her Raza. Was she dreaming, had the sun weakened her brain? Such foolishness. Sakina Bano saw that Hameeda was staring ahead, like the woman on the towel, her eyes squinted because of the glare. Frozen on her full, red lips was a hesitant smile.

Once again Sakina Bano sought her son's figure among the throng near the water's edge. At first the brightness of the sun blinded her and she couldn't see where he was. She strained her eyes, shielding them from the sun with a hand on her forehead. And finally she spotted him. He and Jamil were talking to some people. A dark man and a dark girl. The son and daughter-in-law of the woman in the *sari*. Were they acquaintances then, perhaps friends? The four of them laughed like old friends, the girl standing so close to Raza he must surely be able to see her half-naked breasts. The poor boy!

They had begun to walk toward where she and Hameeda were seated. Raza was going to introduce his friends to his mother. How was she to conceal her discomfort at the woman's mode of dress?

"*Ama*, I want you to meet Ajit and Kamla. Ajit works at Ethan Allen with me. Kamla wants you to come to their house for dinner next Sunday."

Both Ajit and Kamla lifted their hands and said "*Namaste*,"[10] and she nodded and smiled. What does one say in answer to *namaste*, anyway?

Hameeda was also introduced. Kamla made a joke about "the shy new bride," Hameeda showed her pretty teeth in a smile, and then Kamla said, "You have to come, Auntie." Sakina Bano wondered why Raza appeared so comfortable in the presence of a woman who was nearly all naked. Even

[10] A Hindu greeting, accompanied by folding the hands together.

her loincloth was flimsy. Granted it wasn't as bad as some of the others she had been seeing around her, but it was flimsy nonetheless.

"Yes, it's very nice of you to invite us. It's up to Raza. He's usually so busy. But if he is free . . ."

"Of course I'm free next Sunday. We'd love to come, Kamla."

Kamla said, "Good! I'll introduce you and Auntie to my mother-in-law after a swim. Coming?" She laid a hand on Raza's arm and Sakina Bano glanced away, just in time to catch Hameeda's smile of surprise. Well, one's son can become a stranger too, even a good son like Raza.

"Sure. *Yar*,[11] Ajit, are you and Kamla planning to go to the late show?"

"Yes we are. You? Do you have tickets?" Ajit wasn't a bad looking boy. But he didn't measure up to Raza. No, Raza's nose was straight and to the point, his forehead wide and his eyes well-illuminated. But he had changed somehow; she felt she was distanced from him. A son is always a son, she thought and smiled and nodded again as Ajit and Kamla uttered their *Namaste's* and returned to the water with Raza and Jamil.

"*Khalaji*, why don't we wet our feet before we go?" Hameeda suddenly asked her.

"Wet our feet?"

"Yes, *Khala*.[12] Just dip our feet in sea water. Come on. You're not afraid of the water, are you?"

"No, child." She wasn't afraid. Her mind was playing tricks with her, filling her head with thoughts that had no place there. A change was welcome. "Yes, why not?" she said, as if speaking to herself. When she attempted to get up she found that her joints had stiffened painfully. "Here, girl, give me your hand." She extended an arm toward Hameeda. Why not, especially since they had come so far and she had suffered the heat for what had seemed like a very long time.

Hameeda had rolled up her *shalwar* almost to the level of her knees. How pretty her legs are, the skin hairless and shiny, like a baby's, and not skinny at all, Sakina Bano mused in surprise, and how quick she is to show them.

She must do the same, she realized. Otherwise Hameeda would think she was afraid. She pulled up one leg of her *shalwar* tentatively, tucked it at the waist with one swift movement of her right hand, then looked about her sheepishly. Hameeda was laughing.

"The other one too, *Khala!*"

Who would want to look at her aged and scrawny legs? And her husband was not around to glare at her in remonstration. Gingerly the other leg of the *shalwar* was also lifted and tucked in. How funny her legs looked, the hair on them all gray now and curly, the calves limp. Now both women giggled like schoolgirls. And Raza would be amused, he would think she was having a good time, Sakina Bano told herself.

Raza and Jamil burst into laughter when they saw the women approach. They waved. Sakina Bano waved back.

---

[11] An informal term used in addressing a close friend, *buddy*.

[12] A formal term used in addressing an elder member of a family.

Holding the front folds of her *shalwar* protectively, Sakina Bano strode toward the water. As she went past the other woman in the *sari* she smiled at her. The woman gave her a startled look, and then, dropping the hand with which she had been shielding her eyes from the sun, she let her arm fall away from her knees, and following Sakina Bano with her gaze, she returned her smile.

"Wait for me," Sakina Bano called to Hameeda in a loud, happy voice, "wait, girl."

[1989]

The Heart of the Flower

Georgiana Valoyce Sanchez

IT WAS THURSDAY, MARCH 8, 1973. WORD HAD COME TO US SLOWLY AND in confused fragments from across the nation. The siege at Wounded Knee on the Pine Ridge Reservation in South Dakota had been underway for nearly a week before the full drama of what was happening there began to unfold on the West Coast. The siege at Wounded Knee was now into its ninth day.

I went through all the familiar rituals. Putting on the morning coffee. Two slices of bread in the toaster. Frying the eggs. Standing by the door as my husband Ed drove off to work. But, now, changing the sheets on our unmade bed, I daydreamed about joining the American Indian Movement activists at Wounded Knee. I sidestepped my way between bed and dresser to tuck one corner of the bottom sheet secure; sidestep, echoing the rhythm of some distant dance around the drum. A dance that took place in spite of, because of, the United States Army troops and artillery that surrounded the village of Wounded Knee. I snapped the top sheet out over the bed and it swept upward—a bird's wide wing against the sky—before the slow settling to earth.

Outside, beyond the shadowed frame of my front porch, mountains had bloomed. Distant fire trails were as clear as the lifeline on the palm of my hand. Brush stubbled sides caught the light, the shade. A strong wind had come up during the night, clearing the Los Angeles basin of the gray smog that made us forget the mountains had ever existed.

The air breathed. Everywhere was movement and the crisp feel of March wind. Across the street, neat rows of stucco houses sat complacent as cows beneath the restless trees. And I saw feathered prayer sticks, eagle-winged petitions of victory vibrating through the air, planted in my front yard; only not. For fear of cries of blasphemy from Mrs. Johnson across the street, or eyesore or blight, or calling attention to myself as no proper Indian woman should. But mostly because Ed would be embarrassed and angry. I leaned against the door frame and rested my hand against the screen. Beyond the housetops and telephone poles and electric wires, beyond the distant mountains, far to the northeast, lay Wounded Knee.

The child within my womb fluttered. A small movement like a butterfly's wing against the wind. I placed my hand on the small mound of my belly and stood very still, listening with every nerve of my body for the next movement. Again, the small lonely movement. I was filled with wonder at the thought of a child growing, moving inside me. Separate, and yet, so mine. I turned from the open front door and closed it.

I made my way into the kitchen and sat down at the table, waiting for the next movement. None came. The child was still. I cleared the plates of dried egg and toast, collecting the leftover food for the dog. The window next to the kitchen table was sunlit and alive with the patterns of leaf shadows moving in the wind. The wind was a living presence on the Morongo Indian Reservation where I had been raised—where my parents were buried. Sometimes, the wind would come up the Pass between the San Gorgonio and San Jacinto mountain ranges sounding like an old woman singing a wailing song for the dead. Times like that my parents would gather the family together in the warm old house and Mama would make hot fry bread over the wood stove and serve it with honey and mugs of good strong coffee. And we would sit close and tell jokes and stories.

Shadows flitted back and forth across the kitchen table like large gray moths. I leaned forward in my chair and rubbed the pain in my lower back. Leaf branches played against the window, making soft scratching sounds like field mice in an acorn shed. I sat there a few minutes more, watching the shadows dance in the wind. Finally, I took the dishes to the sink and washed them.

On Friday, March 9, I called Doctor Bergman and told him of the low back pain I was feeling. He told me to stay off my feet and to come in the next day if I was not feeling better. I hung up the phone. Bowls of limp cereal adrift waited patiently on the kitchen table for rescue. I wiped up the soggy wake of our breakfast and carried the bowls to the sink. There was so much to be done. The books on my nightstand were piled so high they nearly obscured the small gooseneck reading lamp Ed had bought me for Christmas. The books would have to be sorted and put back into the large walnut bookcase that quietly ruled the living room.

Above the sink an eagle flew over wheat fields of gold and rust. Two orange butterfly plaques hung beside it. I ran warm water into the sink, the water warm as the pain in my lower back, each sting of the water-rush on bowls and spoons an echo of the persistent radiating wave within.

That night, Ed made dinner while I lay blanketed on the couch watching the Five O'Clock News. One commentator reported that the United States Government had issued an order that everyone was to leave the village of Wounded Knee or it would "come in shooting." The National Council of

Churches had sent representatives who pledged to stand between the besieged Indians and the Federal Marshals when the shooting began.

I raised myself on my elbow and called to Ed. "Quick, come and listen to this. They're going to start shooting if the people don't leave."

Ed stepped into the livingroom, wiping his hands on his faded work jeans. His dark face was lined and haggard. He planted his legs apart next to the television set and folded his arms—Geremino, *Goyaathle*, embattled—looking much like a photograph he had once sent me from one of the rural settlements along the Mekong Delta, except, now, his hair was longer and there were no fair-haired buddies grinning over his shoulders, no deserted village in the background.

A reporter was interviewing a group of Onondagas that had traveled to Wounded Knee from upstate New York. "Those crazy AIM bastards are dragging everyone into this," Ed said. "What right have they got to call themselves the 'American Indian Movement'? They have no right to speak for us." The Onondagas moved on. Ed turned his head in my general direction, a side glance, his eyes still on the television screen. "You should hear the guys at work. It sounds like they're just itching for another Indian war."

"It's about time someone spoke up and took a stand," I said, knowing I would anger him. Not caring.

Ed turned fully toward me. His eyes a dark fire. "You're a dreamer, Joanna. You'd think with all that reading you do you'd understand. The old days are gone. There's no bringing them back. This is the *real* world we're living in. We've got enough trouble just trying to make it through the day."

On the television screen there were lines of Indian people walking and cars, bumper to bumper, trying to get to Wounded Knee. There was snow on the ground and many of the Indian people walking had only thin blankets as covering against the cold. Federal Marshals in fur-fringed parkas were blockading the roads to the Pine Ridge Reservation. I pulled the blanket up around my shoulders and straightened my pillow. Ed turned from me and went back into the kitchen. Pregnant or not, if I could, I would be there, now, walking the roads to Wounded Knee.

My bedroom was a dark cave. I lay in the large bed, isolated in the darkness. From beyond the open doorway came the low murmur of the television set. The flickering light from the screen was a campfire that danced shadows against the cave wall. Wounded Knee was far away. I was suspended in time and space, not fully realizing what was happening to me.

It was a strange sensation; the knowing and not knowing. My mind was like a small alert bird perched atop the headboard, watching. As my mind watched and marked the darkness, the flickering light of the television, the shadows on the wall, my body knew the subdued bands of pain, the moontide and the blood flow. And when the water bag broke, warm and gushing between my legs, the small bird perched atop the headboard flew quickly to my side, and I knew. I knew with the clear mind of the bird that the fetus within my womb was being carried on the tide.

I made my way out of the warm cave into the cold light of the white bathroom. I locked the door. No Grandmothers in the birthing hut. Alone. I sat on the toilet seat and reached between my legs to catch the child, denying it even as it happened. My silent screams deafened me, blurred the stillbirth of the fetus. I didn't question that the child was not attached to the placenta, didn't question the break of so vital a link, only felt the small wet body cradled in the palm of my hand. Saw the child's eyes closed, swollen, its hands reaching as if to be held. Its strange sad dignity.

I began to tremble, violently.

I carefully placed the fetus on a flower of pale pink bathroom tissue and rested the tissue on the clothes hamper. I tried to clean myself, flushing away all evidence. Finally, I stood and pulled the rose-colored towel from the towel ring and wiped the floor with it, calming myself in the doing. I threw the dirty towel into the bathtub and called Ed.

What could I say? I should have rested more? I should have dreamed less? I should not have harbored thoughts of death and killing?—of eagle feathers trailing in the wind?

I unlocked the door and let Ed in. I pointed to the fetus and, again, the sense of separation came over me. Small bird eyes noted the concerned look on his face, the shock that rippled through his body and settled in his eyes—and that instant of curiosity at the small dead thing.

Ed cried, hurting man sobs, and I held him, my body weeping but straight and still. From where his sorrow welled I could not say, for I was separate, holding him. There and not there. A wavering ghost, my long white night-gown stained with blood.

The next morning, the bedroom was flooded with light. It was not a clean light. It poured through the smudged windows and reflected off the mirror, dust flecked and hazy. The house was still for a Saturday. Quiet. From the direction of the kitchen came the soft clatter of dishes. Like the tick tock of a clock in an empty room it had the effect of intensifying the silence. Ed.

He had been so kind the night before, anxious to do whatever was needed. I had wrapped the dead fetus in the bathroom tissue and had carried it to the hospital in my purse. I could feel the small body, the heat of its near-life faintly warm and fading, through the tissue, the thin cloth purse. I did not cry the long drive to the hospital. Ed was silent.

They took the child from me. A young nurse's assistant picked the fetus from the tissue with a pair of steel tongs. She placed the fetus in a steel bowl and carried it from the room. It was like the tearing of a limb. Flesh and bone and muscle ripped from my body. And all I could do was cry, deep wrenching sobs.

Now, lying in bed, grief seeped through my pores and clung to the bed, the blankets, the walls. A gray film of a shroud that touched everything. It was inside of me and outside of me. It would not leave. And there was anger, too. A cold deadly fire.

Minute specks of dust drifted in the sunlight. A memory from my childhood assaulted me: me, walking up the stairs of a museum with my parents. Walking through a maze of rooms, looking for a special display of Indian artwork; beads and baskets and old deer hoof rattles. For some reason we did not ask for directions. We came across a dark windowless corner of the museum where a long shelf was stocked with jars of preserved fetuses in different stages of growth. The fluid in the jars had reflected the light of an overhead bulb and the fetuses had seemed to float in the hazy light. The larger babies were perfect—every finger and fingernail, every toe, the two small ears like flower petals, the closed dreaming eyes. I could not grasp the meaning of why dead babies would be bottled for all to see. The act seemed to contain within it a violence so profound, so calculated, that there could be no possible defense against it. At the same time that I was horribly fascinated, I was repulsed and very afraid. My parents had rushed me out of the museum, my mother visibly shaken and my father grim and silent.

I turned away from the hazy drifting light, curling my body around the remembering, the hurt, the anger. But no matter how tightly I shut my eyes, the light seeped through.

I could not sleep. I could not rest. I was an open throbbing wound. I sat up in bed and put on my robe and slippers. As I passed the large dresser, I caught a glimpse of an old woman in turquoise looking at me from the mirror. I smoothed back my hair and continued into the kitchen.

Ed was standing at the stove, frying eggs. I turned away. "You okay?" Ed asked. Stupid, stupid question. "I'm fine," I said.

I sat down at the table and looked out the window. The wind had stopped blowing. "You know," I said, "we're like those fetuses scientists put into bottles." I felt Ed's wondering look. He brought me my breakfast. Two eggs, sunnyside up. Sausages. I pushed the plate away. "Did you hear what I said?"

"Yes," Ed said. He sat down beside me. "Why do you want to talk about things like that?"

"Because that baby is nothing to them." I started to cry. "Don't you see? Don't you see, that's what they're doing to us."

Ed moved his chair closer to mine. He pulled me towards him and held me close. His strong arms were a shaded mountain place; tobacco and sage. Our legs touched. "It's okay," he said. "It's okay."

I pulled away from him. "It's not okay. Can't you see that? What's wrong with you?" I wiped the tears from my face, dim tapes of anger at my father playing; times when he could not ease the pain, make things better.

Ed leaned his elbow on the table and rubbed at his forehead. "Honey, you're tired. You've been through hell. I know that."

"Aren't you listening to what I'm saying? They bottle dead babies for God's sake. I'm dying inside and you just sit there." Ed made a move to hug me again, but I pushed him away. "What are we doing here? What kind of life is this? Right now, there are men, strong Indian men, at Wounded Knee, trying to do something for all of us. And what do you do—fry eggs like an old woman." I pushed hard at the plate of eggs and sausages and sent it flying across the table. Yes: the flying sausages, the sharp thud of plate on wall, the hollow cracking of dish and splatter of egg, Ed's startled face in the foreground. Yes.

I nearly stumbled over my robe as I ran out of the kitchen. I locked the bedroom door and leaned against it, a strange triumph drumming.

On Sunday, March 11, Dennis Banks of the American Indian Movement at Wounded Knee announced on national television that the Oglala Sioux Nation was to determine its own borders, as defined by the Treaty of 1868 with the United States, and that it would stop anyone who violated its borders.

Ed found me in my nightgown, packing canned goods and beans and macaroni into two large shopping bags. He leaned against the doorway. "You planning on going someplace?"

I stood up and braced myself against the cupboard door, lightheaded and dizzy from bending over. "You know perfectly well what I'm doing," I said.

Ed came and stood by me. His face was troubled.

I started rearranging the canned goods still left in the cupboard. Peas with peas. Corn with corn. "I know you think I'm crazy. I've tried to make you understand how important this is, but you're blind and deaf to me." I faced him. "Indian people from all over the nation are sending food and blankets and . . ."

"Guns," Ed said. His eyes were hard, his mouth set against me.

I wanted to slap him. "I don't want killing. I don't think anyone really wants killing. There's something bigger going on there. For the first time since I was a little girl I feel good about being Indian. Most of the time I don't really know what that means. I'd like to think it means something." My hands and legs were shaking. I walked over to the table and sat down.

Ed stood by the cupboard, looking down at the shopping bags. He pushed at his hair and smoothed it behind his ear; there were strands of gray in the raven blackness. "How in the hell do you intend to get this stuff to them?"

I folded my hands in my lap, steadying them. "There's an AIM regional office in L.A. I thought we could take it there."

"You're really determined to get us into this thing, aren't you?" Ed shook his head. "I don't know. Yesterday, when you were so upset, I thought it was because of the baby." He looked fully at me. There was a pleading in his eyes, a weary sorrow. "There are no clean lines, Joanna. Sometimes it's hard to know who the enemy is."

I looked away toward the empty stove to the right of him. "We can't pretend anymore that everything is fine. It's not." Surely, I had explained the years of hurting inside, the slow dying that had begun as far back as my first day of public school. All of the years when I walked close to the edge of a dark abyss where surely I would fall and die because teachers and white students and everyone with power in the outside world told me, in word and action, that I was dirty, stupid, of no worth.

Ed nudged at a bag of groceries with his foot. "And you think that this will make everything right?" The pleading had gone from his eyes. His hands were clenched.

"It's something. It's better than sitting back and letting everything run over us. Every day we lose a little bit more. I see you. The conflict. Wanting to be accepted by the guys at work. Putting up with their stupid jokes. Hating yourself for pretending if we don't do something, if we don't enter into a stream that takes us away from this lie we're living, we'll die inside." I blinked back the tears. "And then what have we got to give to each other"—I hesitated—"to our children?"

Ed turned his back to me. He gripped the edge of the sink with both hands, his arms straight out, head down. Above his head the eagle flew. Butterflies trailed. "Don't do this to me," he said, his voice husky, muffled. "It's not as simple as you make it seem."

He pushed himself away from the sink and walked slowly over to the table. He stood over me; an outcropping of desert rock against the yellow sky walls of our kitchen. "You talk as if I've given you nothing," he said. "As if all I've worked for has been some kind of a lie." He looked away, over my head, toward the window. "All I could think about in Viet Nam was our life together. The kids we'd have. The home I'd buy you." He turned back to me. "Is that so wrong?"

"Not wrong, Ed. Good. Everything I wanted, too." My voice faltered. "But just not enough."

"Not enough." He shook his head, the edge of a bitter laugh in his throat. "Not enough." He pointed his finger at me. "Okay, you win. I won't stop you from doing what you have to do. But don't expect me to take any part in this."

For a moment we were equals, looking into each other's eyes, acknowledging our separateness. If not understanding, at least accepting the other's stand. It was a brief moment of union. Before the eyes looked away. Before we fell back into the hurting bones of ourselves, of our roles as husband, as wife.

Ed carried the groceries to the car. He was tight-lipped and silent. An echo of the night he had driven me to the hospital. His sorrow contained to the point where it seemed he had no sorrow. It was as if his helping me pack the trunk with groceries for Wounded Knee was a form of collusion he deeply regretted but from which he could not free himself. He arranged the groceries in the trunk, propping up the bags with the tool box so they would not spill. He closed the trunk and looked up to where I stood on the porch. "Ready?" he said.

"Ready," I said. I gathered my jacket around me and walked down the porch steps toward the car. Ed stepped aside as I reached for the front door handle. It was an awkward moment. A shifting, somehow, of reins. Before the turn. The leap. "I'll call you when I get there," I said, waiting for his move; the kiss goodbye. Ed nodded.

"The roads are being blockaded," he said, retelling what we both knew.

All vehicles were being searched out of California. Chances were the Los Angeles AIM members would never make it through the check points.

"I have to try," I said. Again, the awkwardness, the unspoken words that even refused to form. Only the stand, the position, sure on either side. I opened the car door and got in.

Ed bent over the open door. I reached for his hand. It was calloused and deeply ingrained with years of dirt and grease and getting up early to take some other man's orders, to fight some other man's wars. No amount of soap could wash away the stain. And I started to cry because it was what he thought he knew and his way of loving me and there I was going off on some maybe hopeless vision quest only I couldn't pull out because the child had died. Would never be born. And, oh God, I had to do something. I kissed the palm of his hand and he reached around with the same hand and wiped the tears from my cheek with his finger.

"Better get going," he said, pulling his hand away. He stepped back and closed the door. He hit the car with the palm of his hand, as if to spark a horse to run, and walked up the porch steps and into the house.

By now I could hardly see from crying. I started the car and backed it out of the driveway. Mrs. Johnson was on her front porch, sweeping it clean. She looked up, solid in her gray housedress, all neat white hair and cool niceness.

I drove away from the house, wiping the tears from my face. At the corner, I turned the car into the slow rush of traffic that flowed by. The car parted the air stream and the wind currents that flowed over and around the car entered the window and touched my hair, my face.

A meadowlark called from a burst of weed-flowers growing in a vacant lot, but clear as the notes were, like the dabs of yellow and lavender blooms that blurred in my passing, the notes echoed within and sang of times when I was a child. Times when the harsh stubble growing on the reservation foothills looked as green and soft as moss. Times when school was out and I would run up the dirt road toward our old house, my shoes in hand, and the earth warm beneath my bare feet.

[1986]

Storyteller

Leslie Marmon Silko

EVERY DAY THE SUN CAME UP A LITTLE LOWER ON THE HORIZON, MOVING more slowly until one day she got excited and started calling the jailer. She realized she had been sitting there for many hours, yet the sun had not moved from the center of the sky. The color of the sky had not been good lately; it had been pale blue, almost white, even when there were no clouds. She told herself it wasn't a good sign for the sky to be indistinguishable from the river ice, frozen solid and white against the earth. The tundra rose up behind the river but all the boundaries between the river and hills and sky were lost in the density of the pale ice.

She yelled again, this time some English words which came randomly into her mouth, probably swear words she'd heard from the oil drilling crews last winter. The jailer was an Eskimo, but he would not speak Yupik[1] to her. She had watched people in the other cells; when they spoke to him in Yupik he ignored them until they spoke English.

He came and stared at her. She didn't know if he understood what she was telling him until he glanced behind her at the small high window. He looked at the sun, and turned and walked away. She could hear the buckles on his heavy snowmobile boots jingle as he walked to the front of the building.

It was like the other buildings that white people, the Gussucks,[2] brought withthem: BIA[3] and school buildings, portable buildings that arrived sliced in halves, on barges coming up the river. Squares of metal panelling bulged out with the layers of insulation stuffed inside. She had asked once what it was and someone told her it was to keep out the cold. She had not laughed then, but she did now. She walked over to the small double-pane window and she laughed out loud. They thought they could keep out the cold with stringy yellow wadding. Look at the sun. It wasn't moving; it was frozen, caught in the middle of the sky. Look at the sky, solid as the river with ice which had trapped the sun. It had not moved for a long time; in a few more hours it would be weak, and heavy frost would begin to appear on the edges and spread across the face of the sun like a mask. Its light was pale yellow, worn thin by the winter.

She could see people walking down the snow-packed roads, their breath steaming out from their parka hoods, faces hidden and protected by deep ruffs of fur. There were no cars or snowmobiles that day so she calculated it was fifty below zero, the temperature which silenced their machines. The metal froze; it split and shattered. Oil hardened and moving parts jammed solidly. She had seen it happen to their big yellow machines and the giant drill last winter when they came to drill their test holes. The cold stopped them, and they were helpless against it.

Her village was many miles upriver from this town, but in her mind she could see it clearly. Their house was not near the village houses. It stood alone on the bank upriver from the village. Snow had drifted to the eaves of the roof on the north side, but on the west side, by the door, the path was almost clear. She had nailed scraps of red tin over the logs last summer. She had done it for the bright red color, not for added warmth the way the

---

[1] A language belonging to the Eskimo-Aleut family and spoken in Siberia and southwestern Alaska.
[2] Eskimo term for "white" people.
[3] Bureau of Indian Affairs.

village people had done. This final winter had been coming down even then; there had been signs of its approach for many years.

II

She went because she was curious about the big school where the Government sent all the other girls and boys. She had not played much with the village children while she was growing up because they were afraid of the old man, and they ran when her grandmother came. She went because she was tired of being alone with the old woman whose body had been stiffening for as long as the girl could remember. Her knees and knuckles were swollen grotesquely, and the pain had squeezed the brown skin of her face tight against the bones; it left her eyes hard like river stone. The girl asked once, what it was that did this to her body, and the old woman had raised up from sewing a sealskin boot, and stared at her.

"The joints," the old woman said in a low voice, whispering like wind across the roof, "the joints are swollen with anger."

Sometimes she did not answer and only stared at the girl. Each year she spoke less and less, but the old man talked more—all night sometimes, not to anyone but himself; in a soft deliberate voice, he told stories, moving his smooth brown hands above the blankets. He had not fished or hunted with the other men for many years although he was not crippled or sick. He stayed in his bed, smelling like dry fish and urine, telling stories all winter; and when warm weather came, he went to his place on the river bank. He sat with a long willow stick, poking at the smoldering moss he burned against the insects while he continued with the stories.

The trouble was that she had not recognized the warnings in time. She did not see what the Gussuck school would do to her until she walked into the dormitory and realized that the old man had not been lying about the place. She thought he had been trying to scare her as he used to when she was very small and her grandmother was outside cutting up fish. She hadn't believed what he told her about the school because she knew he wanted to keep her there in the log house with him. She knew what he wanted.

The dormitory matron pulled down her underpants and whipped her with a leather belt because she refused to speak English.

"Those backwards village people," the matron said, because she was an Eskimo who had worked for the BIA a long time, "they kept this one until she was too big to learn." The other girls whispered in English. They knew how to work the showers, and they washed and curled their hair at night. They ate Gussuck food. She laid on her bed and imagined what her grandmother might be sewing, and what the old man was eating in his bed. When summer came, they sent her home.

The way her grandmother had hugged her before she left for school had been a warning too, because the old woman had not hugged or touched her for many years. Not like the old man, whose hands were always hunting, like ravens circling lazily in the sky, ready to touch her. She was not surprised when the priest and the old man met her at the landing strip, to say that the old lady was gone. The priest asked her where she would like to stay. He referred to the old man as her grandfather, but she did not bother to correct him. She had already been thinking about it; if she went with the priest, he would send her away to a school. But the old man was different. She knew he wouldn't send her back to school. She knew he wanted to keep her.

III

He told her one time, that she would get too old for him faster than he got too old for her; but again she had not believed him because sometimes he lied. He had lied about what he would do with her if she came into his bed. But as the years passed, she realized what he said was true. She was restless and strong. She had no patience with the old man who had never changed his slow smooth motions under the blankets.

The old man was in his bed for the winter; he did not leave it except to use the slop bucket in the corner. He was dozing with his mouth open slightly; his lips quivered and sometimes they moved like he was telling a story even while he dreamed. She pulled on the sealskin boots, the mukluks with the bright red flannel linings her grandmother had sewn for her, and she tied the braided red yarn tassels around her ankles over the gray wool pants. She zipped the wolfskin parka. Her grandmother had worn it for many years, but the old man said that before she died, she instructed him to bury her in an old black sweater, and to give the parka to the girl. The wolf pelts were creamy colored and silver, almost white in some places, and when the old lady had walked across the tundra in the winter, she disappeared into the snow.

She walked toward the village, breaking her own path through the deep snow. A team of sled dogs tied outside a house at the edge of the village leaped against their chains to bark at her. She kept walking, watching the dusky sky for the first evening stars. It was warm and the dogs were alert. When it got cold again, the dogs would lie curled and still, too drowsy from the cold to bark or pull at the chains. She laughed loudly because it made them howl and snarl. Once the old man had seen her tease the dogs and he shook his head. "So that's the kind of woman you are," he said, "in the wintertime the two of us are no different from those dogs. We wait in the cold for someone to bring us a few dry fish."

She laughed out loud again, and kept walking. She was thinking about the Gussuck oil drillers. They were strange; they watched her when she walked near their machines. She wondered what they looked like underneath their quilted goosedown trousers; she wanted to know how they moved. They would be something different from the old man.

The old man screamed at her. He shook her shoulders so violently that her head bumped against the log wall. "I smelled it!" he yelled, "as soon as I woke up! I am sure of it now. You can't fool me!" His thin legs were shaking inside the baggy wool trousers; he stumbled over her boots in his bare feet. His toe nails were long and yellow like bird claws; she had seen a gray crane last summer fighting another in the shallow water on the edge of the river. She laughed out loud and pulled her shoulder out of his grip. He stood in front of her. He was breathing hard and shaking; he looked weak. He would probably die next winter.

"I'm warning you," he said, "I'm warning you." He crawled back into his bunk then, and reached under the old soiled feather pillow for a piece of dry fish. He lay back on the pillow, staring at the ceiling, and chewed dry strips of salmon. "I don't know what the old woman told you," he said, "but there will be trouble." He looked over to see if she was listening. His face suddenly relaxed into a smile, his dark slanty eyes were lost in wrinkles of brown skin. "I could tell you, but you are too good for warnings now. I can smell what you did all night with the Gussucks."

She did not understand why they came there, because the village was small and so far upriver that even some Eskimos who had been away to school would not come back. They stayed downriver in the town. They said the village was too quiet. They were used to the town where the boarding school was located, with electric lights and running water. After all those years away at school, they had forgotten how to set nets in the river and where to hunt seals in the fall. Those who left did not say it, but their confidence had been destroyed. When she asked the old man why the Gussucks bothered to come to the village, his narrow eyes got bright with excitement.

"They only come when there is something to steal. The fur animals are too difficult for them to get now, and the seals and fish are hard to find. Now they come for oil deep in the earth. But this is the last time for them." His breathing was wheezy and fast; his hands gestured at the sky. "It is approaching. As it comes, ice will push across the sky." His eyes were open wide, and he stared at the low ceiling rafters for hours without blinking. She remembered all this clearly because he began the story that day, the story he told from that time on. It began with a giant bear which he described muscle by muscle, from the curve of the ivory claws to the whorls of hair at the top of the massive skull. And for eight days he did not sleep, but talked continuously of the giant bear whose color was pale blue glacier ice.

IV

The snow was dirty and worn down in a path to the door. On either side of the path, the snow was higher than her head. In front of the door there were jagged yellow stains melted into the snow where men had urinated. She stopped in the entry way and kicked the snow off her boots. The room was dim, a kerosene lantern by the cash register was burning low. The long wooden shelves were jammed with cans of beans and potted meats. On the bottom shelf a jar of mayonnaise was broken open, leaking oily white clots on the floor. There was no one in the room except the yellowish dog sleeping in front of the long glass display case. A reflection made it appear to be lying on the knives and ammunition inside the case. Gussucks kept dogs inside their houses with them; they did not seem to mind the odors which seeped out of the dogs. "They tell us we are dirty for the food we eat—raw fish and fermented meat. But we do not live with dogs," the old man once said. She heard voices in the back room, and the sound of bottles set down hard on tables.

They were always confident. The first year they waited for the ice to break up on the river, and then they brought their big yellow machines up river on barges. They planned to drill their test holes during the summer to avoid the freezing. But the imprints and graves of their machines were still there, on the edge of the tundra above the river, where the summer mud had swallowed them before they ever left sight of the river. The village people had gathered to watch the white men, and to laugh as they drove the giant machines, one by one, off the steel ramp into the bogs; as if sheer numbers of vehicles would somehow make the tundra solid. But the old man said they behaved like desperate people, and they would come back again. When the tundra was frozen solid, they returned.

Village women did not even look through the door to the back room. The priest had warned them. The storeman was watching her because he didn't let Eskimos or Indians sit down at the tables in the back room. But she knew he couldn't throw her out if one of his Gussuck customers invited her to sit with him. She walked across the room. They stared at her, but she had the feeling she was walking for someone else, not herself, so their eyes did not matter. The red-haired man pulled out a chair and motioned for her to sit down. She looked back at the storeman while the red-haired man poured her a glass of red sweet wine. She wanted to laugh at the storeman the way she laughed at the dogs, straining against their chains, howling at her.

The red-haired man kept talking to the other Gussucks sitting around the table, but he slid one hand off the top of the table to her thigh. She looked over at the storeman to see if he was still watching her. She laughed out loud at him and the red-haired man stopped talking and turned to her. He asked if she wanted to go. She nodded and stood up.

Someone in the village had been telling him things about her, he said as they walked down the road to his trailer. She understood that much of what he was saying, but the rest she did not hear. The whine of the big generators at the construction camp sucked away the sound of his words. But English was of no concern to her anymore, and neither was anything the Christians in the village might say about her or the old man. She smiled at the effect of the subzero air on the electric lights around the trailers; they did not shine. They left only yellow holes in the darkness.

It took him a long time to get ready, even after she had undressed for him. She waited in the bed with the blankets pulled close, watching him. He adjusted the thermostat and lit candles in the room, turning out the electric lights. He searched through a stack of record albums until he found the right one. She was not sure about the last thing he did: he taped something on the wall behind the bed where he could see it while he laid on top of her. He was shrivelled and white from the cold; he pushed against her body for warmth. He guided her hands to his thighs; he was shivering.

She had returned a last time because she wanted to know what it was he stuck on the wall above the bed. After he finished each time, he reached up and pulled it loose, folding it carefully so that she could not see it. But this time she was ready; she waited for his fast breathing and sudden collapse on top of her. She slid out from under him and stood up beside the bed. She looked at the picture while she got dressed. He did not raise his face from the pillow, and she thought she heard teeth rattling together as she left the room.

She heard the old man move when she came in. After the Gussuck's trailer, the log house felt cool. It smelled like dry fish and cured meat. The room was dark except for the blinking yellow flame in the mica window of the oil stove. She squatted in front of the stove and watched the flames for a long time before she walked to the bed where her grandmother had slept. The bed was covered with a mound of rags and fur scraps the old woman had saved. She reached into the mound until she felt something cold and solid wrapped in a wool blanket. She pushed her fingers around it until she felt smooth stone. Long ago, before the Gussucks came, they had burned whale oil in the big stone lamp which made light and heat as well. The old woman had saved everything they would need when the time came.

In the morning, the old man pulled a piece of dry caribou meat from under the blankets and offered it to her. While she was gone, men from the village had brought a bundle of dry meat. She chewed it slowly, thinking about the way they still came from the village to take care of the old man and his stories. But she had a story now, about the red-haired Gussuck. The old man knew what she was thinking, and his smile made his face seem more round than it was.

"Well," he said, "what was it?"

"A woman with a big dog on top of her."

He laughed softly to himself and walked over to the water barrel. He dipped the tin cup into the water.

"It doesn't surprise me," he said.

V

"Grandma," she said, "there was something red in the grass that morning I remember." She had not asked about her parents before. The old woman stopped splitting the fish bellies open for the willow drying racks. Her jaw muscles pulled so tightly against her skull, the girl thought the old woman would not be able to speak.

"They bought a tin can full of it from the storeman. Late at night. He told them it was alcohol safe to drink. They traded a rifle for it." The old woman's voice sounded like each word stole strength from her. "It made no difference about the rifle. That year the Gussuck boats had come, firing big guns at the walrus and seals. There was nothing left to hunt after that anyway. So," the old lady said, in a low soft voice the girl had not heard for a long time, "I didn't say anything to them when they left that night."

"Right over there," she said, pointing at the fallen poles, half buried in the river sand and tall grass, "in the summer shelter. The sun was high half the night then. Early in the morning when it was still low, the policeman came around. I told the interpreter to tell him that the storeman had poisoned them." She made outlines in the air in front of her, showing how their bodies laid twisted on the sand; telling the story was like laboring to walk through deep snow; sweat shone in the white hair around her forehead. "I told the priest too, after he came. I told him the storeman lied." She turned away from the girl. She held her mouth even tighter, set solidly, not in sorrow or anger, but against the pain, which was all that remained. "I never believed," she said, "not much anyway. I wasn't surprised when the priest did nothing."

The wind came on the river and folded the tall grass into itself like river waves. She could feel the silence the story left, and she wanted to have the old woman go on.

"I heard the sounds that night, grandma. Sounds like someone was singing. It was light outside. I could see something red on the ground." The old woman did not answer her; she moved to the tub full of fish on the ground beside the work bench. She stabbed her knife into the belly of a whitefish and lifted it onto the bench. "The Gussuck storeman left the village right after that," the old woman said as she pulled the entrails from the fish, "otherwise, I could tell you more." The old woman's voice flowed with the wind blowing off the river; they never spoke of it again.

When the willows got their leaves and the grass grew tall along the river banks and around the sloughs, she walked early in the morning. While the sun was still low on the horizon, she listened to the wind off the river; its sound was like the voice that day long ago. In the distance, she could hear the engines of the machinery the oil drillers had left the winter before, but she did not go near the village or the store. The sun never left the sky and the summer became the same long day, with only the winds to fan the sun into the brightness or allow it to slip into twilight.

She sat beside the old man at his place on the river bank. She poked the smoky fire for him, and felt herself growing wide and thin in the sun as if she had been split from belly to throat and strung on the willow pole in preparation for the winter to come. The old man did not speak anymore. When men from the village brought him fresh fish he hid them deep in the river grass where it was cool. After he went inside, she split the fish open and spread them to dry on the willow frame the way the old woman had done. Inside, he dozed and talked to himself. He had talked all winter, softly and incessantly about the giant polar bear stalking a lone man across Bering Sea ice. After all the months the old man had been telling the story, the bear was within a hundred feet of the man; but the ice fog had closed in on them now and the man could only smell the sharp ammonia odor of the bear, and hear the edge of the snow crust crack under the giant paws.

One night she listened to the old man tell the story all night in his sleep, describing each crystal of ice and the slightly different sounds they made under each paw; first the left and then the right paw, then the hind feet. Her grandmother was there suddenly, a shadow around the stove. She spoke in her low wind voice and the girl was afraid to sit up to hear more clearly. Maybe what she said had been to the old man because he stopped telling the story and began to snore softly the way he had long ago when the old woman had scolded him for telling his stories while others in the house were trying to sleep. But the last words she heard clearly: "It will take a long time, but the story must be told. There must not be any lies." She pulled the blankets up around her chin, slowly, so that her movements would not be seen. She thought her grandmother was talking about the old man's bear story; she did not know about the other story then.

She left the old man wheezing and snoring in his bed. She walked through river grass glistening with frost; the bright green summer color was already fading. She watched the sun move across the sky, already lower on the horizon, already moving away from the village. She stopped by the fallen poles of the summer shelter where her parents had died. Frost glittered on the river sand too; in a few more weeks there would be snow. The predawn light would be the color of an old woman. An old woman sky full of snow. There had been something red lying on the ground the morning they died. She looked for it again, pushing aside the grass with her foot. She knelt in the sand and looked under the fallen structure for some trace of it. When she found it, she would know what the old woman had never told her. She squatted down close to the gray poles and leaned her back against them. The wind made her shiver.

The summer rain had washed the mud from between the logs; the sod blocks stacked as high as her belly next to the log walls had lost their square-cut shape and had grown into soft mounds of tundra moss and stiff-bladed grass bending with clusters of seed bristles. She looked at the northwest, in the direction of the Bering Sea. The cold would come down from there to find narrow slits in the mud, rainwater holes in the outer layer of sod which protected the log house. The dark green tundra stretched away flat and continuous. Somewhere the sea and the land met, she knew by their dark green colors there were no boundaries between them. That was how the cold would come: when the boundaries were gone the polar ice would range across the land into the sky. She watched the horizon for a long time. She would stand in that place on the north side of the house and she would keep watch on the northwest horizon, and eventually she would see it come. She would watch for its approach in the stars, and hear it come with the wind. These preparations were unfamiliar, but gradually she recognized them as she did her own footprints in the snow.

She emptied the slop jar beside his bed twice a day and kept the barrel full of water melted from river ice. He did not recognize her anymore, and when he spoke to her, he called her by her grandmother's name and talked about people and events from long ago, before he went back to telling the story. The giant bear was creeping across the new snow on its belly, close enough now that the man could hear the rasp of its breathing. On and on in a soft singing voice, the old man caressed the story, repeating the words again and again like gentle strokes.

The sky was gray like a river crane's egg; its density curved into the thin crust of frost already covering the land. She looked at the bright red color of the tin against the ground and the sky and she told the village men to bring the pieces for the old man and her. To drill the test holes in the tundra, the Gussucks had used hundreds of barrels of fuel. The village people split open the empty barrels that were abandoned on the river bank, and pounded the red tin into flat sheets. The village people were using the strips of tin to mend walls and roofs for winter. But she nailed it on the log walls for its color. When she finished, she walked away with the hammer in her hand, not turning around until she was far away, on the ridge above the river banks, and then she looked back. She felt a chill when she saw how the sky and the land were already losing their boundaries, already becoming lost in each other. But the red tin penetrated the thick white color of earth and sky; it defined the boundaries like a wound revealing the ribs and heart of a great caribou about to bolt and be lost to the hunter forever. That night the wind howled and when she scratched a hole through the heavy frost on the inside of the window, she could see nothing but the impenetrable white; whether it was blowing snow or snow that had drifted as high as the house, she did not know.

It had come down suddenly, and she stood with her back to the wind looking at the river, its smoky water clotted with ice. The wind had blown the snow over the frozen river, hiding thin blue streaks where fast water ran under ice translucent and fragile as memory. But she could see shadows of boundaries, outlines of paths which were slender branches of solidity reaching out from the earth. She spent days walking on the river, watching the colors of ice that would safely hold her, kicking the heel of her boot into the snow crust, listening for a solid sound. When she could feel the paths through the soles of her feet, she went to the middle of the river where the fast gray water churned under a thin pane of ice. She looked back. On the river bank in the distance she could see the red tin nailed to the log house, something not swallowed up by the heavy white belly of the sky or caught in the folds of the frozen earth. It was time.

The wolverine fur around the hood of her parka was white with the frost from her breathing. The warmth inside the store melted it, and she felt tiny drops of water on her face. The storeman came in from the back room. She unzipped the parka and stood by the oil stove. She didn't look at him, but stared instead at the yellowish dog, covered with scabs of matted hair, sleeping in front of the stove. She thought of the Gussuck's picture, taped on the wall above the bed and she laughed out loud. The sound of her laughter was piercing, the yellow dog jumped to its feet and the hair bristled down its back. The storeman was watching her. She wanted to laugh again because he didn't know about the ice. He did not know that it was prowling the earth, or that it had already pushed its way into the sky to seize the sun. She sat down in the chair by the stove and shook her long hair loose. He was like a dog tied up all winter, watching while the others got fed. He remembered how she had gone with the oil drillers, and his blue eyes moved like flies crawling over her body. He held his thin pale lips like he wanted to spit on her. He hated the people because they had something of value, the old man said, something which the Gussucks could never have. They thought they could take it, suck it out of the earth or cut it from the mountains; but they were fools.

There was a matted hunk of dog hair on the floor by her foot. She thought of a yellow insulation coming unstuffed: their defense against the freezing going to pieces as it advanced on them. The ice was crouching on the northwest horizon like the old man's bear. She laughed out loud again. The sun would be down now; it was time.

The first time he spoke to her, she did not hear what he said, so she did not answer or even look up at him. He spoke to her again but his words were only noises coming from his pale mouth, trembling now as his anger began to unravel. He jerked her up and the chair fell over behind her. His arms were shaking and she could feel his hands tense up, pulling the edges of the parka tighter. He raised his fist to hit her, his thin body quivering with rage; but the fist collapsed with the desire he had for the valuable things, which, the old man had rightly said, was the only reason they came. She could hear his heart pounding as he held her close and arched his hip against her, groaning and breathing in spasms. She twisted away from him and ducked under his arms.

She ran with a mitten over her mouth, breathing through the fur to protect her lungs from the freezing air. She could hear him running behind her, his heavy breathing, the occasional sound of metal jingling against metal. But he ran without his parka or mittens, breathing the frozen air; its fire squeezed the lungs against the ribs and it was enough that he could not catch her near his store. On the river bank he realized how far he was from his stove, and the wads of yellow stuffing that held off the cold. But the girl was not able to run very fast through the deep drifts at the edge of the river. The twilight was luminous and he could still see clearly for a long distance; he knew he could catch her so he kept running.

When she neared the middle of the river she looked over her shoulder. He was not following her tracks; he went straight across the ice, running the shortest distance to reach her. He was close then; his face was twisted and scarlet from the exertion and the cold. There was satisfaction in his eyes; he was sure he could outrun her.

She was familiar with the river, down to the instant the ice flexed into hairline fractures, and the cracking bone-sliver sounds gathered momentum with the opening ice until the sound of the churning gray water was set free. She stopped and turned to the sound of the river and the rattle of swirling ice fragments where he fell through. She pulled off a mitten and zipped the parka to her throat. She was conscious then of her own rapid breathing.

She moved slowly, kicking the ice ahead with the heel of her boot, feeling for sinews of ice to hold her. She looked ahead and all around herself; in the twilight, the dense white sky had merged into the flat snow-covered tundra. In the frantic running she had lost her place on the river. She stood still. The east bank of the river was lost in the sky; the boundaries had been swallowed by the freezing white. And then, in the distance, she saw something red, and suddenly it was as she had remembered it all those years.

VI

She sat on her bed and while she waited, she listened to the old man. The man had found a small jagged knoll on the ice. He pulled his beaver fur cap off his head; the fur inside it steamed with his body heat and sweat. He left it upside down on the ice for the great bear to stalk, and he waited downwind on top of the ice knoll; he was holding the jade knife.

She thought she could see the end of his story in the way he wheezed out the words; but still he reached into his cache of dry fish and dribbled water into his mouth from the tin cup. All night she listened to him describe each breath the man took, each motion of the bear's head as it tried to catch the sound of the man's breathing, and tested the wind for his scent.

The state trooper asked her questions, and the woman who cleaned house for the priest translated them into Yupik. They wanted to know what happened to the storeman, the Gussuck who had been seen running after her down the road onto the river late last evening. He had not come back, and the Gussuck boss in Anchorage was concerned about him. She did not answer for a long time because the old man suddenly sat up in his bed and began to talk excitedly, looking at all of them—the trooper in his dark glasses and the housekeeper in her corduroy parka. He kept saying, "The story! The story! Eh-ya! The great bear! The hunter!"

They asked her again, what happened to the man from the Northern Commercial store. "He lied to them. He told them it was safe to drink. But I will not lie." She stood up and put on the gray wolfskin parka. "I killed him," she said, "but I don't lie."

The attorney came back again, and the jailer slid open the steel doors and opened the cell to let him in. He motioned for the jailer to stay to translate for him. She laughed when she saw how the jailer would be forced by this Gussuck to speak Yupik to her. She liked the Gussuck attorney for that, and for the thinning hair on his head. He was very tall, and she liked to think about the exposure of his head to the freezing; she wondered if he would feel the ice descending from the sky before the others did. He wanted to know why she told the state trooper she had killed the storeman. Some village children had seen it happen, he said, and it was an accident. "That's all you have to say to the judge: it was an accident." He kept repeating it over and over again to her, slowly in a loud but gentle voice: "It was an accident. He was running after you and he fell through the ice. That's all you have to say in court. That's all. And they will let you go home. Back to your village." The jailer translated words sullenly, staring down at the floor. She shook her head. "I will not change the story, not even to escape this place and go home. I intended that he die. The story must be told as it is." The attorney exhaled loudly; his eyes looked tired. "Tell her that she could not have killed him that way. He was a white man. He ran after her without a parka or mittens. She could not have planned that." He paused and turned toward the cell door. "Tell her I will do all I can for her. I will explain to the judge that her mind is confused." She laughed out loud when the jailer translated what the attorney said. The Gussucks did not understand the story; they could not see the way it must be told, year after year as the old man had done, without lapse or silence.

She looked out the window at the frozen white sky. The sun had finally broken loose from the ice but it moved like a wounded caribou running on strength which only dying animals find, leaping and running on bullet-shattered lungs. Its light was weak and pale; it pushed dimly through the clouds. She turned and faced the Gussuck attorney.

"It began a long time ago," she intoned steadily, "in the summertime. Early in the morning, I remember, something red in the tall river grass . . ."

The day after the old man died, men from the village came. She was sitting on the edge of her bed, across from the woman the trooper hired to watch her. They came into the room slowly and listened to her. At the foot of her bed they left a king salmon that had been split open wide and dried last summer. But she did not pause or hesitate; she went on with the story, and she never stopped, not even when the woman got up to close the door behind the village men.

The old man would not change the story even when he knew the end was approaching. Lies could not stop what was coming. He thrashed around on the bed, pulling the blankets loose, knocking bundles of dried fish and meat on the floor. The man had been on the ice for many hours. The freezing winds on the ice knoll had numbed his hands in the mittens, and the cold had exhausted him. He felt a single muscle tremor in his hand that he could not suppress, and the jade knife fell; it shattered on the ice, and the blue glacier bear turned slowly to face him.

[1980]

Two Kinds

Amy Tan

MY MOTHER BELIEVED YOU COULD BE ANYTHING YOU WANTED TO BE IN America. You could open a restaurant. You could work for the government and get good retirement. You could buy a house with almost no money down. You could become rich. You could become instantly famous.

"Of course you can be prodigy, too," my mother told me when I was nine. "You can be best anything. What does Auntie Lindo know? Her daughter, she is only best tricky."

America was where all my mother's hopes lay. She had come here in 1949 after losing everything in China: her mother and father, her family home, her first husband, and two daughters, twin baby girls. But she never looked back with regret. There were so many ways for things to get better.

We didn't immediately pick the right kind of prodigy. At first my mother thought I would be a Chinese Shirley Temple. We'd watch Shirley's old movies on TV as though they were training films. My mother would poke my arm and say, "*Ni kan*"—You watch. And I would see Shirley tapping her feet, or singing a sailor song, or pursing her lips into a very round O while saying, "Oh my goodness."

"*Ni kan*," said my mother as Shirley's eyes flooded with tears. "You already know how. Don't need talent for crying!"

Soon after my mother got this idea about Shirley Temple, she took me to a beauty training school in the Mission district and put me in the hands of a student who could barely hold the scissors without shaking. Instead of getting big fat curls, I emerged with an uneven mass of crinkly black fuzz. My mother dragged me off to the bathroom and tried to wet down my hair.

"You look like Negro Chinese," she lamented, as if I had done this on purpose.

The instructor of the beauty training school had to lop off those soggy clumps to make my hair even again. "Peter Pan is very popular these days," the instructor assured my mother. I now had hair the length of a boy's, with straight-across bangs that hung at a slant two inches above my eyebrows. I liked the haircut and it made me actually look forward to my future fame.

In fact, in the beginning, I was just as excited as my mother, maybe even more so. I pictured this prodigy part of me as many different images, trying each one on for size. I was a dainty ballerina girl standing by the curtains, waiting to hear the right music that would send me floating on my tiptoes. I was like the Christ Child lifted out of the straw manger, crying with holy indignity. I was Cinderella stepping from her pumpkin carriage with sparkly cartoon music filling the air.

In all of my imaginings, I was filled with a sense that I would soon become *perfect*. My mother and father would adore me. I would be beyond reproach. I would never feel the need to sulk for anything.

But sometimes the prodigy in me became impatient. "If you don't hurry up and get me out of here, I'm disappearing for good," it warned. "And then you'll always be nothing."

Every night after dinner, my mother and I would sit at the Formica kitchen table. She would present new tests, taking her examples from stories of amazing children she had read in *Ripley's Believe It or Not*, or *Good Housekeeping*, *Reader's Digest*, and a dozen other magazines she kept in a pile in our bathroom. My mother got these magazines from people whose houses she cleaned. And since she cleaned many houses each week, we had a great assortment. She would look through them all, searching for stories about remarkable children.

The first night she brought out a story about a three-year-old boy who knew the capitals of all the states and even most of the European countries. A teacher was quoted as saying the little boy could also pronounce the names of the foreign cities correctly.

"What's the capital of Finland?" my mother asked me, looking at the magazine story.

All I knew was the capital of California, because Sacramento was the name of the street we lived on in Chinatown. "Nairobi!" I guessed, saying the most foreign word I could think of. She checked to see if that was possibly one way to pronounce "Helsinki" before showing me the answer.

The tests got harder—multiplying numbers in my head, finding the queen of hearts in a deck of cards, trying to stand on my head without using my hands, predicting the daily temperatures in Los Angeles, New York, and London.

One night I had to look at a page from the Bible for three minutes and then report everything I could remember. "Now Jehoshaphat had riches and honor in abundance and . . . that's all I remember, Ma," I said.

And after seeing my mother's disappointed face once again, something inside of me began to die. I hated the tests, the raised hopes and failed expectations. Before going to bed that night, I looked in the mirror above the bathroom sink and when I saw only my face staring back—and that it would always be this ordinary face—I began to cry. Such a sad, ugly girl! I made high-pitched noises like a crazed animal, trying to scratch out the face in the mirror.

And then I saw what seemed to be the prodigy side of me—because I had never seen that face before. I looked at my reflection, blinking so I could see more clearly. The girl staring back at me was angry, powerful. This girl and I were the same. I had new thoughts, willful thoughts, or rather thoughts filled with lots of won'ts. I won't let her change me, I promised myself. I won't be what I'm not.

So now on nights when my mother presented her tests, I performed listlessly, my head propped on one arm. I pretended to be bored. And I was. I got so bored I started counting the bellows of the foghorns out on the bay while my mother drilled me in other areas. The sound was comforting and reminded me of the cow jumping over the moon. And the next day, I played a game with myself, seeing if my mother would give up on me before eight bellows. After a while I usually counted only one, maybe two bellows at most. At last she was beginning to give up hope.

Two or three months had gone by without any mention of my being a prodigy again. And then one day my mother was watching "The Ed Sullivan Show" on TV. The TV was old and the sound kept shorting out. Every time my mother got halfway up from the sofa to adjust the set, the sound would go back on and Ed would be talking. As soon as she sat down, Ed would go silent again. She got up, the TV broke into loud piano music. She sat down. Silence. Up and down, back and forth, quiet and loud. It was like a stiff embraceless dance between her and the TV set. Finally she stood by the set with her hand on the sound dial.

She seemed entranced by the music, a little frenzied piano piece with this mesmerizing quality, sort of quick passages and then teasing lilting ones before it returned to the quick playful parts.

"Ni kan," my mother said, calling me over with hurried hand gestures. "Look here."

I could see why my mother was fascinated by the music. It was being pounded out by a little Chinese girl, about nine years old, with a Peter Pan haircut. The girl had the sauciness of a Shirley Temple. She was proudly modest like a proper Chinese child. And she also did this fancy sweep of a curtsy, so that the fluffy skirt of her white dress cascaded slowly to the floor like the petals of a large carnation.

In spite of these warning signs, I wasn't worried. Our family had no piano and we couldn't afford to buy one, let alone reams of sheet music and piano lessons. So I could be generous in my comments when my mother bad-mouthed the little girl on TV.

"Play note right, but doesn't sound good! No singing sound," complained my mother.

"What are you picking on her for?" I said carelessly. "She's pretty good. Maybe she's not the best, but she's trying hard." I knew almost immediately I would be sorry I said that.

"Just like you," she said. "Not the best. Because you not trying." She gave a little huff as she let go of the sound dial and sat down on the sofa.

The little Chinese girl sat down also to play an encore of "Anitra's Dance" by Grieg. I remember the song, because later on I had to learn how to play it.

Three days after watching "The Ed Sullivan Show," my mother told me what my schedule would be for piano lessons and piano practice. She had talked to Mr. Chong, who lived on the first floor of our apartment building. Mr. Chong was a retired piano teacher and my mother had traded house-cleaning services for weekly lessons and a piano for me to practice on every day, two hours a day, from four until six.

When my mother told me this, I felt as though I had been sent to hell. I whined and then kicked my foot a little when I couldn't stand it anymore.

"Why don't you like me the way I am? I'm *not* a genius! I can't play the piano. And even if I could, I wouldn't go on TV if you paid me a million dollars!" I cried.

My mother slapped me. "Who ask you be genius?" she shouted. "Only ask you be your best. For you sake. You think I want you be genius? Hnnh? What for! Who ask you!"

"So ungrateful," I heard her mutter in Chinese. "If she had as much talent as she has temper, she would be famous now."

Mr. Chong, whom I secretly nicknamed Old Chong, was very strange, always tapping fingers to the silent music of an invisible orchestra. He looked ancient in my eyes. He had lost most of the hair on top of his head and he wore thick glasses and had eyes that always looked tired and sleepy. But he must have been younger than I thought, since he lived with his mother and was not yet married.

I met Old Lady Chong once and that was enough. She had this peculiar smell like a baby that had done something in its pants. And her fingers felt like a dead person's, like an old peach I once found in the back of the refrigerator; the skin just slid off the meat when I picked it up.

I soon found out why Old Chong had retired from teaching piano. He was deaf. "Like Beethoven!" he shouted to me. "We're both listening only in our head!" And he would start to conduct his frantic silent sonatas.

Our lessons went like this. He would open the book and point to different things, explaining their purpose: "Key! Treble! Bass! No sharps or flats! So this is C major! Listen now and play after me!"

And then he would play the C scale a few times, a simple chord, and then, as if inspired by an old, unreachable itch, he gradually added more notes and running trills and a pounding bass until the music was really something quite grand.

I would play after him, the simple scale, the simple chord, and then I just played some nonsense that sounded like a cat running up and down on top of garbage cans. Old Chong smiled and applauded and then said, "Very good! But now you must learn to keep time!"

So that's how I discovered that Old Chong's eyes were too slow to keep up with the wrong notes I was playing. He went through the motions in half-time. To help me keep rhythm, he stood behind me, pushing down on my right shoulder for every beat. He balanced pennies on top of my wrists so I would keep them still as I slowly played scales and arpeggios. He had me curve my hand around an apple and keep that shape when playing chords. He marched stiffly to show me how to make each finger dance up and down, staccato like an obedient little soldier.

He taught me all these things, and that was how I also learned I could be lazy and get away with mistakes, lots of mistakes. If I hit the wrong notes because I hadn't practiced enough, I never corrected myself. I just kept playing in rhythm. And Old Chong kept conducting his own private reverie.

So maybe I never really gave myself a fair chance. I did pick up the basics pretty quickly, and I might have become a good pianist at that young age. But I was so determined not to try, not to be anybody different that I learned to play only the most earsplitting preludes, the most discordant hymns.

Over the next year, I practiced like this, dutifully in my own way. And then one day I heard my mother and her friend Lindo Jong both talking in a loud bragging tone of voice so others could hear. It was after church, and I was leaning against the brick wall wearing a dress with stiff white petticoats. Auntie Lindo's daughter, Waverly, who was about my age, was standing farther down the wall about five feet away. We had grown up together and shared all the closeness of two sisters squabbling over crayons and dolls. In other words, for the most part, we hated each other. I thought she was snotty. Waverly Jong had gained a certain amount of fame as "Chinatown's Littlest Chinese Chess Champion."

"She bring home too many trophy," lamented Auntie Lindo that Sunday. "All day she play chess. All day I have no time do nothing but dust off her winnings." She threw a scolding look at Waverly, who pretended not to see her.

"You lucky you don't have this problem," said Auntie Lindo with a sigh to my mother.

And my mother squared her shoulders and bragged: "Our problem worser than yours. If we ask Jing-mei wash dish, she hear nothing but music. It's like you can't stop this natural talent."

And right then, I was determined to put a stop to her foolish pride.

A few weeks later, Old Chong and my mother conspired to have me play in a talent show which would be held in the church hall. By then, my parents had saved up enough to buy me a second-hand piano, a black Wurlitzer spinet with a scarred bench. It was the showpiece of our living room.

For the talent show, I was to play a piece called "Pleading Child" from Schumann's *Scenes from Childhood*. It was a simple, moody piece that sounded more difficult than it was. I was supposed to memorize the whole thing, playing the repeat parts twice to make the piece sound longer. But I dawdled over it, playing a few bars and then cheating, looking up to see what notes followed. I never really listened to what I was playing. I day-dreamed about being somewhere else, about being someone else.

The part I liked to practice best was the fancy curtsy: right foot out, touch the rose on the carpet with a pointed foot, sweep to the side, left leg bends, look up and smile.

My parents invited all the couples from the Joy Luck Club to witness my debut. Auntie Lindo and Uncle Tin were there. Waverly and her two older brothers had also come. The first two rows were filled with children both younger and older than I was. The littlest ones got to go first. They recited simple nursery rhymes, squawked out tunes on miniature violins, twirled Hula Hoops, pranced in pink ballet tutus, and when they bowed or curtsied, the audience would sigh in unison, "Awww," and then clap enthusiastically.

When my turn came, I was very confident. I remember my childish excitement. It was as if I knew, without a doubt, that the prodigy side of me really did exist. I had no fear whatsoever, no nervousness. I remember thinking to myself, This is it! This is it! I looked out over the audience, at my mother's blank face, my father's yawn, Auntie Lindo's stiff-lipped smile, Waverly's sulky expression. I had on a white dress layered with sheets of lace, and a pink bow in my Peter Pan haircut. As I sat down I envisioned people jumping to their feet and Ed Sullivan rushing up to introduce me to eveyone on TV.

And I started to play. It was so beautiful. I was so caught up in how lovely I looked that at first I didn't worry how I would sound. So it was a surprise to me when I hit the first wrong note and I realized something didn't sound quite right. And then I hit another and another followed that. A chill started at the top of my head and began to trickle down. Yet I couldn't stop playing, as though my hands were bewitched. I kept thinking my fingers would adjust themselves back, like a train switching to the right track. I played this strange jumble through two repeats, the sour notes staying with me all the way to the end.

When I stood up, I discovered my legs were shaking. Maybe I had just been nervous and the audience, like Old Chong, had seen me go through the right motions and had not heard anything wrong at all. I swept my right foot out, went down on my knee, looked up and smiled. The room was quiet, except for Old Chong, who was beaming and shouting, "Bravo! Bravo! Well done!" But then I saw my mother's face, her stricken face. The audience clapped weakly, and as I walked back to my chair, with my whole face quivering as I tried not to cry, I heard a little boy whisper loudly to his mother, "That was awful," and the mother whispered back, "Well, she certainly tried."

And now I realized how many people were in the audience, the whole world it seemed. I was aware of eyes burning into my back. I felt the shame of my mother and father as they sat stiffly throughout the rest of the show.

We could have escaped during intermission. Pride and some strange sense of honor must have anchored my parents to their chairs. And so we watched it all: the eighteen-year-old boy with a fake mustache who did a magic show and juggled flaming hoops while riding a unicycle. The breasted girl with white makeup who sang from *Madame Butterfly* and got honorable mention. And the eleven-year-old boy who won first prize playing a tricky violin song that sounded like a busy bee.

After the show, the Hsus, the Jongs, and the St. Clairs from the Joy Luck Club came up to my mother and father.

"Lots of talented kids," Auntie Lindo said vaguely, smiling broadly.

"That was somethin' else," said my father, and I wondered if he was referring to me in a humorous way, or whether he even remembered what I had done.

Waverly looked at me and shrugged her shoulders. "You aren't a genius like me," she said matter-of-factly. And if I hadn't felt so bad, I would have pulled her braids and punched her stomach.

But my mother's expression was what devastated me: a quiet, blank look that said she had lost everything. I felt the same way, and it seemed as if everybody were now coming up, like gawkers at the scene of an accident, to see what parts were actually missing. When we got on the bus to go home, my father was humming the busy-bee tune and my mother was silent. I kept thinking she wanted to wait until we got home before shouting at me. But when my father unlocked the door to our apartment, my mother walked in and then went to the back, into the bedroom. No accusations. No blame. And in a way, I felt disappointed. I had been waiting for her to start shouting, so I could shout back and cry and blame her for all my misery.

I assumed my talent-show fiasco meant I never had to play the piano again. But two days later, after school, my mother came out of the kitchen and saw me watching TV.

"Four clock," she reminded me as if it were any other day. I was stunned, as though she were asking me to go through the talent-show torture again. I wedged myself more tightly in front of the TV.

"Turn off TV," she called from the kitchen five minutes later.

I didn't budge. And then I decided. I didn't have to do what my mother said anymore. I wasn't her slave. This wasn't China. I had listened to her before and look what happened. She was the stupid one.

She came out of the kitchen and stood in the arched entryway of the living room. "Four clock," she said once again, louder.

"I'm not going to play anymore," I said nonchalantly. "Why should I? I'm not a genius."

She walked over and stood in front of the TV. I saw her chest was heaving up and down in an angry way.

"No!" I said, and I now felt stronger, as if my true self had finally emerged. So this was what had been inside me all along.

"No! I won't!" I screamed.

She yanked me by the arm, pulled me off the floor, snapped off the TV. She was frighteningly strong, half pulling, half carrying me toward the piano as I kicked the throw rugs under my feet. She lifted me up and onto the hard bench. I was sobbing by now, looking at her bitterly. Her chest was heaving even more and her mouth was open, smiling crazily as if she were pleased I was crying.

"You want me to be someone that I'm not!" I sobbed. "I'll never be the kind of daughter you want me to be!"

"Only two kinds of daughters," she shouted in Chinese. "Those who are obedient and those who follow their own mind! Only one kind of daughter can live in this house. Obedient daughter!"

"Then I wish I wasn't your daughter. I wish you weren't my mother," I shouted. As I said these things I got scared. I felt like worms and toads and slimy things were crawling out of my chest, but it also felt good, as if this awful side of me had surfaced, at last.

"Too late change this," said my mother shrilly.

And I could sense her anger rising to its breaking point. I wanted to see it spill over. And that's when I remembered the babies she had lost in China, the ones we never talked about. "Then I wish I'd never been born!" I shouted. "I wish I were dead! Like them."

It was as if I had said the magic words. Alakazam!—and her face went blank, her mouth closed, her arms went slack, and she backed out of the room, stunned, as if she were blowing away like a small brown leaf, thin, brittle, lifeless.

It was not only disappointment my mother felt in me. In the years that followed, I failed her so many times, each time asserting my own will, my right to fall short of expectations. I didn't get straight A's. I didn't become class president. I didn't get into Stanford. I dropped out of college.

For unlike my mother, I did not believe I could be anything I wanted to be. I could only be me.

And for all those years, we never talked about the disaster at the recital or my terrible accusations afterward at the piano bench. All that remained unchecked, like a betrayal that was now unspeakable. So I never found a way to ask her why she had hoped for something so large that failure was inevitable.

And even worse, I never asked her what frightened me the most: Why had she given up hope?

For after our struggle at the piano, she never mentioned my playing again. The lessons stopped. The lid to the piano was closed, shutting out the dust, my misery, and her dreams.

So she surprised me. A few years ago, she offered to give me the piano, for my thirtieth birthday. I had not played in all those years. I saw the offer as a sign of forgiveness, a tremendous burden removed.

"Are you sure?" I asked shyly. "I mean, won't you and Dad miss it?"

"No, this your piano," she said firmly. "Always your piano. You only one can play."

"Well, I probably can't play anymore," I said. "It's been years."

"You pick up fast," said my mother, as if she knew this was certain. "You have natural talent. You could been genius if you want to."

"No, I couldn't."

"You just not trying," said my mother. And she was neither angry nor sad. She said it as if to announce a fact that could never be disproved. "Take it," she said.

But I didn't at first. It was enough that she had offered it to me. And after that, every time I saw it in my parents' living room, standing in front of the bay windows, it made me feel proud, as if it were a shiny trophy I had won back.

Last week I sent a tuner over to my parents' apartment and had the piano reconditioned, for purely sentimental reasons. My mother had died a few months before and I had been getting things in order for my father, a little bit at a time. I put the jewelry in special silk pouches. The sweaters she had knitted in yellow, pink, bright orange—all the colors I hated—I put those in moth-proof boxes. I found some old Chinese silk dresses, the kind with little slits up the sides. I rubbed the old silk against my skin, then wrapped them in tissue and decided to take them home with me.

After I had the piano tuned, I opened the lid and touched the keys. It sounded even richer than I remembered. Really, it was a very good piano. Inside the bench were the same exercise notes with handwritten scales, the same secondhand music books with their covers held together with yellow tape.

I opened up the Schumann book to the dark little piece I had played at the recital. It was on the left-hand side of the page, "Pleading Child." It looked more difficult than I remembered. I played a few bars, surprised at how easily the notes came back to me.

And for the first time, or so it seemed, I noticed the piece on the right-hand side. It was called "Perfectly Contented." I tried to play this one as well. It had a lighter melody but the same flowing rhythm and turned out to be quite easy. "Pleading Child" was shorter but slower; "Perfectly Contented" was longer but faster. And after I played them both a few times, I realized they were two halves of the same song.

[1989]

Miss Clairol

Helena María Viramontes

ARLENE AND CHAMP WALK TO K-MART. THE STORE IS FULL OF BINS mounted with bargain buys from T-shirts to rubber sandals. They go to aisle 23, Cosmetics. Arlene, wearing bell bottom jeans two sizes too small, can't bend down to the Miss Clairol boxes, asks Champ.

—Which one amá—asks Champ, chewing her thumb nail.

—Shit, mija,[1] I dunno.—Arlene smacks her gum, contemplating the decision.—Maybe I need a change, tú sabes. What do you think?—She holds up a few blond strands with black roots. Arlene has burned the softness of her hair with peroxide; her hair is stiff, breaks at the ends and she needs plenty of Aqua Net hairspray to tease and tame her ratted hair, then folds it back into a high lump behind her head. For the last few months she has been a platinum "Light Ash" blond, before that a Miss Clairol "Flame" redhead, before that Champ couldn't even identify the color—somewhere between orange and brown, a "Sun Bronze." The only way Champ knows her mother's true hair color is by her roots which, like death, inevitably rise to the truth.

[1] An abbreviation of *mi hija*, or *my daughter*, this is a term of endearment used by women when addressing friends or younger women.

–I hate it, tú sabes, when I can't decide.–Arlene is wearing a pink, strapless tube top. Her stomach spills over the hip hugger jeans. Spits the gum onto the floor.–Fuck it.–And Champ follows her to the rows of nailpolish, next to the Maybelline rack of make-up, across the false eyelashes that look like insects on display in clear, plastic boxes. Arlene pulls out a particular color of nailpolish, looks at the bottom of the bottle for the price, puts it back, gets another. She has a tatoo of purple XXX's on her left finger like a ring. She finally settles for a purple-blackish color, Ripe Plum, that Champ thinks looks like the color of Frankenstein's nails. She looks at her own stubby nails, chewed and gnawed.

Walking over to the eyeshadows, Arlene slowly slinks out another stick of gum from her back pocket, unwraps and crumbles the wrapper into a little ball, lets it drop on the floor. Smacks the gum.

–Grandpa Ham used to make chains with these gum wrappers–she says, toeing the wrapper on the floor with her rubber sandals, her toes dotted with old nailpolish.–He started one, tú sabes, that went from room to room. That was before he went nuts–she says, looking at the price of magenta eyeshadow.–Sabes que? What do you think?–lifting the eye shadow to Champ.

–I dunno know–responds Champ, shrugging her shoulders the way she always does when she is listening to something else, her own heartbeat, what Gregorio said on the phone yesterday, shrugs her shoulders when Miss Smith says OFELIA, answer my question. She is too busy thinking of things people otherwise dismiss like parentheses, but sticks to her like gum, like a hole on a shirt, like a tattoo, and sometimes she wishes she weren't born with such adhesiveness. The chain went from room to room, round and round like a web, she remembers. That was before he went nuts.

–Champ. You listening? Or in lala land again?–Arlene has her arms akimbo on a fold of flesh, pissed.

–I said, I dunno know.–Champ whines back, still looking at the wrapper on the floor.

–Well you better learn, tú sabes, and fast too. Now think, will this color go good with Pancha's blue dress?–Pancha is Arlene's comadre. Since Arlene has a special date tonight, she lent Arlene her royal blue dress that she keeps in a plastic bag at the end of her closet. The dress is made of chiffon, with satin-like material underlining, so that when Arlene first tried it on and strutted about, it crinkled sounds of elegance. The dress fits too tight. Her plump arms squeeze through, her hips breathe in and hold their breath, the seams do all they can to keep the body contained. But Arlene doesn't care as long as it sounds right.

–I think it will–Champ says, and Arlene is very pleased.

–Think so? So do I mija.–

They walk out the double doors and Champ never remembers her mother paying.

It is four in the afternoon, but already Arlene is preparing for the date. She scrubs the tub, Art Labo on the radio, drops crystals of Jean Nate into the running water, lemon scent rises with the steam. The bathroom door ajar, she removes her top and her breasts flop and sag, pushes her jeans down with some difficulty, kicks them off, and steps in the tub.

–Mija. MIJA–she yells.–Mija, give me a few bobby pins.–She is worried about her hair frizzing and so wants to pin it up.

Her mother's voice is faint because Champ is in the closet. There are piles of clothes on the floor, hangers thrown askew and tangled, shoes all piled up or thrown on the top shelf. Champ is looking for her mother's special dress. Pancha says every girl has one at the end of her closet.

–Goddamn it Champ.–

Amidst the dirty laundry, the black hole of the closet, she finds nothing.

–NOW–

–Alright, ALRIGHT. Cheeze amá, stop yelling–says Champ, and goes in the steamy bathroom, checks the drawers, hairbrushes jump out, rollers, strands of hair, rummages through bars of soap, combs, eyeshadows, finds nothing; pulls open another drawer, powder, empty bottles of oil, manicure scissors, kotex, dye instructions crinkled and botched, finally, a few bobby pins.

After Arlene pins up her hair, she asks Champ,–Sabes que? Should I wear my hair up? Do I look good with it up?–Champ is sitting on the toilet.

–Yea, amá, you look real pretty.–

–Thanks mija–says Arlene, Sabes que? When you get older I'll show you how you can look just as pretty–and she puts her head back, relaxes, like the Calgon commercials.

Champ lays on her stomach, T.V. on to some variety show with pogo stick dancers dressed in outfits of stretchy material and glitter. She is wearing one of Gregorio's white T-shirts, the ones he washes and bleaches himself so that the whiteness is impeccable. It drapes over her deflated ten year old body like a dress. She is busy cutting out Miss Breck models from the stacks of old magazines Pancha found in the back of her mother's garage. Champ collects the array of honey colored haired women, puts them in a shoe box with all her other special things.

Arlene is in the bathroom, wrapped in a towel. She has painted her eyebrows so that the two are arched and even, penciled thin and high. The magenta shades her eyelids. The towel slips, reveals one nipple blind from a cigarette burn, a date to forget. She rewraps the towel, likes her reflection, turns to her profile for additional inspection. She feels good, turns up the radio to . . . your love. For your loveeeee, I will do anything, I will do anything, forrr your love. For your kiss . . .

Champ looks on. From the open bathroom door, she can see Arlene, anticipation burning like a cigarette from her lips, sliding her shoulders to the ahhhh ahhhh, and pouting her lips until the song ends. And Champ likes her mother that way.

Arlene carefully stretches black eyeliner, like a fallen question mark, outlines each eye. The work is delicate, her hand trembles cautiously, stops the process to review the face with each line. Arlene the mirror is not Arlene the face who has worn too many relationships, gotten too little sleep. The last touch is the chalky, beige lipstick.

By the time she is finished, her ashtray is full of cigarette butts, Champ's variety show is over, and Jackie Gleason's dancing girls come on to make kaleidoscope patterns with their long legs and arms. Gregorio is still not home, and Champ goes over to the window, checks the houses, the streets, corners, roams the sky with her eyes.

Arlene sits on the toilet, stretches up her nylons, clips them to her girdle. She feels good thinking about the way he will unsnap her nylons, and she will unroll them slowly, point her toes when she does.

Champ opens a can of Campbell soup, finds a perfect pot in the middle of a stack of dishes, pulls it out to the threatening rumbling of the tower. She washes it out, pours the contents of the red can, turns the knob. After it boils, she puts the pan on the sink for it to cool down. She searches for a spoon.

Arlene is romantic. When Champ begins her period, she will tell her things that only women can know. She will tell her about the first time she made love with a boy, her awkwardness and shyness forcing them to go under the house, where the cool, refined soil made a soft mattress. How she closed her eyes and wondered what to expect, or how the penis was the softest skin she had ever felt against her, how it tickled her, searched for a place to connect. She was eleven and his name was Harry.

She will not not tell Champ that her first fuck was a guy named Puppet who ejaculated prematurely, at the sight of her apricot vagina, so plump and fuzzy.—Pendejo—she said—you got it all over me.—She rubbed the gooey substance off her legs, her belly in disgust. Ran home to tell Rat and Pancha, her mouth open with laughter.

Arlene powder puffs under her arms, between her breasts, tilts a bottle of *Love Cries* perfume and dabs behind her ears, neck and breasts for those tight caressing songs which permit them to grind their bodies together until she can feel a bulge in his pants and she knows she's in for the night.

Jackie Gleason is a bartender in a saloon. He wears a black bow tie, a white apron, and is polishing a glass. Champ is watching him, sitting in the radius of the gray light, eating her soup from the pot.

Arlene is a romantic. She will dance until Pancha's dress turns a different color, dance until her hair becomes undone, her hips jiggering and quaking beneath a new pair of hosiery, her mascara shadowing under her eyes from the perspiration of the ritual dance, spinning herself into Miss Clairol, and stopping only when it is time to return to the sewing factory, time to wait out the next date, time to change hair color. Time to remember or to forget.

Champ sees Arlene from the window. She can almost hear Arlene's nylons rubbing against one another, hear the crinkling sound of satin when she gets in the blue and white shark-finned Dodge. Champ yells goodbye. It all sounds so right to Arlene who is too busy cranking up the window to hear her daughter.

[1987]

Wilshire Bus

Hisaye Yamamoto

WILSHIRE BOULEVARD BEGINS SOMEWHERE NEAR THE HEART OF DOWN-
town Los Angeles and, except for a few digressions scarcely worth mentioning, goes straight out to the edge of the Pacific Ocean. It is a wide
boulevard and traffic on it is fairly fast. For the most part, it is bordered on
either side with examples of the recent stark architecture which favors a
great deal of glass. As the boulevard approaches the sea, however, the
landscape becomes a bit more pastoral, so that the university and the soldiers'
home there give the appearance of being huge country estates.

Esther Kuroiwa got to know this stretch of terrotory quite well while her
husband Buro was in one of the hospitals at the soldiers' home. They had
been married less than a year when his back, injured in the war, began
troubling him again, and he was forced to take three months of treatments
at Sawtelle before he was able to go back to work. During this time, Esther
was permitted to visit him twice a week and she usually took the yellow bus
out on Wednesdays because she did not know the first thing about driving
and because her friends were not able to take her except on Sundays. She
always enjoyed the long bus ride very much because her seat companions
usually turned out to be amiable, and if they did not, she took vicarious
pleasure in gazing out at the almost unmitigated elegance along the fabulous
street.

It was on one of these Wednesday trips that Esther committed a grave
sin of omission which caused her later to burst into tears and which caused
her acute discomfort for a long time afterwards whenever something reminded her of it.

The man came on the bus quite early and Esther noticed him briefly as
he entered because he said gaily to the driver, "You robber. All you guys
do is take money from me every day, just for giving me a short lift!"

Handsome in a red-faced way, greying, medium of height, and dressed
in a dark grey sport suit with a yellow-and-black flowered shirt, he said this
in a nice, resonant, carrying voice which got the response of a scattering of
titters from the bus. Esther, somewhat amused and classifying him as a
somatotonic, promptly forgot about him. And since she was sitting alone in
the first regular seat, facing the back of the driver and the two front benches
facing each other, she returned to looking out the window.

At the next stop, a considerable mass of people piled on and the last two
climbing up were an elderly Oriental man and his wife. Both were neatly
and somberly clothed and the woman, who wore her hair in a bun and
carried a bunch of yellow and dark red chrysanthemums, came to sit with
Esther. Esther turned her head to smile a greeting (well, here we are,
Orientals together on a bus), but the woman was watching, with some
concern, her husband who was asking directions of the driver.

His faint English was inflected in such a way as to make Esther decide he was probably Chinese, and she noted that he had to repeat his question several times before the driver could answer it. Then he came to sit in the seat across the aisle from his wife. It was about then that a man's voice, which Esther recognized soon as belonging to the somatotonic, began a loud monologue in the seat just behind her. It was not really a monologue, since he seemed to be addressing his seat companion, but this person was not heard to give a single answer. The man's subject was a figure in the local sporting world who had a nice fortune invested in several of the shining buildings the bus was just passing.

"He's as tight-fisted as they make them, as tight-fisted as they come," the man said. "Why, he wouldn't give you the sweat of his . . ." He paused here to rephrase his metaphor, ". . . wouldn't give you the sweat off his palm!"

And he continued in this vein, discussing the private life of the famous man so frankly that Esther knew he must be quite drunk. But she listened with interest, wondering how much of this diatribe was true, because the public legend about the famous man was emphatic about his charity. Suddenly, the woman with the chrysanthemums jerked around to get a look at the speaker and Esther felt her giving him a quick but thorough examination before she turned back around.

"So you don't like it?" the man inquired, and it was a moment before Esther realized that he was now directing his attention to her seat neighbor.

"Well, if you don't like it," he continued, "why don't you get off this bus, why don't you go back where you came from? Why don't you go back to China?"

Then, his voice growing jovial, as though he were certain of the support of the bus in this at least, he embroidered on this theme with a new eloquence, "Why don't you go back to China, where you can be coolies working in your bare feet out in the rice fields? You can let your pigtails grow and grow in China. Alla samee, mama, no tickee no shirtee. Ha, pretty good, no tickee no shirtee!"

He chortled with delight and seemed to be looking around the bus for approval. Then some memory caused him to launch on a new idea "Or why don't you go back to Trinidad? They got Chinks running the whole shebang in Trinidad. Every place you go in Trinidad . . ."

As he talked on, Esther, pretending to look out the window, felt the tenseness in the body of the woman beside her. The only movement from her was the trembling of the chrysanthemums with the motion of the bus. Without turning her head, Esther was also aware that a man, a mild-looking man with thinning hair and glasses, on one of the front benches was smiling at the woman and shaking his head mournfully in sympathy, but she doubted whether the woman saw.

Esther herself, while believing herself properly annoyed with the speaker and sorry for the old couple, felt quite detached. She found herself wondering whether the man meant her in his exclusion order or whether she was identifiably Japanese. Of course, he was not sober enough to be interested in such fine distinctions, but it did matter, she decided, because she was

Japanese, not Chinese, and therefore in the present case immune. Then she was startled to realize that what she was actually doing was gloating over the fact that the drunken man had specified the Chinese as the unwanted.

Briefly, there bobbled on her memory the face of an elderly Oriental man whom she had once seen from a streetcar on her way home from work. (This was not long after she had returned to Los Angeles from the concentration camp in Arkansas and been lucky enough to get a clerical job with the Community Chest.) The old man was on a concrete island at Seventh and Broadway, waiting for his streetcar. She had looked down on him benignly as a fellow Oriental, from her seat by the window, then been suddenly thrown for a loop by the legend on a large lapel button on his jacket. I AM KOREAN, said the button.

Heat suddenly rising to her throat, she had felt angry, then desolate and betrayed. True, reason had returned to ask whether she might not, under the circumstances, have worn such a button herself. She had heard rumors of I AM CHINESE buttons. So it was true then; why not I AM KOREAN buttons, too? Wryly, she wished for an I AM JAPANESE button, just to be able to call the man's attention to it. "Look at me!" But perhaps the man didn't even read English, perhaps he had been actually threatened, perhaps it was not his doing—his solicitous children perhaps had urged him to wear the badge.

Trying now to make up for her moral shabbiness, she turned towards the little woman and smiled at her across the chrysanthemums, shaking her head a little to get across her message (don't pay any attention to that stupid old drunk, he doesn't know what he's saying, let's take things like this in our stride). But the woman, in turn looking at her, presented a face so impassive yet cold, and eyes so expressionless yet hostile, that Esther's overture fell quite flat.

Okay, okay, if that's the way you feel about it, she thought to herself. Then the bus made another stop and she heard the man proclaim ringingly, "So clear out, all of you, and remember to take every last one of your slant-eyed pickaninnies with you!" This was his final advice as he stepped down from the middle door. The bus remained at the stop long enough for Esther to watch the man cross the street with a slightly exploring step. Then, as it started up again, the bespectacled man in front stood up to go and made a clumsy speech to the Chinese couple and possibly to Esther. "I want you to know," he said, "that we aren't all like that man. We don't all feel the way he does. We believe in an America that is a melting pot of all sorts of people. I'm originally Scotch and French myself." With that, he came over and shook the hand of the Chinese man.

"And you, young lady," he said to the girl behind Esther, "you deserve a Purple Heart or something for having to put up with that sitting beside you."

Then he, too, got off.

The rest of the ride was uneventful and Esther stared out the window with eyes that did not see. Getting off at last at the soldiers' home, she was aware of the Chinese couple getting off after her, but she avoided looking at them. Then, while she was walking towards Buro's hospital very quickly, there arose in her mind some words she had once read and let stick in her craw: People say, do not regard what he says, now he is in liquor. Perhaps it is the only time he ought to be regarded.

These words repeated themselves until her saving detachment was gone every bit and she was filled once again in her life with the infuriatingly helpless, insidiously sickening sensation of there being in the world nothing solid she could put her finger on, nothing solid she could come to grips with, nothing solid she could sink her teeth into, nothing solid.

When she reached Buro's room and caught sight of his welcoming face, she ran to his bed and broke into sobs that she could not control. Buro was amazed because it was hardly her first visit and she had never shown such weakness before, but solving the mystery handily, he patted her head, looked around smugly at his roommates, and asked tenderly, "What's the matter? You've been missing me a whole lot, huh?" And she, finally drying her eyes, sniffed and nodded and bravely smiled and answered him with the question, yes, weren't women silly?

[1988]

I write to show myself showing people
who show me my own showing.

TRINH T. MINH-HA

Woman, Native, Other

Denise Chávez

LIST OF CHARACTERS

(in order of appearance)

María Isabel González, *the narrator*
Jesusita Rael, *a storeowner and spinster*
Esperanza González, *the wife of a Vietnam veteran*
Minda Mirabal, *a foster child*
Magdalena Telles, *the mother of seven children*
Tomasa Pacheco, *a nursing home resident*
Juana Martínez, *a factory employee*
Pauline Mendoza, *a Chicana teenager*
Corrine, "La Cory" Delgado, *a bag lady*

THE SET:

A tall chest, covered by a lace mantel. On it stands a statue of La Virgen de Guadalupe. On either side of the Virgen are two tall candles, and fanning out in front are nine small votive candles, unlit. Nearby is a table and a chair. The space is untidy, scattered with paper; the props, a blanket draped over the chair.

AT RISE:

ISABEL *comes in breathlessly, with a bag of groceries that she sets down on the table. She leaves the food in the bag and organizes the area. The lights come down, and she throws the blanket on the floor, then lays down on it. She is tired and wants to meditate a while. It has been a busy day and she wants to relax. On the floor near her is a large pile of papers, some collated, some not. After a long silence, in the darkness, she turns the lights up slightly and begins to exercise. She does various yoga positions, stretching slowly, first on the floor, then in a seated position. With her back to the audience she begins talking.*

Isabel

Somebody asked me what I do for a living. I am an artist I said. I write. I am a writer . . . (*Stretching, she grabs a foot, then jumps up, yelling*) Green tennis shoes! That's it, I forgot the shoes! (*Turning up lights, she goes to a pile of papers on the desk and jots down the note*) . . . JESUSITA RAEL, *green tennies* . . . (*Back to floor, adjusting self, with* JESUSITA's *voice*) Buenos días le dé Dios, hermana[1] . . . (*Practicing, trying to get voice just right, high, with an S lisp*) Buenos días le dé Dios . . . (*In a shoulder stand, struggling, then falling back and laying there, she turns to one side and begins to collate papers. She talks and collates*) Jesusita, Esperanza, Minda, Magdalena, Tomasa, Juana, Pauline and Corrine; Jesusita, Esperanza, Minda, Magdalena, Tomasa, Juana, Pauline, and La Cory, one, two, three, four, five, six, seven, eight. . . .

(ISABEL *does this for awhile, then goes to the bag, finds juice, has a sip; she takes out a can of peas and leaves it on the chest, near the altar. On her way back, she picks up a pile of bills, opens them, and then places them face down on the table. She starts to put out the prop pieces; we follow her, as she mumbles and works out the play. She talks as she puts out the props, which include:* JESUSITA's *lace collar,* ESPERANZA's *peas,* MINDA's *doll and blanket,* TOMASA's *wig and cane,* JUANA's *goggles, feathers and cedar,* MAGDA-LENA's *comb, brush, makeup and robe,* PAULINE's *jacket and red headband, and* CORRINE's *bag. She goes into snippets of the characters' speech*)

Adrede iba a bailar![2] (*Dancing around the room singing "El Rancho Grande"*) . . . I didn't care with who! (*Sitting down and hunching over, she becomes* TOMASA) I'm going to live to a ripe old age! (*Then sitting up straight, as herself*) My name is María Isabel González . . . (*Sighing*) When people tell me it's an easy time to be a woman, me río! As far as I'm concerned, when you're a woman, no time is easy. And when you're an artist, it's worse. Those born rich suffer as much as those born poor. But I'm not complaining. I might worry, but then I either sing or pray or laugh. Ríanse, as my gramita used to say.[3] And love! One of the greatest powers we all possess is the ability to love.

(*Getting up and beginning to set the altar*) Just last week I was cleaning up in here, you can imagine what it was like, and I ran across a letter from my mom. She's been dead for years. I sat down and read it, and it was as if she was talking to me. Isabel, Isabel, what are your priorities? Mija, you need some lipstick, you're so pale, are you wearing a bra? It was as though she was right here next to me telling me how much she loved me, how proud of me she was, and to keep on working.

(ISABEL *is moved, she pauses in her work. She goes and lights a candle for her mother's spirit*) When I feel alone, I remember behind me stand my grandmother, my mother, all the women who have come before me. Their spirits are always near, watching over me, guiding me, constantly teaching me. Today, when I went out for groceries, I heard one woman telling another, "La vida es una canción."[4] I could have sworn I heard my grama's voice. And then I thought: this woman is a thread that connects me to all

[1] Good morning and God bless you, sister.
[2] I was determined I was going to dance!
[3] Laugh, as my grandmother used to say.
[4] Life is a song.

women, everywhere. Wherever I go, I *know* the women. I know their deepest joys and pains.

(*Setting things on chest*) Jesusita, Minda, Esperanza, the others . . . They are familiar to me. On the surface, their lives are really different from mine. And yet, when I look at them, I see a light shining from and through them, and in that light I recognize my gramita, my mom, my sister, my friends and myself as well. I understand the passion of their lives. I see that it has made them strong, patient and faithful. They have come full circle to that place of peace we all move toward when we pray or sit in silence.

(*Stretching*) Ay . . . Look, I've really been talking, qué habladero![5] I have to get back to work, I have a deadline, excuse me . . .

(*Becoming* JESUSITA, *she puts on the collar* JESUSITA *wears. Throughout the play,* ISABEL *will become the characters, donning costume pieces and assuming the posture and voice of characters. All is done on stage, without a curtain, in full view of the audience. Each character should have one or two costume pieces that identify them. A basic black turtleneck with pants and skirt should serve as the primary costume*)

Jesusita

(*A mouse-like spinster, she speaks in a high reedy voice, with a certain lisp. She runs a store of curiosities, sells thread and needles and little yellow candles that are so old that when you lift them, they break. The store has ceased to really serve the public, but* JESUSITA *would not dare think of closing it. She wears her funny little hat, green tennies and dusts as she talks*)

Buenos días le dé Dios, Hermana Dioses. Muchísimas gracias por la manzanilla que me trajo la última vez. Siéntese, hermana, a platicar.[6] Not too many customers yet. Todo ha cambiado. ¿Por qué? La gente se levanta tarde, come demasiado, y nobody va a misa anymore, y por qué? EL H-B-O. HBO! La television! Pues sí, tengo cable, falta de esa novela desgraciada, *Seducción.*[7] (*Pause*)

Oh, I been pretty good. I'm not dead yet, gracias a Dios! (*Sighing*) People don't need different colors of thread anymore, nobody sews. And ahora nadie usa dedales![8] My mother always used a thimble. She thought anyone who didn't was a fool. One time in this very room, bárbara, she was working on a dress and she yelled to me, "Jesusita, ven pronto!" She had stabbed herself with a small needle and it was moving up her arm into the blood-

---

[5] . . . boy, can I talk!

[6] Thank you very much for the chamomile tea you brought the last time you were here. Sit down, Sister, let's talk.

[7] Everything's changed. Why? People wake up late, they eat too much, and no one goes to mass anymore. Why? . . . Television! Well, I have cable [TV] too, but it's because of that cursed soap opera, *Seduction*. (*Note: Here she's rationalizing why she has television and cable.*)

[8] Now no one uses thimbles.

stream. Oh, yes, she finally got it out. And then she sat down and cried. If she'd lost it, it would have gone through her blood, gone to her heart, and killed her! Bárbara! Have you heard of anything? That was mamá.

(*Looking around*) Rael's Tienda de Abarrotes.[9] Someday it will just disappear. If I'd gotten married . . . Oh, tuve chansa. His name was Prudencio Sifuentes. El Ermitaño,[10] they called him, for his role in *Los Pastores*. Oh, I was too busy with the store. Finally, Prudy moved to Santa Barbara, California. And about a year later, he drowned in the ocean. Bárbaro! No, no, no tuve ganas de casarme con él. Era muy chapito.[11] His ears were small as well. I could never marry anyone with ears smaller than my own. Ni lo permite mi Dios![12] Oh, I missed having children, but then I started with the Foster Children's Program. They became my kids. Rosella, she lives in Roswell, Rini's in Tucumcari, and Donacio's a dentist in Downey, California. All the kids . . . They call me mamá and everything. And they always send me cards pa' Crismes, you know?

(*Confidentially*) Pero ya me cansé.[13] I'm ready to devote more time to the church. I take communion to the prisoners and up to the Four Directions Nursing Home. Vi a la hermana Tomasa. Bárbara![14] She don't look too good, that's what I say. Tenía una peluca güera.[15] She was never a blond! But what can you say? (*With resignation*) I'm too busy with God to be worrying about people.

(*Hedging a bit*) La muchachita?[16] She's still with me. Pobrecita Minda. Me da lástima con ella. Es que her father wants her back, ni lo mande Dios.[17] And Magdalena says she'll take her, ni lo mande Dios. And she can't stay here, ni lo mande Dios! (*Crossing herself*) Pobrecita niña,[18] all she really wants is a mother and to be close to God, if God's not a man! (*High, nervous laughter*).

No, I never married . . .

(*Rearranging things on the altar*) ¿No necesita unas velas, hermana? Cera de abeja.[19] They don't make them like they used to, you know?

(*Sighing*) Nobody buys thread anymore. Or buttons. Or needles.

(*Swatting at a fly*) ¡Malditas moscas![20] Oh, I understand, hermana, you have to go. Lleve esta velita a la hermana Tomasa,[21] if she ain't dead yet,

---

[9] Rael's Grocery Store.

[10] The hermit.

[11] Unbelievable . . . I don't want to marry him, he's too short.

[12] My God won't allow it!

[13] But I've grown tired.

[14] I saw Sister Tomasa. Unbelievable!

[15] She had on a blond wig.

[16] The little girl?

[17] I feel sorry for her. It's that her father wants her back, God forbid.

[18] Poor girl.

[19] Don't you need some candles, sister? Bee's wax.

[20] Damned flies!

[21] Take this candle to Sister Tomasa . . .

pobrecita. El cancer. I'll see you next week at the Third Order Meeting of Las Franciscanas! Vaya con Dios, Hermana María. ¡Adiós!

(*Going back to altar to light a candle and rearrange a little bit more*) Pobrecito Prudy! Como me contaba del amor de California . . . del mar de California.[22] (*She shakes her head as a look of fondness, sadness, almost regret comes to her face*) No era porque era chapito . . . not really . . . eran esas orejitas![23] Pobrecito Prudy. Que mi madrecita lo tenga descansando en paz. . . .[24]

(ISABEL *sheds* JESUSITA *and becomes* ESPERANZA)

Esperanza

(*A plain-looking, tired woman; she goes to the altar and lights a candle immediately*)

No tengo mucho tiempo, Madrecita.[25] I have to rush back to work. I just came to check the mail and to eat lunch. (*Making the sign of the cross*) You know my needs better than I do myself. Take care of José, bring him home and help him to stop drinking. Take care of Isabel, ¡ay Isabel, her and her art! She's a wonderful girl, a beautiful woman, Madrecita. Make her strong like all the other women of her family. Take care of everyone else in the family, tía Panchita, Reis and the twins, my ahijado,[26] el Jerry . . .

(*A bit sadder*) Take care of all my hijitos who are already with you in Heaven. El Hector, pobrecito, ni tuvo chansa para vivir.[27] Take care of all the others who were killed in Vietnam, and all the others who suffered from it, like my José, who never got over that terrible war. Take care of todos los alcohólicos y los que sufren de las drogas y mueren de las drogas! Take care of our men and all the women who love them. ¡Cuídalos, Madrecita! Lift them to your loving heart, hold them in the palm of your hand, have mercy on them.

(*Tiredly, to La Virgencita*) Ay, sometimes I'm so tired I can't even pray. All I can do is sit. Sit and be quiet.

(*Getting up and opening a can of peas with a can opener*) I don't have much time, excuse me, Madrecita. Voy a comer mi lonche.[28] Con su permiso, mi Reina.[29]

---

[22] Poor Prudy. How he used to tell me of his love of California . . . of the ocean.
[23] It wasn't because he was short . . . it was those little ears!
[24] May my Holy Mother [the Virgin Mary] keep him resting in peace.
[25] I don't have much time, Holy Mother.
[26] Aunt Pancha . . . my son-in-law
[27] Hector, poor thing, he didn't have a chance to live.
[28] I am going to eat my lunch.
[29] Excuse me, my queen.

(ISABEL *transforms into the character of* MINDA, *a seven-year-old girl who sits on the floor playing with her doll and blanket*)

Minda

I have a little friend. Her name is uh . . . uh . . . Jennifer . . . Marie . . . something. Something anglo. She's seven-years-old, like me. No! She's not fat! She's real pretty. It's not me, I told you, it's my friend, Jennifer Marie. Anyway, it can't be me 'cause she has a mom. And a real father. And she doesn't live where there's garbage and broken beer bottles all over the place! She doesn't have to take short-cuts through Mrs. Ruiz' faded towels and stinky baby diapers or Mr. Ruiz' baggedy-raggedy shorts on the line! (*Giggling hysterically*)

(*Whispering confidentially to the doll and pulling the blanket over her and the door to make a tent*) Now, you can't tell anyone, okay? This is a secret for always and forever. You can't even tell God, understand? Jennifer's father hurts little girls. He beats her and does ugly, dirty things to her. What he does is bad! And he told her if she ever told anybody, he would kill her! (*Crying hysterically*)

(*Dramatic change into the present and herself*) I never even told God. I didn't even know God until Miss Rael took me to church.

(*Does switch-over to* JESUSITA RAEL, *with a high voice*) ¡Minda, Minda, Minda, buenos días le dé Dios!

(*Back to herself*) I can't talk to Miss Rael. Her voice is too high and her bones stick out, real sharp! And she never even had a baby! But I can talk to you, mi'jita. You're my best bestest friend! And I can talk to Magdalena, the neighbor. She tells me, "Don't be afraid of your body, Minda. All women are the same that way. It's beautiful! A gift from God the Mother. The female thing won't kill you, or your mother being dead. All things have to die. It's natural."

(*To her doll*) Come on, let's you and me and Miss Rael go to church. (*Pretending to be in church*) Shhh. We have to sit back here with the other old ladies and Miss Rael.

(*Looking around and daydreaming. She then becomes attentive and begins to imitate the way the old ladies sing*) Bendito, bendito, bendito sea Dios. Los ángeles cantan y alaban a Dios.[30] Los ángeles cantan y alaban a Dios . . .

(*Daydreaming again and having a conversation with the doll*) I want a dog. But Miss Rael says, "No. It will only die." Oh, let it! It's natural! Ay, ouch! Don't pinch me. I wasn't daydreaming! I know I have a lot to be grateful for! I'm not fat and ugly! (*To doll*) Miss Rael always pinches me when I talk in church . . .

(*Pointing*) See God on the altar? He's got big black strange eyes and silver lightning coming out of his head. Look the other way!

---

[30] Blessed be God. The angels sing and praise God.

(*Pointing the other direction*) And that's the God Mother. She's not old and ugly. She's real pretty! I never had a mother, except when I was born and was real sick and almost died. That was when the tubes were in my mouth and nose and the doctors said, "She'll probably die. If she lives, don't expect much."

(*Suddenly changing, becoming violent with the doll*) You're retarded, retarded! That's what Jennifer's father says to her all the times.

(*Back to earlier conversational tone*) The funny thing is that I lived and my mother died. (*Pause*) Her name was Carmen.

(*Seeing that* RAEL *is after her again, she prays fervently*) Dear Mother of God, save me from the fires of Miss Rael's Hell! I don't want to be afraid of the dark or of God the Man, or spiders, or tunnels that never end, or having babies . . . I want to be a mother someday, when I'm not afraid anymore, okay?

(*As if saying to herself, "Is this a prayer?"*) I wish I had a mother . . .

(*An idea just dawned on her, with a sense of wonder*) Mary, if you become my mother, I'll become a nun, and then a saint . . .

(*Getting pinched again*) Ouch! Maybe I won't become a saint . . . Dear mother God, let me forget everything! Everything! Except love . . . like in a fairy tale . . .

Magdalena

(*A youngish-looking woman in her late forties comes out carrying a makeup case, fixing her face and hair as she speaks to someone behind the screen*)

¡Duérmete, mi amor![31] It's still early, about four. I'm sorry I woke you up. Yes, I'm going. I told you I was. ¿Por qué no vas conmigo?[32] You promised me before Johnny was born that you would climb with me every year as a thank you to la Virgencita. That was seven kids and no marriage license ago!

(*Laughing coyly*) Okay so I'm plenty married now! When you left, I climbed to bring you back. And one year I climbed for el Señor Gallegos, el vecino.[33] It just happened, Mikey, like I told you. Una noche se presentó.[34] His wife, Chila, se estaba muriendo de cancer.[35] He was lonely. Me dio lástima con él.[36] No, I didn't tell him about the baby. He was on the school board, pobrecito. Then there was the climb for el Compadre Juanito.[37] When his wife, Dora, left him with the four kids to run off with his cousin, Humberto, he didn't know what to do. So I told them to move in. There's

[31] Go to sleep, my love.
[32] Why don't you come with me?
[33] the neighbor
[34] One night he showed up.
[35] was dying of cancer.
[36] I felt sorry for him.
[37] . . . Godfather [or a close friend] John.

always room for more. Don't worry about it, Mikey. She missed him and they got back together. They're very happy now. I climbed for them that year. And then one year I climbed for el poeta, Maggie's sobrino, from Portales. Se llamaba Toribio.[38] He was a poet looking for construction work. He didn't have no money and I was getting food stamps, so no problem. But you were the only one I loved, Miguel, you know that!

(*Continuing with conviction*) And then I climbed for all my kids. Yes, and for all their fathers too. They were all good men. And now you've come back. So today I'm climbing for you. And for the baby . . . (*Patting her stomach*)

(*Falling over imaginary shoes*) ¡Ay, Mikey, mi amor, cuidado donde pones los zapatos![39] It's so good to have you home. Put your shoes under the bed, where you used to keep them? ¡Cómo te extrañé! ¿Por qué no me llamaste?[40] Why didn't you at least write? They don't let you write in prison. Duérmete, mi amor[41] . . . Okay, okay, it's all right.

(*Putting on coat and hat*) There's food in the icebox. Me and the kids will be back tonight after the mass. I have to go, mi amor! Es mi manda.[42] Mikey, mi amor, I love you so much. You don't know. I love life so much! I just want to help people. That's the way it is with me. I see the good in all the men. Me dio lástima con el señor Gallegos. Y también con el compadre Juanito. Y especialmente con el poeta, pobrecito, ni tenía barbas, lleno de espinillas.[43] But you're the only one I've ever loved, mi amor! You gonna stay? I'll get my food stamps anyday. When the kids get bigger I'll get a job. The rent is low. We'll get back on our feet, mi amor, you'll see. (*With resignation*) We'll stay together, you and me and the kids.

(*Going to the altar*) Sometimes when I think about you, mi amor, and then I look at you, I love you so much I want to cry. Que la Virgencita me perdone.[44] She understands everything. Everything. And she forgives everything. That's why I have to go on this pilgrimage today, mi amor, that's why . . .

Tomasa

(*A 78-year-old woman wearing a tousled blond wig and hospital gown, walking with a cane; she sits*)

¡Ay, Esperanza, qué bueno que viniste a visitarme![45] Take me home,

---

[38] the poet, Maggie's nephew . . . His name was Toribio.
[39] . . . be careful where you put your shoes.
[40] How I missed you! Why didn't you call me?
[41] Go to sleep, my love.
[42] Religious vow, or promise.
[43] I felt sorry for Mr. Gallegos. And also for Juanito. And especially for the poet, poor thing. [His face] full of pimples, and he didn't even have a beard.
[44] May the Virgin Mother forgive me.
[45] Oh, Esperanza, how nice of you to come visit me!

hermanita, please! (*Starts to cry but quickly snaps out of it.*) You never come to see me anymore! Oh, you came last Thursday. We went outside and sat in the sun . . .

(*With terror*) What's going to happen to me? (*Petulantly*) I want to go home!

(*Seriously*) Can I walk? What's today? Saturday? Already? Crismes? That's a long time off. I'll be dead by then.

(*Angrily*) I don't want to go outside! We just came in! ¡Acuéstame, por favor![46] They never do what I tell them. Where's Ida, she's the one who put me here.

(*Crying again*) Oh, I'm better. Except for my head. I can't think anymore. (*Patting her hair*) Well, at least I still have all my hair.

(*Testily*) No, no quiero nada.[47] Today's Monday. That's right. I forgot. What did you say today was? My daughter Ida never comes to see me. She's got her family, I'm in the way. (*Hopelessly*) ¿Qué me va a pasar?[48]

(*Planning*) Llévame al banco.[49] How much money do I have? It should be enough to get me out of here. I'm moving to San Diego. Ahí tengo unas primitas.[50] Gussie and Tenoria.

(*Suddenly deflated, crying*) ¿Por qué no me he muerto? Diosito, Diosito, ten misericordia.[51] I know, I know. It's not my time. I'm going to live to a ripe old age. That's what Elena, la flaquita,[52] tells me. I don't feel old. 78? I'm not that old!

(*Angry again, hitting the air*) ¡Acuéstame! I want to go to sleep and never wake up!

(*Suddenly getting a dreamy, faraway look, she softens with wonder*) ¿Mamá? ¿Mamá? ¿Comó está?

(*Quietly, sober*) Oh, that's right. She's dead. It's my head! What time is it? ¿Ya te vas? ¿Tan pronto?[53] You're the only one who comes to see me. You and la monjita ratoncita Rael.[54] She brings me communion. Antes que te vayas, ¡acuéstame![55]

(*As if grabbing someone's arm*) ¿Qué me va a pasar? I'm going to live to a ripe old age. That's what la gordita,[56] Elena, tells me. Dale gracias a la Hermana Rael por las velitas. Vuelve, Esperanza.[57]

---

[46] Put me in bed, please!
[47] No, I don't want anything.
[48] What's going to happen to me?
[49] Take me to the bank.
[50] I have a couple of cousins there.
[51] Why haven't I died? God, God have mercy on me.
[52] the skinny one.
[53] You're leaving already? So soon?
[54] . . . mousey-looking nun Rael.
[55] Before you go, put me in bed!
[56] the fat one.
[57] Thank Sister Rael for the candles. Come again, Esperanza.

(*Alone now, she sinks into remembering*) Esperanza! Esperanza, I forgot to tell you. ¡Mamá me vino a visitar![58]

(*Like a little girl, she sits up with her eyes shining beautifully*) Me acuerdo de mi altarcito. Con la Virgencita tan bella. Con su vestido de blanco y su manta de azul. Su carita tan linda, su boca cantando.[59]

(*She gets up, lights a candle and sings*) ¡Oh, María, Madre mía! El consuelo del mortal, ampárame y guíame a la patria celestial.[60]

(*Watching the candle and Virgencita in wonder for a while, she breaks out of her reverie and turns to her mother, who she imagines is next to her*) ¡Mamá! ¡Mire que bonita se ve la Virgen![61]

Juana

(*A 56-year-old factory worker, a nativa. She wears goggles, a scarf, apron, and holds a pair of pantyhose in her hands*)

En esta fábrica hay mexicanos, anglos, vietnameses, latinos, and everybody else ain't got a job. Si no fuera pantyhose, it would be boots or jeans or moccasins . . . or turquoise jewelry . . . algo pa' los turistas.[62]

(*Motioning*) The work starts back there. Little by little it moves to me. I do the inside seams. People don't like you to talk about pantyhose. ¡Yo ni las uso![63]

(*Pausing to place a bingo chip on an imaginary card on a nearby table*) I used to work in the hospital, in the kitchen throwing away the garbage. ¡Ese era trabajo![64] I had to wear unas botitas verdes, de plástico,[65] como los niños. ¡Todos creían que yo era doctora![66] When I told them I worked in the kitchen, their faces got sad . . .

(*Suddenly animated as she places a chip on the imaginary bingo card*) Bingo! Bingo! B-12. Over here! Bingo! I just won ten bucks! A month ago I won fifty! See, we have this bingo goes on all the time. "Something for you to think about," nos dice el Señor Wiley, el patrón. No es de estas partes.[67] Ever notice they always bring in the boss from other places? Me conoce. Me dice,[68] "Wuanita, how you doing this fine day?" "Oh, pretty good, pretty good," le digo. "Mucho bueno," me dice. Le gusta hablar

---

[58] Mama came to visit me!

[59] I remember my little altar with the beautiful statue of the Virgin, with her white dress and blue blanket, her face so pretty, her mouth singing.

[60] Oh, Mary, my Mother, consolation of mortals, protect and guide me to my celestial home.

[61] Mother! Look, how pretty the Virgin looks!

[62] . . . something for the tourists.

[63] And I don't even use them!

[64] That was work!

[65] those green plastic boots.

[66] like the ones children wear. Everyone thought I was a doctor!

[67] says Mr. Wiley, the boss. He's not from around here.

[68] He knows me. He says, . . .

español.[69] "Wuanita, you're the best inside seamer I've got. Keep up the good work and one of these days, one of these days, I'm gonna raise you . . . to $3.50!!" "Oh, thank you, Mr. Wiley, thank you!" "Okey, dokey, Wuanita, now git along . . ."

(*Suddenly a change takes place and she becomes quiet, moving in slow motion as she begins to remove her goggles, apron, etc.*) One of these days, the noise gonna stop! It won't be so long. Tengo cincuenta y seis años.[70] 56 years of my hands working. Making tortillas, changing pañales, burning dyes and lyes, boiling water and stabbing needles.

(*Pause*) Mi abuelita me enseñó a trabajar.[71] She taught me the healing life of the herbs, what to do with cota and osha, como sobar con aceite[72] while praying. Cuando se murió,[73] I took her ashes to the pueblo and I scattered them in the wind. She was the only person I had in the world. Estas manos son mi herencia.[74]

(*She has been redressing herself by taking off the scarf and putting on a medicine wheel necklace. Now she lights cedar and picks up macaw feathers*) I remember my abuelita telling me, "Acuérdate que eres india, y que la Virgen María, la mestiza, es tu madre querida.[75] The Mother's Mother is your mother as well. Never forget that. You are a child of many worlds: say your prayers, praise the sun, glorify the moon, and send your spirit in the wind." (*She ends with a chant, singing to the Virgen and the four directions*)

Hey oh hey, hey ya no
Hey oh hey, hey ya no
Hey oh hey
Hey oh hey.

Pauline

(*Transformation to a 14-year-old girl who sits facing away from the audience responding to an imaginary teacher's questions and demands*)

(*Facing the back wall*) Pauline Mendoza.
(*Turns partly towards the audience*) Pauline Mendoza.
(*Turns full face to the audience*) Pauline Mendoza.
(*Mad*) Pauline Mendoza!
(*Sulkily*) Taos.

---

[69] He likes to speak Spanish.
[70] I am fifty-six years old.
[71] My grandmother taught me to work.
[72] how to rub [the skin] with oil while praying.
[73] When she died.
[74] These hands are my inheritance.
[75] Remember that you are Indian, and the Virgin Mary, the colored [or mixed] one, is your loving mother.

(*Told to say everything again loudly, she yells out*) Pauline Mendoza. Taos. 6th Grade. Fourteen years-old.

(*Bitterly*) I'm a freak.

(*Naming things she likes, staccato-like*) Boys. Cars. Makeup. My leather bracelet. My red headband. Black T-shirts. My jean jacket. My hair cut long in back and short on the sides and front. Tattoos. Can I sit down now?

(*In response to a question*) I made all the tattoos. Myself.

(*Withdrawn*) I'm working on one now. No, you can't see. Can I go back to my desk? Okay, okay. So what do you want to know for anyway? I already told you what I liked! I don't want to be nothin'! My teacher, Mrs. Espinoza, makes me sit behind the screen, in the corner, facing the wall. I'm jittery, she says. Hell, so I work on my tattoos. Nothing better to do. I can't barely read or write. I'm dumb. I'm a freak. Don't yell at me!

(*Yelling*) She always yells at me! It's embarrassing!

(*Trying to get back to her seat*) I've got work to do, okay? (*Sits*) 9 × 8? How the hell should I know? Okay, okay. (*Stands*) Yeah, I like my mom. She's pretty young for a mom. I hate school. I hate homework! Thinking? I hate thinking! Maybe I could like it. You want me to read that book? I can't read the whole thing! Don't you understand? I thought substitutes are supposed to know everything! I'm dumb. I'm a freak. I sit in the corner all the time. Can I sit down now? (*Sits*) I been in 6th grade three years. I'm going to move next year. (*Stands*) Okay, okay.

(*Picking up book, trying to read*) Thee . . . his—hist—history of a . . . ah . . . a . . . p-e-o-p-l-e.

(*Angrily*) Yeah, I know the word people! Don't you, or what? The history of people . . . This is boring! People are boring. I don't know. I don't know. I can't read, I told you. I just can't. Can I sit down?

(*Exasperated*) You still want me to talk about myself? Mrs. Espinoza never makes me read out loud. She lets me sit in the corner and be quiet. That's all she wants from me. Yeah! I try to read in church . . . I try to read the prayer books. One . . . one . . . one . . . ho—ly . . . that's as far as I get. I'm a freak even there. So I look at the statues and pictures and I feel better. A freak? What's a freak? A freak is someone who wears a you-know-what in the sixth grade. A freak is someone that has already started their you-know-what in the 6th grade. That's a freak!

(*Off-guard*) That? Oh, that's my tattoo. No. Oh, okay, since you asked. It's Our Lady of Guadalupe. It don't look like a lady on fire; that's rays of gold, stupid! Don't you know nothing? I just started working on it. Yeah, I told you, I go to church. Why do I like tattoos? I don't talk good. I don't think good. It's something cool. A picture like in church, you know, one . . . holy . . . okay . . . the history of a people, okay? Pictures, pictures!

(*Not so harsh now*) I'm working on my tattoos, back there see, where nobody bothers me. It's my art work. I'm working on my tattoos and my drawings. I'm gonna be an artist.

(*More confidentially, but still hard*) My girlfriend, Gloria, she says I'm changing. I don't want to go out and get rowdy and drunk all the time now. Ever since this lady came to our school. She made me stand up and talk.

She's an artist. Her name is Isabel Martínez. She's Chicana. I never known anybody . . . a lady and a chicana and an artist . . . It surprised me, you know?

(*Stands up straight and takes a deep breath as she moves to light the candle*) Pauline. My name is Pauline Mendoza. I do tattoos. And I draw. Next year I'm going to move to a new school. And someday . . . someday . . . I'm gonna be an artist!

Corrine

(*An aging, very tough bag-lady. She drags around a big and colorful bag which she empties on the floor. Throughout the scene she will put on clothing from the bag*)

Antes me importaban las cosas, pero ahora,[76] sss—I take every day as it comes. Some good, some pretty bad! Like the weather. If it looks like rain or snow, I head down to the Holy Bible Rescue Mission para agarrar mi espacio.[77] I stay there or at the Good Faith Shelter, or one of my other spots. Near the Interstate, that over-hang with the old colchón[78] . . . that's my bedroom! Or behind Bennie's La Paloma Bar, by the vents. No te apenes![79] No sweat! Rain or shine, Corrine got it covered, ésa![80] Ssss.

(*Taking a drink from her wine bottle in the bag*) I don't want your stupid pity, okay? I got enough problems of my own, you start worrying me about your shag rug and your color t.v. . . . I don't need it, okay? I had a family once . . . kids . . . the whole . . . But don't get me wrong, ésa, it's never as good as it looks. I got into writing bad checks. I needed things, you know? I got sent up. That was when they still had the women in the pinta in Santa.[81] Anyway, I was in my 30's ésa, and they took it all away—the kids, the house—and then el tonturio[82] went to live with his novia[83] in Belén. They all disappeared. Yeah, I tried to find them, but my family didn't want to have anything to do with me. So, I did my time. Met me my Sophia. Ay, Sophia, Sophia! ¡Que corazonada![84] We wanted to get married. We did, in our hearts. Later we got separated; she started seeing somebody else, you know? So, I said, okay, anyway, I was getting out. The kids in Belén, the jefita[85] in 'Burque, you think she's gonna welcome me back a la vecindad?

---

[76] Before, things were important to me, but now . . .
[77] to get my space.
[78] mattress.
[79] Don't you worry!
[80] girl!
[81] in the penitentiary in Santa [a city].
[82] the idiot.
[83] girlfriend.
[84] So impulsive!
[85] mother.

¡Tattoos hasta el copete! María and Jesús[86] on my knuckles, my hair dyed blond, my eyebrows shaved and then painted black . . . Una pinta jotita, no less. ¡Niel, ésa![87] Nobody wanted me back the way I was. So I took to the streets. Oh, yeah, I got me a little, here and there, you know, just enough to spend a night, take a shower, get some beer. But didn't last. I was getting old . . . that was over 20 years ago! Pero no te preocupes,[88] ésa, I got it covered!

(*Takes another swig*) Met this lady wanted me to take care of her jefito. Uh-ummmmm! He got this and that wrong with him. Used to be a big man, now look at him. Pobrecito, medio muerto.[89] Anyway, she tried to give me her mother's old clothes to wear. And I said, I don't want them, dammit! You keep your dead woman's things! You think because you're a Mexican with a little bit of money you can treat me like hell? I'm not your slave! Keep your damn job and house and clothes and car and leave me alone. I oughta report you to the authorities—IRA, INS, NBC, CBS—for cruelty to an old woman! I don't need your pity! They think they can give you the slop once they see you in the streets. ¡Qué va! Lo que necesitamos en este estado es una gobernadora como esa Madre Teresa, no?[90] Anyway, I left her holding the clothes and walked over to the Senior Citizens pa' mis enchiladas.[91] It was Friday and I decided to stick around for the baile.[92] Johnny and the Huipiles were playing. Siempre me ha gustado tirar chancla, ¿sabes?[93] Anyway, I went up to this cute viejita[94] to ask her to dance—that's all it was, I swear—y se puso medio weird.[95] So I went up to this dude then, adrede iba a bailar,[96] and I didn't care with who. The dance was over at 5:30 so I walked over to the Holy Bible to see what was happening, you know? It was too late. From there I went over to the Good Faith. ¡Estaba lleno![97] The mattress was gone and Bennie's was taken. So me fui al bus depot a ver a mi novela, *María de Nadie*.[98] And from there, I came over here. I thought maybe the padrecito[99] would let me sit in the portal . . . (*The actress may name any place she is performing*) ¿Quién sabe?[100]

---

[86] neighborhood? Tattoos up to my forehead! Mary and Jesus . . .
[87] A ———ing whore, no less. No bull, girl!
[88] But don't worry, I got it covered.
[89] Poor thing, he's half dead.
[90] Forget it! What we need in this state is a governor like Mother Theresa, right?
[91] for my enchiladas.
[92] dance.
[93] I've always liked to kick up my heels, you know?
[94] cute old woman.
[95] She got a little weird.
[96] I was determined to dance.
[97] It was full!
[98] So I went to the bus depot to see my soap opera, *Mary Who Belongs to No One*.
[99] the Father (priest).
[100] Who knows?

(*Goes over to the Virgencita to light a candle*) Mi Madrecita sabe, no? Me conoce.[101] She know that when Cory got it, she got it! And when she don't got it . . . ssss . . . it don't matter!

(*Fondly touches the face of the Virgencita*) Te debo,[102] eh, Madrecita? Next time.

(*Opening umbrella as she turns away*) Jesús y María . . . (*motioning to the tattoos on her knuckles that spell out these names*) I got it covered, ésa!

Isabel

(ISABEL *takes off* CORRINE's *clothes, putting them in the bag. She rearranges herself a bit; as herself, excited*)

All this time I've been thinking about what that lady at the grocery store said, about life being a song. Well, it's true. Life really is a song. ¡La vida es una canción! The song of childhood, the song of love, the song of parting, the song of death . . . Each of our lives is a song, or a prayer, like a novena.

(*Picking up some of the papers*) When life gets to be too much, I simply lift my hands to the Virgencita and the Heavens and I just pray—or sing! Or I sit quietly at my desk thinking about all the lives that pass before me. Sometimes I have to control myself from reaching out and grabbing someone . . .

(*Excited again*) And in total love and acceptance and friendship saying to them, "Sigue adelante, Hermana![103] Keep going forward! And keep on singing that unending song of love and life—in the fullest, strongest, most beautiful voice you have!"

(*Looking around with joy*) ¡Ay! Qué familia de mujeres, no?[104] What dreams! What hopes! It makes me want to sing!

(*Isabel sings "El Corrido de Las Mujeres."[105] After she finishes singing, she picks a few things and goes out, the pages still on the floor*)

[1987]

---

[101] My Holy Mother [the Virgin Mary] knows, right? She knows me.

[102] I owe you.

[103] Keep going forward, Sister!

[104] Wow! What a family of woman, don't you agree?

[105] "The sufferings of women."

Hospice
A Play in One Act

Pearl Cleage

CAST

Alice Anderson, *a black woman, age 47*
Jenny Anderson, *her daughter, age 30*

(The time is early morning. The set is a small house with upstairs and downstairs. The downstairs area is the main playing space, but the upstairs must be large enough to accommodate the bed, dresser with mirror, etc. This is ALICE's *bedroom.* JENNY *sleeps downstairs, but her bed is not visible. The house is small and crowded with the accumulated paraphernalia of a lifetime. The walls are full of framed photos of dead family. There is a couch with a comforter or soft, warm coverlet of some sort thrown across the back. A coffee table in front is piled high with newspapers, books, mail, papers and medicine bottles. On the table also is a vase holding a dozen beautiful, long-stemmed red roses. In the corner of the room is a small table piled almost as high as the coffee table with papers of various kinds. Somewhere in the middle is a typewriter. This is the area where* JENNY *writes. Tucked next to the table is a small suitcase. There is also a record player surrounded by record albums in and out of their covers. It is not an expensive, modern stereo, but has surprisingly good quality sound for its age and size. There are several brimming bookcases, some potted plants in various states of well-being, etc. The feeling of the room is cluttered, but not claustrophobic.*

An elaborately carved wooden cane sits against the record player. It is morning. Early. The light is that thin early morning kind that lets you know the sun is still undecided. As the lights come up, we hear the sound of a typewriter clicking away. The daughter, JENNY, *is hunched over her work. There is a floor lamp burning over her, creating a small pool of light in the eerie morning gloom.* JENNY *is thirty years old and very pregnant. She is frowning at the page which is still dangling from her typewriter. Re-reading over what she has just typed, she rips the page out and adds it to the small pile of crumpled balls at her feet. She shifts uncomfortably in her straight-back chair, and placing both hands behind her, arches her back, massaging the kinks out of her spine. She has been up for awhile. She shakes her head, and resumes her typing. Upstairs, her mother stirs and turns over in her bed restlessly with a soft moan. Hearing the noise,* JENNY *stops typing suddenly, listening. There is no immediate movement upstairs. She leans back to her work and is suddenly irritated by the fact that her very pregnant belly keeps her from getting as close to the table as she wants to. It is awkward. She tries turning sideways which means she has to type across her stomach. This is even more awkward. She tries several more approaches, but nothing works. During this process, the mother, ALICE, sits up slowly. She is in obvious pain. The upstairs light is always blue and dim. The impression is of silhouette and shadow. ALICE almost doubles over when she sits up, but straightens slowly and with great effort. She is thin and very frail. She is dying of cancer and her head is bald or very lightly fuzzed over with hair from chemotherapy. Her head should not be covered during the course of the play. Slowly and painfully her back straightens, her shoulders are square, and she finds the strength to push the covers off and slowly swing her legs over the side of the bed. She is wearing a long cotton nightgown with sleeves. The effort of sitting up has been very great. She remains motionless, seated on the edge of the bed.)*

JENNY (*loudly*): Well, damn! (*She has spoken more loudly than she meant to and looks guiltily upstairs. ALICE's head looks up in the direction of the curse. When there is no follow-up sound, she droops again. JENNY rises and goes to the bottom of the stairs, listening. No sound from ALICE. JENNY seems obviously relieved and crosses back to sit down at her typewriter. She pours herself a cup of tea from the pot near her. She sips the tea slowly, reading over the page that is in the typewriter and absentmindedly stroking her belly. Suddenly, JENNY drops the pages and begins to pant rapidly. She is having a contraction. When it ends, she checks her watch and crosses slowly to the phone. She is excited, but trying to contain it. She dials quietly.*) Alexis? I'm sorry! I know it's early, but I think it's happening! Yes! Since early this morning . . . No. I'm okay . . . Yes . . . Alright . . . I'll call you later.

(*Upstairs, ALICE stands quietly and walks to the dresser. It is an old-fashioned wardrobe with a full-length mirror on the door. She slowly takes off her nightgown and looks at herself naked in the mirror. We see her in shadow, but it is clear that she is gazing at her body. She folds the nightgown and lays it on the bed. Downstairs, JENNY finishes her tea and resumes typing. ALICE dresses slowly. Underwear, long socks, long skirt, sweater buttoned over it all. She slips on her shoes and makes her slow, painful, laborious way down the stairs. Holding the bannister tightly, she manages it, but the effort to do it with such a straight back and measured gait is immense. JENNY is typing loudly, continuously, and is thoroughly absorbed in her work. She does not look up when ALICE reaches the bottom of the stairs and stops to catch her breath. After a moment, ALICE turns to look at JENNY. JENNY, typing furiously, is oblivious. ALICE walks slowly over to the record player and puts the needle down on the record already on the turntable. It is not the first cut on the album, but she goes right to the spot as if she'd done it a thousand times before. With sudden and unexpected richness, the strains of Leontyne Price singing Puccini's "Madame Butterfly" fill the room. It is "Un Bel Di." JENNY jumps, startled out of her reverie by the blast of music. ALICE moves slowly but with determination over to the couch and sits down slowly, eyes closed, listening to the music and trying not to give in to the pain.*)

JENNY: God! You scared me! (*She moves to turn down the record. No word from* ALICE.) I thought I heard you get up. (JENNY *moves to her desk and carefully takes her work out of the typewriter and puts it face down on her desk. No response from* ALICE. *Her eyes are closed. She is listening intently.*) Are you okay? (ALICE *looks at her, and* JENNY *looks a little guilty at what could be a loaded question.*)

ALICE (*sarcastic*): Never been better. What were you cussing about?

JENNY: What? Oh. I'm sorry. I got stuck in the middle of something. You know . . .

ALICE: I didn't mean to startle you. I wasn't ready to wake up yet.

JENNY: Did you sleep much?

ALICE: No.

JENNY: Me neither. I try to lie on my back, but after awhile, she gets so heavy, I feel like I'm smothering.

ALICE: Well, it won't be long now, as they say.

JENNY: As they say. You want some tea? I just made it a few minutes ago. (ALICE *nods but doesn't answer. She is listening. Eyes closed.* JENNY *goes for the tea.*)

ALICE: Turn it up a little, will you? (JENNY *stops at the record player and turns it up. The rest of "Un Bel Di" is sung by Leontyne Price as* JENNY *gets the tea and* ALICE *leans back, eyes closed, while she listens.* JENNY *brings the tea, standing quietly until the song finishes and then turns off the record.* ALICE *sits motionless for a few moments as if in a trance, then comes back to reality and sits fully erect, eyes open, back in touch with the world around her.* JENNY *hands* ALICE *her tea and goes back to her work.*) Deadline?

JENNY: Not really. I told them I wasn't going home to work. I was going home to have a baby! (*Laughs at her own determination.*) I knew I could get away with it. They've never had a black film critic before. (*Evasively.*) I'm working on a couple of things, but it's hard when the only deadlines are self-imposed.

ALICE: I've always found those to be the hardest ones to miss. Well, I hope you're not blaming this lack of discipline on me. This is your choice, you know. Just keep that in mind.

JENNY: Don't worry. I accept full responsibility.

ALICE: You should.

JENNY: I have.

ALICE (*a beat*): I envy your confidence, but I wish it didn't make you start typing quite so early in the morning.

JENNY (*very controlled*): I think you completed your bad night by getting up on the wrong side of the bed this morning. I said I'm sorry I woke you. I'll say it again, only because I really mean it. I'm sorry.

ALICE: Me too.

(JENNY *rises, stretches, and sits down Indian style on the floor. She has the soles of her feet together and is bouncing her knees toward the floor, pushing them down closer with every bounce. She continues as she speaks, trying to make "neutral conversation.")*

JENNY: Daddy laughed when I first started doing movie reviews. He thought it was the perfect job for me. We used to go to the movies all the time. It gave us something neutral to talk about. No matter how many demonstrators the police locked up, Katherine Hepburn was going to marry Cary Grant; Norma Shearer was going to smile that sweet, sad smile; and Natalie Wood was gonna do Juliet all over Spanish Harlem.

ALICE (*putting her cup down with a smash, irritated by* JENNY's *chatter and her bouncing knees*): Do you have to talk about that now? (JENNY *stops abruptly and sits perfectly still.* ALICE *winces, recovers quickly, and looks fully into* JENNY's *face.)*

JENNY (*softly*): You ought to take something.

ALICE: Like what?

JENNY: Like something for the pain. There's no shame in that.

ALICE: Shame? (*She laughs and shakes her head.*) You've been watching too many of those Hollywood movies. No real sick person gives a damn about shame.

JENNY (*reaching for the medicine*): Then take something. (ALICE's *hand on hers stops her abruptly and with finality.*)

ALICE: I'm not myself when I take something.

JENNY: Then, by all means, take two.

ALICE: Touche, Sister. Touche! (JENNY *extends a pill and pours a small glass of water from a pitcher on the table.* ALICE *relents and swallows the pill and several more. She leans back again, waiting for the medication to take effect.* JENNY *lays down on her back near the couch and takes a long, deep Lamaze cleansing breath. She sucks in as much air as she can, holds it, then lets it out with an extended "whoosh!"* ALICE *opens her eyes and watches her.* JENNY *places her hands very lightly on either side of her stomach and breathes in and out, using the Lamaze method.*) What is that supposed to do?

(JENNY *holds up a finger to indicate that she has to complete the cycle before breaking the breathing to respond. She accelerates her breathing until she is panting rapidly and loudly. She stops after a minute, takes another deep cleansing breath, and lets it out.*)

JENNY: I've tried to explain all of this to you before. Why do you always wait until I'm in the middle of it to decide you want to listen?

ALICE: I'm easily distracted.

JENNY: It's supposed to minimize pain during labor. Redirect your energy or something.

ALICE: It's not your energy you're going to be concerned about. Trust me.

JENNY: No horror stories please! I can't stand it when people tell a pregnant woman horror stories, especially when I'm the pregnant woman!

ALICE: You've already heard all the horror stories I know. You've probably written them all down, too.

JENNY: You're very closemouthed with your stories, now that you mention it. Horror or otherwise.

ALICE: But the few gems I've let slip have not escaped your attention. You've probably made a few notes, just in case.

JENNY: I probably have. Would you mind?

ALICE: I'm not sure. I guess not. It's not like I'm going to use them for anything. You're not, are you?

JENNY: Going to write about you? (ALICE *waits but does not answer.*) Probably.

ALICE (*laughs*): God! That isn't really fair, is it? Why write about me now? Another dreary tale of a cancer-ridden mother attended by her long lost, but dutiful, daughter. The last days of Acid Alice. (*Laughs bitterly.*) Not the stuff best sellers are made of, Sister. Not this year. Not this color.

JENNY: I'll risk it.

ALICE: Don't fool yourself. You're not risking anything. It would probably be great therapy at the very least. (*A beat.*) I'm sorry. I'll be better in a minute. Soon as this pill decides which pain to concentrate on first. Is there any more of that sweet wine we had around here the other day?

JENNY: I stuck it away someplace.

ALICE: What are you writing about that makes you start cussin' so early in the morning?

JENNY (*hedging; sheepishly*): I'm trying to create a portrait of "the new woman."

ALICE: Is there such a creature?

JENNY (*laughingly*): That's the problem. I've read endless magazine articles about her. I've gone to conferences dedicated to her and read novels supposedly written by her about herself. But . . .

ALICE: Different costumes, Sister, same character.

JENNY: Voila!

ALICE: I can't stand the taste of sweet wine. I've never liked it, but it's the only kind that doesn't upset my stomach. Probably just another part of the penance. It's true, you know.

JENNY: What's true?

ALICE: About your not risking anything. It's true. I don't want you to fool yourself about that.

JENNY: I'll try not to. (JENNY *hands* ALICE *her wine and drinks some herself.*) Cheers! Getting pretty decadent around here, aren't we? It's not even nine o'clock in the morning, and we're already drinking wine.

ALICE (*draining her glass*): I'm your mother. It's okay.

JENNY (*suddenly concerned*): Is this okay for you to be drinking that with your medicine? (*She looks on the bottle label for possible warning label.*)

ALICE: Probably not. But what's the worst that can happen? It might kill me.

JENNY: I don't want all of our conversations to be about dying!

ALICE (*very quietly*): Then get out.

(JENNY looks stunned as if ALICE had struck her.)

JENNY *(looking for a neutral subject)*: What happened to all of those old Billie Holiday records you used to have?

ALICE *(still calm and quiet)*: I don't think you should be here, Jenny. I don't want you here.

JENNY: Your timing is lousy, mother. I'm having a baby any minute now, remember?

ALICE: I'm not asking you to go to the moon, Sister. It is my understanding that Prince Charming resides just across town.

JENNY: That's not open for discussion! And what difference does it make? I had a man and I don't have him anymore.

ALICE: I'm old-fashioned. I believe that if you ever have them, you always have them.

JENNY *(wearily)*: We're not all as lucky as you are.

ALICE: Alright, Sister. Let's get the ground rules straight. This is my house. It was left to me, not to you, by my mother, not yours! I own it. Lock, stock and mothballs, and I came a very long way to get here in time enough to die in it.

JENNY: I wouldn't have moved in here if I had known you would be coming. It never occurred to me. It's not like you have a history of dropping in.

ALICE: It's not like I have a history at all as far as you're concerned, so why not just go wherever it was you would have gone if it had occurred to you that I might drop in.

JENNY: I want to stay.

ALICE: No, you don't. You think you ought to stay. Nobody wants to bring a new baby home to a death house!

JENNY: This is not a death house! I'm here, and I'm very much alive!

ALICE: I'm looking for a hospice, Sister. A place to die in peace, not in pieces. *(A beat. Wearily.)* It's just that I get so tired . . .

JENNY *(very gently)*: I want to help you.

ALICE *(angered at her own vulnerability)*: Why are you alone?

JENNY: Because I choose to be.

ALICE: Nobody chooses to be alone. You might choose your sanity, or your freedom, or some other wild thing that results in your being alone, but that's the fallout. The unavoidable consequences. Not the choice.

JENNY: Why can't you let me help you?

ALICE: You're not here to help. You're here to hide.

JENNY: I haven't got any reason to hide. I'm not ashamed of anything.

ALICE: Well, that's something we have in common. Shamelessness.

JENNY: I want to make the best of it.

ALICE: The best of *this*?

JENNY: The best of the time we have together.

ALICE: That's not one of my strong points, making the best of it.

JENNY: It's my specialty . . .

ALICE: You want to make a fairy tale out of it! You want me to tell you the secret of life and give you my motherly blessing. You want me to make up for twenty years of silence in two weeks. You want the two of us to play mother and daughter.

JENNY (*hurt and angry*): We *are* mother and daughter! (*Frustrated and confused.*) This is crazy! This doesn't make any sense!

ALICE: Is it supposed to make sense?

JENNY: Isn't it? I'm not a child anymore! We are two grown women!

ALICE: My mother used to tell me that once she was sure I understood what being grown meant, she'd never have to worry about me again.

JENNY: Is that why you came here? To see if I was grown?

ALICE: No. To see if I was. (*A beat.*) I'm dying, Sister. I'm only forty-seven years old, and I'm dying. I don't have the energy to figure out what you need to know and tell it to you.

JENNY: What are you talking about?

ALICE: You've been sitting around with that hopeful look on your face ever since I got here. You want too much, Sister.

JENNY: I don't want anything from you! You're my mother, and I'm your daughter. Isn't that enough?

ALICE: Yes, you are my daughter. (*A beat. The medication and the wine make her a little drowsy.*) My very own baby daughter. (*A beat.*) I'd like to have been better at this, Sister. But I just don't have any energy left for it now. I need all my energy for myself. I have to pay very close attention to what's happening up here. (*Taps her temple lightly.*)

JENNY: I understand . . .

ALICE (*sarcastic*): Do you?

JENNY: I think I do. (*She resumes her Lamaze exercises quietly.*)

ALICE: Well, then, you don't need any advice from me. You've got everything under control here, Sister. You've got it all organized. You've found a way to redirect your energies and feel no pain. You've even taken the guessing out of boys and girls.

JENNY: It's safer, that's all. I just wanted to be careful since she's my first one.

ALICE: It's a violation.

JENNY: No, mother. Nothing so dramatic as that. It's a simple test that lets you know in advance if your baby is going to have two heads and by the way reveals the gender. It just gives Alexis a little more information to work with. There's a certain amount of risk in having a baby when you're as old as I am.

ALICE: I can't tell you anything about that. You and my eighteenth birthday arrived neck and neck. Is thirty late? Women used to have babies from nine to ninety.

JENNY: It's late for a first one. What are you talking about anyway? (*Laughs.*) You sound like a pioneer woman. "Nine to ninety."

ALICE: It's all different now. Your doctor doesn't even sound like a doctor.

JENNY: Alexis?

ALICE: How can you call your doctor Alexis?

JENNY: That's her name, mother. Don't act so shocked. You're not so old that ought to shock you.

ALICE: No, I guess not. (*A beat.*) I don't even know if the doctor who delivered you had a first name. Dr. Stewart. I never heard anybody call him anything else. Young Dr. Stewart. That was it.

JENNY: "Young Dr. Stewart" . . . sounds like a soap opera doctor.

ALICE: He only delivered babies at the Catholic hospital. The whole time I was in labor with you I had to look at all these bleeding crucifixes. Nails in the palms, a sword in the side, and a great big bleeding valentine right in the middle of his chest.

JENNY: Want some more wine?

ALICE: No. Yes, I guess so. I'm on to you, Sister. You think I'll get high and reveal those secrets you think I'm guarding so closely.

JENNY: No, I don't. I'm hoping you'll get a little high and remember where you put those Billie Holiday records.

ALICE (*irritated*): They're down there with the rest of the records, or they should be. Where else would I put them? Upstairs in my room? It's been awhile since I was in any condition to be playing Billie Holiday in my bedroom!

(JENNY *rummages through the records looking for Billie Holiday.*)

JENNY: I told someone once that the music of Billie Holiday ran through my early life like a leitmotiv.

ALICE: What did he say?

JENNY: Why do you assume I was talking to a man?

ALICE: It's a seduction line, Sister. I'm not that sick. What did he say?

JENNY: He said, "What's a leitmotiv?"

(*They both laugh.*)

ALICE: You know what your father said when you were born?

JENNY: What?

ALICE: I thought he might be disappointed because you weren't a boy, so I said I'd heard that sometimes kings divorce their wives if the firstborn is female. And he laughed and shook his head. "Not in my tribe," he said. "Not in my tribe."

JENNY (*delighted*): He never told me that!

ALICE: It's not a man's story. That's a story women tell each other. (*A beat.*) You see how you're looking at me? You're doing it again! I shouldn't have told you anything! It's only going to make you think you were right about those secrets. Forget it, Sister! It's only the way this medicine (*holding up the wine*) and this medicine (*taps medication bottle*) make my mind wander. There are no secrets. (*A beat.*) Well, maybe one.

JENNY: And what's that?

ALICE: That there are no secrets! (*A beat.* ALICE *is exhausted. She closes her eyes.*) How was it . . . for your grandmother?

JENNY: I think the memory loss was the worst part, for her and for me. She thought the nurse's aides were her daughters. Once when I went to visit, two of them were helping her pick out the earrings she was going to wear that day. She had about five pairs spread out on the sheet, and they were talking as seriously as if she had been getting ready for a night at the opera. (*A beat.*) Sometimes she would make me sit right in front of her and hold my face in her hands and look real hard. (*A beat.*) Sometimes she would remember that I was her granddaughter. Sometimes she could remember my name, but all of that went after awhile.

ALICE: What did they decide?

JENNY: Decide about what?

ALICE: The earrings.

JENNY: A pair of carved gold hoops with ram's heads. They were so heavy they pulled her earlobes down long. Stretched them out like a Watusi woman. She laughed when they held up a mirror so she could see herself. "There now," she said. "That's better."

ALICE: I gave her those.

JENNY: I wondered what she was doing with earrings like that.

ALICE: She used to tell me that the only women who wore big gold hoops in their ears were gypsies or prostitutes.

JENNY: She kept tossing her head so they would bump against her neck. They were very beautiful.

ALICE: When I sent them, I wrote and told her she was too prim ever to be mistaken for a gypsy and too old to be mistaken for a prostitute, so I thought it was safe for her to wear them. She wrote me back and said she was still my mother, and some things didn't change.

JENNY: God! I wish I knew what those things were!

ALICE (*sarcastic, but gently*): Oh, you know, Sister. The right way and the wrong way of doing things. What makes a "lady" and what does not.

JENNY (*finds the record*): Well, here's the only Lady that matters . . . in full gardenia!

ALICE: Don't play that now!

JENNY: Why not? (ALICE *does not respond. A beat.*) When she died, the paper said it was a drug overdose, and you were furious. You told me it wasn't the drugs that killed her. She died because she had to feel everything. Every time. You said nobody could live that way. Not for long.

ALICE: I was wrong, Sister. It's the only way you can tell you're still alive. (*A beat.*) Your father never liked Billie Holiday.

JENNY: I know. He said she made him feel lonesome.

ALICE: He wasn't the only one. You know she had a song that they made them stop playing on the radio because every time they did, the suicide rate in the city would go through the ceiling.

JENNY: Which one was that?

ALICE: "Gloomy Monday." Is it on there?

JENNY (*checks the label*): Yep.

ALICE: Well, don't play it! Lord knows we don't need any additional depression around here.

JENNY: What do you want to hear?

ALICE: How about a poem or two?

JENNY (*startled, covering*): I'm a journalist. You're the poet, remember?

ALICE: There's no journalist in the world who gets up at six in the morning to work. Journalists work late at night. Poets work at dawn. Don't fool yourself.

JENNY: That's the second time you've said that this morning.

ALICE: If I say it three times, believe me. That probably means it's good advice.

JENNY (*hesitantly*): Well, I have been working on something new.

ALICE (*raising eyebrow*): You're writing poems now?

JENNY (*nervously, fingering the pages*): Well . . . sometime . . . I hardly ever show them to anybody though. They can't help comparing mine to yours. (*She laughs ruefully.*) You're a hard act to follow.

ALICE: Then don't try it. And on second thought, don't read anything to me either. If I'm a tough act, I'm probably an impossible audience. Where's Butterfly?

JENNY (*disappointed*): Again?

ALICE: Indulge me. If you're going to stay and keep watch at my death bed, the least you can do is indulge me.

JENNY: I should have told that kid Puccini ran through my life like a leit motiv.

ALICE: No. That would only have added insult to injury.

JENNY: I used to be so embarrassed when you played this stuff.

ALICE: You have no shame about being the unwed mother of a fatherless child, and you were embarrassed at lovely Leontyne singing "Un Bel Di?"

JENNY: She has a father. Besides, you have to admit that Puccini was not exactly the dominant musical influence in our neighborhood. Our driveway was the only place where you had to be careful or you might get hit by a blast of "La Boheme" in the middle of a serious handball game. Everybody else was playing The Supremes! (*Laughing at the memory.*) I remember one day I was trying to get you to at least turn it down a little, and you made me listen to "Un Bel Di" all the way through. You told me to see if I could hear the same thing in it that made me love Smokey Robinson. You said forget about Italians and operas and just try to hear the passion.

ALICE: You looked at me like I was crazy, but you closed your eyes and listened. (*A beat.*) Ten years old . . . trying to hear the passion.

JENNY: I used your analogy a couple of weeks later when Dwan Johnson asked me what was playing at our house. I told him it was "Un Bel Di," and when he asked what it meant, I said, "one fine day." And he said, oh yeah? Just like the Chiffons!

ALICE (*laughs gingerly*): You know I hate the idea of taking these damn pills, but they do help.

JENNY (*a beat*): You know, when I got to college half the girls in my dorm had your books. It was a weird feeling. I had never seen them before, and they would come up to me and ask me about you. It was like some of them knew more about you than I did!

ALICE (*a beat*): I guess I should eat something.

JENNY: What would you like?

ALICE: There's some jello in there, I think. (*She shudders at the thought.*)

JENNY: How about some soup?

ALICE: I don't think so.

JENNY: It's just broth. I don't think it will upset your stomach.

ALICE: Maybe later. It's bad enough to be babbling like this without being nauseated too!

JENNY: There should be something in there that will appeal to you. Let me take a look. I'll put this on to entertain you while I'm gone.

ALICE: I don't want to be entertained. That's what I've been trying to tell you!

JENNY: Alright, alright. I stand corrected.

ALICE: Oh, hell. What's the difference? (JENNY *sets the record on and exits to the kitchen. It is "In My Solitude."* ALICE *winces a little in pain now that she is alone, but she quickly straightens and takes several more pills rapidly.*)

JENNY (*calling from the kitchen*): I've got some plain yogurt too. What do you think? (ALICE *leans back listening, eyes closed. She reaches out to touch the beautiful roses.* JENNY *enters with a small tray. She has to balance it precariously on the pile of stuff already on the coffee table. She fusses over the food until the song ends.*) If I thought taking heroin could make me sing like that, I'd be a junkie with no regrets.

ALICE: You can't sing like that without some regrets, Sister. Don't you know that yet? You better put some sugar in these roses.

JENNY: Sugar? Why?

ALICE: Flowers always live longer if you put some sugar in the water.

JENNY: I guess everything does better with a little sweetening.

ALICE: The woman who told me that was a fiend for roses. She was beautiful, and her boyfriends always sent her roses. Red only! Her apartment was full of them. The scent would choke you when you went to see her. She had so many roses she used to float their petals on her bath water.

JENNY: I tried that once. It sounds beautiful, but it feels like a tub full of hot, sticky rose petals.

ALICE: You know, this place looks very different.

JENNY: It needed a lot of work. Renovations, repairs. I did most of it myself. It took longer than I thought it would. I made a lot of mistakes. Do you like it?

ALICE: I'm not sure yet. (*A beat.*) I sure went the long way around to end up sleeping in the house I was born in.

JENNY (*a beat*): I can't believe you're really here.

ALICE: That makes two of us, Sister. (*A beat.*) The quiet in this house used to be so strong it was a part of the conversation. Mother and Daddy were so calm about everything. They never raised their voices. (*A beat.*) I used to wonder if I was their natural child. I used to study them, looking for clues. They were so damn certain! (ALICE *closes her eyes and leans back.* JENNY *watches her and then suddenly has a contraction. She handles it calmly, blowing out for a few seconds Lamaze style.* ALICE *speaks without opening her eyes.*)

ALICE: You're not going to start that again, are you?

JENNY (*out of breath*): No. I'm going to pack. (*She begins putting things in the large suitcase near her desk.* ALICE *opens her eyes and watches.*)

ALICE: What all are you taking to the hospital, Sister?

JENNY (*laughing*): Not much. This is the only bag I have.

ALICE: I've got a carpetbag. Very bohemian. I guarantee there'll be nothing like it on the ward.

JENNY: Sounds wonderful. Where is it?

ALICE: Look upstairs.

(JENNY *goes upstairs and rummages around to find the carpetbag, still talking.*)

JENNY: I wish I had a bed jacket to take with me. I love those scenes in the movies where the new mother is always propped up on lace pillows in a pink satin bed jacket. (*As* JENNY *rummages and talks,* ALICE *rises stiffly and wanders rather aimlessly around the room. She stops to touch a picture frame here, a piece of furniture, but all very absently. She is not looking for anything. She is simply moving around restlessly. She moves to* JENNY's *desk and sees the two pages* JENNY *was working on this morning. She picks up the pages slowly and reads a little. Upstairs,* JENNY *finds the carpetbag and opens it to look inside.*) They don't hardly make bed jackets like that anymore. I guess they . . . (*She seems to be surprised by what she sees and reaches in to withdraw a cheap wig. She realizes that* ALICE *may have worn it as a concession to vanity when her hair started to fall out.* JENNY *is embarrassed to have found it.* ALICE *is aware that* JENNY *has stopped in mid-sentence. She breaks off her reading and looks upstairs.* JENNY *puts the wig back in the closet and starts talking again nervously, coming downstairs.*) I always like that scene in "The Women" where Joan Crawford and Norma Shearer are getting ready to have it out and the store lingerie model keeps sweeping through saying "Try our new one-piece foundation. Zips up the back and no bones."

ALICE (*watches* JENNY *with irritation as she crosses to sit down again, wincing slightly*): I don't care, you know?

JENNY: About what?

ALICE: About what you think. About your crude efforts to capture my madcap phase in your schoolgirl poetry. Hardly a fitting memorial. (*A beat.*) It just doesn't matter, Sister. Can't you see that?

JENNY (*stung and hurt*): What does matter to you?

ALICE: My own heartbeat. The way my blood feels rushing through my veins. The parts of my body that are going to start hurting again in a few minutes. All of that matters. (ALICE *winces, and* JENNY *moves toward her.*)

JENNY: Are you okay?

ALICE: Stop asking me that! I'm not anywhere in the vicinity of okay, and I'm not going to be for the rest of the time you know me. (ALICE *leans back and takes a pill wearily.* JENNY *has retreated and started transferring her things from her big bag to the carpetbag. She realizes there is still something in it. She withdraws a small packet of things: papers, photo-graphs, etc., bound up with string.*)

JENNY (*cautiously, but curious*): What's this?

ALICE (*wearily*): What?

JENNY: All this "stuff"? (JENNY *hands the packet to* ALICE *who holds it delicately in her hands.*)

ALICE: Some old photographs. A poem or two. Your father's letters.

JENNY (*startled*): He wrote you?

ALICE: Yes.

JENNY (*surprised*): When?

ALICE: For years.

JENNY: He never showed me your letters!

ALICE: I didn't say that I wrote to him. I said he wrote to me.

JENNY: You never wrote back?

ALICE: No.

JENNY: Not once?

ALICE: Not once. If I had had anything left to say to your father, I wouldn't have been in Paris.

JENNY: How long did he write to you?

ALICE: I told you for years.

JENNY: But how many? How many years?

ALICE: Until he died.

JENNY: Where are the rest of them?

ALICE: I burned them.

JENNY: You burned them? God! Don't you ever think about anybody but yourself? You could have given them to me!

ALICE: He asked me to burn them! Besides, they were my letters. Nobody else's.

(JENNY, *knowing this is true, but still hurt by the secret, turns away.*)

JENNY: What did he say about me?

ALICE: He never wrote about you. When I left he told me he wanted to write to me. I told him he could, but not to expect answers to his letters and that if he ever referred to you in any way, I would never open another letter that he sent to me.

JENNY: And he believed you?

ALICE: That's a child's question, Sister. Children can never imagine that their parents could sustain exchanges of over five seconds without discussing them. (JENNY *turns away, and* ALICE *begins to talk almost to herself.*) He wrote about almost everything. Books and politics. Gossip about people we knew and what they were doing. What he was thinking; ideas.

JENNY: He used to talk to me like that, too. Sometimes I felt like listening to Daddy talking was as close as words could ever hope to get to being music. He could start off with Langston Hughes, move to Stokely Carmichael, swoop down long enough to touch on whoever I fancied myself to be in love with at the time and finish up with Duke Ellington without ever taking a breath.

ALICE: He wrote me when Malcolm was shot down. He must have sensed how hard it was to be in Paris then. When something like that happens, you want to be around your own. It seemed like we all heard the news at the same time. We ended up gathering at the cafe where we spent half our lives, crying in our Pernod and trying not to feel so black and helpless and far away from home. But then we looked up the street and here comes this young brother who we know works at the American Embassy. That's all we knew about him because he never hung around with us, but here he comes in his dark blue, pin-striped suit with a step ladder under his arm.

JENNY: A step ladder?

ALICE: He walked right up in front of the cafe, opened the thing up and cleared his throat. Speaking the most perfect, diplomatic corps French, he invited us to express ourselves on the death of "our shining black prince." Then he stepped about halfway up that ladder, left the flawless French behind, and told us in good old Southside Chicago English how his heart was broken by what he had heard happened in the Audobon Ballroom. When he got done, somebody else got up and talked about hearing Malcolm at the Temple in Detroit, way back when, and I told about another meeting where he brought us all to our feet. Everybody had a memory of the man. (*A beat.*) We must have been there a couple of hours. When everybody had had their say, the young brother from the Embassy thanked us, folded up his ladder, and went on up the street.

JENNY: What was his name?

ALICE: I don't remember. I don't think I ever knew, really. He killed himself . . .

JENNY (*distracting* ALICE *from death*): What about pictures?

ALICE (*bemused*): Just some ancient snaps of the ex-patriot colored poetess in her prime. (*She hands the photos to* JENNY *who looks through them eagerly.*)

JENNY: Look at that dress! You look wonderful! Where were you going?

ALICE: Who knows? We are always . . . (*She catches herself suddenly, suspicious of being so unguarded.*) When are you planning to have this baby anyway?

JENNY: Any minute now!

ALICE: I want you to make other arrangements for after she is born.

JENNY: What?

ALICE: I don't want you to bring her back here. I don't want to see her.

JENNY: Not at all?

ALICE: No. Not at all.

JENNY: She's your granddaughter!

ALICE: We've been all through this, Sister. Why don't you just go home?

JENNY: This is home!

ALICE: Why don't you go to where home was before this was home?

JENNY: Because I can't.

ALICE: There's a big difference between can't and won't.

JENNY: Yes. I know. (*Picking up the snapshots again, hoping to resume the conversation.*) Who were you playing here?

ALICE: Probably a cross between Josephine Baker and Anais Nin. I had a lover who loved my "leetle 'ead." He had a lot of money, and it amused him to keep a black American poet. Poetess! That was the phase when I started calling myself Simone and wrapping my head round and around with silver ribbons. (*A beat. She looks at the photo.*) They told me my hair was going to fall out when they started the chemotherapy. They explain everything to sick people, you know, so we won't be surprised when the awful things that are going to happen actually start happening. They explain everything as they take you into those little dark rooms and sit you down. Then they ask you if you've got any more questions, and since they've just described the horrors of hell to you, you probably don't want to hear any more, so you say no, thank you. Then they ease the needles into your arm so that the poison can drip into you for an hour or so, and that's it. Sometimes you feel okay. A little weak, but pretty good. You might even eat something, which is usually a mistake because then you start throwing up. And your hair starts falling out, and pretty soon they tell you it didn't work, and you've still got the cancer, and they're real sorry about . . . your . . . hair. (*A beat.*) He used to love to rub my head, this European fool. I told him that in the United States, black folks didn't tolerate white folks rubbing their heads because we knew they thought it gave them good luck and we needed all our good luck for our damn selves. He just laughed. He didn't know what I was talking about. "You have such a perfectly shaped leetle 'ead," he used to tell me. "Such a leetle 'ead."

JENNY: I shaved my head once.

ALICE: Bald?

JENNY: Completely.

ALICE: If there isn't a good story associated with that kind of madness, there is no excuse for it.

JENNY: It's not much of a story at all really. It was during a time when all the white girls at school were ironing their hair, morning, noon and night. You couldn't walk into the laundry room without bumping into Mary Jo or Susie Q. in their drawers with their hair thrown over the ironing boards.

ALICE: Why didn't you tell them about Madame Walker and her straightening comb?

JENNY: They weren't interested. I think in some weird way they thought the ironing board thing was some kind of ethnic beauty secret.

ALICE: Ethnic, maybe. But not black. There aren't enough of us with hair long enough to throw across an ironing board.

JENNY: After a couple of months, things moved from fad to fetish. All anybody talked about was ironing hair. The best temperatures to use. The advantage of steam over no steam. Techniques to do it yourself and tips on doing with a friend. It was silly, but it started to get on my nerves. One day at dinner, I told them all I thought hair—ironed or otherwise—was the most boring subject in the world and to prove it I was going upstairs and shave all of mine off. And I did.

ALICE: How did you like it?

JENNY: The look or the feeling?

ALICE: Both.

JENNY: It felt great. Cool and strange. Sensual. The look took some getting used to, though.

ALICE: My Frenchman would have loved you! "Such a lovely leetle 'ead!"

JENNY: I liked what it did to those girls though. It made them keep their distance. They were intimidated by whatever it was that made me do it.

ALICE: Ordinary people often mistake courage for insanity. It frightens them. (*A beat.*) What did your father say?

JENNY: He never saw it completely bald. It had grown in some before I went home. It was still too short to suit him though. He looked at me real hard and then he said, "I don't think you've got the face for it."

ALICE: Your father never was one for the avant garde.

JENNY (*pulls some other papers from the packet*): What are these?

ALICE: Poems, Sister. Those are the poems. (*A beat.*) You recognize a poem when you see one, don't you?

JENNY: Can I read them?

ALICE: I should have burned them, too.

JENNY: Why?

ALICE: Because some things are better left unsaid.

JENNY: Are they about Daddy?

ALICE: Yes.

JENNY: All of them?

ALICE: Yes, Sister. They are all about Daddy. (*A beat.*) I was so young when I met your father that he was not just the only man I'd ever slept with, he was the only man I'd ever fantasized about. He was very gentle with me. Very tender. He knew I was a very young girl. He had been a man out in the world longer than I had been alive!

JENNY: "A man out in the world . . ." Listen to how old-fashioned that sounds!

ALICE: Those were different times. Black folks were a little more prim in the fifties just like white folks. Besides, I was only seventeen. I graduated from high school on Wednesday and married your father in the sanctuary of Plymouth Church on Friday night.

JENNY: Daddy said you looked so young to him when he looked into your face to say his vows that he was afraid you had lied and he was marrying a child.

ALICE: When we first got married, I used to write two or three serious love poems everyday. I used to write them on little tiny pieces of paper and put them under his pillow. Whenever he reached under there and found one, I'd read it to him. One night, I told him I wanted to send one of them to a magazine and he ate it!

JENNY: He did what?

ALICE: He ate it. Rolled it up in a little ball, popped it in his mouth, chewed a couple of times, and swallowed it right down.

JENNY: Was it your only copy?

ALICE: That's hardly the point, Sister. He told me those poems were a gift from me to him. He said my words went all down inside him and made him stronger. So I said, that's all very fine, but why did you eat my poem? And he just laughed and said, so the white folks wouldn't get it.

JENNY: Is that when you stopped writing them?

ALICE: No. I wrote them for awhile after that. I just had to memorize them, too. I didn't stop writing them until you were born. Then I didn't have . . . time. (*A beat.*) You want to know what I learned in Paris? Almost twenty years abroad and you know what I learned, Sister? (*She does not give* JENNY *a chance to respond.*) I learned that my name is Alice and not Simone and that the Left Bank is not as far from the West Side of Detroit as I was hoping it would be.

JENNY: It was as far away as another planet to me.

ALICE (*a beat*): I just don't have the energy to figure out what you need to know and tell it to you, Sister. I don't have enough time, and I won't pretend that I do.

JENNY: You never would pretend. Even when it hurt to tell the truth.

ALICE: It hurt you. It hurt me to lie.

JENNY: To lie about *what?*

ALICE: There was a voice screaming inside my head, Sister. After awhile, the only thing that mattered was to make her stop shouting.

JENNY: Did she tell you to go to Paris?

ALICE: She told me to go!

JENNY: Did she tell you not to take me with you?

ALICE: She never considered you at all.

JENNY (*recoils from this statement, but is silent for a moment. She stares at* ALICE): Is it such a crime? To want to know the things your mother knows?

ALICE: And what if I tell you that I don't know anything at all? What if I tell you that running around Europe playing the exotic . . . playing god knows what . . . What if I told you it didn't teach me a damn thing?

JENNY: I wouldn't believe you.

ALICE: Now you do sound like your father. Confront the man directly with an unassailable truth—a provable reality—and he would look calmly into your face and say, "I don't believe you."

JENNY: There's more than one reality.

ALICE: Multiple truths? No. Multiple fantasy, but only one truth.

JENNY: You're making this so hard on me.

ALICE: Join the club. Membership is absolutely voluntary.

JENNY: Even now, you just can't let it go, can you?

ALICE: Let what go? You're talking movie-speak again. Hollywood alone has created the myth of a secret guilt that torments the dying. Forget it, Sister. I let it go. I let it all go. Your father . . . the poems . . .

JENNY: Well, that's nothing new, is it?

ALICE: That's what I've been trying to tell you.

JENNY: I just . . .

ALICE (*interrupting angrily*): . . . you just decided to leave your husband or your lover or your friend and move into your grandmother's house to have a baby, and you liked the whole idea so much you couldn't drag yourself away even when your long lost decaying mother arrived at the door? Give up, Sister! That sepia-tone photograph you've been carrying around in your head for twenty years hasn't got anything to do with me. I wasn't that way then, and I'm not that way now.

JENNY: You don't want to know anything about me at all. You've already drawn your own conclusions.

ALICE: I have drawn no conclusions. I have made no judgements. You are free to do whatever you please.

JENNY: At what price?

ALICE: We all have to pay for something.

JENNY: Why can't you just be my mother for once and not some world-weary, wisecracking, black caricature of a cynical ex-patriot?

ALICE: I am being your mother. This is what your mother is, Sister. A world-weary, wisecracking, black caricature of a cynical ex-patriot.

JENNY (*quietly*): That is not the answer.

ALICE: Don't try for answers, Sister. You don't even understand the questions.

JENNY: That's where you're wrong!

ALICE: Am I?

JENNY: Yes, you are. I understand all the questions. Every single one. (*A beat.*) Right after you left, Daddy sent me away to boarding school. He thought I needed . . . I don't know . . . stability, safety. There had been bombings, threats on his life. So he sent me off to Massachusetts where I'd be safe. I knew he was doing the best he could, so I didn't tell him how much I hated it. I thought that if he really loved me, he would know. Somehow, he would feel it and come and get me. (*A beat.*) But he never did. (*A beat.*) That's one of the questions, isn't it? How come people that love you can't read your mind?

ALICE: Why should they?

JENNY: So that they can love you better!

ALICE: There is no better or worse, Sister. You either do or you don't.

JENNY: You make choices.

ALICE (*outraged*): Choices? Okay, Sister. Take a look! My parting gift to you is a close-up look at the end result of all those choices you're talking about with such enthusiasm. Choices? Take a good, long look at me, and save your reaction to this terrible truth for the labor room. You can scream about the injustice of it all in there, and nobody will pay you the slightest bit of mind. All the ladies do it. They'll never know that your screaming is different. That yours isn't about the pain of your bones separating to let your daughter out. That yours is about the presence of injustice in the world! They'll never suspect a thing. And it doesn't really matter anyway. In spite of their feigned interest, nobody else really gives a damn if you do your birthing and your living and your dying well, or if you shriek and holler and cling to the nurse's arm.

JENNY: You left me?

ALICE: I did not see my future as the dedicated wife of the charismatic leader, dabbling in a little poetry, being indulged at cultural conferences and urged to read that one about the beautiful brothers and sisters in Soweto, or Watts, or Montgomery, Alabama. I just couldn't be that. The world is bigger than that. The world inside my head is bigger than that. Even now . . . I used to watch your father at rallies and in church on Sunday morning, and he'd be so strong and beautiful, it was all I could do to sit still and look prim in my pew. But he was committed to "the movement." He didn't have time anymore to lay in bed with me and improvise. I'd been a wife since I was seventeen, and here I was almost thirty, with a ten-year-old daughter, trying to convince your father to let me publish some love poems! But he couldn't. Or he wouldn't. The kind of love he had to give me now didn't allow for that. And I couldn't do without it. So I left. Not much of a story is it?

JENNY: I could have gone with you. I was old enough.

ALICE: I can tell you the day, the hour, the minute you were conceived. (*A beat.*) I couldn't stand to look at you. (*Changes her tone.*) And I'm selfish! You said it yourself. What was I going to do in Paris with a ten-year-old child? Besides, you were always more your father's child than you ever were mine.

JENNY: I didn't have much choice, did I?

ALICE: Neither did I, Sister. Neither did I. I've spent my life trying to heal a hurt I'm not supposed to have. I got so tired of being trapped inside that tiny little black box. No air, Sister. I couldn't get any air. Everybody was mad at somebody, or about something. (*A beat.*) My mother spent her life catching the bus downtown to the Anis Fur Company. Sitting there in that hot little back room sewing purple silk linings in rich white ladies' sable coats. I went there with her once when I was little. There must have been thirty black women in a room smaller than this one. It was hot and dusty and close. I felt like I was smothering. (*A beat.*) No air, Sister. No goddamn air.

JENNY: Daddy never wanted that.

ALICE: No. He wanted exactly what I was looking for. A way out of that black box. It's just that I was prepared to admit defeat and let the white folks have this particular piece of ground since they wanted it so bad. But your father was different. He was not prepared to give an inch. He was always talking about survival, and I was always talking about love.

JENNY: You were happy once.

ALICE: But the moment passes, Sister.

JENNY: Does that mean it never happened?

ALICE: It means most of the time nobody's even listening.

JENNY: I was listening.

ALICE (*angry*): For what? So you could make up schoolgirl fairy tales about my exotic existence? So you could record my tragic demise for posterity? (*She picks up the poetry and waves it at* JENNY.) Read it to me, why don't you? No? Okay! I'll read it to you then. I used to be good at this. "Pretend it's Paris." (*Her voice is totally sarcastic.*) "For mother . . ."

JENNY: Don't! (JENNY *grabs the poem away and crumples it in her hand.* ALICE *smiles cruelly.*)

ALICE: You're not a poet, Sister. You're a runner. Don't you even understand that? There are people who are runners, Sister. Runners who spend their whole life in flight. Sometimes the speed may have a kind of flash to it—a certain style—but in the end, it's nothing but a hard, scared run, and you end up somewhere panting and hurting and babbling over your shoulder into the dark. (ALICE *turns her back to* JENNY. *She is spent.* JENNY *speaks slowly but with confidence. Something in her tone makes* ALICE *turn as she speaks.*)

JENNY:
"you ration yourself out
like there was a war on.
In Paris, the soldiers threw
chocolate bars and silk stockings.
some people saved the sweets
and hid the stockings in a bureau drawer.
safe and sound.
not me. i was the one
in my stocking feet
with chocolate smeared
across my smile
dancin' and grinnin'
unsafe/unsound/undone.
there's more i can give
if there's more you can take.
the only thing
i wanna do
is make love
and drink champagne
in the middle of the day
and in the middle of the night
and sometimes in the morning
i am the one
in my stocking feet
with chocolate smeared
across my smile
dancin' and grinnin'
i am the one.
oh, yes, i am the one.
close your eyes.
take a deep breath.

pretend it's Paris.
pretend it's Paris.
pretend it's Paris . . .

(*They look at each other for a long moment.*)

ALICE (*quietly*): It's too late to be sorry, Sister, but I . . .
JENNY (*stops her*): Sometimes the love is enough. When it's all you've got.
Sometimes just the possibility is enough. And we don't have to explain
it. We just have to be here together and try. We only have to try! (*A
beat.*) All I ever wanted to tell you was that I understood. I think I always
understood.

(JENNY *and* ALICE *look straight at each other in silence.* JENNY *moves to*
ALICE, *but then stops and winces slightly. She puts her hands to her stomach
lightly, breathing through her mouth.*)

ALICE: What is it?
JENNY (*panting a little*): Contractions! I'd better call Alexis. (JENNY *goes
to the phone and dials quickly.* ALICE *slowly picks up the crumpled pages
of the poem, smoothing them carefully as* JENNY *speaks.*) Alexis? I think
it's . . . Yes. Pretty strong . . . Okay. I'll be ready. (*She hangs up.*) She's
going to come by and pick me up.

(They look at each other. ALICE *touches* JENNY's *cheek lightly.*)

ALICE: I think when I married your father so young, my mother was afraid
she wouldn't have time to get all the women lessons in before I was gone.
JENNY: Did she?
ALICE: She told me what she knew. I guess that's the best anybody can do.
(*Suddenly.*) Forgive me, Sister. I did what I could.

(They embrace each other very gently. Alexis' car horn blows outside.)

ALICE (*breaking the embrace and urging* JENNY *to the door*): Don't try to be
brave now, Sister. Scream as loud as you want.
JENNY (*stops at the door and looks back at* ALICE): I love you, Mamma.
ALICE: And I was always some place loving you, Baby. I was always some
place loving you. (JENNY *exits.* ALICE *sits down slowly in the rocking
chair. She looks down slowly at the poem in her hand and all the energy
seems to leave her body. She drops the pages to the floor.*) Don't fool
yourself, Miss Alice. Just don't fool yourself.

(Lights go down slowly. ALICE *remains in a blue spot in the dark and then
it also fades.* BLACK.)

[1989]

Shango Diaspora*
An African-American Myth of Womanhood and Love

Angela Jackson

CHARACTERS

Watergirl (Ms. Waters), *a brown-skinned Black woman in her early to mid-twenties; warm and intelligent, but learning herself.*

The Three Women, *these three women are like musical energies. #1 and #2 are sopranos, #3 alto, husky, a dreamer. They are three shades and styles of beauty. They are Afros, braids, dreads, nothing extravagant, and nothing too unnatural. They are a trio in different expressions, as the* WOMEN, *the* MAMMIWATERS, *the* VOICES, *the* SISTERS OF SYMPATHY, *and the* WOMEN IN WHITE.

> **Woman #1**, *Black woman from 30 to 45.*
> **Woman #2**, *Black woman a little younger than #1; a shade less aggressive than #1.*
> **Woman #3**, *Black woman from 30 to 45. A Dreamer. A kind woman.*

Woman-along-the-way and Yemoja/Mother, *the first, a Black woman of seniority; crazy, clipped and harsh.* YEMOJA *is a god. Full of jazz and magic. An ageless, lovely, self-acclaiming, absolutely autonomous, arrogant, and tender deity.*

Shango/Fire, *a god. Black man, virile, in his prime—late thirties to mid-forties, apparently. A Black, lean, Yoruba god of thunder, lightning, and fire. He is a scientist, magician, and ruler, thus has great intellect, stature, and dignity. An African-Diaspora man of brilliance and masks.*

The Fan, *Black woman of same age as* MS. WATERS, *she is simpering, manipulative, sharp, shallow, and a little sad.*

The Cats, *three Black women, bitter and sad, of any age. They are primarily dancers. They may have been playing scenery.*

Soldier, *Shango's soldier is preferably male, with a forbidding voice.*

---

* *Shango Diaspora* has been performed across the United States; it was produced in New York in 1982 and most recently in Chicago in 1992. The play appears in print in its entirety here for the first time.

A *Somewhere in the Diaspora. A Black Space.*
TIME:
The Present. What John Wideman calls "African Great Time."

ACT **I**
Scene 1
SETTING:

A *city block.* GIRL *on a porch seated sideways on a bannister, singing along with "Fire," Pointer Sister version.* THREE WOMEN *on the street corner coming from work. In hats or scarves, carrying shopping bag, briefcase, basket.*

WOMAN **#1** (*Yells at* GIRL *aggressively*): Hey, you! Hey, you there singin' "Fire," what you know about it? What you know about Fire?

GIRL (*Turns to her. Defensive but firm*): I know enough. I know about him.

WOMAN **#1:** You know enough to call the Fire Department?

GIRL: I know enough. I learned *something* in school. Isis bathed Osiris in fire for immortality. To build a fire is to burn away the yellow eyes of wolves, to burn the howling out of the night.

GIRL (*Pauses, voice softens*): In the kitchen where love is baked in loaves fire heats the stones.

WOMAN **#2:** Girl, you talking about some kitchen fire. We talking about Fire.

WOMAN **#1** (*Interjects*): Big Fire.

WOMAN **#3** (*Dreamily*): Fire is the first and final fear. I saw Fire once. It was in a dream.

WOMAN **#2** (*Has taken out a Dream Book. Points to a section. Reads*): To dream Fire is to dream prosperity, change, good luck, the sweet sex wish.

WOMAN **#3:** He is a figure of force and fascination in an orange drama.

GIRL (*Saunters down steps. While the women remove hats and baskets, etc.*): Legends I have heard tell of. Stoop-front myths and sermons that made mature women sweat and stir the thick air. Young men shake their heads and touch hands in elaborate fives. Encounters I have watched him through. Flash fire flats housed his concubines. Beautiful and methodical in their wiles. Their kitchens all burned out. Their pots stone cold. I have heard of his hunger. His spirit unharnessed.

WOMAN **#1:** Once, at a dry feast, drought, he ate three thousand trees.

WOMAN **#2:** Once, he set a family outside into a freezing winter drift. Flames licked out through gutted windows like horrible children with their tongues stretched out. While a father stood in snow, barefoot, cursing Fire.

WOMAN **#3:** When he walks he leaves premonitions. When women think of him they store their dreams like secrets poured in Mason Jars, persimmon, marmalade, Sunday morning, and harmonica. They remember the very first fig and the bent heat that swelled from Fire, from him, from them. Delicious!

WOMAN #2: What do you know, girl? You think you an authority on Fire?

WOMAN #3 (*Like a robot mother*): Children should not play with Fire.

WOMAN #1 (*Bossy*): Give me those matches, that cigarette lighter. Stand back from that stove. That fire'll fall on you.

WOMAN #3 (*To imaginary children*): If you are bad you will burn!

WOMAN #2: Listen at what the mothers tell you. Be careful, girl.

WOMAN #1, 2, AND 3: Hot! Hot! Hot!

GIRL (*Ignores them*): I'll be alright.

WOMAN #1: Oh, really? Just who do you think you are?

GIRL: It's too late. I already am who I am.

WOMAN #2: Who are you?

WOMAN #3 (*Looking into a hand mirror. Curious and crazy*): I know who you are.

(*The women get busy. #3 begins to braid #2's hair. #1 begins to wash and hang up clothes; she uses a scrub board. All fixtures are imaginary.*)

GIRL (*Centerstage*): I am the little girl who plays with the god of Fire. He bites my lips, and scars my hands. "Little girl," he tells me, "Don't you know I'd run through you like a silver knife? Burn down all your trembling houses."

WOMAN #1 (*An aside*): That sound like a warning to me.

GIRL: "Yes," I tell him. "I have watched you a long, long time without winking. I know the cruelty of your ember. I have read your mark on women's eyes."

GIRL (*Gestures*): I touch him without squinting. He bites my lips and scars my hands. Full height he draws himself up. He is one flame that flares. Red and blue against the trees. Lightning. Over the sand. Over the houses. "Listen, when I tell you, I am Fire, Little Girl. I am son and father of the sun. I will make you ash and curling smoke."

WOMAN #2 (*An aside*): That sound like warning number two.

GIRL: "I know," I whisper into the deep blue flame. My lips are red with him. "God of Fire who burns poison out of wounds. Son of Fire who bites the ice and makes it sweet. Father of Fire who watches the earth, you are a god of mercy. Have mercy on me. Be tender with my meat." I look into his light and wink.

WOMAN #1 (*An aside*): You better been trying to wink.

GIRL: "Little Girl," he says, "Who owns you? Where is your home?"

WOMAN #1 (*An aside*): He say, "Where this fool come from?"

GIRL: "I am only a child. Water. Early to bed."

WOMAN #2: Early to bed!

WOMAN #1: She ready!

GIRL: River of invisible rises. The beautiful daughter of many people. I strike fire back at the sun and it is glass. Have you never seen the water that holds the fire? Cradles it and rocks it into weaving smoke? You must have something soft against you. You are more child than I. You are thirsty. And will burn yourself out.

WOMAN #1 AND #2: You a bold little miss . . .

GIRL: "No," he snaps and hisses. He is full of caprice. He bites my lips and scars my hands. Curses me with thunder. I am too still, without a murmur. He is wary. A muscle of contempt. We watch each other. And we wait. (GIRL *stops, pauses. Doesn't want to reveal the rest.*)

WOMAN #3 (*Kindly*): Well, then what happened? You not just gone leave us hanging. What happened? Turn yo head around the other way so I can get this part. (*Addresses* GIRL, *then* WOMAN *between her knees.*)

GIRL (*Getting up enough nerve. Begins quickly, abruptly*): Suddenly. He laughed. He held me up and opened his hand. Seven kinds of stone. Alight. I brushed the flame and fled. Wing-singed. Transformed into a trembling bird: a black wave flying from the sun. Breasts heaving and eyes broken open like lips. Now I know hunger and I am mouths. Who curved dizzy in his palm. I touched his flint and fled.

WOMAN #1 (*Sticks clothespin under* GIRL's *nose*): I coulda told you it woulda ended up that way.

WOMAN #3 (*Chastises #1*): See there. That's not right. Be telling somebody I told you so. She don't want to hear that. (*To* GIRL.) Go on, honey, what was it like when he touched you?

GIRL: Something struck me when he touched me. A déjà vu overwhelming. You were there . . . women ripping their corded hair, shouting my lost name.

WOMAN #3: Did it hurt? His touch.

GIRL: It was like a palmtree hard fell with the fist of its hand; while the earth pit swallowed its own green seeds, all my futures were absorbed by a toothless mouth; everything moving with centrifugal force: this body, a brown paperbag doll, flattened against his wall. It was this terrible, terrible déjà vu I tore loose from, yet could not elude. So here I go down the line of women wounded like a row of moons. And we all look alike crying the same blues.

WOMAN #1 (*Working with the clothespin again*): Did you think you'd be any different? Did you think he'd treat you any different than he treated them other women? Did you think you had gold between your legs? And that would make him want you?

GIRL: I didn't think I had anything between my legs because he ain't been between my legs.

WOMAN #2: That's what's wrong with you.

GIRL: He just touched me.

WOMAN #3: Why did you run away?

GIRL: I don't know. I don't remember. I just remember the flirtation dance. The hesitation . . .

WOMAN #3: You were afraid. Weren't you?

GIRL: I guess. The feeling was picking me up. Carrying me away.

WOMAN #3: Why didn't you go with it? You only wishing you *had* gone. You look tired.

GIRL: Every night sleep break me in two. Opens and spreads across the cold. I loiter with my limbs askew and curve around a central heat.

WOMAN #1: Still trying to get next to that heat, huh?

GIRL: "Classic," my sister shakes her head when I tell her. "I did not know such cases were still found." She is not sad for me but marvels at the possibility: a woman so intense, so besieged. The heat a recurring tropical disease. "Tell me who he is." Someone curious inquires. Even though they don't know. They just assume it's got to be a man. How they know it's a man? Got me sleepless. It might be *money*. It just might be lack of money keeping me awake at night. *It might be inflation!*

WOMAN #1: Inflated loneliness.

WOMAN #2: Inflated lust.

WOMAN #3: Love. There is somebody who's stricken you. You're in his aura. He wakes you in the middle of the night. He colors your forehead purple like a royal anointment or a bruise.

WOMAN #2: Valerie Simpson say it's like a mark on you.

WOMAN #1: Then she say, "Don't go, can it wait until tomorrow." Twenty-four more hours before the misery stop or start.

WOMAN #2: Misery stop or start. Miserable he there. You miserable when he gone.

GIRL *(To* WOMAN #3*)*: What can I do?

WOMAN #1: Take some valium and sleep it off.

WOMAN #2: Do quickies and t.m.

WOMAN #3: You have to go to him. Go to him with a sacrifice. You have to give something up. Go singing. Don't listen to them two filling you with fear. You have to dream with him. Or else you'll be left by yourself. Which wouldn't be bad to be a dreamer by yourself if you didn't want *him. (Sends her on her way.)* You have such a pretty voice. Go singing to him.

WOMAN #2: Girl, he is really gonna get you this time.

WOMAN #1: Girl, he is gonna kick your emotional ass.

(WOMAN #3 *takes up imaginary broom. Sweeps. Humming.*)

(To WOMAN #3*.)*: Now, why you send that child on that wild goose chase so he can cook her goose for her?

WOMAN #3: Wasn't no wild goose chase. Something she has to do.

WOMAN #2: She need to be trying to avoid pain.

WOMAN #3: How you avoid pain without avoiding feeling? It's all part of the ritual.

WOMAN #1 AND #2: What ritual?

WOMAN #3 *(Goes dreamy again)*: In autumns what I remember is my father and uncles gathering buckets and rakes doing the earth's duty with a calm and ritual therapy. They worked the wrinkled, sunset leaves into mountains like a sacrifice of lovely and faded women. The men gave leaves to fire. The smoke would rise black and full of husky, sexual smell. The men would lean on their rakes and watch. Their children would flutter and swirl around the smoke and bodies. My father would gather the ashes into buckets and discard them. Now his daughter is fallen, sunsets, and gathering her body for giving. It is a new time, for life, and fire must be fed.

(Fade out on THREE WOMEN.*)*

ACT I
Scene 2
SETTING:

> Enroute to FIRE. *Travel is suggested by the dance movements of the* GIRL, *and by, possibly, having trees move. Stones move. A fence moves. Road-signs move. Dancers may take these parts. She stops at a fence. An old* WOMAN *is working in a garden behind a low fence. She wears a huge* sunhat, *carries a cane, is initially on her knees. Rises.*

GIRL *(Friendly. Respectful)*: Morning. I hate to disturb you. You look so busy. Your garden is so beautiful. Okra, tomatoes, bright sun corn, look like you growing a pot of gumbo right out of the ground. You must have a special gift.

WOMAN-ALONG-THE-WAY *(Abrupt, but not unkind)*: It's a hot day. I suppose you want water? Where you on your way to?

(Goes to a pail of water.)

> My plantings know I love them. Not everything responds the way fruits and vegetables do to good loving. *(Hands* GIRL *dipper.)* Here's water. Nice and chilly.

GIRL: Oh, it's well water. Good. Thank you. *(Drinks politely.)*

WOMAN-ALONG-THE-WAY: Not everybody like well water. Some say they can taste the rust in it. I shouldn't have asked. I know where you going. *(Works with spade or hoe all the while.)*

GIRL: You do?

WOMAN-ALONG-THE-WAY: You going to see Him. Ain't you? Don't answer. I know you are.

GIRL: How do you know when I haven't even said so. And who is *Him?*

WOMAN-ALONG-THE-WAY *(Mumbles)*: They come and go. *(Aloud.)* I can tell these things. You got that look about you. You got fire in your eyes. Flame in yo cheeks. No use blushing all over.

GIRL: I can't help it.

WOMAN-ALONG-THE-WAY: Well, if you blushing that means you ain't been to his firebed yet. It's soft as feathers that burn to the bone. He ain't made you his. Yet. You can still turn around and high tail it out of here.

GIRL: O, I think I know best what I have to do.

WOMAN-ALONG-THE-WAY: Girl, O.K. I was hard-headed too. Just like you. Nobody could tell me anything. I was under his spell. *(Is overtaken by memory.)* I was one entranced. Violated by flame. I stared too long into the roar. Music took my hands. I circled myself in wild paint and watched my body move into heat. I was hungry all the time. Fire was delicious: an inflammatory statement. You know he was. I loved his devastation, continuing combustion. I indulged him too much. He raged unchecked, petulant, spoiled. I swear. His language was abusive. His expressions cruel grimace and scowls. Let me give you a caution: give him only the animal exchange of energy. He doesn't know the sacrament of the heart. His is a bleeding ulcer. But who am I to say a thing or two? I have grown old. I have a loose mouth. Once my cheeks were round and fire swelled inside me until I burst.

GIRL (*Disbelieving*): Nobody tells the same story twice. Tell it to me again.

WOMAN-ALONG-THE-WAY: O.K., I'll put it to you simply. Woman is a language of no more than tree; he roots, he branches, he breaks, he leaves.

GIRL: How he leave after he breaks? Nothing leaves after it's broken.

WOMAN-ALONG-THE-WAY: You know what I mean. What is man will lay you waste. Gods such as they are. Will open you, rotate a crop of jubilee and suicide, then will lay you waste, will lay you waste. Am I right or wrong?

GIRL: I don't like to make general statements about love. Every love don't turn sour in the mouth.

WOMAN-ALONG-THE-WAY: When you come back here spitting out the insides of a used vinegar douche bag you'll be whistling another tune.

GIRL: I have to go. Thank you for the drink. (*Prepares to continue her journey. Walks.*)

WOMAN-ALONG-THE-WAY (*Hollers after her*): Answer me this, Miss Fearless-won't-listen-at-good-advice-know-it-all: Who is gone pick up your body? (*Mumbles to self.*) I probably have to call the Fire Department. Where is that number for the Burn Unit? (*Goes about her tasks.*) Why don't they listen? Why don't the young ones listen to the old ones? Why didn't I listen when they tried to tell me? Well, we'll see. We shall see. Where is that number for the Burn Unit?

(*Fade on scene.*)

ACT I

Scene 3

SETTING:

Smoke in the distance from a high place. That is SHANGO's *lair/palace. The* GIRL *is journeying. Again, trees walk and stones move. Birds in flight. Bird signal songs. Flight from a big wind, a movement.*

GIRL (*Watching the signs of animal flight. Worried. Muses*): When Fire struts/ bewildered beasts scurry. From miles away birds set out a flurry of fear.

(*A flurry among the trees. She cringes.*)

I smell the skin of smoke. I sense his presence near. His teeth that mark the barks of trees; his eyes peeling a path of leaves leaving the bones of slow bedazzled beasts settled beneath his feet. (*Hesitantly approaches a gate at the foot of a suggested stairwell. The stairwell has steps that are really landings. The steps curve. The steps are in darkness. She listens.*) I hear his breathing. The soft rending of cloth. The soft tearing of the hair of air. *(She looks around her, warily.)* A craziness of atmosphere, near his lair of brilliance and intrigue. *(Measures herself to meet the task.)* My heart wide as a child's. A woman's aroma at my wrists, at my temples, behind my ears. *(Takes out perfume from her carrying basket. Carrying basket is full of goodies.)* This craziness of atmosphere. I want to run. I want to stay. I'm wise enough to fear. Fool enough to linger here.

(GIRL, having decided to face FIRE, prepares by dressing up. Adds a skirt of bright-colored veils, jewelry. All this from her basket of goodies. A bowl is also in the basket.)

A VOICE *(A warning voice, deep and stern, comes from nowhere and every-where)*: Who enters his electromagnetic field is polarized, pulled apart, limb from limb, shocked, wild in the head.

(GIRL pauses with hand outstretched toward the suggestion of a door/gate.)

VOICE OF WOMAN #3: You must go to him with a sacrifice. Go singing. If you don't you'll never be free.

(GIRL still hesitates.)

You want a good night's sleep, don't you?

(GIRL opens door/gate. GIRL mounts the long, wide steps that are more like platforms. Lights go up on SHANGO on high. He is close to a cloud. Clouds are stones. SHANGO FIRE DIASPORA sits in a Huey P. Newton, big-backed, bamboo chair. He reclines. Arrogantly. He remains in shadow, although all around him is illuminated. Perhaps he is flanked by drummers who are at a distance. He has one SOLDIER, at least. He is being fanned by a woman. All in SHANGO's palace wear African dress. Flamboyant fire colors. A great glaring light falls on the GIRL's face. Blinds her.)

SOLDIER: Who comes?
GIRL: Only . . . a girl sleepless with praises. *(Shields her eyes.)*
SOLDIER: Then praise.

(Light softens as GIRL kneels and bows deeply.)

GIRL *(Begins tremulously. Gains confidence. It gets good to her. She is downright cocky by the end)*: Most Excellent Lord Shango. You were a god before music/ fell and broke/ into voices. Before the tribes were marked limb from limb, eye from eye, skin from skin, heart from heart, and brain before desire was formed out of hormone, mucus, and marrow. Before Osiris/ you were a god. Before the market of salt, and spices and trade/ beads before rice rose out of mud. Before brute force/ you were a god before the death howl/ before the Chain/ before the Coffle . . .
THE FAN *(Bored and jealous)*: My. My. My girl is so extravagant. Sweet child.
GIRL *(Loud and determined)*: You were born before Hallelujah, as old as Hosanna! Before the plain and orange breasted lizard made marriage patterns in the sand./ Before the funeral of justice, before mercy, before

'27, the flood, when the house was torn from its roots and twins were birthed on the roof./ Before the river ran wild before the anger of water/ before the beacon, and the lighthouse. (*Is so excited she rises in her speech.* SOLDIER *and* THE FAN *gesture her down. She ignores them.*) You were a being before the Hawk and the Holy Ghost danced as one on the corner of Celebration and Sanctuary, before women of the creme sachet and toilet water lay with porcelain gods and works of art./ You were there in the Time of the North Star/ in the Time of Moss that hugs the Tree of Memory. You are as old as the longing for Messiah. Your lifeline equatorial and your heart bleeds back from the long tunnel of the First God. You have accumulated more pain than I. I have heard of you. I know that I am young. Magician of two thousand smoke screens, griot of light years, people say that I am aglow, a star has set upon me. And I am patient as the moon.

SHANGO (*In shadow. Bored. Matter-of-factly*): You are a fool.

GIRL (*Before he can complete the sentence*): Beyond a shadow . . . I am ready for giving. I have come singing. I know that I am young.

THE FAN: Is that all, *little girl?*

GIRL (*Feisty*): I wasn't talking to you. (*To* FIRE.) May we have privacy? I have brought an offering. (SHANGO *snaps his fingers. All retreat to lower platforms. They watch and listen.*)

(THE FAN *takes centerstage. She narrates the actions of the* GIRL *and* FIRE. FIRE *and the* GIRL *do dance actions in the shadows. A hot, hot, hot dance done in shadows with sparks shooting out.*)

THE FAN (*Blasé. Delighting in the* GIRL's *fate*): She prepared a lamb for him. A sacrifice floating in herbs and blood and water seasoned with salt of camouflaged tears, onions, and three kinds of peppers, enough to kill a goat. (*She fans herself all the while.*) Her mouth shaped half a plate of triumph. She held murder in her hands. He sat on his throne, a luxuriating storm. His neck was stiff as an eagle's. He watched the sway of her hips, heavy, widened as she walked with design. He took the dish and tasted it. He ground West African pepper with his teeth. He lulled his tongue inside the heat. Then he said, "This is not sweet enough. There is not enough salt." (*Gleefully.*) He crushed her eyes for salt. He opened her veins for syrup and let her laughter over lamb. Devoured it. *His teeth cracked bone.* Devoured it. *He sucked the marrow.* Then, he roared for more. She gave him her mouth. He pulled her kisses til she was gaunt. Her joints grew thin as spider tapestries. Still. He said he was not satisfied. She fell behind her mask. Inscrutable. Wall of water. Silent hieroglyphic of hurt. Reflecting, she watched his fine teeth glisten while he laughed.

(*A deep bass growl-laugh descends from the shadow and sparks. The two figures now tangled in erotic and subtly violent embrace. A low fade on couple coupling. Then* GIRL *descends. Like a sleepwalker. She is off her center.*)

GIRL (*More to self than to others. Disoriented*): Fire is absolute. You were absolutely right. I should have known. I had no ways. I had no means enough to know. I, who have always been water. More or less. Fire burns. Grates the eyes. Peels/ flesh and sears. (*Gestures back toward* FIRE. *Turns to shout to Him.*) Fire: you are absolute. There is no defense. A woman who loves Fire/ who meddles with flame/ who flirts with tongues/ will burn/ will be/ consumed.

(*On a lower platform the village women appear. They are doing a Fire Dance.* GIRL *descends toward them.*)

In the village, on the street corners, the women raised their skirts and only fanned the flame. Fire rose around their thighs. Went through them and blossomed between their breasts. Fire licked their ankles and they danced. Fire: you are music/ nobody has business listening to alone. *And when I touched you you were warm. I cupped the heat and laughed into the colored shadows you cast across my skin.* I was laughing, people say. Not like a little girl. They say, I raised my skirts delicately, like a lady, and danced. Til they only saw the smoke.

(GIRL *goes up in fire and smoke.* THE FAN *fans on like this happens everyday.*)

(*Black out. Quick.*)

ACT **II**
Scene 1
SETTING:
    Same as initial setting. The GIRL's *porch is lighted but past it, within the house, is in darkness. The* THREE WOMEN *are outside. Doing woman's work, i.e., household service chores that women usually get stuck with.*

WOMAN **#1:** How's that singing girl doin'? I ain't seen her in a while.
WOMAN **#2:** Ask her. She in the know. (*Points to* WOMAN #3.)
WOMAN **#1:** How's that girl doin'? She takin' it bad?
WOMAN **#3:** How else can she take it? I know it was for me. I didn't think it would be that way for her. I don't know exactly how it was for her. She don't talk. I know how it was for me. After a session of such sorcery: the tongue becomes a feather dipped in blood. The bones begin to dance. In leave of reason. The body goes bare and all of the air is familiar. Is a house of flesh as warm as breath is. His loa. His spirit. His power turns tongues to feathers. Bones to dance. Body to bare familiar air. Fire finds his house of flesh. What tongue once feather will speak again? What bones be still after the dance? What body be clothed in the stranger house of cold after his loa has taken hold . . . ?

(*While she is talking #1 and #2 spice her monologue with* "Here she go again. . . ." "You'd think that burned out memory be cold by now.")

WOMAN **#2:** You make too much of it. It was only *sex*. Birds do it. Bees do it. Hippopotamuses . . .
WOMAN **#1:** Hippopota*mi* . . .

WOMAN #2: Yeah, well, they do and ain't got to cry about it.

WOMAN #3: How you know they don't cry about it? And if they don't, why shouldn't I? Or *her*?

WOMAN #1: (*Hesitating at first step of* GIRL's *home*): How long is she gone stay in that room suffering so? That night-cryin' is drivin' me crazy. Some nights I stay awake on the other side of the wall. She be night-cryin' and tears come standin' in my eyes like some soldiers of some goddamned misery warring with my good sense. I thought they was dead. She raisin' my tears from the dead. Why don't she come out? How long is this National Day of Mourning going on?

WOMAN #3: I don't know. Seems like the pain goes up and down like a pot over a gas flame. Flame going up and down.

WOMAN #2: How long can anything sit on the stove and still be good?

WOMAN #1: I'm tired of cryin' for that girl. I told her not to go. Though I hoped deep inside it would turn out a happy ending. I need a happy ending.

WOMAN #2: Well, I ain't gone cry her tears for her. Shit, my eyes allergic to my own tears.

WOMAN #3 (*Angry. Distressed, turns on* #2): I guess you happy now. When she sit in a circle of women, now she can show off her wounds, a review of miseries like cats shedding hair. Don't shed on me, she-cat.

(*Fade on the group as light opens on* GIRL *and her surroundings.*)

ACT II
Scene 2
SETTING:
> The GIRL's *house. Porch is illuminated. So is inside. There is only a bed. The* GIRL *is on it. Smoke rises from the bed suggesting smouldering ashes. The* THREE WOMEN *appear transformed into benevolent spirits all. They are the* SISTERS OF SYMPATHY. *All in dresses and headrags and/or gelees of royal blue, sky blue, and turquoise. There is little initial dialogue. Intense movement. They sweep into the* GIRL's *house. They make a semicircle around her. Shaking their heads. One ministers to the* GIRL. *One goes to sweep the porch. Another builds a fire with a pot over it. They begin throwing things into the fire. Reciting.*

SISTER #1 (*As she throws said item into pot*): Black cat bones. Mojo root. Essence of Van Van. Jasmine Perfume.

SISTER #2 (*Accepts an invisible something from* #3 *who ministers to the* GIRL. #2 *gives the invisible thing to* #1): Pining from a young girl's heart. And bad news.

(SISTER #1 *stirs the mixture. Then all move swiftly to* GIRL.)

GIRL (*Sitting up in bed. Watching amazed and looking scared*): Who are you?

(*The* SISTERS *speak almost simultaneously. One behind the other. They could be one person.*)

SISTER #1: Sisters of

SISTER #2: Sympathy

SISTER #3: But not too much.

ALL SISTERS: Too much sympathy not good for you.

SISTER #1: We interested in curing.

SISTER #2: Self-sufficiency.

SISTER #3: We have come to cure impurities. We've mixed water and magic over a tame fire. Anything can happen. We are in control.

SISTER #2: You have been out of your element.

SISTER #3: You have taken leave of your senses.

SISTER #1: Let Fire get the best of you, huh?

SISTER #3: He was a sweet child.

SISTER #2: Known him since he was a boy.

SISTER #1: But look at you random with assault. Disconcerted. Nearly anonymous with the fate's surprise, and such fabulous, fabulous misery.

SISTER #3: Hair all over your head!

SISTER #2: Eyes looking like hot peppers!

SISTER #1: You are tone-deaf and stupid. While he has danced inside your inner mirror. Settled his sediment. You can't see.

SISTER #3: You would see if you knew *your* eyes, your central equations, your orisha, your deity.

SISTER #2: You must go to meet her.

GIRL (*Reluctantly*): Is this another wild goose chase?

SISTER #1: Do you want a good night's sleep?

(*Light begins to fade and* GIRL *rises and they help her prepare for her journey. Whispering all the while.*)

ALL SISTERS: Believe her. Believe only her.

(*Light continues to fade.*)

SISTER #3: How you gone sing for him if you don't know your own song?

ALL SISTERS: Believe her.

GIRL: Who is she?

ALL SISTERS: You'll know.

(*Total fade as* GIRL *stands on porch. Ready to go. Black stage. Except for one spot on* GIRL, *a blue spot, on* GIRL *at centerstage. She sing-speaks.*)

GIRL (*Half singing. Half talking*):
He's a deep sea diver/ c.c. rider.
He's a deep sea diver/ c.c. rider.
Dipped his hand in water/ turned to cider.

Heard of a woman/ hoodoo in her hand.
Heard of a woman/ hoodoo in her hand.
She live across forest/ and burning sand.

I am the one with a burn/ in my throat.

I am the woman/ a burn in my throat.
Lightning scorched my music/ couldn't save a note.

I simmered my gumbo/ seasoned it hot.
I simmered my gumbo/ seasoned it hot.
Dipped his hand in gumbo/ stuck to the pot.

Heard of a woman/ hoodoo in her hand.
Heard of a woman/ hoodoo in her hand.
Her house past bamboo/ and glistening sand.

(Slow fade on GIRL.*)*

ACT **II**
Scene 3
SETTING:

> A *swamp area. Leafy. Steamy. Initially, the* MAMMIWATERS *are camou-flaged. They reveal themselves. They look downright whorish, villainous, powerful. They wear wet satin that clings. They smoke reefer through cigarette holders. They are portrayed by the* THREE WOMEN.

> *Because they hate elegantly, and are slinkily powerful and above everything including themselves, they narrate their own actions like malicious observers. They punctuate their narration with awful laughter.* GIRL *appears, weary, and confused, talking to herself.*

GIRL: Past bamboo boulevards and neon avenues, icy moons and madness . . . and it is so far! Where is this elusive Water Mother-Hoodoo Woman-Deity who gone make it all right? Am I on another wild goose chase?

MAMMIWATER #1: *(Comes as a voice from behind* GIRL. *Startling as it is meant to be)*: Could be. Could be a wild goose chase.

MAMMIWATER #2: Could be the goose that laid the golden egg.

*(*MAMMIWATERS *all laugh happily.)*

GIRL: Who are you?

MAMMIWATER #3: Who are who?

GIRL: You. Three. The three of you.

MAMMIWATER #1 *(Begins narration of their action)*: The MammiWaters crossed/ their legs were scarred by crocodile teeth. And when they cried/ they cried crocodile tears.

MAMMIWATER #2: Three figurines they sat/ one/ she see no evil. One/ she hear no evil. One/ she speak no evil. They all do a little of each.

MAMMIWATER #3: One/ she played a waterreed. Two/ made nets of water-weeds/ chanting/ while they worked.

GIRL: Who are you? Your voices sound like the worst nightwinds on a cold, cold night. Your faces nearly hidden behind a costume of temptations, bull rushes, and lily leaves.

(GIRL *touches* MAMMIWATER #1's *frock*.)

MAMMIWATER #1 (*Slaps* GIRL's *hand back*): If you please! Don't touch the fabric.

MAMMIWATER #2: Yeah. Hands off the merchandise. Some poor sucker worked his fingers down to the bone to pay for these happy rags.

MAMMIWATER #3: Even the clothes on we back is happy cause they on we back!

MAMMIWATER #2: (*Leans her head toward* GIRL): Feel we do. Madame Ag Onee. Dare you. Touch it.

MAMMIWATER #1 (*Again narrates*): They dare a man to lay with them, and he will disappear. Be devoured by their hidden faces. Their taboo embraces.

MAMMIWATER #3 (*Continues narration*): They drain his scrotum, and seal the veins that make his memory his dream. They draw him down like quicksand, like whirlpool with poisons of the stagnant pool they/ lay wait for him.

ALL MAMMIWATERS (*Almost as one voice, more like a double echo chamber*): They are sisters of tragedy, accomplices, for grief they remove their masks and smile.

MAMMIWATER #2 (*Leans over again*): You look plum tuckered out, girlie. Where you from?

MAMMIWATER #3: She don't know. She don't know where she comin' from.

MAMMIWATER #1: Well, where you been, bitch?

GIRL (*Intimidated. Momentarily despairing. Feeling a little sorry for herself.*): It was through a rainforest I travelled. This is how old my heart is: it is broken in the numbers of rice and rain.

MAMMIWATER #2 (*An aside*): This broad is poetic.

GIRL: My eyes form flat faced leaves/ traces with chains around their ankles. Welts. (*The MammiWaters are unruly all the while she speaks. She really doesn't notice. She is all wrapped up in her journey.*): I watched the earth unwind. Blackbirds that spun like arrows. Insects of a fat season of appendages and poisons.

MAMMIWATER #1 (*To other MammiWaters.*): What this fool talkin' about?

GIRL: It was through a rain forest I travelled. The path cut through anguish and wish so ripe to be rank, spoiled. Sprawling insurmountable, insatiably wanton, a garden of funeral and soiled solitudes.

MAMMIWATER #3: Hard times, huh?

MAMMIWATER #2: The hoe is cracked.

(*The* MAMMIWATERS *come to phoney sympathetic attention.*)

MAMMIWATER #1 (*Snaps to attention*): Who sent you?

GIRL: Friends with their good advice. A coterie of women. A chorus of sympathy grown weary of me. And who exactly are you? Are you the one the sisters sent me to? The three of you? They sent me to *you*? You smelling like rainy autumns, asafetida Grandmama wrapped around my neck to keep out the cold virus and everything else alive. You smelling like perpetual reefer smell your sex simply hovers. And your eyes—faithless, castaway, and cunning . . . Can I trust you?

(MAMMIWATERS *laugh until they cry.*)

MAMMIWATER #2: You trusted *him!*

GIRL: Who?

MAMMIWATER #3: The S.O.B. got you in this sorry way in the first place.

GIRL (*Whispers*): Fire.

MAMMIWATER #3: Yeah, sweet piece, we know about him.

ALL MAMMIWATERS (*Sensuously. Obscenely*): *Fire!*

MAMMIWATER #1: Longed/ to wrap their thighs around him. Fire! To pull him down into wet hurricanes, whirlpools, to eat his echo and chew his maleness. Longed/ to pull him down into the dank forest of forever. To swallow him whole.

MAMMIWATER #2: Well, you gone join us?

MAMMIWATER #3: The pickings is good.

MAMMIWATER #1: Or you gone be a pretty, pious EarthMother, Good Sister, or whatever. Getting fire in yo face at the drop of a hat.

MAMMIWATER #2: Getting *peed* on in the name of Water.

GIRL: I don't think I can hang. I ain't got the proper attitude. I don't believe this was meant for me.

MAMMIWATER #1: Worst that can happen is folks talk bad about you.

MAMMIWATER #2: Yeah, we just a lot of evil rumor, mythologizing, and hypothetomizing on femininity.

MAMMIWATER #3: Yeah. In other words, they talking about yo mama.

MAMMIWATER #1: (*Talking about the other two* MAMMIWATERS): Girl, don't mind them. They on they period.

MAMMIWATER #2: Unh. Uh. Labor pains. We breedin' discontent and fomenting revolution.

GIRL: I heard that! But, tell me, how do you sleep at night?

ALL MAMMIWATERS: Who sleeps at night?

(GIRL *is moving away. Still fascinated by, aware of their madness.*)

MAMMIWATER #1: Reconsider.

MAMMIWATER #2: Send that fire here, to rest, ours is the deep hotel.

MAMMIWATER #3: We'll give him a sleep.

(*The awful laughter of the* MAMMIWATERS *reverberates.*)

(*Slow fade.*)

ACT II
Scene 4
SETTING:
    The moon hangs in the sky. Is replaced by sun. Sun descends. The GIRL *travels through a field. A pool of water is at centerstage.* GIRL *enters. Very much alone.*

GIRL (*Looking around wonderingly*): Now where in the world am I? I shouldn't be far. I should be almost there. Shouldn't I?

VOICE #1 (*A voice from an unseen source. Frail. Timid*): Ask me anything. I am only ash. A product of burn. Set into a hollowed out hole.

GIRL: Who is that?

VOICE #1: Here. Behind this tree.

(GIRL *runs to tree. Finds nothing.*)

GIRL: Where?

VOICE #1, #2, AND #3: Ask us, we balance on nothing. We laugh on nothing. Shadow. And indifferent act. Vacant image in a dark man's eye. A movie image. Mammie, Mamie, Sapphire. Empty idea in lipstick and headrag.

GIRL: Where are you?

VOICE #2: Here beneath this rock.

VOICE #1, #2, AND #3: Here. Here. Here. The heart hurts.

GIRL: Who are you? I feel like a stupid owl always asking "Who?"

VOICE #1: Call me anything. He is not the only hurt in the world.

GIRL: Who is he? Are you talking about Fire? Are you talking about me? Now where are you?

VOICE #1, #2, AND #3: Our face is wind opening its hand. There are other women-mysteries besides the MammiWaters who have their drink of murder and laughter. Our face is wind, voice the edge of nothing. Strictly a product of burn and pale, indifferent imagination. Give us a glass of sparkling pity. We thirst like, better than, bearded Jesus on the cross.

GIRL: Where are you? Maybe I can help you . . .

VOICE #1, #2, AND #3: We're nowhere. Don't you know? We don't exist.

GIRL (*First kneels, then sits at the pool. Worn out. Talking into the pool.*): I give up. Talking to crazy women want me to come wallow in the swamp with them. Now here come some women so pitiful they don't even exist. I just want to find the WaterMother. That's all. Water. I'm thirsty. Look at me. I need to wash my face and hands. Look at me. Embers eaten my eyes. I just want to see. And sleep whole at night. Have a good night's rest. Replenish my heart fibrillating, and womb like a broken silken bubble, frail and frivolous with my female trouble. (GIRL *goes to sleep.*)

(*Enter* WOMEN *in ritual dress, all white, carrying baskets on their heads. They circle* GIRL. *Entrap her. It is the* THREE WOMEN *again.*)

WOMEN IN WHITE (*Whispering. A sonorous chant*): Oba. Water. Oya. Water. Oshun. Water. Omi.

(*They make washing gestures over the* GIRL, *who is still sleeping.*)

WOMAN IN WHITE #1 (*Over the head of the sleeping* GIRL, *makes gestures*): The washing of the beads. The washing of her leaves. The washing of the whispers of her name. The plucking of the eyes of the sorrow.

(GIRL *opens eyes. Is unafraid. Submissive to ritual.*)

The shaving of the head til her hair is an ebony skullcap, shorn immaculate. The washing of the herbs. The washing of the whisper-ring, white-gowned circling. Til the air sings nutmeg and perfumes unknown/ the girl unknown to herself/ fingers the beads/ washes her prayers/ into immaculate sleep.

(GIRL *again sleeps. Fade out on smiling* WOMEN *still circling her.*)

ACT **III**
Scene 1
SETTING:

A *ritual line. Seven women bearing gifts. All in immaculate white. The* GIRL, *however, wears color, perhaps brilliant green. The scene is only blue—indigo, royal blue, azure. Sky, water large and looming. Three male drummers.* GIRL *brings up the rear of the line with her arms full of gifts. She also wears an ivory mask.*

WOMAN IN WHITE #3: I'm taking all my cares to Yemoja, Yemanja, the WaterMother.

WOMAN IN WHITE #2: What you bring her?

WOMAN IN WHITE #3: A fertility doll to bring me babies. A bag of Susan B. Anthony dollars spending like quarters. I'm prayin' she'll multiply my cash.

WOMAN IN WHITE #2: What you bring for her to eat? The orisha must be fed.

WOMAN IN WHITE #3: Red, Black, and Green beans over Brown and wild rice.

WOMAN IN WHITE #2: That'll please her. The national dish. *(She calls back to the* GIRL.*)* And what are you bringing Yemoja, Yemanja, The WaterMother, besides your problems, girl?

GIRL *(Looks into her basket)*: A dish of okra and dried shrimp, many colored beads of sweat, a rosary, perfume, honey, avocado, broken melons, and groundnuts. Ointments and perennial blood.

WOMAN IN WHITE #2: That should definitely please her. She'll look on you with favor. She'll know you serious about fixin' your problem.

WOMAN IN WHITE #3: *(To* GIRL *solicitously)*: Tell me this, honey, why you got on that mask of ivory serenity made of white clay. You not gonna fool her. Everything is not cool.

WOMAN IN WHITE #2: Girl, she just gonna break yo face.

WOMAN IN WHITE #1: Silence. The gift giving begins.

(*All in turn take gifts to the water's edge. They pray at the water's edge. The* GIRL *is last to come forward. When she sets down her offerings and looks out into the suggested sea, something begins to happen. A sparkling mist lifts from the water. It spreads out. A* WOMAN *is shrouded in the sparkling mist. Jazz music comes up with her. She is it!*)

YEMOJA: Girl, you look like death.

(GIRL *draws back.*)

You wearin' that white like death. Child, like a hurt on you. Step out from behind the mask and be a woman. The Mardi Gras of Pain is over. Let me see your hands.

(GIRL *extends hands.*)

Let me see your face.

(GIRL *drops mask. Lifts face.*)

Uh huh. You come just to the right place. Glad you passed the test.

GIRL: What test? There was a test?

YEMOJA: Why you think you have to walk this far to find me? Anybody, whining and worthless, cain't come to me. Very few/ but people/ know my address. Know where I can be reached. Very few/ have crossed the bridge my mouth makes or swings shut. Know how to get past the water that swallows blues. Only a select few recognize my call letters—W-O-M-A-N or W-A-T-E-R, whichever you please. Very few/ outside of human beings, know how to get in touch with me or touch me past a laugh of tea leaves loose in the bottom in the cup of the water that swallows blues.

(*All the worshippers become involved with her talk. They clap and sway.* WOMAN IN WHITE *#2 praisefully mimics the gestures of Yemoja. The* WOMEN *are all joyful and sassy like the* MOTHER.)

WOMAN IN WHITE #1 (*Pleased with* GIRL. *At* GIRL's *shoulder*): She laughs fat and fabulous!

GIRL (*Mesmerized*): Tender. Like a wish inside a cage. So beautiful. Her face—what I can see, is an instrument of music.

WOMAN IN WHITE #1: But isn't her face familiar.

YEMOJA: Music, huh? Thank you, child. But do you really know who I am? I know you don't because you don't know who you are.

WOMAN IN WHITE #1: She is the first birthfluid and the last afterbirth. She is the root of the watertree.

YEMOJA: So you're a child of mine.

GIRL (*Shyly*): I think so. I believe we're related.

YEMOJA (*Amused*): Tell me how.

GIRL: By way of the river and the man who grows dreams that are plucked before winter, yet frostbitten. From the bluesdelta by way of cousins and kitchenette whippings. I have seen the falling sunsets and the Mammi-Waters.

YEMOJA: My lost daughters!

WOMEN IN WHITE ALL: Those creatures. She has seen the MammiWaters.

YEMOJA (*Raises her hand and all is silence*): Let me see your hands again. Yes. You have touched fire. The trauma of the burn is over. Mother's here now. This is the mass dedicated to you. The mass of the snake newly wise finding skin.

(The encounter between YEMOJA *and the* GIRL *is lengthy. The static quality is broken by the activity of the other* WOMEN. *They make preparations for a ritual. Bring candles, etc. There is a surreal, quick quality to their movements. They pantomime water activities: washing, bathing, etc. One boils water . . .)*

You've been held by Fire. I know his name.

GIRL: How do you know?

YEMOJA: His flame still flickers in your eyes. I know his name is Fire. I know him well. And what's he done for you?

GIRL: He infected me with laughing sickness. He taught me the miracle of death. I walked the third rail. He put his eyes on me. I'm in his hot shadow. I can't get a good night's sleep.

YEMOJA: Come here.

(GIRL hesitates.)

WOMAN IN WHITE #1: She will rinse you in cool water and medicines. She will bandage you in honey and herbs.

(YEMOJA throws a net/shawl which may be imaginary over the GIRL's shoulders.)

YEMOJA: That's a net of sympathy. But, not too much. Giving or getting. Too much sympathy not good for you. You have to understand . . .

(Light fades . . .)

Let's talk about him first. Get him out the way. You know what's wrong with Fire?

GIRL: He crazy!

(GIRL wails.)

YEMOJA *(Matter-of-factly)*: Besides the obvious. He's walking in the danger zone and he got his sentry up twenty-four hours a day. He's got his guard up and it ain't standing against you alone.

GIRL: Who?

YEMOJA: I don't wanna name no names. They're afraid he'll break out of his diamond and burn their greedy fingers.

GIRL: If he broke out for me would he burn me—again?

YEMOJA: If you let him. He got some bad habits he gotta break. He think all that actin' out is interestin'.

GIRL: It's too much. All this is keeping me awake nights.

YEMOJA: He sleepin' like a baby.

GIRL: With his mama no doubt.

YEMOJA: Uh uh. The baby sitter.

(GIRL begins to laugh.)

YEMOJA: I knew I could get a laugh outta you. Honey, that story he tellin' is funny. You have to holler. He jumpin' around acting out like he got his penis caught in a zipper.

GIRL: I hope he didn't break it.

YEMOJA: What?

YEMOJA (*Laughs*): Now you got it. But you know he know better than the way he acts. He an adult. He know his childhood is over, but he hanging on. Anyway, you know what I'm about to do? I'm getting ready to jump in this dish of Red, Black, and Green beans, with that okra and shrimp ya brought me on the side. You know talking about these men is that old nervous talk, make you hungry. (GIRL *nods.* YEMOJA *yells to* WOMAN IN WHITE #1.) Bring this child a plate!

(*Black out. Scene does not end. Slowly the setting that the* WOMEN *have arranged comes alive. A circle of candles is lighted. A strong female singing, a wailing and a scatting. The* WOMEN *are dancing in a half-circle. The* YEMOJA *leads their chanting.*)

YEMOJA: Woman, child, you were born before his touch. Listen. Listen. You were born before his touch.

WOMAN IN WHITE #1: Centuries.

WOMAN IN WHITE #2: Millenniums.

WOMAN IN WHITE #3: Eons before.

YEMOJA: His is the theater. Showboat and star stage. He calls down exclamations and hawks applause.

WOMEN IN WHITE ALL: It is you. It is you. The power rests with.

YEMOJA: Yours is subtle and sophisticated. The massive understatement. The magic that moves too slow for the eye. The eloquence of the curve and the deep.

WOMAN IN WHITE #1: It is the weight of you

WOMAN IN WHITE #2: and the waiting, heavy holding,

WOMAN IN WHITE #3: the body of water that can put him still.

YEMOJA: Don't cup your hand too heavy on him. You have the mother's power to caress and smother. He presides over his fear of your extinguishing love and loathing.

WOMAN IN WHITE #1: God/woman, what you can do to him.

WOMAN IN WHITE #2: God/woman, what you can do to him.

YEMOJA: He goes out in the image of a snake, smoke in the hiss before it strikes the abyss that holds all things that are gone. You go over him. Hold, in hungry folds.

WOMEN IN WHITE ALL AND YEMOJA: Do not cup your hand too heavy on him.

(*All* WOMEN *withdraw. Leaving only* GIRL *centerstage. The rest linger in the darkness. Spotlight on* GIRL, *blue, green, yellow, red.*)

GIRL: My face of accusatory eyes. Steam me. Polish me. Mist, take me, til I unfold my eyes that know the language of the high rains that wore grooves in mountains til they bled roads that rose like singers in the sun. My face of lullabye eyes, mist, take me, til I unfold my eyes so soft so on the edge of water and rose so knowing, so soft so on the edge of water and rose so knowing.

(The WOMEN *return. They encircle* GIRL *again. They bow to her, or they genuflect, kneel.*)

YEMOJA: She knows. This one. She knows, and becomes and is and was. She was.

GIRL *(To* YEMOJA, *the WaterMother)*: I am as you are. My face is your face. Your face is my power and my grace. *(To others.)* I am a simple being believing in small rituals. Bathwater flung out of tubs into the streets of Soweto. The child's Saturday night gaiety, a lake, in the cold flat. I am a simple being believing in small rituals. Lovers who bathe after Creation. Mine is a merciful killing/ the cotton chillsoft cloth, unwanted kittens hidden in my blue velvet gelee. Out of each family I have taken a son, testing his method, his trim muscle against the drift, I taste his marrow. And hold his music in my eyes. Until I untie the tides and old slave bones sing while scavengers swoop and swallow songless air. Mine is a merciful killing. The serious suicide's quiet celebration. Ballooning lungs that fatten the chest to bursting. Feel the water fill the mouth. Feel the water fill the nostrils. Feel the water rise, cover the black iris of the eyes.

(*This testimony must be a dance as well as a talk. A church scene of fierce, powerful, swift movements.*)

GIRL *(To All)*: I've learned the word, the key, the tone, and sealed it here *(Points to her own chest.)* to breathe into his mouth.

(*Some* WOMEN *are weeping for joy. Dancing.* GIRL *gathers herself, triumphantly, prepares to leave.*)

YEMOJA: Wait. One last lesson before you forget. Don't meet that fool more than half way. He has to learn to reach. He gotta be above where he is and brave enough to show it. Remember? Let him take a risk.

(GIRL *nods.*)

Fold this leaf of music between the lifted bridges of your breast, above the uncalibrated heartbeat. Listen to this one note: If he ever said something crazy like "No." If he acted like he was loving as a favor to a friend; or he a member of an anti-cruelty society; or if he has nothing in him or sees nothing in you he wants or needs—never mind. You need you. You have some thing for yourself. Poor thing. He out of luck.

(YEMOJA *and* GIRL *exchange farewell embrace.*)

(*Blackout.*)

ACT III
Scene 2
SETTING:
    On the way home. WOMEN IN WHITE *accompany* GIRL. *Each* WOMAN IN

WHITE *wears an identifying band of color—red, yellow, purple.* GIRL *is now Omi Oshun Oba Oya, or* MS. WATERS *for short.*

WOMAN IN WHITE #1: Wooo. My goodness! This is one traveling woman!
WOMAN IN WHITE #2: Where are we now, Ms. Waters.
MS. WATERS: Not far from the strain of the MammiWaters. Can't you smell them?

(MS. WATERS *and* WOMEN *pause. Cat sounds are heard.* MS. WATERS *and* WOMEN *are mystified.* CAT *dancers appear, making cat noises. Dancers wear eye patches over one eye. They parade before the* WOMEN. *They are similar to the* MAMMIWATERS *in their outcast quality, but they lack personal power.*)

CHIEF CAT: Welcome to the Festival of the One Eye.
ALL CATS: He open her nose. He got her mind. He piss in her bread. He mess with her head.

(*All* CATS *cry through their one eye.*)

WOMAN IN WHITE #2: We better move on. I don't like the smell of things here.
WOMAN IN WHITE #3 (*Horrified*): How do they spend their nights?
CHIEF CAT: We suck our solitudes and our whiskey. We sleep a slippery eyed dream. Most of all we lick our wounds miserably. Join us.
MS. WATERS: The Mardi Gras of Pain is over. Haven't you heard? At the festival of widows, wives of complaint, and 3:30 A.M. weepers I will not perform.
CHIEF CAT: Well, you ain't got to be snooty about it.
SECOND CAT: Hey, you! Wipe that smile off yo face!
MS. WATERS: Don't you get tired of crying the blues, crying the blues, instead of weeping and laughing yo personal joy? My sisters, I share your pain but don't you grow weary of wasting yo water in a whiskey glass?
CHIEF CAT (*To other* CATS, *then* MS. WATERS): Listen at her. She think she free. Who you on yo way to see now, Mama, since you been baptized? What you gone do if he, whoever he be, don't want you?
SECOND CAT: Yeah, you gone shout for joy?
MS. WATERS: No. Yes. Why, Yes, I will! I will just be me and . . .
CHIEF CAT: Shit. . . .
ALL CATS (*Chanting*): You a female you can't be free. You a woman you can't be free. You a womb, girl, you can't be free. You a female you can't be free.

(WOMEN IN WHITE *having withdrawn, resurge, form a line behind* MS. WATERS.)

MS. WATERS: I got a line of believers behind me to prove you a lie. My genealogy speaks in butt strut, under satin slightly wrinkled, like one of Duke's songs in this rough, dry material of my African tongue.

(*Snaps out a gorgeous fan. All* WOMEN *fan.*)

WOMEN IN WHITE ALL: Smoke it, Mama. You sizzling, woman. Go head on.

MS. WATERS: I'm so happy I wanta sing for everybody. (*Embraces each* WOMAN.) I love, love, love, I even love his Mama. She a sister. I bear her bowls of African mimosa and violet. I have charity for her and her husband and hers . . .

WOMEN IN WHITE: Woman, you just loving everybody.

MS. WATERS: That's cause I love me. I am about love. I ain't all giving, either. I want some receiving. I have traveled in the name of love, to find love to beget love.

(CATS *are licking their wounds as lights fade.*)

ACT **III**

Scene 3

SETTING:

> SHANGO *in his palace is mixing pots and potions. He is doing math, magic, and science. He is busy and talking to himself;* THE FAN *thinks he's talking to her. She is rapping.*

THE FAN: Feel the breeze? I am only here to please. Am I too high? I don't want to trouble the flame. I am only here to please.

SHANGO (*Musing while working*): In my ordinary life as a man, before I tamed thunder and caught lightning in a jar like lightning bugs and sealed it. In that life I was just a man.

THE FAN: You are man. You are all man.

SHANGO: Without my divine complexity, I was all that I am now and less wise. Oba and man of science, magic, and mathematics. In that life in my land we celebrated the first yam and plantains grew long and thick as Eshu's member. (SHANGO *gestures vaguely.*)

THE FAN (*Coy and coolly lascivious*): How big is Eshu's member? Feel the breeze. I am only here to please.

SHANGO (*Ignores her*): In that time of the giant baobab before I messed in the magic pots of Creation I made love and war. Three wives loved me and I husbanded them. I savored each one of them and listened to the music they spread throughout my house.

THE FAN: There is music in this breeze. Listen. (*She fans furiously.*)

SHANGO: No. Not my house. It was *our* house. (*Having finished mixing, he pours his mixture in a tall chalice. Moves to his throne and begins to sip pensively.*) I poured myself into three women and they grew children from the vines of their bellies. A field of children, a harvest of honey and blackberry flesh and laughter high as grasses. Children. (*He begins to laugh.*) I remember when Awotunde hid in the belly of the old baobab and his mothers could not find him for a day. When he stepped out into the sunlight they reached out for him singing. All three singing. Oya, Oba, Oshun. Three wives.

(*Shadows beside and behind his throne dance as three women.*)

THE FAN (*Sarcastic*): What perfection rested in the palm of your hand.

SHANGO: What perfect peace! I lost it and them. I didn't know my magic, the second face it could turn. (*Rises, looks at* THE FAN *directly for the first time. Puts down chalice. Takes centerstage, looks up, flings out arms, as if he were trying to reach the sun.*) I didn't say my prayers before I joined in the feast, I simply gorged myself like a barbarian. Taking knowledge, pleasure, and plenty without a word of thanks. I messed up. At last, the pulse of the Ancestors beat against me because I did not bless them.

THE FAN (*Bored*): Feel the breeze? The only aim is to please.

SHANGO: And it all went up in the last magic that raged against me. Lightning shaped in a terrible boomerang. I lost it all. I lost it all. Wives, children. What was left but Death? I took Death. Death is the teacher the Ancestors sent me to.

THE FAN (*Interested*): Teaching what?

SHANGO: Loss. I learned loss. You know what lessons I have brought to this lifetime? Never to have what it hurts too much to lose. So I see a dish and I taste. I taste but not too much. (*He is trying to convince himself.*)

THE FAN: Taste. Taste me.

SHANGO: Go away.

THE FAN: My only aim is to please. (*All over him. Whining.*)

SHANGO: Is that all?

THE FAN: Yes. Oh. Yes. Only to please you.

SHANGO (*A slow realization*): Your only aim is me? Do you sing?

(THE FAN *shakes her head.*)

You don't have a life song to sing for yourself? Don't you have a god of your own inside you, flowing like the rivers of Oba, or Oya, or Oshun?

THE FAN: I am a tame breeze at your holy feet. (*She falls to his feet.*)

SHANGO: Get up. I'm too old for this. I know the treachery of all this servility. There were other women after my three.

THE FAN: My veins are fragile glass tubes hot and breaking from the heat.

SHANGO: Woman, are you empty?

THE FAN: I'm filled only with you.

SHANGO: Or whoever is available to . . . What is your name?

THE FAN: I have no *name*. I am only The Fan, handle me. Feel the breeze, my only aim is to please. (*She backs away into darkness.*)

SHANGO (*Back on his throne. Talks to himself*): Three wives—they were. Oba, the first and always ready for battle; Oya, the loyal always at my side even into Death who went with me to face the Ancestors; Oshun, the coy and beautiful, playful one dancing behind her own fan.

(*Three shadows again.*)

And then, after these centuries and so many mistakes . . . a girl with lush, fruit-filled hips, breasts, mouth, and eyes wide open, always for giving. A girl singing self-sacrifice she should have saved. After all . . . What do I have to give? What did I give besides anger and loss? Oba,

Oya, Oshun—that girl I tasted, (admit it, man!) I devoured her and demanded more, the delicacy was so tender. I wonder, that girl, who came singing, does she have a name?

(*Slow fade into black.*)

ACT **III**
Scene 4
SETTING:

> WOMEN *arrive at* SHANGO's *gate.* MS. WATERS *is in foreground, we see shadow of* FIRE *busy on high.*

WOMAN IN WHITE #1: He has sent away his sentry.
WOMAN IN WHITE #2: And his fan.
WOMAN IN WHITE #3: Are you sure . . . ? And what if he?
MS. WATERS: Then I am Ms. Waters. I'm still Ms. Waters. And I'll always sing. (*Knocking at gate/door. Yelling.*) I believe good things are in you. Beyond your fire. Things with no passion in them, torn things of the child you once were, and the hidden face of the god you are. (*Pauses to watch his reaction. He is being coy.*) Tho fire is good I will touch you without heat, remarking only on the simple bone of air you are.
WOMAN IN WHITE #1: (*In background*): He ain't changed. What good is her change if he ain't changed too. She just be broke. He still the same.

(FIRE *is acting like he hears none of this.*)

MS. WATERS: Listen, open this door, fool.

(*He opens door majestically, forcefully.*)

WOMAN IN WHITE #3: She has come singing. Singing.
SHANGO (*Sullen. Reserved. Watching her*): Well. I'm busy. I got a lot ta do.
MS. WATERS: That's fine. I do too. I was on my way home. Thought I'd drop you a line . . . How's tricks? (*She takes his seat. Crosses her legs.*) I want to speak to him.
SHANGO: Only person here is me.
MS. WATERS: Fine. I want to speak to your secret face.
SHANGO: I ain't got no secrets. My business is in the streets.
MS. WATERS (*Rises. Stands on side of seat*): Have a seat.

(*He sits. Tries to assume his original stance. She toys with him. Touches him.*)

> I am willing to be kind. Call a truce. I'll keep it. I am absolutely fierce with honey on the verge of falling. I have forever been one who has given/ charity I found delicious. Too much giving. The ceremony of gifts I was enchanted with. Now I want to receive. I am hungry for draughts of blood and fire.

(*She caresses him.*)

> Now I am the Fire Eater. Nourish me. Here is the painted vase that holds

your soulpiece. I break you, sunder, and carefully collect: I pull out your organs, the suggestion of mango and papaya. My teeth go deep. I suck your crystals of strength. Now I am the Fire Eater. Nourish me.

SHANGO (*His talk counters hers. They speak in turns*): I know the treacheries of waters. Dark sailors who set sail across centuries. Men lost in sudden squalls at sea.

MS. WATERS: Now I am the Fire Eater. Nourish me.

WOMEN IN WHITE (*Husky whispers*): Now she is the Fire Eater. Nourish her.

SHANGO: I know the hunger of the fishing villages that turned to scratch the rocks when the ocean gave up empty nets. I know the treacheries of waters. Men are lost in sudden squalls at sea.

MS. WATERS: I part the fur on your chest. Split your chords of thunder and treble. You are a disembodied voice, hidden, aloof, I claim you, Flamboyant Flame, Fastidious Deity. Now I am the Fire Eater.

WOMEN IN WHITE: Nourish her. Nourish her.

SHANGO: I know the mysteries of waters. A man losing his voice in the fog. The storm, sudden and evil, breaking the body, taking the soul away . . .

(FIRE *tries to break away.*)

I've aged and been through many lives. Wives. I know the *under*-side of oceans.

WOMEN IN WHITE (*Disgustedly*):
So you been a poor judge of character?
Don't judge her by your error.
Listen to her, my brother.

MS. WATERS: Have you never seen the fire reflected in the water? Its edges are softened, blur into a flame easy on the eye.

SHANGO: I've seen rivers rise over their banks. Wash away flesh and dream until every valley is filled with missing links that cannot connect, again. I know the treacheries of water. I never swim alone.

MS. WATERS: Take this thigh bone for wish. And this mouth to sail inside. Mouth made of mist. Break my breasts like bread. I am the end of all drought and famine. (*She rises.*)

WOMEN IN WHITE:
She is sincere as spring water.
She is the movement of honey and the passion of fruit.
Be tender with her.

MS. WATERS: I am the end of all drought and famine. Don't fool around and miss this, brother. There's only one *me* per lifetime.

SHANGO: Only one, huh?

MS. WATERS: Only one smile.

SHANGO: One smile. Milk and easy.

MS. WATERS: One kiss.

SHANGO: One kiss. Like berries breaking.

MS. WATERS: One touch.

SHANGO: One touch. Cool. A dance of feathers.

MS. WATERS: One faith. Believe me.

SHANGO: One faith.

MS. WATERS: One hope. One purpose.

SHANGO: One hope.

MS. WATERS: One charity.

SHANGO: One charity. That means love.

MS. WATERS: Uh huh.

SHANGO: One love. By the way. What's your name, woman?

(They circle around and around each other tentatively acting out each other's spoken promises and hesitations. Barriers are breaking as they do. They mesmerize each other.)

MS. WATERS: Omi. Omi Oya Oba Oshun. Ms. Waters for short.

SHANGO *(Secretly joyous)*: That's enough name for three women. How can you be three women?

MS. WATERS: I'm a riddle like the sphinx. Only one.

SHANGO: Only one. *(Issues his last resistance.)* I'm not looking to be hurt by no woman. This is the way it's gonna be . . . I get restless some time. I gotta have money to burn . . . I flare up now and then. *(He draws her into his lap.)*

MS. WATERS: Fire, hush.

(Spotlight on the circle of their faces.)

RECESSIONAL

SETTING:

An African wedding. Much color. SHANGO *and* MS. WATERS *are at the head of a reception area.* MS. WATERS *is sing-speaking. This scene is used to spotlight the players for applause. It is inside and outside the play proper.*

MS. WATERS: Three wives I come to you. Three wise. My lord he comes like the lightning. My love he is the thunder king.

(She and SHANGO receive the guests.)

WOMAN #1: Watch him, Ms. Waters. Don't let him get too high and mighty.

WOMAN #2: Be tender with him. Tender never hurt nobody, Omi.

WOMAN #3: Be yourself. Just be yourself and you two will make it.

WOMAN #2 *(Looking off stage)*: Did somebody call the Fire Department? Burn Unit? They outside.

WOMAN #3: Tell them to go away. We just burning bad bridges here. We have crossed over to the other side.

WOMAN #1 *(To* MS. WATERS*)*: Woman, just be strong and love that man. Ain't no harm in that. And be sure he got hisself together when he go in the water.

(All laugh.)

SHANGO: I'm always together.

WOMAN #2: We hate for somethin' to happen to him.

WOMAN #3: Water can be dangerous. Like he say.

MS. WATERS: My love he calls me. He calls me by the love of God.

WOMAN #2: You know this don't guarantee no happy ending.

WOMAN #3: How come it don't?

WOMAN #1: Well, I hope she don't put him out when she get tired of his high jinks.

WOMAN #3: What high jinks? He looks right secure to me.

WOMAN #1: Water can be dangerous.

WOMAN #2: So can Fire.

SHANGO: Women, hush.

MS. WATERS (To SHANGO): Three wives of love are singing to you. Three women singing as one.

[1980]

The Day of the Swallows
A Drama in Three Acts

Estela Portillo

THE CHARACTERS
(in order of appearance)

Alysea
Clemencia
Josefa
Tomás
Eduardo
Clara
Don Esquinas
Father Prado

(The tierra of Lago de San Lorenzo is within memory of mountain-sweet pine. Then the maguey thickens with the ferocity of chaotic existence; here the desert yawns. Here it drinks the sun in madness.

The village of Lago de San Lorenzo is a stepchild; it is a stepchild to the Esquinas hacienda, for the hacienda has been a frugal mother and a demanding father. Its name comes from the yearly ritual of the saint-day of San Lorenzo when all the young women gather around the lake to wash their hair and bathe in promise of a future husband. The tempo of life, unbroken, conditioned, flavors its heartbeat with dreams and myths. The *hacienda is the fiber upon which existence hangs. The church, the fluid rose, assures the future promise of Elysian fields. No one dares ask for life.*

What is this footfall beyond ritual, beyond livelihood? What is this faint unknown ache in the heart? It's more than just the rasp of hope. . . . The young know this; and they go to the spring with lyrical intimacy. By the lake, eyes burn and feet dig the mud of the spring; someone traces mountain against sky and gulf expands, drowning, drowning. The obligation is remembered back in the village; the toll of the church bell offering sanctuary is a relief; the lake becomes too much for them.

At daybreak the fiesta day is sanctified with a misa *at sunrise; the choir rejoices the promise of day. A holy procession is led by the priest and an "honored member" of the church. Offerings to the patron saint are generous amidst frugality. The animals are blessed; the people are blessed; all is washed clean.*

Perhaps secretly each villager senses the werewolf moon inside him; the bite into passions will be hard and fierce after sunset.

On the day of San Lorenzo, in the heat of July, everybody goes to the lake; this day the lake is invaded by village life. When the church bells toll eleven in the sun, the late morning is the sole witness to the bathing of the virgins. The lake becomes a sacred temple. The high priestesses talk of hopes, lovers, and promises. In earnest belief, they wash their hair in spring water to insure future marriages made in heaven. It is true, no one has seen a marriage made in heaven, but each girl hugs the private truth that hers will be the one.

Two hundred years before the Esquinas family had settled in Lago de San Lorenzo on a Spanish grant of fifty thousand acres, the Indians were pushed out further into the desert. This was the way of the bearded ga-chupín, with his hot grasp and his hot looks. Their greedy vitality was a wonder to the Indian. It was also death.

But now the barrio clustered itself around the hacienda. The conquered conquered the conquerors.

There is a house, the only house close to the edge of the lake. Here our story begins. . . .)

ACT I

Scene 1

(JOSEFA's *sitting room; it is an unusually beautiful room, thoroughly feminine and in good taste; the profusion of lace everywhere gives the room a safe, homey look. The lace pieces are lovely, needlepoint, hairpin, limerick, the work of patience and love. Upstage left is a large French window; from it one can view a large tree. On the tree is a freshly painted tree house of unusual size and shape. It is an orb that accommodates a great number of birds. The room faces south, so it is flooded with light; the light, the lace, the open window all add to the beauty of the room, a storybook beauty of serenity. To the right is a door leading to the kitchen; there is another door leading to a bedroom; downstage left there is a door leading to the outside.*

ALYSEA *is sitting on the floor when the curtain rises. It is before dawn; but a few minutes after the curtain rises, light begins to fill the room.* ALYSEA *is cleaning the sitting room carpet, an unusual task for this hour. Next to her is a pail; she uses a piece of cloth with quick, frantic movements, rinses, and continues the scrubbing. After a while she looks at the cloth in her hand intently, as in realization of what she is doing. Suddenly she drops it, seemingly in horror. She looks helpless and lost. Still sitting on the floor she leans her head against a chair and cries silently, staring up into the now streaming light from the window. There is the sound of the milk bell. It is* CLEMENCIA *delivering. When she hears it,* ALYSEA *jumps up, wipes away traces of tears with her apron, then opens the French window and looks out.)*

ALYSEA: She'll come right in if I'm not at the door to pay her.

(She looks around the room. Her eyes fall on a small side table next to the couch. She goes to the table and stares at a long kitchen knife with traces of blood on it. Hurriedly, she picks up the cleaning cloth, and uses it to pick up the knife gingerly. She wraps the cloth around the knife and places it in a side table drawer. During this interval, CLEMENCIA's *noisy arrival is heard. The kitchen door is opened; there is a tug of milk can, then a pouring of milk. Several sighs and ejaculations about hard work are heard.* ALYSEA *looks around the room one last time as* CLEMENCIA *walks in.)*

CLEMENCIA: Josefa! Alysea! My centavos for the week are not on the kitchen table. *Hombre* . . . do I have to beg for my money? *Oye* . . . *¿dónde están?*

ALYSEA: *Buenos días,* Clemencia . . . early?

CLEMENCIA *(staring at* ALYSEA*)*: *Que horror!* What is the matter? You look terrible. Have you been up all night?

ALYSEA *(smooths her hair; looks at her hands guiltily)*: Yes . . . I stayed up late. A new pattern in lace.

CLEMENCIA: You work hard to please Josefa, don't you? *(She notices* ALYSEA *looking at her hands.)* What's the matter with your hands? Not rheumatism . . . you're just a girl. . . . Look at mine! Life has eaten them up. . . . I feel pain . . . ay! . . . it is my destiny to suffer. . . . You owe me seven pesos.

ALYSEA: Yes, of course. *(She goes to the household money box, takes a set of keys from her apron pocket and opens it. She counts out the money.)* *Cinco* . . . *seis* . . . *siete.*

CLEMENCIA: *Gracias* . . . *(Looks at* ALYSEA *again and shakes her head)* Rest in the afternoon . . . you look all in. You can in this house. There is a beautiful peace here.

ALYSEA: Yes . . . here it stretches itself out to breathe. . . .

CLEMENCIA: You begin to talk like Josefa now . . . you like her . . . eh? She doesn't want you to work yourself to death . . . she is too kind.

ALYSEA: The most considerate of persons . . . but there is so much to do.

CLEMENCIA: Of course, San Lorenzo . . . *mañana* . . . Josefa will be so grand leading the procession with the Father to the church . . . a happy day for the barrio . . . we all share Josefa's honor like we have shared her goodness . . . a great lady.

ALYSEA: I had forgotten . . . the procession tomorrow.

CLEMENCIA: What's the matter with you? Forgotten?

ALYSEA: Don't mind me. . . . I'm not myself today . . . Clemencia.

CLEMENCIA: Doña Josefa is an angel. All her life, she goes around . . . with that walking stick of hers . . . always she goes . . . like an avenging angel . . . helping . . . what a sight she must be . . . pounding with her stick on those evil people. . . . One, two . . . that's for wickedness! (*She makes motions of one pounding away.*) She takes care of the devil all right . . . eh? Yes . . . she saved you from the sickness. . . .

ALYSEA: Saved me . . . from the sickness . . . what is shadow? What is sickness?

CLEMENCIA: Talk sense, child! . . . you need rest. (*She looks at lace work on table.*) My . . . you are making lace as beautiful as Josefa's! You are lucky.

ALYSEA: Lucky? (*She goes to the window.*) This room is beautiful . . . isn't it? I'm lucky to be here . . . aren't I? (*Pause*) Appearances . . . they are very funny! Tomorrow the church will honor Josefa . . . how very funny! (*She begins to laugh; then the laugh is eventually lost in sobbing.*) Oh, God!

CLEMENCIA: What is the matter? (*She looks around.*) Where is Josefa. . . . Josefa! (*She goes to* ALYSEA *and feels her forehead.*) Are you feverish?

(*At this point* JOSEFA *enters. She is a tall, regal woman about thirty-five. Her bones are Indian's; her coloring is Aryan. She wears her hair back severely. Her movements are graceful and quiet. The cuffs and collar of her dress are of exquisite lace. She walks up to* ALYSEA *and puts her arm around her.*)

JOSEFA: Alysea, quiet! (*She turns to* CLEMENCIA.) She's not feeling well, I suppose.

CLEMENCIA: She worked all night.

JOSEFA: Oh?

CLEMENCIA: You must make her rest.

JOSEFA: You're right, of course. . . .

CLEMENCIA: Well . . . I must be going. . . . I'm late on my rounds . . . (*She sighs.*) I wish I could stay here. (*She looks around.*) What heavenly peace . . .

JOSEFA (*smiling*): You are welcome . . . this is your home . . .

CLEMENCIA: Doña Josefa . . . you are an angel!

JOSEFA: No . . . just happy! . . . Did you get your money?

(JOSEFA *escorts* CLEMENCIA *to the door.* CLEMENCIA *gives a last anxious look at* ALYSEA.)

CLEMENCIA: She'll be all right in your hands, Josefa.

JOSEFA: I'll see that she rests.

(CLEMENCIA *leaves through the kitchen door.* JOSEFA *remains silent as the sounds of departure from the kitchen are heard.*)

JOSEFA: You should rest. . . . Clemencia's right.

(ALYSEA *shakes her head.*)

JOSEFA: Do you think it's wise? . . .

ALYSEA: Wise! the way you word it . . . wise!

JOSEFA: Very well, I'll put it another way . . . is this the time to break down? Beautiful days demand our strength. . . . We must be faithful to loveliness.

ALYSEA (*incredulously*): You believe that? (*She walks up to* JOSEFA *almost menacingly.*) How can you justify in that way? You!

JOSEFA (*softly*): There are things we must do . . . to keep a sanity . . . to make the moment clear. (*Pause*) Any signs of the swallows? Isn't the tree lovely?

ALYSEA: Have you forgotten? . . . how can you! . . . Josefa, last night. . . .

(ALYSEA *is overwhelmed with the memory; she runs out of the room.* JOSEFA *looks for a moment after her; then she touches the lace curtains on the window.*)

JOSEFA: We pattern our lives for one beautiful moment . . . like this lace . . . little bits and pieces come together . . . to make all this . . . my world . . . a crystal thing of light; Alysea must understand . . . she must!

(*There is a knock at the door leading outside.* JOSEFA *goes to the door; she opens it; it is* TOMÁS, *her shiftless uncle.*)

TOMÁS: Oh . . . it is you, Josefa! You're not at the hacienda this morning.

JOSEFA: What are you doing here?

TOMÁS: The pump . . .

JOSEFA: You fixed that already. . . . I've told you not to come around here at this time of day. . . .

TOMÁS: You do not appreciate . . . always suspicious. . . .

JOSEFA: I don't want you bothering Alysea . . . ever. . . .

TOMÁS: It is like you . . . to think the worst of me.

JOSEFA (*with resignation*): How are the children? Your wife Anita?

TOMÁS: They manage better than me . . . thanks to you. . . . There is little steady work. . . . I need a few centavos . . . Josefa. . . . you're rich!

JOSEFA: What for. . . tequila?

TOMÁS: Just a little money . . . look, my hands . . . they shake. . . . I need it, Josefa . . . please!

JOSEFA: Don't beg!

TOMÁS: You let Clara have all she wants. . . .

JOSEFA: That is none of your business.

TOMÁS (*noticing the pail*): Eh . . . what's this? Looks like blood!

JOSEFA: Go to the kitchen . . . help yourself to meal and beans . . . for the family.

(TOMÁS *is still staring at the pail.*)

JOSEFA: Did you hear me?

TOMÁS: Yes . . . yes, Doña Perfecta . . . Doña Perfecta . . . so charitable . . . ha! ha!

JOSEFA: I'm not in the mood for your sarcasm.

TOMÁS: You will lead the procession tomorrow like the queen of the world . . . eh? You can spare a few centavos? a bottle? Do you keep some in the house when you get it for Clara?

JOSEFA: You're not getting any money.

TOMÁS (*starting to leave*): What's in that pail?

JOSEFA (*indignant*): I don't have to satisfy your curiosity.

TOMÁS: *Cálmate.* . . . I was just asking. . . .

(JOSEFA *turns her back to him; he leaves through the kitchen door; his grumbling is heard as he helps himself to the food offered by* JOSEFA. JOSEFA *stares at the contents of the pail; she looks away and touches her temples with her fingertips. She sits in a rocking chair, leans back, closes her eyes, and grips the arms of the chair. She rocks back and forth.*)

JOSEFA: There is no desert here . . . only light . . . to live each day with nothing . . . to sink . . . (*She closes her eyes and rocks.*) The lonely, lonely struggle . . . then to emerge . . . to find the light . . . I have so much now. . . . I want to give so much now . . . Alysea must understand! We must keep this world of light at all costs. . . .

(*She rises and walks to the window and stands absorbing the light; one can sense an obvious union between the light and* JOSEFA.)

JOSEFA (*softly*): How moist your lips, my light. . . . Through me . . . through me . . . you live. (*She comes back from her intimate world and looks at the birdhouse with pleasure.*) The long flight . . . how tired they will be; how thirsty after the desert . . . here my swallows will find peace . . . home. (*As she looks at the tree,* TOMÁS *comes through the patio outside the window. He has a sack over his shoulder.* JOSEFA *does not seem to be mindful of him.* TOMÁS *calls.*)

TOMÁS: Hey, Josefa! Are you casting a spell . . . so early? You don't scare me . . . I know you, *querida* . . . I know many things . . . you burn inside. . . .

(JOSEFA *stares at him unbelievingly, as if he has destroyed a beauty; then she turns away from the window.*)

TOMÁS: Hey, Josefa . . . don't run away . . . the great Doña Perfecta runs away from her good-for-nothing uncle . . . that's funny . . . ha, ha!

JOSEFA (*firmly, but in an ominous tone*): Go home, Tomás, go home.

(*She closes the window and walks to an unfinished damask close to the window. She sits down, unhooks the needle, and begins to work on it. Her concentration is a fiery intensity; this is obvious in her finger movements.* ALYSEA *comes back into the room; she is now composed and refreshed; she has put on a pretty dress. She sees the pail and removes it, taking it into the kitchen; all this time* JOSEFA *remains absorbed in the damask.* ALYSEA *comes back.* JOSEFA *looks up.*)

JOSEFA: You look so nice! Every morning now . . . you look like the garden. . . .

ALYSEA: Nothing is as beautiful as your garden . . . paradise must look like that.

JOSEFA: A garden of light . . . perhaps it has a sense of paradise. . . .

ALYSEA: Tomás was here?

JOSEFA: Sneaking around as usual . . . (*Pause*) the pretty dress . . . for Eduardo again?

ALYSEA: Yes . . . I'll bring in the morning coffee . . . scones?

JOSEFA: Fine . . . and honey . . . suddenly I'm hungry . . . (*She leaves the damask and begins to clear the coffee table.*) By the way . . . ask Eduardo to have some morning coffee with us today . . . don't run off for your usual morning walk.

ALYSEA: May I? Thank you . . . he's been coaxing me . . . he's absolutely fascinated by you.

JOSEFA: Do invite him.

(ALYSEA *seems to be holding back tears, although she has pretended calm through the conversation.*)

JOSEFA: What's the matter?

(ALYSEA *is not able to answer; she just shakes her head.* JOSEFA *walks up to her.* ALYSEA *stands still and helpless.* JOSEFA *takes* ALYSEA'S *face in her hands.*)

JOSEFA: You are so dear to me . . . I don't like to see you like this . . . Alysea, don't dwell on what happened . . . things will be all right. Haven't I always made things all right?

(ALYSEA *still doesn't answer.*)

JOSEFA: The tragic things in my life taught me one thing . . . calm. The waiting . . . that is harder than struggle. . . . Alysea, learn how . . . to find a strength . . . this loveliness here . . . our world . . . isn't it worth it?

(ALYSEA *begins to cry gently.* JOSEFA *comforts her.* ALYSEA *becomes limp; she places her head on* JOSEFA'S *shoulder like a child.* JOSEFA *strokes her hair.*)

JOSEFA: Your hair . . . your beautiful hair . . . here, let me comb it. . . .

(*Suddenly* ALYSEA *breaks away. She seems at a loss, then remembers the coffee.*)

ALYSEA: I'll get things started in the kitchen . . . Eduardo will be here any moment now.

JOSEFA: About last night, Alysea . . . we must have a story.

ALYSEA (*she seems to shiver*): Story?

JOSEFA: When I took David to the hospital . . . the doctors . . . everyone was sympathetic . . . I told them someone had broken in . . .

ALYSEA: And David?

JOSEFA: He will be all right.

ALYSEA: I can never believe that. . . .

JOSEFA: I will take care of him always. . . .

ALYSEA: You killed him!

JOSEFA: Don't! He'll be back with us in a few weeks . . . I will make a fine life for him always. . . .

ALYSEA: He'll never . . . he'll never . . .

(*She is overcome by emotion; she walks out of the room into the kitchen. JOSEFA looks after her. She remains standing for a moment; then she picks up a book of poetry from the lamp table.*)

JOSEFA: Santa Teresita . . .
"*El hombre toma . . . toma y hiere,
La flor desnuda . . . temblorosa . . .*"
("Man takes . . . he takes and wounds
The tremulous . . . naked flower")
In her world of God . . . she saw what I see . . . she knew the light . . . beauty . . . truth . . . yes . . . in a cloister.

(*She looks around the room. Then she walks up to a workbasket and picks up a piece of lace. She holds it to the light and intently traces the pattern.*)

JOSEFA: The web . . . the beautiful web we weave! Anything . . . anything is worth this!

ACT I
Scene 2
(*A few minutes later; ALYSEA comes from the kitchen with a morning tray; coffee, scones, juice. She places the tray on the coffee table. There is a knock. ALYSEA goes to the door. It is EDUARDO.*)

EDUARDO (*a young man of mixed heritage*): I came through the path. . . .

ALYSEA (*drawing him in*): I'm glad. Josefa wants you to have morning coffee . . . in here . . . with her. You always come for me in such a hurry . . . you hadn't seen this room . . . had you?

EDUARDO: No . . . never! (*Looking around*) Well . . . you were right . . . what a room! . . . for women.

ALYSEA: What do you mean?

EDUARDO: It is a dream of gentleness . . . peace; it is not a man's room . . . but it is beautiful.

ALYSEA: You're right . . . Josefa made this haven . . . away from the world of men.

EDUARDO (*looking at her quizzically*): You like that?

ALYSEA: After what I've lived through . . . yes; this was heaven . . . when she brought me here. Sit down . . . she'll be here any moment.

(EDUARDO *watches* ALYSEA *as she arranges napkins, spoons.*)

EDUARDO: Have you told her . . . about our plans?

ALYSEA: No . . . she suspects something between us.

EDUARDO: And?

ALYSEA: It is hard to understand her feelings . . . there is a stillness in her.

EDUARDO: She dotes on you . . . I don't think she will be pleased . . . after all, I'm taking you away to a wilderness . . . mountain, pines. My squaw . . . living and loving in the open.

(*He goes to her, gathers her in his arms; they kiss,* ALYSEA *clings to him.*)

EDUARDO: It won't be like this . . . you know!

ALYSEA: I'll be with you . . . isn't that everything?

EDUARDO: And the gentle life you love?

ALYSEA: What you will share with me . . . will be so much more.

(*They embrace again.*)

EDUARDO: Say! Have you seen the morning? It is a conspiracy . . . sun, clouds, green fields . . . and the pines from the distance . . . I can hardly wait. Let's leave right now . . . pack the horses . . . take the mountain trail past the lake . . . the way of my people.

ALYSEA: Not now . . . you crazy Indian!

EDUARDO: We'll find a clearing . . . plow . . . build a cabin . . . have babies. . . .

ALYSEA: Sometimes I think you have to be out in the open . . . no matter what . . .

EDUARDO: That's where my God is.

(EDUARDO *sits down;* ALYSEA *stands behind his chair and gently traces his cheek.*)

ALYSEA: Your world! A beautiful God exists . . . in your world . . . when you talk . . . He is free . . . green . . . open. You know something?

EDUARDO (*catching her hand and kissing it*): What?

ALYSEA: Father Prado understands your God too. At confession . . . I told him about not attending mass because we go exploring . . . to find the tallest pines . . . I told him about your God . . . he smiled and told me I had found a holier temple.

EDUARDO: Let's take him with us.

ALYSEA (*laughing*): You know better . . . his life is the barrio . . . the people.

EDUARDO: He will marry us . . . before we leave. . . .

ALYSEA (*pulling away*): No . . . we must wait . . .

EDUARDO: Why? Listen, woman . . . no one in her right mind turns down a marriage proposal. . . .

ALYSEA: I want you to be sure . . . after a while . . . after we have shared. . . .

EDUARDO (*in jest*): You shameless hussy . . . you wish to live in sin, eh?

ALYSEA: Don't jest . . . . there was so much ugliness . . . before Josefa brought me here . . . I remember . . . they brought a bunch of us from the country . . . they promised jobs as seamstresses; my barrio was poor . . . we went hungry . . . so I came . . . the city was a nightmare . . . they locked us up in an old house . . . they gave us disgusting soiled dresses to wear . . . then we found out.

EDUARDO: Stop torturing yourself.

ALYSEA: No . . . let me finish . . . I've never told you . . . I hid in the closet of the room; an ugly man with fat hands asked the girls where I was . . . they didn't know . . . he cursed; I was trembling underneath a pile of dirty dresses suffering with the sweat of lust . . . I closed my eyes. Then, I decided to run . . . I simply got up . . . and ran . . . down the stairs . . . into an open hall . . . where men . . . men with hard, dead looks stared . . . no one expected me to try and escape through the front door . . . but I did . . . I got as far as the street . . . then he caught up with me; his hands were at my throat. . . .

EDUARDO: That's enough. . . .

ALYSEA: All of a sudden . . . Josefa appeared . . . with her walking stick. She raised it over her head and beat the man . . . he cried out in pain . . . she never faltered . . . then she brought me to this world of light . . .

EDUARDO: We shall marry tomorrow night . . . that's it!

ALYSEA: No . . . no . . . there's something else . . . (*She becomes very agitated.*) Eduardo . . . last night . . . (JOSEFA *enters.*)

JOSEFA: Good morning . . . am I late? Is the coffee cold?

ALYSEA: No . . . no . . . you are just in time.

EDUARDO (*drawing out a chair for her*): Our great lady! (ALYSEA *becomes busy with the food.*)

ALYSEA (*to* JOSEFA): Juice?

JOSEFA: Yes . . . thank you. Eduardo, what are you up to . . . charming the women so early in the morning?

EDUARDO: What better time?

JOSEFA: You are different! Alysea . . . give Eduardo . . . some of this orange . . . it's delicious . . .

EDUARDO: No! No! just coffee . . . and what's this? (*He picks up a scone, tastes it.*) Wonderful! I had heard about all your wonders . . . but . . . cooking too!

JOSEFA: Alysea baked them . . . from an old recipe of mine. . . .

(ALYSEA *hands* EDUARDO *some coffee.*)

EDUARDO: Thank you, *linda.* . . .

(ALYSEA *serves herself.* JOSEFA *looks intently from one to the other.*)

JOSEFA: All these walks you two take . . . into forbidden country . . .

EDUARDO: How can beauty be forbidden? . . .

JOSEFA: I feel the same way . . . but the desert mind forbids it . . . many times.

ALYSEA: It won't be forbidden tomorrow . . . all the young girls will bathe in the lake at noontime . . . the promise of a perfect love. . . .

EDUARDO: I hear it is your year, Josefa . . . you will lead the church procession . . .

JOSEFA: My people enjoy planning for it . . .

ALYSEA: Josefa is as bad as Father Prado about the barrio people . . . all is to please them . . . .

EDUARDO: And what pleases you, Josefa?

JOSEFA: To make them happy!

EDUARDO: I can see why they talk of you with awe . . . .

JOSEFA: I am Indian, you know . . . yet not of desert, not of them, in a way. Yet . . . totally theirs.

ALYSEA (*rising*): Well . . . I shall leave you for a few moments; Josefa . . . the lace for the capitol . . . must make the morning express . . . excuse me.

(ALYSEA *leaves.* EDUARDO *finishes his coffee.*)

JOSEFA: She's falling in love with you . . .

EDUARDO: It's mutual . . . .

JOSEFA: For how long, Eduardo?

EDUARDO (*stands, hands in pockets, somewhat ill-at-ease*): Love is not timed.

JOSEFA: Isn't it?

EDUARDO: What do you mean?

JOSEFA: Clara.

EDUARDO: You know?

JOSEFA: She has described to me . . . your every mood . . . your every gesture . . . in love . . . .

EDUARDO: I don't know what to say!

JOSEFA: Guilt?

EDUARDO: Ridiculous . . . there's no guilt in love!

JOSEFA (*laughing as if to herself*): The way you men justify . . . the word "love" doesn't it really mean . . . take? . . . destroy?

EDUARDO: It isn't that . . . .

JOSEFA: Of course not! Disguised in a man's words . . . in a man's promises . . . . oh, I know, you make a dream of your deadly game.

EDUARDO: Alysea's happy.

JOSEFA: Is she? For how long . . . until you find another fancy?

EDUARDO: What I feel for her is different . . . .

JOSEFA: I remember Clara telling me the same things about you and her . . . how easily you put her out of your life.

EDUARDO: Clara understands.

JOSEFA: No, Eduardo . . . she just accepts . . . she knows nothing else.

EDUARDO: You make me feel guilty . . . why?

JOSEFA: I'll tell you why . . . Alysea has love here; she is happy . . . she has found her place in the world . . . safe with me . . . there is a constancy here . . .

EDUARDO: All right! I don't think one should have conditions . . . I know I love her now . . . I want to love her forever . . . but it is not for me to know. . . .

JOSEFA: She belongs here . . . with me . . . You men explain away all your indiscretions, so easily . . . after all, you make the rules and enjoy the abuses!

EDUARDO: That's not fair . . .

JOSEFA: That's funny . . . . When has a man been fair to . . . women?

EDUARDO: You are distorting . . . .

JOSEFA: What I offer her is not a violence. . . . Man's love is always a violence.

EDUARDO: I'm sorry.

JOSEFA: For what . . . the evil in the world?

EDUARDO: I love Alysea.

JOSEFA: Oh, yes . . . you love, he loves, they love . . . how convenient the word "love!"

(EDUARDO *remains silent.* JOSEFA *suddenly realizes he is a guest.*)

JOSEFA (*in an even, pleasant voice*): Come, Eduardo, you must forgive me for such an outburst. . . . What a terrible hostess I am! Don't mind me, when there is concern for the people you love . . . Here, let me refill your cup! (*She pours him some coffee and hands it to him.*) There is a special happiness in this house, you know. . . .

EDUARDO (*reassured*): I know . . . it is the soaring sea in you.

JOSEFA: What?

EDUARDO: You carry things, people with you . . . when your strength is washed away . . . you leave beauty behind.

JOSEFA: How lovely . . . you are easy to fall in love with. . . .

EDUARDO: So are you . . . if a man is brave enough.

JOSEFA: Brave?

EDUARDO: You are a whirlwind. . . .

JOSEFA: I have always sought the calm. . . .

EDUARDO: Ah . . . but your depths! Josefa, I sense them . . . you are not the barrio.

JOSEFA (*amused*): Such discernment! . . . but then, you are right. . . . I am of the lake.

EDUARDO: I've heard . . . I hear you dare the lake alone . . . in solitude. . . .

JOSEFA: The barrio stories are myth . . . primitive fears . . . what most of the people fear is instinctive. . . .

EDUARDO: In what way?

JOSEFA: Out in the lake . . . out in the pines . . . they see themselves too

well . . . they have become the desert . . . it is too much to accept . . .
so monsters are created . . . . but for me . . . ah . . . for me!

EDUARDO: Tell me. . . .

JOSEFA: When I was young . . . when I refused to go bathe on San Lorenzo's
day, when I chose the moonlight in any season . . . it was defiance . . .

EDUARDO: What did you defy?

JOSEFA: What defied me . . . the world! Yes, I would go . . . to defy . . .
then . . . but it became something else.

EDUARDO (*looking at her intently*): Why didn't you ever marry? No one
good enough?

JOSEFA (*shrugs it off*): I never saw the dream . . . I never felt the
hope . . . there was always too much clarity for me . . . (*Pause*) . . .
Do you think me beautiful?

EDUARDO: Yes . . . very . . . mixed in with a dangerous excitement. . . .

JOSEFA: You are making love to me . . .

EDUARDO: I make love to all things beautiful . . . don't you?

JOSEFA (*in a whisper*): Yes . . . oh, yes. . . .

(ALYSEA *comes in breathless.*)

ALYSEA: Well . . . you two . . . that wasn't long was it? (*Looks at both of
them.*) You two must have found marvelous things to talk about . . . it
shows!

JOSEFA: I tell you, Eduardo . . . this girl has possibilities. . . .

EDUARDO: I know. . . .

ALYSEA: Did she tell you about her magicians?

EDUARDO: She was about to . . . when you came.

JOSEFA (*looking at him intently*): How did you know . . . I was about to?

EDUARDO: The light in your eyes . . . the sudden magic in you. . . .

ALYSEA: I know what you mean, Eduardo . . . such a mystical thing. . . .

JOSEFA: You have laid the setting . . . so kindly. (*She walks to the window
and looks out with her eyes closed as she speaks.*)

JOSEFA: The magicians are real, you know! I found them . . . long
ago . . . the night of the Festival of San Lorenzo. The virgins had bathed
by the noon-day sun . . . I . . . I went after the Rosary bell . . . I went
when they were all celebrating; the silence was perfumed . . . desire was
heavy . . . painful. Does it surprise you that I speak of desire? Oh, yes
. . . I felt it . . . to my fingertips . . . it was so real, the beautiful need
. . . the lights of the barrio were far off in another world . . . this always
affected me . . . I became another being far from my kind . . . even my
desire was a special suffering. . . .

EDUARDO: You still did not marry.

JOSEFA: What does that have to do with desire? My desire . . . like my
being . . . became a purer grain. It was more than someone to see or
touch . . . or embrace . . . it was a need for a pouring of self . . . a
gentleness . . . a faith. I did not want the callous Indian youth . . . with
hot breath and awkward hands . . . a taking without feeling . . . no, not
that! I wanted so much more. . . .

(JOSEFA *turns to look at* ALYSEA *and* EDUARDO, *caught in her spell.*)

JOSEFA: Look at you . . . children . . . listening to fairy tales. . . .
EDUARDO: Children believe. . . .
JOSEFA: So do I! . . . isn't it funny?
EDUARDO: No . . . it is like that with some people.
JOSEFA: For me . . . it came true! . . . the wonder was my magicians. That night at the lake there was a different music . . . the stillness sung inside me . . . the moonlight grew in me . . . it became my lover. . . . There by the lake, I felt the light finding its way among the pines . . . to me . . . It took me . . . then . . . perhaps it was my imagination . . . it said to me . . . "We are one . . . make your beauty . . . make your truth." Deep, I felt a burning spiral . . . it roared in my ears . . . my heart . . . (*Pause*) It was too much to bear . . . so I ran and ran and ran until I fell . . . not knowing where; I lay there in utter quiet . . . then I opened my eyes and found myself calmly looking up at the stars . . . sisters of my love! The moon had followed me; it lay a lake around me, on the grass. . . .
EDUARDO: Were you afraid?
JOSEFA: Afraid? There was no room . . . the joy was too great. I had the secret of the magicians . . . the wine of love . . . the light was me; I knew that I would bear the children of light . . . the moon . . . the burning lake.
ALYSEA (*in a whisper*): I believe her . . . look around you, the children of light . . . her garden . . . the lace . . . her love for the barrio people . . . her bright, bright calm. . . .
EDUARDO (*taking up the pace*): Her person. . . .
JOSEFA: Hush . . . you two . . . don't go on so!

(*The voice of* TOMÁS *from the outside window breaks the spell.*)

TOMÁS: Josefa! . . . David's horse! . . . I found it out in the pasture . . . without a bridle . . . Josefa!
JOSEFA (*goes to the window*): David's horse?
EDUARDO (*going to the window*): Need any help?
JOSEFA: He didn't hear you . . . he's coming in. . . .

(ALYSEA *all of a sudden loses all her brightness; she seems frightened and lost. She looks at* JOSEFA's *every move;* JOSEFA *shows no reaction; she calmly begins to pick up cups, napkins.*)

JOSEFA: It is getting late . . . my! The morning has flown . . . such a wonderful time . . . I hope it isn't too late for you two to go for your walk.
EDUARDO: No . . . no . . . there's plenty of time.

(TOMÁS *comes in through the kitchen door.*)

TOMÁS: He must have broken out from the stable . . . I thought I would tell you before I took him back to the hacienda. . . .

JOSEFA: Yes . . . take him back . . . horses will do that.

(EDUARDO *takes* ALYSEA *by the hands. He looks at her intently.*)

EDUARDO: What on earth is the matter? You need some morning air . . . I'll tell you what . . . I'll take you to a place where I can trace the path of the swallows any day now. . . .

(ALYSEA *doesn't seem to be listening to him;* JOSEFA *notices this and promptly suggests.*)

JOSEFA: Yes . . . I insist on it . . . take her; right now . . . enjoy this lovely day. . . .

(EDUARDO *takes* ALYSEA *by the shoulder.*)

EDUARDO: Come on. . . .

(*He steers her to the door;* ALYSEA *does not resist. They exit.*)

TOMÁS (*slyly*): I guess she feels bad about David . . . what happened last night. . . .

JOSEFA: What?

TOMÁS: I heard the talk in the barrio . . . someone broke into the house . . . that is . . . that is what you claim.

JOSEFA: What do you mean?

TOMÁS: You didn't tell me earlier. . . .

JOSEFA: Tell you? Why should I tell you anything?

TOMÁS: The blood in the pail . . . you didn't tell me anything about that either . . .

JOSEFA: So?

TOMÁS: Well . . . I remember . . . all those times . . . you save the poor, innocent, helpless ones . . . you never say anything . . . it's always the barrio who puts the story together . . . you are clever. . . .

JOSEFA: Don't be ridiculous. . . .

TOMÁS: Yes . . . people have no idea how clever you really are . . . la Doña Perfecta! You saved Alysea from the evil man . . . you saved David from a drunken father, the barrio tells the story of an angel . . . but it's funny . . . somehow . . . they never remember to tell that you crippled one man and the other died on the road where you left him. . . .

JOSEFA: You are pitiful . . . like those two men . . . destructive and pitiful. . . .

TOMÁS: Perhaps you'll get your hands on me too.

JOSEFA (*calmly, with disdain*): Hadn't you better see about that horse?

TOMÁS: Now the town is busy making you out a heroine . . . an intruder? That's hard to believe . . . the girl looked too guilty a while ago . . . (*He studies* JOSEFA *who is straightening up.*) But you . . . it's amazing! . . . such grace . . . such pious silence . . . yes . . . you are a dangerous one, all right!

JOSEFA: All this . . . this foolishness, I know, is leading up to some sort of blackmail . . . you want money . . . don't you?

TOMÁS: You know me so well! . . . after all, I'm on your side . . . we are of the same blood. . . .

JOSEFA: Get out of here . . . and be careful about what you say . . . you clown! . . . who's going to believe anything you say? Be careful . . . or I may let you starve.

TOMÁS: Didn't work . . . eh? No money?

JOSEFA: You've tried my patience long enough . . . I have better things to do with my time . . . go and see about that horse. . . .

(JOSEFA *picks up the tray and starts toward the kitchen.*)

TOMÁS: Not even a few pesos?

(JOSEFA *looks at him contemptuously and walks out into the kitchen without a word.*)

TOMÁS: She'll break! She'll break . . . once I lay all my cards on the table . . . stupid women! . . . (*He looks around the room.*) I know they keep the household money somewhere around here . . . yes.

(*He begins to look in the drawers.*)

ACT I
Scene 3
(*Later the same morning. The room is empty, full of light, when* CLARA *enters. She is the wife of* DON ESQUINAS, *owner of the hacienda. She has the grace and elegance of good living. But, at closer scrutiny, one can see that this once beautiful woman is dissipated. Her blond beauty, although meticulously enhanced by great care, has the flavor of fading youth. She carries a knitting bag. Although she has been in this room many times, she is each time overwhelmed by the unusual light. She walks up to the table, lays her bag on it, opens it, searches for a cigarette; she finds one, lights it, and draws its flavor leisurely. She catches sight of* JOSEFA's *workbasket; she also sees the damask; she traces the design; then she picks up a piece of lace from the workbasket and examines it admiringly.*)

CLARA: Angel filigree . . . how lovely . . . it's unearthly. . . .

(*As she examines the lace,* ALYSEA *walks into the room breathlessly. Her arms are full of freshly cut flowers. She glances at* DOÑA CLARA *apologetically.*)

ALYSEA: Doña Clara . . . am I late?

CLARA: No, no . . . I just got here.

ALYSEA (*going to the vase and setting the flowers next to it*): I always linger too long in the garden. . . .

CLARA: What a garden . . . what incantations does Josefa use?

ALYSEA: It's marvelous, the way she does it . . .

CLARA: She talks to the flowers. . . .

ALYSEA: She talks to all living things. . . .

CLARA (*looking at* ALYSEA *as she arranges the flowers in the vase*): You too . . . how you have blossomed in this house.

ALYSEA: Me?

CLARA (*in a deliberately contained voice*): Of course, this time it could be Eduardo . . . I hear he loves you.

ALYSEA: Love does that . . . doesn't it?

CLARA: It's true then! . . . and you love him too?

ALYSEA: Yes.

CLARA: Well . . . (*She puts out her cigarette.*) That's that! . . . where is my dress?

ALYSEA (*coming out of her reverie*): Oh, I'm sorry . . . of course, your fitting.

(ALYSEA *goes to a wardrobe and takes out a simple gown. She hands it to* CLARA. CLARA *goes behind the screen.*)

CLARA: I suppose you'll go away with him?

ALYSEA: He wants me to . . . I haven't quite decided. . . .

CLARA: About love?

ALYSEA: Am I good enough for him? I have to use reason. . . .

CLARA (*almost impatiently*): You don't have to reason love . . . my God!

ALYSEA: Will it be fair to him!

CLARA: What love there is . . . you take . . . don't reason it away . . . take it!

(*She comes from around the screen and gives her back to* ALYSEA *so* ALYSEA *will fasten the dress. Both are facing the mirror.* CLARA *looks* ALYSEA *directly in the eyes.*)

CLARA: Love is always fair just because it is. (*She can't look in the mirror any longer.*) What's the matter with me . . . look at me . . . an expert on love . . . ha! (*She bites her lip.*)

ALYSEA: You are beautiful and wise. (CLARA *doesn't answer; she deliberately becomes absorbed with the gown. She surveys herself in the mirror.*)

CLARA: It seems to lack something . . . Alysea . . . what do you think?

ALYSEA: Of course . . . Josefa made something very special for it . . . (*She looks around.*) Where is it? Oh, yes . . . I'll be back in a minute.

(ALYSEA *goes through the bedroom door.* CLARA *goes to the mirror and traces the lines on her face. She then walks up to her knitting bag, takes a flask, opens it.*)

CLARA (*bitterly*): Here's to youth! (*She drinks long draughts. She does it three times; then she puts the flask away. She walks up to the mirror again.*)

CLARA: Well, my girl . . . what's in store for you? He's left you . . . you always knew he would leave you . . . what is there now, my girl . . . except time? . . . (*She covers her face with her hands.*)

(ALYSEA *comes in from the bedroom with a beautiful lace shawl.* CLARA *quickly recovers and looks at the shawl.*)

ALYSEA: Look . . . isn't it beautiful . . . a *duende* design.

CLARA: Andalusian?

ALYSEA: Yes . . . Josefa copied it!

CLARA: Superb!

(ALYSEA *drapes it over one shoulder and clasps it on* CLARA's *waist.*)

CLARA: Oh, thank you . . . but . . . these days I need the right lights . . . not all things are kind to me anymore. . . . Yes, it is beautiful. . . .

(*She turns and contemplates* ALYSEA.)

CLARA: Look at you . . . you are so young . . . your beauty so sharp . . . only yesterday, my dear, only yesterday, I was young like you . . . mark that well!

(JOSEFA *comes in through the outside door.* CLARA *sees her. She goes to* JOSEFA *and kisses her cheek.*)

CLARA: I missed you this morning . . . you didn't come.
JOSEFA: Didn't I tell you? . . . there's a million things to do before to-morrow.
CLARA: The shawl . . . it's beautiful . . . only Josefa!
JOSEFA (*surveying her handiwork*): The design . . . the delicacy against the dark dress . . . it is impressive . . . you wear it well.

(JOSEFA *notices that* CLARA *is somewhat too gay; a little bit unsteady.*)

ALYSEA: Shall I get the combs?
CLARA: Combs?
JOSEFA: Mantilla combs . . . made by the gypsies. . . .
CLARA: To go with the gown.
ALYSEA: I'll get them.

(*She walks back to the bedroom.* JOSEFA *looks at* CLARA *realizing what the matter is.*)

JOSEFA: You must have started early . . .
CLARA: What? (*She busies herself at the mirror.*) You worry too much . . . just a little courage . . . I needed a little courage . . .
JOSEFA: Eduardo?
CLARA (*turns and faces* JOSEFA; *pain in her eyes*): He loves her.
JOSEFA: I know. . . .
CLARA: You see . . . I needed a little courage this morning.
JOSEFA: If you start again . . . promise me you won't!
CLARA (*with false gaiety*): I promise. (*She closes her eyes.*) I wish . . . I wish I were young for one day . . . just one day . . . so he would love me the way I love him.
JOSEFA: Men don't love . . . they take . . . haven't you learned that by now?
CLARA: Oh, Josefa . . . you are wrong . . . you are wrong . . . a woman was made to love a man . . . to love is enough for a woman . . . if only they would let us love them without negating, without negating. . . .
JOSEFA: Why, Clara? Why must you give . . . so easily? Not to them . . . Clara . . . not to men!

CLARA (*shrugs*): My downfall? (*In a whisper*) My life?

JOSEFA: Here . . . enough of that . . . there are beautiful things to love . . .

(ALYSEA *returns with the combs. She hands them to* JOSEFA *who goes to* CLARA *and expertly places them in her hair.*)

CLARA: Without mantilla?

JOSEFA: It would be too much with the shawl. . . .

CLARA: Yes . . . of course . . . you're right . . . a gypsy with majesty!

ALYSEA: Yes . . . That's what you look like . . . a gypsy queen.

JOSEFA: *El espíritu duende.* . . .

CLARA: Like your magicians?

JOSEFA: Perhaps. . : .

(*The church bell rings midday; suddenly two swallows are seen outside the window.*)

ALYSEA: Look!

JOSEFA: They're coming . . . the advance guard . . . every year.

CLARA: You love them . . . don't you? . . . your magicians let you find so many things to love . . . lucky . . . lucky Josefa.

JOSEFA: The swallows are safe here . . . after the long, long, lonely flight. . . .

CLARA: Lonely? . . . they come in droves. . . .

(*The three look outside the window for a minute. Choir practice begins.*)

JOSEFA: Look at the lake . . . it shimmers with love . . . (*Turns to* CLARA) I said lonely, Clara, because finding direction . . . is lonely . . . it is too personal a thing. . . .

CLARA: I see what you mean . . . Josefa (*Looks out the window pensively*), why don't I see the love shimmering in your lake?

(JOSEFA *smiles.*)

ALYSEA: Her magicians . . . isn't it, Josefa?

JOSEFA: Yes . . . my magicians.

ACT **II**

(*It is early afternoon of the same day.* JOSEFA *comes through the outside door. There is a small injured bird in her hands. She cradles it gently and examines it.*)

JOSEFA: You poor little thing . . . a broken wing . . . don't worry, you'll be fine in a little while . . . (*She puts the soft piece of life against her cheek.*) There will be no second pain . . . Alysea!

ALYSEA (*comes in through the kitchen door*): Yes?

JOSEFA: Look . . . I found it in the garden . . . it lay there . . . small, helpless . . . look, he's thirsty . . . quick, get some water and an eye-dropper.

(ALYSEA *goes into the bedroom.* JOSEFA *sits in her rocking chair and places the bird gently on her lap* . . . . ALYSEA *comes back with a cup and an eye-dropper.* JOSEFA *picks up the bird, fills the eye-dropper, and patiently feeds the bird water. The bird drinks.*)

JOSEFA: See . . . oh, he has life . . . this one!
ALYSEA: Just a baby . . . let us set the wing . . . I'll get some small twigs and a bandage. . . .

(*She leaves again;* JOSEFA *continues feeding the bird.*)

JOSEFA: How did you find the birdhouse . . . eh? My magicians must have led you here . . . before the others . . . every year . . . the sky is black with their wings . . . here they rest . . . and eat . . . you will be safe . . . until you join your brothers and sisters . . . yes. . . .

(ALYSEA *comes back; together they carefully set the small wing.*)

JOSEFA: There!
ALYSEA: Let's put him in the birdhouse . . . he's tired . . .

(JOSEFA *kisses the bird; then both of them go to the window, lean out to the tree, and place the bird in the tree house. Satisfied,* JOSEFA *and* ALYSEA *look at each other.* JOSEFA *reaches out and begins to stroke* ALYSEA's *hair.*)

JOSEFA (*softly*): We share so much . . . just wait . . . the magicians will come to you . . . I know. . . .
ALYSEA: What?
JOSEFA: Remember how much you wished for the magicians?
ALYSEA: No . . . no . . . I don't want them anymore. . . .
JOSEFA: But . . .
ALYSEA: When you brought me here . . . all that's happened . . . it is so unreal . . . a year of mists and deep sinking dreams . . . but not anymore!
JOSEFA: Hush . . . you're just upset . . . that's all. . . .
ALYSEA: No . . . last night . . . no . . . never again. . . .
JOSEFA: Poor little girl . . . you've tired yourself out all morning . . . I forgot . . . I don't know why . . . but I just forgot about . . . about last night.
ALYSEA (*looking at her with horror*): Josefa . . . no! Forgot? How could you?
JOSEFA (*becoming slightly agitated*): Habit . . . to keep strong . . . since I was little . . . to keep strong . . . I put ugliness away.
ALYSEA: Where? Where?
JOSEFA: What do you mean?
ALYSEA: If you have a conscience . . . where could you put it away?
JOSEFA: There will be atonement. . . .
ALYSEA: No . . . that's impossible . . . you think . . . it will . . . disappear? The blood . . . the knife . . . (*She runs to the table where she had placed the knife.*) Look . . . I'll show you . . . you make it disappear! (*She opens the drawer and stares unbelievingly.*)
ALYSEA: The knife . . . it's gone!

(*She begins to look frantically everywhere.*)

ALYSEA: Did you hear me?

(JOSEFA *seems almost unaware of* ALYSEA's *frenzy.*)

JOSEFA: Yes . . . of course. . . .

(ALYSEA *begins to look again and this time finds the money box gone.*)

ALYSEA: The money box . . . it's gone too.
JOSEFA: Tomás . . . of course . . . he took the money and the knife.

(ALYSEA *collapses into a chair and covers her face with her hands.* TOMÁS' *voice is heard singing a barrio love song;* ALYSEA *looks up in fright.* JOSEFA *goes to the door of the kitchen and calls out into the patio behind the kitchen.*)

JOSEFA: Tomás! Come in here. . . .

(TOMÁS *comes into the kitchen still singing. He walks into the room.* JOSEFA *watches him warily,* ALYSEA *in terror.*)

TOMÁS: Well . . . well . . . Did you call me, *querida?* (*He strokes* JOSEFA's *arm intimately. She breaks away.*)
JOSEFA: Don't you ever put your hands on me!
TOMÁS: Ha! ha! ha! . . . Doña Perfecta . . . (*He looks around the room.*) You know . . . I think I'll move over here . . . I like this house . . . ah! . . . it is time I had a little elegance in my life . . . yes. (*He sprawls out in a chair.*)
JOSEFA: You've been drinking. . . .
TOMÁS: Yes . . . I have been drinking . . . and I shall drink some more . . . you can afford it. . . .

(ALYSEA *begins to cry.*)

TOMÁS: What's the matter with her?
JOSEFA: She is tired . . . and I . . . have had enough of your insolence. . . .
TOMÁS: *Que maravilla* . . . How long . . . Josefa . . . how long . . . can you keep it up? (*He paces in front of her; she remains calm.*)
TOMÁS (*practically shouting in her face*): I took the knife! Do you understand . . . I took the knife! . . . aren't you afraid, Josefa?

(ALYSEA *begins to cry desperately.* JOSEFA *goes to her. She tries to comfort her.*)

JOSEFA: Don't, Alysea . . . remember . . . it's late . . . we have to pack for David . . . he'll need his things in the hospital . . . compose yourself . . . Why don't you go and start packing . . . I'll talk to Tomás.

(ALYSEA *nods her head in agreement; she rises and leaves as if she wanted escape.*)

JOSEFA (*turns and faces* TOMÁS): Have you ever . . . have you ever . . . done anything kind for anybody?

TOMÁS (*sarcastically*): No . . . just you . . . *querida* . . . you are the angel . . .

JOSEFA: All right . . . what do you intend to do?

TOMÁS: Nothing . . . you see . . . we . . . you and I . . . must have a clearer understanding. . . . I know much more than you think . . . about you and (*nods toward bedroom*) her!

(JOSEFA *stiffens.*)

JOSEFA: All right . . . you win . . . I'll give you money. . . .

TOMÁS: No more crumbs . . . dear niece . . . I call the play . . . from now on.

JOSEFA: You're bluffing . . . lying . . . as usual.

TOMÁS: Am I?

(*There is a knock at the door; with alacrity* TOMÁS *springs up and goes to the door and opens it. It is* DON ESQUINAS, CLARA's *husband.*)

TOMÁS: Ah . . . Don Esquinas, won't you come in?

(DON ESQUINAS *brushes past* TOMÁS, *totally ignoring him.* TOMÁS *makes a mock gesture of humility.*)

DON ESQUINAS: Josefa . . . the worst has happened. . . . I warned you!

JOSEFA (*placing her hands on her heart*): Clara . . . let me go to her. (*She starts to go;* DON ESQUINAS *stops her.*)

DON ESQUINAS: It's too late. . . .

JOSEFA (*savagely*): It isn't . . . I can take care of her.

DON ESQUINAS: How? By giving her more drink . . . you've done enough harm. . . .

JOSEFA: Harm? I have been her sole companion for years . . . I have suffered with her . . . nursed her . . . Harm?

DON ESQUINAS: Do you know how I found my wife this afternoon when I got home? She was lying in bed . . . stark naked . . . screaming about crawling . . . crawling, dark . . . she slashed everything in sight . . . broke the mirror . . . there were bottles . . . everywhere. . . .

JOSEFA: My poor, poor darling. . . .

DON ESQUINAS: I . . . the servants . . . we were helpless . . . it was dreadful . . . she kept screaming and sobbing that your magicians had . . . had no faces. . . .

JOSEFA: She's so alone. . . .

DON ESQUINAS: Your lies . . . the liquor and your lies . . . both supplied by you! I'm taking her to the sanatorium . . . this time for good.

JOSEFA: She is so alone. . . .

DON ESQUINAS: Stop saying that! You . . . you supplied her with liquor. . . .

JOSEFA: All that unhappiness . . . she is so lost . . . there was nothing else . . . She promised me this afternoon.

DON ESQUINAS: Promised? You stupid woman . . . you knew she wouldn't keep the promise. . . .

JOSEFA (*suddenly in anger*): I tell you . . . you won't listen . . . . you men never listen . . . all she had was hopelessness. . . .

DON ESQUINAS: You don't know what you are talking about . . . . She always had everything . . . since the day she was born . . . never, never, did she have to lift a finger . . . anything she desires. . . .

JOSEFA: Except her husband!

DON ESQUINAS: What in damnation?

JOSEFA: She wanted you to love her. . . .

DON ESQUINAS: Love her? You women are insane! I married her . . . didn't I?

JOSEFA: She knew all about your . . . your women. . . .

DON ESQUINAS: That is a man's way! You have no right to question . . . Tell me, how much liquor did you give her? When did you give it to her?

(JOSEFA *remains silent.*)

DON ESQUINAS: Well?

JOSEFA: She wanted a baby . . . .

DON ESQUINAS: Nonsense! We settled that long ago . . . that was past and forgotten. . . .

JOSEFA: No . . . it was never forgotten . . . she cried every night. . . .

DON ESQUINAS: Silly tears of a drunken woman . . . adopt a baby . . . a baby not of the Esquinas blood? For my heir? absurd!

JOSEFA (*bitterly*): Which of your bastards are you going to choose as your heir?

DON ESQUINAS: You ungrateful peasant . . . let me tell you . . . you influenced her too much . . . this is probably all your fault . . . I don't want you around the hacienda now that she is gone . . . do you hear?

(JOSEFA *turns her back on him;* DON ESQUINAS *is somewhat at a loss. Her calm toward his anger is disconcerting. He stands for a moment, then he walks out of the room. On his way out,* TOMÁS *follows him, still assuming a pose of mock humility.*)

TOMÁS: It is terrible, Don Esquinas, what my niece has done . . . if I can make up for it in any way . . . please call on me. . . .

(DON ESQUINAS *ignores him and leaves.* TOMÁS *turns to* JOSEFA.)

TOMÁS: See what you have done to your friend . . . the wife of our Don?

(JOSEFA *too ignores him,* TOMÁS' *attitude of humility is now gone. His attitude is again cunning and sly. He walks up to* JOSEFA.)

TOMÁS: Tch, tch, tch, . . . Doña Perfecta is not perfecta . . . eh?

JOSEFA (*not listening to him*): She's gone . . . the light of my magicians never came to her . . . poor, poor lost child.

TOMÁS: You are insane about those magicians. (JOSEFA *walks away from him;* TOMÁS *grabs her arm angrily.*) I'm sick and tired of you ignoring me! You think I'm scum? I don't matter . . . do I? Well, you listen, Doña Perfecta, you listen to me!

(JOSEFA *waits silently for him to let go of her arm. When he does, she touches her temples with her fingertips.*)

JOSEFA: I have a headache. . . .

TOMÁS: None of your tricks . . . listen to me! I saw you . . . do you hear . . . I saw you. Last San Lorenzo's day, I remember. I left the fiesta . . . I was too drunk; I walked toward the lake . . . I remember, it was a clear, clear night; the moon lighted everything . . . as I came near the lake past the back of this house . . . I saw two figures come from the water's edge . . . they ran . . . one caught up with the other!

(TOMÁS *watches her maliciously and intently, wishing to get a reaction. Her surface is still calm as he scrutinizes her face.*)

JOSEFA: What are you trying to do?

TOMÁS (*laughing slyly and triumphantly*): It was you and the girl . . . you and the girl . . . wasn't it? Now . . . I begin to put things together . . . it all fits!

JOSEFA: Your drunken hallucinations. . . .

TOMÁS: I know better, *reina del barrio* . . . you are a. . . .

JOSEFA: If you have nothing else to threaten me with. . . . (*She walks away from him with disdain.*)

TOMÁS (*practically screaming with exasperation*): You think you can always win, with your calm; you're not made of stone . . . you'll break, milady . . . I'll be back. Inside you're trembling with fear. . . .

(*She turns abruptly and faces him haughtily.* TOMÁS *falters first; he turns and leaves. As* JOSEFA *looks after him,* ALYSEA *comes from the bedroom wearing street clothes.*)

JOSEFA (*turns and sees her*): Finished?
ALYSEA: Yes, I'm ready.

(JOSEFA *walks up to her and puts her arm around her.*)

JOSEFA: The ride will do you good; after you come back from the hospital . . . after you see my little David, we'll have supper here . . . then, we can have one of our little chats.

ALYSEA (*gently breaks away from* JOSEFA): I'm not coming back.

JOSEFA: Not coming back?

ALYSEA: I meant to tell you earlier . . . I'm going away with Eduardo.

JOSEFA: Because of what happened last night?

ALYSEA: Many reasons, but mostly because I want to be with him.

JOSEFA: You are like all the rest . . . you insist on being a useless, empty sacrifice!

ALYSEA: I love him.

JOSEFA: Love him? Tell me, how long will your precious Eduardo love you? (*Pause*) You know who was here? Don Esquinas! Clara drank herself insane because your Eduardo left her. What do you think he'll do to you?

ALYSEA: I can't believe that . . . there's more to love.

JOSEFA (*ironically and bitterly*): Love! remember the brothel? No different . . . you choose darkness . . . all your pains are still to come! Haven't I taught you anything?

ALYSEA: It all fell apart . . . last night. All I can remember are David's eyes. (*She breaks down sobbing.*)

JOSEFA: He'll be all right . . . I'll take care of my little love . . . as long as he lives . . .

ALYSEA: His eyes told me. You and I were all the terror in the world.

JOSEFA: No . . . the terror is in the world out there . . . don't say that!

ALYSEA: The violence . . . the useless violence. . . .

JOSEFA: I forbid you to go on like this.

(*She walks to the window and reaches into the birdhouse until she finds the crippled bird. She picks him up, fondles him, and holds him against her cheek.*)

JOSEFA (*with eyes closed*): Remember how he came . . . crippled, starved, half dead?

ALYSEA: The way I came?

JOSEFA: It will be safe here and happy. You have always been safe and happy! We have so much, Alysea.

(ALYSEA *remains silent.*)

JOSEFA: You know why I built the birdhouse?

(*She seems to be remembering something painful. She goes to the rocking chair, places the bird on her lap, and strokes it gently.*)

JOSEFA: When I was seven . . . the swallows came . . . they came one hot dry dawn . . . and continued all day . . . on the edge of the desert that still hotter afternoon . . . I saw noisy boys with desert time on their hands . . . playing . . . I watched the playing become a violence . . . they were catching birds . . . now it became a killing . . . they stoned them . . . plucked them . . . laughing with a fearful joy . . . the sand was a sea of dead birds . . . I . . . I . . . couldn't stand it . . . I ran . . . I hit them . . . I said, "Stop! Stop!" (*Pause*) They laughed; then for a joke . . . for a joke they said . . . they held me down, the burning sand against my back . . . . In spite of all my terror, I opened my eyes . . . a boy . . . a big boy . . . held a swallow over me; he took a knife . . . cut the bird . . . Oh, God! so much blood . . . all that blood. (JOSEFA *strokes the bird gently and shakes her head, closes her eyes.*) It spilled . . . spilled into my face . . . ran into my mouth . . . warm . . . warm . . . salt warm . . . was it my tears? the blood?

(*She stands and goes to the window still with the bird; she caresses the bird with her cheek and places it gently in the birdhouse. The Rosary bell begins to toll. It is sunset.* JOSEFA *looks out in silence.*)

JOSEFA: Alysea, . . . look, the lake is screaming with life . . . look . . . the colors of love . . . then . . . the day went . . . (*She turns to* ALYSEA.)

Out there . . . the beauty is lost in fears . . . what do you expect out there? Stay with the radiance . . . Alysea, stay with me!

ALYSEA: I won't be coming back.

(ALYSEA *turns and leaves, going into the bedroom;* JOSEFA *looks after her for a moment, seems to start after* ALYSEA, *then changes her mind. She turns to the unfinished damask. She unhooks the needle and begins to work on it in deep concentration.* ALYSEA *returns with a suitcase.* JOSEFA *does not look up although she is aware of* ALYSEA. ALYSEA *comes close to* JOSEFA *rather hesitantly.* JOSEFA *looks up and smiles.*)

JOSEFA (*in a casual tone*): Look . . . do you think I ought to give the design a name? I saw it in a dream the other night . . . so vivid! perhaps I should call it "Swallow Song." What do you think?

ALYSEA (*looking intently at the design over* JOSEFA's *shoulder*): It looks like flowing grain . . . with . . . with a streak of lightning . . . so well intermingled . . . how strange! . . . beauty and terror as one . . . see? (*She traces the pattern with her finger.*)

JOSEFA: How foolish of you . . . that is not lightning . . . it is . . . it is sweet rain.

(ALYSEA *looks intently at the pattern, then at* JOSEFA.)

ALYSEA (*softly*): Lovely Josefa . . . no, no . . . you could never see the lightning . . . only your gentle lights. (*She picks up her suitcase and starts to leave.*) Goodbye, sweet lady of light!

(JOSEFA *looks up but does not answer.* ALYSEA *moves toward the outside door.*)

JOSEFA (*as if in afterthought*): Alysea?

ALYSEA: Yes?

JOSEFA: On the way . . . please stop by the rectory . . . will you? Tell Father Prado I cannot make Rosary tonight. Tell him . . . if he would be so kind . . . to come later this evening. . . .

ALYSEA: Of course. (*She hesitates for a moment, as if at a loss for words. Then with one last look of love for* JOSEFA *and the room, she departs. After* ALYSEA *leaves,* JOSEFA *continues putting the final stitches on the damask.*)

JOSEFA: There! Finished . . . another birth of light!

(*She stands and stretches as if very tired. She rubs the back of her neck and breathes deep. She goes to the window again. It is now dark.*)

JOSEFA: My lover! You look morning crystal in the water . . . so still . . . so deep . . . I ache for you so! you beckon me shamelessly . . .

(*She stands at the window as the curtain drops for Act II.*)

ACT III

(*Late the same evening. The church bells are announcing the end of Rosary.* JOSEFA *is sitting in her rocking chair saying her prayer beads. Every so often she pauses in thought. There is a knock at the door.* JOSEFA *rises and goes to the door.* FATHER PRADO *enters.)*

FATHER PRADO (*kissing her on the cheek*): My dear . . . how are you this evening? We missed you at Rosary . . . you always lead prayer with the confidence of an angel . . . a hundred things to do before tomorrow . . . eh?

JOSEFA: It's good to see you! (*She leads him by the arm to a settee.*)

FATHER PRADO: Tell me . . . can I help with anything?

JOSEFA: You are here . . . that is more than enough.

FATHER PRADO: You must give me a chance . . . you do so much for the church, for me . . . now let me do something for you.

JOSEFA: Father . . . you are my kindred spirit . . . the oasis in the middle of the desert.

FATHER PRADO: You spoil me. . . .

JOSEFA: I finished the boys' surplices for tomorrow. . . .

FATHER PRADO: See what I mean? Your lovely little hands (*Kisses them*) produce such lovely wondrous things for us . . . (*Looks around*) And this place! A sanctuary . . . who would think? To find such a place as this in our desert barrio? Ah . . . all things and all people here are too mindful of the desert . . . except you.

JOSEFA: My magicians, Father!

FATHER PRADO (*in jest*): Of course, your magicians!

JOSEFA: I wonder if you take me seriously? Come . . . would you like some coffee? Tea?

FATHER PRADO: No . . . no, it is late; I ate too much at supper . . . I tell myself every night it seems . . . but I go on eating just the same.

JOSEFA: The way you work for the barrio people! Every church festival is such a chore for you . . . you work yourself to death. . . .

FATHER PRADO: So do you!

JOSEFA: We can't help it . . . can we, Father? You love the people as much as I do.

FATHER PRADO: It means so much to them . . . these festivals . . . they are just ritual to you . . . aren't they?

JOSEFA: Maybe . . . but what blossoms from the barrio people because of the festival . . . that is not ritual . . . there is a rebirth . . . they come to life for a little while.

FATHER PRADO: Tomorrow will be very special for them . . . a day to honor their Josefa. Such a legend you are!

JOSEFA: If it makes them happy.

(FATHER PRADO *looks at her intently.*)

FATHER PRADO: Are you feeling all right? You look a little pale . . . of course! How stupid of me . . . so many things have been happening today . . . even in the rectory life seeps in . . . .

JOSEFA: You know about Clara?

FATHER PRADO: Unfortunate . . . *pobrecita* . . . such a beautiful child.

JOSEFA: She won't be coming back this time.

(JOSEFA *begins to cry softly. She brushes a tear from her cheek.*)

FATHER PRADO: There . . . there, don't cry! (*Comforts her*) I know how
you feel . . . you two were so close . . . she depended on you so!

JOSEFA: When life is a farce . . .

FATHER PRADO: In her own way . . . there was so much meaning . . .
Alysea has found something special too . . . she and Eduardo stopped
by the rectory.

JOSEFA: One by one . . . like leaves from a tree . . .

FATHER PRADO: I know! Then . . . the terrible thing . . . I heard in the
village . . . the terrible thing that happened to David . . . I hope they
catch——

(JOSEFA *interrupts violently.*)

JOSEFA: Father!

FATHER PRADO: What is it, child?

JOSEFA: May I have confession now?

FATHER PRADO (*puzzled*): Here?

JOSEFA: Please, Father!

FATHER PRADO: Of course, if that's what you want. . . .

(*He comes near her; as he does, she falls to her knees and leans her head
against his body.*)

FATHER PRADO: What is wrong?

JOSEFA: Forgive me, Father, for I have sinned . . . . (FATHER *remains
silent.*) I have sinned . . . I have sinned. . . .

FATHER PRADO: God forgives. . . .

JOSEFA: Oh, Father . . . I'm lost! I'm lost. . . .

FATHER PRADO: All of us . . . at one time . . .

JOSEFA: I am guilty of grievous sins . . . they are beyond forgiveness . . .
people will judge them so! Father . . .before I tell you . . . you must
know . . . I do not feel sorry . . . I want . . . I need . . . the calm . . .
to keep things as they are.

(FATHER *simply nods his head.*)

JOSEFA: David was hurt last night . . . I lied about the intruder. There was
no intruder . . . I was the one.

FATHER PRADO (*incredulously*): You . . . did that to David?

JOSEFA: Yes . . . (*She braces herself as if to accept the fact.*) I did that to
David.

FATHER PRADO: I can't believe it . . . you! Not you!

JOSEFA: Me, Father, me!

FATHER PRADO: It was inhuman. . . .

JOSEFA: Oh, Father! I . . . I don't know . . . why? why?

FATHER PRADO: Tell me, my child, there must have been a reason . . .

JOSEFA: Last night . . . last night . . . after supper . . . David helped

Alysea and me put the last touches on the birdhouse. David was so excited
. . . (*Pause*) The moon . . . the reflection of diamonds in the lake . . .
life . . . all were too much for me . . . I was overflowing . . . I felt the
sweetness of the night with every fiber . . . every fiber . . . (*Lost in
memory; then she resumes her story.*) David didn't want to go to bed . . .
he insisted on staying up all night to wait for the swallows . . . Of course
I said "No!" He left for bed reluctantly . . . (*Pause*) Father?

FATHER PRADO: Yes?

JOSEFA: Have you ever felt as if you were one total yearning . . . it roars
and spills. . . .

(FATHER PRADO *remains silent.*)

JOSEFA: Alysea and I are lovers.

FATHER PRADO: What?

JOSEFA: A year ago tonight we became lovers . . . if you remember she
had been with me for some months before San Lorenzo's day . . . she
was something new in my life . . . she felt and responded to my every
mood . . . my every act . . . Oh! To have someone in your life! I had
repulsed all the men in the barrio . . . the coarseness! The taking! No
. . . no . . . I could never surrender to that . . . but when she came,
she filled my life in so many ways . . . so many ways . . . it was natural
that the yearning grow for more . . . the body too is master. . . .

FATHER PRADO: Yes, my child, of course it is!

JOSEFA: A year ago I took Alysea to the lake on the eve of San Lorenzo
. . . She had heard about the Bathing of the Virgins at noon the next
day . . . Could she go . . . she asked! I was angry . . . I knew all the
hope . . . all the dreams of those girls would turn to jagged violence . . .
it was a lie . . . The whole ritual is a lie!

FATHER PRADO: No . . . no, Josefa . . . to those girls the dream of a perfect
love is true as long as it gives meaning to their lives. . . .

JOSEFA: I know what men are!

(FATHER PRADO *remains silent.*)

JOSEFA: I told her . . . go with me when the moon comes out . . . when
the lake waits for just me . . . it is my lover! (*Pause*) She believed me
. . . It is true, Father . . . the lake is my lover. . . .

FATHER PRADO: Oh, my child!

JOSEFA: We bathed . . . and then . . . it happened . . . (*Pause*) Last night
after David went to bed . . . I felt the nymph magic . . . I took Alysea
. . . Suddenly . . . there was David . . . in the middle of the room. The
horror in his eyes . . . Why? why? There was horror in his eyes. . . .

FATHER PRADO: He did not understand. . . .

JOSEFA: Oh, Father! Now . . . I can see why . . . now! But . . . last night
. . . it was not the Josefa he loved that David saw . . . I could not stand
what he saw! I could not!

FATHER PRADO: God forgive you!

JOSEFA: Something happened in me . . . I don't know what it was . . . I ran . . . I ran into the kitchen and found a kitchen knife . . . Somehow . . . somehow I knew David would tell . . . the barrio people would look at me that way too. . . .

FATHER PRADO: I never thought you would care about what people . . .

JOSEFA: Oh, Father . . . until last night I never knew my fears . . . I went back to where Alysea was holding the frightened child . . . then . . . then I made Alysea hold him tight . . . Father, it was not her fault! There have been so many furies in her life . . . she drowned in my agony . . . she trusted me . . . what else could she do? (*She goes to the window, looks out at the lake for a moment.*) Father . . . look . . . come look at the lake . . . maybe you can understand the power it has over me . . . Look . . .

(FATHER PRADO *goes somewhat reluctantly to the window. He also looks out, but remains silent.*)

JOSEFA: I took the knife and cut David's tongue. . . .

FATHER PRADO: *Jesucristo, perdona a tu hija.* . . .

JOSEFA: I was silencing the world from reprimand . . . I knew I had to silence the world from reprimand . . . I felt no guilt . . . all I knew . . . the life I had . . . the faith of the barrio people . . . this house of light . . . must be preserved . . . I silenced all reprimand with my terrible deed . . . (*She covers her face for a moment. Then she gathers strength and continues talking.*) With the light of day . . . I knew better . . . others had not my eyes . . . others had not my eyes . . . others had not my reasons . . . or my magicians . . . (*She looks at* FATHER PRADO *intently.*) Can you ever understand?

FATHER PRADO (*as if talking to himself*): I don't understand . . . I don't understand why I didn't see . . . detect what was happening to you . . . .

JOSEFA (*puzzled*): Happening to me?

FATHER PRADO: All your beauty . . . your calm . . . your giving was . . . your talent . . . what a splendid canopy for the twisted fears of so many years . . . so many years . . . I'm an old fool . . . forgive me, my daughter, I have never really seen you . . . I pride myself in knowing you so well . . . I claimed I loved you . . . how blind . . . how blind . . .

JOSEFA: Don't blame yourself, Father . . . I am what you see . . . that is really what I am . . . Not what you discovered this moment. . . .

FATHER PRADO: My poor, poor child. . . .

JOSEFA: No . . . Father . . . don't pity me . . . anything but that! That is one thing I shall never suffer. . . .

FATHER PRADO: I have never seen you cry . . . Josefa . . . until tonight . . .

JOSEFA: The past . . . the dark gnawing . . . such hungers! I must not be a desert . . . now they are harmless ghosts. . . .

FATHER PRADO: Are they?

JOSEFA: You don't understand . . . do you?

FATHER PRADO: I want to. . . .

JOSEFA: The magicians created "me!" . . . the blight of meniality never touched me . . . The magicians gave me the purity of light . . . and the wisp of beauties at my fingertips . . . so . . . I really am . . . what you always thought I was. . . .

FATHER PRADO: There is so much God in you! . . .

JOSEFA: God in me? . . . no, Father . . . no . . . I failed goodness . . . I wanted, I prayed . . . to save my soul as the church instructed . . . as your faith believed. . . .

FATHER PRADO (*somewhat taken aback*): But . . . you are the most pious . . . the most constant . . . in the barrio . . . Faith shines in you . . . all the beauty you create. . . .

JOSEFA: Faith? Oh, no, Father . . . no . . . It was not faith, it was the light of my magicians . . . I bear the children of light! I am its high priestess. . . .

FATHER PRADO: I . . . I . . .

(*He can't go on; he sits down and places his head in his hands.* JOSEFA *looks at him and is full of concern. She goes to comfort him.*)

JOSEFA (*she says this as if she does not believe it herself*): Don't grieve for me, Father . . . for what I have done, I am willing to atone . . . David will be my whole life . . . I will create beauty for him . . . for you . . . for the barrio people . . . longings will fade away with commitment. . . . Father . . . Father (*She kneels in front of him.*) Forgive me, Father, for I have sinned . . . I have grievously sinned.

(*With tears in his eyes,* FATHER PRADO *strokes her hair in silence.*)

FINAL SCENE

(*Dawn the next morning; the sitting room is a pastel paradise; there is life in the birdhouse, a roar of bird sounds;* JOSEFA *comes from the bedroom with a white gown over her arm. It is the gown to be worn at the procession. She goes to the window and looks at the tree with great happiness.*)

JOSEFA: I waited for you . . . before dawn I heard the flurry of the sea . . . oh, what a sight you were over my burning lake . . . straight . . . straight . . . you came to me . . . to this temple of peace . . . no more songs of pain for you. . . .

(*Church bells sound morning vigil. The procession will follow in the freshness of the early morning.* JOSEFA *remembers the barrio world.*)

JOSEFA: My day . . . my day . . . but, oh my people! . . . it was not meant to be shared with you . . . my day was planned by my magicians . . . long before you planned this one for me . . . I must get ready. . . .

(*She goes behind the screen, puts on her gown, comes back and looks in the mirror. Her dress is white. She looks unusually young and beautiful. All of a sudden she touches her rather severe hairdo. Then she lets down her hair.*)

JOSEFA (*looking at herself in the mirror*): Yes . . . yes . . . this way . . . there is a wildness in me . . . (*She laughs in joyous delirium.*)

(*Then she becomes the usual* JOSEFA *for a moment. She remembers the boys' surplices. She goes to the wardrobe and takes them out. She lays them carefully over a chair.*)

JOSEFA: There . . . something of me will be at the procession . . . yes, even that . . . the boys will find them here. . . .

(*She takes a final look in the mirror, then she goes to the window and looks out to the lake.*)

JOSEFA: So still your water . . . but I know your passions underneath . . . deep . . . deep . . . for all time . . . Hush! I'm coming. . . .

(*As she turns to leave, she touches the lace, the damask now finished, the fresh flowers on the table . . . with love . . . with a tender regret . . . but a secret within her . . .*)

JOSEFA: My magicians will let me come back as light . . . yes, yes!

(*She goes to the door and gives the room one final glance.*)

JOSEFA (*in a whisper*): Wait for me. . . .

(*Church bells begin to toll for the gathering of the procession. Voices are heard outside the window.*)

VOICES: "Here! the starting will be here . . . in front of Josefa's garden." "Has anyone seen Josefa this morning?"

(*The sitting room seems alive even without people; then two boys enter. They have come for the surplices.*)

1ST BOY: Hey . . . look . . . they're over there. (*Each of the boys takes one.*)
2ND BOY: Aren't they something . . . grand . . . like at the cathedral . . .
1ST BOY: That's what he said. . . .
2ND BOY: Who said?
1ST BOY: Father Prado . . . he said Josefa was like a cathedral . . .
2ND BOY: 'Cause she makes all this grand stuff?
1ST BOY: I guess so . . . 'cause she's different . . . don't you think?
2ND BOY: Ah . . . ha! She made all the altar linen. . . .
1ST BOY: Yeah . . . Father Prado said she was like the silence of the cathedral . . . and you know those glass-stained windows?
2ND BOY: Yeah. . . .
1ST BOY: That's her soul. . . .
2ND BOY: You think something is wrong with Father Prado?

(*They laugh in jest; shove each other around in horseplay, then stop when the church bells ring again.*)

1ST BOY: Hey, come on . . . the procession is going to start. . . .

(The room is empty again; this time the voices of the choir beginning the procession hymns are heard . . . They are as ethereal as the room. Combined, the room and the voices have a cathedral-like awesomeness. CLEMENCIA *breaks the atmosphere. She is in her Sunday best.)*

CLEMENCIA: Josefa! . . . Where are you? *(She looks in the bedroom; then she peeks through the kitchen door.)* Mnnnn . . . where could she be? Everybody's waiting. Josefa! Oh, dear, oh dear! They've started without her . . . . *(She goes to the window.)* Look at those birds! Every year! . . . they come straight to this tree. Ah . . . God's morning . . . the lake . . . the green pines . . . *(Suddenly something out in the lake catches her eye.)* What is that . . . floating in the lake? Mmmmmmmm . . . looks like a girl dressed in white . . . That's foolish! It is too early for the Bathing of the Virgins, yet . . . yes . . . wearing clothes?

(As she hears the choir, she loses interest and goes to the mirror and straightens her hat.)

CLEMENCIA *(with a sigh)*: Why do we all end up looking like scarecrows? *(She turns to leave and catches sight of the open window.)* I better close the window . . . the room will be covered with birds!

(She goes to the window again; as she starts to close it, she gazes out into the lake again fascinated by what she saw before.)

CLEMENCIA: Yes . . . it is a body! A body floating in the lake . . . I'm sure of it!

(She gasps, but at this moment the church bells ring again. Out of habit, she starts to hurry off, shrugging off what she has seen.)

CLEMENCIA: The sun is too bright . . . it is my imagination! I better hurry . . . what a day this will be. . . .

(She leaves the room. The voices of the choir, the church bell, the birds on the tree in full life, and the almost unearthly light streaming through the windows gives the essence of a presence in the room . . . of something beautiful.)

[1973]

And the Soul Shall Dance

Wakako Yamauchi

ACT I

Scene 1

(*Interior of the Murata house, afternoon. The set is spare. There is a kitchen table, four chairs, a bed, and on the wall, a calendar indicating the year and month: June, 1935. There is a doorway leading to the other room. Props are: a bottle of sake, two cups, a dish of chiles, a phonograph, and two towels hanging on pegs on the wall. A wide wooden bench sits outside.*

The bathhouse has just burned to the ground due to the carelessness of MASAKO, Nisei *daughter, eleven. Offstage there are sounds of* MURATA, *forty,* Issei *farmer, putting out the fire.*

Inside the house HANA MURATA, Issei *wife, in a drab house dress, confronts* MASAKO, *who is wearing a summer dress of the era.* MASAKO *is sullen and somewhat defiant.* HANA *breaks the silence.*)

HANA: How could you be so careless, Masako? You know you should be extra careful with fire. How often have I told you? Now the whole bathhouse is gone. I told you time and again, when you stoke a fire, you should see that everything is swept into the fireplace.

(MURATA *enters. He's dressed in old work clothes. He suffers from heat and exhaustion.*)

MURATA (*Coughing*): Shack went up like a matchbox. . . . This kind of weather dries everything . . . just takes a spark to make a bonfire out of dry timber.

HANA: Did you save any of it?

MURATA: No. Couldn't . . .

HANA (*To* MASAKO): How many times have I told you . . .

(MASAKO *moves nervously.*)

MURATA: No use crying about it now. *Shikata ga nai.* It's gone now. No more bathhouse. That's all there is to it.

HANA: But you've got to tell her. Otherwise she'll make the same mistake. You'll be building a bathhouse every year.

(MURATA *removes his shirt and wipes off his face. He throws his shirt on a chair and sits at the table.*)

MURATA: *Baka!* Ridiculous!

MASAKO: I didn't do it on purpose. (*She goes to the bed, opens a book!*)

HANA (*Follows* MASAKO): I know that but you know what this means? It means we bathe in a bucket . . . inside the house. Carry water in from the pond, heat it on the stove . . . We'll use more kerosene.

MURATA: Tub's still there. And the fireplace. We can still build a fire under the tub.

HANA (*Shocked*): But no walls! Everyone in the country can see us!

MURATA: Wait till dark then. Wait till dark.

HANA: We'll be using a lantern. They'll still see us.

MURATA: Angh! Who? Who'll see us? You think everyone in the country waits to watch us take a bath? Hunh! You know how stupid you sound? Ridiculous!

HANA (*Defensively*): It'll be inconvenient.

(HANA *is saved by a rap on the door.* OKA, Issei *neighbor, forty-five, enters. He is short and stout, dressed in faded work clothes.*)

OKA: Hello! Hello! Oi! What's going on here? Hey! Was there some kind of fire?

(HANA *rushes to the door to let* OKA *in. He stamps the dust from his shoes and enters.*)

HANA: Oka-san! You just wouldn't believe. . . . We had a terrible thing happen.

OKA: Yeah. Saw the smoke from down the road. Thought it was your house. Came rushing over. Is the fire out?

(MURATA *half rises and sits back again. He's exhausted.*)

MURATA (*Gesturing*): Oi, oi. Come in . . . sit down. No big problem. It was just our bathhouse.

OKA: Just the *furoba*, eh?

MURATA: Just the bath.

HANA: Our Masako was careless and the *furoba* caught fire. There's nothing left of it but the tub.

(MASAKO *looks up from her book, pained. She makes a very small sound.*)

OKA: Long as the tub's there, no problem. I'll help you with it. (*He starts to roll up his sleeves.* MURATA *looks at him*)

MURATA: What . . . now? Now?

OKA: Long as I'm here.

HANA: Oh, Papa. Aren't we lucky to have such friends?

MURATA (*To* HANA): Hell, we can't work on it now. The ashes are still hot. I just now put the damned fire out. Let me rest awhile. (*To* OKA) Oi, how about a little sake? (*Gesturing to* HANA) Make sake for Oka-san.

(OKA *sits at the table.* HANA *goes to prepare the sake. She heats it, gets out the cups and pours it for the men.*)

I'm tired . . . I am *tired*.

HANA: Oka-san has so generously offered his help . . .

(OKA *is uncomfortable. He looks around and sees* MASAKO *sitting on the bed.*)

OKA: Hello, there, Masako-chan. You studying?

MASAKO: No, it's summer vacation.

MURATA (*Sucking in his breath*): Kids nowadays . . . no manners . . .
HANA: She's sulking because I had to scold her.

(MASAKO *makes a small moan.*)

MURATA: Drink Oka-san.
OKA (*Swallowing*): Ahhh, that's good.
MURATA: Eh, you not working today?
OKA: No . . . no . . . I took the afternoon off today. I was driving over to
    Nagatas' when I saw this big black cloud of smoke coming from your
    yard.
HANA: It went up so fast . . .
MURATA: What's up at Nagatas'? (*To* HANA) Get the chiles out. Oka-san
    loves chiles.

(HANA *opens a jar of chiles and puts them on a plate. She serves the men
and gets her mending basket and walks to* MASAKO. MASAKO *makes room for
her on the bed.*)

OKA (*Helping himself*): Ah, chiles. (MURATA *looks at him, the question
    unanswered*) Well, I want to see him about my horse. I'm thinking of
    selling my horse.
MURATA: Sell your horse!
OKA (*Scratches his head*): The fact is, I need some money. Nagata-san's the
    only one around made money this year, and I'm thinking he might want
    another horse.
MURATA: Yeah, he made a little this year. And he's talking big . . . big!
    Says he's leasing twenty more acres this fall.
OKA: Twenty acres?
MURATA: Yeah. He might want another horse.
OKA: Twenty acres, eh?
MURATA: That's what he says. But you know his old woman makes all the
    decisions.

(OKA *scratches his head.*)

HANA: They're doing all right.
MURATA: Henh. Nagata-kun's so hen-pecked, it's pathetic. *Peko-peko.* (*He
    makes motions of a hen pecking*)
OKA: (*Feeling the strain*): I better get over there.
MURATA: Why the hell you selling your horse?
OKA: I need cash.
MURATA: Oh, yeah. I could use some too. Seems like everyone's getting
    out of the depression but the poor farmers. Nothing changes for us. We
    go on and on planting our tomatoes and summer squash and eating
    them. . . . Well, at least it's healthy.
HANA: Papa, do you have lumber?
MURATA: Lumber? For what?
HANA: The bath.
MURATA (*Impatiently*): Don't worry about that. We need more sake now.

(HANA *rises to serve him.*)

OKA: You sure Nagata-kun's working twenty more acres?

MURATA: Last I heard. What the hell; if you need a few bucks, I can loan you . . .

OKA: A few hundred. I need a few hundred dollars.

MURATA: Oh, a few hundred. But what the hell you going to do without a horse? Out here a man's horse is as important as his wife.

OKA (*Seriously*): I don't think Nagata will buy my wife.

(*The men laugh, but* HANA *doesn't find it so funny.* MURATA *glances at her. She fills the cups again.* OKA *makes a half-hearted gesture to stop her.* MASAKO *watches the pantomime carefully.* OKA *swallows his drink in one gulp.*)

I better get moving.

MURATA: What's the big hurry?

OKA: Like to get the horse business done.

MURATA: Ehhh . . . relax. Do it tomorrow. He's not going to die, is he?

OKA (*Laughing*): Hey, he's a good horse. I want to get it settled today. If Nagata-kun won't buy, I got to find someone else. You think maybe Kawaguchi . . . ?

MURATA: Not Kawaguchi. . . . Maybe Yamamoto.

HANA: What is all the money for, Oka-san? Does Emiko-san need an operation?

OKA: Nothing like that . . .

HANA: Sounds very mysterious.

OKA: No mystery, Mrs. No mystery. No sale, no money, no story.

MURATA (*Laughing*): That's a good one. "No sale, no money, no. . . ." Eh, Mama.

(*He points to the empty cups.* HANA *fills the cups and goes back to* MASAKO.)

HANA (*Muttering*): I see we won't be getting any work done today. (*To* MASAKO) Are you reading again? Maybe we'd still have a bath if you—

MASAKO: I didn't do it on purpose.

MURATA (*Loudly*): I sure hope you know what you're doing, Oka-kun. What'd you do without a horse?

OKA: I was hoping you'd lend me yours now and then . . . (*He looks at* HANA) I'll pay for some of the feed.

MURATA (*Emphatically waving his hand*): Sure! Sure!

OKA: The fact is, I need that money. I got a daughter in Japan and I just got to send for her this year.

(*Coming to life,* HANA *puts down her mending and sits at the table.*)

HANA: A daughter? You have a daughter in Japan? Why, I didn't know you had children. Emiko-san and you . . . I thought you were childless.

OKA (*Scratching his head*): We are. I was married before.

MURATA: You son-of-a-gun!

HANA: Is that so? How old is your daughter?

OKA: Kiyoko must be . . . fifteen now. Yeah, fifteen.

HANA: Fifteen! Oh, that *would* be too old for Emiko-san's child. Is Kiyoko-san living with relatives in Japan?

OKA (*Reluctantly*): Yeah, with grandparents. With Shizue's parents. Well, the fact is, Shizue, that's my first wife, and Emiko were sisters. They come from a family with no sons. I was a boy when I went to work for the family . . . as an apprentice . . . they're blacksmiths. Later I married Shizue and took on the family name—you know, *yoshi*—because they had no sons. My real name is Sakakihara.

MURATA: Sakakihara! That's a great name!

HANA: A magnificent name!

OKA: No one knows me by that here.

MURATA: Should have kept that . . . Sakakihara.

OKA (*Muttering*): I don't even know myself by that name.

HANA: And Shizue-san passed away and you married Emiko-san?

OKA: Oh, yeah. Well, Shizue and I lived with the family for a while and we had the baby . . . that's, you know, Kiyoko. . . . (*The liquor has affected him and he's become less inhibited*) Well, while I was serving apprentice with the family, they always looked down their noses at me. After I married, it got worse. . . . That old man . . . angh! He was terrible! Always pushing me around, making me look bad in front of my wife and kid. That old man was mean . . . ugly!

MURATA: Yeah, I heard about that apprentice work—*detchi-boko*. . . . Heard it was damned humiliating.

OKA: That's the God's truth!

MURATA: Never had to do it myself. I came to America instead. They say *detchi-boko* is bloody hard work.

OKA: The work's all right. I'm not afraid of work. It's the humiliation! I hated them! Pushing me around like I was still a boy. . . . Me, a grown man! And married to their daughter! (MURATA *groans in sympathy*) Well, Shizue and I talked it over and we decided the best thing was to get away. We thought if I came to America and made some money . . . you know, send her money until we had enough, I'd go back and we'd leave the family . . . you know, move to another province . . . start a small business, maybe in the city, a noodle shop or something.

MURATA: That's everyone's dream. Make money, go home and live like a king.

OKA: I worked like a dog. Sent every penny to Shizue. And then she died. She died on me!

(HANA *and* MURATA *observe a moment of silence in respect for* OKA's *anguish.*)

HANA: And you married Emiko-san.

OKA: I didn't marry her. They married her to me! Right after Shizue died.

HANA: But Oka-san, you were lucky . . .

OKA: Before the body was cold! No respect! By proxy. The old man wrote me they were arranging a marriage by proxy for me and Emiko. They said she'd grown to be a beautiful woman and would serve me well.

HANA: Emiko-san *is* a beautiful woman.

OKA: And they sent her to me. Took care of everything! Immigration, fare, everything.

HANA: But she's your sister-in-law—Kiyoko's aunt. It's good to keep the family together.

OKA: That's what I thought. But hear this: Emiko was the favored one. Shizue was not so pretty, not so smart. They were grooming Emiko for a rich man—his name was Yamoto—lived in a grand house in the village. They sent her to schools, you know, the culture thing: tea ceremony, you know, all that. They didn't even like me, and suddenly they married her to me.

MURATA: Yeah. You don't need all that formal training to make it over here. Just a strong back.

HANA: And a strong will.

OKA: It was all arranged. I couldn't do anything about it.

HANA: It'll be all right. With Kiyoko coming . . .

OKA (*Dubiously*): I hope so . . . I never knew human beings could be so cruel. You know how they mistreated my daughter? You know after Emiko came over, things got from bad to worse and I *never* had enough money to send to Kiyoko.

MURATA: They don't know what it's like here. They think money's picked off the ground here.

OKA: And they treated Kiyoko so bad. They told her I forgot about her. They told her I didn't care—they said I abandoned her. Well, she knew better. She wrote to me all the time and I always told her I'd send for her . . . soon as I got the money. (*He shakes his head*) I just got to do something this year.

HANA: She'll be happier here. She'll know her father cares.

OKA: Kids tormented her for not having parents.

MURATA: Kids are cruel.

HANA: Masako will help her. She'll help her get started at school. She'll make friends . . . she'll be all right.

OKA: I hope so. She'll need friends. (*He considers he might be making a mistake after all*) What could I say to her? Stay there? It's not what you think over here? I can't help her? I just have to do this thing. I just have to do this one thing for her.

MURATA: Sure . . .

HANA: Don't worry. It'll work out fine.

(MURATA *gestures to* HANA. *She fills the cups.*)

MURATA: You talk about selling your horse, I thought you were pulling out.

OKA: I wish I could. But there's nothing else I can do.

MURATA: Without money, yeah . . .

OKA: You can go into some kind of business with money, but a man like me . . . no education . . . there's no kind of job I can do. I'd starve in the city.

MURATA: Dishwashing, maybe. Janitor . . .

OKA: At least here we can eat. Carrots, maybe, but we can eat.

MURATA: All the carrots we been eating 'bout to turn me into a rabbit.

(*They laugh.* HANA *starts to pour more wine for* OKA *but he stops her.*)

OKA: I better not drink any more. Got to drive to Nagata-san's yet. (*He rises and walks over to* MASAKO) You study hard, don't you? You'll teach Kiyoko English, eh? When she gets here . . .

HANA: Oh, yes. She will.

MURATA: Kiyoko-san could probably teach her a thing or two.

OKA: She won't know about American ways . . .

MASAKO: I'll help her.

HANA: Don't worry, Oka-san. She'll have a good friend in our Masako.

(*They move toward the door.*)

OKA: Well, thanks for the sake. I guess I talk too much when I drink. (*He scratches his head and laughs*) Oh. I'm sorry about the fire. By the way, come to my house for your bath . . . until you build yours again.

HANA (*Hesitantly*): Oh, uh . . . thank you. I don't know if . . .

MURATA: Good! Good! Thanks a lot. I need a good hot bath tonight.

OKA: Tonight, then.

MURATA: We'll be there.

HANA (*Bowing*): Thank you very much. Sayonara.

OKA (*Nodding*): See you tonight.

(OKA *leaves.* HANA *faces her husband as soon as the door closes.*)

HANA: Papa, I don't know about going over there.

MURATA (*Surprised*): Why?

HANA: Well, Emiko-san . . .

MURATA (*Irritated*): What's the matter with you? We need a bath and Oka's invited us over.

HANA (*To* MASAKO): Help me clear the table.

(MASAKO *reluctantly leaves her book and begins to clear the table.*)

Papa, you know we've been neighbors already three, four years and Emiko-san's never been very hospitable.

MURATA: She's shy, that's all.

HANA: Not just shy . . . she's strange. I feel like she's pushing me off . . . she makes me feel like—I don't know—like I'm prying or something.

MURATA: Maybe you are.

HANA: And never puts out a cup of tea. . . . If she had all that training in the graces . . . why, a cup of tea . . .

MURATA: So, if you want tea, ask for it.

HANA: I can't do that, Papa. She's strange . . . I don't know . . . (*To* MASAKO) When we go there, be very careful not to say anything wrong.

MASAKO: I never say anything anyway.

HANA (*Thoughtfully*): Would you believe the story Oka-san just told? Why, I never knew . . .

MURATA: There're lot of things you don't know. Just because a man don't . . . talk about them, don't mean he don't feel . . . don't think about . . .

HANA (*Looking around*): We'll have to take something. . . . There's nothing to take. . . . Papa, maybe you can dig up some carrots.

MURATA: God, Mama, be sensible. They got carrots. Everybody's got carrots.

HANA: Something . . . maybe I should make something.

MURATA: Hell, they're not expecting anything.

HANA: It's not good manners to go empty-handed.

MURATA: We'll take the sake.

(HANA *grimaces.* MASAKO *sees the record player.*)

MASAKO: I know, Mama. We can take the Victrola! We can play records for Mrs. Oka. Then nobody has to talk.

(MURATA *laughs. Fade-out.*)

Scene 2

(*That evening. We see the exterior wall of Oka's weathered house. There is a workable screen door and a large screened window. Outside there is a wide wooden bench that can accommodate three or four people. There is one separate chair and a lantern stands against the house.*

The last rays of the sun light the area in a soft golden glow. This light grows gray as the scene progresses and it is quite dark at the end of the scene.

Through the screened window, EMIKO OKA, *Issei woman, thirty, can be seen walking erratically back and forth. She wears a drab cotton dress but her grace and femininity come through. Her hair is in a bun, in the style of Issei women of the era.*

OKA *sits cross-legged on the bench. He wears a yukata [summer robe] and fans himself with a round Japanese fan.*

The Muratas enter. MURATA *carries towels and a bottle of sake.* HANA *carries the Victrola, and* MASAKO *a package containing their yukatas.*)

OKA (*Standing to receive the Muratas*): Oh, you've come. Welcome!

MURATA: Yah. . . . Good of you to ask us.

HANA (*Bowing*): Yes, thank you very much. (*To* MASAKO) Say "hello," Masako.

MASAKO: Hello.

HANA: And "thank you."

MASAKO: Thank you.

(OKA *makes motion of protest. Emiko stops her pacing and watches from the window.*)

HANA (*Glancing briefly at the window*): And how is Emiko-san this evening?

OKA (*Turning toward the house*): Emi! Emiko!

HANA: That's all right. Don't call her out. She must be busy.

OKA (*Half-rising*): Emiko!

(EMIKO *comes to the door.* HANA *starts a deep bow toward the door.*)

MURATA: *Konbanwa* (Good evening)!

HANA: *Konbanwa*, Emiko-san. I feel so bad about this intrusion. Your husband has told you, our bathhouse was destroyed by fire and he graciously invited us to come use yours.

(EMIKO *shakes her head.*)

OKA: I didn't have a chance to . . .

HANA (*Recovering and nudging* MASAKO): Say hello to Mrs. Oka.

MASAKO: Hello, Mrs. Oka.

(HANA *lowers the Victrola onto the bench.*)

OKA: What's this? You brought a phonograph?

MASAKO: It's a Victrola.

HANA (*Laughing indulgently*): Yes. Masako wanted to bring this over and play some records.

MURATA (*Extending the wine*): Brought a little sake too.

OKA (*Taking the bottle*): Ah, now that I like. Emiko, bring out the cups.

(*He waves at his wife, but she doesn't move. He starts to ask again, but decides to get them himself. He enters the house and returns with two cups.* EMIKO *seats herself on the single chair. The Muratas unload their paraphernalia;* OKA *pours the wine, the men drink,* HANA *chatters and sorts the records.* MASAKO *stands by, helping her.*)

HANA: Yes, our Masako loves to play records. I like records too . . . and Papa, he . . .

MURATA (*Watching* EMIKO): They take me back home. The only way I can get there . . . in my mind.

HANA: Do you like music, Emiko-san? (EMIKO *looks vague but smiles faintly*) Oka-san, you like them, don't you?

OKA: Yeah. But I don't have a player. No chance to hear them.

MURATA: I had to get this for them. They wouldn't leave me alone until I got it. Well . . . a phonograph . . . what the hell, they got to have *some* fun.

HANA: We don't have to play them, if you'd rather not . . .

OKA: Play. Play them.

HANA: I thought we could listen to them and relax. (*She extends some records to* EMIKO) Would you like to look through these, Emiko-san?

(EMIKO *doesn't respond. She pulls out a sack of Bull Durham and starts to roll a cigarette.* HANA *pushes* MASAKO *to her.*)

Take these to her.

(MASAKO *moves toward* EMIKO *with the records.* MASAKO *stands watching her as she lights her cigarette.*)

Some of these are very old. You might know them, Emiko-san. (*She sees*

MASAKO *watching* EMIKO) Masako, bring those over here. (*She laughs uncomfortably*) You might like this one, Emiko-san . . . (*She starts the player*) Do you know it?

(*The record whines out "Kago No Tori."* EMIKO *listens with her head cocked. She smokes her cigarette. She becomes wrapped in nostalgia and memories of the past.* MASAKO *watches her carefully.*)

MASAKO (*Whispering*): Mama, she's crying.

(*Startled,* HANA *and* MURATA *look toward* EMIKO.)

HANA (*Pinching* MASAKO): Shhh. The smoke is in her eyes.
MURATA: Did you bring the record I like, Mama?

(EMIKO *rises abruptly and enters the house.*)

MASAKO: They were tears, Mama.
HANA: From yawning, Masako. (*Regretfully, to* OKA) I'm afraid we've offended her.
OKA (*Unaware*): Hunh? Aw . . . no . . . pay no attention . . . no offense . . .

(MASAKO *looks toward the window.* EMIKO *stands forlornly and slowly drifts into a dance.*)

HANA: I'm very sorry. Children, you know . . . they'll say anything, anything that's on their minds.
MURATA (*Notices* MASAKO *watching* EMIKO *through the window and tries to divert her attention*): The needles. Masako, where're the needles?
MASAKO (*Still watching*): I forgot them.

(HANA *sees what's going on.* OKA *is unaware.*)

HANA: Masako, go take your bath now. Masako . . .

(MASAKO *reluctantly picks up her towel and leaves.*)

OKA: Yeah, yeah . . . take your bath.
MURATA (*Sees* EMIKO *still dancing*): Change the record, Mama.
OKA (*Still unaware*): That's kind of sad.
MURATA: No use to get sick over a record. We're supposed to enjoy.

(HANA *stops the record.* EMIKO *disappears from the window.* HANA *selects a lively* ondo (*folk dance*)—*"Tokyo Ondo."*)

HANA: We'll find something more fun.

(*The three begin to tap their feet to the music.*)

Can't you just see the festival? The dancers, the bright kimonos, the paper lanterns bobbing in the wind, the fireflies . . . how nostalgic. . . . Oh, how nostalgic . . .

(*From the side of the house,* EMIKO *appears. Her hair is down, she wears an old straw hat. She dances in front of the Muratas. They're startled. After the first shock, they watch with frozen smiles. They try to join* EMIKO's *mood but something is missing.* OKA *is grieved. He finally stands as though he's had enough.* EMIKO, *now close to the door, ducks into the house.*)

That was pretty . . . very nice . . .

(OKA *settles down and grunts.* MURATA *clears his throat and* MASAKO *returns from her bath.*)

MURATA: You're done already? (*He's glad to see her*)
MASAKO: I wasn't very dirty. The water was too hot.
MURATA: Good! Just the way I like it.
HANA: Not dirty?
MURATA (*Picking up his towel*): Come on, Mama . . . scrub my back.
HANA (*Laughing embarrassedly*): Oh, oh . . . well . . . (*She stops the player*) Masako, now don't forget . . . crank the machine and change the needle now and then.
MASAKO: I didn't bring them.
HANA: Oh. Oh . . . all right. I'll be back soon . . . don't forget . . . crank.

(*She leaves with her husband.* OKA *and* MASAKO *are alone.* OKA *is awkward and falsely hearty.*)

OKA: So! So you don't like hot baths, eh?
MASAKO: Not too hot.
OKA (*Laughing*): I thought you like it real hot. Hot enough to burn the house down. That's a little joke.

(MASAKO *busies herself with the records to conceal her annoyance.*)

I hear you're real good in school. Always top of the class.
MASAKO: It's a small class. Only two of us.
OKA: When Kiyoko comes, you'll help her in school, yeah? You'll take care of her . . . a favor for me, eh?
MASAKO: Okay.
OKA: You'll be her friend, eh?
MASAKO: Okay.
OKA: That's good. That's good. You'll like her. She's a nice girl too. (*He stands, yawns, and stretches*) I'll go for a little walk now. (*He touches his crotch to indicate his purpose*)

(MASAKO *turns her attention to the records and selects one—"The Soul Shall Dance"—and begins to sway to the music. The song draws* EMIKO *from the house. She looks out the window, sees* MASAKO *is alone and begins to slip into a dance.*)

EMIKO: Do you like that song, Masa-chan?

(MASAKO *is startled and draws back. She remembers her mother's warning. She doesn't know what to do. She nods.*)

That's one of my favorite songs. I remember in Japan I used to sing it so often . . . my favorite song . . . (*She sings along with the record*)
Akai kuchibiru
Kappu ni yosete
Aoi sake nomya
Kokoro ga odoru . . .
Do you know what that means, Masa-chan?

MASAKO: I think so . . . The soul will dance?

EMIKO: Yes, yes, that's right.
The soul shall dance.
Red lips against a glass
Drink the green . . .

MASAKO: Wine?

EMIKO (*Nodding*): Drink the green wine.

MASAKO: Green? I thought wine is purple.

EMIKO (*Nodding*): Wine is purple . . . but this is a green liqueur. (*She holds up one of the china cups as though it were crystal, and looks at it as though the light were shining through it and she sees the green liquid*) It's good . . . it warms your heart.

MASAKO: And the soul dances.

EMIKO: Yes.

MASAKO: What does it taste like? The green wine . . .

EMIKO: Oh, it's like . . . it's like . . .

(*The second verse starts.* "Kurai yoru no yume/ Setsunasa yo/ Aoi sake nomya/ Yume mo odoru. . . .")

MASAKO: In the dark night . . .

EMIKO: Dreams are unbearable . . . insufferable . . . (*She turns sad*)

MASAKO: Drink the . . .

EMIKO (*Nodding*): Drink the green wine . . .

MASAKO: And the dreams will dance.

EMIKO (*Softly*): I'll be going back one day . . .

MASAKO: To where?

EMIKO: My home . . . Japan . . . my real home. I'm planning to go back.

MASAKO: By yourself?

EMIKO (*Nodding*): Oh, yes. It's a secret. You can keep a secret?

MASAKO: Uh-huh. I have lots of secrets . . . all my own . . .

(*The music stops.* EMIKO *sees* OKA *approaching and disappears into the house.* MASAKO *attends to the record and does not know* EMIKO *is gone.*)

Secrets I never tell anyone.

OKA: Secrets? What kind of secrets? What did she say?

MASAKO: Oh. Nothing.

OKA: What did you talk about?

MASAKO: Nothing. . . . Mrs. Oka was talking about the song. She was telling me what it meant . . . about the soul.

OKA (*Scoffing*): Heh! What does she know about soul? (*Calming down*) Ehhh . . . some people don't have them . . . souls.

MASAKO (*Timidly*): I thought . . . I think everyone has a soul. I read in a book . . .

OKA (*Laughing*): Maybe . . . maybe you're right. I'm not an educated man, you know . . . I don't know too much about books. When Kiyoko comes you can talk to her about it. Kiyoko is very . . .

(*From inside the house, we hear* EMIKO *begin to sing loudly at the name Kiyoko as though trying to drown it out.* OKA *stops talking. Then resumes.*)

Kiyoko is very smart. You'll have a good time with her. She'll learn your language fast. How old did you say you are?

MASAKO: Almost twelve.

(*By this time* OKA *and* MASAKO *are shouting, trying to be heard above* EMIKO's *singing.*)

OKA: Kiyoko is fifteen. . . . Kiyoko . . .

(OKA *is exasperated. He rushes into the house seething.* MASAKO *hears* OKA's *muffled rage: "Behave yourself," and "kitchigai" come through.* MASAKO *slinks to the window and looks in.* OKA *slaps* EMIKO *around.* MASAKO *reacts to the violence.* OKA *comes out.* MASAKO *returns to the bench in time. He pulls his fingers through his hair and sits next to* MASAKO. *She very slightly draws away.*)

Want me to light a lantern?

MASAKO (*Shaken*): No . . . ye—. . . okay . . .

OKA: We'll get a little light here . . .

(*He lights the lantern as the Muratas return from their bath. They are in good spirits.*)

MURATA: Ahhhh. . . . Nothing like a good hot bath.

HANA: So refreshing . . .

MURATA: A bath should be taken hot and slow. Don't know how Masako gets through so fast.

HANA: She probably goesn't get in the tub.

MASAKO: I do.

(*Everyone laughs.*)

Well I do.

(EMIKO *comes out. She has a large purple welt on her face. She sits on the separate chair, hands folded, quietly watching the Muratas. They look at her with alarm.* OKA *engages himself with his fan.*)

HANA: Oh! Emiko-san . . . what . . . ah-ah . . . whaa . . . (*She draws a deep breath*) What a nice bath we had . . . such a lovely bath. We do appreciate your hos . . . pitality. Thank you so much.

EMIKO: Lovely evening, isn't it?

HANA: Very lovely. Very. Ah, a little warm, but nice. . . . Did you get a chance to hear the records? (*Turning to* MASAKO) Did you play the records for Mrs. Oka?

MASAKO: Ye—. . . no. . . . The needle was . . .

EMIKO: Yes, she did. We played the records together.

MURATA: Oh, you played the songs together?

EMIKO: Yes . . . yes . . .

MURATA: That's nice. . . . Masako can understand pretty good, eh?

EMIKO: She understands everything . . . everything I say.

MURATA (*Withdrawing*): Oh, yeah? Eh, Mama, we ought to be going . . . (*He closes the player*) Hate to bathe and run but . . .

HANA: Yes, yes. Tomorrow is a busy day. Come, Masako.

EMIKO: Please . . . stay a little longer.

MURATA: Eh, well, we got to be going.

HANA: Why, thank you, but . . .

EMIKO: It's still quite early.

OKA (*Indicating he's ready to say good-bye*): Enjoyed the music. And the sake.

EMIKO: The records are very nice. Makes me remember Japan. I sang those songs . . . those very songs. . . . Did you know I used to sing?

HANA (*Politely*): Why, no . . . no. I didn't know that. You must have a very lovely voice.

EMIKO: Yes.

HANA: No, I didn't know that. That's very nice.

EMIKO: Yes, I sang. My parents were very strict . . . they didn't like it. They said it was frivolous. Imagine?

HANA: Yes, I can imagine. Things were like that . . . in those days singing was not considered proper or nice . . . I mean, only for women in the profess—. . .

MURATA: We better get home, Mama.

HANA: Yes, yes. What a shame you couldn't continue with it.

EMIKO: In the city I did do some classics: the dance, and the *koto*, and the flower, and of course, the tea . . . (*She makes the proper gesture for the different disciplines*) All those. Even some singing . . . classics, of course.

HANA (*Politely*): Of course.

EMIKO: All of it is so disciplined . . . so disciplined. I was almost a *natori*.

HANA: Oh! How nice.

EMIKO: But everything has changed.

HANA: Oh!

EMIKO: I was sent here to America. (*She glares at* OKA)

HANA: Oh, too bad . . . I mean, too bad about your *natori*.

MURATA (*Loudly to* OKA): So did you see Nagata today?

OKA: Oh, yeah. Yeah.

MURATA: What did he say? Is he interested?

OKA: Yeah. Yeah. He's interested.

MURATA: He likes the horse, eh?

OKA: Ah . . . yeah.

MURATA: I knew he'd like him. I'd buy him myself if I had the money.

OKA: Well, I have to take him over tomorrow. He'll decide then.

MURATA: He'll buy . . . he'll buy. You'd better go straight over to the ticket office and get that ticket. Before you—ha-ha—spend the money.

OKA: Ha-ha. Yeah.

HANA: It'll be so nice when Kiyoko-san comes to join you. I know you're looking forward to it.

EMIKO (*Confused*): Oh . . . oh . . .

HANA: Masako is so happy. It'll be good for her too.

EMIKO: I had more freedom in the city . . . I lived with an aunt and she let me. . . . She wasn't so strict.

(MURATA *and* MASAKO *have their gear together and stand ready to leave.*)

MURATA: Good luck on the horse tomorrow.

OKA: Yeah, thanks.

HANA (*Bowing*): Many, many thanks.

OKA (*Nodding toward the sake*): Thanks for the sake.

HANA (*Bowing again*): Good night, Emiko-san. We'll see you again soon. We'll bring the records too.

EMIKO (*Softly*): Those songs . . . those very songs . . .

MURATA: Let's go, Mama.

(*The Muratas pull away. Light follows them and grows dark on the Okas. The Muratas begin walking home.*)

HANA: That was uncomfortable.

MASAKO: What's the matter with—

HANA: Shhhh!

MURATA: I guess Oka has his problems.

MASAKO: Is she really *kitchigai?*

HANA: Of course not. She's not crazy. Don't say that word, Masako.

MASAKO: I heard Mr. Oka call her that.

HANA: He called her that?

MASAKO: I . . . I think so.

HANA: You heard wrong, Masako. Emiko-san isn't crazy. She just likes her drinks. She had too much to drink tonight.

MASAKO: Oh.

HANA: She can't adjust to this life. She can't get over the good times she had in Japan. Well, it's not easy . . . but one has to know when to bend . . . like the bamboo. When the winds blow, bamboo bends. You bend or crack. Remember that, Masako.

MURATA (*Laughing wryly*): Bend, eh? Remember that, Mama.

HANA (*Softly*): You don't know . . . it isn't ever easy.

MASAKO: Do you want to go back to Japan, Mama?

HANA: Everyone does.

MASAKO: Do you, Papa?

MURATA: I'll have to make some money first.

MASAKO: I don't. Not me. Not Kiyoko . . .

HANA: After Kiyoko-san comes, Emiko will have company and things will straighten out. She has nothing to live on but memories. She doesn't have any friends. At least I have my friends at church . . . at least I have that. She must get awful lonely.

MASAKO: I know that. She tried to make friends with me.

HANA: She did? What did she say?

MASAKO: Well, sort of . . .

HANA: What did she say?

MASAKO: She didn't say anything. I just felt it. Maybe you should be her friend, Mama.

MURATA: Poor woman. We could have stayed longer.

HANA: But you wanted to leave. I tried to be friendly. You saw that. It's not easy to talk to Emiko. She either closes up, you can't pry a word from her, or else she goes on and on . . . all that . . . that . . . about the *koto* and tea and the flower . . . I mean, what am I supposed to say? She's so unpredictable. And the drinking . . .

MURATA: All right, all right, Mama.

MASAKO: Did you see her black eye?

HANA (*Calming down*): She probably hurt herself. She wasn't very steady.

MASAKO: Oh, no. Mr. Oka hit her.

HANA: I don't think so.

MASAKO: He hit her. I saw him.

HANA: You saw that? Papa, do you hear that? She saw them. That does it. We're not going there again.

MURATA: Aww . . . Oka wouldn't do that. Not in front of a kid.

MASAKO: Well, they didn't do it in front of me. They were in the house.

MURATA: You see . . .

HANA: That's all right. You just have to fix the bathhouse. Either that or we're going to bathe at home . . . in a bucket. We're not going . . . we'll bathe at home. (MURATA *mutters to himself*) What?

MURATA: I said all right, it's the bucket then. I'll get to it when I can.

(HANA *passes* MURATA *and walks ahead.*)

Scene 3
(*Same evening. Lights cross-fade to the exterior of the Oka house. The Muratas have just left.* EMIKO *sits on the bench. Her back is to* OKA. OKA, *still standing, looks at her contemptuously as she takes the bottle and one of the cups to pour herself a drink.*)

OKA: Nothing more disgusting than a drunk woman. (EMIKO *ignores him*) You made a fool of yourself. *Washi baka ni shite!* You made a fool of me!

(EMIKO *doesn't move.*)

EMIKO: One can only make a fool of oneself.

OKA: You learn that in the fancy schools, eh? (EMIKO *examines the pattern on her cup*) Eh? Eh? Answer me! (EMIKO *ignores him*) I'm talking to you. Answer me! (*Menacing*) You don't get away with that. You think you're so fine . . .

(EMIKO *looks off into the horizon.* OKA *turns her roughly around.*)

When I talk, you listen!

(EMIKO *turns away again.* OKA *pulls the cup from her hand.*)

Goddamnit! What'd you think my friends think of you? What kind of ass they think I am? (*He grabs her shoulders*)

EMIKO: Don't touch me . . . don't touch me.

OKA: Who the hell you think you are? "Don't touch me, don't touch me." Who the hell! High and mighty, eh? Too good for me, eh? Don't put on the act for me . . . I know who you are.

EMIKO: Tell me who I am, Mister Smart Peasant.

OKA: Shut your fool mouth, goddamnit! Sure! I'll tell you. I know all about you . . . Shizue told me. The whole village knows.

EMIKO: Shizue!

OKA: Yeah! Shizue. Embarrassed the hell out of her, your own sister.

EMIKO: Embarrassed? I have nothing to be ashamed of. I don't know what you're talking about.

OKA (*Derisively*): You don't know what I'm talking about. I know. The whole village knows. They're all laughing at you. At me! Stupid Oka got stuck with a secondhand woman. I didn't say anything because . . .

EMIKO: I'm not secondhand!

OKA: Who you trying to fool? I know. Knew long time ago. . . . Shizue wrote me all about your affairs in Tokyo. The men you were mess—

EMIKO: Affairs? Men?

OKA: That man you were messing with . . . I knew all along. I didn't say anything because you . . . I . . .

EMIKO: I'm not ashamed of it.

OKA: You're not ashamed! What the hell! Your father thought he was pulling a fast one on me . . . thought I didn't know nothing . . . thought I was some kind of dumb ass . . . I didn't say nothing because Shizue's dead . . . Shizue's dead. I was willing to give you a chance.

EMIKO (*Laughing*): A chance?

OKA: Yeah! A chance! Laugh! Give a *joro* another chance. Sure, I'm stupid . . . dumb.

EMIKO: I'm not a whore. I'm true . . . he knows I'm true.

OKA: True! Ha!

EMIKO: You think I'm untrue just because I let . . . let you. . . . There's only one man for me.

OKA: (*Obscene gesture*) you? I can do what I want with you. Your father palmed you off on me—like a dog or cat—an animal . . . couldn't do nothing with you. Even that rich dumb Yamoto wouldn't have you. Your father—greedy father—so proud . . . making big plans for you . . . for himself. Ha! The whole village laughing at him . . . (EMIKO *hangs her head*) Shizue told me. And she was working like a dog . . . trying to keep your goddamn father happy . . . doing my work and yours.

EMIKO: My work?

OKA: Yeah, your work too! She killed herself working! She killed herself . . . (*He has tender memories of his dull, uncomplaining wife*) Up in the morning getting the fires started, working the bellows, cleaning the furnace, cooking, and late at night working with the sewing . . . tending the baby. . . . (*He mutters*) The goddamn family killed her. And you . . . you out there in Tokyo with the fancy clothes, doing the (*He sneers*) dance, the tea, the flower, the *koto*, and the . . . (*Obscene gesture*)

EMIKO (*Hurting*): Achhhh . . .

OKA: Did you have fun? Did you have fun on your sister's blood? (EMIKO *doesn't answer*) Did you? He must have been a son-of-a-bitch. . . . What would make that goddamn greedy old man send his prize mare to a plow horse like me? What kind of bum was he that your father—

EMIKO: He's not a bum . . . he's not a bum.

OKA: Was he Korean? Was he *Etta*? That's the only thing I could figure.

EMIKO: I'm true to him. Only him.

OKA: True? You think he's true to you? You think he waits for you? Remembers you? *Aho!* Think he cares?

EMIKO (*Nodding quietly*): He does.

OKA: And waits ten years? *Baka!* Go back to Japan and see. You'll find out. Go back to Japan. *Kaire!*

EMIKO: In time.

OKA: In time? How about now?

EMIKO: I can't now.

OKA: Ha! Now! Go now! Who needs you? Who needs you? You think a man waits ten years for a woman? You think you're some kind of . . . of . . . diamond . . . treasure . . . he's going to wait his life for you? Go to him. He's probably married with ten kids. Go to him. Get out! Goddamn *joro*. . . . Go! Go!

(*He sweeps* EMIKO *off the bench.*)

EMIKO (*Hurting*): Ahhhh! I . . . I don't have the money. Give me money to—

OKA: If I had money I would give it to you ten years ago. You think I been eating this *kuso* for ten years because I like it?

EMIKO: You're selling the horse. . . . Give me the—

OKA (*Scoffing*): That's for Kiyoko. I owe you nothing.

EMIKO: Ten years, you owe me.

OKA: Ten years of what? Misery? You gave me nothing. I give you nothing. You want to go, pack your bag and start walking. Try cross the desert. When you get dry and hungry, think about me.

EMIKO: I'd die out there.

OKA: Die? You think I didn't die here?

EMIKO: I didn't do anything to you.

OKA: No, no you didn't. All I wanted was a little comfort and . . . you . . . no, you didn't. No. So you die. We all die. Shizue died. If she was here, she wouldn't treat me like this. . . . (*He thinks of his poor dead wife*) Ah, I should have brought her with me. She'd be alive now. We'd be poor but happy . . . like . . . like Murata and his wife . . . and the kid . . .

EMIKO: I wish she were alive too. I'm not to blame for her dying. I didn't know . . . I was away. I loved her. I didn't want her to die . . . . I . . .

OKA (*Softening*): I know that. I'm not blaming you for that. . . . And it's not my fault what happened to you either . . .

(EMIKO *is silent and he mistakes that for a change in attitude. He is encouraged.*)

You understand that, eh? I didn't ask for you. It's not my fault you're here in this desert . . . with . . . with me . . .

(EMIKO *weeps.* OKA *reaches out.*)

I know I'm too old for you. It's hard for me too . . . but this is the way it is. I just ask you be kinder . . . understand it wasn't my fault. Try make it easier for me . . . for yourself too.

(OKA *touches her and she shrinks from his touch.*)

EMIKO: Ach!

OKA (*Humiliated again*): Goddamn it! I didn't ask for you! *Aho!* If you were smart you'd done as your father said . . . cut out that *saru shibai* with the *Etta* . . . married the rich Yamoto. Then you'd still be in Japan. Not here to make my life so miserable. (EMIKO *is silent*) And you can have your *Etta* . . . and anyone else you want. Take them all on . . . (*He is worn out. It's hopeless*) God, why do we do this all the time? Fighting, fighting all the time. There must be a better way to live . . . there must be another way.

(OKA *waits for a response, gives up, and enters the house.* EMIKO *watches him leave and pours herself another drink. The storm has passed, the alcohol takes over. She turns to the door* OKA *disappeared into.*)

EMIKO: Because I must keep the dream alive . . . the dream is all I live for. I am only in exile now. Because if I give in, all I've lived before . . . will mean nothing . . . will be for nothing. . . . Because if I let you make me believe this is all there is to my life, the dream would die . . . I would die . . . (*She pours another drink and feels warm and good*)

(*Fade-out.*)

ACT **II**

Scene 1

(Muratas' kitchen, afternoon. The calendar reads September. MASAKO is at the kitchen table with several books. She thumbs through a Japanese magazine. HANA is with her, sewing.)

MASAKO: Do they always wear kimonos in Japan, Mama?

HANA: Most of the time.

MASAKO: I wonder if Kiyoko will be wearing a kimono like this?

HANA (Peering into MASAKO's magazine): They don't dress like that . . . not for everyday.

MASAKO: I wonder what she's like.

HANA: Probably a lot like you. What do you think she's like?

MASAKO: She's probably taller.

HANA: Mr. Oka isn't tall.

MASAKO: And pretty . . .

HANA (Laughing): Mr. Oka. . . . Well, I don't suppose she'll look like her father.

MASAKO: Mrs. Oka is pretty.

HANA: She isn't Kiyoko-san's real mother, remember.

MASAKO: Oh. That's right.

HANA: But they are related. Well, we'll soon see.

MASAKO: I thought she was coming in September. It's already September.

HANA: Papa said Oka-san went to San Pedro a few days ago. He should be back soon with Kiyoko-san.

MASAKO: Didn't Mrs. Oka go too?

HANA (Glancing toward the Oka house): I don't think so. I see lights in their house at night.

MASAKO: Will they bring Kiyoko over to see us?

HANA: Of course. First thing, probably. You'll be very nice to her, won't you?

MASAKO (Leaves the table and finds another book): Sure. I'm glad I'm going to have a friend. I hope she likes me.

HANA: She'll like you. Japanese girls are very polite, you know.

MASAKO: We have to be or our mamas get mad at us.

HANA: Then I should be getting mad at you more often.

MASAKO: It's often enough already, Mama. (She opens a hardback book) Look at this, Mama . . . I'm going to show her this book.

HANA: She won't be able to read at first.

MASAKO: I love this story. Mama, this is about people like us—settlers—it's about the prairie. We live in a prairie, don't we?

HANA: Prairie? Does that mean desert?

MASAKO: I think so.

HANA (Nodding and looking bleak): We live in a prairie.

MASAKO: It's about the hardships and the floods and droughts and how they have nothing but each other.

410   AND THE SOUL SHALL DANCE

HANA (*Nodding*): We have nothing but each other. But these people—they're white people.

MASAKO (*Nodding*): Sure, Mama. They come from the East. Just like you and Papa came from Japan.

HANA: We come from the Far Far East. That's different. White people are different from us.

MASAKO: I know that.

HANA: White people among white people . . . that's different from Japanese among white people. You know what I'm saying?

MASAKO: I know that. How come they don't write books about us . . . about Japanese people?

HANA: Because we're nobodies here.

MASAKO: If I didn't read these, there'd be nothing for me . . .

HANA: Some of the things you read, you're never going to know.

MASAKO: I can dream though.

HANA (*Sighing*): Sometimes the dreaming makes the living harder. Better to keep your head out of the clouds.

MASAKO: That's not much fun.

HANA: You'll have fun when Kiyoko-san comes. You can study together, you can sew, and sometimes you can try some of those fancy American recipes.

MASAKO: Mama, you have to have chocolate and cream and things like that.

HANA: We'll get them.

(*We hear the putt-putt of* OKA's *old car.* MASAKO *and* HANA *pause and listen.* MASAKO *runs to the window.*)

MASAKO: I think it's them!

HANA: The Okas?

MASAKO: It's them! It's them!

(HANA *stands and looks out. She removes her apron and puts away her sewing.*)

HANA: Two of them. Emiko-san isn't with them. Let's go outside.

(OKA *and* KIYOKO, *fourteen, enter.* OKA *is wearing his going-out clothes; a sweater, white shirt, dark pants, but no tie.* KIYOKO *walks behind him. She is short, chunky, broad-chested and very self-conscious. Her hair is straight and banded into two shucks. She wears a conservative cotton dress, white socks and two-inch heels.* OKA *is proud. He struts in, his chest puffed out.*)

OKA: Hello, hello. . . . We're here. We made it! (*He pushes Kiyoko forward*) This is my daughter, Kiyoko. (*To* KIYOKO) Murata-san . . . remember I was talking about? My friends . . .

KIYOKO (*Barely audible as she speaks a standard formal greeting, bowing deeply*): Hajime mashite yoroshiku onegai shimasu . . .

HANA (*Also bowing formally*): I hope your journey was pleasant.

OKA (*While the women are still bowing, he pushes* KIYOKO *toward* MASAKO): This is Masako-chan; I told you about her . . .

(MASAKO *is shocked at* KIYOKO's *appearance. The girl she expected is already a woman. She stands with her mouth agape and withdraws noticeably.* HANA *rushes in to fill the awkwardness.*)

HANA: Say hello, Masako. My goodness, where are your manners? (*She laughs apologetically*) In this country they don't make much to-do about manners. (*She stands back to examine* KIYOKO) My, my, I didn't picture you so grown up. My, my. . . . Tell me, how was your trip?

OKA (*Proudly*): We just drove in from Los Angeles just this morning. We spent the night in San Pedro and the next two days we spent in Los Angeles . . . you know, Japanese town.

HANA: How nice!

OKA: Kiyoko was so excited. Twisting her head this way and that—couldn't see enough with her big eyes. (*He imitates her fondly*) She's from the country, you know . . . just a big country girl. Got all excited about the Chinese dinner—we had a Chinese dinner. She never ate it before.

(KIYOKO *covers her mouth and giggles.*)

HANA: Chinese dinner!

OKA: Oh, yeah. Duck, *pakkai*, chow mein, seaweed soup . . . the works!

HANA: A feast!

OKA: Oh, yeah. Like a holiday. Two holidays. Two holidays in one.

HANA (*Pushes* MASAKO *forward*): Two holidays in one! Kiyoko-san, our Masako has been looking forward to meeting you.

KIYOKO (*Bowing again*): Hajime mashite . . .

HANA: She's been thinking of all sorts of things she can do with you: sewing, cooking . . .

MASAKO: Oh, Mama.

(KIYOKO *covers her mouth and giggles.*)

HANA: It's true, Kiyoko-san. She's been looking forward to having a best friend.

(KIYOKO *giggles again and* MASAKO *pulls away.*)

OKA: Kiyoko, you shouldn't be so shy. The Muratas are my good friends and you should feel free with them. Ask anything, say anything . . . right?

HANA: Of course, of course. (*She is slightly annoyed with* MASAKO) Masako, go in and start the tea.

(MASAKO *enters the house.*)

I'll call Papa. He's in the yard. Papa! Oka-san is here! (*To* KIYOKO) Now tell me, how was your trip? Did you get seasick?

KIYOKO (*Bowing and nodding*): Eh [Yes]. A little . . .

OKA: Tell her. Tell her how sick you got.

(KIYOKO *covers her mouth and giggles.*)

HANA: Oh, I know, I know. I was too. That was a long time ago. I'm sure things are improved now. Tell me about Japan . . . what is it like now? They say it's so changed . . . modern . . .

OKA: Kiyoko comes from the country . . . backwoods. Nothing changes much there from century to century.

HANA: Ah! That's true. That's why I love Japan. And you wanted to leave. It's unbelievable. To come here!

OKA: She always dreamed about it.

HANA: Well, it's not really that bad.

OKA: No, it's not that bad. Depends on what you make of it.

HANA: That's right. What you make of it. I was just telling Masako today . . .

(MURATA *enters. He rubs his hands to take off the soil and comes in grinning. He shakes* OKA's *hand.*)

MURATA: *Oi, oi* . . .

OKA: Yah . . . I'm back. This is my daughter.

MURATA: No! She's beautiful!

OKA: Finally made it. Finally got her here.

MURATA (*To* KIYOKO): Your father hasn't stopped talking about you all summer.

HANA: And Masako too.

KIYOKO (*Bowing*): *Hajime mashite* . . .

MURATA (*Acknowledging with a short bow*): Yah. How'd you like the trip?

OKA: I was just telling your wife—had a good time in Los Angeles. Had a couple of great dinners, took in the cinema—Japanese pictures, bought her some American clothes.

HANA: Oh, you bought that in Los Angeles.

MURATA: Got a good price for your horse, eh? Lots of money, eh?

OKA: Nagata's a shrewd bargainer. Heh. It don't take much money to make her happy. She's a country girl.

MURATA: That's all right. Country's all right. Country girl's the best.

OKA: Had trouble on the way back.

MURATA: Yeah?

OKA: Fan belt broke.

MURATA: That'll happen.

OKA: Lucky I was near a gasoline station. We were in the mountains. Waited in a restaurant while it was getting fixed.

HANA: Oh, that was good.

OKA: Guess they don't see Japanese much. Stare? Terrible! Took them a long time to wait on us. Dumb waitress practically threw the food at us. Kiyoko felt bad.

HANA: Ah! That's too bad . . . too bad. That's why I always pack a lunch when we take trips.

MURATA: They'll spoil the day for you . . . those barbarians!

OKA: Terrible food too. Kiyoko couldn't swallow the dry bread and bologna.

HANA: That's the food they eat!

MURATA: Let's go in . . . have a little wine. Mama, we got wine? This is a celebration.

HANA: I think so . . . a little . . .

(*They enter the house talking.* MASAKO *has made the tea, and* HANA *begins to serve the wine.*)

How is your "mother"? Was she happy to see you?

KIYOKO: Oh, she . . . yes . . .

HANA: I just know she was surprised to see you so grown up. Of course, you remember her from Japan, don't you?

KIYOKO (*Nodding*): Eh. I can barely remember. I was very young . . .

HANA: Of course. But you do, don't you?

KIYOKO: She was gone most of the time . . . at school in Tokyo. She was very pretty, I remember that.

HANA: She's still very pretty.

KIYOKO: *Eh.* She was always laughing. She was much younger then.

HANA: Oh now, it hasn't been that long ago.

(MASAKO *leaves the room to go outside. The following dialogue continues muted as light goes dim in the house and focuses on* MASAKO. EMIKO *enters, is drawn to the Murata window and listens.*)

OKA: We stayed at an inn on East First Street. *Shizuokaya.* Whole inn filled with Shizuoka people . . . talking the old dialect. Thought I was in Japan again.

MURATA: That right?

OKA: Felt good. Like I was in Japan again.

HANA (*To* KIYOKO): Did you enjoy Los Angeles?

KIYOKO (*Nodding*): *Eh.*

OKA: That's as close as I'll get to Japan.

MURATA: *Mattakuna!* That's for sure.

(*Outside* MASAKO *becomes aware of* EMIKO.)

MASAKO: Why don't you go in?

EMIKO: Oh. Oh. Why don't you?

MASAKO: They're all grownups in there. I'm not grown up.

EMIKO (*Softly*): All grownups. . . . Maybe I'm not either. (*Her mood changes*) Masa-chan, do you have a boyfriend?

MASAKO: I don't like boys. They don't like me.

EMIKO: Oh, that will change. You will change. I was like that too.

MASAKO: Besides, there're none around here . . . Japanese boys. . . . There are some at school, but they don't like girls.

HANA (*Calling from the kitchen*): Masako . . .

(MASAKO *doesn't answer.*)

EMIKO: Your mother is calling you.

MASAKO (*Answering her mother*): *Nani* (What)?

HANA (*From the kitchen*): Come inside now.

EMIKO: You'll have a boyfriend one day.

MASAKO: Not me.

EMIKO: You'll fall in love one day. Someone will make the inside of you light up, and you'll know you're in love. (*She relives her own experience*) Your life will change . . . grow beautiful. It's good, Masa-chan. And this feeling you'll remember the rest of your life . . . will come back to you . . . haunt you . . . keep you alive . . . five, ten years . . . no matter what happens . . . keep you alive.

HANA (*From the kitchen*): Masako. . . . Come inside now.

(MASAKO *turns aside to answer and* EMIKO *slips away.*)

MASAKO: What, Mama?

HANA (*Coming outside*): Come inside. Don't be so unsociable. Kiyoko wants to talk to you.

MASAKO (*Watching* EMIKO *leave*): She doesn't want to talk to me. You're only saying that.

HANA: What's the matter with you? Don't you want to make friends with her?

MASAKO: She's not my friend. She's your friend.

HANA: Don't be so silly. She's only fourteen.

MASAKO: Fifteen. They said fifteen. She's your friend. She's an old lady.

HANA: Don't say that.

MASAKO: I don't like her.

HANA: Shhh! Don't say that.

MASAKO: She doesn't like me either.

HANA: Ma-chan. Remember your promise to Mr. Oka? You're going to take her to school, teach her the language, teach her the ways of Americans.

MASAKO: She can do it herself. You did.

HANA: That's not nice, Ma-chan.

MASAKO: I don't like the way she laughs. (*She imitates* KIYOKO *holding her hand to her mouth and giggling and bowing*)

HANA: Oh, how awful! Stop that. That's the way the girls do in Japan. Maybe she doesn't like your ways either. That's only a difference in manners. What you're doing now is considered very bad manners. (*She changes tone*) Ma-chan . . . just wait—when she learns to read and speak, you'll have so much to say to each other. Come on, be a good girl and come inside.

MASAKO: It's just old people in there, Mama. I don't want to go in.

(HANA *calls* KIYOKO *away from the table and speaks confidentially to her.*)

HANA: Kiyoko-san, please come here a minute. Maybe it's better for you to talk to Masako alone.

(KIYOKO *leaves the table and walks to* HANA *outside.*)

Masako has a lot of things to tell you about . . . what to expect in school and things . . .

MURATA (*Calling from the table*): Mama, put out something . . . chiles . . . for Oka-san.

(HANA *leaves the two girls and enters the house.* KIYOKO *and* MASAKO *stand awkwardly,* KIYOKO *glancing shyly at* MASAKO.)

MASAKO: Do you like it here?
KIYOKO (*Nodding*): Eh.

(*There's an uncomfortable pause.*)

MASAKO: School will be starting next week . . .
KIYOKO (*Nodding*): Eh.
MASAKO: Do you want to walk to school with me?
KIYOKO (*Nodding*): Ah.
MASAKO (*Rolls her eyes and tries again*): I leave at 7:30.
KIYOKO: Ah.

(*There's a long pause.* MASAKO *finally gives up and moves offstage.*)

MASAKO: I have to do something.

(KIYOKO *watches her leave and uncertainly moves back to the house.* HANA *looks up at* KIYOKO *coming in alone, sighs, and quietly pulls out a chair for her. Fade-out.*)

Scene 2
(*November, night. Interior of the Murata house. Lamps are lit. The family is at the kitchen table.* HANA *sews,* MASAKO *does her homework,* MURATA *reads the paper. They're dressed in warm robes and having tea. Outside, thunder rolls in the distance and lightning flashes.*)

HANA: It'll be *ohigan* (an autumn festival) soon.
MURATA: Something to look forward to.
HANA: We will need sweet rice for *omochi* (rice cakes).
MURATA: I'll order it next time I go to town.
HANA (*To* MASAKO): How is school? Getting a little harder?
MASAKO: Not that much. Sometimes the arithmetic is hard.
HANA: How is Kiyoko-san doing? Is she getting along all right?
MASAKO: She's good in arithmetic. She skipped a grade already.
HANA: Already? That's good news. Only November and she skipped a grade! At this rate she'll be through before you.
MASAKO: Well, she's older.
MURATA: Sure, she's older, Mama.
HANA: Has she made any friends?
MASAKO: No. She follows me around all day. She understands okay, but she doesn't talk. She talks like, you know . . . she says "ranchi" for lunch

416   AND THE SOUL SHALL DANCE

and "ranchi" for ranch too, and like that. Kids laugh and copy behind her back. It's hard to understand her.

HANA: You understand her, don't you?

MASAKO: I'm used to it.

(MURATA *smiles secretly.*)

HANA: You should tell the kids not to laugh; after all, she's trying. Maybe you should help her practice those words . . . show her what she's doing wrong.

MASAKO: I already do. Our teacher told me to do that.

MURATA (*Looking up from his paper*): You ought to help her all you can.

HANA: And remember when you started school you couldn't speak English either.

MASAKO: I help her.

(MURATA *rises and goes to the window. The night is cold. Lightning flashes and the wind whistles.*)

MURATA: Looks like a storm coming up. Hope we don't have a freeze.

HANA: If it freezes, we'll have another bad year. Maybe we ought to start the smudge pots.

MURATA (*Listening*): It's starting to rain. Nothing to do now but pray.

HANA: If praying is the answer, we'd be in Japan now . . . rich.

MURATA (*Wryly*): We're not dead yet. We still have a chance. (HANA *glares at this small joke*) Guess I'll turn in.

HANA: Go to bed . . . go to bed. I'll sit up and worry.

MURATA: If worrying was the answer, we'd be around the world twice and in Japan. Come on, Mama. Let's go to bed. It's too cold tonight to be mad.

(*There's an urgent knock on the door. The family react to it.*)

Dareh da! (*Goes to the door and pauses*) Who is it!

KIYOKO (*Weakly*): It's me . . . help me . . .

(MURATA *opens the door and* KIYOKO *enters. She's dressed in a kimono with a shawl thrown over. Her legs are bare except for a pair of straw* zori. *Her hair is stringy from the rain and she trembles from the cold.*)

MURATA: My God! Kiyoko-san! What's the matter?

HANA: Kiyoko-san! What is it?

MURATA: What happened?

KIYOKO (*Gasping*): They're fighting . . . they're fighting.

MURATA: Ah . . . don't worry . . . those things happen. No cause to worry. Mama, make tea for her. Sit down and catch your breath. I'll take you home when you're ready.

HANA: Papa, I'll take care of it.

MURATA: Let me know when you're ready to go home.

HANA: It must be freezing out there. Try to get warm. Try to calm yourself.

MURATA: Kiyoko-san . . . don't worry.

(HANA *waves* MASAKO *and* MURATA *off.* MURATA *leaves.* MASAKO *goes to her bed in the kitchen.*)

HANA: Papa, I'll take care of it.

KIYOKO (*Looking at* MURATA's *retreating form*): I came to ask your help.

HANA: You ran down here without a lantern? You could have fallen and hurt yourself.

KIYOKO: I don't care . . . I don't care.

HANA: You don't know, Kiyoko-san. It's treacherous out there . . . snakes, spiders . . .

KIYOKO: I must go back . . . I . . . I . . . you . . . please come with me.

HANA: First, first, we must get you warm. . . . Drink your tea.

KIYOKO: But they might kill each other. They're fighting like animals. Help me stop them!

HANA (*Goes to the stove to warm a pot of soup*): I cannot interfere in a family quarrel.

KIYOKO: It's not a quarrel . . . it's a . . .

HANA: That's all it is. A family squabble. You'll see. Tomorrow . . .

KIYOKO (*Rises and puts her hand on* HANA's *arm*): Not just a squabble . . . please!

(*She starts toward the door but* HANA *restrains her.*)

HANA: Now listen. Listen to me, Kiyoko-san. I've known your father and mother a little while now. I suspect it's been like this for years. Every family has some kind of trouble.

KIYOKO: Not like this . . . not like this.

HANA: Some have it better—some worse. When you get married, you'll understand. Don't worry. Nothing will happen. (*She takes a towel from the wall and dries* KIYOKO's *hair*) You're chilled to the bone. You'll catch your death . . .

KIYOKO: I don't care . . . I want to die.

HANA: Don't be silly. It's not that bad.

KIYOKO: They started drinking early in the afternoon. They make some kind of brew and hide it somewhere in the desert.

HANA: It's illegal to make it. That's why they hide it. That home brew is poison to the body . . . and the mind too.

KIYOKO: It makes them crazy. They drink it all the time and quarrel constantly. I was in the other room studying. I try so hard to keep up with school.

HANA: We were talking about you just this evening. Masako says you're doing so well . . . you skipped a grade?

KIYOKO: It's hard . . . hard . . . I'm too old for the class and the children . . . (*She remembers all her problems and starts to cry again*)

HANA: It's always hard in a new country.

KIYOKO: They were bickering and quarreling all afternoon. Then something happened. All of a sudden I saw them on the floor . . . hitting and . . .

and. . . . He was hitting her in the stomach, the face. . . . I tried to stop them, but they were so . . . drunk.

HANA: There, there . . . . It's probably all over now.

KIYOKO: Why does it happen like this? Nothing is right. Everywhere I go . . . Masa-chan is so lucky. I wish my life was like hers. I can hardly remember my real mother.

HANA: Emiko-san is almost a real mother to you. She's blood kin.

KIYOKO: She hates me. She never speaks to me. She's so cold. I want to love her but she won't let me. She hates me.

HANA: I don't think that's true, Kiyoko-san.

KIYOKO: I know it's true.

HANA: No. I don't think you have anything to do with it. It's this place. She hates it. This place is so lonely and alien.

KIYOKO: Then why didn't she go back? Why did they stay here?

HANA: You don't know. It's not so simple. Sometimes I think—

KIYOKO: Then why don't they make the best of it here? Like you?

HANA: That isn't easy either. Believe me. (*She goes to the stove to stir the soup*) Sometimes . . . sometimes the longing for homeland fills me with despair. Will I never return again? Will I never see my mother, my father, my sisters again? But what can one do? There are responsibilities here . . . children . . . (*She draws a sharp breath*) And another day passes . . . another month . . . another year. Eventually everything passes. (*She takes the soup to* KIYOKO) Did you have supper tonight?

KIYOKO (*Bowing gratefully*): Ah. When my . . . my aunt gets like this, she doesn't cook. No one eats. I don't get hungry anymore.

HANA: Cook for yourself. It's important to keep your health.

KIYOKO: I left Japan for a better life here . . .

HANA: It isn't easy for you, is it? But you must remember your filial duty.

KIYOKO: It's so hard.

HANA: But you can make the best of it here, Kiyoko-san. And take care of yourself. You owe that to yourself. Eat. Keep well. It'll be better, you'll see. And sometimes it'll seem worse. But you'll survive. We do, you know . . . we do . . . (*She looks around*) It's getting late.

KIYOKO (*Apprehensively*): I don't want to go back.

HANA: You can sleep with Masako tonight. Tomorrow you'll go back. And you'll remember what I told you.

(*She puts her arms around* KIYOKO, *who is overcome with self-pity and begins to weep quietly.*)

Life is never easy, Kiyoko-san. Endure. Endure. Soon you'll be marrying and going away. Things will not always be this way. And you'll look back on this . . . this night and you'll—

(*There is a rap on the door.* HANA *exchanges glances with* KIYOKO *and goes to answer it. She opens it a crack.* OKA *has come looking for* KIYOKO. *He's dressed in an overcoat and holds a wet newspaper over his head.*)

OKA: Ah! I'm sorry to bother you so late at night . . . the fact is . . .

HANA: Oka-san . . .

OKA (*Jovially*): Good evening, good evening . . . (*He sees* KIYOKO) Ah . . . there you are. . . . Did you have a nice visit?

HANA (*Irritated*): Yes, she's here.

OKA (*Still cheerful*): Thought she might be. Ready to come home now?

HANA: She came in the rain.

OKA (*Ignoring* HANA's *tone*): That's foolish of you, Kiyoko. You might catch cold.

HANA: She was frightened by your quarreling. She came for help.

OKA (*Laughing with embarrassment*): Oh! Kiyoko, that's nothing to worry about. It's just we had some disagreement . . .

HANA: That's what I told her, but she was frightened all the same.

OKA: Children are—

HANA: Not children, Oka-san. Kiyoko. Kiyoko was terrified. I think that was a terrible thing to do to her.

OKA (*Rubbing his head*): Oh, I . . . I . . .

HANA: If you had seen her a few minutes ago . . . hysterical . . . shaking . . . crying . . . wet and cold to the bone . . . out of her mind with worry.

OKA (*Rubbing his head*): Oh . . . I . . . don't know what she was so worried about.

HANA: You. You and Emiko fighting like you were going to kill each other.

OKA (*There's nothing more to hide. He lowers his head in penitence*): Aaaaaachhhhhhh . . .

HANA: I know I shouldn't tell you this, but there're one or two things I have to say: You sent for Kiyoko-san and now she's here. You said yourself she had a bad time in Japan, and now she's having a worse time. It isn't easy for her in a strange new country; the least you can do is try to keep her from worrying . . . especially about yourselves. I think it's terrible what you're doing to her . . . terrible!

OKA (*Bowing in deep humility*): I am ashamed . . .

HANA: I think she deserves better. I think you should think about that.

OKA (*Still in his bow*): I thank you for this reminder. It will never happen again. I promise.

HANA: I don't need that promise. Make it to Kiyoko-san.

OKA (*To* KIYOKO): Come with Papa now. He did a bad thing. He'll be a good papa from now. He won't worry his little girl again. All right? All right?

(*They move to the door.*)

KIYOKO: Thank you so much.

(HANA *puts* MURATA's *robe around* KIYOKO, *who tries to return it.*)

OKA: Madam. I thank you again.

HANA (*To* KIYOKO): That's all right. You can bring it back tomorrow. (*Aside to* KIYOKO) Remember . . . remember what we talked about. (*Loudly*) Good night, Oka-san.

(*They leave.* HANA *goes to* MASAKO, *who lies on the bed, and covers her.* MURATA *appears from the bedroom. He's heard it all. He and* HANA *exchange a glance and together they retire to their room. Fade-out.*)

Scene 3

(*The next morning. The Murata house and yard.* HANA *and* MURATA *have already left the house to examine the rain damage in the fields.* MASAKO *prepares to go to school. She puts on a coat and picks up her books and lunch bag. Meanwhile,* KIYOKO *slips quietly into the yard. She wears a coat and carries Murata's robe. She sets it on the outside bench.* MASAKO *walks out and is surprised to see* KIYOKO.)

MASAKO: Hi. I thought you'd be . . . sick today.
KIYOKO: Oh. I woke up late.
MASAKO (*Scrutinizing* KIYOKO's *face*): Your eyes are red.
KIYOKO (*Averting her eyes*): Oh, I . . . got . . . sand in it. Yes.
MASAKO: Do you want to use eye drops? We have eye drops in the house.
KIYOKO: Oh . . . no. That's all right.
MASAKO: That's what you call bloodshot.
KIYOKO: Oh.
MASAKO: My father gets it a lot. When he drinks too much.
KIYOKO: Oh . . .
MASAKO (*Notices Kiyoko doesn't have her lunch*): Where's your lunch bag?
KIYOKO: I . . . forgot it.
MASAKO: Did you make your lunch today?
KIYOKO: Yes. Yes, I did. But I forgot it.
MASAKO: Do you want to go back and get it?
KIYOKO: No, that's all right.

(*They are silent for a while.*)

We'll be late.

MASAKO: Do you want to practice your words?
KIYOKO (*Thoughtfully*): Oh . . .
MASAKO: Say, "My."
KIYOKO: My?
MASAKO: Eyes . . .
KIYOKO: Eyes.
MASAKO: Are . . .
KIYOKO: Are.
MASAKO: Red.
KIYOKO: Red.
MASAKO: Your eyes are red. (KIYOKO *doesn't repeat it*) I . . . (KIYOKO *doesn't cooperate*) Say, "I."
KIYOKO: I.
MASAKO: Got . . .
KIYOKO: Got.
MASAKO: Sand . . . (KIYOKO *balks*) Say, "I."

KIYOKO (*Sighing*): I.

MASAKO: Reft . . .

KIYOKO: Reft.

MASAKO: My . . .

KIYOKO: My.

MASAKO: Runch . . .

KIYOKO: Run . . . lunch. (*She stops*) Masako-san, you are mean. You are hurting me.

MASAKO: It's a joke! I was just trying to make you laugh!

KIYOKO: I cannot laugh today.

MASAKO: Sure you can. You can laugh. Laugh! Like this! (*She makes a hearty laugh.*)

KIYOKO: I cannot laugh when you make fun of me.

MASAKO: Okay, I'm sorry. We'll practice some other words then, okay? (KIYOKO *doesn't answer*) Say, "Okay."

KIYOKO (*Reluctantly*): Okay . . .

MASAKO: Okay, then . . . um . . . um . . . (*She still teases and talks rapidly*) Say . . . um . . . "She sells sea shells on the sea shore."

(KIYOKO *turns away indignantly*.)

Aw, come on, Kiyoko! It's just a joke. Laugh!

KIYOKO (*Imitating sarcastically*): Ha-ha-ha! Now you say, "*Kono kyaku wa yoku kaki ku kyaku da* (This guest eats a lot of persimmons)!"

MASAKO: Sure! I can say it! *Kono kyaku waki ku kyoku kaku* . . .

KIYOKO: That's not right.

MASAKO: *Koki kuki kya* . . .

KIYOKO: No.

MASAKO: Okay, then. You say, "Sea sells she shells . . . shu . . . sss . . ."

(*They both laugh*, KIYOKO *with her hands over her mouth*. MASAKO *takes* KIYOKO's *hands from her mouth*.)

Not like that! Like this! (*She gives a big belly laugh*)

KIYOKO: Like this? (*She imitates* MASAKO)

MASAKO: Yeah, that's right! You're not mad anymore?

KIYOKO: I'm not mad anymore.

MASAKO: Okay. You can share my lunch today because we're . . .

KIYOKO: "Flends?"

(MASAKO *looks at* KIYOKO, *they giggle and move on*. HANA *and* MURATA *come in from assessing the storm's damage. They are dressed warmly*. HANA *is depressed*. MURATA *tries hard to be cheerful*.)

MURATA: It's not so bad, Mama.

HANA: Half the ranch is flooded . . . at least half.

MURATA: No-no. A quarter, maybe. It's sunny today . . . it'll dry.

HANA: The seedlings will rot.

MURATA: No, no. It'll dry. It's all right—better than I expected.

HANA: If we have another bad year, no one will lend us money for the next crop.

MURATA: Don't worry. If it doesn't drain by tomorrow, I'll replant the worst places. We still have some seed left. Yeah, I'll replant . . .

HANA: More work.

MURATA: Don't worry, Mama. It'll be all right.

HANA (*Quietly*): Papa, where will it end? Will we always be like this—always at the mercy of the weather—prices—always at the mercy of the gods?

MURATA (*Patting* HANA's *back*): Things will change. Wait and see. We'll be back in Japan by . . . in two years . . . guarantee. . . . Maybe sooner.

HANA (*Dubiously*): Two years . . .

MURATA (*Finds the robe on the bench*): Ah, look, Mama. Kiyoko-san brought back my robe.

HANA (*Sighing*): Kiyoko-san . . . poor Kiyoko-san . . . and Emiko-san.

MURATA: Ah, Mama. We're lucky. We're lucky, Mama.

(HANA *smiles sadly at* MURATA. *Fade-out.*)

Scene 4

(*The following spring, afternoon. Exterior of the Oka house.* OKA *is dressed to go out. He wears a sweater, long-sleeved white shirt, dark pants, no tie. He puts his foot on the bench to wipe off his shoe with the palm of his hand. He straightens his sleeve, removes a bit of lint, and runs his fingers through his hair. He hums under his breath.* KIYOKO *comes from the house. Her hair is frizzled with a permanent wave, she wears a gaudy new dress and a pair of new shoes. She carries a movie magazine—Photoplay or Modern Screen.*)

OKA (*Appreciatively*): Pretty. Pretty.

KIYOKO (*Turning for him*): It's not too *hadeh?* I feel strange in colors.

OKA: Oh no. Young girls should wear bright colors. There's time enough to wear gray when you get old. Old-lady colors. (KIYOKO *giggles*) Sure you want to go to the picture show? It's such a nice day . . . shame to waste in a dark hall.

KIYOKO: Where else can we go?

OKA: We can go to the Muratas.

KIYOKO: All dressed up?

OKA: Or Nagatas. I'll show him what I got for my horse.

KIYOKO (*Laughing*): Oh, I love the pictures.

OKA: We don't have many nice spring days like this. Here the season is short. Summer comes in like a dragon . . . right behind . . . breathing fire . . . like a dragon. You don't know the summers here. They'll scare you. (*He tousles* KIYOKO's *hair and pulls a lock of it. It springs back. He shakes his head in wonder*) Goddamn. Curly hair. Never thought curly hair could make you so happy.

KIYOKO (*Giggling*): All the American girls have curly hair.

OKA: Your friend Masako like it?

KIYOKO (*Nodding*): She says her mother will never let her get a permanent wave.

OKA: She said that, eh? Bet she's wanting one.

KIYOKO: I don't know about that.

OKA: Bet she's wanting some of your pretty dresses too.

KIYOKO: Her mother makes all her clothes.

OKA: Buying is just as good. Buying is better. No trouble that way.

KIYOKO: Masako's not so interested in clothes. She loves the pictures, but her mother won't let her go. Someday, can we take Masako with us?

OKA: If her mother lets her come. Her mother's got a mind of her own . . . a stiff back.

KIYOKO: But she's nice.

OKA (*Dubiously*): Oh, yeah. Can't be perfect, I guess. Kiyoko, after the harvest I'll have money and I'll buy you the prettiest dress in town. I'm going to be lucky this year. I feel it.

KIYOKO: You're already too good to me . . . dresses, shoes, permanent wave . . . movies . . .

OKA: That's nothing. After the harvest, just wait . . .

KIYOKO: Magazines. . . . You do enough. I'm happy already.

OKA: You make me happy too, Kiyoko. You make me feel good . . . like a man again. . . . (*That statement bothers him*) One day you're going to make a young man happy. (KIYOKO *giggles*) Someday we going to move from here.

KIYOKO: But we have good friends here, Papa.

OKA: Next year our lease will be up and we got to move.

KIYOKO: The ranch is not ours?

OKA: No. In America, Japanese cannot own land. We lease and move every two, three years. Next year we going to go someplace where there's young fellows. There's none good enough for you here. (*He watches* KIYOKO *giggle*) Yeah. You going to make a good wife. Already a good cook. I like your cooking.

KIYOKO (*A little embarrassed*): Shall we go now?

OKA: Yeah. Put the magazine away.

KIYOKO: I want to take it with me.

OKA: Take it with you?

KIYOKO: Last time, after we came back, I found all my magazines torn in half.

OKA (*Looking toward the house*): Torn?

KIYOKO: This is the only one I have left.

OKA (*Not wanting to deal with it*): All right. All right.

(*The two prepare to leave when the door opens.* EMIKO *stands there, her hair is unkempt and she looks wild. She holds an empty can in one hand, the lid in the other.*)

EMIKO: Where is it?

(OKA *tries to make a hasty departure.*)

KIYOKO: Where is what?

(OKA *pushes* KIYOKO *ahead of him, still trying to make a getaway.*)

EMIKO: Where is it? Where is it? What did you do with it?

(EMIKO *moves toward* OKA. *He can't ignore her and he stops.*)

OKA (*With false unconcern to* KIYOKO): Why don't you walk on ahead to the
    Muratas?
KIYOKO: We're not going to the pictures?
OKA: We'll go. First you walk to the Muratas. Show them your new dress.
    I'll meet you there.

(KIYOKO *picks up a small package and exits.* OKA *sighs and shakes his head.*)

EMIKO (*Shaking the can*): Where is it? What did you do with it?
OKA (*Feigning surprise*): With what?
EMIKO: You know what. You stole it. You stole my money.
OKA: *Your* money?
EMIKO: I've been saving that money.
OKA: Yeah? Well, where'd you get it? Where'd you get it, eh? You stole it
    from me! Dollar by dollar. . . . You stole it from me! Out of my pocket!
EMIKO: I saved it!
OKA: From my pocket!
EMIKO: It's mine! I saved for a long time. . . . Some of it I brought from
    Japan.
OKA: *Bakayuna!* What'd you bring from Japan? Nothing but some useless
    kimonos.

(OKA *starts to leave but* EMIKO *hangs on to him.*)

EMIKO: Give back my money! Thief!
OKA (*Swings around and balls his fists but doesn't strike*): Goddamn! Get
    off me!
EMIKO (*Now pleading*): Please give it back . . . please . . . please . . .

(She starts to stroke him. OKA *pulls her hands away and pushes her from
him.*)

    Oni!

OKA (*Seething*): Oni? What does that make you? *Oni baba?* Yeah, that's
    what you are . . . a devil!
EMIKO: It's mine! Give it back . . .
OKA: The hell! You think you can live off me and steal my money too? How
    stupid you think I am?
EMIKO (*Tearfully*): But I've paid . . . I've paid . . .
OKA: With what?
EMIKO: You know I've paid.
OKA (*Scoffing*): You call that paying?
EMIKO: What did you do with it?

OKA: I don't have it.

EMIKO: It's gone? It's gone?

OKA: Yeah! It's gone. I spent it. The hell! Every last cent.

EMIKO: The new clothes . . . the curls . . . restaurants . . . pictures . . . shoes. . . . My money . . . my going-home money . . .

OKA: You through?

EMIKO: What will I do? What will—

OKA: I don't care what you do. Walk. Use your feet. Swim to Japan. I don't care. I give you no more than you gave me. Now I don't want anything. I don't care what you do. (*He walks away*)

(EMIKO *still holds the empty can. Offstage we hear* OKA's *car door slam and the sound of his old car starting off. Accustomed to crying alone, she doesn't utter a sound. Her shoulders begin to shake, her dry soundless sobs turn to a silent laugh. She wipes the dust gently from the can as though comforting a friend. Her movements become sensuous, her hands move on to her own body, around her throat, over her breasts, to her hips, caressing, soothing, reminding her of her lover's hands. Fade-out.*)

Scene 5

(*Same day, late afternoon. Exterior of the Murata house. The light is soft.* HANA *is sweeping the yard;* MASAKO *hangs a glass wind chime on the exposed wall.*)

HANA (*Directing* MASAKO): There . . . there. That's a good place.

MASAKO: Here?

HANA (*Nodding*): It must catch the slightest breeze. (*Sighing and listening*) It brings back so much. . . . That's the reason I never hung one before. I guess it doesn't matter much anymore . . .

MASAKO: I thought you liked to think about Japan.

HANA (*Laughing sadly*): I didn't want to hear that sound so often . . . get too used to it. Sometimes you hear something too often, after a while you don't hear it anymore. . . . I didn't want that to happen. The same thing happens to feelings too, I guess. After a while you don't feel anymore. You're too young to understand that yet.

MASAKO: I understand, Mama.

HANA: Wasn't it nice of Kiyoko-san to give us the *furin*?

MASAKO: I love it. I don't know anything about Japan, but it makes me feel something too.

HANA: Maybe someday when you're grown up, gone away, you'll hear it and remember yourself as this little girl . . . remember this old house, the ranch, and . . . your old mama . . .

MASAKO: That's kind of scary.

(EMIKO *enters unsteadily. She carries a bundle wrapped in a* furoshiki [*colorful scarf*]. *In the package are two beautiful kimonos.*)

HANA: Emiko-san! What a pleasant surprise! Please sit down. We were just hanging the *furin*. It was so sweet of Kiyoko-san to give it to Masako. She loves it.

(EMIKO *looks mildly interested. She acts as normal as she can throughout the scene, but at times drops her facade, revealing her desperation.*)

EMIKO: Thank you. (*She sets her bundle on the bench but keeps her hand on it*)

HANA: Your family was here earlier. (EMIKO *smiles vaguely*) On their way to the pictures, I think. (*To* MASAKO) Make tea for us, Ma-chan.

EMIKO: Please don't . . .

HANA: Kiyoko-san was looking so nice—her hair all curly. . . . Of course, in our day, straight black hair was desirable. Of course, times change.

EMIKO: Yes.

HANA: But she did look fine. My, my, a colorful new dress, new shoes, a permanent wave—looked like a regular American girl. Did you choose her dress?

EMIKO: No . . . I didn't go.

HANA: You know, I didn't think so. Very pretty though. I liked it very much. Of course, I sew all Masako's clothes. It saves money. It'll be nice for you to make things for Kiyoko-san too. She'd be so pleased. I know she'd be pleased . . .

(*While* HANA *talks,* EMIKO *plucks nervously at her package. She waits for* HANA *to stop talking.*)

Emiko-san, is everything all right?

EMIKO (*Smiling nervously*): Yes.

HANA: Masako, please go make tea for us. See if there aren't any more of those crackers left. Or did you finish them? (*To* EMIKO) We can't keep anything in this house. She eats everything as soon as Papa brings it home. You'd never know it, she's so skinny. We never have anything left for company.

MASAKO: We hardly ever have company anyway.

(HANA *gives her daughter a strong look, and* MASAKO *goes into the house.* EMIKO *is lost in her own thoughts. She strokes her package.*)

HANA: Is there something . . . I can help you with? (*Very gently*) Emiko-san?

EMIKO (*Suddenly frightened*): Oh no. I was thinking . . . Now that . . . now that . . . Masa-chan is growing up . . . older . . .

HANA (*Relieved*): Oh, yes. She's growing fast.

EMIKO: I was thinking . . . (*She stops, puts the package on her lap and is lost again*)

HANA: Yes, she *is* growing. Time goes so fast. I think she'll be taller than me soon. (*She laughs weakly, stops and looks puzzled*)

EMIKO: Yes.

(EMIKO'*s depression pervades the atmosphere.* HANA *is affected by it. The two women sit in silence. A small breeze moves the wind chimes. For a moment light grows dim on the two lonely figures.* MASAKO *comes from the house with a tray of tea. The light returns to normal again.*)

HANA (*Gently*): You're a good girl.

(MASAKO *looks first to* EMIKO *then to her mother. She sets the tray on the bench and stands near* EMIKO, *who seems to notice her for the first time.*)

EMIKO: How are you?

HANA (*Pours the tea and serves her*): Emiko-san, is there something I can do for you?

EMIKO: There's . . . I was . . . I . . . Masa-chan will be a young lady soon . . .

HANA: Oh, well, now I don't know about "lady."

EMIKO: Maybe she would like a nice . . . nice . . . (*she unwraps her package*) I have kimonos . . . I wore in Japan for dancing . . . maybe she can . . . if you like, I mean. They'll be nice on her . . . she's so slim . . .

(EMIKO *shakes out a robe.* HANA *and* MASAKO *are impressed.*)

HANA: Ohhhh! Beautiful!

MASAKO: Oh, Mama! Pretty!

(HANA *and* MASAKO *finger the material.*)

Gold threads, Mama.

HANA: Brocade!

EMIKO: Maybe Masa-chan would like them. I mean for her school programs . . . Japanese school . . .

HANA: Oh, no! Too good for country. People will be envious of us . . . wonder where we got them.

EMIKO: I mean for festivals . . . *Obon, Hana Matsuri* . . .

HANA: Oh, but you have Kiyoko-san now. You should give them to her. Has she seen them?

EMIKO: Oh . . . no . . .

HANA: She'll love them. You should give them to her . . . not our Masako.

EMIKO: I thought . . . I mean I was thinking of . . . if you could give me a little . . . if you could pay . . . manage to give me something for . . .

HANA: But these gowns, Emiko-san—they're worth hundreds.

EMIKO: I know, but I'm not asking for that. Whatever you can give . . . only as much as you can give.

MASAKO: Mama?

HANA: Masako, Papa doesn't have that kind of money.

EMIKO: Anything you can give . . . anything . . .

MASAKO: Ask Papa.

HANA: There's no use asking. I know he can't afford it.

EMIKO (*Looking at* MASAKO): A little at a time.

MASAKO: Mama?

HANA (*Firmly*): No, Masako. This is a luxury.

(HANA *folds the gowns and puts them away.* MASAKO *is disappointed.* EMIKO *is devastated.* HANA *sees this and tries to find some way to help.*)

Emiko-san, I hope you understand . . . (EMIKO *is silent, trying to gather her resources*) I know you can sell them and get the full price somewhere. Let's see . . . a family with a lot of growing daughters . . . someone who did well last year. . . . Nagatas have no girls. . . . Umedas have girls but no money. . . . Well, let's see. . . . Maybe not here in this country town. Ah. . . . You can take them to the city, Los Angeles, and sell them to a store . . . or Terminal Island . . . lots of wealthy fishermen there. Yes, that would be the place. Why, it's no problem, Emiko-san. Have your husband take them there. I know you'll get your money. He'll find a buyer. I know he will.

EMIKO: Yes. (*She finishes folding and ties the scarf. She sits quietly*)

HANA: Please have your tea. I'm sorry . . . I really would like to take them for Masako but it just isn't possible. You understand, don't you? (EMIKO *nods*) Please don't feel so . . . so bad. It's not really a matter of life or death, is it? Emiko-san?

(EMIKO *nods again.* HANA *sips her tea.*)

MASAKO: Mama? If you could ask Papa . . .

HANA: Oh, the tea is cold. Masako, could you heat the kettle?

EMIKO: No more. I must be going. (*She picks up her package and rises slowly*)

HANA (*Looking helpless*): So soon? Emiko-san, please stay.

(EMIKO *starts to go.*)

Masako will walk with you. (*She pushes* MASAKO *forward*)

EMIKO: It's not far.

HANA: Emiko-san? You'll be all right?

EMIKO: Yes . . . yes . . . yes . . . (*She goes*)

HANA (*Calling after her*): I'm sorry, Emiko-san.

EMIKO: Yes . . .

(MASAKO *and* HANA *watch as* EMIKO *leaves. The light grows dim as though a cloud passes over.* EMIKO *is gone.* HANA *strokes* MASAKO's *hair.*)

HANA: Your hair is so black and straight . . . nice . . .

(*They stand close. The wind chimes tinkle; light grows dim. Light returns to normal.* MURATA *enters. He sees this tableau of mother and child and is puzzled.*)

MURATA: What's going on here?

(*The two women part.*)

HANA: Oh . . . nothing . . . nothing . . .

MASAKO: Mrs. Oka was here. She had two kimo—

HANA (*Putting her hand on* MASAKO's *shoulder*): It was nothing . . .

MURATA: *Eh?* What'd she want?

HANA: Later, Papa. Right now, I'd better fix supper.

MURATA (*Looking at the sky*): Strange how that sun comes and goes. Maybe I didn't need to irrigate—looks like rain. (*He remembers and is exasperated*) Ach! I forgot to shut the water.

MASAKO: I'll do it, Papa.

HANA: Masako, that gate's too heavy for you.

MURATA: She can handle it. Take out the pin and let the gate fall all the way down. All the way. And put the pin back. Don't forget to put the pin back.

HANA: And be careful. Don't fall in the canal.

(MASAKO *leaves.*)

MURATA: What's the matter with that girl?

HANA: Nothing. Why?

MURATA: Usually have to beg her to do . . .

HANA: She's growing up.

MURATA: Must be that time of the month.

HANA: Oh, Papa, she's too young for that yet.

MURATA (*Genially as they enter the house*): Got to start sometime. Looks like I'll be outnumbered soon. I'm outnumbered already.

(HANA *glances at him and quietly sets about preparations for supper.* MURATA *removes his shirt and sits at the table with a paper. Light fades slowly.*)

Scene 6

(*Same evening. Exterior, desert. There is at least one shrub.* MASAKO *appears, walking slowly. From a distance we hear* EMIKO *singing the song* "And the Soul Shall Dance." MASAKO *looks around, sees the shrub and crouches under it.* EMIKO *appears. She's dressed in one of her beautiful kimonos tied loosely at her waist. She carries a branch of sage. Her hair is loose.*)

EMIKO: *Akai kichibiru*
Kappu ni yosete
Aoi sake nomya
Kokoro ga odoru . . .
Kurai yoru no yume
Setsu nasa yo . . .

(*She breaks into a dance, laughs mysteriously, turns round and round, acting out a fantasy.* MASAKO *stirs uncomfortably.* EMIKO *senses a presence. She stops, drops her branch and walks offstage, singing as she goes.*

Aoi sake nomya
Yume mo odoru . . .

MASAKO *watches as* EMIKO *leaves. She rises slowly and picks up the branch* EMIKO *has left. She looks at the branch, moves forward a step and looks off to the point where* EMIKO *disappeared. Light slowly fades until only the image of* MASAKO'S *face remains etched in the mind.*)

[1990]

Now we are the "betrayers of the lie." In our speaking and writing, we betray what has harmed us and held us down. We tell on those who hurt us. We give away the truths of oppression, and we betray our own denial by allowing our art and literature, our often unconscious internal creative processes, to express what we ourselves have held in.

LINDA HOGAN

"Women: Doing and Being,"
The Stories We Hold Secret

CULTURAL NARRATIVES

Cultural Narratives and
Critical Perspectives

The material gathered in these last two sections requires a word of introduction. Although I have divided these nonfiction pieces into Cultural Narratives and Critical Perspectives, these categories overlap because many of the essays are formally experimental. In the selections that follow, the writers embody the complex tensions and weavings together of two cultures and two symbol systems: the American and the indigenous cultures of color. This new symbolic territory requires new forms to map it.

The forms and styles in which the writers of these selections speak are varied—sometimes lyrical and symbolic, sometimes subjective, sometimes analytical and academic, sometimes vernacular. This variety of formal "textures" reflects the growing awareness by contemporary women writers of color of the uniqueness of their cultural experience. These pieces are arguments, but they are also testimonials, monologues, and reflections by women whose words and forms emerge from their own cultural idioms and narrative traditions. New forms express the powerful liberation a recognition of difference can bring.

Generally, the writings included in the Cultural Narratives section are meditations on what it means to be a woman speaking from an ethnic identity of color; the selections in the Critical Perspectives section turn that angle of vision toward literary texts and literary theories. These critical essays often subvert, question, and augment dominant scholarly critical discourse as they illuminate the depths of experience of women of color, and they express what Cherríe Moraga and Gloria Anzaldúa call "a theory of the flesh." In *This Bridge Called My Back*, their collection of writing by women of color, Moraga and Anzaldúa explain their ideas about the function of criticism:

> A theory of the flesh means one where the physical realities of our lives—our skin color, the land or concrete we grew up on, our sexual longings—all fuse to create a politic born out of necessity. Here we attempt to bridge the contradictions in our experience:
>
> > We are the colored in a white feminist movement.
> > We are the feminists among the people of our culture.
> > We are often the lesbians among the straight.
> > We do this bridging by naming our selves and by telling stories in our own words.[1]

---

[1] Cherríe Moraga and Gloria Anzaldúa, eds., *This Bridge Called My Back: Writings by Radical Women of Color* (New York: Kitchen Table Women of Color, 1984), 23.

You're Short, Besides!

Sucheng Chan

WHEN ASKED TO WRITE ABOUT BEING A PHYSICALLY HANDICAPPED ASIAN American woman, I considered it an insult. After all, my accomplishments are many, yet I was not asked to write about any of them. Is being handicapped the most salient feature about me? The fact that it might be in the eyes of others made me decide to write the essay as requested. I realized that the way I think about myself may differ considerably from the way others perceive me. And maybe that's what being physically handicapped is all about.

I was stricken simultaneously with pneumonia and polio at the age of four. Uncertain whether I had polio of the lungs, seven of the eight doctors who attended me—all practitioners of Western medicine—told my parents they should not feel optimistic about my survival. A Chinese fortune teller my mother consulted also gave a grim prognosis, but for an entirely different reason: I had been stricken because my name was offensive to the gods. My grandmother had named me "grandchild of wisdom," a name that the fortune teller said was too presumptuous for a girl. So he advised my parents to change my name to "chaste virgin." All these pessimistic predictions notwithstanding, I hung onto life, if only by a thread. For three years, my body was periodically pierced with electric shocks as the muscles of my legs atrophied. Before my illness, I had been an active, rambunctious, precocious, and very curious child. Being confined to bed was thus a mental agony as great as my physical pain. Living in war-torn China, I received little medical attention; physical therapy was unheard of. But I was determined to walk. So one day, when I was six or seven, I instructed my mother to set up two rows of chairs to face each other so that I could use them as I would parallel bars. I attempted to walk by holding my body up and moving it forward with my arms while dragging my legs along behind. Each time I fell, my mother gasped, but I badgered her until she let me try again. After four nonambulatory years, I finally walked once more by pressing my hands against my thighs so my knees wouldn't buckle.

My father had been away from home during most of those years because of the war. When he returned, I had to confront the guilt he felt about my condition. In many East Asian cultures, there is a strong folk belief that a person's physical state in this life is a reflection of how morally or sinfully he or she lived in previous lives. Furthermore, because of the tendency to view the family as a single unit, it is believed that the fate of one member can be caused by the behavior of another. Some of my father's relatives told him that my illness had doubtless been caused by the wild carousing he did in his youth. A well-meaning but somewhat simple man, my father believed them.

Throughout my childhood, he sometimes apologized to me for having to suffer retribution for his former bad behavior. This upset me; it was bad enough that I had to deal with the anguish of not being able to walk, but to have to assuage his guilt as well was a real burden! In other ways, my father was very good to me. He took me out often, carrying me on his shoulders or back, to give me fresh air and sunshine. He did this until I was too large and heavy for him to carry. And ever since I can remember, he has told me that I am pretty.

After getting over her anxieties about my constant falls, my mother decided to send me to school. I had already learned to read some words of Chinese at the age of three by asking my parents to teach me the sounds and meaning of various characters in the daily newspaper. But between the ages of four and eight, I received no education since just staying alive was a full-time job. Much to her chagrin, my mother found no school in Shanghai, where we lived at the time, which would accept me as a student. Finally, as a last resort, she approached the American School, which agreed to enroll me only if my family kept an *amah* (a servant who takes care of children) by my side at all times. The tuition at the school was twenty U.S. dollars per month—a huge sum of money during those years of runaway inflation in China—and payable only in U.S. dollars. My family afforded the high cost of tuition and the expense of employing a full-time *amah* for less than a year.

We left China as the Communist forces swept across the country in victory. We found an apartment in Hong Kong across the street from a school run by Seventh-Day Adventists. By that time I could walk a little, so the principal was persuaded to accept me. An *amah* now had to take care of me only during recess when my classmates might easily knock me over as they ran about the playground.

After a year and a half in Hong Kong, we moved to Malaysia, where my father's family had lived for four generations. There I learned to swim in the lovely warm waters of the tropics and fell in love with the sea. On land I was a cripple; in the ocean I could move with the grace of a fish. I liked the freedom of being in the water so much that many years later, when I was a graduate student in Hawaii, I became greatly enamored with a man just because he called me a "Polynesian water nymph."

As my overall health improved, my mother became less anxious about all aspects of my life. She did everything possible to enable me to lead as normal a life as possible. I remember how once some of her colleagues in the high school where she taught criticized her for letting me wear short skirts. They felt my legs should not be exposed to public view. My mother's response was, "All girls her age wear short skirts, so why shouldn't she?"

The years in Malaysia were the happiest of my childhood, even though I was constantly fending off children who ran after me calling, "*Baikah! Baikah!*" ("Cripple! Cripple!" in the Hokkien dialect commonly spoken in Malaysia). The taunts of children mattered little because I was a star pupil. I won one award after another for general scholarship as well as for art and public speaking. Whenever the school had important visitors my teacher always called on me to recite in front of the class.

A significant event that marked me indelibly occurred when I was twelve.

That year my school held a music recital and I was one of the students chosen to play the piano. I managed to get up the steps to the stage without any problem, but as I walked across the stage, I fell. Out of the audience, a voice said loudly and clearly, "Ayah! A *baikah* shouldn't be allowed to perform in public." I got up before anyone could get on stage to help me and, with tears streaming uncontrollably down my face, I rushed to the piano and began to play. Beethoven's "Für Elise" had never been played so fiendishly fast before or since, but I managed to finish the whole piece. That I managed to do so made me feel really strong. I never again feared ridicule.

In later years I was reminded of this experience from time to time. During my fourth year as an assistant professor at the University of California at Berkeley, I won a distinguished teaching award. Some weeks later I ran into a former professor who congratulated me enthusiastically. But I said to him, "You know what? I became a distinguished teacher by *limping* across the stage of Dwinelle 155!" (Dwinelle 155 is a large, cold, classroom that most colleagues of mine hate to teach in.) I was rude not because I lacked graciousness but because this man, who had told me that my dissertation was the finest piece of work he had read in fifteen years, had nevertheless advised me to eschew a teaching career.

"Why?" I asked.

"Your leg . . ." he responded.

"What about my leg?" I said, puzzled.

"Well, how would you feel standing in front of a large lecture class?"

"If it makes any difference, I want you to know I've won a number of speech contests in my life, and I am not the least bit self-conscious about speaking in front of large audiences. . . . Look, why don't you write me a letter of recommendation to tell people how brilliant I am, and let *me* worry about my leg!"

This incident is worth recounting only because it illustrates a dilemma that handicapped persons face frequently: those who care about us sometimes get so protective that they unwittingly limit our growth. This former professor of mine had been one of my greatest supporters for two decades. Time after time, he had written glowing letters of recommendation on my behalf. He had spoken as he did because he thought he had my best interests at heart; he thought that if I got a desk job rather than one that required me to be a visible, public person, I would be spared the misery of being stared at.

Americans, for the most part, do not believe as Asians do that physically handicapped persons are morally flawed. But they are equally inept at interacting with those of us who are not able-bodied. Cultural differences in the perception and treatment of handicapped people are most clearly expressed by adults. Children, regardless of where they are, tend to be openly curious about people who do not look "normal." Adults in Asia have no hesitation in asking visibly handicapped people what is wrong with them, often expressing their sympathy with looks of pity, whereas adults in the United States try desperately to be polite by pretending not to notice.

One interesting response I often elicited from people in Asia but have never encountered in America is the attempt to link my physical condition to the state of my soul. Many a time while living and traveling in Asia people would ask me what religion I belonged to. I would tell them that my mother is a devout Buddhist, that my father was baptized a Catholic but has never practiced Catholicism, and that I am an agnostic. Upon hearing this, people would try strenuously to convert me to their religion so that whichever God they believed in could bless me. If I would only attend this church or that temple regularly, they urged, I would surely get cured. Catholics and Buddhists alike have pressed religious medallions into my palm, telling me if I would wear these, the relevant deity or saint would make me well. Once while visiting the tomb of Muhammad Ali Jinnah in Karachi, Pakistan, an old Muslim, after finishing his evening prayers, spotted me, gestured toward my legs, raised his arms heavenward, and began a new round of prayers, apparently on my behalf.

In the United States adults who try to act "civilized" toward handicapped people by pretending they don't notice anything unusual sometimes end up ignoring handicapped people completely. In the first few months I lived in this country, I was struck by the fact that whenever children asked me what was the matter with my leg, their adult companions would hurriedly shush them up, furtively look at me, mumble apologies, and rush their children away. After a few months of such encounters, I decided it was my responsibility to educate these people. So I would say to the flustered adults, "It's okay, let the kid ask." Turning to the child, I would say, "When I was a little girl, no bigger than you are, I became sick with something called polio. The muscles of my leg shrank up and I couldn't walk very well. You're much luckier than I am because now you can get a vaccine to make sure you never get my disease. So don't cry when your mommy takes you to get a polio vaccine, okay?" Some adults and their little companions I talked to this way were glad to be rescued from embarrassment; others thought I was strange.

Americans have another way of covering up their uneasiness: they become jovially patronizing. Sometimes when people spot my crutch, they ask if I've had a skiing accident. When I answer that unfortunately it is something less glamorous than that they say, "I bet you *could* ski if you put your mind to it!" Alternately, at parties where people dance, men who ask me to dance with them get almost belligerent when I decline their invitation. They say, "Of course you can dance if you *want* to!" Some have given me pep talks about how if I would only develop the right mental attitude, I would have more fun in life.

Different cultural attitudes toward handicapped persons came out clearly during my wedding. My father-in-law, as solid a representative of middle America as could be found, had no qualms about objecting to the marriage on racial grounds, but he could bring himself to comment on my handicap only indirectly. He wondered why his son, who had dated numerous high school and college beauty queens, couldn't marry one of them instead of me. My mother-in-law, a devout Christian, did not share her husband's prejudices, but she worried aloud about whether I could have children. Some Chinese friends of my parents, on the other hand, said that I was lucky to have found such a noble man, one who would marry me despite my handicap. I, for my part, appeared in church in a white lace wedding dress I had designed and made myself—a miniskirt!

How Asian Americans treat me with respect to my handicap tells me a great deal about their degree of acculturation. Recent immigrants behave just like Asians in Asia; those who have been here longer or who grew up in the United States behave more like their white counterparts. I have not encountered any distinctly Asian American pattern of response. What makes the experience of Asian American handicapped people unique is the duality of responses we elicit.

Regardless of racial or cultural background, most handicapped people have to learn to find a balance between the desire to attain physical independence and the need to take care of ourselves by not overtaxing our bodies. In my case, I've had to learn to accept the fact that leading an active life has its price. Between the ages of eight and eighteen, I walked without using crutches or braces but the effort caused my right leg to become badly misaligned. Soon after I came to the United States, I had a series of operations to straighten out the bones of my right leg; afterwards though my leg looked straighter and presumably better, I could no longer walk on my own. Initially my doctors fitted me with a brace, but I found wearing one cumbersome and soon gave it up. I could move around much more easily—and more important, faster—by using one crutch. One orthopedist after another warned me that using a single crutch was a bad practice. They were right. Over the years my spine developed a double-S curve and for the last twenty years I have suffered from severe, chronic back pains, which neither conventional physical therapy nor a lighter work load can eliminate.

The only thing that helps my backaches is a good massage, but the soothing effect lasts no more than a day or two. Massages are expensive, especially when one needs them three times a week. So I found a job that pays better, but at which I have to work longer hours, consequently increasing the physical strain on my body—a sort of vicious circle. When I was in my thirties, my doctors told me that if I kept leading the strenuous life I did, I would be in a wheelchair by the time I was forty. They were right on target: I bought myself a wheelchair when I was forty-one. But being the incorrigible character that I am, I use it only when I am *not* in a hurry!

It is a good thing, however, that I am too busy to think much about my handicap or my backaches because pain can physically debilitate as well as cause depression. And there are days when my spirits get rather low. What has helped me is realizing that being handicapped is akin to growing old at an accelerated rate. The contradiction I experience is that often my mind races along as though I'm only twenty while my body feels about sixty. But fifteen or twenty years hence, unlike my peers who will have to cope with aging for the first time, I shall be full of cheer because I will have already fought, and I hope won, that battle long ago.

Beyond learning how to be physically independent and, for some of us, living with chronic pain or other kinds of discomfort, the most difficult thing a handicapped person has to deal with, especially during puberty and early adulthood, is relating to potential sexual partners. Because American culture places so much emphasis on physical attractiveness, a person with a shriveled limb, or a tilt to the head, or the inability to speak clearly, experiences great uncertainty—indeed trauma—when interacting with someone to whom he or she is attracted. My problem was that I was not only physically handicapped, small, and short, but worse, I also wore glasses and was smarter than all the boys I knew! Alas, an insurmountable combination. Yet somehow I have managed to have intimate relationships, all of them with extraordinary men. Not surprisingly, there have also been countless men who broke my heart—men who enjoyed my company "as a friend," but who never found the courage to date or make love with me, although I am sure my experience in this regard is no different from that of many able-bodied persons.

The day came when my backaches got in the way of having an active sex life. Surprisingly that development was liberating because I stopped worrying about being attractive to men. No matter how headstrong I had been, I, like most women of my generation, had had the desire to be alluring to men ingrained into me. And that longing had always worked like a brake on my behavior. When what men think of me ceased to be compelling, I gained greater freedom to be myself.

I've often wondered if I would have been a different person had I not been physically handicapped. I really don't know, though there is no question that being handicapped has marked me. But at the same time I usually do not *feel* handicapped—and consequently, I do not *act* handicapped. People are therefore less likely to treat me as a handicapped person. There is no doubt, however, that the lives of my parents, sister, husband, other family members, and some close friends have been affected by my physical condition. They have had to learn not to hide me away at home, not to feel embarrassed by how I look or react to people who say silly things to me, and not to resent me for the extra demands my condition makes on them. Perhaps the hardest thing for those who live with handicapped people is to know when and how to offer help. There are no guidelines applicable to all situations. My advice is, when in doubt, ask, but ask in a way that does not smack of pity or embarrassment. Most important, please don't talk to us as though we are children.

So, has being physically handicapped been a handicap? It all depends on one's attitude. Some years ago, I told a friend that I had once said to an affirmative action compliance officer (somewhat sardonically since I do not believe in the head count approach to affirmative action) that the institution which employs me is triply lucky because it can count me as non-white, female and handicapped. He responded, "Why don't you tell them to count you four times? . . . Remember, you're short, besides!"

[1989]

"You May Consider Speaking about Your Art"

Elizabeth Cook-Lynn

EVER SINCE I LEARNED TO READ, I HAVE WANTED TO BE A WRITER.

I was born in the Government Hospital at Fort Thompson, South Dakota, in 1930, and when I was a "child of prairie hawks" (*Seek the House of Relatives*), I lived out on the Crow Creek (a tributary of the James and the Missouri) in what anthropologists like to call "an extended family." And I loved to read.

Reading, if it is not too obvious to say so, precedes writing, though I teach college students today who are examples of an apparently opposing point of view. They have read nothing.

On the contrary, I read everything: the Sears catalog, *Faust*, Dick and Jane, *Tarzan of the Apes*, *The Scarlet Letter*, the First Letter to the Corinthians, *David Copperfield*, "The Ancient Mariner," Dick Tracy, "Very Like a Whale," *Paradise Lost*, *True Confessions*, and much more. I went to whatever libraries were available as often as I went anywhere.

But I read nothing about the Dakotapi. Much later I took a history course at South Dakota State College called "The Westward Movement," and there was not one mention of Indian Nations! I keep the text for that course on my own library shelf as a marvelous example of scholarly ineptitude and/ or racism.

Wanting to write comes out of that deprivation, though, for we eventually have to ask, what happens to a reasonably intelligent child who sees him or herself excluded from a world which is created and recreated with the obvious intent to declare him or her *persona non grata?* Silence is the first reaction. Then there comes the development of a mistrust of that world. And, eventually, anger.

That anger is what started me writing. Writing, for me, then, is an act of defiance born of the need to survive. I am me. I exist. I am a Dakotah. I write. It is the quintessential act of optimism born of frustration. It is an act of courage, I think. And, in the end, as Simon Ortiz says, it is an act that defies oppression.

In those early days, even though I had a need to write—that is, survive—I lived in a world in which the need to write was not primary. The need "to tell," however, was. And so I listened and heard about a world that existed in the flesh and in the imagination, too, and in the hearts and minds of real people. In those days I thought the world was made up of "Siouxs" and "Wasichus."

It is this dichotomous nature of the real world and the literary world and, yes, the present world that accounts for the work I do. It is the reason I call myself a Dakotah poet, however hesitantly I accept the label, however unclear the responsibilities that come with that label.

The best way to begin a philosophical discussion concerning the nature and substance of the work of a contemporary Dakotah poet is to admit, oddly enough, to a certain kind of timidity and lack of confidence and to conclude by saying that I do not speak for my people.

First of all, one must be timid because there is the consideration that poets have a tendency to think too much of themselves. It is quite possible that we poets think we are more significant, more important than we are; that the events we choose to signal as important for one reason or another are, after all, something else; that the statements and interpretations we have given to these events are mistaken and/or irrelevant.

Second, the idea that poets can speak for others, the idea that we can speak for the dispossessed, the weak, the voiceless, is indeed one of the great burdens of contemporary American Indian poets today, for it is widely believed that we "speak for our tribes." The frank truth is that I don't know very many poets who say, "I speak for my people." It is not only unwise; it is probably impossible, and it is very surely arrogant, for We Are Self-Appointed and the self-appointedness of what we do indicates that the responsibility is ours and ours alone.

Therein lies another dichotomy: I claim to be a Dakotah poet by disclaiming that I speak for my people.

I am not greatly surprised that this dichotomy does not exist for the "real" poets of our tribes, the men and women who sit at the drum and sing the old songs and create new ones. That is an entirely different matter, for it remains communal. Thus, when I hear the poetry of the Crown Butte Singers, the Porcupine Travelers, and the Wahpekute Singers, I have every confidence that they speak in our own language for the tribes, Oyate.

"A Poet's Lament: Concerning the Massacre of American Indians at Wounded Knee" is a good example to use to discuss and illustrate the problems that I see involved in the matter of responsibility for a poet like me, one who writes English, using contemporary forms.

This poem describes what was and is a very public event. Yet as a self-appointed poet I bring my own perceptions into this tribal event even as I am aware of the public nature of the event and the history that surrounds it. The private histories which do not rely upon the written word, research, and text are a part of that perception.

> All things considered, they said,
> Crow Dog should be removed.
> With Sitting Bull dead
> It was easier said.
>
> And so the sadly shrouded songs of poets,
> Ash-yellowed, crisp with age
> arise from drums to mark in fours
> three times the sacred ways
> that prayers are listened for; an infant girl stares
> past the night, her beaded cap of buckskin brightens
> Stars and Stripes that pierce

her mother's breast; Hokshina, innocent
as snow birds, tells of Ate's blood as red as plumes
that later decorate the posts of death.

"Avenge the slaughtered saints," beg mad-eyed
poets everywhere as if the bloody Piemontese are real
and really care for liberty of creed; the blind
who lead the blind will consecrate the Deed, indeed!

All things considered, they said,
Crow Dog should be removed.
With Sitting Bull dead
It was easier said.

In this specific case I mean to suggest that it is the responsibility of a poet like me to "consecrate" history and event, survival and joy and sorrow, the significance of ancestors and the unborn; and I use one of the most infamous crimes in all of human history, which took place against a people who did not deserve to be butchered, to make that responsibility concrete. Only recently has the mainstream of American society been confronted with the monstrous nature of this historical act and others like it, but Indians have always known it.

The ceremony I describe in the second stanza really did occur, I'm told; the people and the warriors gathered within hours after the dreadful killing, and they swept into the grounds and guarded their dead, placing twelve red-draped markers at the perimeters of the site. I don't know if this is "true." I wasn't a witness. I have not read any account of it. Surely, though, in the memories of the people, this ceremony took place in order to consecrate the event. And the poem that I write in English and in contemporary form, and the songs that continue to rise from drums in Dakota and in traditional forms a century later, recreate that consecration. That is what I mean to hold on to when I talk of responsibility in the creative process.

It is no accident that I refer to the number "twelve" to record this event in sacred terms, for that number figures prominently in sacred ritual. It is no accident that I begin and end with the names of Sitting Bull and Crow Dog, both religious leaders of the people, because I mean to deliberately place this event which is usually described in military terms into the religious context to which it speaks.

Ceremony, in literary terms, can be said to be that body of creative expression which accounts for the continued survival and development of a people, a nation. In this instance, it relies upon ancient symbols which are utilized spontaneously in a communal effort to speak with the givers of prayers, to recall the knowledge about life and death that has its origins in mythology and imagination.

The people who gathered to perform this ceremony a hundred years ago did so at risk of their lives. It was then and remains now an important commitment to nationhood and culture. They imagined the grief of the Unktechies who arose from the water, hundreds, perhaps thousands of years ago, to give the people a religion and then went deep into the Earth to listen for the sounds of our drums, songs, poetry, and prayers. The people wept and sang of their own grief and sorrow.

Years ago when I was twenty and I first started sending out my poems, an editor wrote on an acceptance letter a question that has haunted me for the rest of my so-called career as a poet. She asked, "WHY is Native American poetry so incredibly sad?"

Now I recognize it as a tactless question asked out of astounding ignorance. It reflects the general American attitude that American Indians should have been happy to have been robbed of their lands and murdered. I am no longer intimidated, as I once was, by that question, and I make no excuses for the sorrow I feel in my heart concerning recent history. I do not apologize for returning to those historical themes, for that is part of the ceremonial aspect of being a Dakotah poet.

Attending to ceremonial matters as a writer does not mean, however, that I am not writing about myself. Quite the opposite is true. There is a self-absorption in my work which is inherent in my survival as a person, and my identity as a Dakotah. This self-absorption has always been a part of tradition, I think, for Dakotahs, in spite of the pervasive articulation in recent times of the idea that the Indian "self" was somehow unimportant; that Indians have been absorbed in the contemplation of the natural world, readily giving themselves up to it, mastered by it philosophically as well as physically; that submission to environment dominates American Indian life and belief.

This overstatement has been handy for the perpetuation of the longed-for nineteenth-century idea concerning the ultimate and expected disappearance of Natives and Native America from this continent. It is convenient to suggest from this imagined obsession with the natural world that the American Indian would become an artifact, too unreal and obsolete for survival in the modern world. The Indian's "journey," then, as a race of people, would be concluded.

The function of contemporary American poetry is to disavow that false notion.

One of what I consider my best poems is entitled "Journey," and it is an attempt to express that disavowal:

I. Dream

Wet, sickly
smells of cattle yard silage fill the prairie air
far beyond the timber; the nightmare only just
begun, a blackened cloud moves past the sun
to dim the river's glare, a malady of modern times.
We prayed
to the giver of prayers and traveled to the spirit
mounds we thought were forever; awake, we feared that
hollow trees no longer hid the venerable ones we were taught
to believe in.

II. Memory

Dancers with cane whistles,
the prairie's wise and knowing kinsmen
They trimmed their deer skins
in red down feathers,
made drum sticks from the gray grouse,
metaphorically speaking, and knocked on doors
which faced the East.
Dancers with cane whistles,
born under the sign of hollow stems,
after earth and air and fire and water
you conjure faith to clear the day.
Stunningly, blessedly you pierce the sky
with sound so clear each winged creature soars.

In my mind Grandmothers, those old partisans of faith
who long for shrill and glowing rituals of the past,
recall the times they went on long communal
buffalo hunts; because of this they tell the
lithe and lissome daughters:
   look for men who know the sacred ways
   look for men who wear the white-striped quill
   look for dancers with cane whistles
   and seek the house of relatives to stay the night.

III. Sacristans

This journey through another world, beyond bad dreams
beyond the memories of a murdered generation,
cartographed in captivity by bare survivors
makes sacristans of us all.

The old ones go our bail, we oblate preachers of our tribes.
Be careful, they say, don't hock the beads of
kinship agonies; the moire-effect of unfamiliar hymns
upon our own, a change in pitch or shrillness of the voice
transforms the ways of song to words of poetry or prose
and makes distinctions
no one recognizes.
Surrounded and absorbed, we tread like Etruscans
on the edge of useless law; we pray
to the giver of prayer, we give the cane whistle
in ceremony, we swing the heavy silver chain
of incense burners. Migration makes
new citizens of Rome.

    The journey theme is pervasive in contemporary Native American poetry. The oral traditions from which these expressions emerge indicate a self-absorption essential to our lives. They follow the traditions of native literatures which express as a foremost consideration the survival of the individual, thus the tribe, thus the species, a journey of continuing life and human expectancy.

The final responsibility of a writer like me, and an essential reason to move on from "wanting to be a writer" to actually writing, is to commit something to paper in the modern world which supports this inexhaustible legacy left us by our ancestors. Grey Cohoe, the Navajo poet and artist, once said to a group of Native American students we were working with: "Have confidence in what you know."

That is difficult when we ordinarily see ourselves omitted from the pages of written histories, but not impossible.

[1987]

Some Lines for a Younger Brother . . .

Sue Kunitomi Embrey

I STILL REMEMBER THE DAY HE WAS BORN. IT WAS EARLY APRIL AND PAPA came into the kitchen with a smile on his face. He said we had a baby brother. In the months to follow, we were busy carrying and cuddling the brother who was many years younger than the rest of us. When he cried from hunger and Mama was busy, one of us would run into the bedroom and rock the bed or pick him up and quiet him.

We were a family of five sons and three daughters. Money was scarce. My father ran a moving and transfer business in L'il Tokyo, the Japanese community in the shadow of City Hall in Los Angeles, but people had little money to pay him. He came home with boxes of books bartered for his services, and we spent many hours curled up in a corner reading some popular fiction story.

Tets, as we called him, was eight years old when Papa was killed in an automobile accident a week before Christmas. Tets cried because he could not give his dad the present he had made at school. The bullies would beat him up now that he had no father, he said.

Pearl Harbor was attacked by the Japanese when Tets was in elementary school. Rumors of sabotage couldn't be separated from the facts. Soon there was a clamor on the West Coast for wholesale evacuation of all Japanese into inland camps. The democratic process was lost in hysteria. The grocery store which we had purchased only a year before was sold at a loss. All the furniture we couldn't sell, the plants my mother had tenderly cared for, our small personal treasures went to a neighborhood junk dealer. Tears came when we saw the truck being loaded.

On the first Sunday in May, 1942, Manzanar Relocation Center became our war-time home. Before breakfast, we walked around the dry, dusty land, to get acquainted with the landscape. The sun sparkled against the Sierra Nevada mountains to the west. The brown Inyo hills were high-rising barriers, more formidable than the barbed wire which was soon to enclose us. As we wondered how the pioneers had crossed over the Sierras, someone asked, "How long do we have to stay here?" and someone quoted from the military instructions, "For the duration of the war and six months thereafter." Six months are forever, and forever is a long, long time.

Some order became evident within a few months after the fear, confusion and shock of transplantation from the big city to the arid land of Manzanar. Catholic nuns, who had joined the evacuees, found empty barracks and started a school. The War Relocation Authority recruited teachers from the "outside." Many of them were Quakers with a real desire to serve their fellow man.

When I asked Tets what he was studying, he shrugged his shoulders. There were no chairs, no desks, no supplies, he said. "What's the use of studying American history when we're behind barbed wires?" he asked. I tried to tell him that it would matter some day, but I was not sure any more. "Someday," I said, "the government would realize it had made a mistake and would try to correct it." His eyes were narrow against the noon sun, his whole body positioned badly to the right as he looked at me and said, "You 'da kind'? I lose fight." The colloquial speech was everywhere among the second generation. "Da kind" categorically placed me among those who argued for and defended American democracy. The second expression was used constantly, but it meant different things to different people.

"Try walking out that gate," he added. "See if they don't shoot you in the back." With that, he walked away.

The rest of us managed to get out of confinement—to Chicago, to Madison, Wisconsin. Three brothers entered the United States Army. Tets was left with his aging mother and he was to spend almost three years behind barbed wires.

By 1948 when the family was partially reunited and settled in Los Angeles, Tets was in high school, or we thought he was. One day a school counselor came to the door. He reported that Tets had not been in school for several weeks and that he had been missing school sporadically for several months. He saw the shock on our faces. We had been too busy working to be suspicious.

"I'm looking for a job," Tets said, when confronted.

"But you can't find a job without a high school diploma," I protested.

"So I found out," he answered. "Learning to say 'isn't' instead of 'ain't' doesn't get you a job. They want us to have experience to land a job, but how can we get experience if we can't get a job?"

I asked him what he was going to do.

"I'm going to join the Army," was his reply.

Day in and day out, this was his argument. "I'm going to join the Army when I'm eighteen. You won't have me around to bother you and I'll be doing some traveling. I'm tired of holding up the buildings in L'il Tokyo. There's nothing to do and no place to go where I can be with my friends."

He was sure that wars were over for a while and there would be no danger. He signed up one day and was gone the next. He came home on furlough, husky and tanned, a lot taller and more confident than when he had left. He had been in training camp in Louisiana and had seen much of the country. Before he left, he broke the news to us that he had signed up for another three years so he wouldn't have to serve in the reserves. He was transferred to the West Coast and we saw him often when he hitch-hiked home on weekends. One day he phoned collect from San Jose. He was being shipped out to Japan and it would probably be a year before he would be back.

His hitch was almost over when the Korean War broke out. Soon after his 22nd birthday, he wrote that he hoped to be home for Christmas. He explained that he had not been sleeping well lately since some veterans had been brought into his barracks. They had nightmares and they screamed in the night. The stories of war they told could not be shut out of his mind. There was a rumor going around that his company might be going over to replace the first groups. He hoped his timetable for discharge would not change. He was worried and that was why he had not written.

Tets came home before Christmas. He came home in a flag-draped coffin, with one of his buddies as military escort. The funeral at the Koyasan Buddhist Church was impressive. There was a change of guards every few minutes. Their soft-spoken orders mixed with the solemn chants. The curling incense smoke made hazy halos of the young faces who came mourning a dead friend.

On December 27, 1969, I joined several hundred young people who made a day-long pilgrimage to the Manzanar cemetery. While I helped clean out the sagebrush and manzanita, pulled tumbleweeds out of my boots, I was interrupted many times to recall facts and figures for the NBC and CBS television camera crews who were there to record the event.

Mt. Williamson's peak crested somewhere in the grey clouds that drew menacingly closer as the hours passed. Soon there was no sun. No seven-mile shadow lay across Owens Valley.

Dedication services ended that freezing, windswept and emotional day. I looked beyond the crowd and the monument. Out of the painful memories my mind dusted out of the past, I saw again the blurred impressions of the barbed-wire fence, the sentry towers and the tar-papered barracks. For a moment I saw again the 12-year-old boy with his head cocked, his shoulders sagging, his eyes fighting to keep open in the sun, while the long and lonely desert stretched out behind him.

[1980]

Homeplace
(a site of resistance)

bell hooks

WHEN I WAS A YOUNG GIRL THE JOURNEY ACROSS TOWN TO MY GRAND-mother's house was one of the most intriguing experiences. Mama did not like to stay there long. She did not care for all that loud talk, the talk that was usually about the old days, the way life happened then—who married whom, how and when somebody died, but also how we lived and survived as black people, how the white folks treated us. I remember this journey not just because of the stories I would hear. It was a movement away from the segregated blackness of our community into a poor white neighborhood. I remember the fear, being scared to walk to Baba's (our grandmother's house) because we would have to pass that terrifying whiteness—those white faces on the porches staring us down with hate. Even when empty or vacant, those porches seemed to say "danger," "you do not belong here," "you are not safe."

Oh! that feeling of safety, of arrival, of homecoming when we finally reached the edges of her yard, when we could see the soot black face of our grandfather, Daddy Gus, sitting in his chair on the porch, smell his cigar, and rest on his lap. Such a contrast, that feeling of arrival, of homecoming, this sweetness and the bitterness of that journey, that constant reminder of white power and control.

I speak of this journey as leading to my grandmother's house, even though our grandfather lived there too. In our young minds houses belonged to women, were their special domain, not as property, but as places where all that truly mattered in life took place—the warmth and comfort of shelter, the feeding of our bodies, the nurturing of our souls. There we learned dignity, integrity of being; there we learned to have faith. The folks who made this life possible, who were our primary guides and teachers, were black women.

Their lives were not easy. Their lives were hard. They were black women who for the most part worked outside the home serving white folks, cleaning their houses, washing their clothes, tending their children—black women who worked in the fields or in the streets, whatever they could do to make ends meet, whatever was necessary. Then they returned to their homes to make life happen there. This tension between service outside one's home, family, and kin network, service provided to white folks which took time and energy, and the effort of black women to conserve enough of themselves to provide service (care and nurturance) within their own families and communities is one of the many factors that has historically distinguished the lot of black women in patriarchal white supremacist society from that of black men. Contemporary black struggle must honor this history of service just as it must critique the sexist definition of service as women's "natural" role.

Since sexism delegates to females the task of creating and sustaining a home environment, it has been primarily the responsibility of black women to construct domestic households as spaces of care and nurturance in the face of the brutal harsh reality of racist oppression, of sexist domination. Historically, African-American people believed that the construction of a homeplace, however fragile and tenuous (the slave hut, the wooden shack), had a radical political dimension. Despite the brutal reality of racial apartheid, of domination, one's homeplace was the one site where one could freely confront the issue of humanization, where one could resist. Black women resisted by making homes where all black people could strive to be subjects, not objects, where we could be affirmed in our minds and hearts despite poverty, hardship, and deprivation, where we could restore to ourselves the dignity denied us on the outside in the public world.

This task of making homeplace was not simply a matter of black women providing service; it was about the construction of a safe place where black people could affirm one another and by so doing heal many of the wounds inflicted by racist domination. We could not learn to love or respect ourselves in the culture of white supremacy, on the outside; it was there on the inside, in that "homeplace," most often created and kept by black women, that we had the opportunity to grow and develop, to nurture our spirits. This task of making a homeplace, of making home a community of resistance, has been shared by black women globally, especially black women in white supremacist societies.

I shall never forget the sense of shared history, of common anguish, I felt when first reading about the plight of black women domestic servants in South Africa, black women laboring in white homes. Their stories evoked vivid memories of our African-American past. I remember that one of the black women giving testimony complained that after traveling in the wee hours of the morning to the white folks' house, after working there all day, giving her time and energy, she had "none left for her own." I knew this story. I had read it in the slave narratives of African-American women who, like Sojourner Truth, could say, "When I cried out with a mother's grief none but Jesus heard." I knew this story. I had grown to womanhood hearing about black women who nurtured and cared for white families when they longed to have time and energy to give to their own.

I want to remember these black women today. The act of remembrance is a conscious gesture honoring their struggle, their effort to keep something for their own. I want us to respect and understand that this effort has been and continues to be a radically subversive political gesture. For those who dominate and oppress us benefit most when we have nothing to give our own, when they have so taken from us our dignity, our humanness that we have nothing left, no "homeplace" where we can recover ourselves. I want us to remember these black women today, both past and present. Even as I speak there are black women in the midst of racial apartheid in South Africa, struggling to provide something for their own. "We . . . know how our sisters suffer" (Quoted in the petition for the repeal of the pass laws, August 9, 1956). I want us to honor them, not because they suffer but because they continue to struggle in the midst of suffering, because they continue to resist. I want to speak about the importance of homeplace in the midst of oppression and domination, of homeplace as a site of resistance and liberation struggle. Writing about "resistance," particularly resistance to the Vietnam war, Vietnamese Buddhist monk Thich Nhat Hahn says:

> . . . resistance, at root, must mean more than resistance against war. It is a resistance against all kinds of things that are like war. . . . So perhaps, resistance means opposition to being invaded, occupied, assaulted and destroyed by the system. The purpose of resistance, here, is to seek the healing of yourself in order to be able to see clearly . . . I think that communities of resistance should be places where people can return to themselves more easily, where the conditions are such that they can heal themselves and recover their wholeness.

Historically, black women have resisted white supremacist domination by working to establish homeplace. It does not matter that sexism assigned them this role. It is more important that they took this conventional role and expanded it to include caring for one another, for children, for black men, in ways that elevated our spirits, that kept us from despair, that taught some of us to be revolutionaries able to struggle for freedom. In his famous 1845 slave narrative, Frederick Douglass tells the story of his birth, of his enslaved black mother who was hired out a considerable distance from his place of residence. Describing their relationship, he writes:

> I never saw my mother, to know her as such more than four or five times in my life; and each of these times was very short in duration, and at night. She was hired by Mr. Stewart, who lived about twelve miles from my house. She made her journeys to see me in the night, traveling the whole distance on foot, after the performance of her day's work. She was a field hand, and a whipping is the penalty of not being in the field at sunrise . . . I do not recollect of ever seeing my mother by the light of day. She was with me in the night. She would lie down with me and get me to sleep, but long before I waked she was gone.

After sharing this information, Douglass later says that he never enjoyed a mother's "soothing presence, her tender and watchful care" so that he received the "tidings of her death with much the same emotions I should have probably felt at the death of a stranger." Douglass surely intended to impress upon the consciousness of white readers the cruelty of that system of racial domination which separated black families, black mothers from their children. Yet he does so by devaluing black womanhood, by not even registering the quality of care that made his black mother travel those twelve miles to hold him in her arms. In the midst of a brutal racist system, which did not value black life, she valued the life of her child enough to resist that system, to come to him in the night, just to hold him.

Now I cannot agree with Douglass that he never knew a mother's care. I want to suggest that his mother, who dared to hold him in the night, gave him at birth a sense of value that provided a groundwork, however fragile, for the person he later became. If anyone doubts the power and significance of this maternal gesture, they would do well to read psychoanalyst Alice Miller's book, *The Untouched Key: Tracing Childhood Trauma in Creativity and Destructiveness.* Holding him in her arms, Douglass' mother provided, if only for a short time, a space where this black child was not the subject of dehumanizing scorn and devaluation but was the recipient of a quality of care that should have enabled the adult Douglass to look back and reflect on the political choices of this black mother who resisted slave codes, risking her life, to care for her son. I want to suggest that devaluation of the role his mother played in his life is a dangerous oversight. Though Douglass is only one example, we are currently in danger of forgetting the powerful role black women have played in constructing for us homeplaces that are the site for resistance. This forgetfulness undermines our solidarity and the future of black liberation struggle.

Douglass's work is important, for he is historically identified as sympathetic to the struggle for women's rights. All too often his critique of male domination, such as it was, did not include recognition of the particular circumstances of black women in relation to black men and families. To me one of the most important chapters in my first book, *Ain't I a Woman: Black Women and Feminism*, is one that calls attention to "Continued Devaluation of Black Womanhood." Overall devaluation of the role black women have played in constructing for us homeplaces that are the site for resistance undermines our efforts to resist racism and the colonizing mentality which promotes internalized self-hatred. Sexist thinking about the nature of domesticity has determined the way black women's experience in the home is perceived. In African-American culture there is a long tradition of "mother worship." Black autobiographies, fiction, and poetry praise the virtues of the self-sacrificing black mother. Unfortunately, though positively motivated, black mother worship extols the virtues of self-sacrifice while simultaneously implying that such a gesture is not reflective of choice and will, rather the perfect embodiment of a woman's "natural" role. The assumption then is that the black woman who works hard to be a responsible caretaker is only doing what she should be doing. Failure to recognize the realm of choice, and the remarkable re-visioning of both woman's role and the idea of "home" that black women consciously exercised in practice, obscures the political commitment to racial uplift, to eradicating racism, which was the philosophical core of dedication to community and home.

Though black women did not self-consciously articulate in written discourse the theoretical principles of decolonization, this does not detract from the importance of their actions. They understood intellectually and intuitively the meaning of homeplace in the midst of an oppressive and dominating social reality, of homeplace as site of resistance and liberation struggle. I know of what I speak. I would not be writing this essay if my mother, Rosa Bell, daughter to Sarah Oldham, granddaughter to Bell Hooks, had not created homeplace in just this liberatory way, despite the contradictions of poverty and sexism.

In our family, I remember the immense anxiety we felt as children when mama would leave our house, our segregated community, to work as a maid in the homes of white folks. I believe that she sensed our fear, our concern that she might not return to us safe, that we could not find her (even though she always left phone numbers, they did not ease our worry). When she returned home after working long hours, she did not complain. She made an effort to rejoice with us that her work was done, that she was home, making it seem as though there was nothing about the experience of working as a maid in a white household, in that space of Otherness, which stripped her of dignity and personal power.

Looking back as an adult woman, I think of the effort it must have taken for her to transcend her own tiredness (and who knows what assaults or wounds to her spirit had to be put aside so that she could give something to her own). Given the contemporary notions of "good parenting" this may seem like a small gesture, yet in many post-slavery black families, it was a gesture parents were often too weary, too beaten down to make. Those of us who were fortunate enough to receive such care understood its value. Politically, our young mother, Rosa Bell, did not allow the white supremacist culture of domination to completely shape and control her psyche and her familial relationships. Working to create a homeplace that affirmed our beings, our blackness, our love for one another was necessary resistance. We learned degrees of critical consciousness from her. Our lives were not without contradictions, so it is not my intent to create a romanticized portrait. Yet any attempts to critically assess the role of black women in liberation struggle must examine the way political concern about the impact of racism shaped black women's thinking, their sense of home, and their modes of parenting.

An effective means of white subjugation of black people globally has been the perpetual construction of economic and social structures that deprive many folks of the means to make homeplace. Remembering this should enable us to understand the political value of black women's resistance in the home. It should provide a framework where we can discuss the development of black female political consciousness, acknowledging the political importance of resistance effort that took place in homes. It is no accident that the South African apartheid regime systematically attacks and destroys black efforts to construct homeplace, however tenuous, that small private reality where black women and men can renew their spirits and recover themselves. It is no accident that this homeplace, as fragile and as transitional as it may be, a makeshift shed, a small bit of earth where one rests, is always subject to violation and destruction. For when a people no longer have the space to construct homeplace, we cannot build a meaningful community of resistance.

Throughout our history, African-Americans have recognized the subversive value of homeplace, of having access to private space where we do not directly encounter white racist aggression. Whatever the shape and direction of black liberation struggle (civil rights reform or black power movement), domestic space has been a crucial site for organizing, for forming political solidarity. Homeplace has been a site of resistance. Its structure was defined less by whether or not black women and men were conforming to sexist behavior norms and more by our struggle to uplift ourselves as a people, our struggle to resist racist domination and oppression.

That liberatory struggle has been seriously undermined by contemporary efforts to change that subversive homeplace into a site of patriarchal domination of black women by black men, where we abuse one another for not conforming to sexist norms. This shift in perspective, where homeplace is not viewed as a political site, has had negative impact on the construction of black female identity and political consciousness. Masses of black women, many of whom were not formally educated, had in the past been able to play a vital role in black liberation struggle. In the contemporary situation, as the paradigms for domesticity in black life mirrored white bourgeois norms (where home is conceptualized as politically neutral space), black people began to overlook and devalue the importance of black female labor in teaching critical consciousness in domestic space. Many black women, irrespective of class status, have responded to this crisis of meaning by imitating leisure-class sexist notions of women's role, focusing their lives on meaningless compulsive consumerism.

Identifying this syndrome as "the crisis of black womanhood" in her essay, "Considering Feminism as a Model for Social Change," Sheila Radford-Hill points to the mid-sixties as that historical moment when the primacy of black woman's role in liberation struggle began to be questioned as a threat to black manhood and was deemed unimportant. Radford-Hill asserts:

> Without the power to influence the purpose and the direction of our collective experience, without the power to influence our culture from within, we are increasingly immobilized, unable to integrate self and role identities, unable to resist the cultural imperialism of the dominant culture which assures our continued oppression by destroying us from within. Thus, the crisis manifests itself as social dysfunction in the black community—as genocide, fratricide, homicide, and suicide. It is also manifested by the abdication of personal responsibility by black women for themselves and for each other . . . The crisis of black womanhood is a form of cultural aggression: a form of exploitation so vicious, so insidious that it is currently destroying an entire generation of black women and their families.

This contemporary crisis of black womanhood might have been avoided had black women collectively sustained attempts to develop the latent feminism expressed by their willingness to work equally alongside black men in black liberation struggle. Contemporary equation of black liberation struggle with the subordination of black women has damaged collective black solidarity. It has served the interests of white supremacy to promote the assumption that the wounds of racist domination would be less severe were black women conforming to sexist role patterns.

We are daily witnessing the disintegration of African-American family life that is grounded in a recognition of the political value of constructing homeplace as a site of resistance; black people daily perpetuate sexist norms that threaten our survival as a people. We can no longer act as though sexism in black communities does not threaten our solidarity; any force which estranges and alienates us from one another serves the interests of racist domination.

Black women and men must create a revolutionary vision of black liberation that has a feminist dimension, one which is formed in consideration of our specific needs and concerns. Drawing on past legacies, contemporary black women can begin to reconceptualize ideas of homeplace, once again considering the primacy of domesticity as a site for subversion and resistance. When we renew our concern with homeplace, we can address political issues that most affect our daily lives. Calling attention to the skills and resources of black women who may have begun to feel that they have no meaningful contribution to make, women who may or may not be formally educated but who have essential wisdom to share, who have practical experience that is the breeding ground for all useful theory, we may begin to bond with one another in ways that renew our solidarity.

When black women renew our political commitment to homeplace, we can address the needs and concerns of young black women who are groping for structures of meaning that will further their growth, young women who are struggling for self-definition. Together, black women can renew our commitment to black liberation struggle, sharing insights and awareness, sharing feminist thinking and feminist vision, building solidarity.

With this foundation, we can regain lost perspective, give life new meaning. We can make homeplace that space where we return for renewal and self-recovery, where we can heal our wounds and become whole.

[1990]

Learning from the 6os*

Audre Lorde

MALCOLM X IS A DISTINCT SHAPE IN A VERY PIVOTAL PERIOD OF MY LIFE. I stand here now—Black, Lesbian, Feminist—an inheritor of Malcolm and in his tradition, doing my work, and the ghost of his voice through my mouth asks each one of you here tonight: Are you doing yours?

There are no new ideas, just new ways of giving those ideas we cherish breath and power in our own living. I'm not going to pretend that the moment I first saw or heard Malcolm X he became my shining prince,

---

* Transcript of a talk given at Harvard University's Malcolm X Weekend, February 1982.

because it wouldn't be true. In February 1965 I was raising two children and a husband in a three-room flat on 149th Street in Harlem. I had read about Malcolm X and the Black Muslims. I became more interested in Malcolm X after he left the Nation of Islam, when he was silenced by Elijah Muhammad for his comment, after Kennedy's assassination, to the effect that the chickens had come home to roost. Before this I had not given much thought to the Nation of Islam because of their attitude toward women as well as because of their nonactivist stance. I'd read Malcolm's autobiography, and I liked his style, and I thought he looked a lot like my father's people, but I was one of the ones who didn't really hear Malcolm's voice until it was amplified by death.

I had been guilty of what many of us are still guilty of—letting the media, and I don't mean only the white media—define the bearers of those messages most important to our lives.

When I read Malcolm X with careful attention, I found a man much closer to the complexities of real change than anything I had read before. Much of what I say here tonight was born from his words.

In the last year of his life, Malcolm X added a breadth to his essential vision that would have brought him, had he lived, into inevitable confrontation with the question of difference as a creative and necessary force for change. For as Malcolm X progressed from a position of resistance to, and analysis of, the racial status quo, to more active considerations of organizing for change, he began to reassess some of his earlier positions. One of the most basic Black survival skills is the ability to change, to metabolize experience, good or ill, into something that is useful, lasting, effective. Four hundred years of survival as an endangered species has taught most of us that if we intend to live, we had better become fast learners. Malcolm knew this. We do not have to live the same mistakes over again if we can look at them, learn from them, and build upon them.

Before he was killed, Malcolm had altered and broadened his opinions concerning the role of women in society and the revolution. He was beginning to speak with increasing respect of the connection between himself and Martin Luther King, Jr., whose policies of nonviolence appeared to be so opposite to his own. And he began to examine the societal conditions under which alliances and coalitions must indeed occur.

He had also begun to discuss those scars of oppression which lead us to war against ourselves in each other rather than against our enemies.

As Black people, if there is one thing we can learn from the 60s, it is how infinitely complex any move for liberation must be. For we must move against not only those forces which dehumanize us from the outside, but also against those oppressive values which we have been forced to take into ourselves. Through examining the combination of our triumphs and errors, we can examine the dangers of an incomplete vision. Not to condemn that vision but to alter it, construct templates for possible futures, and focus our rage for change upon our enemies rather than upon each other. In the 1960s, the awakened anger of the Black community was often expressed, not vertically against the corruption of power and true sources of control over our lives, but horizontally toward those closest to us who mirrored our own impotence.

We were poised for attack, not always in the most effective places. When we disagreed with one another about the solution to a particular problem, we were often far more vicious to each other than to the originators of our common problem. Historically, difference had been used so cruelly against us that as a people we were reluctant to tolerate any diversion from what was externally defined as Blackness. In the 60s, political correctness became not a guideline for living, but a new set of shackles. A small and vocal part of the Black community lost sight of the fact that unity does not mean unanimity—Black people are not some standardly digestible quantity. In order to work together we do not have to become a mix of indistinguishable particles resembling a vat of homogenized chocolate milk. Unity implies the coming together of elements which are, to begin with, varied and diverse in their particular natures. Our persistence in examining the tensions within diversity encourages growth toward our common goal. So often we either ignore the past or romanticize it, render the reason for unity useless or mythic. We forget that the necessary ingredient needed to make the past work for the future is our energy in the present, metabolizing one into the other. Continuity does not happen automatically, nor is it a passive process.

The 60s were characterized by a heady belief in instantaneous solutions. They were vital years of awakening, of pride, and of error. The civil rights and Black power movements rekindled possibilities for disenfranchised groups within this nation. Even though we fought common enemies, at times the lure of individual solutions made us careless of each other. Sometimes we could not bear the face of each other's differences because of what we feared those differences might say about ourselves. As if everybody can't eventually be too Black, too white, too man, too woman. But any future vision which can encompass all of us, by definition, must be complex and expanding, not easy to achieve. The answer to cold is heat, the answer to hunger is food. But there is no simple monolithic solution to racism, to sexism, to homophobia. There is only the conscious focusing within each of my days to move against them, wherever I come up against these particular manifestations of the same disease. By seeing who the *we* is, we learn to use our energies with greater precision against our enemies rather than against ourselves.

In the 60s, White america—racist and liberal alike—was more than pleased to sit back as spectator while Black militant fought Black Muslim, Black Nationalist badmouthed the nonviolent, and Black women were told that our only useful position in the Black Power movement was prone. The existence of Black lesbian and gay people was not even allowed to cross the public consciousness of Black America. We know in the 1980s, from documents gained through the Freedom of Information Act, that the FBI and CIA used our intolerance of difference to foment confusion and tragedy in segment after segment of Black communities of the 60s. Black was beautiful, but still suspect, and too often our forums for debate became stages for playing who's-Blacker-than-who or who's-poorer-than-who games, ones in which there can be no winners.

The 60s for me was a time of promise and excitement, but the 60s was also a time of isolation and frustration from within. It often felt like I was working and raising my children in a vacuum, and that it was my own fault—if I was only Blacker, things would be fine. It was a time of much wasted energy, and I was often in a lot of pain. Either I denied or chose between various aspects of my identity, or my work and my Blackness would be unacceptable. As a Black lesbian mother in an interracial marriage, there was usually some part of me guaranteed to offend everybody's comfortable prejudices of who I should be. That is how I learned that if I didn't define myself for myself, I would be crunched into other people's fantasies for me and eaten alive. My poetry, my life, my work, my energies for struggle were not acceptable unless I pretended to match somebody else's norm. I learned that not only couldn't I succeed at that game, but the energy needed for that masquerade would be lost to my work. And there were babies to raise, students to teach. The Vietnam War was escalating, our cities were burning, more and more of our school kids were nodding out in the halls, junk was overtaking our streets. We needed articulate power, not conformity. There were other strong Black workers whose visions were racked and silenced upon some imagined grid of narrow Blackness. Nor were Black women immune. At a national meeting of Black women for political action, a young civil rights activist who had been beaten and imprisoned in Mississippi only a few years before, was trashed and silenced as suspect because of her white husband. Some of us made it and some of us were lost to the struggle. It was a time of great hope and great expectation; it was also a time of great waste. That is history. We do not need to repeat these mistakes in the 80s.

The raw energy of Black determination released in the 60s powered changes in Black awareness and self-concepts and expectations. This energy is still being felt in movements for change among women, other peoples of Color, gays, the handicapped—among all the disenfranchised peoples of this society. That is a legacy of the 60s to ourselves and to others. But we must recognize that many of our high expectations of rapid revolutionary change did not in fact occur. And many of the gains that did are even now being dismantled. This is not a reason for despair, nor for rejection of the importance of those years. But we must face with clarity and insight the lessons to be learned from the oversimplification of any struggle for self-awareness and liberation, or we will not rally the force we need to face the multidimensional threats to our survival in the 80s.

There is no such thing as a single-issue struggle because we do not live single-issue lives. Malcolm knew this. Martin Luther King, Jr. knew this. Our struggles are particular, but we are not alone. We are not perfect, but we are stronger and wiser than the sum of our errors. Black people have been here before us and survived. We can read their lives like signposts on the road and find, as Bernice Reagon says so poignantly, that each one of us is here because somebody before us did something to make it possible. To learn from their mistakes is not to lessen our debt to them, nor to the hard work of becoming ourselves, and effective.

We lose our history so easily, what is not predigested for us by the *New*

York Times, or the *Amsterdam News,* or *Time* magazine. Maybe because we do not listen to our poets or to our fools, maybe because we do not listen to our mamas in ourselves. When I hear the deepest truths I speak coming out of my mouth sounding like my mother's, even remembering how I fought against her, I have to reassess both our relationship as well as the sources of my knowing. Which is not to say that I have to romanticize my mother in order to appreciate what she gave me—Woman, Black. We do not have to romanticize our past in order to be aware of how it seeds our present. We do not have to suffer the waste of an amnesia that robs us of the lessons of the past rather than permit us to read them with pride as well as deep understanding.

We know what it is to be lied to, and we know how important it is not to lie to ourselves.

We are powerful because we have survived, and that is what it is all about—survival and growth.

Within each one of us there is some piece of humanness that knows we are not being served by the machine which orchestrates crisis after crisis and is grinding all our futures into dust. If we are to keep the enormity of the forces aligned against us from establishing a false hierarchy of oppression, we must school ourselves to recognize that any attack against Blacks, any attack against women, is an attack against all of us who recognize that our interests are not being served by the systems we support. Each one of us here is a link in the connection between antipoor legislation, gay shootings, the burning of synagogues, street harassment, attacks against women, and resurgent violence against Black people. I ask myself as well as each one of you, exactly what alteration in the particular fabric of my everyday life does this connection call for? Survival is not a theory. In what way do I contribute to the subjugation of any part of those who I define as my people? Insight must illuminate the particulars of our lives: who labors to make the bread we waste, or the energy it takes to make nuclear poisons which will not biodegrade for one thousand years; or who goes blind assembling the micro-transistors in our inexpensive calculators?

We are women trying to knit a future in a country where an Equal Rights Amendment was defeated as subversive legislation. We are Lesbians and gay men who, as the most obvious target of the New Right, are threatened with castration, imprisonment, and death in the streets. And we know that our erasure only paves the way for erasure of other people of Color, of the old, of the poor, of all of those who do not fit that mythic dehumanizing norm.

Can we really still afford to be fighting each other?

We are Black people living in a time when the consciousness of our intended slaughter is all around us. People of Color are increasingly expendable, our government's policy both here and abroad. We are functioning under a government ready to repeat in El Salvador and Nicaragua the tragedy of Vietnam, a government which stands on the wrong side of every single battle for liberation taking place upon this globe; a government which has invaded and conquered (as I edit this piece) the fifty-three square mile sovereign state of Grenada, under the pretext that her 110,000 people pose a threat to the U.S. Our papers are filled with supposed concern for human rights in white communist Poland while we sanction by acceptance and military supply the systematic genocide of apartheid in South Africa, of murder and torture in Haiti and El Salvador. American advisory teams bolster repressive governments across Central and South America, and in Haiti, while *advisory* is only a code name preceding military aid.

Decisions to cut aid for the terminally ill, for the elderly, for dependent children, for food stamps, even school lunches, are being made by men with full stomachs who live in comfortable houses with two cars and umpteen tax shelters. None of them go hungry to bed at night. Recently, it was suggested that senior citizens be hired to work in atomic plants because they are close to the end of their lives anyway.

Can any one of us here still afford to believe that efforts to reclaim the future can be private or individual? Can any one here still afford to believe that the pursuit of liberation can be the sole and particular province of any one particular race, or sex, or age, or religion, or sexuality, or class?

Revolution is not a one-time event. It is becoming always vigilant for the smallest opportunity to make a genuine change in established, outgrown responses; for instance, it is learning to address each other's difference with respect.

We share a common interest, survival, and it cannot be pursued in isolation from others simply because their differences make us uncomfortable. We know what it is to be lied to. The 60s should teach us how important it is not to lie to ourselves. Not to believe that revolution is a one-time event, or something that happens around us rather than inside of us. Not to believe that freedom can belong to any one group of us without the others also being free. How important it is not to allow even our leaders to define us to ourselves, or to define our sources of power to us.

There is no Black person here who can afford to wait to be led into positive action for survival. Each one of us must look clearly and closely at the genuine particulars (conditions) of his or her life and decide where action and energy is needed and where it can be effective. Change is the immediate responsibility of each of us, wherever and however we are standing, in whatever arena we choose. For while we wait for another Malcolm, another Martin, another charismatic Black leader to validate our struggles, old Black people are freezing to death in tenements, Black children are being brutalized and slaughtered in the streets, or lobotomized by television, and the percentage of Black families living below the poverty line is higher today than in 1963.

And if we wait to put our future into the hands of some new messiah, what will happen when those leaders are shot, or discredited, or tried for murder, or called homosexual, or otherwise disempowered? Do we put our future on hold? What is that internalized and self-destructive barrier that keeps us from moving, that keeps us from coming together?

We who are Black are at an extraordinary point of choice within our lives. To refuse to participate in the shaping of our future is to give it up. Do not be misled into passivity either by false security (they don't mean me) or by despair (there's nothing we can do). Each of us must find our work and do it. Militancy no longer means guns at high noon, if it ever did. It means actively working for change, sometimes in the absence of any surety that change is coming. It means doing the unromantic and tedious work necessary to forge meaningful coalitions, and it means recognizing which coalitions are possible and which coalitions are not. It means knowing that coalition, like unity, means the coming together of whole, self-actualized human beings, focused and believing, not fragmented automatons marching to a prescribed step. It means fighting despair.

And in the university, that is certainly no easy task, for each one of you by virtue of your being here will be deluged by opportunities to misname yourselves, to forget who you are, to forget where your real interests lie. Make no mistake, you will be courted; and nothing neutralizes creativity quicker than tokenism, that false sense of security fed by a myth of individual solutions. To paraphrase Malcolm—a Black woman attorney driving a Mercedes through Avenue Z in Brooklyn is still a "nigger bitch," two words which never seem to go out of style.

You do not have to be me in order for us to fight alongside each other. I do not have to be you to recognize that our wars are the same. What we must do is commit ourselves to some future that can include each other and to work toward that future with the particular strengths of our individual identities. And in order to do this, we must allow each other our differences at the same time as we recognize our sameness.

If our history has taught us anything, it is that action for change directed only against the external conditions of our oppressions is not enough. In order to be whole, we must recognize the despair oppression plants within each of us—that thin persistent voice that says our efforts are useless, it will never change, so why bother, accept it. And we must fight that inserted piece of self-destruction that lives and flourishes like a poison inside of us, unexamined until it makes us turn upon ourselves in each other. But we can put our finger down upon that loathing buried deep within each one of us and see who it encourages us to despise, and we can lessen its potency by the knowledge of our real connectedness, arcing across our differences.

Hopefully, we can learn from the 60s that we cannot afford to do our enemies' work by destroying each other.

What does it mean when an angry Black ballplayer—this happened in Illinois—curses a white heckler but pulls a knife on a Black one? What better way is there to police the streets of a minority community than to turn one generation against the other?

Referring to Black lesbians and gay men, the student president at Howard University says, on the occasion of a Gay Student Charter on campus, "The Black community has nothing to do with such filth—we will have to abandon *these people*." [italics mine] Abandon? Often without noticing, we absorb the racist belief that Black people are fitting targets for everybody's anger. We are closest to each other, and it is easier to vent fury upon each other than upon our enemies.

Of course, the young man at Howard was historically incorrect. As part of the Black community, he has a lot to do with "us." Some of our finest writers, organizers, artists and scholars in the 60s as well as today, have been lesbian and gay, and history will bear me out.

Over and over again in the 60s I was asked to justify my existence and my work, because I was a woman, because I was a Lesbian, because I was not a separatist, because some piece of me was not acceptable. Not because of my work but because of my identity. I had to learn to hold on to all the parts of me that served me, in spite of the pressure to express only one to the exclusion of all others. And I don't know what I'd say face to face with that young man at Howard University who says I'm filth because I identify women as my primary source of energy and support, except to say that it is my energy and the energy of other women very much like me which has contributed to his being where he is at this point. But I think he would not say it to my face because name-calling is always easiest when it is removed, academic. The move to render the presence of lesbians and gay men invisible in the intricate fabric of Black existence and survival is a move which contributes to fragmentation and weakness in the Black community.

In academic circles, as elsewhere, there is a kind of name-calling increasingly being used to keep young Black women in line. Often as soon as any young Black woman begins to recognize that she is oppressed as a woman as well as a Black, she is called a lesbian no matter how she identifies herself sexually. "What do you mean you don't want to make coffee take notes wash dishes go to bed with me, you a lesbian or something?" And at the threat of such a dreaded taint, all too often she falls meekly into line, however covertly. But the word *lesbian* is only threatening to those Black women who are intimidated by their sexuality, or who allow themselves to be defined by it and from outside themselves. Black women in struggle from our own perspective, speaking up for ourselves, sharing close ties with one another politically and emotionally, are not the enemies of Black men. We are Black women who seek our own definitions, recognizing diversity among ourselves with respect. We have been around within our communities for a very long time, and we have played pivotal parts in the survival of those communities: from Hat Shep Sut through Harriet Tubman to Daisy Bates and Fannie Lou Hamer to Lorraine Hansberry to your Aunt Maydine to some of you who sit before me now.

In the 60s Black people wasted a lot of our substance fighting each other. We cannot afford to do that in the 80s, when Washington, D.C. has the highest infant mortality rate of any U.S. city, 60 percent of the Black community under twenty is unemployed and more are becoming unemployable, lynchings are on the increase, and less than half the registered Black voters voted in the last election.

How are you practicing what you preach—whatever you preach, and who exactly is listening? As Malcolm stressed, we are not responsible for our oppression, but we must be responsible for our own liberation. It is not going to be easy, but we have what we have learned and what we have been given that is useful. We have the power those who came before us have given us, to move beyond the place where they were standing. We have the trees, and water, and sun, and our children. Malcolm X does not live in the dry texts of his words as we read them; he lives in the energy we generate and use to move along the visions we share with him. We are making the future as well as bonding to survive the enormous pressures of the present, and that is what it means to be a part of history.

[1984]

Grandma's Story

Trinh T. Minh-ha

See all things howsoever they flourish
Return to the root from which they grew
This return to the root is called Quietness

—Lao Tzu, *Tao-te-ching*, 16 (tr. A. Waley)

Truth and Fact: Story and History

Let me tell you a story. For all I have is a story. Story passed on from generation to generation, named Joy. Told for the joy it gives the storyteller and the listener. Joy inherent in the process of storytelling. Whoever understands it also understands that a story, as distressing as it can be in its joy, never takes anything away from anybody. Its name, remember, is Joy. Its double, Woe Morrow Show.

> Let the one who is diseuse, one who is mother who waits nine days and nine nights be found. Restore memory. Let the one who is diseuse, one who is daughter restore spring with her each appearance from beneath the earth. The ink spills thickest before it runs dry before it stops writing at all. (Theresa Hak Kyung Cha)[1]

Something must be said. Must be said that has not been *and* has been said before. "It will take a long time, but the story must be told. There must not be any lies" (Leslie Marmon Silko). It will take a long time for living cannot be told, not merely told: living is not livable. Understanding, however, is creating, and living, such an immense gift that thousands of people benefit from each past or present life being lived. The story depends upon every one of us to come into being. It needs us all, needs our remembering, understanding, and creating what we have heard together to keep on coming into being. The story of a people. Of us, peoples. Story, history, literature (or religion, philosophy, natural science, ethics)—all in one. They call it the tool of primitive man, the simplest vehicle of truth. When history separated itself from story, it started indulging in accumulation and facts. Or it thought it could. It thought it could build up to History because the Past, unrelated to the Present and the Future, is lying there in its entirety, waiting to be revealed and related. The act of revealing bears in itself a magical (not factual) quality—inherited undoubtedly from "primitive" storytelling—for the Past perceived as such is a well-organized past whose organization is already given. Managing to identify with History, history (with a small letter h) thus manages to oppose the factual to the fictional (turning a blind eye to the "magicality" of its claims); the story-writer—the historian—to the story-teller. As long as the transformation, manipulations, or redistributions inherent in the collecting of events are overlooked, the division continues its course, as sure of its itinerary as it certainly dreams to be. Story-writing becomes history-writing, and history quickly sets itself apart, consigning story to the realm of tale, legend, myth, fiction, literature. Then, since fictional and factual have come to a point where they mutually exclude each other, fiction, not infrequently, means lies, and fact, truth. DID IT REALLY HAPPEN? IS IT A TRUE STORY?

> I don't want to listen to any more of your stories [Maxine Hong Kingston screamed at her champion-story-talker mother]; they have no logic. They scramble me up. You lie with stories. You won't tell me a story and then say, "This is a true story," or "This is just a story." I can't tell the difference. I don't even know what your real names are. I can't tell what's real and what you made up.[2]

Which truth? the question unavoidably arises. The story has been defined as "a free narration, not necessarily factual but truthful in character. . . . [It] gives us human nature in its bold outlines; history, in its individual details."[3] Truth. Not one but two: truth and fact, just like in the old times when queens were born and kings were made in Egypt. (Queens and princesses were then "Royal Mothers" from birth, whereas the king wore the crown of high priest and did not receive the Horus-name until his coronation.) Poetry, Aristotle said, is truer than history. Storytelling as literature (narrative poetry) must then be truer than history. If we rely on history to tell us what happened at a specific time and place, we can rely on the story to tell us not only what might have happened, but also what is happening at an unspecified time and place. No wonder that in old tales storytellers are very often women, witches, and prophets. The African griot and griotte are well known for being poet, storyteller, historian, musician, and magician—all at once. But why truth at all? Why this battle for truth and on behalf of truth? I do not remember having asked grand mother once whether the story she was telling me was true or not. Neither do I recall her asking me whether the story I was reading her was true or not. We knew we could make each other cry, laugh, or fear, but we never thought of saying to each other, "This is just a story." A story is a story. There was no need for clarification—a need many adults considered "natural" or imperative among children—for there was no such thing as "a blind acceptance of the story as literally true." Perhaps the story has become *just* a story when I have become adept at consuming truth as fact. Imagination is thus equated with falsification, and I am made to believe that if, accordingly, I am not told or do not establish in so many words what is true and what is false, I or the listener may no longer be able to differentiate fancy from fact (sic). Literature and history once were/still are stories: this does not necessarily mean that the space they form is undifferentiated, but that this space can articulate on a different set of principles, one which may be said to stand outside the hierarchical realm of facts. On the one hand, each society has its own politics of truth; on the other hand, being truthful is being in the in-between of all regimes of truth. Outside specific time, outside specialized space: "Truth embraces with it all other abstentions other than itself" (T. Hak Kyung Cha).

Keepers and Transmitters

Truth is when it is itself no longer. Diseuse, Thought-Woman, Spider-Woman, griotte, storytalker, fortune-teller, witch. If you have the patience to listen, she will take delight in relating it to you. An entire history, an entire vision of the world, a lifetime story. Mother always has a mother. And Great Mothers are recalled as the goddesses of all waters, the sources of diseases and of healing, the protectresses of women and of childbearing. To listen carefully is to preserve. But to preserve is to burn, for understanding means creating.

> Let the one who is diseuse, Diseuse de bonne aventure. Let her call forth. Let her break open the spell cast upon time upon time again and again. (T. Hak Kyung Cha)[4]

The world's earliest archives or libraries were the memories of women. Patiently transmitted from mouth to ear, body to body, hand to hand. In the process of storytelling, speaking and listening refer to realities that do not involve just the imagination. The speech is seen, heard, smelled, tasted, and touched. It destroys, brings into life, nurtures. Every woman partakes in the chain of guardianship and of transmission. In Africa it is said that every griotte who dies is a whole library that burns down (a "library in which the archives are not classified but are completely inventoried" [A. Hampate Ba]). Phrases like "I sucked it at my mother's breast" or "I have it from Our Mother" to express what has been passed down by the elders are common in this part of the world. Tell me and let me tell my hearers what I have heard from you who heard it from your mother and your grandmother, so that what is said may be guarded and unfailingly transmitted to the women of tomorrow, who will be our children and the children of our children.

These are the opening lines she used to chant before embarking on a story. I owe that to you, her and her, who owe it to her, her and her. I memorize, recognize, and name my source(s), not to validate my voice through the voice of an authority (for we, women, have little authority in the History of Literature, and wise women never draw their powers from authority), but to evoke her and sing. The bond between women and word. Among women themselves. To produce their full effect, words must, indeed, be chanted rhythmically, in cadences, off cadences.

> My great-grandmama told my grandmama the part she lived through that my grandmama didn't live through and my grandmama told my mama what they both lived through and my mama told me what they all lived through and we were supposed to pass it down like that from generation to generation so we'd never forget. Even though they'd burned everything to play like it didn't ever happen. (Gayl Jones)[5]

In this chain and continuum, I am but one link. The story is me, neither me nor mine. It does not really belong to me, and while I feel greatly responsible for it, I also enjoy the irresponsibility of the pleasure obtained through the process of transferring. Pleasure in the copy, pleasure in the reproduction. No repetition can ever be identical, but my story carries with it their stories, their history, and our story repeats itself endlessly despite our persistence in denying it. *I don't believe it. That story could not happen today.* Then someday our children will speak about us here present, about those days when things like that could happen . . . .

> It was like I didn't know how much was me and Mutt and how much was Great Gram and Corregidora—like Mama when she had started talking like Great Gram. But was what Corregidora had done to *her,* to *them,* any worse than what Mutt had done to me, than what we had done to each other, than what Mama had done to Daddy, or what he had done to her in return. . . . (Gayl Jones)[6]
>
> Upon seeing her you know how it was for her. You know how it might have been. You recline, you lapse, you fall, you see before you what you have seen before. Repeated, without your even knowing it. It is you standing there. It is you waiting outside in the summer day. (T. Hak Kyung Cha)[7]

Every gesture, every word involves our past, present, and future. The body never stops accumulating, and years and years have gone by mine without my being able to stop them, stop it. My sympathies and grudges appear at the same time familiar and unfamiliar to me; I dwell in them, they dwell in me, and we dwell in each other, more as guest than as owner. My story, no doubt, is me, but it is also, no doubt, older than me. Younger than me, older than the humanized. Unmeasurable, uncontainable, so immense that it exceeds all attempts at humanizing. But humanizing we do, and also overdo, for the vision of a story that has no end—no end, no middle, no beginning; no start, no stop, no progression; neither backward nor forward, only a stream that flows into another stream, an open sea—is the vision of a madwoman. "The unleashed tides of muteness," as Clarice Lispector puts it. We fear heights, we fear the headless, the bottomless, the boundless. And we are in terror of letting ourselves be engulfed by the depths of muteness. This is why we keep on doing violence to words: to tame and cook the wild-raw, to adopt the vertiginously infinite. Truth does not make sense; it exceeds meaning and exceeds measure. It exceeds all regimes of truth. So, when we insist on telling over and over again, we insist on repetition in re-creation (and vice versa). On distributing the story into smaller proportions that will correspond to the capacity of absorption of our mouths, the capacity of vision of our eyes, and the capacity of bearing of our bodies. Each story is at once a fragment and a whole; a whole within a whole. And the same story has always been changing, for things which do not shift and grow cannot continue to circulate. Dead. Dead times, dead words, dead tongues. Not to repeat in oblivion.

> Sediment. Turned stone. Let the one who is diseuse dust breathe away the distance of the well. Let the one who is diseuse again sit upon the stone nine days and nine nights. thus. Making stand again, Eleusis. (T. Hak Kyung Cha)[8]

Storytelling in the "Civilized" Context

The simplest vehicle of truth, the story is also said to be "a phase of communication," "the natural form for revealing life." Its fascination may be explained by its power both to give a vividly felt insight into the life of other people and to revive or keep alive the forgotten, dead-ended, turned-into-stone parts of ourselves. To the wo/man of the West who spends time recording and arranging the "data" concerning storytelling as well as "the many rules and taboos connected with it," this tool of primitive wo/man has provided primitive peoples with opportunities "to train their speech, formulate opinions, and express themselves" (Anna Birgitta Rooth). It gives "a sympathetic understanding of their limitations in knowledge, and an appreciation of our privileges in civilization, due largely to the struggles of the past" (Clark W. Hetherington). It informs of the explanations they invented for "the things [they] did not understand," and represents their religion, "a religion growing out of fear of the unknown" (Katherine Dunlap Cather). In summary, the story is either a mere practice of the art of rhetoric or "a repository of obsolete customs" (A. Skinner). It is mainly valued for its artistic potential and for the "religious beliefs" or "primitive-mind"-revealing superstitions mirrored by its content. (Like the supernatural, is the superstitious another product of the Western mind? For to accept even temporarily Cather's view on primitive religion, one is bound to ask: which [institutionalized] religion does not grow out of fear of the unknown?) Associated with backwardness, ignorance, and illiteracy, storytelling in the more "civilized" context is therefore relegated to the realm of children. "The fact that the story is the product of primitive man," wrote Herman H. Horne, "explains in part why the children hunger so for the story."[9] "Wherever there is no written language, wherever the people are too unlettered to read what is written," Cather equally remarked, "they still believe the legends. They love to hear them told and retold. . . . As it is with unlettered peasants today, as it was with tribesmen in primitive times and with the great in medieval castle halls, it still is with the child."[10] Primitive means elementary, therefore infantile. No wonder then that in the West storytelling is treasured above all for its educational force in the kindergarten and primary school. The mission of the storyteller, we thus hear, is to "teach children the tales their *fathers* knew," to mold ideals, and to "illuminate facts." For children to gain "right feelings" and to "think true," the story as a pedagogical tool must inform so as to keep their opinion "abreast of the scientific truth of the time, instead of dragging along in the superstitions of the past." But for the story to be well-told information, it must be related "in as fascinating a form as [in] the old myths and fables."[11] Patch up the content of the new and the form of the old, or impose one on the other. The dis-ease lingers on. With (traditional but non-superstitious?) formulas like "once upon a time" and "long, long ago," the storyteller can be reasonably sure of making "a good beginning." For many people truth has the connotation of uniformity and prescription. Thinking true means thinking in conformity with a certain scientific (read "scientistic") discourse produced by certain institutions. Not only has the "civilized" mind classified many of the realities it *does not understand* in the categories of the untrue and the superstitious, it has also turned the story—as total event of a community, a people—into a *fatherly* lesson for children of a certain age. Indeed, in the "civilized" context, only children are allowed to indulge in the so-called fantastic or the fantastic-true. They are perceived as belonging to a world apart, one which adults (compassionately) control and populate with toys—that is to say, with false human beings (dolls), false animals, false objects (imitative, diminutive versions of the "real"). "Civilized" adults fabricate, structure, and segregate the children's world; they invent toys for the latter to *play* with and stories of a specially adapted, more digestive kind to absorb, yet they insist on molding this world according to the scientifically true—the real, obviously not in its full scale, but in a reduced scale: that which is supposed to be the (God-like-) child's scale. Stories, especially "primitive-why stories" or fairy tales, must be carefully sorted and graded, for children should neither be "deceived" nor "duped" and "there should never be any doubt in [their] mind as to what is make-believe and what is real." In other words, the difference "civilized" adults recognize in the little people's world is a mere matter of scale. The forms of constraint that rule these bigger people's world and allow them to distinguish with certainty the false from the true must, unquestionably, be exactly the same as the ones that regulate the smaller people's world. The apartheid type of difference continues to operate in all spheres of "civilized" life. There does not seem to be any possibility either as to the existence of such things as, for example, two (or more) different realms of make-believe or two (or more) different realms of truth. The "civilized" mind is an indisputably clear-cut mind. If once upon a time people believed in the story and thought it was true, then why should it be false today? If true and false keep on changing with the times, then isn't it true that what is "crooked thinking" today may be "right thinking" tomorrow? What kind of people, we then wonder, walk around asking obstinately: "Is there not danger of making liars of children by feeding them on these [fairy] stories?" What kind of people set out for northern Alaska to study storytelling among the Indians and come round to writing: "What especially impressed me was their eagerness to make me understand. To me this eagerness became a proof of the high value they set on their stories and what they represented"?[12] What kind of people, indeed, other than the very kind for whom the story is "*just* a story"?

A Regenerating Force

An oracle and a bringer of joy, the storyteller is the living memory of her time, her people. She composes on life but does not lie, for composing is not imagining, fancying, or inventing. When asked, "What is oral tradition?" an African "traditionalist" (a term African scholars consider more accurate than the French term "griot" or "griotte," which tends to confuse traditionalists with mere public entertainers) would most likely be nonplussed. As A. Hampate Ba remarks, "[s/he] might reply, after a lengthy silence: 'It is total knowledge,' and say no more."[13] She might or might not reply so, for what is called here "total knowledge" is not really nameable. At least it cannot be named (so) without incurring the risk of sliding right back into one of the many slots the "civilized" discourse of knowledge readily provides it with. The question "What is oral tradition?" is a question-answer that needs no answer at all. Let the one who is civilized, the one who invents "oral tradition," let him define it for himself. For "oral" and "written" or "written" versus "oral" are notions that have been as heavily invested as the notions of "true" and "false" have always been. (If writing, as mentioned earlier, does not express language but encompasses it, then where does the written stop? The line distinguishing societies with writing from those without writing seems most ill-defined and leaves much to be desired . . .) Living is neither oral nor written—how can the living and the lived be contained in the merely oral? Furthermore, when she composes on life she not only gives information, entertains, develops, or expands the imagination. Not only educates. Only practices a craft. "Mind breathes mind," a civilized man wrote, "power feels power, and absorbs it, as it were. The telling of stories refreshes the mind as a bath refreshes the body; it gives exercise to the intellect and its powers; it tests the judgment and the feelings."[14] Man's view is always reduced to man's mind. For this is the part of himself he values most. THE MIND. The intellect and its powers. Storytelling allows the "civilized" narrator above all to renew his mind and exercise power through his intellect. Even though the motto reads "Think, act, and feel," his task, he believes, is to ease the passage of the story *from mind to mind*. She, however, who sets out to revive the forgotten, to survive and supersede it ("From stone. Layers. Of stone upon stone between the layers, dormant. No more" [T. Hak Kyung Cha].[15]), she never speaks of and cannot be content with mere matters of the mind—such as mind transmission. The storyteller has long been known as a personage of power. True, she partakes in this living heritage of power. But her powers do more than illuminate or refresh the mind. They extinguish as quickly as they set fire. They wound as easily as they soothe. And not necessarily the mind. Abraham Lincoln accurately observed that "the sharpness of a refusal, or the edge of a rebuke, may be blunted by an appropriate story, so as to save wounded feeling and yet serve the purpose . . . story-telling as an emollient saves me much friction and distress."[16] Yet this is but one more among the countless functions of storytelling. Humidity, receptivity, fecundity. Again, her speech is seen, heard, smelled, tasted, and touched. Great Mother is the goddess of all waters, the protectress of women and of childbearing, the unweary sentient hearer, the healer and also the bringer of diseases. She who gives always accepts, she who wishes to preserve never fails to refresh. Regenerate.

> She was already in her mid-sixties
> when I discovered that she would listen to me
> to all my questions and speculations.
> I was only seven or eight years old then. (Leslie Marmon Silko)[17]

Salivate, secrete the words. No water, no birth, no death, no life. No speech, no song, no story, no force, no power. The entire being is engaged in the act of speaking-listening-weaving-procreating. If she does not cry she will turn into stone. Utter, weep, wet, let it flow so as to break through (it). Layers of stone amidst layers of stone. Break with her own words. The interrelation of woman, water, and word pervades African cosmogonies. Among the Dogon, for example, the process of regeneration which the eight ancestors of the Dogon people had to undergo was carried out in the waters of the womb of the female Nummo (the Nummo spirits form a male and female Pair whose essence is divine) *while she spoke* to herself and to her own sex, accompanied by the male Nummo's voice. "The spoken Word entered into her and wound itself round her womb in a spiral of eight turns . . . the spiral of the Word gave to the womb its regenerative movement." Of the fertilizing power of words and their transmissions through women, it is further said that:

> the first Word had been pronounced [read "scanned"] in front of the genitalia of a woman. . . . The Word finally came from the ant-hill, that is, from the mouth of the seventh Nummo [the seventh ancestor and master of speech], which is to say from a woman's genitalia.
> The Second Word, contained in the craft of weaving, emerged from a mouth, which was also the primordial sex organ, in which the first childbirths took place.[18]

Thus, as a wise Dogon elder (Ogotemmêli) pointed out, "issuing from a

woman's sexual part, the Word enters another sexual part, namely the ear."
(The ear is considered to be bisexual, the auricle being male and the auditory
aperture, female.) From the ear, it will, continuing the cycle, go to the
sexual part where it encircles the womb. African traditions conceive of
speech as a gift of God/dess and a force of creation. In Fulfulde, the word for
"speech" (haala) has the connotation of "giving strength," and by extension
of "making material." Speech is the materialization, externalization, and
internalization of the vibrations of forces. That is why, A. Hampate Ba
noted, "every manifestation of a force in any form whatever is to be regarded
as its speech . . . everything in the universe speaks. . . . If speech is
strength, that is because it creates a *bond of coming-and-going* which generates *movement and rhythm* and therefore *life and action* [my italics]. This
movement to and fro is symbolized by the weaver's feet going up and down
. . . (the symbolism of the loom is entirely based on creative speech in
action)."[19] Making material: spinning and weaving is a euphonious heritage
of wo/mankind handed on from generation to generation of weavers within
the clapping of the shuttle and the creaking of the block—which the Dogon
call "the creaking of the Word." "The cloth was the Word"; the same term,
soy, is used among the Dogon to signify both the woven material and the
spoken word. Life is a perpetual to and fro, a dis/continuous releasing and
absorbing of the self. Let her weave her story within their stories, her life
amidst their lives. And while she weaves, let her whip, spur, and set them
on fire. Thus making them sing again. Very softly a-new a-gain.

At Once "Black" and "White" Magic

"The witch is a woman; the wizard is a male imitation" (Robert Briffault).
In many parts of the world, magic (and witchcraft) is regarded as essentially
a woman's function. It is said that "in primitive thought every woman is
credited with the possession of magic powers." Yet she who possesses that
power is always the last one to credit it. Old Lao Tzu warned: the wo/man
of virtue is not virtuous; the one who never fails in virtue has no virtue at
all. Practicing power for the sake of power—an idea implied in the widely
assumed image of the witch as exclusively an evil-doer—is an inheritance,
I suspect, of the "civilized" mind. She who brings death and disease also
brings life and health. The line dividing the good and the evil, magic and
witchcraft, does not always seem to be as clear-cut as it should be. In
the southern Celebes, for example, "All the deities and spirits from whom
sorcerers, whether male or female, derive their power are spoken of as their
'grandmothers.'" Throughout Africa, priestesses are called "Mothers," and
the numerous female fetishes served exclusively by women are known as
the "Mother fetishes." Among the Butwa, the female hierophants are named
"the mothers of the Butwa mysteries." Among the Bir, the women are those
who perform the essential ritual of maintaining the sacred fire. In Indonesia,
America, northern Asia, and northern Europe, it has been demonstrated

that "magical practices and primitive priestly functions formerly belonged to the exclusive sphere of women and that they were taken up [appropriated] by men at a comparatively late epoch." Thus, the adoption of female attire by male shamans and priests is a widespread phenomenon that still prevails in today's religious contexts. Imitating women and wearing women's clothes—priestly robes, skirts, aprons, sottanas, woven loincloches—are regarded as bestowing greater power: the Mothers' power.[20] Of making material. Of composing on life. Her speech, her storytelling is at once magic, sorcery, and religion. It enchants. It animates, sets into motion, and rouses the forces that lie dormant in things, in beings. It is "bewitching." At once "black" and "white" magic. Which, however, causes sickness and death? which brings joy into life? For white, remember, is the color for mourning in many cultures. The same "medicines," the same dances, the same sorcery are said to be used in both. As occasion arises, the same magic may serve for beneficent *and* maleficent ends. This is why her power is so dreaded; because it can be used for harm; because when it is wielded by one sex, it arouses alarm in the other. The (wizard's) game dates from the times when every practice of this art by women became a threat to men and was automatically presumed to be malignant in intention; when every magic woman must necessarily be a witch—no longer a fairy who works wonders nor a Mother-priestess-prophetess who nurtures, protects, restores, and warns against ill-will. Ill assumption leads to ill action. Men appropriate women's power of "making material" to themselves and, not infrequently, corrupt it out of ignorance. The story becomes *just a* story. It becomes a good or bad lie. And in the more "civilized" contexts where women are replaced and excluded from magico-religious functions, adults who still live on storytelling become bums who spend their time feeding on lies, "them big old lies we tell when we're jus' sittin' around here on the store porch doin' nothin'." When Zora Neale Hurston came back to Eatonville, Florida, to collect old stories, her home folks proudly told her: "Zora, you come to de right place if lies is what you want. Ah'm gointer lie up a nation"; or "Now, you gointer hear lies above suspicion"; or else "We kin tell you some lies most any ole time. We never run outer lies and lovin'."[21] All right, let them call it lie, let us smile and call it lie too if that satisfies them, but "let de lyin' go on!" For we do not *just* lie, we lie and love, we "lie up a nation," and our lies are "above suspicion." How can they be otherwise when they derive their essence from that gift of God: speech? Speech, that active agent in our Mothers' magic; speech, which owes its fertilizing power to . . . who else but the Mother of God?

The Woman Warrior: She Who Breaks Open the Spell

"Thought-Woman / is sitting in her room / and whatever she thinks about / appears. / She thought of her sisters, / . . . / and together they created the Universe / . . . / Thought-Woman, the spider, / named things and / as she named them / they appeared (Leslie Marmon Silko).[22] The touch infinitely delicate awakens, restores them to life, letting them surge forth in their own measures and their own rhythms. The touch infinitely attentive of a fairy's wand, a woman's voice, or a woman's hand, which goes to meet things in the dark and pass them on without deafening, without extinguishing in the process. Intense but gentle, it holds words out in the direction of things or lays them down nearby things so as to call them and breathe new life into them. Not to capture, to chain them up, nor to be mean. Not to instruct nor to discipline. But to kindle that zeal which hibernates within each one of us. "Speech may create peace, as it may destroy it. It is like fire," wrote A. Hampate Ba, "One ill-advised word may start a war just as one blazing twig may touch off a great conflagration. . . . Tradition, then, confers on . . . the Word not only creative power but a double function of saving and destroying."[23] Her words are like fire. They burn and they destroy. It is, however, only by burning that they lighten. Destroying and saving, therefore, are here one single process. Not two processes posed in opposition or in conflict. They would like to order everything around hierarchical oppositions. They would like to cut her power into endless opposing halves or cut herself from the Mothers' powers—setting her against either her mother, her godmother, her mother-in-law, her grandmother, her daughter, or her granddaughter. One of them has to be wicked so as to break the network of transmission. This is cleverly called jealousy among women, the jealousy of the woman who cannot suffer seeing her daughter or another woman take more pleasure in life than herself. For years and years, centuries and centuries, they have devoted their energies to breaking bonds and spreading discords and confusion. Divide and conquer. Mothers fighting mothers. Here is what an Indian witch has to say on "white skin people / like the belly of a fish / covered with hair":

> . . . . They see no life
> When they look
> they see only objects.
> . . . . They fear
> They fear the world.
> They destroy what they fear.
> They fear themselves.
> . . . . Stolen rivers and mountains
> the stolen land will eat their hearts
> and jerk their mouths from the Mother.
> The people will starve.[24]

These are excerpts of a story passed on by Leslie Marmon Silko. The story is the vision of a witch who, a long time ago, at a contest of witches from all the pueblos, "didn't show off any dark thunder charcoals or red anthill beads" like the other witches, but only asked them to listen: "What I have is a story. . . . laugh if you want to / but as I tell the story / it will begin to happen." Scanned by the refrain "set in motion now / set in motion / to work for us" the story thus unfolds, naming as it proceeds the killing, the destruction, the foul deed, the loss of the white man, and with it, the doom of the Indian people. "It isn't so funny. . . . Take it back. Call that story back," said the audience by the end of the story, but the witch answered: "It's already turned loose / It's already coming. / It can't be called back." A story is *not* just a story. Once the forces have been aroused and set into motion, they can't simply be stopped at someone's request. Once told, the story is bound to circulate; humanized, it may have a temporary end, but its effects linger on and its end is never truly an end. Who among us has not, to a certain extent, felt what George Ebers, for example, felt toward his mother's stories: "When the time of rising came, I climbed joyfully into my mother's warm bed, and never did I listen to more beautiful fairy tales than at those hours. They became instinct with life to me and have always remained so. . . . It is a singular thing that actual events which happened in those early days have largely vanished from my memory, but the fairy tales I heard and secretly experienced became firmly impressed on my mind."[25] The young beautiful fairy and the old ugly witch, remember, have the same creative power, the same decisive force of speech. As she names them, they appear . . . The story tells us not only what might have happened, but also what *is happening* at an unspecified time and place. Whenever Ebers had the slightest doubt in mind, he would immediately appeal to his mother, for he thought "she could never be mistaken and knew that she always told the truth." Lying is not a mother's attribute. Or else, if lying is what you think she does, then she will "never run outer lies and lovin'."

> When we Chinese girls listened to the adult talk-story, we learned that we failed if we grew up to be but wives or slaves. We could be heroines, swordswomen. . . . Night after night my mother would talk-story until we fell asleep. I couldn't tell where the stories left off and the dreams began, her voice the voice of the heroines in my sleep. . . . At last I saw that I too had been in the presence of great power, my mother talking-story. . . . She said I would grow up a wife and a slave, but she taught me the song of the warrior woman, Fa Mu Lan. I would have to grow up a warrior woman. (Maxine Hong Kingston)[26]

She fires her to achievement and she fires her with desire to emulate. She fires her with desire to emulate the heroines of whom she told and she fires her with desire to emulate the heroine who tells of the other heroines, "I too had been in the presence of great power, my mother talking-story." What is transmitted from generation to generation is not only the stories, but the very power of transmission. The stories are highly inspiring, and so is she, the untiring storyteller. She, who suffocates the codes of lie and truth. She, who loves to tell and retell and loves to hear them told and retold night after night again and again. Hong Kingston grows up a warrior woman and a warrior-woman-storyteller herself. She is the woman warrior who continues to fight in America the fight her mothers fought in China. Even though she is often "mad at the Chinese for lying so much," and blames her mother for lying with stories, she happily *lets the lying go on* by retelling us her mother's "lies" and offering us versions of her stories that can be called lies themselves. Her brother's version of a story, she admits it herself, "may be better than mine because of its bareness, not twisted into designs." Her brother, indeed, is no woman warrior-storyteller. Hong Kingston's apparent confusion of story and reality is, in fact, no confusion at all since it is an unending one; her parents often accuse her of not being able to "tell a joke from real life" and to understand that Chinese "like to say the opposite." Even the events described by her relatives in their letters from China she finds suspect: "I'd like to go to China and see those people and find out what's cheat story and what's not." The confusion she experienced in her girlhood is the confusion we all experience in life, even when we think, as adults, that we have come up with definite criteria for the true and the false. What is true and what is not, and who decides so if we wish not to have this decision made *for* us? When, for example, Hong Kingston yells at her mother: "You can't stop me from talking. You tried to cut off my tongue, but it didn't work," we not only know she is quite capable of telling "fancy" from "facts," we are also carried a step further in this differentiation by her mother's answer: "I cut it to make you talk more, not less, you dummy."[27] (Her mother has already affirmed elsewhere that she cut it so that her daughter would not be "tongue-tied.") The opening story of *The Woman Warrior* is a forbidden story ("No Name Woman") that begins with Hong Kingston's mother saying: "You must not tell anyone what I am about to tell you." Twenty years after she heard this story about her father's sister who drowned herself and her baby in the family well, not only has Hong Kingston broken open the spell cast upon her aunt by retelling the story—"I alone devote pages of paper to her"—but she has done it in such a way as to reach thousands and thousands of listeners and readers. Tell it to the world. To preserve is to pass on, not to keep for oneself. A story told is a story bound to circulate. By telling her daughter not to tell it to anyone, the mother knew what she was supposed to say, for "That's what Chinese say. We like to say the opposite." She knew she was in fact the first before her daughter to break open the spell. The family cursed her, she who committed adultery and was such a spite suicide (the aunt); the men (her brothers) tabooed her name and went on living "as if she had never been born"; but the women (Hong Kingston's mother and those who partook in this aunt's death) would have to carry her with(in) them for life and pass her on, even though they condemned her no less. For every woman is the woman of all women, and this one died first and foremost for being a woman. ("Now that you have started to menstruate," the mother warned her daughter, "what happened to her could happen to you. Don't humiliate us.") Hong Kingston has, in her own way, retained many of the principles of her mother's storytelling. If, in composing with "fancy" and "fact," the latter knows when she should say "white is white" and when she should say "white is black" in referring to the same thing, her daughter also knows when to dot her i's and when not to. Her writing, neither fiction nor nonfiction, constantly invites the reader either to drift naturally from the realm of imagination to that of actuality or to live them both without ever being able to draw a clear line between them yet never losing sight of their differentiation. What Hong Kingston does *not* tell us about her mother but allows us to read between the lines and in the gaps of her stories reveals as much about her mother as what she *does* tell us about her. This, I feel, is the most "truthful" aspect of her work, the very power of her storytelling. *The Woman Warrior* ends with a story Hong Kingston's mother told her, not when she was young, she says, "but recently, when I told her I also talk-story." The beginning of the story, which relates how the family in China came to love the theater through the grandmother's passion for it and her generosity, is the making of the mother. The ending of the story, which recalls one of the songs the poetess Ts'ai Yen composed while she was a captive of the barbarians and how it has been passed down to the Chinese, is the making of the daughter—Hong Kingston herself. Two powerful woman storytellers meet at the end of the book, both working at strengthening the ties among women while commemorating and transmitting the powers of our foremothers. At once a grandmother, a poetess, a storyteller, and a woman warrior.

A Cure and a Protection from Illness

> I grew up with storytelling. My earliest memories are of my grandmother telling me stories while she watered the morning-glories in her yard. Her stories were about incidents from long ago, incidents which occurred before she was born but which she told as certainly as if she had been there. The chanting or telling of ancient stories to effect certain cures or protect from illness and harm have always been part of the Pueblo's curing ceremonies. I feel the power that the stories still have to bring us together, especially when there is loss and grief. (Leslie Marmon Silko)[28]

Refresh, regenerate, or purify. Telling stories and watering morning-glories both function to the same effect. For years and years she has been renewing her forces with regularity to keep them intact. Such ritual ablutions—the telling and retelling—allow her to recall the incidents that occurred before she was born with as much certainty as if she had witnessed them herself. The words passed down from mouth to ear (one sexual part to another sexual part), womb to womb, body to body are the remembered ones. S/He whose belly cannot contain (also read "retain") words, says a Malinke song, will succeed at nothing. The further they move away from the belly, the more liable they are to be corrupted. (Words that come from the MIND and are passed on directly "from mind to mind" are, consequently, highly suspect . . .) In many parts of Africa, the word "belly" refers to the notion of occult power. Among the Basaa of Cameroon, for example, the term *hu*, meaning (a human being's) "stomach," is used to designate "a thing whose origin and nature nobody knows," but which is unanimously attributed to women and their powers. A Basaa man said he heard from his fathers that "it was the woman who introduced the *hu*" into human life. In several myths of the Basaa's neighboring peoples, *evu*, the equivalent of the Basaa's *hu*, is said to have requested that it be carried in the woman's belly at the time it first met her and to have entered her body through her sexual part. Thus associated with women, the *hu* or *evu* is considered both maleficent and beneficent. It is at times equated with devil and sorcery, other times with prophecy and anti-sorcery. S/He who is said to "have a *hu*" is both feared and admired. S/He is the one who sees the invisible, moves with ease in the night-world as if in broad daylight, and is endowed with uncommon, exceptional intelligence, penetration, and intuition.[29] Woman and magic. Her power resides in her belly—Our Mother's belly—for her cure is not an isolated act but a total social phenomenon. Sorcery, according to numerous accounts, is hereditary solely within the matrilineal clan; and a man, in countless cases, can only become a sorcerer (a wizard) through the transmission of power by a sorceress (witch). He who understands the full power of woman and/in storytelling also understands that life is not to be found in the mind nor in the heart, but there where she carries it:

> I will tell you something about stories, [he said]
> They aren't just entertainment.
> Don't be fooled.
> They are all we have, you see,
> all we have to fight off
> illness and death.
>
> You don't have anything
> if you don't have the stories. . . .
> He rubbed his belly.
> I keep them here [he said]
> Here, put your hand on it
> See, it is moving
> There is life here
> for the people.[30]

The story as a cure and a protection is at once musical, historical, poetical, ethical, educational, magical, and religious. In many parts of the world, the healers are known as the living memories of the people. Not only do they hold esoteric and technical knowledge, but they are also kept closely informed of the problems of their communities and are entrusted with all family affairs. In other words, they know everyone's story. Concerned with the slightest incident, they remain very alert to their entourage and heedful of their patients' talks. They derive their power from *listening* to the others and *absorbing* daily realities. While they cure, they take into them their patients' possessions and obsessions and let the latter's illnesses become theirs. Their actions imply a personal investment of which the healing technics form only a part and are a reflection. "I see the patient's psychic life," many of them say, "nothing is hidden from me." Dis-ease breeds dis-ease; life engenders life. The very close relationship these healers maintain with their patients remains the determining factor of the cure. Curing means re-generating, for understanding is creating. The principle of healing rests on *reconciliation*, hence the necessity for the family and/or the community to cooperate, partake in, and witness the recovery, de-possession, regeneration of the sick. The act of healing is therefore a socio-cultural act, a collective, motherly undertaking. (Here, it is revealing to remember that male healers often claim to be wedded to at least two wives: a terrestrial one *and* a spiritual one. The spiritual wife or the "woman spirit" protects the healer and is the source of his powers. She is the one who "has knowledge" and from whom he seeks advice in all matters. When she becomes too demanding and too possessive, it is said that only one person can send her away: the healer's own mother.)[31] The storyteller, besides being a great mother, a teacher, a poetess, a warrior, a musician, a historian, a fairy, and a witch, is a healer and a protectress. Her chanting or telling of stories, as Marmon Silko notices, has the power of bringing us together, especially when there is sickness, fear, and grief. "'When they look / they see only objects,' / They fear / they never stop fearing / but they see not fear the living thing. / They follow not its movements / for they fear not to fear. / 'They destroy what they fear. / They fear themselves.' / They destroy the stories / let these be confused or forgotten / let these be only stories / They would like that . . ."

> Stolen rivers and mountains
> the stolen land will eat their hearts
> and jerk their mouths from the Mother.
> The people will starve.[32]

"Tell It the Way They Tell It"

It is a commonplace for those who consider the story to be just a story to believe that, in order to appropriate the "traditional" storytellers' powers and to produce the same effects as theirs, it suffices to "look for the structure of their narratives." *See them as they see each other*, so goes the (anthropological) creed. "Tell it the way *they* tell it instead of imposing *our* structure," they repeat with the best of intentions and a conscience so clear that they pride themselves on it. Disease breeds disease. Those who function best within definite structures and spend their time structuring their own or their peers' existences must obviously "look for" that which, according to their "findings" and analyses, is supposed to be "the structure of their [the storytellers'] narratives." What we "look for" is un/fortunately what we shall find. The anthropologist, as we already know, does not *find* things; s/he *makes* them. And makes them up. The structure is therefore not something given, entirely external to the person who structures, but a projection of that person's way of handling realities, here narratives. It is perhaps difficult for an analytical or analytically trained mind to admit that recording, gathering, sorting, deciphering, analyzing and synthesizing, dissecting and articulating are already "imposing our [/a] structure," a structural activity, a structuring of the mind, a whole mentality. (Can one "look for a structure" without structuring?) But it is particularly difficult for a dualistic or dualistically trained mind to recognize that "looking for the structure of their narratives" already involves the separation of the structure from the narratives, of the structure from that which is structured, of the narrative from the narrated, and so on. It is, once more, as if form and content stand apart; as if the structure can remain fixed, immutable, independent of and unaffected by the changes the narratives undergo; as if a structure can only function as a standard mold within the old determinist schema of cause and product. Listen, for example, to what a man of the West had to say on the form of the story:

> Independent of the content which the story carries, and which may vary from history to nonsense, is the form of the story which is practically the same in all stories. The content is varied and particular, the form is the same and universal. Now there are four main elements in the form of each story, viz. the beginning, the development, the climax, and the end.[33]

Just like the Western drama with its four or five acts. A drama whose naïve claim to universality would not fail to make this man of the West our laughingstock. "A good story," another man of the West asserted, "must have a beginning that rouses interest, a succession of events that is orderly and complete, a climax that forms the story's point, and an end that leaves the mind at rest."[34] No criteria other than those quoted here show a more thorough investment of the Western mind. *Get them*—children, story-believers—*at the start; make your point* by ordering events to a definite *climax;* then *round out to completion;* descend to a rapid close—not one, for example, that puzzles or keeps them puzzling over the story, but one that *leaves the mind at rest.* In other words, to be "good" a story must be built in conformity with the ready-made idea some people—Western adults—have of reality, that is to say, a set of prefabricated schemata (prefabricated by whom?) they value out of habit, conservatism, and ignorance (of other ways of telling and listening to stories). If these criteria are to be adopted, then countless non-Western stories will fall straight into the category of "bad" stories. Unless one makes it up or invents a reason for its absence, one of these four elements required always seems to be missing. The stories in question either have no development, no climax that forms the story's point, or no end that leaves the mind at rest. (One can say of the majority of these stories that their endings precisely refute such generalization and rationale for they offer no security of this kind. An example among endless others is the moving story of "The Laguna People" passed on by Marmon Silko, which ends with a little girl, her sister, and the people turning into stone while they sat on top of a mesa, after they had escaped the flood in their home village below. Because of the disquieting nature of the resolution here, the storytellers

[Marmon Silko and her aunt] then add, as a compromise to the fact-oriented mind of today's audience: "The story ends there. / Some of the stories / Aunt Susi told / have this kind of ending. / There are no explanations."[35] There is no point [to be] made either.) "Looking for the structure of *their* narratives" so as to "tell it the way *they* tell it" is an attempt at remedying this ignorance of other ways of telling and listening (and, obviously, at re-validating the nativist discourse). In doing so, however, rare are those who realize that what they come up with is not "structure of *their* narratives" but a reconstruction of the story that, at best, makes a number of its functions appear. Rare are those who acknowledge the unavoidable transfer of values in the "search" and admit that "the attempt will remain largely illusory: we shall never know if the other, into whom we cannot, after all, dissolve, fashions from the elements of [her/]his social existence a synthesis exactly superimposable on that which we have worked out."[36] The attempt will remain illusory as long as the controlled succession of certain mental operations which constitutes the structural activity is not made explicit and dealt with—not just mentioned. Life is not a (Western) drama of four or five acts. Sometimes it just drifts along; it may go on year after year without development, without climax, without definite beginnings or endings. Or it may accumulate climax upon climax, and if one chooses to mark it with beginnings and endings, then everything has a beginning and an ending. There are, in this sense, no good or bad stories. In life, we usually don't know when an event is occurring; we think it is starting when it is already ending; and we don't see its in/significance. The present, which saturates the total field of our environment, is often invisible to us. The structural activity that does not carry on the cleavage between form and content but emphasizes the interrelation of the material and the intelligible is an activity in which structure should remain an unending question: one that speaks him/her as s/he speaks it, brings it to intelligibility.

"The Story Must Be Told.
There Must Not Be Any Lies"

"Looking for the structure of their narratives" is like looking for the pear shape in Erik Satie's musical composition *Trois Pièces en Forme de Poire* (Three Pieces in a Pear Shape). (The composition was written after Satie met with Claude Debussy, who criticized his music for "lacking of form.") If structure, as a man (R. Barthes) pertinently defines it, is "the residual deposit of duration," then again, rare are those who can handle it by letting it come, instead of hunting for it or hunting it down, filling it with their own marks and markings so as to consign it to the meaningful and lay claim to it. *"They see no life / When they look / they see only objects."* The ready-made idea they have of reality prevents their perceiving the story as a living thing, an organic process, a way of life. What is taken for stories, only stories, are fragments of/in life, fragments that never stop interacting while being complete in themselves. A story in Africa may last three months. The storyteller relates it night after night, continually, or s/he starts it one night and takes it up again from that point three months later. Meanwhile, as the occasion arises, s/he may start on yet another story. Such is life . . . . :

> The gussucks [the Whites] did not understand the story; they could not see the way it must be told, year after year as the old man had done, without lapse or silence. . . .
> "It began a long time ago," she intoned steadily . . . she did not pause or hesitate; she went on with the story, and she never stopped. . . .[37]

"Storyteller," from which these lines are excerpted, is another story, another gift of life passed on by Marmon Silko. It presents an example of multiple storytelling in which story and life merge, the story being as complex as life and life being as simple as a story. The story of "Storyteller" is the layered making of four storytellers: Marmon Silko, the woman in the story, her grandmother, and the person referred to as "the old man." Except for Marmon Silko who plays here the role of the coordinator, each of these three storytellers has her/his own story to live and live with. Despite the differences in characters or in subject matter, their stories closely interact and constantly overlap. The woman makes of her story a continuation of her grandmother's, which was left with no ending—the grandmother being thereby compelled to bear it (the story) until her death, her knees and knuckles swollen grotesquely, "swollen with anger" as she explained it. She bore it, knowing that her granddaughter will have to bear it too: "It will take a long time," she said, "but the story must be told. There must not be any lies." Sometime after her death, exactly when does not matter, when the time comes, the granddaughter picks up the story where her grandmother left it and carries it to its end accordingly, the way "it must be told." She carries it to a certain completion by bringing in death where she intends to have it in her story: the white storeman who lied in her grandma's story and was the author of her parents' death would have to pay for his lies, but his death would also have to be of his own making. The listener/reader does not (have to) know whether the storeman in the granddaughter's story is the same as the one who, according to the grandmother, "left right after that [after he lied and killed]" (hence making it apparently impossible for the old woman to finish her story). A storeman becomes *the* storeman, the man in the store, the man in the story. (The truthfulness of the story, as we already know, does not limit itself to the realm of facts.) Which story? *The* story. What grandma began, granddaughter completes and passes on to be further completed. As a storyteller, the woman (the granddaughter) does not directly kill; she decides when and where that storeman will find death, but she does not carry out a hand-to-hand fight and her murder of him is no murder in the common, factual sense of the term: all she needs to do is set in motion the necessary forces and let them act on their own.

They asked her again, what happened to the man from the Northern Commercial Store. "He lied to them. He told them it was safe to drink. But I will not lie. . . . I killed him," she said, "but I don't lie."

When she is in jail, the Gussuck attorney advises her to tell the court the *truth*, which is that it was an accident, that the storeman ran after her in the cold and fell through the ice. That's all what she has to say—then "they will let [her] go home. Back to [her] village."

She shook her head. "I will not change the story, not even to escape this place and go home. I intended that he die. The story must be told as it is." The attorney exhaled loudly; his eyes looked tired. "Tell her that she could not have killed him that way. He was a white man. He ran after her without a parka or mittens. She could not have planned that."[38]

When the helpful, conscientious (full-of-the-white-man's-complex-of-superiority) attorney concludes that he will do "all [he] can for her" and will explain to the judge that "her mind is confused," she laughs out loud and finally decides to tell him the story anew: "*It began a long time ago . . .*" (my italics). He says she could not have killed that white man because, again, for him the story is just a story. But Thought-Woman, Spider-Woman is a fairy and a witch who protects her people and tells stories to effect cures. As she names Death, Death appears. The spell is cast. Only death gives an ending to the stories in "Storyteller." (The old man's story of the giant bear overlaps with the granddaughter's story and ends the moment the old man—the storyteller—dies.) Marmon Silko as a storyteller never loses sight of the difference between truth and fact. Her naming retains the accuracy and magic of our grand mothers' storytelling without ever confining itself to the realm of factual naming. It is accurate because it is at once extremely flexible and rigid, not because it wishes to stick to certain rules of correctness for reasons of mere conservatism (scholars studying traditional storytelling are often impressed by the storyteller's "necessity of telling the stories correctly," as they put it). It is accurate because it partakes in the setting into motion of forces that lie dormant in us. Because, as African storytellers sing, "the tongue that falsifies the word / taints the blood of [her/]him that lies."[39] Because she who bears it in her belly cannot cut herself off from herself. Off from the bond of coming-and-going. Off from her great mothers.

"May my story be beautiful and unwind like a long thread . . . , she recites as she begins her story. Here she chants the time-honored formula that opens the tales of Kabyle folksingers, but what she chants, in a way, is a variant of what her African griotte-sisters chant every time they set about composing on life: tell me so that I can tell my hearers what I have heard from you who heard it from your mother and your great mother. . . . Each woman, like each people, has her own way of unrolling the ties that bind. Storytelling, the oldest form of building historical consciousness in community, constitutes a rich oral legacy, whose values have regained all importance recently, especially in the context of writings by women of color. She who works at un-learning the dominant language of "civilized" missionaries also has to learn how to un-write and write anew. And she often does so by re-establishing the contact with her foremothers, so that living tradition can never congeal into fixed forms, so that life keeps on nurturing life, so that what is understood as the Past continues to provide the link for the Present and the Future. As our elder Lao Tzu says, "Without allowance for filling, a valley will run dry; / Without allowance for growing, creation will stop functioning." Tradition as on-going commitment, and in women's own terms. The story is beautiful, because or therefore it unwinds like a thread. A long thread, for there is no end in sight. Or the end she reaches leads actually to another end, another opening, another "residual deposit of duration." Every woman partakes in the chain of guardianship and of transmission—in other words, of creation. Every griotte who dies is a whole library that burns down. Tell it so that they can tell it. So that it may become larger than its measure, always larger than its own in/significance. In this horizontal and vertical vertigo, she carries the story on, motivated at once by the desire to finish it and the necessity to remind herself and others that "it's never finished." A lifetime story. More than a lifetime. One that will be picked up where it is left; when, it does not matter. For the time is already set. "It will take a long time . . . ," the grandmother ends; "it began long ago . . . ," the granddaughter starts. The time is set, she said; not in terms of when exactly but of what: what exactly must be told, and how. "There must not be any lies." Like Maxine Hong Kingston who decided to tell the world the forbidden story of her tabooed aunt, the "No Name Woman," Marmon Silko's granddaughter-storyteller opens the spell cast upon her people, by re-setting into motion what was temporarily delayed in the story of her grandmother. The burden of the story-truth. She knew that during her own lifetime the moment would come when she would be able to assume her responsibility and resume the grandmother's interrupted story-trajectory. She killed the one who lied to her people, who actively participated in the slow extinction of her race. She killed Him. She killed the white storeman in "her story" which is not "just a story": "I intended that he die. The story must be told as it is." To ask, like the white attorney, whether the story she tells makes any sense, whether it is factually possible, whether it is true or not is to cause confusion by an incorrect question. Difference here is not understood as difference. Her (story) world remains therefore irreducibly foreign to Him. The man can't hear it the way she means it. He sees her as victim, as unfortunate object of hazard. "Her mind is confused," he concludes. She views herself as the teller, the un-making subject, the agent of the storeman's death, the moving force of the story. She didn't know when exactly she would be able to act in concordance with fate (she is also fate), but she planned and waited for the ripe moment to come, so that what appeared as an accident was carefully matured. Her sense of the story overflows the boundaries of patriarchal time and truth. It overflows the notion of story as finished product ("just a story")—one neatly wrapped, that rounds off with a normative finale and "leaves the mind at rest." Marmon

Silko's "Storyteller" keeps the reader puzzling over the story as it draws to a close. Again, truth does not make sense. It exceeds measure: the woman storyteller sees her vouching for it as a defiance of a whole system of the white man's lies. She values this task, this responsibility over immediate release (her being freed from imprisonment through the attorney's advice), over immediate enlightenment and gratification (vengeance for the sake of vengeance). Even if the telling condemns her present life, what is more important is to (re-)tell the story as she thinks it should be told; in other words, to maintain the difference that allows (her) truth to live on. The difference. He does not hear or see. He cannot give. Never the given, for there is no end in sight.

There are these stories that just have to be told in the same way the wind goes blowing across the mesa

    —Leslie Marmon Silko, "Stories and Their Tellers"

A Bedtime Story

> Once upon a time,
> an old Japanese legend
> goes as told
> by Papa,
> an old woman traveled through
> many small villages
> seeking refuge
> for the night.
> Each door opened
> a sliver
> in answer to her knock
> then closed.
> Unable to walk
> any further
> she wearily climbed a hill
> found a clearing
> and there lay down to rest
> a few moments to catch
> her breath.
>
> The villagetown below
> lay asleep except
> for a few starlike lights.
> Suddenly the clouds opened
> and a full moon came into view
> over the town.
>
> The old woman sat up
> turned toward

the village town
and in supplication
called out
Thank you people
of the village,
if it had not been for your
kindness
in refusing me a bed
for the night
these humble eyes would never
have seen this
memorable sight.

Papa paused, I waited.
In the comfort of our
hilltop home in Seattle
overlooking the valley,
I shouted
"That's the END?"

—Mitsuye Yamada, *Camp Notes*

References

1. Theresa Hak Kyung Cha, *Dictée* (New York: Tanam Press, 1982), p. 133.
2. Maxine Hong Kingston, *The Woman Warrior* (1975, rpt. New York: Vintage Books, 1977), p. 235.
3. Herman Harrell Horne, *Story-telling, Questioning and Studying* (New York: Macmillan, 1917), pp. 23–24.
4. *Dictée*, p. 123.
5. Gayl Jones, *Corregidora* (New York: Random House, 1975), p. 9.
6. Ibid., p. 184.
7. *Dictée*, p. 106.
8. Ibid., p. 130.
9. Horne, p. 34.
10. Katherine Dunlap Cather, *Educating by Story-telling* (New York: World Book Company, 1926), pp. 5–6.
11. Clark W. Hetherington, introduction in ibid., pp. xiii–xiv.
12. Anna Birgitta Rooth, *The Importance of Storytelling: A Study Based on Field Work in Northern Alaska* (Uppsala, Sweden: Almqvist & Wiksell, 1976), p. 88.
13. A. Hampate Ba, "The Living Tradition," *General History of Africa, I. Methodology and African Prehistory*, ed. J. Ki Zerbo (UNESCO, Heineman, Univ. of California Press, 1981), p. 167.
14. Froebel quoted in Horne, p. 29.
15. *Dictée*, p. 150.
16. Quoted in Horne, p. 30.

17. Leslie Marmon Silko, "Aunt Susie," *Storyteller* (New York: Seaver Books, 1981), p. 4.

18. Marcel Griaule, *Conversations with Ogotemmêli* (1965, rpt. New York: Oxford Univ. Press, 1975), pp. 26, 138–39.

19. Ba, "The Living Tradition," pp. 170–71.

20. On the part played by women in religious cults and their powers, see Robert Briffault, *The Mothers* (1927, rpt. New York: Atheneum, 1977), especially the chapter on "The Witch and the Priestess," pp. 269–88.

21. Zora Neale Hurston, *Mules and Men*, excerpts in *I Love Myself*, ed. A. Walker (Old Westbury, N.Y.: Feminist Press, 1979), pp. 85, 93, 89.

22. Leslie Marmon Silko, *Ceremony* (New York: Viking Press, 1977), p. 1.

23. "The Living Tradition," p. 171.

24. *Ceremony*, pp. 132–38, or *Storyteller*, pp. 130–37.

25. Quoted in Cather, p. 22.

26. *Woman Warrior*, pp. 23–24.

27. Ibid., pp. 189, 237, 240, 235.

28. *Ceremony*, back cover page.

29. For more information on the *hu* and its relation to women, see Meinrad P. Hebga, *Sorcellerie—Chimère dangereuse . . . ?* (Abidjan, Ivory Coast: INADES, 1979), pp. 87–115, 258–65.

30. *Ceremony*, p. 2.

31. Maurice Dorès, *La Femme village* (Paris: L'Harmattan, 1981), pp. 20–25.

32. *Ceremony*, pp. 132–38.

33. Horne, p. 26.

34. E. P. St. John, *Stories and Story-telling*, quoted in Horne, p. 26.

35. *Storyteller*, pp. 38–42.

36. Claude Lévi-Strauss, *The Scope of Anthropology*, tr. S. Ortner Paul & R. A. Paul (1967, rpt. London: Jonathan Cape, 1971), p. 14.

37. *Storyteller*, pp. 31–32.

38. Ibid.

39. "The Living Tradition," p. 172.

[1989]

La Güera

Cherríe Moraga

It requires something more than personal experience to gain a philosophy or point of view from any specific event. It is the quality of our response to the event and our capacity to enter into the lives of others that help us to make their lives and experiences our own.

Emma Goldman[1]

I AM THE VERY WELL-EDUCATED DAUGHTER OF A WOMAN WHO, BY THE standards in this country, would be considered largely illiterate. My mother was born in Santa Paula, Southern Caifornia, at a time when much of the central valley there was still farm land. Nearly thirty-five years later, in 1948, she was the only daughter of six to marry an anglo, my father.

I remember all of my mother's stories, probably much better than she realizes. She is a fine story-teller, recalling every event of her life with the vividness of the present, noting each detail right down to the cut and color of her dress. I remember stories of her being pulled out of school at the ages of five, seven, nine, and eleven to work in the fields, along with her brothers and sisters; stories of her father drinking away whatever small profit she was able to make for the family; of her going the long way home to avoid meeting him on the street, staggering toward the same destination. I remember stories of my mother lying about her age in order to get a job as a hat-check girl at Agua Caliente Racetrack in Tijuana. At fourteen, she was the main support of the family. I can still see her walking home alone at 3 a.m., only to turn all of her salary and tips over to her mother, who was pregnant again.

The stories continue through the war years and on: walnut-cracking factories, the Voit Rubber factory, and then the computer boom. I remember my mother doing piecework for the electronics plant in our neighborhood. In the late evening, she would sit in front of the T.V. set, wrapping copper wires into the backs of circuit boards, talking about "keeping up with the younger girls." By that time, she was already in her mid-fifties.

Meanwhile, I was college-prep in school. After classes, I would go with my mother to fill out job applications for her, or write checks for her at the supermarket. We would have the scenario all worked out ahead of time. My mother would sign the check before we'd get to the store. Then, as we'd approach the checkstand, she would say—within earshot of the cashier—"oh honey, you go 'head and make out the check," as if she couldn't be bothered with such an insignificant detail. No one asked any questions.

I was educated, and wore it with a keen sense of pride and satisfaction, my head propped up with the knowledge, from my mother, that my life would be easier than hers. I was educated; but more than this, I was "la güera": fair-skinned. Born with the features of my Chicana mother, but the skin of my Anglo father, I had it made.

No one ever quite told me this (that light was right), but I knew that being light was something valued in my family (who were all Chicano, with the exception of my father). In fact, everything about my upbringing (at least what occurred on a conscious level) attempted to bleach me of what color I did have. Although my mother was fluent in it, I was never taught much Spanish at home. I picked up what I did learn from school and from over-heard snatches of conversation among my relatives and mother. She often called other lower-income Mexicans "braceros," or "wet-backs," refer-ring to herself and her family as "a different class of people." And yet, the real story was that my family, too, had been poor (some still are) and farmworkers. My mother can remember this in her blood as if it were yesterday. But this is something she would like to forget (and rightfully), for to her, on a basic economic level, being Chicana meant being "less." It was through my mother's desire to protect her children from poverty and illiteracy that we became "anglocized"; the more effectively we could pass in the white world, the better guaranteed our future.

From all of this, I experience, daily, a huge disparity between what I was born into and what I was to grow up to become. Because (as Goldman suggests) these stories my mother told me crept under my "güera" skin. I had no choice but to enter into the life of my mother. *I had no choice.* I took her life into my heart, but managed to keep a lid on it as long as I feigned being the happy, upwardly mobile heterosexual.

When I finally lifted the lid to my lesbianism, a profound connection with my mother reawakened in me. It wasn't until I acknowledged and confronted my own lesbianism in the flesh, that my heartfelt identification with and empathy for my mother's oppression—due to being poor, uneducated, and Chicana—was realized. My lesbianism is the avenue through which I have learned the most about silence and oppression, and it continues to be the most tactile reminder to me that we are not free human beings.

You see, one follows the other. I had known for years that I was a lesbian, had felt it in my bones, had ached with the knowledge, gone crazed with the knowledge, wallowed in the silence of it. Silence *is* like starvation. Don't be fooled. It's nothing short of that, and felt most sharply when one has had a full belly most of her life. When we are not physically starving, we have the luxury to realize psychic and emotional starvation. It is from this starvation that other starvations can be recognized—if one is willing to take the risk of making the connection—if one is willing to be responsible to the result of the connection. For me, the connection is an inevitable one.

What I am saying is that the joys of looking like a white girl ain't so great since I realized I could be beaten on the street for being a dyke. If my sister's being beaten because she's Black, it's pretty much the same principle. We're both getting beaten any way you look at it. The connection is blatant; and in the case of my own family, the difference in the privileges attached to looking white instead of brown are merely a generation apart.

In this country, lesbianism is a poverty—as is being brown, as is being a woman, as is being just plain poor. The danger lies in ranking the oppressions. *The danger lies in failing to acknowledge the specificity of the oppression.* The danger lies in attempting to deal with oppression purely from a theoretical base. Without an emotional, heartfelt grappling with the source of our own oppression, without naming the enemy within ourselves and outside of us, no authentic, non-hierarchical connection among oppressed groups can take place.

When the going gets rough, will we abandon our so-called comrades in a flurry of racist/heterosexist/what-have-you panic? To whose camp, then, should the lesbian of color retreat? Her very presence violates the ranking and abstraction of oppression. Do we merely live hand to mouth? Do we merely struggle with the "ism" that's sitting on top of our own heads?

The answer is: yes, I think first we do; and we must do so thoroughly and deeply. But to fail to move out from there will only isolate us in our own oppression—will only insulate, rather than radicalize us.

To illustrate: a gay male friend of mine once confided to me that he continued to feel that, on some level, I didn't trust him because he was male; that he felt, really, if it ever came down to a "battle of the sexes," I might kill him. I admitted that I might very well. He wanted to understand the source of my distrust. I responded, "You're not a woman. Be a woman for a day. Imagine being a woman." He confessed that the thought terrified him because, to him, being a woman meant being raped by men. He *had* felt raped by men; he wanted to forget what that meant. What grew from that discussion was the realization that in order for him to create an authentic alliance with me, he must deal with the primary source of his own sense of oppression. He must, first, emotionally come to terms with what it feels like to be a victim. If he—or anyone—were to truly do this, it would be impossible to discount the oppression of others, except by again forgetting how we have been hurt.

And yet, oppressed groups are forgetting all the time. There are instances of this in the rising Black middle class, and certainly an obvious trend of such "unconsciousness" among white gay men. Because to remember may mean giving up whatever privileges we have managed to squeeze out of this society by virtue of our gender, race, class, or sexuality.

Within the women's movement, the connections among women of different backgrounds and sexual orientations have been fragile, at best. I think this phenomenon is indicative of our failure to seriously address ourselves to some very frightening questions: How have I internalized my own oppression? How have I oppressed? Instead, we have let rhetoric do the job of poetry. Even the word "oppression" has lost its power. We need a new language, better words that can more closely describe women's fear of and resistance to one another; words that will not always come out sounding like dogma.

What prompted me in the first place to work on an anthology by radical women of color was a deep sense that I had a valuable insight to contribute, by virtue of my birthright and background. And yet, I don't really understand first-hand what it feels like being shitted on for being brown. I understand much more about the joys of it—being Chicana and having family are synonymous for me. What I know about loving, singing, crying, telling stories, speaking with my heart and hands, even having a sense of my own soul comes from the love of my mother, aunts, cousins . . .

But at the age of twenty-seven, it is frightening to acknowledge that I have internalized a racism and classism, where the object of oppression is not only someone outside of my skin, but the someone inside my skin. In fact, to a large degree, the real battle with such oppression, for all of us, begins under the skin. I have had to confront the fact that much of what I value about being Chicana, about my family, has been subverted by anglo culture and my own cooperation with it. This realization did not occur to me overnight. For example, it wasn't until long after my graduation from the private college I'd attended in Los Angeles, that I realized the major reason for my total alienation from and fear of my classmates was rooted in class and culture. CLICK.

Three years after graduation, in an apple-orchard in Sonoma, a friend of mine (who comes from an Italian Irish working-class family) says to me, "Cherríe, no wonder you felt like such a nut in school. Most of the people there were white and rich." It was true. All along I had felt the difference, but not until I had put the words "class" and "color" to the experience, did my feelings make any sense. For years, I had berated myself for not being as "free" as my classmates. I completely bought that they simply had more guts than I did—to rebel against their parents and run around the country hitch-hiking, reading books and studying "art." They had enough privilege to be atheists, for chrissake. There was no one around filling in the disparity for me between their parents, who were Hollywood filmmakers, and my parents, who wouldn't know the name of a filmmaker if their lives depended on it (and precisely because their lives didn't depend on it, they couldn't be bothered). But I knew nothing about "privilege" then. White was right. Period. I could pass. If I got educated enough, there would never be any telling.

Three years after that, another CLICK. In a letter to Barbara Smith, I wrote:

I went to a concert where Ntozake Shange was reading. There, everything exploded for me. She was speaking a language that I knew—in the deepest parts of me—existed, and that I had ignored in my own feminist studies and even in my own writing. What Ntosake caught in me is the realization that in my development as a poet, I have, in many ways, denied the voice of my brown mother—the brown in me. I have acclimated to the sound of a white language which, as my father represents it, does not speak to the emotions in my poems—emotions which stem from the love of my mother.

The reading was agitating. Made me uncomfortable. Threw me into a week-long terror of how deeply I was affected. I felt that I had to start all over again. That I turned only to the perceptions of white middle-class women to speak for me and all women. I am shocked by my own ignorance.

Sitting in that auditorium chair was the first time I had realized to the core of me that for years I had disowned the language I knew best—ignored the words and rhythms that were the closest to me. The sounds of my mother and aunts gossiping—half in English, half in Spanish—while drinking cerveza in the kitchen. And the hands—I had cut off the hands in my poems. But not in conversation; still the hands could not be kept down. Still they insisted on moving.

The reading had forced me to remember that I knew things from my roots. But to remember puts me up against what I don't know. Shange's reading agitated me because she spoke with power about a world that is both alien and common to me: "the capacity to enter into the lives of others." But you can't just take the goods and run. I knew that then, sitting in the

Oakland auditorium (as I know in my poetry), that the only thing worth writing about is what seems to be unknown and, therefore, fearful.

The "unknown" is often depicted in racist literature as the "darkness" within a person. Similarly, sexist writers will refer to fear in the form of the vagina, calling it "the orifice of death." In contrast, it is a pleasure to read works such as Maxine Hong Kingston's *Woman Warrior*, where fear and alienation are described as "the white ghosts." And yet, the bulk of literature in this country reinforces the myth that what is dark and female is evil. Consequently, each of us—whether dark, female, or both—has in some way *internalized* this oppressive imagery. What the oppressor often succeeds in doing is simply *externalizing* his fears, projecting them into the bodies of women, Asians, gays, disabled folks, whoever seems most "other."

> call me
> roach and presumptuous
> nightmare on your white pillow
> your itch to destroy
> the indestructible
> part of yourself

> Audre Lorde[2]

But it is not really difference the oppressor fears so much as similarity. He fears he will discover in himself the same aches, the same longings as those of the people he has shitted on. He fears the immobilization threatened by his own incipient guilt. He fears he will have to change his life once he has seen himself in the bodies of the people he has called different. He fears the hatred, anger, and vengeance of those he has hurt.

This is the oppressor's nightmare, but it is not exclusive to him. We women have a similar nightmare, for each of us in some way has been both oppressed and the oppressor. We are afraid to look at how we have failed each other. We are afraid to see how we have taken the values of our oppressor into our hearts and turned them against ourselves and one another. We are afraid to admit how deeply "the man's" words have been ingrained in us.

To assess the damage is a dangerous act. I think of how, even as a feminist lesbian, I have so wanted to ignore my own homophobia, my own hatred of myself for being queer. I have not wanted to admit that my deepest personal sense of myself has not quite "caught up" with my "woman-identified" politics. I have been afraid to criticize lesbian writers who choose to "skip over" these issues in the name of feminism. In 1979, we talk of "old gay" and "butch and femme" roles as if they were ancient history. We toss them aside as merely patriarchal notions. And yet, the truth of the matter is that I have sometimes taken society's fear and hatred of lesbians to bed with me. I have sometimes hated my lover for loving me. I have sometimes felt "not woman enough" for her. I have sometimes felt "not man enough." For a lesbian trying to survive in a heterosexist society, there is no easy way around these emotions. Similarly, in a white-dominated world, there is little getting around racism and our own internalization of it. It's always there, embodied in some one we least expect to rub up against.

When we do rub up against this person, *there* then is the challenge. *There* then is the opportunity to look at the nightmare within us. But we usually shrink from such a challenge.

Time and time again, I have observed that the usual response among white women's groups when the "racism issue" comes up is to deny the difference. I have heard comments like, "Well, we're open to *all* women; why don't they (women of color) come? You can only do so much . . ." But there is seldom any analysis of how the very nature and structure of the group itself may be founded on racist or classist assumptions. More importantly, so often the women seem to feel no loss, no lack, no absence when women of color are not involved; therefore, there is little desire to change the situation. This has hurt me deeply. I have come to believe that the only reason women of a privileged class will dare to look at *how* it is that *they* oppress, is when they've come to know the meaning of their own oppression. And understand that the oppression of others hurts them personally.

The other side of the story is that women of color and working-class women often shrink from challenging white middle-class women. It is much easier to rank oppressions and set up a hierarchy, rather than take responsibility for changing our own lives. We have failed to demand that white women, particularly those who claim to be speaking for all women, be accountable for their racism.

The dialogue has simply not gone deep enough.

I have many times questioned my right to even work on an anthology which is to be written "exclusively by Third World women." I have had to look critically at my claim to color, at a time when, among white feminist ranks, it is a "politically correct" (and sometimes peripherally advantageous) assertion to make. I must acknowledge the fact that, physically, I have had a *choice* about making that claim, in contrast to women who have not had such a choice, and have been abused for their color. I must reckon with the fact that for most of my life, by virtue of the very fact that I am white-looking, I identified with and aspired toward white values, and that I rode the wave of that Southern Californian privilege as far as conscience would let me.

Well, now I feel both bleached and beached. I feel angry about this—the years when I refused to recognize privilege, both when it worked against me, and when I worked it, ignorantly, at the expense of others. These are not settled issues. That is why this work feels so risky to me. It continues to be discovery. It has brought me into contact with women who invariably know a hell of a lot more than I do about racism, as experienced in the flesh, as revealed in the flesh of their writing.

I think: what is my responsibility to my roots—both white and brown, Spanish-speaking and English? I am a woman with a foot in both worlds; and I refuse the split. I feel the necessity for dialogue. Sometimes I feel it urgently.

But one voice is not enough, nor two, although this is where dialogue begins. It is essential that radical feminists confront their fear of and resistance to each other, because without this, there *will* be no bread on the table. Simply, we will not survive. If we could make this connection in our heart of hearts, that if we are serious about a revolution—better—if we seriously believe there should be joy in our lives (real joy, not just "good times"), then we need one another. We women need each other. Because my/your solitary, self-asserting "go-for-the-throat-of-fear" power is not enough. The real power, as you and I well know, is collective. I can't afford to be afraid of you, nor you of me. If it takes head-on collisions, let's do it: this polite timidity is killing us.

As Lorde suggests in the passage I cited earlier, it is in looking to the nightmare that the dream is found. There, the survivor emerges to insist on a future, a vision, yes, born out of what is dark and female. The feminist movement must be a movement of such survivors, a movement with a future.

References

1. Alix Kates Shulman, "Was My Life Worth Living?" *Red Emma Speaks* (New York: Random House, 1972), p. 388.
2. From "The Brown Menace or Poem to the Survival of Roaches," *The New York Head Shop and Museum* (Detroit: Broadside, 1974), p. 48.

[1981]

Rootedness: The Ancestor as Foundation

Toni Morrison

THERE IS A CONFLICT BETWEEN PUBLIC AND PRIVATE LIFE, AND IT'S A conflict that I think ought to remain a conflict. Not a problem, just a conflict. Because they are two modes of life that exist to exclude and annihilate each other. It's a conflict that should be maintained now more than ever because the social machinery of this country at this time doesn't permit harmony in a life that has both aspects. I am impressed with the story of—probably Jefferson, perhaps not, who walked home alone after the presidential inauguration. There must have been a time when an artist could be genuinely representative *of* the tribe and *in* it; when an artist could have a tribal or racial sensibility and an individual expression of it. There were spaces and places in which a single person could enter and behave as an individual within the context of the community. A small remnant of that you can see sometimes in Black churches where people shout. It is a very personal grief and a personal statement done among people you trust. Done within the context of the community, therefore safe. And while the shouter is performing some rite that is extremely subjective, the other people are performing as a community in protecting that person. So you have a public and a private expression going on at the same time. To transfer that is not possible. So I just do the obvious, which is to keep my life as private as possible; not because it is all that interesting, it's just important that it be private. And then, whatever I do that is public can be done seriously.

The autobiographical form is classic in Black American or Afro-American literature because it provided an instance in which a writer could be representative, could say, "My single solitary and individual life is like the lives of the tribe; it differs in these specific ways, but it is a balanced life because it is both solitary and representative." The contemporary autobiography tends to be "how I got over—look at me—alone—let me show you how I did it." It is inimical, I think, to some of the characteristics of Black artistic expression and influence.

The label "novel" is useful in technical terms because I write prose that is longer than a short story. My sense of the novel is that it has always functioned for the class or the group that wrote it. The history of the novel as a form began when there was a new class, a middle class, to read it; it was an art form that they needed. The lower classes didn't need novels at that time because they had an art form already: they had songs, and dances, and ceremony, and gossip, and celebrations. The aristocracy didn't need it because they had the art that they had patronized, they had their own pictures painted, their own houses built, and they made sure their art separated them from the rest of the world. But when the industrial revolution began, there emerged a new class of people who were neither peasants nor aristocrats. In large measure they had no art form to tell them how to behave in this new situation. So they produced an art form: we call it the novel of manners, an art form designed to tell people something they didn't know. That is, how to behave in this new world, how to distinguish between the good guys and the bad guys. How to get married. What a good living was. What would happen if you strayed from the fold. So that early works such as *Pamela*, by Samuel Richardson, and the Jane Austen material provided social rules and explained behavior, identified outlaws, identified the people, habits, and customs that one should approve of. They were didactic in that sense. That, I think, is probably why the novel was not missed among the so-called peasant cultures. They didn't need it, because they were clear about what their responsibilities were and who and where was evil, and where was good.

But when the peasant class, or lower class, or what have you, confronts the middle class, the city, or the upper classes, they are thrown a little bit into disarray. For a long time, the art form that was healing for Black people was music. That music is no longer *exclusively* ours; we don't have exclusive rights to it. Other people sing it and play it; it is the mode of contemporary music everywhere. So another form has to take that place, and it seems to me that the novel is needed by African-Americans now in a way that it was not needed before—and it is following along the lines of the function of novels everywhere. We don't live in places where we can hear those stories anymore; parents don't sit around and tell their children those classical, mythological archetypal stories that we heard years ago. But new information has got to get out, and there are several ways to do it. One is in the novel. I regard it as a way to accomplish certain very strong functions—one being the one I just described.

It should be beautiful, and powerful, but it should also *work*. It should have something in it that enlightens; something in it that opens the door and points the way. Something in it that suggests what the conflicts are, what the problems are. But it need not solve those problems because it is not a case study, it is not a recipe. There are things that I try to incorporate into my fiction that are directly and deliberately related to what I regard as the major characteristics of Black art, wherever it is. One of which is the ability to be both print and oral literature: to combine those two aspects so that the stories can be read in silence, of course, but one should be able to hear them as well. It should try deliberately to make you stand up and make you feel something profoundly in the same way that a Black preacher requires his congregation to speak, to join him in the sermon, to behave in a certain way, to stand up and to weep and to cry and to accede or to change and to modify—to expand on the sermon that is being delivered. In the same way that a musician's music is enhanced when there is a response from the audience. Now in a book, which closes, after all—it's of some importance to me to try to make that connection—to try to make that happen also. And, having at my disposal only the letters of the alphabet and some punctuation, I have to provide the places and spaces so that the reader can participate. Because it is the affective and participatory relationship between the artist or the speaker and the audience that is of primary importance, as it is in these other art forms that I have described.

To make the story appear oral, meandering, effortless, spoken—to have the reader *feel* the narrator without *identifying* that narrator, or hearing him or her knock about, and to have the reader work *with* the author in the construction of the book—is what's important. What is left out is as important as what is there. To describe sexual scenes in such a way that they are not clinical, not even explicit—so that the reader brings his own sexuality to the scene and thereby participates in it in a very personal way. And owns it. To construct the dialogue so that it is heard. So that there are no adverbs attached to them: "loudly," "softly," "he said menacingly." The menace should be in the sentence. To use, even formally, a chorus. The real presence of a chorus. Meaning the community or the reader at large, commenting on the action as it goes ahead.

In the books that I have written, the chorus has changed but there has always been a choral note, whether it is the "I" narrator of *Bluest Eye*, or the town functioning as a character in *Sula*, or the neighborhood and the community that responds in the two parts of town in *Solomon*. Or, as extreme as I've gotten, all of nature thinking and feeling and watching and responding to the action going on in *Tar Baby*, so that they are in the story: the trees hurt, fish are afraid, clouds report, and the bees are alarmed. Those are the ways in which I try to incorporate, into that traditional genre the novel, unorthodox novelistic characteristics—so that it is, in my view, Black, because it uses the characteristics of Black art. I am not suggesting that some of these devices have not been used before and elsewhere—only the reason why I do. I employ them as well as I can. And those are just some; I wish there were ways in which such things could be talked about in the criticism. My general disappointment in some of the criticism that my work has received has nothing to do with approval. It has something to do with the vocabulary used in order to describe these things. I don't like to find my books condemned as bad or praised as good, when that condemnation or that praise is based on criteria from other paradigms. I would much prefer that they were dismissed or embraced based on the success of their accomplishment within the culture out of which I write.

I don't regard Black literature as simply books written *by* Black people, or simply as literature written *about* Black people, or simply as literature that uses a certain mode of language in which you just sort of drop *g*'s. There is something very special and very identifiable about it and it is my struggle to *find* that elusive but identifiable style in the books. My joy is when I think that I have approached it; my misery is when I think I can't get there.

[There were times when I did.] I got there in several separate places when I knew it was exactly right. Most of the time in *Song of Solomon*, because of the construction of the book and the tone in which I could blend the acceptance of the supernatural and a profound rootedness in the real world at the same time with neither taking precedence over the other. It is indicative of the cosmology, the way in which Black people looked at the world. We are very practical people, very down-to-earth, even shrewd people. But within that practicality we also accepted what I suppose could be called superstition and magic, which is another way of knowing things. But to blend those two worlds together at the same time was enhancing, not limiting. And some of those things were "discredited knowledge" that Black people had; discredited only because Black people were discredited therefore what they *knew* was "discredited." And also because the press toward upward social mobility would mean to get as far away from that kind of knowledge as possible. That kind of knowledge has a very strong place in my work.

I have talked about function in that other question, and I touched a little bit on some of the other characteristics [or distinctive elements of African-American writing], one of which was oral quality, and the participation of the reader and the chorus. The only thing that I would add for this question is the presence of an ancestor; it seems to me interesting to evaluate Black literature on what the writer does with the presence of an ancestor. Which is to say a grandfather as in Ralph Ellison, or a grandmother as in Toni Cade Bambara, or a healer as in Bambara or Henry Dumas. There is always an elder there. And these ancestors are not just parents, they are sort of timeless people whose relationships to the characters are benevolent, instructive, and protective, and they provide a certain kind of wisdom.

How the Black writer responds to that presence interests me. Some of them, such as Richard Wright, had great difficulty with that ancestor. Some of them, like James Baldwin, were confounded and disturbed by the presence or absence of an ancestor. What struck me in looking at some contemporary fiction was that whether the novel took place in the city or in the country, the presence or absence of that figure determined the success or the happiness of the character. It was the absence of an ancestor that was frightening, that was threatening, and it caused huge destruction and disarray in the work itself. That the solace comes, not from the contemplation of serene nature as in a lot of mainstream white literature, nor from the regard in which the city was held as a kind of corrupt place to be. Whether the character was in Harlem or Arkansas, the point was there, this timelessness was there, this person who represented this ancestor. And it seemed to be one of those interesting aspects of the continuum in Black or African-American art, as well as some of the things I mentioned before: the deliberate effort, on the part of the artist, to get a visceral, emotional response as well as an intellectual response as he or she communicates with the audience.

The treatment of artists by the people for whom they speak is also of some interest. That is to say, when the writer is one of them, when the voice is not the separate, isolated ivory tower voice of a very different kind of person but an implied "we" in a narration. This is disturbing to people and critics who view the artist as the supreme individual. It is disturbing because there is a notion that that's what the artist is—always in confrontation with his own society, and you can see the differences in the way in which literature is interpreted. Whether or not Sula is nourished by that village depends on your view of it. I know people who believe that she was destroyed by it. My own special view is that there was no other place where she could live. She would have been destroyed by any other place; she was permitted to "be" only in that context, and no one stoned her or killed her or threw her out. Also it's difficult to see who the winners are if you are not looking at it from that point of view. When the hero returns to the fold—returns to the tribe—it is seen by certain white critics as a defeat, by others as a triumph, and that is a difference in what the *aims* of the art are.

In *Song of Solomon* Pilate is the ancestor. The difficulty that Hagar [youngest of the trio of women in that household] has is how far removed she is from the experience of her ancestor. Pilate had a dozen years of close, nurturing relationships with two males—her father and her brother. And that intimacy and support was in her and made her fierce and loving because she had that experience. Her daughter Reba had less of that and related to men in a very shallow way. Her daughter had even less of an association with men as a child, so that the progression is really a diminishing of their abilities because of the absence of men in a nourishing way in their lives. Pilate is the apogee of all that: of the best of that which is female and the best of that which is male, and that balance is disturbed if it is not nurtured, and if it is not counted on and if it is not reproduced. That is the disability we must be on guard against for the future—the female who reproduces the female who reproduces the female. You know there are a lot of people who talk about the position that men hold as of primary importance, but actually it is if we don't keep in touch with the ancestor that we are, in fact, lost.

The point of the books is that it is *our* job. When you kill the ancestor you kill yourself. I want to point out the dangers, to show that nice things don't always happen to the totally self-reliant if there is no conscious historical connection. To say, see—this is what will happen.

I don't have much to say about that [the necessity to develop a specific Black feminist model of critical inquiry] except that I think there is more danger in it than fruit, because any model of criticism or evaluation that excludes males from it is as hampered as any model of criticism of Black literature that excludes women from it. For critics, models have some function. They like to talk in terms of models and developments and so on, so maybe it's of some use to them, but I suggest that even for them there is some danger in it.

If anything I do, in the way of writing novels (or whatever I write) isn't about the village or the community or about you, then it is not about anything. I am not interested in indulging myself in some private, closed exercise of my imagination that fulfills only the obligation of my personal dreams—which is to say yes, the work must be political. It must have that as its thrust. That's a pejorative term in critical circles now: if a work of art has any political influence in it, somehow it's tainted. My feeling is just the opposite: if it has none, it is tainted.

The problem comes when you find harangue passing off as art. It seems to me that the best art is political and you ought to be able to make it unquestionably political and irrevocably beautiful at the same time.

[1984]

Landscape, History, and the Pueblo Imagination

Leslie Marmon Silko

From a High Arid Plateau
in New Mexico

You see that after a thing is dead, it dries up. It might take weeks or years, but eventually if you touch the thing, it crumbles under your fingers. It goes back to dust. The soul of the thing has long since departed. With the plants and wild game the soul may have already been borne back into bones and blood or thick green stalk and leaves. Nothing is wasted. What cannot be eaten by people or in some way used must then be left where other living creatures may benefit. What domestic animals or wild scavengers can't eat will be fed to the plants. The plants feed on the dust of these few remains.

The ancient Pueblo people buried the dead in vacant rooms or partially collapsed rooms adjacent to the main living quarters. Sand and clay used to construct the roof make layers many inches deep once the roof has collapsed. The layers of sand and clay make for easy gravedigging. The vacant room fills with cast-off objects and debris. When a vacant room has filled deep enough, a shallow but adequate grave can be scooped in a far corner. Archaeologists have remarked over formal burials complete with elaborate funerary objects excavated in trash middens of abandoned rooms. But the rocks and adobe mortar of collapsed walls were valued by the ancient people. Because each rock had been carefully selected for size and shape, then chiseled to an even face. Even the pink clay adobe melting with each rainstorm had to be prayed over, then dug and carried some distance. Corn cobs and husks, the rinds and stalks and animal bones were not regarded by the ancient people as filth or garbage. The remains were merely resting at a midpoint in their journey back to dust. Human remains are not so different. They should rest with the bones and rinds where they all may benefit living creatures—small rodents and insects—until their return is completed. The remains of things—animals and plants, the clay and the stones—were treated with respect. Because for the ancient people all these things had spirit and being.

The antelope merely consents to return home with the hunter. All phases of the hunt are conducted with love. The love the hunter and the people have for the Antelope People. And the love of the antelope who agree to give up their meat and blood so that human beings will not starve. Waste of meat or even the thoughtless handling of bones cooked bare will offend the antelope spirits. Next year the hunters will vainly search the dry plains for antelope. Thus it is necessary to return carefully the bones and hair, and the stalks and leaves to the earth who first created them. The spirits remain close by. They do not leave us.

The dead become dust, and in this becoming they are once more joined with the Mother. The ancient Pueblo people called the earth the Mother Creator of all things in this world. Her sister, the Corn Mother, occasionally merges with her because all succulent green life rises out of the depths of the earth.

Rocks and clay are part of the Mother. They emerge in various forms, but at some time before, they were smaller particles or great boulders. At a later time they may again become what they once were. Dust.

A rock shares this fate with us and with animals and plants as well. A rock has being or spirit, although we may not understand it. The spirit may differ from the spirit we know in animals or plants or in ourselves. In the end we all originate from the depths of the earth. Perhaps this is how all beings share in the spirit of the Creator. We do not know.

From the Emergence Place

Pueblo potters, the creators of petroglyphs and oral narratives, never conceived of removing themselves from the earth and sky. So long as the human consciousness remains *within* the hills, canyons, cliffs, and the plants, clouds, and sky, the term *landscape*, as it has entered the English language, is misleading. "A portion of territory the eye can comprehend in a single view" does not correctly describe the relationship between the human being and his or her surroundings. This assumes the viewer is somehow *outside* or *separate from* the territory he or she surveys. Viewers are as much a part of the landscape as the boulders they stand on. There is no high mesa edge or mountain peak where one can stand and not immediately be part of all that surrounds. Human identity is linked with all the elements of Creation through the clan: you might belong to the Sun Clan or the Lizard Clan or the Corn Clan or the Clay Clan.* Standing deep within the natural world, the ancient Pueblo understood the thing as it was—the squash blossom, grasshopper, or rabbit itself could never be created by the human hand. Ancient Pueblos took the modest view that the thing itself (the landscape) could not be improved upon. The ancients did not presume to tamper with what had already been created. Thus *realism*, as we now recognize it in painting and sculpture, did not catch the imaginations of Pueblo people until recently.

The squash blossom itself is *one thing*: itself. So the ancient Pueblo potter abstracted what she saw to be the key elements of the squash blossom—the

---

* Clan—A social unit composed of families sharing common ancestors who trace their lineage back to the Emergence where their ancestors allied themselves with certain plants or animals or elements.

four symmetrical petals, with four symmetrical stamens in the center. These key elements, while suggesting the squash flower, also link it with the four cardinal directions. By representing only its intrinsic form, the squash flower is released from a limited meaning or restricted identity. Even in the most sophisticated abstract form, a squash flower or a cloud or a lightning bolt became intricately connected with a complex system of relationships which the ancient Pueblo people maintained with each other, and with the populous natural world they lived within. A bolt of lightning is itself, but at the same time it may mean much more. It may be a messenger of good fortune when summer rains are needed. It may deliver death, perhaps the result of manipulations by the Gunnadeyahs, destructive necromancers. Lightning may strike down an evil-doer. Or lightning may strike a person of good will. If the person survives, lightning endows him or her with heightened power.

Pictographs and petroglyphs of constellations or elk or antelope draw their magic in part from the process wherein the focus of all prayer and concentration is upon the thing itself, which, in its turn, guides the hunter's hand. Connection with the spirit dimensions requires a figure or form which is all-inclusive. A "lifelike" rendering of an elk is too restrictive. Only the elk *is* itself. A *realistic* rendering of an elk would be only one particular elk anyway. The purpose of the hunt rituals and magic is to make contact with *all* the spirits of the Elk.

The land, the sky, and all that is within them—the landscape—includes human beings. Interrelationships in the Pueblo landscape are complex and fragile. The unpredictability of the weather, the aridity and harshness of much of the terrain in the high plateau country explain in large part the relentless attention the ancient Pueblo people gave the sky and the earth around them. Survival depended upon harmony and cooperation not only among human beings, but among all things—the animate and the less animate, since rocks and mountains were known to move, to travel occasionally.

The ancient Pueblos believed the Earth and the Sky were sisters (or sister and brother in the post-Christian version). As long as good family relations are maintained, then the Sky will continue to bless her sister, the Earth, with rain, and the Earth's children will continue to survive. But the old stories recall incidents in which troublesome spirits or beings threaten the earth. In one story, a malicious ka'tsina, called the Gambler, seizes the Shiwana, or Rainclouds, the Sun's beloved children.* The Shiwana are snared in magical power late one afternoon on a high mountain top. The Gambler takes the Rainclouds to his mountain stronghold where he locks them in the north room of his house. What was his idea? The Shiwana were beyond value. They brought life to all things on earth. The Gambler wanted a big stake to wager in his games of chance. But such greed, even on the part of only one being, had the effect of threatening the survival of all life

---

* Ka'tsina—Ka'tsinas are spirit beings who roam the earth and who inhabit kachina masks worn in Pueblo ceremonial dances.

on earth. Sun Youth, aided by old Grandmother Spider, outsmarts the Gambler and the rigged game, and the Rainclouds are set free. The drought ends, and once more life thrives on earth.

Through the Stories We Hear
Who We Are

All summer the people watch the west horizon, scanning the sky from south to north for rain clouds. Corn must have moisture at the time the tassels form. Otherwise pollination will be incomplete, and the ears will be stunted and shriveled. An inadequate harvest may bring disaster. Stories told at Hopi, Zuni, and at Acoma and Laguna describe drought and starvation as recently as 1900. Precipitation in west-central New Mexico averages fourteen inches annually. The western pueblos are located at altitudes over 5,600 feet above sea level, where winter temperatures at night fall below freezing. Yet evidence of their presence in the high desert plateau country goes back ten thousand years. The ancient Pueblo people not only survived in this environment, but many years they thrived. In A.D. 1100 the people at Chaco Canyon had built cities with apartment buildings of stone five stories high. Their sophistication as sky-watchers was surpassed only by Mayan and Inca astronomers. Yet this vast complex of knowledge and belief, amassed for thousands of years, was never recorded in writing.

Instead, the ancient Pueblo people depended upon collective memory through successive generations to maintain and transmit an entire culture, a world view complete with proven strategies for survival. The oral narrative, or "story," became the medium in which the complex of Pueblo knowledge and belief was maintained. Whatever the event or the subject, the ancient people perceived the world and themselves within that world as part of an ancient continuous story composed of innumerable bundles of other stories.

The ancient Pueblo vision of the world was inclusive. The impulse was to leave nothing out. Pueblo oral tradition necessarily embraced all levels of human experience. Otherwise, the collective knowledge and beliefs comprising ancient Pueblo culture would have been incomplete. Thus stories about the Creation and Emergence of human beings and animals into this World continue to be retold each year for four days and four nights during the winter solstice. The "humma-hah" stories related events from the time long ago when human beings were still able to communicate with animals and other living things. But, beyond these two preceding categories, the Pueblo oral tradition knew no boundaries. Accounts of the appearance of the first Europeans in Pueblo country or of the tragic encounters between Pueblo people and Apache raiders were no more and no less important than stories about the biggest mule deer ever taken or adulterous couples surprised in cornfields and chicken coops. Whatever happened, the ancient people instinctively sorted events and details into a loose narrative structure. Everything became a story.

Traditionally everyone, from the youngest child to the oldest person, was expected to listen and to be able to recall or tell a portion, if only a small detail, from a narrative account or story. Thus the remembering and retelling were a communal process. Even if a key figure, an elder who knew much more than others, were to die unexpectedly, the system would remain intact. Through the efforts of a great many people, the community was able to piece together valuable accounts and crucial information that might otherwise have died with an individual.

Communal storytelling was a self-correcting process in which listeners were encouraged to speak up if they noted an important fact or detail omitted. The people were happy to listen to two or three different versions of the same event or the same humma-hah story. Even conflicting versions of an incident were welcomed for the entertainment they provided. Defenders of each version might joke and tease one another, but seldom were there any direct confrontations. Implicit in the Pueblo oral tradition was the awareness that loyalties, grudges, and kinship must always influence the narrator's choices as she emphasizes to listeners this is the way *she* has always heard the story told. The ancient Pueblo people sought a communal truth, not an absolute. For them this truth lived somewhere within the web of differing versions, disputes over minor points, outright contradictions tangling with old feuds and village rivalries.

A dinner-table conversation, recalling a deer hunt forty years ago when the largest mule deer ever was taken, inevitably stimulates similar memories in listeners. But hunting stories were not merely after-dinner entertainment. These accounts contained information of critical importance about behavior and migration patterns of mule deer. Hunting stories carefully described key landmarks and locations of fresh water. Thus a deer-hunt story might also serve as a "map." Lost travelers, and lost piñon-nut gatherers, have been saved by sighting a rock formation they recognize only because they once heard a hunting story describing this rock formation.

The importance of cliff formations and water holes does not end with hunting stories. As offspring of the Mother Earth, the ancient Pueblo people could not conceive of themselves without a specific landscape. Location, or "place," nearly always plays a central role in the Pueblo oral narratives. Indeed, stories are most frequently recalled as people are passing by a specific geographical feature or the exact place where a story takes place. The precise date of the incident often is less important than the place or location of the happening. "Long, long ago," "a long time ago," "not too long ago," and "recently" are usually how stories are classified in terms of time. But the places where the stories occur are precisely located, and prominent geographical details recalled, even if the landscape is well-known to listeners. Often because the turning point in the narrative involved a peculiarity or special quality of a rock or tree or plant found only at that place. Thus, in the case of many of the Pueblo narratives, it is impossible to determine which came first: the incident or the geographical feature which begs to be brought alive in a story that features some unusual aspect of this location.

There is a giant sandstone boulder about a mile north of Old Laguna, on the road to Paguate. It is ten feet tall and twenty feet in circumference. When I was a child, and we would pass this boulder driving to Paguate village, someone usually made reference to the story about Kochininako, Yellow Woman, and the Estrucuyo, a monstrous giant who nearly ate her. The Twin Hero Brothers saved Kochininako, who had been out hunting rabbits to take home to feed her mother and sisters. The Hero Brothers had heard her cries just in time. The Estrucuyo had cornered her in a cave too small to fit its monstrous head. Kochininako had already thrown to the Estrucuyo all her rabbits, as well as her moccasins and most of her clothing. Still the creature had not been satisfied. After killing the Estrucuyo with their bows and arrows, the Twin Hero Brothers slit open the Estrucuyo and cut out its heart. They threw the heart as far as they could. The monster's heart landed there, beside the old trail to Paguate village, where the sandstone boulder rests now.

It may be argued that the existence of the boulder precipitated the creation of a story to explain it. But sandstone boulders and sandstone formations of strange shapes abound in the Laguna Pueblo area. Yet most of them do not have stories. Often the crucial element in a narrative is the terrain—some specific detail of the setting.

A high dark mesa rises dramatically from a grassy plain fifteen miles southeast of Laguna, in an area known as Swanee. On the grassy plain one hundred and forty years ago, my great-grandmother's uncle and his brother-in-law were grazing their herd of sheep. Because visibility on the plain extends for over twenty miles, it wasn't until the two sheepherders came near the high dark mesa that the Apaches were able to stalk them. Using the mesa to obscure their approach, the raiders swept around from both ends of the mesa. My great-grandmother's relatives were killed, and the herd lost. The high dark mesa played a critical role: the mesa had compromised the safety which the openness of the plains had seemed to assure. Pueblo and Apache alike relied upon the terrain, the very earth herself, to give them protection and aid. Human activities or needs were maneuvered to fit the existing surroundings and conditions. I imagine the last afternoon of my distant ancestors as warm and sunny for late September. They might have been traveling slowly, bringing the sheep closer to Laguna in preparation for the approach of colder weather. The grass was tall and only beginning to change from green to a yellow which matched the late-afternoon sun shining off it. There might have been comfort in the warmth and the sight of the sheep fattening on good pasture which lulled my ancestors into their fatal inattention. They might have had a rifle whereas the Apaches had only bows and arrows. But there would have been four or five Apache raiders, and the surprise attack would have canceled any advantage the rifles gave them.

Survival in any landscape comes down to making the best use of all available resources. On that particular September afternoon, the raiders made better use of the Swanee terrain than my poor ancestors did. Thus the high dark mesa and the story of the two lost Laguna herders became inextricably linked. The memory of them and their story resides in part with the high black mesa. For as long as the mesa stands, people within the family and clan will be reminded of the story of that afternoon long ago. Thus the continuity and accuracy of the oral narratives are reinforced by the landscape—and the Pueblo interpretation of that landscape is *maintained*.

The Migration Story: An Interior Journey

The Laguna Pueblo migration stories refer to specific places—mesas, springs, or cottonwood trees—not only locations which can be visited still, but also locations which lie directly on the state highway route linking Paguate village with Laguna village. In traveling this road as a child with older Laguna people I first heard a few of the stories from that much larger body of stories linked with the Emergence and Migration.* It may be coincidental that Laguna people continue to follow the same route which, according to the Migration story, the ancestors followed south from the Emergence Place. It may be that the route is merely the shortest and best route for car, horse, or foot traffic between Laguna and Paguate villages. But if the stories about boulders, springs, and hills are actually remnants from a ritual that retraces the creation and emergence of the Laguna Pueblo people as a culture, as the people they became, then continued use of that route creates a unique relationship between the ritual-mythic world and the actual, everyday world. A journey from Paguate to Laguna down the long incline of Paguate Hill retraces the original journey from the Emergence Place, which is located slightly north of the Paguate village. Thus the landscape between Paguate and Laguna takes on a deeper significance: the landscape resonates the spiritual or mythic dimension of the Pueblo world even today.

Although each Pueblo culture designates a specific Emergence Place—usually a small natural spring edged with mossy sandstone and full of cattails and wild watercress—it is clear that they do not agree on any single location or natural spring as the one and only true Emergence Place. Each Pueblo group recounts its own stories about Creation, Emergence, and Migration, although they all believe that all human beings, with all the animals and plants, emerged at the same place and at the same time.†

---

* The Emergence—All the human beings, animals, and life which had been created emerged from the four worlds below when the earth became habitable.
  The Migration—The Pueblo people emerged into the Fifth World, but they had already been warned they would have to travel and search before they found the place they were meant to live.
† Creation—Tse'itsi'nako, Thought Woman, the Spider, thought about it, and everything she thought came into being. First she thought of three sisters for herself, and they helped her think of the rest of the Universe, including the Fifth World and the four worlds below. The Fifth World is the world we are living in today. There are four previous worlds below this world.

Natural springs are crucial sources of water for all life in the high desert plateau country. So the small spring near Paguate village is literally the source and continuance of life for the people in the area. The spring also functions on a spiritual level, recalling the original Emergence Place and linking the people and the spring water to all other people and to that moment when the Pueblo people became aware of themselves as they are even now. The Emergence was an emergence into a precise cultural identity. Thus the Pueblo stories about the Emergence and Migration are not to be taken as literally as the anthropologists might wish. Prominent geographical features and landmarks which are mentioned in the narratives exist for ritual purposes, not because the Laguna people actually journeyed south for hundreds of years from Chaco Canyon or Mesa Verde, as the archaeologists say, or eight miles from the site of the natural springs at Paguate to the sandstone hilltop at Laguna.

The eight miles, marked with boulders, mesas, springs, and river crossings, are actually a ritual circuit or path which marks the interior journey the Laguna people made: a journey of awareness and imagination in which they emerged from being within the earth and from everything included in earth to the culture and people they became, differentiating themselves for the first time from all that had surrounded them, always aware that interior distances cannot be reckoned in physical miles or in calendar years.

The narratives linked with prominent features of the landscape between Paguate and Laguna delineate the complexities of the relationship which human beings must maintain with the surrounding natural world if they hope to survive in this place. Thus the journey was an interior process of the imagination, a growing awareness that being human is somehow different from all other life—animal, plant, and inanimate. Yet we are all from the same source: the awareness never deteriorated into Cartesian duality, cutting off the human from the natural world.

The people found the opening into the Fifth World too small to allow them or any of the animals to escape. They had sent a fly out through the small hole to tell them if it was the world which the Mother Creator had promised. It was, but there was the problem of getting out. The antelope tried to butt the opening to enlarge it, but the antelope enlarged it only a little. It was necessary for the badger with her long claws to assist the antelope, and at last the opening was enlarged enough so that all the people and animals were able to emerge up into the Fifth World. The human beings could not have emerged without the aid of antelope and badger. The human beings depended upon the aid and charity of the animals. Only through interdependence could the human beings survive. Families belonged to clans, and it was by clan that the human being joined with the animal and plant world. Life on the high arid plateau became viable when the human beings were able to imagine themselves as sisters and brothers to the badger, antelope, clay, yucca, and sun. Not until they could find a viable relationship to the terrain, the landscape they found themselves in, could they *emerge*. Only at the moment the requisite balance between human and *other* was realized could the Pueblo people become a culture, a distinct group whose population and survival remained stable despite the vicissitudes of climate and terrain.

Landscape thus has similarities with dreams. Both have the power to seize terrifying feelings and deep instincts and translate them into images—visual, aural, tactile—into the concrete where human beings may more readily confront and channel the terrifying instincts or powerful emotions into rituals and narratives which reassure the individual while reaffirming cherished values of the group. The identity of the individual as a part of the group and the greater Whole is strengthened, and the terror of facing the world alone is extinguished.

Even now, the people at Laguna Pueblo spend the greater portion of social occasions recounting recent incidents or events which have occurred in the Laguna area. Nearly always, the discussion will precipitate the retelling of older stories about similar incidents or other stories connected with a specific place. The stories often contain disturbing or provocative material, but are nonetheless told in the presence of children and women. The effect of these inter-family or inter-clan exchanges is the reassurance for each person that she or he will never be separated or apart from the clan, no matter what might happen. Neither the worst blunders or disasters nor the greatest financial prosperity and joy will ever be permitted to isolate anyone from the rest of the group. In the ancient times, cohesiveness was all that stood between extinction and survival, and, while the individual certainly was recognized, it was always as an individual simultaneously bonded to family and clan by a complex bundle of custom and ritual. You are never the first to suffer a grave loss or profound humiliation. You are never the first, and you understand that you will probably not be the last to commit or be victimized by a repugnant act. Your family and clan are able to go on at length about others now passed on, others older or more experienced than you who suffered similar losses.

The wide deep arroyo near the Kings Bar (located acoss the reservation borderline) has over the years claimed many vehicles. A few years ago, when a Viet Nam veteran's new red Volkswagen rolled backwards into the arroyo while he was inside buying a six-pack of beer, the story of his loss joined the lively and large collection of stories already connected with that big arroyo. I do not know whether the Viet Nam veteran was consoled when he was told the stories about the other cars claimed by the ravenous arroyo. All his savings of combat pay had gone for the red Volkswagen. But this man could not have felt any worse than the man who, some years before, had left his children and mother-in-law in his station wagon with the engine running. When he came out of the liquor store his station wagon was gone. He found it and its passengers upside down in the big arroyo. Broken bones, cuts and bruises, and a total wreck of the car. The big arroyo has a wide mouth. Its existence needs no explanation. People in the area regard the arroyo much as they might regard a living being, which has a certain character and personality. I seldom drive past that wide deep arroyo without feeling a familiarity with and even a strange affection for this arroyo. Because as treacherous as it may be, the arroyo maintains a strong connection between human beings and the earth. The arroyo demands from us the caution and attention that constitute respect. It is this sort of respect the old believers have in mind when they tell us we must respect and love the earth.

Hopi Pueblo elders have said that the austere and, to some eyes, barren plains and hills surrounding their mesa-top villages actually help to nurture the spirituality of the Hopi *way*. The Hopi elders say the Hopi people might have settled in locations far more lush where daily life would not have been so grueling. But there on the high silent sandstone mesas that overlook the sandy arid expanses stretching to all horizons, the Hopi elders say the Hopi people must "live by their prayers" if they are to survive. The Hopi way cherishes the intangible: the riches realized from interaction and interrelationships with all beings above all else. Great abundances of material things, even food, the Hopi elders believe, tend to lure human attention away from what is most valuable and important. The views of the Hopi elders are not much different from those elders in all the Pueblos.

The bare vastness of the Hopi landscape emphasizes the visual impact of every plant, every rock, every arroyo. Nothing is overlooked or taken for granted. Each ant, each lizard, each lark is imbued with great value simply because the creature is there, simply because the creature is alive in a place where any life at all is precious. Stand on the mesa edge at Walpai and look west over the bare distances toward the pale blue outlines of the San Francisco peaks where the ka'tsina spirits reside. So little lies between you and the sky. So little lies between you and the earth. One look and you know that simply to survive is a great triumph, that every possible resource is needed, every possible ally—even the most humble insect or reptile. You realize you will be speaking with all of them if you intend to last out the year. Thus it is that the Hopi elders are grateful to the landscape for aiding them in their quest as spiritual people.

Out under the Sky

My earliest memories are of being outside, under the sky. I remember climbing the fence when I was three years old, and heading for the plaza in the center of Laguna village because other children passing by had told me there were ka'tsinas there dancing with pieces of wood in their mouths. A neighbor woman retrieved me before I ever saw the wood-swallowing ka'tsinas, but from an early age I knew that I wanted to be outside. Outside walls and fences.

My father had wandered all the hills and mesas around Laguna when he was a child. Because the Indian School and the taunts of the other children did not set well with him. It had been difficult in those days to be part Laguna and part white, or *amedicana*. It was still difficult when I attended the Indian School at Laguna. Our full-blooded relatives and clanspeople assured us we were theirs and that we belonged there because we had been born and reared there. But the racism of the wider world we call America had begun to make itself felt years before. My father's response was to head for the mesas and hills with his older brother, their dog, and .22 rifles. They retreated to the sandstone cliffs and juniper forests. Out in the hills they were not lonely because they had all the living creatures of the hills around them, and, whatever the ambiguities of racial heritage, my father and my uncle understood what the old folks had taught them: the earth loves all of us regardlessly, because we are her children.

I started roaming those same mesas and hills when I was nine years old. At eleven I rode away on my horse, and explored places my father and uncle could not have reached on foot. I was never afraid or lonely, although I was high in the hills, many miles from home. Because I carried with me the feeling I'd acquired from listening to the old stories, that the land all around me was teeming with creatures that were related to human beings and to me. The stories had also left me with a feeling of familiarity and warmth for the mesas and hills and boulders where the incidents or action in the stories had taken place. I felt as if I had actually been to those places, although I had only heard stories about them. Somehow the stories had given a kind of being to the mesas and hills, just as the stories had left me with the sense of having spent time with the people in the stories, although they had long since passed on.

It is unremarkable to sense the presence of those long passed at the locations where their adventures took place. Spirits range without boundaries of any sort. Spirits may be called back in any number of ways. The method used in the calling also determines how the spirit manifests itself. I think a spirit may or may not choose to remain at the site of its passing or death. I think they might be in a number of places at the same time. Storytelling can procure fleeting moments to experience who they were and how life felt long ago. What I enjoyed most as a child was standing at the site of an incident recounted in one of the ancient stories Aunt Susie had told us as girls. What excited me was listening to old Aunt Susie tell us an old-time story and then for me to realize that I was familiar with a certain mesa or cave that figured as the central location of the story she was telling. That was when the stories worked best. Because then I could sit there listening and be able to visualize myself as being located *within* the story being told, within the landscape. Because the storytellers did not just tell the stories, they would in their way act them out. The storyteller would imitate voices for vast dialogues between the various figures in the story. So we sometimes say the moment is alive again within us, within our imaginations and our memory, as we listen.

Aunt Susie once told me how it had been when she was a child and her grandmother agreed to tell the children stories. The old woman would always ask the youngest child in the room to go open the door. "Go open the door," her grandmother would say. "Go open the door so our esteemed ancestors may bring us the precious gift of their stories." Two points seem clear: the spirits could be present and the stories were valuable because they taught us how we were the people we believed we were. The myth, the web of memories and ideas that create an identity, a part of oneself. This sense of identity was intimately linked with the surrounding terrain, to the landscape which has often played a significant role in a story or in the outcome of a conflict.

The landscape sits in the center of Pueblo belief and identity. Any narratives about the Pueblo people necessarily give a great deal of attention and detail to all aspects of a landscape. For this reason, the Pueblo people have always been extremely reluctant to relinquish their land for dams or highways. For this reason, Taos Pueblo fought from 1906 until 1973 to win back their sacred Blue Lake, which was illegally taken from them by the creation of Taos National Forest. For this reason, the decision in the early 1950s to begin open-pit mining of the huge uranium deposits north of Laguna, near Paguate village, has had a powerful psychological impact upon the Laguna people. Already a large body of stories has grown up around the subject of what happens to people who disturb or destroy the earth. I was a child when the mining began and the apocalyptic warning stories were being told. And I have lived long enough to begin hearing the stories which verify the earlier warnings.

All that remains of the gardens and orchards that used to grow in the sandy flats southeast of Paguate village are the stories of the lovely big peaches and apricots the people used to grow. The Jackpile Mine is an open pit that has been blasted out of the many hundreds of acres where the orchards and melon patches once grew. The Laguna people have not witnessed changes to the land without strong reactions. Descriptions of the landscape *before* the mine are as vivid as any description of the present-day destruction by the open-pit mining. By its very ugliness and by the violence it does to the land, the Jackpile Mine insures that from now on it, too, will be included in the vast body of narratives which make up the history of the Laguna people and the Pueblo landscape. And the description of what that landscape looked like *before* the uranium mining began will always carry considerable impact.

Landscape as a Character in Fiction

Drought or the disappearance of game animals may signal disharmony or even witchcraft. When the rain clouds fail to appear in time to help the corn plants, or the deer are suddenly scarce, then we know the very sky and earth are telling human beings that all is not well. A deep arroyo continues to claim victims.

When I began writing I found that the plots of my short stories very often featured the presence of elements out of the landscape, elements which directly influenced the outcome of events. Nowhere is landscape more crucial to the outcome than in my short story, "Storyteller." The site is southwest Alaska, near the village of Bethel, on the Kuskokwim River. Tundra country. Here the winter landscape can suddenly metamorphose into a seamless blank white so solid that pilots in aircraft without electronic instruments lose their bearings and crash their planes straight into the frozen tundra, believing down to be up. Here on the Alaska tundra, in mid-February, not all the space-age fabrics, electronics, or engines can ransom human beings from the restless shifting forces of the winter sky and winter earth.

The young Yupik Eskimo woman works out an elaborate yet subconscious plan to avenge the deaths of her parents. After months of baiting the trap, she lures the murderer onto the river ice where he falls through to his death. The murderer is a white man who operates the village trading post. For years the murderer has existed like a parasite, exploiting not only the fur-bearing animals and the fish, but the Yupik people themselves. When the Yupik woman kills him, the white trader has just finished cashing in on the influx of workers for the petroleum exploration and pipeline who have suddenly come to the tiny village. For the Yupik people, souls deserving punishment spend varying lengths of time in a place of freezing. The Yupik see the world's end coming with ice, not fire. Although the white trader possesses every possible garment, insulation, heating fuel, and gadget ever devised to protect him from the frozen tundra environment, he still dies, drowning under the freezing river ice. Because the white man had not reckoned with the true power of that landscape, especially not the power which the Yupik woman understood instinctively and which she used so swiftly and efficiently. The white man had reckoned with the young woman and determined he could overpower her. But the white man failed to account for the conjunction of the landscape with the woman. The Yupik woman had never seen herself as anything but a part of that sky, that frozen river, that tundra. The river ice and the blinding white are her accomplices, and yet the Yupik woman never for a moment misunderstands her own relationship with that landscape. After the white trader has crashed through the river ice, the young woman finds herself a great distance from either shore of the treacherous frozen river. She can see nothing but the whiteness of the sky swallowing the earth. But far away in the distance, on the side of her log and tundra sod cabin, she is able to see the spot of bright red. A bright red marker she had nailed up weeks earlier because she was intrigued by the contrast between all that white and the spot of brilliant red. The Yupik woman knows the appetite of the frozen river. She realizes that the ice and the fog, the tundra and the snow seek constantly to be reunited with the living beings which skitter across it. The Yupik woman knows that inevitably she and all things will one day lie in those depths. But the woman is young and her instinct is to live. The Yupik woman knows how to do this.

Inside the small cabin of logs and tundra sod, the old Storyteller is mumbling the last story he will ever tell. It is the story of the hunter stalking a giant polar bear the color of blue glacier ice. It is a story which the old Storyteller has been telling since the young Yupik woman began to arrange the white trader's death. But a sudden storm develops. The hunter finds himself on an ice floe off shore. Visibility is zero, the scream of the wind blots out all sound. Quickly the hunter realizes he is being stalked. Hunted by all the forces, by all the elements of the sky and earth around him. When at last the hunter's own muscles spasm and cause the jade knife to fall and shatter the ice, the hunter's death in the embrace of the giant ice blue bear is the foretelling of the world's end. When humans have blasted and burned the last bit of life from the earth, an immeasurable freezing will descend with a darkness that obliterates the sun.

[1991]

An Oral History*
(Testimonio)

Sherezada (Chiqui) Vicioso

I STARTED WRITING WHEN I WAS VERY YOUNG AND FOUND OUT THAT THE best way to pass Math was to write a poem to the teacher. . . . I began to become aware of the marginalized people in my country when I was an adolescent and worked in the barrios as part of a Christian youth volunteer group. Basically I am a poet, but I also write criticism about women's literature. I began to write in 1978 and published my first book of poetry, *Viajes desde el agua*, in 1981.

Up until about 1977, I regarded literature as a hobby of the petite bourgeoisie, but when I went to Cuba and spoke there with writers whom I very much admired, they showed me that a writer is also a cultural worker. Whereas I took note of this fact on an intellectual level, I realized it on an emotional one only when I went to Africa in 1978. I started writing criticism from 1982 on and published my second book in 1985 (*Un extraño ulular traía el viento*).

Both my books were written for Dominicans and were published in Santo Domingo. I never thought of publishing in the United States because, as a Latina, I felt unable to deal with the publishing establishment in that country. My first book was presented at the Las Américas bookshop and other places for Latinos in New York. After all, New York is the second most important city for Dominicans. The island has six million inhabitants and half a million live in New York. Economically, it's the most important. I never felt far from Santo Domingo when I lived in New York.

I first came to the United States in April 1967. Initially, I had wanted to be a lay nun and work in the barrios. Marriage repelled me, especially when I looked at my aunts, practically all of whom were divorced. I couldn't stand the idiocy of the whole scene: the danger of getting mixed up with someone when you were thirteen or fourteen, worrying about not having a boyfriend when you were sixteen. To me, becoming a nun was my path to freedom.

* This narrative is the transcript of an interview with Sherezada (Chiqui) Vicioso on November 17, 1987. Translated by Nina M. Scott.

I also wanted to study medicine. The one year I planned to stay eventually became seventeen.

My mother, who had left a year earlier, said I should go to the States in order to improve my English and to get to know the world before embarking on becoming a nun. I was very angry with her at the time, but she was right.

I come from a very special family with an intellectual background. On my father's side, my grandfather was a journalist and a writer, and my father is a poet and a well-known composer. My mother is a better poet than I am, but has never dared to write. She is the daughter of a peasant woman who worked in a tobacco factory and a Dominican oligarch who owned the factory and literally bought her when she was sixteen. My mother is a hybrid of two very distinct classes. I felt this when I went to school in Santiago.

In spite of having studied English in school, I found out, on my arrival in New York, that I didn't know very much. Like most Dominicans who come to the United States, I went to work in a factory: first a hat, and then a button factory (the acetone in which we had to wash the buttons damaged my eyes so that I have had to wear glasses ever since). I went to night school for a while, and then was accepted into a city-sponsored intensive English program, where I was paid to study.

My next job was as a telephone operator, and I quickly acquired a reputation as being extremely courteous to the customers, as my English still wasn't all that good and I said "Thank you" to everyone, even if they insulted me. Then Brooklyn College opened its doors to minority students. They responded to a policy, initiated under the Johnson administration, whereby colleges were paid federal funds to admit minorities. I was one of eight Dominican students admitted to Brooklyn College.

Since there were only eight of us, and it was very tough to survive in such a racist atmosphere, we joined up with other minority students, principally Puerto Ricans, Blacks, other people from the Caribbean—we formed a Third World Alliance.

This was a real threshold for me; I had never known the people from Barbados or Trinidad, etc. My concept of the Caribbean, up to that time, had been limited to the Spanish-speaking part, and I discovered my identity as a *caribeña* in New York.

I was also racially classified at Brooklyn College, which was an interesting experience for me. In Santo Domingo, the popular classes have a pretty clear grasp of racial divisions, but the middle and upper-middle classes are very deluded on this point. People straighten their hair and marry "in order to improve the race," etc., etc., and don't realize the racist connotations of their language or their attitude. In the United States, there is no space for fine distinctions of race, and one goes from being "trigüeño" or "indio" to being "mulatto" or "Black" or "Hispanic." This was an excellent experience for me. From that point on, I discovered myself as a Caribbean *mulata* and adopted the Black identity as a gesture of solidarity. At that time, I deeply admired and identified with Angela Davis, and ever since then, I have kept on identifying myself as a Black woman.

This opened another door; I learned about Frantz Fanon and other Caribbean theoreticians, and that finished Europe for me. I learned about the triangular trade and how we had financed Europe's development. I realized that capitalism was an impossible model to follow in our development. For me, this was discovering a universe. I only became a feminist much later.

When I first became more radical I was very much put off by feminism and people like Gloria Steinem and Betty Friedan—to me they were representatives of the white U.S. middle class who were busy telling us how *we* were being screwed by machismo. In a first stage I rejected this and, up to a point, I also had a false sense of solidarity with our men, who were racially oppressed as well. I felt that if we women criticized our men, we were only providing the racists with ammunition. This created a conflict of loyalties for me.

Discovering myself as a woman came much later. First I had to discover that I was part of a certain geographical area, and then, that I was Latin American. The great majority of the Latin American exiles converged on New York at that time—the Argentinians, the Uruguayans, the Chileans (Allende fell during those years)—so that, for me, New York became a kind of great doorway to this Latin American world.

Being in New York was very essential to my development. I would not be the woman I am today had I not gone to New York. I would have been the classic *fracasada* (failure) in my country because I know that I would not have found happiness in marriage and having children. I would have been frustrated, unhappy in a marriage, or divorced several times over because I would not have understood that within me was a woman who needed to express her own truths, articulate her own words. That, in Santo Domingo, would have been impossible.

Nevertheless, for the first ten years that I lived in New York, I was engulfed by a great silence; I could write nothing at all. The only poem I salvaged from this era was one about two young Puerto Ricans, aged sixteen and seventeen, who were shot by a bartender they had robbed of $100. I saw an article about it in the paper and it made me terribly sad. The poem ends with the line, "sadness has never come so cheaply." New York was, for me, a crushing kind of silence.

Still, all these experiences were being stored up inside of me. It's that kind of a process; things go in stages.

It was going to Africa that restored my essence as a *caribeña* for me. I went for three and a half months to work on coordinating the first meeting of ministers of education of the Portuguese-speaking African nations, and discovered Amílcar Cabral, the outstanding African cultural and revolutionary theoretician. Up to that point, I had never understood the important role that culture plays in effecting change. This was a central experience for me.

When I returned to the States, I was a different person; I suffered from severe depressions, which I now realize marked the death of one Chiqui and the birth of another. I figured the only thing that could save me was to return to the university, so I decided, at that point, to get an M.A. in Education from Columbia. I tried to work one more year in New York, but it was no good, and I returned to Santo Domingo.

I was there for four years, until last year, when I returned to the States. Some very difficult things happened during that time. The man with whom I had planned to restructure my life died of cancer. I was working terribly hard in my job as an educational coordinator. Basically, I had a kind of breakdown. I returned to the States to recuperate, and then went back to Santo Domingo. I've been there three months now.

I have really wanted to be a literary critic, yet once again I am denying my condition as a writer. The African experience had awakened me to the terrible problem of illiteracy in my country; 40% of the population is totally illiterate, another 40%, functionally so. I've always moved in this atmosphere of crisis and tension [between the two drives in my life]. Even now, I am teaching not literature but a course on Dominican education at the university.

I had to go back to Santo Domingo because, after a few years, living in the United States gave me a kind of physical malaise. . . . When you first get here from your country, full of strength and energy, you get involved in a first stage of learning, absorbing, discovering. Then comes a time when you have to go back in order to revitalize yourself. If you stay in New York too long, you begin to get worn down by it. Anyone who is in the least sensitive can't help but feel bruised by the destruction of our people. Really. I saw it all the time in the Dominican community. Even though I had already acquired all sorts of New York rituals—I took perfumed baths in a flowered bathtub, swallowed my B12 vitamins, was into meditation—none of it was doing me any good. I realized I had to leave.

The New York experience, which was so crucial to my discovery of my Caribbean and racial identity, has made me a very, very critical person with respect to my own society. Things I never noticed before, I now see. Like racism, for example. Class differences. Santo Domingo is a very societally structured city. The situation of women is atrocious. I get almost rude about this because I can't stand the kind of sexist behavior that exists in my country. And for that, you pay the price of ostracism. It's really hard. By dint of having lived in the United States, I am considered a "liberated woman," which means that the men feel they have a green light to harass me sexually while the women distrust me. That's the most painful part. You come back to your country with a sense of intimate relationship and find that, for the most part, the principal *machistas* are the women themselves. And that's terrible. You find yourself confronted by an immense hostility that is a product of their own frustration. At first you ask yourself, "what have you done to this woman to have her treat you like this?" And then you realize that you symbolize all the things that she has never been able to do, and perhaps never will: leave the country, study what she wants to. She may find herself tied down by three or four children, a husband that bores her, physical confinement, etc.; and you come along as a woman who can come and go as she wishes, write, be creative and productive, freely elect the man she wants to be with, and you become, for her, an object of hatred. It's really dreadful. And with the men, you represent a challenge to try and get you because you're different, but the real challenge is to dominate you. For the women, you are all they cannot be and that must be destroyed for survival. And you have to understand that so that you don't self-destruct. You can laugh off the first two or three aggressions, but by the fourth time, it really hurts.

As a writer I haven't yet been able to talk about my experiences in the States. At some moment in the future I will. Remember that New York was an experience of great silence for me. I feel that a time will come when I will be able to surmount what happened to me in New York and will be able to write about it. Remember, too, that the things I'm telling you in such a light vein today were wrenching experiences for me, especially discrimination. I still can't talk about it, but because I now have a better understanding of the creative process, I have learned not to push the creative instincts so that they won't become artificial. I know I have to let things come to the surface. The time will come when I'll be able to do it. I've written some sociological essays and some journalistic pieces on New York for a Santo Domingo paper in order to let my people know what's happening there, but in terms of literature I haven't yet been able to draw out what I have inside.

Because so many of my potential readers live in New York, I am definitely moving more and more toward publishing in the United States. I think people on the island would be interested as well. . . . We cannot avoid the "invasion" of the Dominicans from the U.S. The whole country is changing: English is spoken all over—you feel the influence of the Dominicans who come back everywhere. I also think there will be interest in my writing in the States, first of all, because there are so many of us there, and second, because I will approach things with the particular viewpoint of a woman. I have a lot to tell about what New York did to my family. I had to assume a kind of paterfamilias role with respect to my siblings. A lot of it was very traumatic.

However, for the moment I'm more interested in women's issues, and especially in testimonials by Dominican women. I'm working on a book that is a collection of women's testimonials from the four years when I was here earlier. I've collected testimonials from all classes of women: peasants, factory workers, etc. I would like to be the voice of those who have no voice. Later, I'll be able to speak about New York.

In Santo Domingo there is a need to create a market for women's literature. As women, we have not yet discovered our power as consumers of books, but some day, when we discover this, perhaps we'll manifest this power by supporting women who write.

[1989]

In Search of Our Mothers' Gardens

Alice Walker

> I described her own nature and temperament. Told how they needed a larger life for their expression. . . . I pointed out that in lieu of proper channels, her emotions had overflowed into paths that dissipated them. I talked, beautifully I thought, about an art that would be born, an art that would open the way for women the likes of her. I asked her to hope, and build up an inner life against the coming of that day. . . . I sang, with a strange quiver in my voice, a promise song.
>
> —JEAN TOOMER, "Avey," Cane

The poet speaking to a prostitute who falls asleep while he's talking—

When the poet Jean Toomer walked through the South in the early twenties, he discovered a curious thing: black women whose spirituality was so intense, so deep, so *unconscious*, that they were themselves unaware of the richness they held. They stumbled blindly through their lives: creatures so abused and mutilated in body, so dimmed and confused by pain, that they considered themselves unworthy even of hope. In the selfless abstractions their bodies became to the men who used them, they became more than "sexual objects," more even than mere women: they became "Saints." Instead of being perceived as whole persons, their bodies became shrines: what was thought to be their minds became temples suitable for worship. These crazy Saints stared out at the world, wildly, like lunatics—or quietly, like suicides; and the "God" that was in their gaze was as mute as a great stone.

Who were these Saints? These crazy, loony, pitiful women?

Some of them, without a doubt, were our mothers and grandmothers.

In the still heat of the post-Reconstruction South, this is how they seemed to Jean Toomer: exquisite butterflies trapped in an evil honey, toiling away their lives in an era, a century, that did not acknowledge them, except as "the *mule* of the world." They dreamed dreams that no one knew—not even themselves, in any coherent fashion—and saw visions no one could understand. They wandered or sat about the countryside crooning lullabies to ghosts, and drawing the mother of Christ in charcoal on courthouse walls.

They forced their minds to desert their bodies and their striving spirits sought to rise, like frail whirlwinds from the hard red clay. And when those frail whirlwinds fell, in scattered particles, upon the ground, no one mourned. Instead, men lit candles to celebrate the emptiness that remained, as people do who enter a beautiful but vacant space to resurrect a God.

Our mothers and grandmothers, some of them: moving to music not yet written. And they waited.

They waited for a day when the unknown thing that was in them would be made known; but guessed, somehow in their darkness, that on the day of their revelation they would be long dead. Therefore to Toomer they walked, and even ran, in slow motion. For they were going nowhere immediate, and the future was not yet within their grasp. And men took our mothers and grandmothers, "but got no pleasure from it." So complex was their passion and their calm.

To Toomer, they lay vacant and fallow as autumn fields, with harvest time never in sight: and he saw them enter loveless marriages, without joy; and become prostitutes, without resistance; and become mothers of children, without fulfillment.

For these grandmothers and mothers of ours were not Saints, but Artists; driven to a numb and bleeding madness by the springs of creativity in them for which there was no release. They were Creators, who lived lives of spiritual waste, because they were so rich in spirituality—which is the basis of Art—that the strain of enduring their unused and unwanted talent drove them insane. Throwing away this spirituality was their pathetic attempt to lighten the soul to a weight their work-worn, sexually abused bodies could bear.

What did it mean for a black woman to be an artist in our grandmothers' time? In our great-grandmothers' day? It is a question with an answer cruel enough to stop the blood.

Did you have a genius of a great-great-grandmother who died under some ignorant and depraved white overseer's lash? Or was she required to bake biscuits for a lazy backwater tramp, when she cried out in her soul to paint watercolors of sunsets, or the rain falling on the green and peaceful pasturelands? Or was her body broken and forced to bear children (who were more often than not sold away from her)—eight, ten, fifteen, twenty children—when her one joy was the thought of modeling heroic figures of rebellion, in stone or clay?

How was the creativity of the black woman kept alive, year after year and century after century, when for most of the years black people have been in America, it was a punishable crime for a black person to read or write? And the freedom to paint, to sculpt, to expand the mind with action did not exist. Consider, if you can bear to imagine it, what might have been the result if singing, too, had been forbidden by law. Listen to the voices of Bessie Smith, Billie Holiday, Nina Simone, Roberta Flack, and Aretha Franklin, among others, and imagine those voices muzzled for life. Then you may begin to comprehend the lives of our "crazy," "Sainted" mothers and grandmothers. The agony of the lives of women who might have been Poets, Novelists, Essayists, and Short-Story Writers (over a period of centuries), who died with their real gifts stifled within them.

And, if this were the end of the story, we would have cause to cry out in my paraphrase of Okot p'Bitek's great poem:

> O, my clanswomen
> Let us all cry together!
> Come,
> Let us mourn the death of our mother,

The death of a Queen
The ash that was produced
By a great fire!
O, this homestead is utterly dead
Close the gates
With *lacari* thorns,
For our mother
The creator of the Stool is lost!
And all the young women
Have perished in the wilderness!

But this is not the end of the story, for all the young women—our mothers and grandmothers, *ourselves*—have not perished in the wilderness. And if we ask ourselves why, and search for and find the answer, we will know beyond all efforts to erase it from our minds, just exactly who, and of what, we black American women are.

One example, perhaps the most pathetic, most misunderstood one, can provide a backdrop for our mothers' work: Phillis Wheatley, a slave in the 1700s.

Virginia Woolf, in her book *A Room of One's Own*, wrote that in order for a woman to write fiction she must have two things, certainly: a room of her own (with key and lock) and enough money to support herself.

What then are we to make of Phillis Wheatley, a slave, who owned not even herself? This sickly, frail black girl who required a servant of her own at times—her health was so precarious—and who, had she been white, would have been easily considered the intellectual superior of all the women and most of the men in the society of her day.

Virginia Woolf wrote further, speaking of course not of our Phillis, that "any woman born with a great gift in the sixteenth century [insert "eighteenth century," insert "black woman," insert "born or made a slave"] would certainly have gone crazed, shot herself, or ended her days in some lonely cottage outside the village, half witch, half wizard [insert "Saint"], feared and mocked at. For it needs little skill and psychology to be sure that a highly gifted girl who had tried to use her gift for poetry would have been so thwarted and hindered by contrary instincts [add "chains, guns, the lash, the ownership of one's body by someone else, submission to an alien religion"] that she must have lost her health and sanity to a certainty."

The key words, as they relate to Phillis, are "contrary instincts." For when we read the poetry of Phillis Wheatley—as when we read the novels of Nella Larsen or the oddly false-sounding autobiography of that freest of all black women writers, Zora Hurston—evidence of "contrary instincts" is everywhere. Her loyalties were completely divided, as was, without question, her mind.

But how could this be otherwise? Captured at seven, a slave of wealthy, doting whites who instilled in her the "savagery" of the Africa they "rescued" her from . . . one wonders if she was even able to remember her homeland as she had known it, or as it really was.

Yet, because she did try to use her gift for poetry in a world that made her a slave, she was "so thwarted and hindered by . . . contrary instincts, that she . . . lost her health. . . ." In the last years of her brief life, burdened not only with the need to express her gift but also with a penniless, friendless "freedom" and several small children for whom she was forced to do strenuous work to feed, she lost her health, certainly. Suffering from malnutrition and neglect and who knows what mental agonies, Phillis Wheatley died.

So torn by "contrary instincts" was black, kidnapped, enslaved Phillis that her description of "the Goddess"—as she poetically called the Liberty she did not have—is ironically, cruelly humorous. And, in fact, has held Phillis up to ridicule for more than a century. It is usually read prior to hanging Phillis's memory as that of a fool. She wrote:

> The Goddess comes, she moves divinely fair,
> Olive and laurel binds her *golden* hair.
> Wherever shines this native of the skies,
> Unnumber'd charms and recent graces rise. [My italics]

It is obvious that Phillis, the slave, combed the "Goddess's" hair every morning; prior, perhaps, to bringing in the milk, or fixing her mistress's lunch. She took her imagery from the one thing she saw elevated above all others.

With the benefit of hindsight we ask, "How could she?"

But at last, Phillis, we understand. No more snickering when your stiff, struggling, ambivalent lines are forced on us. We know now that you were not an idiot or a traitor; only a sickly little black girl, snatched from your home and country and made a slave; a woman who still struggled to sing the song that was your gift, although in a land of barbarians who praised you for your bewildered tongue. It is not so much what you sang, as that you kept alive, in so many of our ancestors, *the notion of song.*

Black women are called, in the folklore that so aptly identifies one's status in society, "the *mule* of the world," because we have been handed the burdens that everyone else—*everyone else*—refused to carry. We have also been called "Matriarchs," "Superwomen," and "Mean and Evil Bitches." Not to mention "Castraters" and "Sapphire's Mama." When we have pleaded for understanding, our character has been distorted; when we have asked for simple caring, we have been handed empty inspirational appellations, then stuck in the farthest corner. When we have asked for love, we have been given children. In short, even our plainer gifts, our labors of fidelity and love, have been knocked down our throats. To be an artist and a black woman, even today, lowers our status in many respects, rather than raises it: and yet, artists we will be.

Therefore, we must fearlessly pull out of ourselves and look at and identify with our lives the living creativity some of our great-grandmothers were not allowed to know. I stress *some* of them because it is well known that the majority of our great-grandmothers knew, even without "knowing" it, the reality of their spirituality, even if they didn't recognize it beyond what happened in the singing at church—and they never had any intention of giving it up.

How they did it—those millions of black women who were not Phillis Wheatley, or Lucy Terry or Frances Harper or Zora Hurston or Nella Larsen or Bessie Smith; or Elizabeth Catlett, or Katherine Dunham, either—brings me to the title of this essay, "In Search of Our Mothers' Gardens," which is a personal account that is yet shared, in its theme and its meaning, by all of us. I found, while thinking about the far-reaching world of the creative black woman, that often the truest answer to a question that really matters can be found very close.

In the late 1920s my mother ran away from home to marry my father. Marriage, if not running away, was expected of seventeen-year-old girls. By the time she was twenty, she had two children and was pregnant with a third. Five children later, I was born. And this is how I came to know my mother: she seemed a large, soft, loving-eyed woman who was rarely impatient in our home. Her quick, violent temper was on view only a few times a year, when she battled with the white landlord who had the misfortune to suggest to her that her children did not need to go to school.

She made all the clothes we wore, even my brothers' overalls. She made all the towels and sheets we used. She spent the summers canning vegetables and fruits. She spent the winter evenings making quilts enough to cover all our beds.

During the "working" day, she labored beside—not behind—my father in the fields. Her day began before sunup, and did not end until late at night. There was never a moment for her to sit down, undisturbed, to unravel her own private thoughts; never a time free from interruption—by work or the noisy inquiries of her many children. And yet, it is to my mother—and all our mothers who were not famous—that I went in search of the secret of what has fed that muzzled and often mutilated, but vibrant, creative spirit that the black woman has inherited, and that pops out in wild and unlikely places to this day.

But when, you will ask, did my overworked mother have time to know or care about feeding the creative spirit?

The answer is so simple that many of us have spent years discovering it. We have constantly looked high, when we should have looked high—and low.

For example: in the Smithsonian Institution in Washington, D.C., there hangs a quilt unlike any other in the world. In fanciful, inspired, and yet simple and identifiable figures, it portrays the story of the Crucifixion. It is considered rare, beyond price. Though it follows no known pattern of quilt-making, and though it is made of bits and pieces of worthless rags, it is obviously the work of a person of powerful imagination and deep spiritual feeling. Below this quilt I saw a note that says it was made by "an anonymous Black woman in Alabama, a hundred years ago."

If we could locate this "anonymous" black woman from Alabama, she would turn out to be one of our grandmothers—an artist who left her mark in the only materials she could afford, and in the only medium her position in society allowed her to use.

As Virginia Woolf wrote further, in *A Room of One's Own:*

> Yet genius of a sort must have existed among women as it must have existed among the working class. [Change this to "slaves" and "the wives and daughters of sharecroppers."] Now and again an Emily Brontë or a Robert Burns [change this to "a Zora Hurston or a Richard Wright"] blazes out and proves its presence. But certainly it never got itself on to paper. When, however, one reads of a witch being ducked, of a woman possessed by devils [or "Sainthood"], of a wise woman selling herbs [our root workers], or even a very remarkable man who had a mother, then I think we are on the track of a lost novelist, a suppressed poet, of some mute and inglorious Jane Austen. . . . Indeed, I would venture to guess that Anon, who wrote so many poems without signing them, was often a woman. . . .

And so our mothers and grandmothers have, more often than not anonymously, handed on the creative spark, the seed of the flower they themselves never hoped to see: or like a sealed letter they could not plainly read.

And so it is, certainly, with my own mother. Unlike "Ma" Rainey's songs, which retained their creator's name even while blasting forth from Bessie Smith's mouth, no song or poem will bear my mother's name. Yet so many of the stories that I write, that we all write, are my mother's stories. Only recently did I fully realize this: that through years of listening to my mother's stories of her life, I have absorbed not only the stories themselves, but something of the manner in which she spoke, something of the urgency that involves the knowledge that her stories—like her life—must be recorded. It is probably for this reason that so much of what I have written is about characters whose counterparts in real life are so much older than I am.

But the telling of these stories, which came from my mother's lips as naturally as breathing, was not the only way my mother showed herself as an artist. For stories, too, were subject to being distracted, to dying without conclusion. Dinners must be started, and cotton must be gathered before the big rains. The artist that was and is my mother showed itself to me only after many years. This is what I finally noticed:

Like Mem, a character in *The Third Life of Grange Copeland*, my mother adorned with flowers whatever shabby house we were forced to live in. And not just your typical straggly country stand of zinnias, either. She planted ambitious gardens—and still does—with over fifty different varieties of plants that bloom profusely from early March until late November. Before she left home for the fields, she watered her flowers, chopped up the grass, and laid out new beds. When she returned from the fields she might divide clumps of bulbs, dig a cold pit, uproot and replant roses, or prune branches from her taller bushes or trees—until night came and it was too dark to see.

Whatever she planted grew as if by magic, and her fame as a grower of flowers spread over three counties. Because of her creativity with her flowers, even my memories of poverty are seen through a screen of blooms—sunflowers, petunias, roses, dahlias, forsythia, spirea, delphiniums, verbena . . . and on and on.

And I remember people coming to my mother's yard to be given cuttings from her flowers; I hear again the praise showered on her because whatever rocky soil she landed on, she turned into a garden. A garden so brilliant with colors, so original in its design, so magnificent with life and creativity, that to this day people drive by our house in Georgia—perfect strangers and imperfect strangers—and ask to stand or walk among my mother's art.

I notice that it is only when my mother is working in her flowers that she is radiant, almost to the point of being invisible—except as Creator: hand and eye. She is involved in work her soul must have. Ordering the universe in the image of her personal conception of Beauty.

Her face, as she prepares the Art that is her gift, is a legacy of respect she leaves to me, for all that illuminates and cherishes life. She has handed down respect for the possibilities—and the will to grasp them.

For her, so hindered and intruded upon in so many ways, being an artist has still been a daily part of her life. This ability to hold on, even in very simple ways, is work black women have done for a very long time.

This poem is not enough, but it is something, for the woman who literally covered the holes in our walls with sunflowers:

> They were women then
> My mama's generation
> Husky of voice—Stout of
> Step
> With fists as well as
> Hands
> How they battered down
> Doors
> And ironed
> Starched white
> Shirts
> How they led
> Armies
> Headragged Generals
> Across mined
> Fields
> Booby-trapped
> Kitchens
> To discover books
> Desks
> A place for us
> How they knew what we
> *Must* know
> Without knowing a page
> Of it
> Themselves.

Guided by my heritage of a love of beauty and a respect for strength—in search of my mother's garden, I found my own.

And perhaps in Africa over two hundred years ago, there was just such a mother; perhaps she painted vivid and daring decorations in oranges and yellows and greens on the walls of her hut; perhaps she sang—in a voice like Roberta Flack's—*sweetly* over the compounds of her village; perhaps she wove the most stunning mats or told the most ingenious stories of all the village storytellers. Perhaps she was herself a poet—though only her daughter's name is signed to the poems that we know.

Perhaps Phillis Wheatley's mother was also an artist.

Perhaps in more than Phillis Wheatley's biological life is her mother's signature made clear.

[1984]

Fire and Ice
(Some Thoughts on Property, Appearance, and the Language of Lawmakers)

Patricia J. Williams

LAST JANUARY I WENT TO A GINGERBREAD-MAN-MAKING PARTY. LOTS OF children, popcorn, eggnog, and cookie cutting. The party was in a neighborhood that used to be the Lower East Side but is now struggling for the separate identity of a gentler (and more gentrified) name. It reaches for inspiration to the other side of Broadway, to Soho and the Village, where I was living then. After the party I wandered home, along the Bowery, up Lafayette. It was no temperature at all, zero degrees. I decided to stop in at the dance studio where I took classes and get the latest schedule. It's located in an old warehouse that used to be an informal home for the homeless, an abandoned-factory refuge from the cold. In the old days I would make my way through the littered hallways, the slumped bodies in the foyer, dispensing change upon request, praying for divine protection, both for them and for me. My car was broken into occasionally, but for the most part it was safe for all of us, because so well-trafficked. We were each other's guardians. Then one day all that "empty space" in the building was converted into loft-condominiums, and the old familiar bodies from inside began to be seen slumped on the sidewalk outside the old warehouse.

At any rate there I was, late on a frozen Sunday afternoon, walking through a border-line Bowery neighborhood, toward the factory-condominium that was also my dance studio. As I opened the heavy iron door, I met three angry people stalking down the hallway. The procession was led by a child of about eight who flounced through the door I held open for her, without lifting her eyes from the ground. Her younger sister, about six, followed through the door I continued to hold open, looked me coldly in the eye, and did not say thank you. Their mother followed, a deep furrow between her eyes; as she drew abreast of me, she turned and sharply asked if I were going upstairs to the dance studio. When I said yes, she shouted at me, with the unique intensity of a neurotic New Yorker: "Well, tell them to call the police! There are BUMS in the lobby again!" Then she pushed past, after her little girls.

I let myself cautiously in and walked through the hallway to the staircase. There was one old, bent, toothless black woman huddled under a yellow blanket with holes in it. She was sucking on a cigarette with one hand and pulling at her skirt with the other. She wore black round-toed sneakers with white rubber rims and gray argyle kneesocks. I gave her $1.25 when she asked for spare change; then I went upstairs to get a copy of the dance schedule. No one molested me and I called no police.

Back out on the sidewalk a few minutes later, I saw the angry woman and her two children across the street, waiting to get their car from a garage. In what was clearly the most spontaneous action of my well-ordered day, I jaywalked over to her and said, simply, that if she wanted to call the police for that old woman, she would have to take on the responsibility herself. If I had taken the few seconds that indignation eclipsed, I would have been prepared for her anger. She jumped in her car, locked the doors, and through her window (rolled down two inches) yelled at me about how she was spending "too much goddamned money" to live in that building, how she had been shot at, how she had been mugged, how maybe one woman wasn't dangerous but, where there's one woman, the men will follow and "those men" are dangerous. "Those men" are dangerous, she said over and over again.

I wanted to say more, I wanted to ask her to observe that the warmth of something as simple as fire is no longer free in this city, that the dismantling of the welfare state means people will steal to survive. I wanted to tell her that when people are too tired to be angry, when they lose the will to survive, that only then will the war exit their bodies. When they become sunken, spiritless, haunted by the living, pursued by death, abandoned by all but pathos—then graphic artists will flock to their grave, sad images and proclaim them indomitable human spirits, pietàs, survivors. Then, at last, they will be sympathetic. I wanted to say all of that, but she kept shouting and shouting at me about all the goddamned money she was spending to keep "those people" out of her life and off "her" streets.

Her two young children sat in the back seat through all this, frightened puppies hovering in their mother's shadow—frightened by their mother's fury, frightened by me, who deeply did not wish this confrontation. They stared at me in round-eyed, innocent terror. I hated them for their terror of me more than I hated their mother for her protective rage. When they finally drove off, in a back-wheeled spray of salt and slush, I cried. Unexpectedly I felt exiled, intensely alien, cold and alone, despite the fact that I was only two blocks from home.

Over a year has passed. The neighborhood has continued to change. Japanese restaurants and oriental rug marts abound. There's a security guard in the foyer of the building now; they hired an old black man in a blue suit with a badge, to keep out other old tired black people. The guard smiles and nods benevolently at me when I come and go. I nod back at him. He says I make his day worthwhile; he is paternal, flirtatious. We both enjoy the fantasy that he is protecting me. I walk out into the cold dark winter of New York. I look back through the moist glass doors and see his blackened shape, pot-bellied and alone; a plastic chair; his transistor radio, its tiny antenna raised into the empty space of the stairwell. He is brilliantly backlit, like the wick of a candle. He stays in my mind like that, a burning marker, a flaming signifier.

On October 29, 1984, Eleanor Bumpurs, a 270-pound, arthritic sixty-seven-year-old woman, was shot to death while resisting eviction from her apartment in the Bronx. She was $96.85, or one month, behind in her rent. Mayor Ed Koch and Police Commissioner Benjamin Ward described the struggle that preceded her demise as involving two officers with large plastic shields, one with a restraining hook, one with a shotgun, and at least one other who was supervising. All of these officers also carried service revolvers. During the course of the attempted eviction, Mrs. Bumpurs wielded a knife that Commissioner Ward says was "bent" on one of the plastic shields and escaped the constraint of the restraining hook twice. At some point, Stephen Sullivan, the officer positioned farthest away from her and the one with the shotgun, took aim and fired at her. He missed (mostly—it is alleged that this blast removed half of the hand that held the knife and, according to the Bronx district attorney's office, "it was anatomically impossible for her to hold the knife"), pumped his gun, and shot again, making his mark the second time around.[1]

What has not been made clear in discussion relating to this case is that Mrs. Bumpurs was evicted on a default judgment of possession and warrant of eviction issued without any hearing of any kind. She was never personally served because, allegedly, she was not at home on the two occasions the process server says he called. Since Mrs. Bumpurs did not appear in court to answer the petition for her eviction, the default judgment for possession and warrant for her eviction were signed by the Civil Court judge solely on the papers submitted. From what we know now . . . there is serious doubt about the validity of those papers.

Only last year, in announcing the indictments of five process servers, the Attorney General and the New York City Departments of Consumer Affairs and Investigation issued a report on service of process in Civil Court, finding that at least one-third of all default judgments were based on perjurious affidavits.[2]

The case against Officer Sullivan was not brought to trial until January 1987.

Initially a grand jury indicted him for reckless manslaughter. Two lower courts rejected the indictment, but in 1986 the New York Court of Appeals reversed and ordered a trial regarding the second shot.

In the two-and-a-half-year interval between the incident and the trial, controversy billowed and swirled around the poles of whether Mrs. Bumpurs ought to have brandished a knife or whether the officer ought to have used his gun. In February 1987 a New York Supreme Court justice found Officer Sullivan innocent of manslaughter charges. The case centered on a very narrow use of language pitted against circumstance. District Attorney Mario Merola described the case as follows: "*Obviously* [emphasis added], one shot would have been justified. But if that shot took off part of her hand and rendered her defenseless, whether there was any need for a second shot, which killed her, that's the whole issue of whether you have reasonable force or excessive force."[3] My intention in this chapter is to analyze the task facing judges and lawyers in undoing institutional descriptions of what is "obvious" and what is not; and in resisting the general predigestion of evidence for jury consumption.

Shortly after Merola's statement, Sullivan's attorney expressed eagerness to get the case before a jury. Then, after the heavily publicized attack in Howard Beach, the same attorney decided that a nonjury trial might be better after all. "'I think a judge will be much more likely than a jury to understand the defense that the shooting was justified,' said Officer Sullivan's lawyer, Bruce A. Smiry, when asked why he had requested a nonjury trial. 'The average lay person might find it difficult to understand why the police were there in the first place, and why a shotgun was employed . . . Because of the climate now in the city, I don't want people perceiving this as a racial case.'"[4]

Since 1984 Mayor Koch, Commissioner Ward, and a host of other city officials have repeatedly termed the shooting of Eleanor Bumpurs as completely legal.[5] At the same time, Ward admitted publicly that Mrs. Bumpurs should not have died. Koch admitted that her death had been the result of "a chain of mistakes and circumstances that came together in the worst possible way, with the worst possible consequences."[6] The officers could have waited until she calmed down, or they could have used tear gas or mace, Ward said. But, according to Ward, all that is hindsight (prompting one to wonder how often this term is used as a euphemism for short-circuited foresight). As to whether this white officer's shooting of a black woman had racial overtones, Ward said he had "no evidence of racism." (Against this, it is interesting to note that in New York City, where blacks and Latinos account for close to half the population, "86.8% of police officers are white; 8.6% are black; 4.5% Latino; and 0.1% Asian or American Indian."[7]) The commissioner pointed out that he is sworn to uphold the law, which is "inconsistent with treating blacks differently," and that the shooting was legal because it was "within the code of police ethics."[8] Finally, city officials resisted criticism of the police department's handling of the incident by accusing "outsiders" of not knowing all the facts and not understanding the pressure under which officers labor.

The word *legal* has as its root the Latin *lex*, which meant law in a fairly concrete sense, law as we understand it when we refer to written law, codes, systems of obedience. The word *lex* did not include the more abstract, ethical dimension of law which includes not merely consideration of rules but their purposes and effective implementation. The larger meaning was contained in the Latin *jus* from which we derive the word *justice*. This is not an insignificant semantic distinction: the word of law, whether statutory or judge-made, is a subcategory of the underlying social motives and beliefs from which it is born. It is the technical embodiment of attempts to order society according to a consensus of ideals. When a society loses sight of those ideals and grants obeisance to words alone, law becomes sterile and formalistic; lex is applied without jus and is therefore unjust. A sort of punitive literalism ensues that leads to a high degree of thoughtless conformity; for literalism has, as one of its primary underlying values, order (the ultimate goal may be justice, but it is the ordering of behavior that is deemed the immediate end). Living solely according to the letter of the law means that we live without spirit, that one can do anything one wants to as long as it complies in a technical sense. The cynicism or rebelliousness that infects one's spirit, the enthusiasm or dissatisfaction with which one technically conforms, is unimportant. It implies furthermore that such compliance is in some ways arbitrary, that is to say, inconsistent with the will of the compliant. The law becomes a battleground of wills. But the extent to which technical legalisms are used to obfuscate the human motivations that generate our justice system is the real extent to which we as human beings are disenfranchised.

Cultural needs and ideals change with the momentum of time; the need to redefine our laws in keeping with the spirit of cultural flux is what keeps a society alive and humane. In instances like the Bumpurs case, the words of the law called for nonlethal alternatives to be applied first, but allowed for a degree of police discretion in determining which situations were so immediately life-endangering as to require the use of deadly force. It was this discretionary area that presumably was the basis upon which the claim was founded that Officer Sullivan acted legally. Yet the purpose of the law as written was to prevent unnecessry deaths; it is ironic that a public mandate so unambiguous about its concern and, in this instance, relatively unambiguous about the limits of its application should be used as the justification for this shooting. The law as written permitted shooting in general and therefore, by extension of the city's reasoning, it would be impossible for a police officer ever to shoot someone in a specifically objectionable way.

If our laws are thus piano-wired on the exclusive validity of literalism, if they are picked clean of their spirit, then society risks heightened irresponsibility for the consequence of abominable actions. Jonathan Swift's description of lawyers in *Gulliver's Travels* (part 4, chapter 5) comes weirdly and ironically alive: "there was a society of men among us, bred up from their youth in the art of proving by words multiplied for the purpose, that white is black, and black is white, according as they are paid. To this society all the rest of the people are slaves." We risk as well subjecting ourselves to such absurdly empty rhetoric as Commissioner Ward's comments that Mrs. Bumpurs' death was "unfortunate, but the law says . . ." or that racism is "unfortunate, but the law says . . ." What's worse, this sort of apologizing is the softened inverse of something akin to fascism. Ward's sentiments may as well read: "The law says . . . and therefore the death was unfortunate but irremedial; the law says . . . and therefore there is little that can be done about racism." The law becomes a shield behind which to avoid responsibility for the human repercussions of either governmental or publicly harmful private activity.

A related issue is the degree to which much of the criticism of the police department's handling of this case was devalued as "noisy" or excessively emotional. It is as though passionate protest were a separate crime, a rudeness of such dimension as to defeat altogether any legitimacy of content. As lawyers, we are taught from the moment we enter law school to temper our emotionalism, quash our idealism. Most of us were taught that our heartfelt instincts would subvert the law and defeat the security of a well-ordered civilization; but faithful adherence to the word of law, to *stare decisis* and clearly stated authority, would lead as a matter of course to a bright clear world in which those heartfelt instincts would, like the Wizard of Oz, be waiting. Form was exalted over substance, and cool rationales over heated feelings. Yet being ruled by the cool formality of language is surely as bad as being ruled solely by one's emotions.

But undue literalism is only one brand of sleight of tongue in the attainment of meaningless dialogue. The defense in the Bumpurs case used overgeneralization as an effective linguistic complement to their aversion of the issues; it is an old game, Enlargement of the Stakes, and an ancient tactic of irresponsibility. Allegations that the killing was illegal, unnecessary, and should be prosecuted were met with responses like: "The laws permit police officers to shoot people." "As long as police officers have guns, there will be unfortunate deaths." "The conviction rate in cases like this is very low." (This was part of the basis on which two lower courts had vacated the 1985 grand-jury indictment of Officer Sullivan, before it was finally reinstated in November 1986, and the basis on which the Police Benevolent Association staged a continuing protest against Sullivan's being tried for anything.) The observation that tear gas would have been an effective alternative to shooting drew the dismissive reply that "there were lots of things they could have done."[9]

Privatization of Response as a Justification for Public Irresponsibility is a version of the same game. This method holds up the private self as indistinguishable from the public-duty-self. Public and media commentary is responded to by officials as if it were meant specifically to hurt private, vulnerable feelings; and trying to hold a public official accountable while not hurting his feelings is a skill the acquisition of which could consume time better spent on almost any conceivable issue. Thus, when Commissioner Ward was asked if the internal review board planned to discipline Officer Sullivan, many seemed conditioned to accept as responsive his saying that, while he was personally very sorry she had died, he couldn't understand why the media were focusing so closely on him. "How many other police commissioners," he asked repeatedly, "have gotten as much attention as I have?" (Not that there wasn't truth to that. Ward was the first black commissioner in the history of the New York Police Department; the excessive scrutiny to which he was subjected in the public's search for irony, as opposed to other responsible officials, was glaring.)

Finally, a most cruel form of semantic slipperiness infused Mrs. Bumpurs' death from the beginning: Victim Responsibility. It is the least responsive form of dialogue, yet apparently the easiest to buy into (were we hardened to its fallacy during our helpless, finger-pointing, guilt-ridden childhoods?). The following examples can be found in the answers, from various public officials and law-enforcement personnel, to questions posed by television reporter Gil Noble on the program "Like It Is":

> —*Don't you think this officer was motivated by racism?* "She was psychotic; she said that she saw Reagan coming through her walls."
> —*Wasn't the discharge of the shotgun illegal?* "She waved a knife."
> —*Wasn't shooting her unnecessary?* "She made the officers fear for their lives."
> —*Couldn't the officers have used tear gas?* "Couldn't her children have paid her rent and taken care of her?" (The hypothesized failure of Mrs. Bumpurs' children to look after her actually became a major point in Officer Sullivan's defense attorney's opening and closing statements. Ironically, "a former employee of the Housing Authority said that, three weeks before Mrs. Bumpurs's death . . . her relatives tried to make a payment of about . . . half of the rent she owed . . . But the former Authority employee, Joan Alfredson . . . who was a bookkeeper, said she turned down the payment because she was forbidden to accept partial payment without the written consent of a supervisor."[10])

All these words, from the commissioner, from the mayor, from the media and the public generally, have rumbled and resounded with the sounds of discourse; we want to believe that their symmetrical, pleasing structure adds up to discourse; and if we are not careful, we will hypnotize ourselves into believing that it is discourse. When the whole world gets to that point, I know that I, for one, will see Ronald Reagan, clear and sprightly, coming through my walls as Mrs. Bumpurs alleged he did in her last hours. And I have not yet been able to settle within myself whether that would be the product of psychosis.

The night after the Bumpurs story became public, I dreamed about a black woman who was denied entry to a restaurant because of her color. In response she climbed over the building. The next time she found a building in her way, she climbed over it, and the next time and the next and the next. She became famous, as she roamed the world, traveling in determined straight lines, wordlessly scaling whatever lay in her path, including skyscrapers. Well-meaning white people came to marvel at her and gathered in crowds to watch and applaud. But she never acknowledged their presence and went about her business in unsmiling silence. The white people were annoyed, angry that she did not appreciate their praise and seemed ungrateful for their gift of her fame; they condemned her. I stood somewhere on the periphery of this dream and wondered what unspoken rule, what deadened curiosity, it was that kept anyone from ever asking why.

I have tried to ask myself a progression of questions about the Bumpurs death: my life experiences prepared me to comprehend the animating force behind the outraged, dispossessed knife wielding of Eleanor Bumpurs. I know few blacks who have not had some encounter with police intimidation. My earliest memory of such an instance was when I was about nine, my sister seven. My family was driving to Georgia to see my father's relatives. Two highway patrolmen stopped our car on a deserted stretch of highway in South Carolina. They were attracted by the Massachusetts license plates; they wanted to know what "y'all" were doing in those parts'; they asked about the weather in Boston, they fondled with great curiosity my father's driver's license, they admired the lines of the car. They were extremely polite, their conversation a model of southern hospitality and propriety. Throughout the entire fifteen or twenty minutes of our detention, one officer questioned my mother and father in soothing, honeyed tones; the other held a double-barreled shotgun through the rear window, pointed at my sister and me. If he had "accidently" shot us both, our deaths would have been, like that of Eleanor Bumpurs, entirely legal in the state of South Carolina.

What I found more difficult to focus on was the "why," the animus that inspired such fear and impatient contempt in a police officer that the presence of six other well-armed men could not allay his need to kill a sick old lady fighting off hallucinations with a knife. It seemed to me a fear embellished by something beyond Mrs. Bumpurs herself; something about her that filled the void between her physical, limited presence and the "immediate threat and endangerment to life" in the beholding eyes of the officer. Why was the sight of a knife-wielding woman so fearful to a shotgun-wielding policeman that he had to blow her to pieces as the only recourse, the only way to preserve his physical integrity? What offensive spirit of his past experience raised her presence to the level of a physical menace beyond what it in fact was; what spirit of prejudgment, of prejudice, provided him such a powerful hallucinogen?

However slippery these questions may be on a legal or conscious level, unresponsiveness does not make them go away. Failure to resolve the dilemma of racial violence merely displaces its power. The legacy of killing finds its way into cultural expectations, archetypes, and isms. The echoes of both dead and deadly others acquire an hallucinatory quality; their voices speak of an unwanted past, but also reflect images of the future. Today's world condemns those voices as superstitious, paranoid; neglected, they speak from the shadows of such inattention in garbles and growls, in the tongues of the damned and the insane. The superstitious listen, and perhaps in the silence of their attention they hear and understand. So-called enlightened others who fail to listen to these voices of demonic selves, made invisibly uncivilized, simply make them larger, more barbarously enraged, until the nearsightedness of looking-glass existence is smashed in by the terrible dispossession of dreams too long deferred.

References

1. Ronald Smothers, "Blacks, after Howard Beach, Unite on Goals, Split on Policy," *New York Times*, January 12, 1987, p. B2.
2. Margaret Taylor, "A Court Fails, an Old Woman Dies, and the Police Stand Trial," *New York Times*, March 19, 1987, p. A26.
3. Dennis Heuesi, "Bumpurs Case Charge Reinstated," *New York Times*, November 26, 1986, p. B6.
4. Selwyn Raab, "Trial of Officer in Bumpurs Case Starting with Request for No Jury," *New York Times*, January 12, 1987, p. B2.
5. Remarks of Commissioner Benjamin Ward at City University of New York Law School, November 1985, audiotape on file at CUNY Law School.
6. *New York Times*, November 21, 1987, p. B3.
7. *Fact Sheets on Institutional Racism* (New York: Council on Interracial Books for Children, 1982).
8. Remarks of Ward; Selwyn Raab, "Ward Defends Police Actions in Bronx Death," *New York Times*, November 3, 1984, p. A27.
9. *New York Times*, November 3, 1984, November 21 and 26, 1986; remarks of Ward.
10. Selwyn Raab, "Civilian Describes 'Struggle' before Shooting of Bumpurs," *New York Times*, January 14, 1987, p. B2.

[1991]

Letter to Ma

Merle Woo

Dear Ma,   January, 1980

I was depressed over Christmas, and when New Year's rolled around, do you know what one of my resolves was? Not to come by and see you as much anymore. I had to ask myself why I get so down when I'm with you, my mother, who has focused so much of her life on me, who has endured so much; one who I am proud of and respect so deeply for simply surviving.

I suppose that one of the main reasons is that when I leave your house, your pretty little round white table in the dinette where we sit while you drink tea (with only three specks of Jasmine) and I smoke and drink coffee, I am down because I believe there are chasms between us. When you say,

"I support you, honey, in everything you do except . . . except . . ." I know you mean except my speaking out and writing of my anger at all those things that have caused those chasms. When you say I shouldn't be so ashamed of Daddy, former gambler, retired clerk of a "gook suey" store, because of the time when I was six and saw him humiliated on Grant Avenue by two white cops, I know you haven't even been listening to me when I have repeatedly said that I am not ashamed of him, not you, not who we are. When you ask, "Are you so angry because you are unhappy?" I know that we are not talking to each other. Not with understanding, although many words have passed between us, many hours, many afternoons at that round table with Daddy out in the front room watching television, and drifting out every once in a while to say "Still talking?" and getting more peanuts that are so bad for his health.

We talk and we talk and I feel frustrated by your censorship. I know it is unintentional and unconscious. But whatever I have told you about the classes I was teaching, or the stories I was working on, you've always forgotten within a month. Maybe you can't listen—because maybe when you look in my eyes, you will, as you've always done, sense more than what we're actually saying, and that makes you fearful. Do you see your repressed anger manifested in me? What doors would groan wide open if you heard my words with complete understanding? Are you afraid that your daughter is breaking out of our shackles, and into total anarchy? That your daughter has turned into a crazy woman who advocates not only equality for Third World people, for women, but for gays as well? Please don't shudder, Ma, when I speak of homosexuality. Until we can all present ourselves to the world in our completeness, as fully and beautifully as we see ourselves naked in our bedrooms, we are not free.

After what seems like hours of talking, I realize it is not talking at all, but the filling up of time with sounds that say, "I am your daughter, you are my mother, and we are keeping each other company, and that is enough." But it is not enough because my life has been formed by your life. Together we have lived one hundred and eleven years in this country as yellow women, and it is not enough to enunciate words and words and words and then to have them only mean that we have been keeping each other company. I desperately want you to understand me and my work, Ma, to know what I am doing! When you distort what I say, like thinking I am against all "caucasians" or that I am ashamed of Dad, then I feel anger and more frustration and want to slash out, not at you, but at those external forces which keep us apart. What deepens the chasms between us are our different reactions to those forces. Yours has been one of silence, self-denial, self-effacement; you believing it is your fault that you never fully experienced self-pride and freedom of choice. But listen, Ma, only with a deliberate consciousness is my reaction different from yours.

When I look at you, there are images: images of you as a little ten-year-old Korean girl, being sent alone from Shanghai to the United States, in steerage with only one skimpy little dress, being sick and lonely on Angel

Island for three months; then growing up in a "Home" run by white missionary women. Scrubbing floors on your hands and knees, hauling coal in heavy metal buckets up three flights of stairs, tending to the younger children, putting hot bricks on your cheeks to deaden the pain from the terrible toothaches you always had. Working all your life as maid, waitress, salesclerk, office worker, mother. But throughout there is an image of you as strong and courageous, and persevering: climbing out of windows to escape from the Home, then later, from an abusive first husband. There is so much more to these images than I can say, but I think you know what I mean. Escaping out of windows offered only temporary respites; surviving is an everyday chore. You gave me, physically, what you never had, but there was a spiritual, emotional legacy you passed down which was reinforced by society: self-contempt because of our race, our sex, our sexuality. For deeply ingrained in me, Ma, there has been that strong, compulsive force to sink into self-contempt, passivity, and despair. I am sure that my fifteen years of alcohol abuse have not been forgotten by either of us, nor my suicidal depressions.

Now, I know you are going to think I hate and despise you for your self-hatred, for your isolation. But I don't. Because in spite of your withdrawal, in spite of your loneliness, you have not only survived, but been beside me in the worst of times when your company meant everything in the world to me. I just need more than that now, Ma. I have taken and taken from you in terms of needing you to mother me, to be by my side, and I need, now, to take from you two more things: understanding and support for who I am now and my work.

We are Asian American women and the reaction to our identity is what causes the chasms instead of connections. But do you realize, Ma, that I could never have reacted the way I have if you had not provided for me the opportunity to be free of the binds that have held you down, and to be in the process of self-affirmation? Because of your life, because of the physical security you have given me: my education, my full stomach, my clothed and starched back, my piano and dancing lessons—all those gifts you never received—I saw myself as having worth; now I begin to love myself more, see our potential, and fight for just that kind of social change that will affirm me, my race, my sex, my heritage. And while I affirm myself, Ma, I affirm you.

Today, I am satisfied to call myself either an Asian American Feminist or Yellow Feminist. The two terms are inseparable because race and sex are an integral part of me. This means that I am working with others to realize pride in culture and women and heritage (the heritage that is the exploited yellow immigrant: Daddy and you). Being a Yellow Feminist means being a community activist and a humanist. It does not mean "separatism," either by cutting myself off from non-Asians or men. It does not mean retaining the same power structure and substituting women in positions of control held by men. It does mean fighting the whites and the men who abuse us, straightjacket us and tape our mouths; it means changing the economic class system and psychological forces (sexism, racism, and homophobia) that really hurt all of us. And I do this, not in isolation, but in the community.

We no longer can afford to stand back and watch while an insatiable elite ravages and devours resources which are enough for all of us. The obstacles are so huge and overwhelming that often I do become cynical and want to give up. And if I were struggling alone, I know I would never even attempt to put into action what I believe in my heart, that (and this is primarily because of you, Ma) Yellow Women are strong and have the potential to be powerful and effective leaders.

I can hear you asking now, "Well, what do you mean by 'social change and leadership'? And how are you going to go about it?" To begin with we must wipe out the circumstances that keep us down in silence and self-effacement. Right now, my techniques are education and writing. Yellow Feminist means being a core for change, and that core means having the belief in our potential as human beings. I will work with anyone, support anyone, who shares my sensibility, my objectives. But there are barriers to unity: white women who are racist, and Asian American men who are sexist. My very being declares that those two groups do not share my complete sensibility. I would be fragmented, mutilated, if I did not fight against racism and sexism together.

And this is when the pain of the struggle hits home. How many white women have taken on the responsibility to educate themselves about Third World people, their history, their culture? How many white women really think about the stereotypes they retain as truth about women of color? But the perpetuation of dehumanizing stereotypes is really very helpful for whites; they use them to justify their giving us the lowest wages and all the work they don't want to perform. Ma, how can we believe things are changing when as a nurse's aide during World War II, you were given only the tasks of changing the bed linen, removing bed pans, taking urine samples, and then only three years ago as a retired volunteer worker in a local hospital, white women gave themselves desk jobs and gave you, at sixty-nine, the same work you did in 1943? Today you speak more fondly of being a nurse's aide during World War II and how proud you are of the fact that the Red Cross showed its appreciation for your service by giving you a diploma. Still in 1980, the injustices continue. I can give you so many examples of groups which are "feminist" in which women of color were given the usual least important tasks, the shitwork, and given no say in how that group is to be run. Needless to say, those Third World women, like you, dropped out, quit.

Working in writing and teaching, I have seen how white women condescend to Third World women because they reason that because of our oppression, which they know nothing about, we are behind them and their "progressive ideas" in the struggle for freedom. They don't even look at history! At the facts! How we as Asian American women have always been fighting for more than mere survival, but were never acknowledged because we were in our communities, invisible, but not inaccessible.

And I get so tired of being the instant resource for information on Asian American women. Being the token representative, going from class to class, group to group, bleeding for white women so they can have an easy answer—and then, and this is what really gets to me—they usually leave to never continue their education about us on their own.

To the racist white female professor who says, "If I have to watch everything I say I wouldn't say anything," I want to say, "Then get out of teaching."

To the white female poet who says, "Well, frankly, I believe that politics and poetry don't necessarily have to go together," I say, "Your little taste of white privilege has deluded you into thinking that you don't have to fight against sexism in this society. You are talking to me from your own isolation and your own racism. If you feel that you don't have to fight for me, that you don't have to speak out against capitalism, the exploitation of human and natural resources, then you in your silence, your inability to make connections, are siding with a system that will eventually get you, after it has gotten me. And if you think that's not a political stance, you're more than simply deluded, you're crazy!"

This is the same white voice that says, "I am writing about and looking for themes that are 'universal.'" Well, most of the time when "universal" is used, it is just a euphemism for "white": white themes, white significance, white culture. And denying minority groups their rightful place and time in U.S. history is simply racist.

Yes, Ma, I am mad. I carry the anger from my own experience and the anger you couldn't afford to express, and even that is often misinterpreted no matter how hard I try to be clear about my position. A white woman in my class said to me a couple of months ago, "I feel that Third World women hate me and that *they* are being racist; I'm being stereotyped, and I've never been part of the ruling class." I replied, "Please try to understand. Know our history. Know the racism of whites, how deep it goes. Know that we are becoming ever more intolerant of those people who let their ignorance be their excuse for their complacency, their liberalism, when this country (this world!) is going to hell in a handbasket. Try to understand that our distrust is from experience, and that our distrust is power*less*. Racism is an essential part of the status quo, power*ful*, and continues to keep us down. It is a rule taught to all of us from birth. Is it no wonder that we fear there are no exceptions?"

And as if the grief we go through working with white women weren't enough; so close to home, in our community, and so very painful, is the lack of support we get from some of our Asian American brothers. Here is a quote from a rather prominent male writer ranting on about a Yellow "sister":

. . . I can only believe that such blatant sucking off of the identity is the work of a Chinese American woman, another Jade Snow Wong Pochahontas yellow. Pussywhipped again. Oh, damn, pussywhipped again.

Chinese American woman: "another Jade Snow Wong Pochahontas yellow." According to him, Chinese American women sold out—are contemptuous of their culture, pathetically strain all their lives to be white, hate Asian American men, and so marry white men (the John Smiths)—or just like Pochahontas: we rescue white men while betraying our fathers; then marry white men, get baptized, and go to dear old England to become curiosities of the civilized world. Whew! Now, that's an indictment! (Of all women of color.) Some of the male writers in the Asian American community seem never to support us. They always expect us to support them, and you know what? We almost always do. Anti-Yellow men? Are they kidding? We go to their readings, buy and read and comment on their books, and try to keep up a dialogue. And they accuse us of betrayal, are resentful because we do readings together as Women, and so often do not come to our performances. And all the while we hurt because we are rejected by our brothers. The Pochahontas image used by a Chinese American man points out a tragic truth: the white man and his ideology are still over us and between us. These men of color, with clear vision, fight the racism in white society, but have bought the white male definition of "masculinity": men only should take on the leadership in the community because the qualities of "originality, daring, physical courage, and creativity" are "traditionally masculine."[1]

Some Asian men don't seem to understand that by supporting Third World women and fighting sexism, they are helping themselves as well. I understand all too clearly how dehumanized Dad was in this country. To be a Chinese man in America is to be a victim of both racism and sexism. He was made to feel he was without strength, identity, and purpose. He was made to feel soft and weak, whose only job was to serve whites. Yes, Ma, at one time I was ashamed of him because I thought he was "womanly." When those two white cops said, "Hey, fat boy, where's our meat?" he left me standing there on Grant Avenue while he hurried over to his store to get it; they kept complaining, never satisfied, "That piece isn't good enough. What's the matter with you, fat boy? Don't you have respect? Don't wrap that meat in newspapers either; use the good stuff over there." I didn't know that he spent a year and a half on Angel Island; that we could never have our right names; that he lived in constant fear of being deported; that, like you, he worked two full-time jobs most of his life; that he was mocked and ridiculed because he speaks "broken English." And Ma, I was so ashamed after that experience when I was only six years old that I never held his hand again.

Today, as I write to you of all these memories, I feel even more deeply hurt when I realize how many people, how so many people, because of racism and sexism, fail to see what power we sacrifice by not joining hands.

But not all white women are racist, and not all Asian American men are sexist. And we choose to trust them, love and work with them. And there are visible changes. Real tangible, positive changes. The changes I love to see are those changes within ourselves.

Your grandchildren, my children, Emily and Paul. That makes three generations. Emily loves herself. Always has. There are shades of self-doubt but much less than in you or me. She says exactly what she thinks, most of the time, either in praise or in criticism of herself or others. And at sixteen she goes after whatever she wants, usually center stage. She trusts and loves people, regardless of race or sex (but, of course, she's cautious), loves her community and works in it, speaks up against racism and sexism at school. Did you know that she got Zora Neale Hurston and Alice Walker on her reading list for a Southern Writers class when there were only white authors? That she insisted on changing a script done by an Asian American man when she saw that the depiction of the character she was playing was sexist? That she went to a California State House Conference to speak out for Third World students' needs?

And what about her little brother, Paul? Twelve years old. And remember, Ma? At one of our Saturday Night Family Dinners, how he lectured Ronnie (his uncle, yet!) about how he was a male chauvinist? Paul told me once how he knew he had to fight to be Asian American, and later he added that if it weren't for Emily and me, he wouldn't have to think about feminist stuff too. He says he can hardly enjoy a movie or TV program anymore because of the sexism. Or comic books. And he is very much aware of the different treatment he gets from adults: "You have to do everything right," he said to Emily, "and I can get away with almost anything."

Emily and Paul give us hope, Ma. Because they are proud of who they are, and they care so much about our culture and history. Emily was the first to write your biography because she knows how crucial it is to get our stories in writing.

Ma, I wish I knew the histories of the women in our family before you. I bet that would be quite a story. But that may be just as well, because I can say that *you* started something. Maybe you feel ambivalent or doubtful about it, but you did. Actually, you should be proud of what you've begun. I am. If my reaction to being a Yellow Woman is different than yours was, please know that that is not a judgment on you, a criticism or a denial of you, your worth. I have always supported you, and as the years pass, I think I begin to understand you more and more.

In the last few years, I have realized the value of Homework: I have studied the history of our people in this country. I cannot tell you how proud I am to be a Chinese/Korean American Woman. We have such a proud heritage, such a courageous tradition. I want to tell everyone about that, all the particulars that are left out in the schools. And the full awareness of being a woman makes me want to sing. And I do sing with other Asian Americans and women, Ma, anyone who will sing with me.

I feel now that I can begin to put our lives in a larger framework. Ma, a larger framework! The outlines for us are time and blood, but today there is breadth possible through making connections with others involved in community struggle. In loving ourselves for who we are—American women of color—we can make a vision for the future where we are free to fulfill our human potential. This new framework will not support repression, hatred, exploitation and isolation, but will be a human and beautiful framework, created in a community, bonded not by color, sex or class, but by love and the common goal for the liberation of mind, heart, and spirit.

Ma, today, you are as beautiful and pure to me as the picture I have of you, as a little girl, under my dresser-glass.

I love you,
Merle

Reference

1. *Aiieeeee! An Anthology of Asian American Writers.* editors Frank Chin, Jeffrey Paul Chan, Lawson Fusao Inada. Shawn Wong (Howard University Press, 1974).

[1981]

Invisibility Is an Unnatural Disaster: Reflections of an Asian American Woman

Mitsuye Yamada

LAST YEAR FOR THE ASIAN SEGMENT OF THE ETHNIC AMERICAN Literature course I was teaching, I selected a new anthology entitled *Aiieeeee!* compiled by a group of outspoken Asian American writers. During the discussion of the long but thought-provoking introduction to this anthology, one of my students blurted out that she was offended by its militant tone and that as a white person she was tired of always being blamed for the oppression of all the minorities. I noticed several of her classmates' eyes nodding in tacit agreement. A discussion of the "militant" voices in some of the other writings we had read in the course ensued. Surely, I pointed out, some of these other writings have been just as, if not more, militant as the words in this introduction? Had they been offended by those also but failed to express their feelings about them? To my surprise, they said they were not offended by any of the Black American, Chicano or American Indian writings, but were hard-pressed to explain why when I asked for an explanation. A little further discussion revealed that they "understood" the anger expressed by the Blacks and Chicanos and they "empathized" with the frustrations and sorrow expressed by the American Indian. But the Asian Americans??

Then finally, one student said it for all of them: "It made me angry. *Their* anger made *me* angry, because I didn't even know the Asian Americans felt oppressed. I didn't expect their anger."

At this time I was involved in an academic due process procedure begun as a result of a grievance I had filed the previous semester against the administrators at my college. I had filed a grievance for violation of my rights as a teacher who had worked in the district for almost eleven years. My student's remark "Their anger made me angry . . . I didn't expect their anger," explained for me the reactions of some of my own colleagues as well as the reactions of the administrators during those previous months. The grievance procedure was a time-consuming and emotionally draining process, but the basic principle was too important for me to ignore. That basic principle was that I, an individual teacher, do have certain rights which are given and my superiors cannot, should not, violate them with impunity. When this was pointed out to them, however, they responded with shocked surprise that I, of all people, would take them to task for violation of what was clearly written policy in our college district. They all seemed to exclaim, "We don't understand this; this is so uncharacteristic of her; she seemed such a nice person, so polite, so obedient, so non-trouble-making." What was even more surprising was once they were forced to acknowledge that I was determined to start the due process action, they assumed I was not doing it on my own. One of the administrators suggested someone must have pushed me into this, undoubtedly some of "those feminists" on our campus, he said wryly.

In this age when women are clearly making themselves visible on all fronts, I, an Asian American woman, am still functioning as a "front for those feminists" and therefore invisible. The realization of this sinks in slowly. Asian Americans as a whole are finally coming to claim their own, demanding that they be included in the multicultural history of our country. I like to think, in spite of my administrator's myopia, that the most stereo-typed minority of them all, the Asian American woman, is just now emerging to become part of that group. It took forever. Perhaps it is important to ask ourselves why it took so long. We should ask ourselves this question just when we think we are emerging as a viable minority in the fabric of our society. I should add to my student's words, "because I didn't even know they felt oppressed," that it took this long because we Asian American women have not admitted to ourselves that we *were* oppressed. We, the visible minority that is invisible.

I say this because until a few years ago I have been an Asian American woman working among non-Asians in an educational institution where most of the decision-makers were men[*]; an Asian American woman thriving under the smug illusion that I was *not* the stereotypic image of the Asian woman because I had a career teaching English in a community college. I did not think anything assertive was necessary to make my point. People who know

[*] It is hoped this will change now that a black woman is Chancellor of our college district.

me, I reasoned, the ones who count, know who I am and what I think. Thus, even when what I considered a veiled racist remark was made in a casual social setting, I would "let it go" because it was pointless to argue with people who didn't even know their remark was racist. I had supposed that I was practicing passive resistance while being stereotyped, but it was so passive no one noticed I was resisting; it was so much my expected role that it ultimately rendered me invisible.

My experience leads me to believe that contrary to what I thought, I had actually been contributing to my own stereotyping. Like the hero in Ralph Ellison's novel *The Invisible Man*, I had become invisible to white Americans, and it clung to me like a bad habit. Like most bad habits, this one crept up on me because I took it in minute doses like Mithradates' poison and my mind and body adapted so well to it I hardly noticed it was there.

For the past eleven years I have busied myself with the usual chores of an English teacher, a wife of a research chemist, and a mother of four rapidly growing children. I hadn't even done much to shatter this particular stereotype: the middle class woman happy to be bringing home the extra income and quietly fitting into the man's world of work. When the Asian American woman is lulled into believing that people perceive her as being different from other Asian women (the submissive, subservient, ready-to-please, easy-to-get-along-with Asian woman), she is kept comfortably content with the state of things. She becomes ineffectual in the milieu in which she moves. The seemingly apolitical middle class woman and the apolitical Asian woman constituted a double invisibility.

I had created an underground culture of survival for myself and had become in the eyes of others the person I was trying not to be. Because I was permitted to go to college, permitted to take a stab at a career or two along the way, given "free choice" to marry and have a family, given a "choice" to eventually do both, I had assumed I was more or less free, not realizing that those who are free make and take choices; they do not choose from options proffered by "those out there."

I, personally, had not "emerged" until I was almost fifty years old. Apparently through a long conditioning process, I had learned how *not* to be seen for what I am. A long history of ineffectual activities had been, I realize now, initiation rites toward my eventual invisibility. The training begins in childhood; and for women and minorities, whatever is started in childhood is continued throughout their adult lives. I first recognized just how invisible I was in my first real confrontation with my parents a few years after the outbreak of World War II.

During the early years of the war, my older brother, Mike, and I left the concentration camp in Idaho to work and study at the University of Cincinnati. My parents came to Cincinnati soon after my father's release from Internment Camp (these were POW camps to which many of the Issei* men, leaders in their communities, were sent by the FBI), and worked as

---

* Issei—Immigrant Japanese, living in the U.S.

domestics in the suburbs. I did not see them too often because by this time I had met and was much influenced by a pacifist who was out on a "furlough" from a conscientious objectors' camp in Trenton, North Dakota. When my parents learned about my "boy friend" they were appalled and frightened. After all, this was the period when everyone in the country was expected to be one-hundred percent behind the war effort, and the Nisei* boys who had volunteered for the Armed Forces were out there fighting and dying to prove how American we really were. However, during interminable arguments with my father and overheard arguments between my parents, I was devastated to learn they were not so much concerned about my having become a pacifist, but they were more concerned about the possibility of my marrying one. They were understandably frightened (my father's prison years of course were still fresh on his mind) about repercussions on the rest of the family. In an attempt to make my father understand me, I argued that even if I didn't marry him, I'd still be a pacifist; but my father reassured me that it was "all right" for me to be a pacifist because as a Japanese national and a "girl" *it didn't make any difference to anyone.* In frustration I remember shouting, "But can't you see, *I'm* philosophically committed to the pacifist cause," but he dismissed this with "In my college days we used to call philosophy, foolosophy," and that was the end of that. When they were finally convinced that I was not going to marry "my pacifist," the subject was dropped and we never discussed it again.

As if to confirm my father's assessment of the harmlessness of my opinions, my brother Mike, an American citizen, was suddenly expelled from the University of Cincinnati while I, "an enemy alien," was permitted to stay. We assumed that his stand as a pacifist, although he was classified a 4-F because of his health, contributed to his expulsion. We were told the Air Force was conducting sensitive wartime research on campus and requested his removal, but they apparently felt my presence on campus was not as threatening.

I left Cincinnati in 1945, hoping to leave behind this and other unpleasant memories gathered there during the war years, and plunged right into the politically active atmosphere at New York University where students, many of them returning veterans, were continuously promoting one cause or other by making speeches in Washington Square, passing out petitions, or staging demonstrations. On one occasion, I tagged along with a group of students who took a train to Albany to demonstrate on the steps of the State Capitol. I think I was the only Asian in this group of predominantly Jewish students from NYU. People who passed us were amused and shouted "Go home and grow up." I suppose Governor Dewey, who refused to see us, assumed we were a group of adolescents without a cause as most college students were considered to be during those days. It appears they weren't expecting any results from our demonstration. There were no newspersons, no security persons, no police. No one tried to stop us from doing what we were doing.

---

* Nisei—Second generation Japanese, born in the U.S.

We simply did "our thing" and went back to our studies until next time, and my father's words were again confirmed: it made no difference to anyone, being a young student demonstrator in peacetime, 1947.

Not only the young, but those who feel powerless over their own lives know what it is like not to make a difference on anyone or anything. The poor know it only too well, and we women have known it since we were little girls. The most insidious part of this conditioning process, I realize now, was that we have been trained not to expect a response in ways that mattered. We may be listened to and responded to with placating words and gestures, but our psychological mind set has already told us time and again that we were born into a ready-made world into which we must fit ourselves, and that many of us do it very well.

This mind set is the result of not believing that the political and social forces affecting our lives are determined by some person, or a group of persons, probably sitting behind a desk or around a conference table.

Just recently I read an article about "the remarkable track record of success" of the Nisei in the United States. One Nisei was quoted as saying he attributed our stamina and endurance to our ancestors whose characters had been shaped, he said, by their living in a country which has been constantly besieged by all manner of natural disasters, such as earthquakes and hurricanes. He said the Nisei has inherited a steely will, a will to endure and hence, to survive.

This evolutionary explanation disturbs me, because it equates the "act of God" (i.e., natural disasters) to the "act of man" (i.e., the war, the evacuation). The former is not within our power to alter, but the latter, I should think, is. By putting the "acts of God" on par with the acts of man, we shrug off personal responsibilities.

I have, for too long a period of time, accepted the opinion of others (even though they were directly affecting my life) as if they were objective events totally out of my control. Because I separated such opinions from the persons who were making them, I accepted them the way I accepted natural disasters; and I endured them as inevitable. I have tried to cope with people whose points of view alarmed me in the same way that I had adjusted to natural phenomena, such as hurricanes, which plowed into my life from time to time. I would readjust my dismantled feelings in the same way that we repaired the broken shutters after the storm. The Japanese have an all-purpose expression in their language for this attitude of resigned acceptance: "Shikataganai." "It can't be helped." "There's nothing I can do about it." It is said with the shrug of the shoulders and tone of finality, perhaps not unlike the "those-were-my-orders" tone that was used at the Nuremberg trials. With all the sociological studies that have been made about the causes of the evacuations of the Japanese Americans during World War II, we should know by now that "they" knew that the West Coast Japanese Americans would go without too much protest, and of course, "they" were right, for most of us (with the exception of those notable few), resigned to our fate, albeit bewildered and not willingly. We were not perceived by our government as responsive Americans; we were objects that happened to be standing in the path of the storm.

Perhaps this kind of acceptance is a way of coping with the "real" world. One stands against the wind for a time, and then succumbs eventually because there is no point to being stubborn against all odds. The wind will not respond to entreaties anyway, one reasons; one should have sense enough to know that. I'm not ready to accept this evolutionary reasoning. It is too rigid for me; I would like to think that my new awareness is going to make me more visible than ever, and to allow me to make some changes in the "man made disaster" I live in at the present time. Part of being visible is refusing to separate the actors from their actions, and demanding that they be responsible for them.

By now, riding along with the minorities' and women's movements, I think we are making a wedge into the main body of American life, but people are still looking right through and around us, assuming we are simply tagging along. Asian American women still remain in the background and we are heard but not really listened to. Like Musak, they think we are piped into the airwaves by someone else. We must remember that one of the most insidious ways of keeping women and minorities powerless is to let them only talk about harmless and inconsequential subjects, or let them speak freely and not listen to them with serious intent.

We need to raise our voices a little more, even as they say to us "This is so uncharacteristic of you." To finally recognize our own invisibility is to finally be on the path toward visibility. Invisibility is not a natural state for anyone.

[1981]

"My folk, in other words, have always been a race of theory—though more in the form of the hieroglyph, a written figure which is both sensual and abstract, both beautiful and communicative."

BARBARA CHRISTIAN

from "The Race for Theory" from *Cultural Critique 6*

CRITICAL PERSPECTIVES

Something Sacred Going On out There: Myth and Vision in American Indian Literature

Paula Gunn Allen

IT IS DIFFICULT IF NOT IMPOSSIBLE AT THE PRESENT TIME TO SPEAK coherentlyabout myth because the term has become so polluted by popular misuse. Yet no discussion of American Indian literature is complete without an examination of what mythic narrative and the concept of myth itself mean in a tribal context.

Popularly among Americans, *myth* is synonomous with *lie*; moreover, it implies ignorance or a malicious intent to defraud. Thus, any attitude or idea that does not conform to contemporary western descriptions of reality is termed myth, signifying falsehood. Labeling something a myth merely discredits the perceptual system and world-view of those who are not in accord with the dominating paradigm. Thus, current dictionary definitions of *myth* reinforce a bias that enables the current paradigm of our techno-cratic social science–biased society to prevail over tribal or poetic views just as it enables an earlier Christian biblical paradigm to prevail over the pagan one. Indeed, terms such as *pagan, tribal,* and *poetic*—often used interchangeably—imply ignorance, backwardness, and foolishness. They allow dismissal by western readers, just as their allied term, *myth* does. A definition such as the following makes it clear that any story called a myth is not to be taken seriously.

> 1. a traditional or legendary story, usually concerning some superhuman being or some alleged person or event, with or without a determinable basis of fact or a natural explanation, esp., a traditional or legendary story that is concerned with deities or demigods and the creation of the world and its inhabitants. 2. stories or matter of this kind . . . 3. any invented story, idea or concept . . . 4. an imaginary or fictitious thing or person. 5. an unproved collective belief that is accepted uncritically and is used to justify a social institution.[1]

Essentially, all parts of the definition indicate a prevailing belief in the fictitiousness of myth; such terms as "alleged," "determinable," "factual," and "natural explanation" imply falsity or, at least, questionable accuracy. This meta-myth is deceptive, for it imputes factualness to certain assump-tions that form the basis of western perceptions without acknowledging that it does so. Part of this meta-myth is the belief that there is such a thing as determinable fact, natural—that is, right—explanations, and reality that can be determined outside the human agency of discovery and fact finding.

This attitude falls more along the lines of uncritical acceptance used to justify the social institutions of contemporary societies than of proven belief attested to by many physicists, psychoanalysts, visionary mystics, poets, artists, and Indians as well as human experience of thousands of years and thousands of cultures.

Be that as it may, *myth* has not been considered synonymous with *belief* until recently. Earlier it was synonymous with *fable,* from the Greek, where it had the connotation of moral story. The Greek terms μύ-σ-τησ and μυ-σ-τήρον meant "one who is initiated" and "a mystery, secret (thing muttered)," respectively, and are based on the Indo-Germanic root, MU. Another Greek term, μύ, μῦ, "a sound of muttering," and its Latin forms, *muttum* or *mutum,* meaning "a slight sound," both signify muttering and muteness.[2]

So while μῦϊοσ is translated as "fable," it is more accurately translated as "ritual," that is, as a language construct that contains the power to transform something (or someone) from one state or condition to another. Of course it reflects belief, at least in the sorcerer's or magician's sense, but it is at base a vehicle, a means of transmitting paranormal power.

The mythic narrative as an articulation of thought or wisdom is not expressible in other forms; it must be seen as a necessary dimension of human expression, a dimension that is categorically unique. It is in this sense that facts or explanations of various phenomena such as "how the Loon got its white neck" or "why coyote has a ragged coat" can be incorporated into mythic structures. These pourquoi elements are signals of the kind of reality myth inhabits, rather than statements about social and material reality; their referent is to the sacred world of ritual magic rather than to the external world of machine-verifiable facts.

In this regard, the American psychoanalyst Rollo May defines myth "in its historically accurate sense of a psycho-biological pattern which give meaning and direction to experience."[3] In other words, the mythic dimension of experience—the psychospiritual ordering of nonordinary knowledge—is an experience that all peoples, past, present, and to come, have in common. As Thomas Mann observes, myth and life are identities:

> Life, then—at any rate—significant life—was in ancient times the reconstitution of the myth in flesh and blood; it referred to and appealed to the myth; only through it . . . could it approve itself as genuine and significant. The myth is the legitimization of life; only through and in it does life find self-awareness, sanction, consecration.[4]

Myth may be seen as a teleological statement, a shaped system of reference that allows us to order and thus comprehend perception and knowledge, as Mann suggests. The existence of mythic structures supposes a rational ordering of the universe. The presence of myth in a culture signifies a belief in the teleological nature of existence and indicates that powers other than those of material existence, or what Carlos Castaneda calls "ordinary reality," guide and direct the universe and human participation in it. As such myth stands as an expression of human need for coherence and integration and as the mode whereby human beings might actively fill that need.

Yet myth is more than a statement about how the world ought to work; its poetic and mystic dimensions indicate that it embodies a sense of reality that includes all human capacities, ideal or actual. These, broadly speaking, are the tendency to feel or emotively relate to experience and the tendency to intellectually organize it—the religious, aesthetic, and philosophical aspects of human cultures. Human beings need to belong to a tradition and equally need to know about the world in which they find themselves. Myth is a kind of story that allows a holistic image to pervade and shape consciousness, thus providing a coherent and empowering matrix for action and relationship. It is in this sense that myth is most significant, for it is this creative, ordering capacity of myth that frightens and attracts the rationalistic, other-centered mind, forcing it into thinly veiled pejoration of the mythic faculty, alienistic analysis of it, and counter myth-making of its own.

Myth, then, is an expression of the tendency to make stories of power out of the life we live in imagination; from this faculty when it is engaged in ordinary states of consciousness come tales and stories. When it is engaged in nonordinary states, myth proper—that is, mystery mumblings—occur. It is of course the former relationship between myth and imagination that has caused myth to be regarded as "a wholly fictitious story" as the *Oxford English Dictionary* puts it or, as in the standard *French Dictionary of Littre*, "that which has no real existence."

In the culture and literature of Indian America, the meaning of myth may be discovered, not as speculation about primitive long-dead ancestral societies but in terms of what is real, actual, and viable in living cultures in America. Myth abounds in all of its forms; from the most sacred stories to the most trivial, mythic vision informs the prose and poetry of American Indians in the United States as well as the rest of the Americas.

An American Indian myth is a story that relies preeminently on symbol for its articulation. It generally relates a series of events and uses supernatural, heroic figures as the agents of both the events and the symbols. As a story, it demands the immediate, direct participation of the listener.

American Indian myths depend for their magic on relationship and participation. Detached, analytical, distanced observation of myth will not allow the listener mythopoeic vision. Consequently, these myths cannot be understood more than peripherally by the adding-machine mind; for when a myth is removed from its special and necessary context, it is no longer myth; it is a dead or dying curiosity. It is akin, in that state, to the postcard depictions of American Indian people that abound in the southwestern United States.

Only a participant in mythic magic can relate to the myth, can enter into its meaning on its own terms. This is not to say that only a devout Oglala can comprehend the Myth of White Buffalo Woman or that only a practicing Cheyenne can comprehend the presence of Sweet Medicine. It does mean that only those who experientially accept the nonmaterial or nonordinary reality of existence can hope to comprehend either figure in their own terms; all others are, of necessity, excluded.

I have said that an American Indian myth is a particular kind of story, requiring supernatural or nonordinary figures as characters. Further, a myth relies on mystical or metaphysically charged symbols to convey its significance, and the fact of the mystical and the teleological nature of myth is embodied in its characteristic devices; the supernatural characters, the nonordinary events, the transcendent powers, and the pourquoi elements all indicate that something sacred is going on.

On literal levels of analysis, the myth tells us what kind of story it is. It focuses our attention on the level of consciousness it relates to us and relates us to. Having engaged our immediate participation on its own level, the myth proceeds to re-create and renew our ancient relationship to the universe that is beyond the poverty-stricken limits of the everyday.

Mythologists have long noticed a connection between ritual and myth. Some believe that ritual is an enactment of a myth, while others feel that myth tells about the ritual in story form. Neither explanation seems satisfactory to all parties, and for a very good reason: these speculations are based on Greek and Roman mythologies, the only kind that the Church did not suppress totally, and on extant histories of rituals in Greek and Roman cultures. The materials thus left available for students of the mysteries, coupled with analytical methods developed over two millennia of churchly control of academic research, led to fundamental misperception and misrepresentation of ritual and mythic modes.

> It was precisely because the classics were based upon fictive themes that they survived the mythoclastic rigors of early Christianity. Myths were pagan, and therefore false in the light of true belief—albeit that true belief might today be considered merely another variety of mythopoeic faith. Here is where the game of debunking starts, in the denunciation of myth as falsehood from the vantagepoint of a rival myth.
>
> Classical myths could be rescued by allegory, prefiguration, or other methods of reinterpretation; but they could not be accepted literally.[5]

Other material that has come to light more recently in this regard has been forced to conform to the preconceived theories of Christian enculturated mythologists prior to Sir James Frazer, the Scottish classicist and anthropologist who compiled *The Golden Bough*, his study of magic and religion. But an alternative explanation to those popularly held is possible, based on an examination of actual contemporary Native American practices. This explanation coincides, in some significant ways, with contemporary psychoanalytical observation. Its ultimate proof, of course, lies in the actual practice among mythopoeic peoples around the world.

Briefly stated, myth and ritual are based on visionary experience. This simple observation has apparently escaped notice because generally neither mythologists nor social scientists credit visionary experience with the same validity given them by visionary peoples, including some artists and poets. Yet a careful look at Native American cultures reveals evidence of direct vision as central to religious practice, ritual, and literature. In most Indian societies, the vision is actively pursued and brought back to the people as a gift of power and guidance.

A significant example of the relationship of vision to myth and ritual is in the story of Sweet Medicine, a central figure in the Cheyenne religion. Called a "culture hero" by anthropologists and a prophet and savior by the Cheyenne, Sweet Medicine brought religion, religious rituals, and social laws to the Cheyenne people.[6] He received them from the Sacred Ones who live on the mountain that the Cheyenne call Noahvose (Sacred or Holy Mountain)[7] and is known to whites as Bear Butte, in the Black Hills country. Revealed to him at this place were the religion of the Sacred Arrows, the religious and political organization the Cheyenne would adopt, the proper marriage ritual, the correct way to trap eagles to obtain the emblem feathers the chiefs wore, and many other things. "There was no end to all the things the people learned from him."[8] Sweet Medicine lived to be very old, outlasting four generations of Cheyenne. At his death he told the people how they must live if they wanted to be sure of plenty of game and other food; he prophesied their future, telling them of the coming of the whites and of the horse, the disappearance of the buffalo, and the ultimate loss of the true Cheyenne way. After he died, his body was said to have disappeared. All that remained was the tipi he had died in. The spot was marked with a stone cairn, the historical marker of the Cheyenne.[9]

Sweet Medicine came to the Cheyenne "many centuries ago"; a more recent example of the visionary source of a myth is found in the life and experience of Black Elk. Ultimately, I suppose, Black Elk will be seen as a prophet and a savior of his people, just as Sweet Medicine is seen by his. Presently Black Elk is considered a sage, a prophet, and healer, a wicasa wakan, sacred or holy man. The fact that he has heirs to his visionary power attests to the enormity of his gift.

Black Elk was a very young boy when his vision came to him. The Oglala, along with many eastern, midwestern, northwestern, southwestern, and southern Indians actively seek visions. The ability to achieve a vision is a mark of maturity, a kind of rite of passage. Usually a man or woman goes after a vision by performing a particular ritual called hanblecheya or Lamenting for a Vision. (Actually, there are two separate rituals involved in this rite as purification—inipi—precede the vision quest.)[10] But Black Elk was much younger than the age when hanblecheya is practiced. He was called by the powers that are usually sought, and his vision was bestowed on him without his asking. In this respect also his experience parallels Sweet Medicine, who was also given to vision and miracles before he reached maturity.

In *Black Elk Speaks*,[11] Black Elk tells of his initial vision and the subsequent visions during the years of his growing up. This singularly complete account of a holy man's vision, the ceremonies performed in reenacting the vision, and the powers held by the person who had the vision all indicate the centrality of vision to ritual, song, and myth. In fact, if Black Elk as narrator were removed from his own account and Black Elk as mythic character left in and if the point of view of the narrative were shifted from first-person personal to third-person omniscient, the vision would become identical in form and symbolic content to those great myths that have come down to us not only from the Oglala but from peoples as diverse as the Tlingit of Alaska, the Hopi of Arizona, the Cherokee of the Carolinas and Georgia, and the Iroquois of New York and Canada. Certainly, with the exception of the narrator's presence, the story is in the most proper sense a myth. Consisting of a logical progression of symbol, it is in truth a metaphysical statement that is significant in its cosmological implications, its prophetic content, its narrative sequence, its sense of timelessness, its characters, and, ultimately, its meaning for people all over this country. Seen that way, it is an example of myth at its most sacred and abstract.

Every element in such a story is meaningful on the deepest levels of human understanding. Thus it is that the true significance of Black Elk's vision is yet to be discovered; the meaning of the vision has not yet been explicated in terms of ordinary human consciousness, and the great sweep of history it encompasses has not yet been lived. Yet much of it has been lived, and those parts are undeniably true. This gives us another clue to the true nature of the prophetic aspect of the myth. White researchers have supposed that a myth was a story intended to explain and record events after they had happened so that they would be remembered. Working from this assumption and allied misunderstandings, anthropologists and mythologists have supposed an astounding chain of "facts" about the lives, movements, and ultimate origins of Indian people and about their cultures, world-view, and even their bodies. Yet this primary assumption is false. No Indian who is even peripherally aware of the Indian idea of things can muster much more than contempt for the ideas advanced by the literary curio hunters of the white world. Yet few white investigators who profess to be aware of and concerned with Indian attitudes are willing to listen, even provisionally, to the Indian account of these matters. It is assumed that Indians are "making believe" for religious, political, or existential reasons or that they are simply ignorant of the real truth about how the world works. It is seldom assumed that a given tribal version of its own history is true or that it might be seen as true from some perspective other than the social science paradigm common to western ideas of fact finding.[12]

Black Elk's vision offers an opportunity to demonstrate that the American Indian position is neither romantically primitive nor realistically absurd; and because it is written, the factualness of this account can be examined and verified in time. An examination of its elements and their arrangement can be made to discover the workings of a metaphysical statement and how myth relates to sacred songs, rituals, objects, and ornaments.

The vision begins when Black Elk is guided to the other world by two men who move down through the sky like "arrows slanting down."[13] The long spears they carry emit flashes of "jagged lightning."[14] From the beginning of this vision we are told the kind of vision it will be; visions that include the powers associated with Thunder and the West indicate a highly sacred or powerful vision and signify revelation, introspection, and deep change.[15] Because of these qualities, the Thunder and the West are said to be terrifying because they have the power to "make live" and the power to destroy. These powers are conferred on Black Elk, and are such as to terrify any man.

This vision is of or from the West. Its major symbolic theme is Thunder and what is associated with it: horses, lightning, rainbow, water. The other symbols occur in the context of these. And each action or speech occurs from the West, which is not the usual sequence of Oglala practice.

The directions themselves are the major motif, as they generally are in Oglala rituals. Orienting oneself to the directions is basic to all Native North American peoples and appears to be as important in South America.

The presence of different troops of horses, one troop from each direction, indicates that the vision will be comprehensive. The powers that will derive from it will include war and healing, knowledge and life. The poems and text will, like the actions and sacramental objects, be related to this whole and to these powers. All the powers that a man can possess will be represented here, and Black Elk will carry them back to his people, to use on their behalf. The primary thrust of the vision, in keeping with its western point of view, will be that of revelation, self-awareness and deep personal experience, and supernatural truth.

The Grandfathers of Powers of the Six Directions are the agents of this vision and its power. The First Grandfather, the Power of the West, tells Black Elk what will be given him:

> "Behold them yonder where the sun goes down, the thunder beings! You shall see, and have from them my power; and they shall take you to the high and lonely center of the earth that you may see; even to the place where the sun continually shines, they shall take you there to understand."
>
> And as he spoke of understanding, I looked up and saw the rainbow leap with flames of many colors over me.
>
> Now there was a wooden cup in his hand and it was full of water and in the water was the sky.
>
> "Take this," he said. "It is the power to make live, and it is yours."
>
> Now he had a bow in his hands. "Take this," he said. "It is the power to destroy, and it is yours."[16]

Each of the Grandfathers plays a role in this vision. The Sixth Grandfather represents Black Elk himself. He shows Black Elk the reality of humanity and its true power by transforming himself into a youth:

> and when he had become a boy, I knew that he was myself with all the years that would be mine at last.[17]

He shows himself as Black Elk's body because Black Elk represents all his people; he will be required to take this vision and its powers to his people and use both on their behalf. In no other way can such a vision become actual or positive. Without this sharing of what is conferred on one for the benefit of many, the vision itself will turn on the visionary, making him ill or even killing him, as later events show.

But while the body or person of Black Elk is like that of the Sixth Grandfather, the spirit of Black Elk (the spirit form in which he will experience the rest of the vision) is that of the Power of the West; for after giving Black Elk the power to make live and the power to destroy, the First Grandfather shows him a remarkable thing:

> Then he pointed to himself and said: "Look close at him who is your spirit now, for you are his body and his name is Eagle Wing Stretches."[18]

And in this mystic body, or mythic character, Black Elk goes through the rest of the vision.

The Grandfathers give Black Elk the power to make live, the power to understand and to know, the power to destroy, the power to purify, the power to feed and nurture, and the power to heal. Each of these powers is signified with an emblem or sacramental object, and some are accompanied by a song to be sung when calling on that power.[19] Most of all, he was given the gift of prophecy, the power of the universe itself.

> Now the fifth Grandfather spoke, the oldest of them all, the Spirit of the Sky. "My boy," he said, "I have sent for you and you have come. My power you shall see!" He stretched his arms and turned into a spotted eagle hovering. "Behold," he said, "all the wings of the air shall come to you, and they and the winds and the stars shall be like relatives. You shall go across the earth with my power." Then the eagle soared above my head and fluttered there; and suddenly the sky was full of friendly wings all coming toward me.[20]

In the next sequence, Black Elk learns the immediate future of the Oglala Lakotas. In the person of Eagle Wing Stretches, the Grandfather of the West, he journeys over a "distant landscape," rescuing the people from threatened annihilation by war, disease, and massacre. He restores for them the ancient way, the Path of the Sacred Pipe, the holy tree, the nation's hoop.[21] Then he discovers the farther future of the people, revealed once again symbolically. He is shown the means of saving the people of the earth from the great destructive forces that would overcome them, which is the sacred flower, the "herb of understanding."[22] He learns songs of power and sees the people calling the powers of the cosmos.[23] That power comes to their aid at the end of the fourth ascent in the guise of "the chief of all the horses, and when he snorted, it was a flash of lightning and his eyes were like the sunset star."[24]

> My horses, prancing they are coming;
> My horses, neighing they are coming;
> Prancing, they are coming.
> All over the universe they come.

They will dance; may you behold them.
They will dance; may you behold them.
They will dance; may you behold them.
They will dance; may you behold them.
  A horse nation, they will dance. May you behold them.
  A horse nation, they will dance. May you behold them.
  A horse nation, they will dance. May you behold them.
  A horse nation, they will dance. May you behold them.[25]

The last major sequence of the vision consists of a summarization of the vision and a return to more or less normal consciousness. In it Black Elk, as Eagle Wing Stretches, returns to the sacred tipi of the Six Grandfathers, where his triumph is acknowledged, the nature of his mythic identity, journey, and powers are explained once more, and he is returned to earth. His journey has lasted twelve days, during which the small boy's body had been lying, comatose, in the tipi of his parents.

The vision, which lasted twelve days, is divided into six parts, another indication of the depth of its significance and its inclusiveness: the first part has two aspects, the vision of the Horse Nation and the meeting with the Six Powers of the Universe. The second, broadly speaking the Prophecy, is divided into prophetic vision of the immediate, the near, and the distant future. The first part has since been lived on earth, as has much of the rest. The last major division, divided into two parts, consists of summary and return.

This sequence reveals to Black Elk that his body is painted in a special manner, signifying the kind of vision or kind of power he has had:

> I had not noticed how I was dressed until now, and I saw that I was painted red all over, and my joints were painted black, with white stripes between the joints. My bay had lightning stripes all over him, and his mane was cloud. And when I breathed, my breath was lightning.[26]

He is assured of his triumph after painful experience; his powers are affirmed and their emblems shown again. He learns the songs, the way to dress when acting as an agent of the supernatural, the movements and sequences that will ensure his success in these matters, and, most of all, the meaning of his experience in terms of the people, living and yet unborn.

Had Black Elk had this vision under more normal circumstances, he would have returned from his vision and recounted it to an older holy man, the one who had directed his quest. Then, with the holy man's help, he would have enacted significant portions of that vision in a ceremony for the people. In this way, the power bestowed on him during the vision would have been diffused, confirmed, intensified or amplified, and rendered real and functional on material and human levels. But he was very young. It frightened him, made him feel separated from his family and friends, burdened him with a knowledge that he was not old enough to use or understand. Some Indians feel that the disasters that befell Black Elk's people subsequently were a result of his failure to follow the usual pattern; yet it seems that, had this been necessary or wise, the Grandfathers either would have waited several years before calling Black Elk or would have chosen someone who was of the right age to give that vision to. Eventually Black Elk did what he should have done, and the account of the ceremonies held in enacting the vision (actually parts of it) clarify for us the relation between ritual, myth, and vision.

When Black Elk was sixteen, the time when young Oglalas prepare for their first hanblecheya, he began to be haunted by a fear.[27] The thunder, lightning, and clouds called him continuously; the coyotes and birds reminded him that it was his time. He didn't know what to do, and because of his growing fear and distraction, he became more and more fearful, behaving strangely and worrying those around him. When he was seventeen his parents asked an old medicine man, Black Road, to help Black Elk. Black Elk told the old man about his vision, and the old man arranged a ceremony because Black Elk had to do what the bay horse wanted him to do. The old man said he "must do [his] duty and perform the vision for [his] people upon earth."[28]

The Horse Dance that Black Road and another wise man, Bear Sings, designed with Black Elk incorporated all the symbols and personages in the parts of the vision pertaining to the horses, which are scattered throughout the account.[29] The songs that Black Elk had heard in the vision were sung, and all the people participated in the ceremony. Black Elk was painted red, the color of the earth and of the East, and the color of what is sacred, and black, the color of the West, of truth, revelation, and destruction. The horses were painted to show their relationship to the lightning, and the riders were dressed to indicate the various symbols that the vision horses had carried or worn or that were associated with them. Young women, virgins, enacted the part played by their supernatural counterparts, their faces painted scarlet. Six old men were the Six Grandfathers, and a sacred tipi was erected and painted to conform to the one in Black Elk's vision, a rainbow over the door.

Thus, in particular details of design and ornamentation, in movements and action and in characters, the vision was reconstructed as closely as may be done of the nonordinary in this material plane. The people and Black Elk were reenacting the vision so that its power would be revealed and renewed on earth. Black Elk comments on the strength or truth of this enactment: as they were praying and dancing he once again saw the sacred tipi as in his vision—the rainbow door, the horses, and the Six Grandfathers sitting inside. He even saw himself on the bay in front of the tipi. As the vision faded, it began to storm; wind and hail struck.

> The people of the village ran to fasten down their tipis, while the black horse riders sang to the drums that rolled like thunder . . . And as they sang, the hail and rain were falling yonder just a little way from us, and we could see it, but the cloud stood there and flashed and thundered, and only a little sprinkle fell on us.[30]

That Black Elk's ceremony was true and effective can hardly be doubted: after it was over, the people came up to him and told him how they or their relatives were well again after being sick, and they gave him presents.[31] More significant, perhaps, was what they saw in the tipi they had erected:

> Then the horses were all rubbed down with sacred sage and led away, and we began going into the tepee to see what might have happened there while we were dancing. The Grandfathers had sprinkled fresh soil on the nation's hoop that they had made in there with the red and black roads across it, and all around this little circle of the nation's hoop we saw the prints of tiny pony hoofs as though the spirit horses had been dancing while we danced.[32]

And Black Elk himself felt renewed; the fear that had dogged him for two years was gone. He was accepted as a wicasa wakan by the other holy men.

This reenactment is normal procedure for a vision of this type. Such a ceremony, or at least use of revealed songs, power objects and animals, costume and emblematic designs, is incorporated into the visionary's daily life after a successful hanblecheya. Sometimes these things are kept privately by the seer, sometimes they are made public, in part at least, as in Black Elk's case, but always the mental or spiritual phenomena are made physical.

For example, the vision of Wovoka, the Paiute holy man and prophet, became the Ghost Dance. It was danced all over the Plains during the most destructive years of the wars. Other visions, received during the dancing by participants, were incorporated into the ceremony as it was practiced in any locale, but it was through the agency of direct vision that the clothing worn, the songs sung, the dance itself, the rules for the behavior of the dancers, the articles they carried and the ornamentation they used were determined.[33]

As in the case of Sweet Medicine Man and the religion of the Sacred Arrows, all areas of behavior that were touched on in the vision were incorporated into the religious and social behavior of the people the vision was meant to serve. Because of his vision and his enactment of it, Black Elk became a powerful healer. He also gained invulnerability in battle when he imitated the geese, the symbols or emblems of purification and wisdom.[34]

Presumably he would have achieved the status of a great leader, as did Crazy Horse and Sitting Bull, had not white wars and government systems, rules, and prohibitions intervened. As it is, through the agency of the books he dictated, the personal aid he gave his people, and the heirs he left, his influence extends across the world; his vision was enacted in the Lakota way and recorded in the white man's way, thus reaching far beyond the small hoop of the Lakota across the hoops of many nations, just as the Grandfathers had showed him it would.[35]

Sweet Medicine Man was an ancient, traditional figure, and the dances, societies, laws, and truths he brought have become the traditional ways of the Cheyenne. Black Elk's vision has had neither time nor appropriate circumstances to become embedded in a people's way, but the processes of the transformation of vision into thought and action are the same. Those processes themselves are traditional in Indian America, as attested to in the ethnographies and collections of such people as Ruth Underhill, Alice Marriott, James Mooney, Franz Boas, Natalie Curtis, Jack and Anna Kilpatrick, John Stands-in-Timber, Lame Deer, Paul Radin, and so many more. Their testimony is clear: the Indian way includes ample room for vision translated into meaningful action and custom and thought, and it is because of the centrality of the vision to the life of the peoples of America that the religious life of the tribe endures, even under the most adverse circumstances. Vision is a way of becoming whole, of affirming one's special place in the universe, and myth, song, and ceremony are ways of affirming vision's place in the life of all the people. Thus it renews all: the visionary and his relatives and friends, even the generations long dead and those yet unborn.

The vision, however, as vision, can be experienced only by one person directly. Yet it, like all aspects of Indian life, must be shared; thus myth. Myth is a story of a vision; it is a presentation of that vision told in terms of the vision's symbols, characters, chronology, and import. It is a vehicle of transmission, of sharing, of renewal, and as such plays an integral part in the ongoing psychic life of a people.

In *Love and Will*, Rollo May recounts an experience he had with a Cézanne painting, contending that the painting was "mythic" because it encompassed "near and far, past, present and future, conscious and unconscious in one immediate totality of our relationship to the world."[36] In this way, myth acts as a lens through which we can discover the reality that exists beyond the limits of simple linear perception; it is an image, a verbal construct, that allows truth to emerge into direct consciousness. In this way, myth allows us to rediscover ourselves in our most human and ennobling dimensions. Through it we are allowed to see our own transcendent powers triumphant; we know, experientially, our true identity and our human capacity that is beyond behaviorism, history, and the machine.

Myth functions as an affirmation of self that transcends the temporal. It guides our attention toward a view of ourselves, a possibility, that we might not otherwise encounter. It shows us our own ability to accept and allow the eternal to be part of our selves. It allows us to image a marriage between our conscious and unconscious, fusing the twin dimensions of mind and society into a coherent, meaningful whole. It allows us to adventure in distant, unfamiliar landscapes while remaining close to home. Thus myth shows us that it is possible to relate ourselves to the grand and mysterious universe that surrounds and informs our being; it makes us aware of other orders of reality and experience and in that awareness makes the universe our home. It is a magic: it is the area of relationship between all those parts of experience that commonly divide us from ourselves, our universe, and our fellows. In the myth, and especially the mythopoeic vision that gives it birth, past, present, and future are one, and the human counterparts of these—ancestors, contemporaries, and descendents—are also one. Conscious and unconscious are united through the magic of symbolic progression so that the symbols can convey direct, rational meanings and stir indirect memories and insights that have not been raised to conscious articulation. In mythopoeic vision and its literary counterparts, the near and the far must come together, for in its grasp we stand in a transcendent landscape that incorporates both. Lastly, the mythic heals, it makes us whole. For in relating our separate experiences to one another, in weaving them into coherence and therefore significance, a sense of wholeness arises, a totality which, by virtue of our active participation, constitutes direct and immediate comprehension of ourselves and the universe of which we are integral parts.

References

1. *Random House Dictionary of the English Language*, unabridged (New York: Random House, 1966).

2. Walter W. Skeat, *An Etymological Dictionary of the English Language*, 4th rev. ed. (Oxford: Oxford University Press, 1978), pp. 755–756.

3. Rollo May, *Love and Will* (New York: Random House, 1966), p. 107.

4. Thomas Mann, "Freud and the Future," in Henry A. Murray, ed., *Myth and Mythmakers* (New York: George Braziller, 1960), p. 373.

5. Harry Levin, "Some Meanings of Myth" in Murray, *Myth*, p. 106.

6. John Stands-in-Timber and Margot Liberty, *Cheyenne Memories* (Lincoln: University of Nebraska Press, 1972), p. 27.

7. Stands-in-Timber and Liberty, *Cheyenne Memories*, p. 36.

8. Stands-in-Timber and Liberty, *Cheyenne Memories*, p. 39.

9. Stands-in-Timber and Liberty, *Cheyenne Memories*, pp. 39–41.

10. See John (Fire) Lame Deer and Richard Erdoes, *Lame Deer: Seeker of Visions* (New York: Touchstone, 1972); Black Elk and Joseph Epes Brown, *The Sacred Pipe* (Baltimore: Penguin, 1971), p. 44, for details on inipi and hanblecheya.

11. John G. Neihardt, *Black Elk Speaks* (Lincoln: University of Nebraska Press, 1961).

12. Sitting Bull had a vision before the Battle of the Greasy Grass (Little Big Horn) that foretold Custer's defeat. Yet histories, sometimes mentioning the vision as an example of primitive superstition, I suppose, generally lay the defeat to the "overwhelming" numbers of warriors Custer fought and to ambush tactics. The facts of the matter are quite different, as an earnest student of military strategy can discover: as many Indians as some reports estimate couldn't have watered their horses or found sufficient game to feed themselves, let alone ambush Yellow Hair.

13. Neihardt, *Black Elk Speaks*, p. 22.

14. Neihardt, *Black Elk Speaks*, p. 22.

15. Neihardt, *Black Elk Speaks*, p. 92. There are explanations of the ritual significance of the directions in a number of sources. Hamilton A. Tyler, *Pueblo Gods and Myths* (Norman: University of Oklahoma Press, 1964), is a good source. Few adequate accounts of Indian religions or philosophy can be complete without some discussion of this.

16. Neihardt, *Black Elk Speaks*, pp. 25–26.

17. Neihardt, *Black Elk Speaks*, p. 30.

18. Neihardt, *Black Elk Speaks*, p. 26.

19. Neihardt, *Black Elk Speaks*, pp. 26–29.

20. Neihardt, *Black Elk Speaks*, pp. 29–30.
21. Neihardt, *Black Elk Speaks*, pp. 39–40.
22. Neihardt, *Black Elk Speaks*, pp. 40, 43.
23. Neihardt, *Black Elk Speaks*, p. 40.
24. Neihardt, *Black Elk Speaks*, p. 40.
25. Neihardt, *Black Elk Speaks*, p. 35. I have included all the lines of the songs, as proper, though Neihardt only indicates where the repetitions go.
26. Neihardt, *Black Elk Speaks*, p. 44.
27. Neihardt, *Black Elk Speaks*, pp. 163–165.
28. Neihardt, *Black Elk Speaks*, p. 165.
29. Neihardt, *Black Elk Speaks*, pp. 166–180.
30. Neihardt, *Black Elk Speaks*, p. 180.
31. Neihardt, *Black Elk Speaks*, see pp. 174–179 for entire relevant passage.
32. Neihardt, *Black Elk Speaks*, pp. 178–179.
33. Neihardt, *Black Elk Speaks*, pp. 234–251. See also Stands-in-Timber and Liberty, *Cheyenne Memories*, Natalie Curtis, ed., *The Indians' Book* (New York: Dover, 1968), and especially James Mooney, *The Ghost Dance Religion and the Great Sioux Outbreak of 1890* (Chicago: University of Chicago Press, 1965).
34. Neihardt, *Black Elk Speaks*, p. 169.
35. Neihardt, *Black Elk Speaks*, pp. 42, 43, 44.
36. May, *Love and Will*, p. 124.

[1982]

La conciencia de la mestiza:
Towards a New Consciousness

Gloria Anzaldúa

Por la mujer de mi raza
hablará el espíritu.[1]

JOSE VASCONCELOS, MEXICAN PHILOSOPHER, ENVISAGED UNA RAZA *mestiza, una mezcla de razas afines, una raza de color—la primera raza síntesis del globo.* He called it a cosmic race, *la raza cósmica,* a fifth race embracing the four major races of the world.[2] Opposite to the theory of the pure Aryan, and to the policy of racial purity that white America practices, his theory is one of inclusivity. At the confluence of two or more genetic streams, with chromosomes constantly "crossing over," this mixture of races, rather than resulting in an inferior being, provides hybrid progeny, a mutable, more malleable species with a rich gene pool. From this racial, ideological, cultural and biological cross-pollinization, an "alien" consciousness is presently in the making—a new *mestiza* consciousness, *una conciencia de mujer*. It is a consciousness of the Borderlands.

Una lucha de fronteras/A Struggle of Borders

> Because I, a *mestiza*,
> continually walk out of one culture
> and into another,
> because I am in all cultures at the same time,
> *alma entre dos mundos, tres, cuatro,*
> *me zumba la cabeza con lo contradictorio.*
> *Estoy norteada por todas las voces que me hablan*
> *simultáneamente.*

The ambivalence from the clash of voices results in mental and emotional states of perplexity. Internal strife results in insecurity and indecisiveness. The *mestiza's* dual or multiple personality is plagued by psychic restlessness.

In a constant state of mental nepantilism, an Aztec word meaning torn between ways, *la mestiza* is a product of the transfer of the cultural and spiritual values of one group to another. Being tricultural, monolingual, bilingual or multilingual, speaking a patois, and in a state of perpetual transition, the *mestiza* faces the dilemma of the mixed breed: which collectivity does the daughter of a darkskinned mother listen to?

El chogue de un alma atrapado entre el mundo del espíritu y el mundo de la técnica a veces la deja entullada. Cradled in one culture, sandwiched between two cultures, straddling all three cultures and their value systems, *la mestiza* undergoes a struggle of flesh, a struggle of borders, an inner war. Like all people, we perceive the version of reality that our culture communicates. Like others having or living in more than one culture, we get multiple, often opposing messages. The coming together of two self-consistent but habitually incompatible frames of reference[3] causes *un choque*, a cultural collision.

Within us and within *la cultura chicana*, commonly held beliefs of the white culture attack commonly held beliefs of the Mexican culture, and both attack commonly held beliefs of the indigenous culture. Subconsciously, we see an attack on ourselves and our beliefs as a threat and we attempt to block with a counterstance.

But it is not enough to stand on the opposite river bank, shouting questions, challenging patriarchical, white conventions. A counterstance locks one into a duel of oppressor and oppressed; locked in mortal combat, like the cop and the criminal, both are reduced to a common denominator of violence. The counterstance refutes the dominant culture's views and beliefs, and, for this, it is proudly defiant. All reaction is limited by, and dependent on, what it is reacting against. Because the counterstance stems from a problem with authority—outer as well as inner—it's a step towards liberation from cultural domination. But it is not a way of life. At some point, on our way to a new consciousness, we will have to leave the opposite bank, the split between the two mortal combatants somehow healed so that we are on both shores at once and, at once, see through serpent and eagle eyes. Or perhaps we will decide to disengage from the dominant culture, write it off altogether as a lost cause, and cross the border into a wholly new and separate territory. Or we might go another route. The possibilities are numerous once we decide to act and not react.

A Tolerance for Ambiguity

These numerous possibilities leave *La Mestiza* floundering in uncharted seas. In perceiving conflicting information and points of view, she is subjected to a swamping of her psychological borders. She has discovered that she can't hold concepts or ideas in rigid boundaries. The borders and walls that are supposed to keep the undesirable ideas out are entrenched habits and patterns of behavior; these habits and patterns are the enemy within. Rigidity means death. Only by remaining flexible is she able to stretch the psyche horizontally and vertically. *La mestiza* constantly has to shift out of habitual formations; from convergent thinking, analytical reasoning that tends to use rationality to move toward a single goal (a Western mode), to divergent thinking,[4] characterized by movement away from set patterns and goals and toward a more whole perspective, one that includes rather than excludes.

The new *mestiza* copes by developing a tolerance for contradictions, a tolerance for ambiguity. She learns to be an Indian in Mexican culture, to be Mexican from an Anglo point of view. She learns to juggle cultures. She has a plural personality, she operates in a pluralistic mode—nothing is thrust out, the good, the bad and the ugly, nothing rejected, nothing abandoned. Not only does she sustain contradictions, she turns the ambivalence into something else.

She can be jarred out of ambivalence by an intense, and often painful, emotional event which inverts or resolves the ambivalence. I'm not sure exactly how. The work takes place underground—subconsciously. It is work that the soul performs. That focal point or fulcrum, that juncture where the *mestiza* stands, is where phenomena tend to collide. It is where the possibility of uniting all that is separate occurs. This assembly is not one where severed or separated pieces merely come together. Nor is it a balancing of opposing powers. In attempting to work out a synthesis, the self has added a third element which is greater than the sum of its severed parts. That third element is a new consciousness—a *mestiza* consciousness—and though it is a source of intense pain, its energy comes from a continual creative motion that keeps breaking down the unitary aspect of each new paradigm.

En unas pocas centurias, the future will belong to the *mestiza*. Because the future depends on the breaking down of paradigms, it depends on the straddling of two or more cultures. By creating a new mythos—that is, a change in the way we perceive reality, the way we see ourselves and the ways we behave—*la mestiza* creates a new consciousness.

The work of *mestiza* consciousness is to break down the subject-object duality that keeps her a prisoner and to show in the flesh and through the images in her work how duality is transcended. The answer to the problem between the white race and the colored, between males and females, lies in healing the split that originates in the very foundation of our lives, our culture, our languages, our thoughts. A massive uprooting of dualistic thinking in the individual and collective consciousness is the beginning of a long struggle, but one that could, in our best hopes, bring us to the end of rape, of violence, of war.

La encrucijada/The Crossroads

> A chicken is being sacrificed
> > at a crossroads, a simple mound of earth
> a mud shrine for *Eshu*,
> > *Yoruba* god of indeterminacy,
> who blesses her choice of path.
> > She begins her journey.

Su cuerpo es una bocacalle. La mestiza has gone from being the sacrificial goat to becoming the officiating priestess at the crossroads.

As a *mestiza* I have no country, my homeland cast me out; yet all countries are mine because I am every woman's sister or potential lover. (As a lesbian I have no race, my own people disclaim me; but I am all races because there is the queer of me in all races.) I am cultureless because, as a feminist, I challenge the collective cultural/religious male-derived beliefs of Indo-Hispanics and Anglos; yet I am cultured because I am participating in the creation of yet another culture, a new story to explain the world and our participation in it, a new value system with images and symbols that connect us to each other and to the planet. *Soy un amasamiento*, I am an act of kneading, of uniting and joining that not only has produced both a creature of darkness and a creature of light, but also a creature that questions the definitions of light and dark and gives them new meanings.

We are the people who leap in the dark, we are the people on the knees of the gods. In our flesh, (r)evolution works out the clash of cultures. It makes us crazy constantly, but if the center holds, we've made some kind of evolutionary step forward. *Nuestra alma el trabajo*, the opus, the great alchemical work; spiritual *mestizaje,* a "morphogenesis,"* an inevitable unfolding. We have become the quickening serpent movement.

Indigenous like corn, like corn, the *mestiza* is a product of crossbreeding, designed for preservation under a variety of conditions. Like an ear of corn—a female seed-bearing organ—the *mestiza* is tenacious, tightly wrapped in the husks of her culture. Like kernels she clings to the cob; with thick stalks and strong brace roots, she holds tight to the earth—she will survive the crossroads.

Lavando y remojando el maíz en agua de cal, despojando el pellejo. Moliendo, mixteando, amasando, haciendo tortillas de masa.† She steeps the corn in lime, it swells, softens. With stone roller on *metate,* she grinds the corn, then grinds again. She kneads and moulds the dough, pats the round balls into *tortillas.*

> We are the porous rock in the stone *metate*
> squatting on the ground.
> We are the rolling pin, *el maíz y agua,*
> *la masa harina. Somos el amasijo.*
> *Somos lo molido en el metate.*
> We are the *comal* sizzling hot,
> the hot *tortilla,* the hungry mouth.
> We are the coarse rock.
> We are the grinding motion,
> the mixed potion, *somos el molcajete.*
> We are the pestle, the *comino, ajo, pimienta,*
> We are the *chile colorado,*
> the green shoot that cracks the rock.
> We will abide.

El camino de la mestiza/The *Mestiza* Way

Caught between the sudden contraction, the breath sucked in and the endless space, the brown woman stands still, looks at the sky. She decides to go down, digging her way along the roots of trees. Sifting through the bones, she shakes them to see if there is any marrow in them. Then, touching the dirt to her

---

* To borrow chemist Ilya Prigogine's theory of "dissipative structures." Prigogine discovered that substances interact not in predictable ways as it was taught in science, but in different and fluctuating ways to produce new and more complex structures, a kind of birth he called "morphogenesis," which created unpredictable innovations.[5]

† *Tortillas de masa harina:* corn tortillas are of two types, the smooth uniform ones made in a tortilla press and usually bought at a tortilla factory or supermarket, and *gorditas,* made by mixing *masa* with lard or shortening or butter (my mother sometimes puts in bits of bacon or *chicarrones*).

forehead, to her tongue, she takes a few bones, leaves the rest in their burial place.

She goes through her backpack, keeps her journal and address book, throws away the muni-bart metromaps. The coins are heavy and they go next, then the greenbacks flutter through the air. She keeps her knife, can opener and eyebrow pencil. She puts bones, pieces of bark, *hierbas*, eagle feather, snakeskin, tape recorder, the rattle and drum in her pack and she sets out to become the complete *tolteca*.

Her first step is to take inventory. *Despojando, desgranando, quitando paja.* Just what did she inherit from her ancestors? This weight on her back—which is the baggage from the Indian mother, which the baggage from the Spanish father, which the baggage from the Anglo?

Pero es difícil differentiating between *lo heredado, lo adquirido, lo impuesto.* She puts history through a sieve, winnows out the lies, looks at the forces that we as a race, as women, have been a part of. *Luego bota lo que no vale, los desmientos, los desencuentos, el embrutecimiento. Aguarda el juicio, hondo y enraízado, de la gente antigua.* This step is a conscious rupture with all oppressive traditions of all cultures and religions. She communicates that rupture, documents the struggle. She reinterprets history and, using new symbols, she shapes new myths. She adopts new perspectives toward the darkskinned, women and queers. She strengthens her tolerance (and intolerance) for ambiguity. She is willing to share, to make herself vulnerable to foreign ways of seeing and thinking. She surrenders all notions of safety, of the familiar. Deconstruct, construct. She becomes a *nahual*, able to transform herself into a tree, a coyote, into another person. She learns to transform the small "I" into the total Self. *Se hace moldeadora de su alma. Según la concepción que tiene de sí misma, así será.*

Que no se nos olvide los hombres

"Tú no sirves pa' nada—
you're good for nothing.
Eres pura vieja."

"You're nothing but a woman" means you are defective. Its opposite is to be *un macho.* The modern meaning of the word "machismo," as well as the concept, is actually an Anglo invention. For men like my father, being "macho" meant being strong enough to protect and support my mother and us, yet being able to show love. Today's macho has doubts about his ability to feed and protect his family. His "machismo" is an adaptation to oppression and poverty and low self-esteem. It is the result of hierarchical male dominance. The Anglo, feeling inadequate and inferior and powerless, displaces or transfers these feelings to the Chicano by shaming him. In the Gringo world, the Chicano suffers from excessive humility and self-effacement, shame of self and self-deprecation. Around Latinos he suffers from a sense of language inadequacy and its accompanying discomfort; with Native Americans he suffers from a racial amnesia which ignores our common blood, and from guilt because the Spanish part of him took their land and oppressed them. He has an excessive compensatory hubris when around Mexicans from the other side. It overlays a deep sense of racial shame.

The loss of a sense of dignity and respect in the macho breeds a false machismo which leads him to put down women and even to brutalize them. Coexisting with his sexist behavior is a love for the mother which takes precedence over that of all others. Devoted son, macho pig. To wash down the shame of his acts, of his very being, and to handle the brute in the mirror, he takes to the bottle, the snort, the needle and the fist.

Though we "understand" the root causes of male hatred and fear, and the subsequent wounding of women, we do not excuse, we do not condone and we will not longer put up with it. From the men of our race, we demand the admission/acknowledgement/disclosure/testimony that they wound us, violate us, are afraid of us and of our power. We need them to say they will begin to eliminate their hurtful put-down ways. But more than the words, we demand acts. We say to them: we will develop equal power with you and those who have shamed us.

It is imperative that *mestizas* support each other in changing the sexist elements in the Mexican-Indian culture. As long as woman is put down, the Indian and the Black in all of us is put down. The struggle of the *mestiza* is above all a feminist one. As long as *los hombres* think they have to *chingar mujeres* and each other to be men, as long as men are taught that they are superior and therefore culturally favored over *la mujer*, as long as to be a *vieja* is a thing of derision, there can be no real healing of our psyches. We're halfway there—we have such love of the Mother, the good mother. The first step is to unlearn the *puta/virgen* dichotomy and to see *Coatlapopeuh—Coatlicue* in the Mother, *Guadalupe*.

Tenderness, a sign of vulnerability, is so feared that it is showered on women with verbal abuse and blows. Men, even more than women, are fettered to gender roles. Women at least have had the guts to break out of bondage. Only gay men have had the courage to expose themselves to the woman inside them and to challenge the current masculinity. I've encountered a few scattered and isolated gentle straight men, the beginnings of a new breed, but they are confused, and entangled with sexist behaviors that they have not been able to eradicate. We need a new masculinity and the new man needs a movement.

Lumping the males who deviate from the general norm with man, the oppressor, is a gross injustice. *Asombra pensar que nos hemos quedado en ese pozo oscuro donde el mundo encierra a las lesbianas. Asombra pensar que hemos, como femenistas y lesbianas, cerrado nuestros corazónes a los hombres, a nuestros hermanos los jotos, desheredados y marginales como nosotros.* Being the supreme crossers of cultures, homosexuals have strong bonds with the queer white, Black, Asian, Native American, Latino and with the queer in Italy, Australia and the rest of the planet. We come from all colors, all classes, all races, all time periods. Our role is to link people with each other—the Blacks with Jews with Indians with Asians with whites with extra-terrestrials. It is to transfer ideas and information from one culture to another. Colored homosexuals have more knowledge of other cultures; have always been at the forefront (although sometimes in the closet) of all liberation struggles in this country; have suffered more injustices and have survived them despite all odds. Chicanos need to acknowledge the political and artistic contributions of their queer. People, listen to what your *jotería* is saying.

The *mestizo* and the queer exist at this time and point on the evolutionary continuum for a purpose. We are a blending that proves that all blood is intricately woven together, and that we are spawned out of similar souls.

Somos una genta

> Hay tantísimas fronteras
> que dividen a la gente,
> pero por cada frontera
> existe también un puente.
> —GINA VALDÉS[6]

Divided Loyalties. Many women and men of color do not want to have any dealings with white people. It takes too much time and energy to explain to the downwardly mobile, white middle-class women that it's okay for us to want to own "possessions," never having had any nice furniture on our dirt floors or "luxuries" like washing machines. Many feel that whites should help their own people rid themselves of race hatred and fear first. I, for one, choose to use some of my energy to serve as a mediator. I think we need to allow whites to be our allies. Through our literature, art, *corridos* and folktales we must share our history with them so when they set up committees to help Big Mountain Navajos or the Chicano farmworkers or *los Nicaragüenses* they won't turn people away because of their racial fears and ignorances. They will come to see that they are not helping us but following our lead.

Individually, but also as a racial entity, we need to voice our needs. We need to say to white society: we need you to accept the fact that Chicanos are different, to acknowledge your rejection and negation of us. We need you to own the fact that you looked upon us as less than human, that you stole our lands, our personhood, our self-respect. We need you to make public restitution: to say that, to compensate for your own sense of defectiveness, you strive for power over us, you erase our history and our experience because it makes you feel guilty—you'd rather forget your brutish acts. To say you've split yourself from minority groups, that you disown us, that your dual consciousness splits off parts of yourself, transferring the "negative" parts onto us. (Where there is persecution of minorities, there is shadow projection. Where there is violence and war, there is repression of shadow.) To say that you are afraid of us, that to put distance between us, you wear the mask of contempt. Admit that Mexico is your double, that she exists in the shadow of this country, that we are irrevocably tied to her. Gringo, accept the doppelganger in your psyche. By taking back your collective shadow the intracultural split will heal. And finally, tell us what you need from us.

By Your True Faces We Will Know You

I am visible—see this Indian face—yet I am invisible. I both blind them with my beak nose and am their blind spot. But I exist, we exist. They'd like to think I have melted in the pot. But I haven't, we haven't.

The dominant white culture is killing us slowly with its ignorance. By taking away our self-determination, it has made us weak and empty. As a people we have resisted and we have taken expedient positions, but we have never been allowed to develop unencumbered—we have never been allowed to be fully ourselves. The whites in power want us people of color to barricade ourselves behind our separate tribal walls so they can pick us off one at a time with their hidden weapons; so they can whitewash and distort history. Ignorance splits people, creates prejudices. A misinformed people is a subjugated people.

Before the Chicano and the undocumented worker and the Mexican from the other side can come together, before the Chicano can have unity with Native Americans and other groups, we need to know the history of their struggle and they need to know ours. Our mothers, our sisters and brothers, the guys who hang out on the street corners, the children in the playgrounds, each of us must know our Indian lineage, our afro-*mestisaje*, our history of resistance.

To the immigrant *mexicano* and the recent arrivals we must teach our history. The 80 million *mexicanos* and the Latinos from Central and South America must know of our struggles. Each one of us must know basic facts about Nicaragua, Chile and the rest of Latin America. The Latinoist movement (Chicanos, Puerto Ricans, Cubans and other Spanish-speaking people working together to combat racial discrimination in the market place) is good but it is not enough. Other than a common culture we will have nothing to hold us together. We need to meet on a broader communal ground.

The struggle is inner: Chicano, *indio*, American Indian, *mojado*, *mexicano*, immigrant Latino, Anglo in power, working class Anglo, Black, Asian—our psyches resemble the bordertowns and are populated by the same people. The struggle has always been inner, and is played out in the outer terrains. Awareness of our situation must come before inner changes, which in turn come before changes in society. Nothing happens in the "real" world unless it first happens in the images in our heads.

El día de la Chicana

> I will not be ashamed again
> Nor will I shame myself.

I am possessed by a vision: that we Chicanas and Chicanos have taken back or uncovered our true faces, our dignity and self-respect. It's a validation vision.

Seeing the Chicana anew in light of her history, I seek an exoneration, a seeing through the fictions of white supremacy, a seeing of ourselves in our true guises and not as the false racial personality that has been given to us and that we have given to ourselves. I seek our woman's face, our true features, the positive and the negative seen clearly, free of the tainted biases of male dominance. I seek new images of identity, new beliefs about ourselves, our humanity and worth no longer in question.

Estamos viviendo en la noche de la Raza, un tiempo cuando el trabajo se hace a lo quieto, en el oscuro. El día cuando aceptamos tal y como somos y para en donde vamos y porque—ese día será el día de la Raza. Yo tengo el conpromiso de expresar mi visión, mi sensibilidad, mi percepción dé la revalidación de la gente mexicana, su mérito, estimación, honra, aprecio y validez.

On December 2nd when my sun goes into my first house, I celebrate *el día de la Chicana y el Chicano.* On that day I clean my altars, light my *Coatlalopeuh* candle, burn sage and copal, take *el baño para espantar basura,* sweep my house. On that day I bare my soul, make myself vulnerable to friends and family by expressing my feelings. On that day I affirm who we are.

On that day I look inside our conflicts and our basic introverted racial temperament. I identify our needs, voice them. I acknowledge that the self and the race have been wounded. I recognize the need to take care of our personhood, of our racial self. On that day I gather the splintered and disowned parts of *la gente mexicana* and hold them in my arms. *Todas las partes de nosotros valen.*

On that day I say, "Yes, all you people wound us when you reject us. Rejection strips us of self-worth; our vulnerability exposes us to shame. It is our innate identity you find wanting. We are ashamed that we need your good opinion, that we need your acceptance. We can no longer camouflage our needs, can no longer let defenses and fences sprout around us. We can no longer withdraw. To rage and look upon you with contempt is to rage and be contemptuous of ourselves. We can no longer blame you, nor disown the white parts, the male parts, the pathological parts, the queer parts, the vulnerable parts. Here we are weaponless with open arms, with only our magic. Let's try it our way, the *mestiza* way, the Chicana way, the woman way."

On that day, I search for our essential dignity as a people, a people with a sense of purpose—to belong and contribute to something greater than our *pueblo*. On that day I seek to recover and reshape my spiritual identity. *¡Anímate! Raza, a celebrar el día de la Chicana.*

El retorno

> All movements are accomplished in six stages,
> and the seventh brings return.
> —I CHING[7]

> *Tanto tiempo sin verte casa mía,*
> *mi cuna, mi hondo nido de la huerta.*
> —"SOLEDAD"[8]

I stand at the river, watch the curving, twisting serpent, a serpent nailed to the fence where the mouth of the Rio Grande empties into the Gulf.

I have come back. *Tanto dolor me costó el alejamiento.* I shade my eyes and look up. The bone beak of a hawk slowly circling over me, checking me out as potential carrion. In its wake a little bird flickering its wings, swimming sporadically like a fish. In the distance the expressway and the slough of traffic like an irritated sow. The sudden pull in my gut, *la tierra, los aguaceros.* My land, *el viento soplando la arena, el lagartijo debajo de un nopalito. Me acuerdo como era antes. Una región desértica de vasta llanuras, costeras de baja altura, de escasa lluvia, de chaparrales formados por mesquites y huizaches.* If I look real hard I can almost see the Spanish fathers who were called "the cavalry of Christ" enter this valley riding their burros, see the clash of cultures commence.

Tierra natal. This is home, the small towns in the Valley, *los pueblitos* with chicken pens and goats picketed to mesquite shrubs. *En las colonias* on the other side of the tracks, junk cars line the front yards of hot pink and lavender-trimmed houses—Chicano architecture we call it, self-consciously. I have missed the TV shows where hosts speak in half and half, and where awards are given in the category of Tex-Mex music. I have missed the Mexican cemeteries blooming with artificial flowers, the fields of aloe vera and red pepper, rows of sugar cane, of corn hanging on the stalks, the cloud of *polvareda* in the dirt roads behind a speeding truck, *el sabor de tamales de rez y venado.* I have missed *la yegua colorada* gnawing the wooden gate of her stall, the smell of horse flesh from Carito's corrals. *He hecho menos las noches calientes sin aire, noches de linternas y lechuzas* making holes in the night.

I still feel the old despair when I look at the unpainted, dilapidated, scrap lumber houses consisting mostly of corrugated aluminum. Some of the poorest people in the U.S. live in the Lower Rio Grande Valley, an arid and semi-arid land of irrigated farming, intense sunlight and heat, citrus groves next to chaparral and cactus. I walk through the elementary school I attended so long ago, that remained segregated until recently. I remember how the white teachers used to punish us for being Mexican.

How I love this tragic valley of South Texas, as Ricardo Sánchez calls it; this borderland between the Nueces and the Rio Grande. This land has survived possession and ill-use by five countries: Spain, Mexico, the Republic of Texas, the Confederacy, and the U.S. again. It has survived Anglo-Mexican blood feuds, lynchings, burnings, rapes, pillage.

Today I see the Valley still struggling to survive. Whether it does or not, it will never be as I remember it. The borderlands depression that was set off by the 1982 peso devaluation in Mexico resulted in the closure of hundreds of Valley businesses. Many people lost their homes, cars, land. Prior to 1982, U.S. store owners thrived on retail sales to Mexicans who came across the borders for groceries and clothes and appliances. While goods on the U.S. side have become 10, 100, 1000 times more expensive for Mexican buyers, goods on the Mexican side have become 10, 100, 1000 times cheaper for Americans. Because the Valley is heavily dependent on agriculture and Mexican retail trade, it has the highest unemployment rates along the entire border region; it is the Valley that has been hardest hit.*

"It's been a bad year for corn," my brother, Nune, says. As he talks, I remember my father scanning the sky for a rain that would end the drought, looking up into the sky, day after day, while the corn withered on its stalk. My father has been dead for 29 years, having worked himself to death. The life span of a Mexican farm laborer is 56—he lived to be 38. It shocks me that I am older than he. I, too, search the sky for rain. Like the ancients, I worship the rain god and the maize goddess, but unlike my father I have recovered their names. Now for rain (irrigation) one offers not a sacrifice of blood, but of money.

"Farming is in a bad way," my brother says. "Two to three thousand small and big farmers went bankrupt in this country last year. Six years ago the price of corn was $8.00 per hundred pounds," he goes on. "This year it is $3.90 per hundred pounds." And, I think to myself, after taking inflation into account, not planting anything puts you ahead.

I walk out to the back yard, stare at *los rosales de mamá*. She wants me to help her prune the rose bushes, dig out the carpet grass that is choking

---

* Out of the twenty-two border counties in the four border states, Hidalgo County (named for Father Hidalgo who was shot in 1810 after instigating Mexico's revolt against Spanish rule under the banner of *la Virgen de Guadalupe*) is the most poverty-stricken county in the nation as well as the largest home base (along with Imperial in California) for migrant farmworkers. It was here that I was born and raised, I am amazed that both it and I have survived.

them. *Mamagrande Ramona también tenía rosales.* Here every Mexican grows flowers. If they don't have a piece of dirt, they use car tires, jars, cans, shoe boxes. Roses are the Mexican's favorite flower. I think, how symbolic—thorns and all.

Yes, the Chicano and Chicana have always taken care of growing things and the land. Again I see the four of us kids getting off the school bus, changing into our work clothes, walking into the field with Papí and Mamí, all six of us bending to the ground. Below our feet, under the earth lie the watermelon seeds. We cover them with paper plates, putting *terremotes* on top of the plates to keep them from being blown away by the wind. The paper plates keep the freeze away. Next day or the next, we remove the plates, bare the tiny green shoots to the elements. They survive and grow, give fruit hundreds of times the size of the seed. We water them and hoe them. We harvest them. The vines dry, rot, are plowed under. Growth, death, decay, birth. The soil prepared again and again, impregnated, worked on. A constant changing of forms, *renacimientos de la tierra madre.*

> This land was Mexican once
> was Indian always
> and is.
> And will be again.

References

1. This is my own "take-off" on Jose Vasconcelos' idea. Jose Vasconcelos, *La Raza Cósmica: Missión de la Raza Ibero-Americana* (Mexico: Aguilar S.A. de Ediciones, 1961).

2. Vasconcelos.

3. Arthur Koestler termed this "bisociation." Albert Rothenberg, *The Creative Process in Art, Science, and Other Fields* (Chicago, IL: University of Chicago Press, 1979), 12.

4. In part, I derive my definition for "convergent" and "divergent" thinking from Rothenberg, 12–13.

5. Harold Gilliam, "Searching for a New World View," *This World* (January, 1981), 23.

6. Gina Valdés, *Puentes y Fronteras: Coplas Chicanas* (Los Angeles, CA: Castle Lithograph, 1982), 2.

7. Richard Wilhelm, *The I Ching or Book of Changes*, trans. Cary F. Baynes (Princeton, NJ: Princeton University Press, 1950), 98.

8. "Soledad" is sung by the group Haciendo Punto en Otro Son.

[1987]

The Highs and the Lows of Black Feminist Criticism

Barbara Christian

IN HER ESSAY, "IN SEARCH OF OUR MOTHERS' GARDENS," ALICE WALKER asked the questions, "What is *my* literary tradition? Who are the black women artists who preceded me? Do I have a ground to stand on?" Confronted by centuries of Afro-American women who, but for an exceptional few, lived under conditions antithetical to the creation of Art as it was then defined, how could she claim a creative legacy of foremothers, women who after all had no access to the pen, to paints, or to clay? If American cultural history was accurate, singing was the only art form in which black women participated.

But Walker turned the *idea* of Art on its head. Instead of looking high, she suggested, we should look low. On that low ground she found a multitude of artist-mothers—the women who'd transformed the material to which they'd had access into their conception of Beauty: cooking, gardening, quilting, storytelling. In retrieving that low ground, Walker not only reclaimed her foremothers, she pointed to a critical approach. For she reminded us that Art, and the thought and sense of beauty on which it is based, is the province not only of those with a room of their own, or of those in libraries, universities and literary Renaissances—that *creating* is necessary to those who work in kitchens and factories, nurture children and adorn homes, sweep streets or harvest crops, type in offices or manage them.

In the early seventies, when anyone asked me, "What do you think you're doing anyway? What is this Black Feminist Literary Critic thing you're trying to become?" I would immediately think of Alice's essay.

Like any other critic, my personal history has much to do with what I hear when I read. Perhaps because I am from the Caribbean, Alice's *high* and *low* struck chords in me. I'd grown up with a sharp division between the "high" thought, language, behavior expected in school and in church, and the "low" language that persisted at home and in the yards and the streets.

In school: Proper English, Romanesque sentences, Western philosophy, jargon and exegesis; boys always before girls, lines and lines; *My Country 'Tis of Thee*, the authority of the teacher.

In church: Unintelligible Latin and Greek, the canon, the text, the Virgin Mary and the nuclear family; priests always before nuns; Gregorian chant and tiptoeing.

At home: Bad English, raunchy sayings and stories, the intoning of toasts; women in the kitchen, the parlor *and* the market; kallaloo, loud supper talk, cousins, father, aunts, godmothers.

> *In the yards:* Sashaying and bodies, sweat, calypso, long talk and plenty voices;
> women and men bantering, bad words, politics and bamboo-
> shaying.

What was real? The high, though endured, was valued. The low, though enjoyed, was denigrated even by the lowest of the low.

As I read *Jane Eyre,* I wondered what women dreamt as they gazed at men and at the sea. I knew that women as well as men gazed. My mother and aunts constantly assessed men's bodies, the sea's rhythm. But Charlotte Brontë was in print. She had a language across time and space. I could not find my mother's language, far less her attitude, in any books, despite the fact that her phrasing was as complex and as subtle as Charlotte's.

Because of the 1950s (which for me was not the Eisenhower years but rather the Civil Rights movement, rhythm 'n' blues, and the works of James Baldwin), because of the 1960s (which for me was not the Free Speech Movement and the Weathermen, but rather SNCC, SEEK, the Black Muslims, Aretha and the Black Arts Movement), the *low* began to be valued by some of us. Yet there remained the high and the low for many black women. Camouflaged by the rhetoric of the period, we were, on high ground, a monolithic Harriet Tubman or a silent Queen of Africa; on low ground, we were screaming sapphires or bourgeois bitches.

But what were *we* saying, writing? By the early seventies, I knew some black women had written. I'd read Phillis Wheatley, Gwendolyn Brooks, and Lorraine Hansberry. I'd heard poets like Nikki Giovanni and June Jordan read. I'd known women in my childhood and adolescence who'd written stories. Yet I had never, in my years of formal schooling from kindergarten in the black Virgin Islands through a Ph.D. at white Columbia, heard even the name of *one* black woman writer. That women writers were studied, I knew. I'd had courses in which Jane Austen, George Eliot, Emily Dickinson, and Virginia Woolf appeared like fleeting phantoms. I knew the university knew that black male writers existed. My professors bristled at the names of Richard Wright and James Baldwin and barely acknowledged Langston Hughes and Ralph Ellison.

But what of black women writers? No phantoms, no bristlings—not even a mention. Few of us knew they wrote; fewer of us cared. In fact, who even perceived of us, as late as the early 1970s, as writers, artists, thinkers? Why should anyone want to know what we thought or imagined? What could we tell others, far less show them, that they did not already know? After all, weren't we, as Mister taunts Celie, "black" "pore," woman, and therefore "nothing at all?"

Of course we were telling stories, playing with language, speculating and specifying, reaching for wisdom, transforming the universe in our image.

Who but us could end a harrowing tale with these words to her tormentors?

> Frado has passed from their memories as Joseph from the butler's but she will
> never cease to track them *till* beyond mortal vision. (Harriet Wilson, *Our Nig*)

Who but us could use the image of a Plum Bun for the intersection of racism and sexism in this country? (Jessie Fauset, *Plum Bun*)
Who but us could begin her story with this comment?

Now, women forget all those things they don't want to remember and remember everything they don't want to forget. The dream is the truth. Then they act and do things accordingly. (Zora Neale Hurston, *Their Eyes Were Watching God*)

Who but us could lovingly present women poets in the kitchen? (Paule Marshall, *Poets in the Kitchen*)

Who but us could tell how it was possible to clean the blood off [our] beaten men and yet receive abuse from the victim? (Toni Morrison, *The Bluest Eye*)
Who but us could chant:

momma/momma/mammy/nanny/granny/
woman/mistress/sista luv
(June Jordan, Trying to Get Over)

But who knew that we knew? Even those of us who were telling stories or writing did not always see ourselves as artists of the word. And those of us who did know our genius were so rejected, unheard that we sometimes became crazy women crying in the wind or silenced scarecrows. Who could answer us but us?

For us did need us if only to validate that which we knew, we knew. The publications of first novels, Toni Morrison's *The Bluest Eye*, Alice Walker's *The Third Life of Grange Copeland*, June Jordan's *His Own Where*, heralded the decade of the seventies. While their novels were barely acknowledged in 1970, the movement of women all over the world was highlighted by American women who had some access to the Big Capital Media. Inspired, though sometimes disappointed, by movements of people of color, of blacks in the United States, of liberation struggles of "underdeveloped" nations, some American women began to seek themselves as women and to protest the truncated definition of woman in this society. In this context the literature of women, the critical responses of women were published as never before during a decade when many others were asserting that *The* Movement was dead.

For those of us who came out of the sixties, the vision of women moving all over the world was not solely a claiming of our rights but also the rights of all those who had been denied their humanity. In the space created for us by our foremothers, by our sisters in the streets, the houses, the factories, the schools, we were now able to speak and to listen to each other, to hear our own language, to refine and critique it across time and space, through the written word. For me that dialogue *is* the kernel of what a black feminist literary critic tries to do. We listen to those of us who speak, write, read, to those who have written, to those who may write. We write to those who write, read, speak, may write, and we try to hear the voiceless. We are participants in a many-voiced palaver of thought/feeling, image/language that moves us to *move*—toward a world where, like Alice Walker's revolutionary petunias, all of us can bloom.

We found that in order to move beyond prescribed categories we had to "rememory"—reconstruct our past. But in the literary church of the sixties, such an appeal to history was anathema. Presiding at the altar were the new critic priests, for whom the text was God, unstained by history, politics, experience, the world. Art for them was artifact. So, for example, the literature of blacks could not be literature, tainted as it was by what they called sociology. To the side of the altar were the pretenders, the political revolutionaries and new philosophers for whom creative works were primarily a pretext to expound their own ideas, their world programs. For both groups, women were neither the word nor the world, though sometimes we could be dots on some i's, muses or furies in the service of the text or the idea.

We found that we could not talk to either group unless we talked their talk, which was specialized, abstract—on high ground. So we learned their language only to find that its character had a profound effect on the questions we thought, the images we evoked, and that such thinking recalled a tradition beyond which we had to move if *we* were to be included in any authentic dialogue.

Because language is one (though not the only) way to express what one knows/feels even when one doesn't know one knows it, because storytelling *is* a dynamic form of remembering/recreating, we found that it was often in the relationship between literatures and the world that re-visioning occurred. It is often in the poem, the story, the play, rather than in Western philosophical theorizing, that feminist thought/feeling evolves, challenges and renews itself. So our Sister-bonding was presented and celebrated in novels like *Sula*, our body/spirit/erotic in works like *The Color Purple*, our revision of biography in works like *Zami*. It has often been through our literatures that women have renamed critical areas of human life: mothering, sexuality, bodies, friendship, spirituality, economics, the process of literature itself. And it was to these expressions that many of us turned in order to turn to ourselves as situated in a dynamic rather than a fixed world. For many of us such a turning led us to universities where words, ideas, are, were supposed to be nurtured and valued.

And—ah, here's the rub.

As a result of that gravitation, we *have* moved to excavate the past and restore to ourselves the words of many of our foremothers who were buried in the rumble of distorted history. We have questioned the idea of great works of literature, preferences clearly determined by a powerful elite. We have asked why some forms are not considered literature—for example, the diary, the journal, the letter. We have built journals and presses through which the works of women might be published. We have developed women's studies programs. Using our stories and images, we have taught our daughters and sons about ourselves, our sisters, brothers, and lovers about our desires. And some of us have shared a palaver with our writers/readers that prompts us all to re-vision ourselves.

Yet even as we moved, the high, the low persisted, in fact moved further and further apart. For we now confronted the revelation we always knew, that there is both a She and there are many she's. And that sometimes, in our work we seemed to reduce the *both-and* to *either-or*. That revelation made itself strongly felt in the exclusion that women of color protested when Woman was defined, in the rejection that many working-class women experienced when Woman was described. The awareness that we too seek to homogenize the world of our Sisters, to fix ourselves in boxes and categories through jargon, theory, abstraction, is upon us.

Why so? Has our training led us back to the high ground that had rejected us, our education to the very language that masked our existence? So often feminist literary discussion seems riveted on defining Woman in much the same way that Western medieval scholars tried to define God. Why is it that rather than acknowledging that we are both-and, we persist in seeking the either-or. Might that be because the either-or construction, the either-or deconstruction, is so embedded in our education? Might it be because that language, whether it moves us anywhere or not, is recognized, rewarded as brilliant, intellectual, high, in contrast to the low, vulgar, ordinary language of most creative writers and readers? Is it that we too are drawn to the power that resides on the high ground?

Even as we turned to our literatures, in which language is not merely an object but is always situated in a context, in which the pleasure and emotion of language are as important as its meaning, we have gravitated toward a critical language that is riddled with abstraction and is as distanced as possible from the creative work, and from pleasure. I sometimes wonder if we critics read stories and poems, or, if as our language indicates, our reading fare is primarily that of other critics and philosophers? Do we know our own literatures? Why, for example, does it appear that white feminist critics have abandoned their contemporary novelists? Where is the palaver among them? Or are Freud, Lacan, Barthes, Foucault, Derrida inevitably more appealing? Why are we so riveted on male thinkers, preferably dead or European? Why is it that in refuting essence, we become so fixed on essence? To whom are we writing when we write? Have we turned so far round that we have completed our circle? Is it that we no longer see any connections between the emotion/knowing language of women's literature, the many-voiced sounds of our own language and the re-visioning we seek?

Now when I think of Alice's *high* and *low*, I feel a new meaning. Because I am a black literary/feminist critic, I live in a sharp distinction between the high world of lit crit books, journals, and conferences, the middle world of classrooms and graduate students, and the low world of bookstores, kitchens, communities, and creative writers.

> *In the high world:* Discourse, theory, the canon, the body, the boys (prefera- bly Lacan, Derrida, and Foucault) before the girls; linguis-

	tics, the authority of the critic, the exclusion of creative writings.
In the middle world:	Reading the texts, sometimes of creative writers; negotiating between advancement and appreciation; tropes, research, discourse; now I understand my mother; narrative strategies. What does it mean? The race for theory.
In the low world:	Stories, poems, plays. The language of the folk. Many bodies—the feeling as one with June, Alice, Toni.

I sure know what she's talking about.
I don't want to hear that.
Her words move me.
That poem changed my life.

I dream like that.
That's really disturbing.
God—that's beautiful.
Perhaps I'm not so crazy after all.
I want to write too.
Say what?

Much, of course, can be learned by all of us from all of us who speak, read, write, including those of us who look high. But as we look high, we might also look low, lest we devalue women in the world even as we define *Woman*. In ignoring their voices, we may not only truncate our movement but we may also limit our own process until our voices no longer sound like women's voices to anyone.

[1990]

Defining Black Feminist Thought
Patricia Hill Collins

WIDELY USED YET RARELY DEFINED, BLACK FEMINIST THOUGHT encompasses diverse and contradictory meanings. Two interrelated tensions highlight issues in defining Black feminist thought. The first concerns the thorny question of who can be a Black feminist. One current response, explicit in Patricia Bell Scott's (1982b) "Selected Bibliography on Black Feminism," classifies all African-American women, regardless of the content of our ideas, as Black feminists. From this perspective, living as Black women provides experiences to stimulate a Black feminist consciousness. Yet indiscriminately labeling all Black women in this way simultaneously conflates the terms *woman* and *feminist* and identifies being of African descent—a questionable biological category—as being the sole determinant of a Black feminist consciousness. As Cheryl Clarke points out, "I criticized Scott. Some of the women she cited as 'black feminists' were clearly not feminist at the time they wrote their books and still are not to this day" (1983, 94).

The term *Black feminist* has also been used to apply to selected African-Americans—primarily women—who possess some version of a feminist consciousness. Beverly Guy-Sheftall (1986) contends that both men and women can be "Black feminists" and names Frederick Douglass and William E. B. DuBois as prominent examples of Black male feminists. Guy-Sheftall also identifies some distinguishing features of Black feminist ideas: namely, that Black women's experiences with both racial and gender oppression that result in needs and problems distinct from white women and Black men, and that Black women must struggle for equality both as women and as African-Americans. Guy-Sheftall's definition is helpful in that its use of ideological criteria fosters a definition of Black feminist thought that encompasses both experiences and ideas. In other words, she suggests that experiences gained from living as African-American women stimulate a Black feminist sensibility. But her definition is simultaneously troublesome because it makes the biological category of Blackness the prerequisite for possessing such thought. Furthermore, it does not explain why these particular ideological criteria and not others are the distinguishing ones.

The term Black feminist has also been used to describe selected African-American women who possess some version of a feminist consciousness (Beale 1970; Hooks 1981; Barbara Smith 1983; White 1984). This usage of the term yields the most restrictive notion of who can be a Black feminist. The ground-breaking Combahee River Collective (1982) document, "A Black Feminist Statement," implicitly relies on this definition. The Collective claims that "as Black women we find any type of biological determinism a particularly dangerous and reactionary basis upon which to build a politic" (p. 17). But in spite of this statement, by implying that only African-American women can be Black feminists, they require a biological prerequisite for race and gender consciousness. The Collective also offers its own ideological criteria for identifying Black feminist ideas. In contrast to Beverly Guy-Sheftall, the Collective places a stronger emphasis on capitalism as a source of Black women's oppression and on political activism as a distinguishing feature of Black feminism.

Biologically deterministic criteria for the term *black* and the accompanying assumption that being of African descent somehow produces a certain consciousness or perspective are inherent in these definitions. By presenting race as being fixed and immutable—something rooted in nature—these approaches mask the historical construction of racial categories, the shifting meaning of race, and the crucial role of politics and ideology in shaping conceptions of race (Gould 1981; Omi and Winant 1986). In contrast, much greater variation is afforded the term feminist. Feminists are seen as ranging from biologically determined—as is the case in radical feminist thought, which argues that only women can be feminists—to notions of feminists as individuals who have undergone some type of political transformation theoretically achievable by anyone.

Though the term Black feminist could also be used to describe any individual who embraces Black feminist ideas, the separation of biology from ideology required for this usage is rarely seen in the works of Black women intellectuals. Sometimes the contradictions among these competing definitions can be so great that Black women writers use all simultaneously. Consider the following passage from Deborah McDowell's essay "New Directions for Black Feminist Criticism":

> I use the term here simply to refer to Black female critics who analyze the works of Black female writers from a feminist political perspective. But the term can also apply to any criticism written by a Black woman regardless of her subject or perspective—a book written by a male from a feminist or political perspective, a book written by a Black woman or about Black women authors in general, or any writings by women. (1985, 191)

While McDowell implies that elite white men could be "black feminists," she is clearly unwilling to state so categorically. From McDowell's perspective, whites and Black men who embrace a specific political perspective, and Black women regardless of political perspective, could all potentially be deemed Black feminist critics.

The ambiguity surrounding current perspectives on who can be a Black feminist is directly tied to a second definitional tension in Black feminist thought: the question of what constitutes Black feminism. The range of assumptions concerning the relationship between ideas and their advocates as illustrated in the works of Patricia Bell Scott, Beverly Guy-Sheftall, the Combahee River Collective, and Deborah McDowell leads to problems in defining Black feminist theory itself. Once a person is labeled a "Black feminist," then ideas forwarded by that individual often become defined as Black feminist thought. This practice accounts for neither changes in the thinking of an individual nor differences among Black feminist theorists.

A definition of Black feminist thought is needed that avoids the materialist position that being Black and/or female generates certain experiences that automatically determine variants of a Black and/or feminist consciousness. Claims that Black feminist thought is the exclusive province of African-American women, regardless of the experiences and worldview of such women, typify this position. But a definition of Black feminist thought must also avoid the idealist position that ideas can be evaluated in isolation from the groups that create them. Definitions claiming that anyone can produce and develop Black feminist thought risk obscuring the special angle of vision that Black women bring to the knowledge production process.

The Dimensions of a Black Women's Standpoint

Developing adequate definitions of Black feminist thought involves facing this complex nexus of relationships among biological classification, the social construction of race and gender as categories of analysis, the material conditions accompanying these changing social constructions, and Black women's consciousness about these themes. One way of addressing the definitional tensions in Black feminist thought is to specify the relationship between a Black women's standpoint—those experiences and ideas shared by African-American women that provide a unique angle of vision on self, community, and society—and theories that interpret these experiences.[1] I suggest that Black feminist thought consists of specialized knowledge created by African-American women which clarifies a standpoint of and for Black women. In other words, Black feminist thought encompasses theoretical interpretations of Black women's reality by those who live it.

This definition does not mean that all African-American women generate such thought or that other groups do not play a critical role in its production. Before exploring the contours and implications of this working definition, understanding five key dimensions of a Black women's standpoint is essential.

The Core Themes of a Black Women's Standpoint

All African-American women share the common experience of being Black women in a society that denigrates women of African descent. This commonality of experience suggests that certain characteristic themes will be prominent in a Black women's standpoint. For example, one core theme is a legacy of struggle. Katie Cannon observes, "throughout the history of the United States, the interrelationship of white supremacy and male superiority has characterized the Black woman's reality as a situation of struggle—a struggle to survive in two contradictory worlds simultaneously, one white, privileged, and oppressive, the other black, exploited, and oppressed" (1985, 30). Black women's vulnerability to assaults in the workplace, on the street, and at home has stimulated Black women's independence and self-reliance.

In spite of differences created by historical era, age, social class, sexual orientation, or ethnicity, the legacy of struggle against racism and sexism is a common thread binding African-American women. Anna Julia Cooper,

---

[1] For discussions of the concept of standpoint, see Hartsock (1983a, 1983b), Jaggar (1983), and Smith (1987). Even though I use standpoint epistemologies as an organizing concept in this volume, they remain controversial. For a helpful critique of standpoint epistemologies, see Harding (1986). Haraway's (1988) reformulation of standpoint epistemologies approximates my use here.

a nineteenth-century Black woman intellectual, describes Black women's vulnerability to sexual violence:

> I would beg . . . to add my plea for the *Colored Girls* of the South:—that large, bright, promising fatally beautiful class . . . so full of promise and possibilities, yet so sure of destruction; often without a father to whom they dare apply the loving term, often without a stronger brother to espouse their cause and defend their honor with his life's blood; in the midst of pitfalls and snares, waylaid by the lower classes of white men, with no shelter, no protection. (Cooper 1892, 240)

Yet during this period Black women struggled and built a powerful club movement and numerous community organizations (Giddings 1984, 1988; Gilkes 1985).

Age offers little protection from this legacy of struggle. Far too many young Black girls inhabit hazardous and hostile environments. In 1975 I received an essay entitled "My World" from Sandra, a sixth-grade student who was a resident of one of the most dangerous public housing projects in Boston. Sandra wrote, "My world is full of people getting rape. People shooting on another. Kids and grownups fighting over girlsfriends. And people without jobs who can't afford to get a education so they can get a job . . . winos on the streets raping and killing little girls." Her words poignantly express a growing Black feminist sensibility that she may be victimized by racism and poverty. They also reveal her awareness that she is vulnerable to rape as a gender-specific form of sexual violence. In spite of her feelings about her community, Sandra not only walked the streets daily but managed safely to deliver three younger siblings to school. In doing so she participated in a Black women's legacy of struggle.

This legacy of struggle constitutes one of several core themes of a Black women's standpoint. Efforts to reclaim the Black feminist intellectual tradition are revealing Black women's longstanding attention to a series of core themes first recorded by Maria W. Stewart (Richardson 1987). Stewart's treatment of the interlocking nature of race, gender, and class oppression, her call for replacing denigrated images of Black womanhood with self-defined images, her belief in Black women's activism as mothers, teachers, and Black community leaders, and her sensitivity to sexual politics are all core themes advanced by a variety of Black feminist intellectuals.

Variation of Responses to Core Themes

The existence of core themes does not mean that African-American women respond to these themes in the same way. Diversity among Black women produces different concrete experiences that in turn shape various reactions to the core themes. For example, when faced with stereotypical, controlling images of Black women, some women—such as Sojourner Truth—demand, "ain't I a woman?" By deconstructing the conceptual apparatus of the dominant group, they invoke a Black women's legacy of struggle. In contrast, other women internalize the controlling images and come to believe that they are the stereotypes (Brown-Collins and Sussewell 1986).

A variety of factors explain the diversity of responses. For example, although all African-American women encounter racism, social class differences among African-American women influence how racism is experienced. A young manager who graduated with honors from the University of Maryland describes the specific form racism can take for middle-class Blacks. Before flying to Cleveland to explain a marketing plan for her company, her manager made her go over it three or four times in front of him so that she would not forget *her* marketing plan. Then he explained how to check luggage at an airport and how to reclaim it. "I just sat at lunch listening to this man talking to me like I was a monkey who could remember but couldn't think," the Black female manager recalled. When she had had enough, she responded, "I asked him if he wanted to tie my money up in a handkerchief and put a note on me saying that I was an employee of this company. In case I got lost I would be picked up by Traveler's Aid, and Traveler's Aid would send me back" (Davis and Watson 1985, 86). Most middle-class Black women do not encounter such blatant incidents, but many working-class Blacks do. For both groups the racist belief that African-Americans are less intelligent than whites remains strong.

Sexual orientation provides another key factor. Black lesbians have identified homophobia in general and the issues they face living as Black lesbians in homophobic communities as being a major influence on their angle of vision on everyday events (Shockley 1974; Lorde 1982, 1984; Clarke et al. 1983; Barbara Smith 1983) Beverly Smith describes how being a lesbian affected her perceptions of the wedding of one of her closest friends: "God, I wish I had one friend here. Someone who knew me and would understand how I feel. I am masquerading as a nice, straight, middle-class Black 'girl'" (1983, 172). While the majority of those attending the wedding saw only a festive event, Beverly Smith felt that her friend was being sent into a form of bondage.

Other factors such as ethnicity, region of the country, urbanization, and age combine to produce a web of experiences shaping diversity among African-American women. As a result, it is more accurate to discuss a Black *women's* standpoint than a Black *woman's* standpoint.

The Interdependence of Experience and Consciousness

Black women's work and family experiences and grounding in traditional African-American culture suggest that African-American women as a group experience a world different from that of those who are not Black and female. Moreover, these concrete experiences can stimulate a distinctive Black feminist consciousness concerning that material reality.[2] Being Black and female may expose African-American women to certain common experiences, which in turn may predispose us to a distinctive group consciousness, but it in no way guarantees that such a consciousness will develop among all women or that it will be articulated as such by the group.

Many African-American women have grasped this connection between what one does and how one thinks. Hannah Nelson, an elderly Black domestic worker, discusses how work shapes the perspectives of African-American and white women: "Since I have to work, I don't really have to worry about most of the things that most of the white women I have worked for are worrying about. And if these women did their own work, they would think just like I do—about this, anyway" (Gwaltney 1980, 4). Ruth Shays, a Black inner-city resident, points out how variations in men's and women's experiences lead to differences in perspective. "The mind of the man and the mind of the woman is the same" she notes, "but this business of living makes women use their minds in ways that men don't even have to think about" (Gwaltney 1980, 33).

This connection between experience and consciousness that shapes the everyday lives of all African-American women pervades the works of Black women activists and scholars. In her autobiography, Ida B. Wells describes how the lynching of her friends had such an impact on her worldview that she subsequently devoted much of her life to the antilynching cause (Duster 1970). Sociologist Joyce Ladner's (1972) *Tomorrow's Tomorrow*, a groundbreaking study of Black female adolescence, emerged from her discomfort with the disparity between the teachings of mainstream scholarship and her experiences as a young Black woman in the South. Similarly, the transformed consciousness experienced by Janie, the light-skinned heroine of Zora Neale Hurston's (1937) classic *Their Eyes Were Watching God*, from obedient granddaughter and wife to a self-defined African-American woman, can be directly traced to her experiences with each of her three husbands. In one scene Janie's second husband, angry because she served him a dinner of scorched rice, underdone fish, and soggy bread, hits her. That incident stimulates Janie to stand "where he left her for unmeasured time" and think. Her thinking leads to the recognition that "her image of Jody tumbled down and shattered . . . she had an inside and an outside now and suddenly she knew how not to mix them" (p. 63).

---

[2] Scott (1985) defines consciousness as the symbols, norms, and ideological forms people create to give meaning to their acts. For de Lauretis (1986), consciousness is a process, a "particular configuration of subjectivity . . . produced at the intersection of meaning with experience. . . . Consciousness is grounded in personal history, and self and identity are understood within particular cultural contexts. Consciousness . . . is never fixed, never attained once and for all, because discursive boundaries change with historical conditions" (p. 8).

Consciousness and the Struggle for a
Self-defined Standpoint

African-American women as a group may have experiences that provide us with a unique angle of vision. But expressing a collective, self-defined Black feminist consciousness is problematic precisely because dominant groups have a vested interest in suppressing such thought.[3] As Hannah Nelson notes, "I have grown to womanhood in a world where the saner you are, the madder you are made to appear" (Gwaltney 1980, 7). Ms. Nelson realizes that those who control the schools, media, and other cultural institutions of society prevail in establishing their viewpoint as superior to others.

An oppressed group's experiences may put its members in a position to see things differently, but their lack of control over the ideological apparatuses of society makes expressing a self-defined standpoint more difficult. Elderly domestic worker Rosa Wakefield assesses how the standpoints of the powerful and those who serve them diverge:

> If you eats these dinners and don't cook 'em, if you wears these clothes and don't buy or iron them, then you might start thinking that the good fairy or some spirit did all that. . . . Black folks don't have no time to be thinking like that. . . . But when you don't have anything else to do, you can think like that. It's bad for your mind, though. (Gwaltney 1980, 88)

Ms. Wakefield has a self-defined perspective growing from her experiences that enables her to reject the standpoint of more powerful groups. And yet ideas like hers are typically suppressed by dominant groups. Groups unequal in power are correspondingly unequal in their ability to make their standpoint known to themselves and others.

Individual African-American women have long displayed varying types of consciousness regarding our shared angle of vision. By aggregating and articulating these individual expressions of consciousness, a collective, focused group consciousness becomes possible. Black women's ability to forge these individual, unarticulated, yet potentially powerful expressions of everyday consciousness into an articulated, self-defined, collective standpoint is key to Black women's survival. As Audre Lorde points out, "it is axiomatic that if we do not define ourselves for ourselves, we will be defined by others—for their use and to our detriment" (1984, 45).

[3] The presence of a Black women's culture of resistance (Terborg-Penn 1986; Dodson and Gilkes (1987) that is both Afrocentric and feminist challenges two prevailing interpretations of the consciousness of oppressed groups. One approach claims that subordinate groups identify with the powerful and have no valid independent interpretation of their own oppression. The second assumes the oppressed are less human than their rulers, and are therefore less capable of interpreting their own experiences (Rollins 1985; Scott 1985). Both approaches see any independent consciousness expressed by oppressed groups as being either not of their own making or inferior to that of the dominant group. More important, both explanations suggest that the alleged lack of political activism on the part of oppressed groups stems from their flawed consciousness of their own subordination.

One fundamental feature of this struggle for a self-defined standpoint involves tapping sources of everyday, unarticulated consciousness that have traditionally been denigrated in white, male-controlled institutions. For Black women, the struggle involves embracing a consciousness that is simultaneously Afrocentric and feminist. What does this mean?

Research in African-American Studies suggests that an Afrocentric worldview exists which is distinct from and in many ways opposed to a Eurocentric worldview (Okanlawon 1972; Asante 1987; Myers 1988). Standard scholarly social constructions of blackness and race define these concepts as being either reflections of quantifiable, biological differences among humans or residual categories that emerged in response to institutionalized racism, (Lyman 1972; Bash 1979; Gould 1981; Omi and Winant 1986). In contrast, even though it often relies on biological notions of the "race," Afrocentric scholarship suggests that "blackness" and Afrocentricity reflect longstanding belief systems among African peoples (Diop 1974; Richards 1980; Asante 1987). While Black people were forced to adapt these Afrocentric belief systems in the face of different institutional arrangements of white domination, the continuation of an Afrocentric worldview has been fundamental to African-Americans' resistance to racial oppression (Smitherman 1977; Webber 1978; Sobel 1979; Thompson 1983). In other words, being Black encompasses *both* experiencing white domination *and* individual and group valuation of an independent, long-standing Afrocentric consciousness.

African-American women draw on this Afrocentric worldview to cope with racial oppression. But far too often Black women's Afrocentric consciousness remains unarticulated and not fully developed into a self-defined standpoint. In societies that denigrate African ideas and peoples, the process of valuing an Afrocentric worldview is the result of self-conscious struggle.

Similar concerns can be raised about the issue of what constitutes feminist ideas (Eisenstein 1983; Jaggar 1983). Being a biological female does not mean that one's ideas are automatically feminist. Self-conscious struggle is needed in order to reject patriarchal perceptions of women and to value women's ideas and actions. The fact that more women than men identify themselves as feminists reflects women's greater experience with the negative consequences of gender oppression. Becoming a feminist is routinely described by women (and men) as a process of transformation, of struggling to develop new interpretations of familiar realities.

The struggles of women from different racial/ethnic groups and those of women and men within African-American communities to articulate self-defined standpoints represent similar yet distinct processes. While race and gender are both socially constructed categories, constructions of gender rest on clearer biological criteria than do constructions of race. Classifying African-Americans into specious racial categories is considerably more difficult than noting the clear biological differences distinguishing females from males (Patterson 1982). But though united by biological sex, women do not form the same type of group as do African-Americans, Jews, native Americans, Vietnamese, or other groups with distinct histories, geographic origins, cultures, and social institutions. The absence of an identifiable tradition uniting women does not mean that women are characterized more by differences than by similarities. Women do share common experiences, but the experiences are not generally the same type as those affecting racial and ethnic groups (King 1988). Thus while expressions of race and gender are both socially constructed, they are not constructed in the same way. The struggle for an Afrocentric feminist consciousness requires embracing both an Afrocentric worldview and a feminist sensibility and using both to forge a self-defined standpoint.[4]

The Interdependence of Thought and Action

One key reason that standpoints of oppressed groups are suppressed is that self-defined standpoints can stimulate resistance. Annie Adams, a Southern Black woman, describes how she became involved in civil rights activities:

> When I first went into the mill we had segregated water fountains . . . Same thing about the toilets. I had to clean the toilets for the inspection room and then, when I got ready to go to the bathroom, I had to go all the way to the bottom of the stairs to the cellar. So I asked my boss man, "what's the difference? If I can go in there and clean them toilets, why can't I use them?" Finally, I started to use that toilet. I decided I wasn't going to walk a mile to go to the bathroom. (Byerly 1986, 134)

In this case Ms. Adams found the standpoint of the "boss man" inadequate, developed one of her own, and acted on it. Her actions illustrate the connections among concrete experiences with oppression, developing a self-defined standpoint concerning those experiences, and the acts of resistance that can follow.

This interdependence of thought and action suggests that changes in thinking may be accompanied by changed actions and that altered experiences may in turn stimulate a changed consciousness. The significance of this connection is succinctly expressed by Patrice L. Dickerson, an astute Black feminist college student, who writes, "it is a fundamental contention of mine that in a social context which denies and deforms a person's capacity to realize herself, the problem of self-consciousness is not simply a problem of thought, but also a problem of practice, . . . the demand to end a deficient consciousness must be joined to a demand to eliminate the conditions which caused it" (personal communication 1988). The struggle for a self-defined Afrocentric feminist consciousness occurs through a merger of thought and action.

This dimension of a Black women's standpoint rejects either/or dichotomous thinking that claims that *either* thought *or* concrete action is desirable and that merging the two limits the efficacy of both. Such approaches

---

[4] Even though I will continue to use the term *Afrocentric feminist thought* interchangeably with the phrase *Black feminist thought*, I think they are conceptually distinct.

generate deep divisions among theorists and activists which are more often fabricated than real. Instead, by espousing a both/and orientation that views thought and action as part of the same process, possibilities for new relationships between thought and action emerge. That Black women should embrace a both/and conceptual orientation grows from Black women's experiences living as both African-Americans and women and, in many cases, in poverty.

Very different kinds of "thought" and "theories" emerge when abstract thought is joined with concrete action. Denied positions as scholars and writers which allow us to emphasize purely theoretical concerns, the work of most Black women intellectuals is influenced by the merger of action and theory. The activities of nineteenth-century Black women intellectuals such as Anna J. Cooper, Frances Ellen Watkins Harper, Ida B. Wells, and Mary Church Terrell exemplify this tradition of merging intellectual work and activism. These women both produced analyses of Black women's oppression and worked to eliminate that oppression. The Black women's club movement they created was both an activist and an intellectual endeavor.

Contemporary Black women intellectuals continue to draw on this tradition of using everyday actions and experiences in our theoretical work.[5] Bell Hooks describes the impact working as an operator at the telephone company had on her efforts to write *Ain't I a Woman: Black Women and Feminism* (1981). The women she worked with wanted her to "write a book that would make our lives better, one that would make other people understand the hardships of being black and female" (1989, 152). To Hooks, "it was different to be writing in a context where my ideas were not seen as separate from real people and real lives" (p. 152). Similarly, Black feminist historian Elsa Barkley Brown describes the importance her mother's ideas played in the scholarship she eventually produced on African-American washerwomen. Initially Brown used the lens provided by her training as a historian and assessed her sample group as devalued service workers. But over time she came to understand washerwomen as entrepreneurs. By taking the laundry to whoever had the largest kitchen, they created a community and a culture among themselves. In explaining the shift of vision that enabled her to reassess this portion of Black women's history, Brown notes, "it was my mother who taught me how to ask the right questions—and all of us who try to do this thing called scholarship on a regular basis are fully aware that asking the right questions is the most important part of the process" (1986, 14).

[5] Canadian sociologist Dorothy Smith (1987) also views women's concrete, everyday world as stimulating theory. But the everyday she examines is individual, a situation reflecting in part the isolation of white, middle-class women. In contrast, I contend that the collective values in Afrocentric communities, when combined with the working-class experiences of the majority of Black women, provide a collective as well as an individual concrete.

Rearticulating a Black Women's Standpoint

The existence of a Black women's standpoint does not mean that African-American women appreciate its content, see its significance, or recognize the potential that a fully articulated Afrocentric feminist standpoint has as a catalyst for social change. One key role for Black women intellectuals is to ask the right questions and investigate all dimensions of a Black women's standpoint with and for African-American women.[6] Black women intellectuals thus stand in a special relationship to the community of African-American women of which we are a part, and this special relationship frames the contours of Black feminist thought.

This special relationship of Black women intellectuals to the community of African-American women parallels the existence of two interrelated levels of knowledge (Berger and Luckmann 1966). The commonplace, taken-for-granted knowledge shared by African-American women growing from our everyday thoughts and actions constitutes a first and most fundamental level of knowledge. The ideas that Black women share with one another on an informal, daily basis about topics such as how to style our hair, characteristics of "good" Black men, strategies for dealing with white folks, and skills of how to "get over" provide the foundations for this taken-for-granted knowledge.

Experts or specialists who participate in and emerge from a group produce a second, more specialized type of knowledge. The range of Black women intellectuals discussed in Chapter 1 are these specialists, and their theories clarifying a Black women's standpoint form the specialized knowledge of Black feminist thought. The two types of knowledge are interdependent. While Black feminist thought articulates the taken-for-granted knowledge shared by African-American women as a group, the consciousness of Black women may be transformed by such thought. The actions of educated Black women within the Black women's club movement typify this special relationship between Black women intellectuals and the wider community of African-American women:

> It is important to recognize that black women like Frances Harper, Anna Julia Cooper, and Ida B. Wells were not isolated figures of intellectual genius; they were shaped by and helped to shape a wider movement of Afro-American women.

[6] See Harold Cruse's (1967) analysis of the Black intellectual tradition and John Childs's (1984) discussion of the desired relationship of Black intellectuals to African-American culture. Childs argues against a relationship wherein "the people recede. They become merely the raw energy which the intellectuals must reshape, refine, and give voice to. A temptation for these intellectuals is to see themselves as the core formative force through which culture comes into conscious existence and through which it is returned, now complete, to the people" (p. 69). Like Childs, I suggest that the role of Black women intellectuals is to "illuminate the very intricacy and strength of the peoples' thought" (p. 87).

This is not to claim that they were representative of all black women; they and their counterparts formed an educated, intellectual elite, but an elite that tried to develop a cultural and historical perspective that was organic to the wider condition of black womanhood. (Carby 1987, 115)

The work of these women is important because it illustrates a tradition of joining scholarship and activism, and thus it taps the both/and conceptual orientation of a Black women's standpoint.

The suppression of Black feminist thought in mainstream scholarship and within its Afrocentric and feminist critiques has meant that Black women intellectuals have traditionally relied on alternative institutional locations to produce specialized knowledge about a Black women's standpoint. Many Black women scholars, writers, and artists have worked either alone, as was the case with Maria W. Stewart, or within African-American community organizations, the case for Black women in the club movement. The emergence of Black women's studies in colleges and universities during the 1980s, and the creation of a community of African-American women writers such as Toni Morrison, Alice Walker, and Gloria Naylor, have created new institutional locations where Black women intellectuals can produce specialized thought. Black women's history and Black feminist literary criticism constitute two focal points of this renaissance in Black women's intellectual work (Carby 1987). These are parallel movements: the former aimed at documenting social structural influences on Black women's consciousness; the latter, at exploring Black women's consciousness (self-definitions) through the freedom that art provides.

One danger facing African-American women intellectuals working in these new locations concerns the potential isolation from the types of experiences that stimulate an Afrocentric feminist consciousness—lack of access to other Black women and to a Black women's community. Another is the pressure to separate thought from action—particularly political activism—that typically accompanies training in standard academic disciplines. In spite of these hazards, contemporary Afrocentric feminist thought represents the creative energy flowing between these two focal points of history and literature, an unresolved tension that both emerges from and informs the experiences of African-American women.

The potential significance of Black feminist thought as specialized thought goes far beyond demonstrating that African-American women can be theorists. Like the Black women's activist tradition from which it grows and which it seeks to foster, Black feminist thought can create collective identity among African-American women about the dimensions of a Black women's standpoint. Through the process of rearticulation, Black women intellectuals offer African-American women a different view of themselves and their world from that forwarded by the dominant group (Omi and Winant 1986, 93). By taking the core themes of a Black women's standpoint and infusing them with new meaning, Black women intellectuals can stimulate a new consciousness that utilizes Black women's everyday, taken-for-granted knowledge. Rather than raising consciousness, Black feminist thought affirms and rearticulates a consciousness that already exists. More important, this rearticulated consciousness empowers African-American women and stimulates resistance.

Sheila Radford-Hill stresses the importance of rearticulation as an essential ingredient of an empowering Black feminist theory in her essay "Considering Feminism as a Model for Social Change." In evaluating whether Black women should espouse feminist programs, Radford-Hill suggests, "the essential issue that black women must confront when assessing a feminist position is as follows: If I, as a black woman, 'become a feminist,' what basic tools will I gain to resist my individual and group oppression" (1986, 160)? For Radford-Hill, the relevance of feminism as a vehicle for social change must be assessed in terms of its "ability to factor black women and other women of color into alternative conceptions of power and the consequences of its use" (p. 160). Thus Black feminist thought aims to develop a theory that is emancipatory and reflective and which can aid African-American women's struggles against oppression.

The earlier definition of Black feminist thought can now be reformulated to encompass the expanded definition of standpoint, the relationship between everyday and specialized thought, and the importance of rearticulation as one key dimension of Black feminist thought. Restated, Black feminist thought consists of theories or specialized thought produced by African-American women intellectuals designed to express a Black women's standpoint. The dimensions of this standpoint include the presence of characteristic core themes, the diversity of Black women's experiences in encountering these core themes, the varying expressions of Black women's Afrocentric feminist consciousness regarding the core themes and their experiences with them, and the interdependence of Black women's experiences, consciousness, and actions. This specialized thought should aim to infuse Black women's experiences and everyday thought with new meaning by rearticulating the interdependence of Black women's experiences and consciousness. Black feminist thought is *of* African-American women in that it taps the multiple relationships among Black women needed to produce a self-defined Black women's standpoint. Black feminist thought is *for* Black women in that it empowers Black women for political activism.

At first glance, this expanded definition could be read to mean that only African-American women can participate in the production of Black feminist thought and that only Black women's experiences can form the content of that thought. But this model of Black feminism is undermined as a critical perspective by being dependent on those who are biologically Black and female. Given that I reject exclusionary definitions of Black feminism which confine "black feminist criticism to black women critics of black women artists depicting black women" (Carby 1987, 9), how does the expanded definition of Black feminist thought address the two original definitional tensions?

Who Can Be a Black Feminist?
The Centrality of Black Women
Intellectuals to the Production of
Black Feminist Thought

I aim to develop a definition of Black feminist thought that relies exclusively neither on a materialist analysis—one whereby all African-American women by virtue of biology become automatically registered as "authentic Black feminists"—nor on an idealist analysis whereby the background, worldview, and interests of the thinker are deemed irrelevant in assessing his or her ideas. Resolving the tension between these two extremes involves reassessing the centrality Black women intellectuals assume in producing Black feminist thought. It also requires examining the importance of coalitions with Black men, white women, people of color, and other groups with distinctive standpoints. Such coalitions are essential in order to foster other groups' contributions as critics, teachers, advocates, and disseminators of a self-defined Afrocentric feminist standpoint.

Black women's concrete experiences as members of specific race, class, and gender groups as well as our concrete historical situations necessarily play significant roles in our perspectives on the world. No standpoint is neutral because no individual or group exists unembedded in the world. Knowledge is gained not by solitary individuals but by Black women as socially constituted members of a group (Narayan 1989). These factors all frame the definitional tensions in Black feminist thought.

Black women intellectuals are central to Black feminist thought for several reasons. First, our experiences as African-American women provide us with a unique standpoint on Black womanhood unavailable to other groups. It is more likely for Black women as members of an oppressed group to have critical insights into the condition of our own oppression than it is for those who live outside those structures. One of the characters in Frances Ellen Watkins Harper's 1892 novel, *Iola Leroy*, expresses this belief in the special vision of those who have experienced oppression:

> Miss Leroy, out of the race must come its own thinkers and writers. Authors belonging to the white race have written good books, for which I am deeply grateful, but it seems to be almost impossible for a white man to put himself completely in our place. No man can feel the iron which enters another man's soul. (Carby 1987, 62)

Only African-American women occupy this center and can "feel the iron" that enters Black women's souls, because we are the only group that has experienced race, gender, and class oppression as Black women experience them. The importance of Black women's leadership in producing Black feminist thought does not mean that others cannot participate. It does mean that the primary responsibility for defining one's own reality lies with the people who live that reality, who actually have those experiences.

Second, Black women intellectuals provide unique leadership for Black women's empowerment and resistance. In discussing Black women's involvement in the feminist movement, Sheila Radford-Hill points out the connections among self-definition, empowerment, and taking actions in one's own behalf:

> Black women now realize that part of the problem within the movement was our insistence that white women do for/with us what we must do for/with ourselves: namely, frame our own social action around our own agenda for change. . . . Critical to this discussion is the right to organize on one's own behalf. . . . Criticism by black feminists must reaffirm this principle. (1986, 162)

Black feminist thought cannot challenge race, gender, and class oppression without empowering African-American women. "Oppressed people resist by identifying themselves as subjects, by defining their reality, shaping their new identity, naming their history, telling their story," notes Bell Hooks (1989, 43). Because self-definition is key to individual and group empowerment, using an epistemology that cedes the power of self-definition to other groups, no matter how well-meaning, in essence perpetuates Black women's subordination. As Black feminist sociologist Deborah K. King succinctly states, "Black feminism asserts self-determination as essential" (1988, 72).

Stressing the importance of Black women's centrality to Black feminist thought does not mean that all African-American women exert this leadership. While being an African-American woman generally provides the experiential base for an Afrocentric feminist consciousness, these same conditions suppress its articulation. It is not acquired as a finished product but must continually develop in relation to changing conditions.

Bonnie Johnson emphasizes the importance of self-definition. In her critique of Patricia Bell Scott's bibliography on Black feminism, she challenges both Scott's categorization of all works by Black women as being Black feminist and Scott's identification of a wide range of African-American women as Black feminists: "Whether I think they're feminists is irrelevant. *They* would not call themselves feminist" (Clarke et al. 1983, 94). As Patrice L. Dickerson contends, "a person comes into being and knows herself by her achievements, and through her efforts to become and know herself, she achieves" (personal correspondence 1988). Here is the heart of the matter. An Afrocentric feminist consciousness constantly emerges and is part of a self-conscious struggle to merge thought and action.

Third, Black women intellectuals are central in the production of Black feminist thought because we alone can create the group autonomy that must precede effective coalitions with other groups. This autonomy is quite distinct from separatist positions whereby Black women withdraw from other groups and engage in exclusionary politics. In her introduction to *Home*

Girls, A Black Feminist Anthology, Barbara Smith describes this difference: "Autonomy and separatism are fundamentally different. Whereas autonomy comes from a position of strength, separatism comes from a position of fear. When we're truly autonomous we can deal with other kinds of people, a multiplicity of issues, and with difference, because we have formed a solid base of strength" (1983, xl). Black women intellectuals who articulate an autonomous, self-defined standpoint are in a position to examine the usefulness of coalitions with other groups, both scholarly and activist, in order to develop new models for social change. However, autonomy to develop a self-defined, independent analysis does not mean that Black feminist thought has relevance only for African-American women or that we must confine ourselves to analyzing our own experiences. As Sonia Sanchez points out, "I've always known that if you write from a black experience, you're writing from a universal experience as well . . . I know you don't have to whitewash yourself to be universal" (in Tate 1983, 142).

While Black feminist thought may originate with Black feminist intellectuals, it cannot flourish isolated from the experiences and ideas of other groups. The dilemma is that Black women intellectuals must place our own experiences and consciousness at the center of any serious efforts to develop Black feminist thought yet not have that thought become separatist and exclusionary. Bell Hooks offers a solution to this problem by suggesting that we shift from statements such as "I am a feminist" to those such as "I advocate feminism." Such an approach could "serve as a way women who are concerned about feminism as well as other political movements could express their support while avoiding linguistic structures that give primacy to one particular group" (1984, 30).

By advocating, refining, and disseminating Black feminist thought, other groups—such as Black men, white women, white men, and other people of color—further its development. Black women can produce an attenuated version of Black feminist thought separated from other groups. Other groups cannot produce Black feminist thought without African-American women. Such groups can, however, develop self-defined knowledge reflecting their own standpoints. But the full actualization of Black feminist thought requires a collaborative enterprise with Black women at the center of a community based on coalitions among autonomous groups.

Coalitions such as these require dialogues among Black women intellectuals and within the larger African-American women's community. Exploring the common themes of a Black women's standpoint is an important first step. Moreover, finding ways of handling internal dissent is especially important for the Black women's intellectual community. Evelynn Hammond describes how maintaining a united front for whites stifles her thinking: "What I need to do is challenge my thinking, to grow. On white publications sometimes I feel like I'm holding up the banner of black womanhood. And that doesn't allow me to be as critical as I would like to be" (in Clarke et al. 1983, 104). Cheryl Clarke observes that she has two dialogues: one with the public and the private ones in which she feels free to criticize the work of other Black women. Clarke states that the private dialogues are the ones that "have changed my life, have shaped the way I feel . . . have mattered to me" (p. 103).

Coalitions also require dialogues with other groups. Rather than rejecting our marginality, Black women intellectuals can use our outsider-within stance as a position of strength in building effective coalitions and stimulating dialogue. Barbara Smith suggests that Black women develop dialogues based on a "commitment to principled coalitions based not upon expediency, but upon our actual need for each other" (1983, xxxiii). Dialogues among and coalitions with a range of groups, each with its own distinctive set of experiences and specialized thought embedded in those experiences, form the larger, more general terrain of intellectual and political discourse necessary for furthering Black feminism. Through dialogues exploring how relations of domination and subordination are maintained and changed, parallels between Black women's experiences and those of other groups become the focus of investigation.

Dialogue and principled coalition create possibilities for new versions of truth. Alice Walker's answer to the question of what she felt were the major differences between the literature of African-Americans and whites offers a provocative glimpse of the types of truths that might emerge through an epistemology based on dialogue and coalition. Walker did not spend much time considering this question, since it was not the difference between them that interested her, but, rather, the way Black writers and white writers seemed to be writing one immense story, with different parts of the story coming from a multitude of different perspectives. In a conversation with her mother, Walker refines this epistemological vision: "I believe that the truth about any subject only comes when all sides of the story are put together, and all their different meanings make one new one. Each writer writes the missing parts to the other writer's story. And the whole story is what I'm after" (1983, 49). Her mother's response to Walker's vision of the possibilities of dialogues and coalitions hints at the difficulty of sustaining such dialogues under oppressive conditions: "'Well, I doubt if you can ever get the *true* missing parts of anything away from the white folks,' my mother says softly, so as not to offend the waitress who is mopping up a nearby table; 'they've sat on the truth so long by now they've mashed the life out of it'" (1983, 49).

What Constitutes Black Feminism?
The Recurring Humanist Vision

A wide range of African-American women intellectuals have advanced the view that Black women's struggles are part of a wider struggle for human dignity and empowerment. In an 1893 speech to women, Anna Julia Cooper cogently expressed this alternative worldview:

> We take our stand on the solidarity of humanity, the oneness of life, and the unnaturalness and injustice of all special favoritisms, whether of sex, race, country, or condition. . . . The colored woman feels that woman's cause is one and universal; and that . . . not till race, color, sex, and condition are seen as accidents, and not the substance of life; not till the universal title of humanity to life, liberty, and the pursuit of happiness is conceded to be inalienable to all; not till then is woman's lesson taught and woman's cause won—not the white woman's nor the black woman's, not the red woman's but the cause of every man and of every woman who has writhed silently under a mighty wrong. (Loewenberg and Bogin 1976, 330–31)

Like Cooper, many African-American women intellectuals embrace this perspective regardless of particular political solutions we propose, our fields of study, or our historical periods. Whether we advocate working through separate Black women's organizations, becoming part of women's organizations, working within existing political structures, or supporting Black community institutions, African-American women intellectuals repeatedly identify political actions such as these as a *means* for human empowerment rather than ends in and of themselves. Thus the primary guiding principle of Black feminism is a recurring humanist vision (Steady 1981, 1987).[7]

Alice Walker's preference for the term *womanist*, a term she describes as "womanist is to feminist as purple is to lavender," addresses this notion of the solidarity of humanity. To Walker, one is "womanist" when one is "committed to the survival and wholeness of entire people, male and female." A womanist is "not a separatist, except periodically for health" and is "traditionally universalist, as is 'Mama, why are we brown, pink, and yellow, and our cousins are white, beige, and black?' Ans.: 'Well, you know the colored race is just like a flower garden, with every color flower represented'" (1983, xi). By redefining all people as "people of color," Walker universalizes what are typically seen as individual struggles while simultaneously allowing space for autonomous movements of self-determination.

In assessing the sexism of the Black nationalist movement of the 1960s,

---

[7] My use of the term *humanist* grows from an Afrocentric historical context distinct from that criticized by Western feminists. I use the term to tap an Afrocentric humanism as cited by West (1977–78), Asante (1987) and Turner (1984) and as part of the Black theological tradition (Mitchell and Lewter 1986; Cannon 1988). See Harris (1981) for a discussion of the humanist tradition in the works of three Black women writers. See Richards (1990) for a discussion of African-American spirituality, a key dimension of Afrocentric humanism. Novelist Margaret Walker offers one of the clearest discussions of Black humanism. Walker claims: "I think it is more important now to emphasize humanism in a technological age than ever before, because it is only in terms of humanism that society can redeem itself. I believe that mankind is only one race—the human race. There are many strands in the family of man—many races. The world has yet to learn to appreciate the deep reservoirs of humanism in all races, and particularly in the Black race" (Rowell 1975, 12).

Black feminist lawyer Pauli Murray identifies the dangers inherent in separatism as opposed to autonomy, and also echoes Cooper's concern with the solidarity of humanity:

> The lesson of history that all human rights are indivisible and that the failure to adhere to this principle jeopardizes the rights of all is particularly applicable here. A built-in hazard of an aggressive ethnocentric movement which disregards the interests of other disadvantaged groups is that it will become parochial and ultimately self-defeating in the face of hostile reactions, dwindling allies, and mounting frustrations. . . . Only a broad movement for human rights can prevent the Black Revolution from becoming isolated and can insure ultimate success. (Murray 1970, 102)

Without a commitment to human solidarity, suggests Murray, any political movement—whether nationalist, feminist or antielitist—may be doomed to ultimate failure.

Bell Hooks' analysis of feminism adds another critical dimension that must be considered: namely, the necessity of self-conscious struggle against a more generalized ideology of domination:

> To me feminism is not simply a struggle to end male chauvinism or a movement to ensure that women will have equal rights with men; it is a commitment to eradicating the ideology of domination that permeates Western culture on various levels—sex, race, and class, to name a few—and a commitment to reorganizing U.S. society so that the self-development of people can take precedence over imperialism, economic expansion, and material desires. (Hooks 1981, 194)

Former assemblywoman Shirley Chisholm also points to the need for self-conscious struggle against the stereotypes buttressing ideologies of domination. In "working toward our own freedom, we can help others work free from the traps of their stereotypes," she notes. "In the end, antiblack, antifemale, and all forms of discrimination are equivalent to the same thing—antihumanism. . . . We must reject not only the stereotypes that others have of us but also those we have of ourselves and others" (1970, 181).

This humanist vision is also reflected in the growing prominence of international issues and global concerns in the works of contemporary African-American women intellectuals (Lindsay 1980; Steady 1981, 1987). Economists Margaret Simms and Julianne Malveaux's 1986 edited volume, *Slipping through the Cracks: The Status of Black Women*, contains articles on Black women in Tanzania, Jamaica, and South Africa. Angela Davis devotes an entire section of her 1989 book, *Women, Culture, and Politics*, to international affairs and includes essays on Winnie Mandela and on women in Egypt. June Jordan's 1985 volume, *On Call*, includes essays on South Africa, Nicaragua, and the Bahamas. Alice Walker writes compellingly of the types of links these and other Black women intellectuals see between African-American women's issues and those of other groups: "To me, Central

America is one large plantation; and I see the people's struggle to be free as a slave revolt" (1988, 177).

The words and actions of Black women intellectuals from different historical times and addressing markedly different audiences resonate with a strikingly similar theme of the oneness of all human life. Perhaps the most succinct version of the humanist vision in Black feminist thought is offered by Fannie Lou Hamer, the daughter of sharecroppers, and a Mississippi civil rights activist. While sitting on her porch, Ms. Hamer observed, "Ain' no such thing as I can hate anybody and hope to see God's face" (Jordan 1981, xi).

Taken together, the ideas of Anna Julia Cooper, Pauli Murray, Bell Hooks, Alice Walker, Fannie Lou Hamer, and other Black women intellectuals too numerous to mention suggest a powerful answer to the question "What is Black feminism?" Inherent in their words and deeds is a definition of Black feminism as a process of self-conscious struggle that empowers women and men to actualize a humanist vision of community.

References

Asante, Molefi Kete. 1987. *The Afrocentric Idea*. Philadelphia: Temple University Press.

Bash, Harry H. 1979. *Sociology, Race and Ethnicity*. New York: Gordon and Breach.

Beale, Frances. 1970. "Double Jeopardy: To Be Black and Female." In *The Black Woman: An Anthology*, edited by Toni Cade (Bambara), 90–100. New York: Signet.

Berger, Peter L., and Thomas Luckmann. 1966. *The Social Construction of Reality*. New York: Doubleday.

Brown, Elsa Barkley. 1986. *Hearing Our Mothers' Lives*. Atlanta: Fifteenth Anniversary of African-American and African Studies, Emory University. (unpublished)

Brown-Collins, Alice, and Deborah Ridley Sussewell. 1986. "The Afro-American Women's Emerging Selves." *Journal of Black Psychology* 13(1): 1–11.

Byerly, Victoria. 1986. *Hard Times Cotton Mills Girls*. Ithaca, NY: Cornell University Press.

Cannon, Katie G. 1985. "The Emergence of a Black Feminist Consciousness." In *Feminist Interpretations of the Bible*, edited by Letty M. Russell, 30–40. Philadelphia: Westminster Press.

———. 1988. *Black Womanist Ethics*. Atlanta: Scholars Press.

Clarke, Cheryl. 1983. "The Failure to Transform: Homophobia in the Black Community." In *Home Girls: A Black Feminist Anthology*, edited by Barbara Smith, 197–208. New York: Kitchen Table Press.

Cooper, Anna Julia. 1892. *A Voice from the South; By a Black Woman of the South*. Xenia, OH: Aldine Printing House.

Davis, George, and Glegg Watson. 1985. *Black Life in Corporate America*. New York: Anchor.

Diop, Cheikh. 1974. *The African Origin of Civilization: Myth or Reality*. New York: L. Hill.

Duster, Alfreda M., ed. 1970. *Crusade for Justice: The Autobiography of Ida B. Wells*. Chicago: University of Chicago Press.

Eisenstein, Hester. 1983. *Contemporary Feminist Thought*. Boston: G. K. Hall.

Giddings, Paula. 1984. *When and Where I Enter . . . The Impact of Black Women on Race and Sex in America*. New York: William Morrow.

Gilkes, Cheryl Townsend. 1980. " 'Holding Back the Ocean with a Broom': Black Women and Community Work." In *The Black Woman*, edited by La Frances Rodgers-Rose, 217–32. Beverly Hills, CA: Sage.

Gould, Stephen Jay. 1981. *The Mismeasure of Man*. New York: W. W. Norton.

Guy-Sheftall, Beverly. 1986. "Remembering Sojourner Truth: On Black Feminism." *Catalyst* (Fall): 54–57.

Gwaltney, John Langston. 1980. *Drylongso, A Self-Portrait of Black America*. New York: Vintage.

Hooks, Bell. 1981. *Ain't I a Woman: Black Women and Feminism*. Boston: South End Press.

———. 1984. *From Margin to Center*. Boston: South End Press.

———. 1989. *Talking Back: Thinking Feminist, Thinking Black*. Boston: South End Press.

Hurston, Zora Neale. [1937] 1969. *Their Eyes Were Watching God*. Greenwich, CT: Fawcett.

Jaggar, Alison M. 1983. *Feminist Politics and Human Nature*. Totawa, NJ: Rowman & Allanheld.

Jewell, L. George, Evelyn Hammonds, Bonnie Johnson, and Linda Powell. 1983.

Jordan, June. 1981. *Civil Wars*. Boston: Beacon.

King, Deborah K. 1988. "Multiple Jeopardy, Multiple Consciousness: The Context of a Black Feminist Ideology." *Signs* 14(1): 42–72.

Ladner, Joyce. 1972. *Tomorrow's Tomorrow*. Garden City, NY: Doubleday.

Lindsay, Beverly, ed. 1980. *Comparative Perspectives of Third World Women: The Impact of Race, Sex, and Class*. New York: Praeger.

Lorde, Audre. 1982. *Zami: A New Spelling of My Name*. Trumansberg, NY: The Crossing Press.

McDowell, Deborah E. 1985. "New Directions for Black Feminist Criticism." In *The New Feminist Criticism*, edited by Elaine Showalter, 186–99. New York: Pantheon.

Murray, Pauli. 1970. "The Liberation of Black Women." In *Voices of the New Feminism*, edited by Mary Lou Thompson, 87–102. Boston: Beacon.

Narayan, Uma. 1989. "The Project of Feminist Epistemology: Perspectives from a Nonwestern Feminist." In *Gender/Body/Knowledge: Feminist Reconstructions of Being and Knowing*, edited by Alison M. Jaggar and Susan R. Bordo, 256–69. New Brunswick, NJ: Rutgers University Press.

Okanlawon, Alexander. 1972. "Africanism—A Synthesis of the African World-View." *Black World* 21(9): 40–44, 92–97.

Omi, Michael, and Howard Winant. 1986. *Racial Formation in the United States: From the 1960s to the 1980s*. New York: Routledge & Kegan Paul.

Patterson, Orlando. 1982. *Slavery and Social Death*. Cambridge, MA: Harvard University Press.

Radford-Hill, Sheila. 1986. "Considering Feminism as a Model for Social Change." In *Feminist Studies/Critical Studies*, edited by Teresa de Lauretis, 157–72. Bloomington: Indiana University Press.

Richards, Dona. 1980. "European Mythology: The Ideology of 'Progress.' " In

Contemporary Black Thought, edited by Molefi Kete Asante and Abdulai Sa. Vandi, 59–79. Beverly Hills, CA: Sage.

Richardson, Marilyn, ed. 1987. *Maria W. Stewart, America's First Black Woman Political Writer*. Bloomington: Indiana University Press.

Scott, Patricia Bell. 1982a. "Debunking Sapphire: Toward a Non-Racist and Non-Sexist Social Science." In *But Some of Us Are Brave*, edited by Gloria T. Hull, Patricia Bell Scott, and Barbara Smith, 85–92. Old Westbury, NY: Feminist Press.

———. 1982b. "Selected Bibliography on Black Feminism." In *But Some of Us Are Brave*, edited by Gloria T. Hull, Patricia Bell Scott, and Barbara Smith, 23–36. Old Westbury, NY: Feminist Press.

Shockley, Ann Allen. 1974. *Loving Her*. Tallahassee, FL: Naiad Press.

Smith, Barbara. 1983. "Introduction." In *Home Girls: A Black Feminist Anthology*, edited by Barbara Smith, xix–lvi. New York: Kitchen Table Press.

Smitherman, Geneva. 1977. *Talkin and Testifyin: The Language of Black America*. Boston: Houghton Mifflin.

Sobel, Mechal. 1979. *Trabelin' On: The Slave Journey to an Afro-Baptist Faith*. Princeton: Princeton University Press.

Steady, Filomina Chioma. 1981. "The Black Woman Cross-Culturally: An Overview." In *The Black Woman Cross-Culturally*, edited by Filomina Chioma Steady, 7–42. Cambridge, MA: Schenkman.

———. 1987. "African Feminism: A Worldwide Perspective." In *Women in Africa and the African Diaspora*, edited by Rosalyn Terborg-Penn, Sharon Harley, and Andrea Benton Rushing, 3–24. Washington, DC: Howard University Press.

Tate, Claudia, ed. 1983. *Black Women Writers at Work*. New York: Continuum Publishing.

Thompson, Robert Farris. 1983. *Flash of the Spirit: African and Afro-American Art and Philosophy*. New York: Vintage.

Walker, Alice. 1983. *In Search of Our Mothers' Gardens*. New York: Harcourt Brace Jovanovich.

———. 1988. *Living by the Word*. New York: Harcourt Brace Jovanovich.

Webber, Thomas L. 1978. *Deep Like the Rivers*. New York: W. W. Norton.

White, E. Frances. 1984. "Listening to the Voices of Black Feminism." *Radical America* 18(2–3): 7–25.

[1990]

Defining Asian American Realities through Literature

Elaine H. Kim

THERE WERE SOME LETTERS IN THE "DEAR ABBY" COLUMN RECENTLY that reflect a gulf between Asian Americans and the descendants of European immigrants. Two Irish Americans wrote that they could not understand why an American of "Oriental" descent would complain about being asked "what are you" within five minutes of being introduced to a "Caucasian." One wrote, "I don't think it's rude . . . I think it's a positive component of international understanding." Abby says that the "Oriental" readers, "without exception," responded like the following letter writer:

> . . . What am I? Why, I'm a person like everyone else. . . . 'Where did you come from?' would be an innocent question when one Caucasian asks it of another, but when it is asked of an Asian, it takes on a different tone. . . . When I say, 'I'm from . . . Portland, Oregon!' they are invariably surprised . . . because they find it hard to believe that an Asian-looking person is actually . . . American. . . . Being white is not a prerequisite for being . . . American . . . and . . . it's high time everyone realized it.

Significantly, Abby concludes the column with the other Irish American letter: "The Irish are so proud of being Irish, they tell you before you even ask. Tip O'Neill never tried to hide his Irish ancestry."[1]

So much writing by Asian Americans is focused on the theme of claiming an American, as opposed to Asian, identity that we may begin to wonder if this constitutes accommodation, a collective colonized spirit—the fervent wish to "hide our ancestry," which is impossible for us anyway, to relinquish our marginality, and to lose ourselves in an intense identification with the hegemonic culture. Or is it in fact a celebration of our marginality and a profound expression of protest against being defined by domination?

Today, as we study the power of "otherness" and the celebration of marginality, we must pause to think about the complexity and diversity of minority discourse in order to understand why the political concerns expressed in Asian American literature are unique. Tied to issues of gender, social stratification, racial oppression, and the need to restore the foundations of our history and culture, the most recurrent theme in our writing is what I call claiming America for Asian Americans. That does not mean disappearing like raindrops in the ocean of white America, fighting to become "normal," losing ourselves in the process. It means inventing a new identity, defining ourselves according to the truth instead of a racial fantasy, so that we can be reconciled with one another in order to celebrate our marginality. It is this seeming paradox, the Asian American claim on America, that is the oppositional quality of our discourse.

In this article, I have deliberately chosen to provide a roughly chronological survey of various Asian American literary works, because our literature is still unfamiliar to most scholars and because it represents diverse nationalities and different class backgrounds, nativities, generations, historical moments, and genders, factors that often make quite contradictory demands. In general, though, I think it is fair to say that the literature reflects an overarching collective concern, the invention of an American identity.

Asian Americans may seem squarely placed in the so-called hegemonic stage of domination. Our literature is written primarily by American-born, American-educated Asians whose first language is English, whether we concur and collaborate or resist. The Asian American writer exists on the margins of his or her own marginal community, wedged between the hegemonic culture and the non-English-speaking communities largely unconcerned with self-definition. Nor has the transformation of our communities during the last two decades brought with it a legion of new writers: For the most part, they continue to be second and third generation American born Chinese and Japanese. They cannot be expected to speak in the voices of the vast numbers of immigrants and refugees whose stories have never been well represented in our literature, past or present.

Inscriptions of Asians in U.S. Popular Culture

Although we are no longer under direct colonial domination, clumsy racial fantasies about Asians continue to flourish in the West, and these extend to Asian Americans as well. The Vietnamese in Japanese army uniforms, the sinister villains and brute hordes of faceless masses found in films like "Rambo" are not much different from the business-suited New York Chinatown gangland mobsters in "Year of the Dragon." Familiar representations of Asians—always unalterably alien—as helpless heathens, comical servants, loyal allies and, only in the case of women, exotic sex objects imbued with an innate understanding of how to please, serve, and titillate, extend directly to Asian Americans and exist in all cases to define as their dialectical opposite the Anglo man as heroic, courageous, and physically superior, whether as soldier, missionary, master, or lover.

These racial romances so characteristic of the dominant phase of colonization may be part of the baggage of Western imperialist penetration into Asia; nevertheless they are extended to us, who have not been allowed a separate identity. Asian America is after all itself a creation of white racism that groups nationalities and nativities together, making it possible to blame—and murder—a Chinese American out of frustration over competition from Japanese auto manufacturers.

We can see how the notions about Asians and Asian Americans overlap in the "middleman minority" function for both. British and American scholarship traditionally placed Asians between blacks and whites on a racial continuum: if whites were born to lead, blacks were best at hard labor, and Asians were suited to carry out orders. This notion has been sedimented into our interpretations of economic development in Asia today: the "little tigers," South Korea, Taiwan, and Singapore, are sandwiched between the industrialized nations of the West and the countries of Africa and Latin America. Only Japan presents a classification problem. In this country, Asian America is a buffer zone between whites and blacks or Hispanics: supposedly obedient, docile, efficient at carrying out the mandates of the decision makers, Asian Americans are increasingly visible in low middle management, high clerical, and small business occupations. Ideologically, we occupy the position of "model minority," living proof that racism is not what keeps other people of color down.

Views of the Literary Critics

Racist and culturally hegemonic views of Asians and Asian Americans are inscribed in works by well-known Anglo American writers like Jack London, as well as a plethora of lesser writers, like the creator of Charlie Chan, Earl Derr Biggers, whose caricatures have survived him. That both Biggers and his British counterpart, Arthur Sarsfield Ward, creator of Fu Manchu, received recognition and honorary degrees at Harvard demonstrates how extensive has been the penetration of these views of Asians and Asian Americans into the American intelligentsia. Indeed, it is difficult for Anglo American literary critics to remain unaffected by the same notions embedded in the minds of Dear Abby's readers. Contemporary Chinese American playwright Frank Chin has noted that New York critics of his play, *Chickencoop Chinaman*, complained in the early 1970s that his characters did not speak, dress, or act "like Orientals."

Certainly reviews of our literature by Anglo-American critics reveal that the criteria used to assess their literary merit have been other than literary and aesthetic. Reviewers of Etsu Sugimoto's *A Daughter of the Samurai* (1925) praised the writer because she "pleads no causes, asks no vexing questions"[2] at a time when the controversial issue of Japanese exclusion was being spiritedly discussed. Critics of *The Grass Roof* (1931) lauded Younghill Kang's Korea, which is described as a "planet of death," its brilliant colors, haunting music, and the magic of its being fading into an "infernal twilight" of decay commanded by the inability to modernize. But when Kang depicts the arrogance and race prejudice of the American missionaries in Korea, the critics are indignant:

> Mr. Kang does not, I think, give a full account of American missionaries. Doubtless these are blundering human beings, just like the rest of us. He accuses them of lack of education, yet he longed ardently to come to their country for the kind of education they receive. He was desperately eager to receive the benefit of their escort to America.[3]

During the World War II era, the American public became widely aware of broad distinctions among Asian nationalities, at least between Japanese and all others. China and the Philippines became known as allies in the Pacific, and popular magazines like *Life* and *Time* carried feature articles on how to tell the Chinese from the Japanese. In 1943 and 1950, the first books by second generation Chinese Americans were published by major houses. Promoters of Pardee Lowe's *Father and Glorious Descendant* suggested that the book might be worth reading because Lowe's enlistment in the U.S. Army showed him to be "one of America's loyal minorities."[4] Jade Snow

Wong's *Fifth Chinese Daughter*[5] was valued primarily as evidence that American racial minorities have only themselves to blame for their failure in American life. Such a view, expressed by a member of a racial minority group, was important during the Cold War period, when charges of race discrimination in the United States were circulating in developing countries which, having recently been freed from direct colonial rule, were questioning the value of American world leadership. The U.S. State Department in fact negotiated the rights to publish Wong's book in a number of Asian languages and arranged a tour for her in 1952 to forty-five Asian locales from Tokyo to Karachi, where she was to speak about the benefits of American democracy from the perspective of a Chinese American.

During the Civil Rights movement of the late 1960s and the period of increased ethnic awareness immediately ensuing, several books by Japanese Americans were brought out by major publishers. Critical reception was shaped by political concerns at a time when people of color vociferously seeking justice and equality could be shown the example of the non-militant approach of the "model minority." Jeanne Wakatsuki and James D. Houston's *Farewell to Manzanar*[6] was celebrated for its "lack of bitterness, self-pity, or solemnity,"[7] in portraying the wartime incarceration of Japanese Americans. Daniel Okimoto's *American in Disguise*[8] was appreciated by critics for having been written with "restraint" during "the current racial uproar."[9] One reviewer praised him for talking of "the Negro problem sympathetically and yet not without the racial pride of one from a subculture which always worked hard and had a devotion to education as a spur to achievement."[10] Ironically, what the reviewers call "racial pride" can also be seen as racial self-hatred: *American in Disguise* illustrates that the price for such "success" is rejection of both Japanese and Japanese American identity. Okimoto thus finds white women "personally as well as physically" appealing, because they have the "seductive attraction" of being able to provide him with "[c]rowning evidence of having made it." The "key to final assimilation," Okimoto notes, is intermarriage, and the book ends with the writer's reference to his own children, for whom "[p]hysically, at least, half the disguise I have worn will be lost." Even in the end, his own face is still an unfortunate "disguise."[11]

The barriers to understanding Asian American literature posed by the blinders of culturally hegemonic interpretations can be seen in other non-literary criteria. In *Publisher's Weekly*, one critic praises Maxine Hong Kingston's *The Woman Warrior*[12] for its "myths rich and varied as Chinese brocade" and its prose manifesting "the delicacy and precision of porcelain": "East meets West with . . . charming results" in the book.[13] A closer look would have revealed its deliberately anti-exotic, anti-nostalgic character:

> The old man opened his eyes wide at us and turned in a circle, surrounded. His neck tendons stretched out. "Maggots!" he shouted. "Maggots! Where are my grandsons? I want grandsons! Give me grandsons! Maggots!" He pointed at each one of us, "Maggot! Maggot! Maggot! Maggot! Maggot! Maggot!" Then he dived

into his food, eating fast and getting seconds. "Eat, maggots," he said. "Look at the maggots chew."

"He does that at every meal," the girls told us in English.

"Yeah," we said. "Our old man hates us too. What assholes."[14]

A critic notes with approval that Kingston's name indicates that she is married to an "American," that is, a white, implying that she herself is not "American" and that her marriage has some bearing on the critical approach to her book.[15] In the *National Observer,* one reviewer defends his interpretation by mentioning that his wife is Chinese Canadian. Even Kingston's portrayal of ambiguity as central to the Chinese American woman's experience is misconstrued: "It's hard to tell where her fantasies end and reality begins," the critic complains. He is confused by her depiction of some Chinese women as aggressive and verbal and others as docile, as if there can only be one type of Chinese woman. These confusions are "especially hard for a non-Chinese," he concludes, "and that's the troubling aspect of the book."[16] One of the main points of *The Woman Warrior* is that a marginal person indeed derives power and vision from living with paradoxes. The narrator says, "I learned to make my mind large, as the universe is large, so that there is room for paradoxes."[17]

Though truly universal, Asian American literature exists outside the canon of American literature and is considered narrow and specialized work penned by aliens to whom the English language and the culture it represents can never really belong. Thus, despite the place we are supposed to occupy as an assimilated "model minority," it's hard to think of an Asian American writer who is not immediately identified as such, attesting to the continuing marginality of our literature.

Early Immigrant Writers: A Class Perspective

The first Asian American writers in English were acutely aware of common misconceptions about Asia and Asians. These early immigrant writers were not representative of the general population of Asian Americans, who were predominantly laborers recruited for agricultural and construction work in Hawaii and on the Pacific Coast. Consumed in struggles for their livelihood in a hostile environment and segregated in field labor camps and ethnic urban enclaves, they usually did not speak or write in English. Even Filipino immigrants were mostly illiterate, since recruiters in search of a docile labor force preferred those without formal education. Then too, autobiographical writing and popular fiction were not found in the traditional cultures that produced the first immigrants. In China and Korea, writing and literature were the domain of the literati, who traditionally confined themselves to classical poetry and essays. Autobiography as such was unknown, since for a scholar to write a book about himself would have been deemed egotistical in the extreme. Fiction was considered frivolous and was usually written under pen names. Farmers and peasants performed as master storytellers, dramatic dancers, and singers but rarely expressed themselves through the written word.

Scholars and diplomats, who had been exempted from exclusion legislation aimed at restricting the entry of Asian laborers into the United States, comprised a disproportionately large part of the early Asian American voice. Addressing an Anglo American audience, they tried to win sympathy for the people of the educated elite of which they were part. Their portrayals of Asia are focused on high culture, and their criticisms of American society are tentative and apologetic.

Probably the best known interpreter of Asia to the West is self-styled cultural envoy Lin Yutang, whose *My Country and My People*[18] enjoyed enormous popularity in the West, although Chinese critics have pointed out that Lin was "out of tempo with the Chinese people," indulging as he does in "chitchat on the moon, rocks and gardens, dreams, smoke and incense" while Chinese were dying by the millions in their struggle against foreign domination. "No wonder," writes one critic, "many Chinese called his book 'My Country and My Class' or, resorting to a pun. . . . 'Mai Country and Mai People,' mai being the Chinese word for selling and betraying."[19] Ironically, Lin spent most of his life in the United States as a Chinese expatriate; the place he won for himself here was made possible only if he remained Chinese.

The writings of Younghill Kang and Carlos Bulosan illustrate the transition from sojourner to immigrant searching for a permanent place in America. Kang and Bulosan paint vivid portraits of the lives of Korean and Filipino exiles—their work, their aspirations, their exclusion from American social and intellectual life. Searching for entry into that life, first through books and then through American women, both discover that the America of their aspirations does not yet exist: it must be invented, brought into being.

Not one of the characters in Kang's *East Goes West*[20] achieves his American dream. Reading Shakespeare in his unheated room, the narrator is only able to think of food, and the young American woman he so eagerly hopes to befriend moves away, leaving no forwarding address. The story ends with his dream of being locked in a dark cellar with some black men as torch-bearing whites are about to set them all on fire. His only hope is a Buddhist interpretation of the dream, that he will be reincarnated into a better life.

Bulosan's *America Is in the Heart*[21] describes the lives and work of the Filipino migrant workers who followed the harvest, working in fields and canneries from the Mexican border to Alaska during the 1920s and 1930s. Although Bulosan is attempting to claim America for the thousands of farmworkers and menial laborers for whom he seeks to give voice, it is an America of the heart, a dream, a promise, an ideal forged from loneliness and suffering.

We must be united in the effort to make an America in which our people can find happiness. . . . We are all Americans that have toiled and suffered and known oppression and defeat, from the first Indian that offered peace in Manhattan to the last Filipino pea-pickers. . . . America is a prophecy of a new society of men . . . the nameless foreigner, the homeless refugee, the hungry boy begging for a job and the black body dangling from a tree.[22]

The war era's paternalistically friendly attitudes towards certain Asian nations has passed, Bulosan died in poverty and obscurity, and Asian Americans are eternal aliens once again, periodically reminded that we have no right to "complain" about anything. Instead, we should be grateful. "If you don't like it here," even third generation Asian Americans would be told, "you can always go back."

The contemporary Southeast Asian refugee claim on America is captured in Wendy Law-Yone's *The Coffin Tree*,[23] which is the story of a Burmese refugee woman who can never "go back." The contrast between her life in Burma and America provides us with a profound understanding of why she almost loses her mind. Her brother, who had been the vital one in Burma, fails to thrive here. After he dies and she hears of the death of her father, her last link to Burma, she is totally alone in the world, having lost the continuity between past and future provided by her family in the traditional culture. Unless she can adapt herself to a hostile and terrifying new world, with its bitter loneliness, its telephone answering machines, and its asylums for the insane, unless she can survive the transplant and set down roots in American soil, she will disappear from the face of the earth.

Community Portraits

In our communities, the wish to "disappear" by being fully assimilated into white society has always been resisted in fervent attempts to preserve cultural integrity within the American context. Although Louis Chu's *Eat a Bowl of Tea*[24] never achieved popularity or financial success during his lifetime, the novel is now viewed as a cornerstone in the Asian American literary tradition. The book is set in New York Chinatown in the late 1940s, the characters aging men who have spent their lives in laundry and restaurant labor. Their contacts with American society are limited to harassment by police and immigration officials and brief encounters with American prostitutes. Their lives have been sustained by fantasies about China and by the profound warmth of their friendships with each other. The central contradiction is the conflict between the old community of bachelor sojourners and the young immigrants who will make America their permanent home. Chu's Chinese American community is on the threshold of change: forced by the Chinese Revolution to face the likelihood that they may never return to their homeland after all, the old men find that the community structure they have built in New York is all that is left to them. The uncertain future belongs to the youth, represented by Ben Loy, whose sexual impotence is a reflection of the social powerlessness of generations of Chinatown bachelors constricted by genocidal American laws and policies. The bitter tea he must drink is his willingness to compromise in order to obtain a new life in America. The tea is Chinese medicine, and the move he makes is from New York to San Francisco Chinatown. Although he will not raise his son as he was raised, he will not forsake his Chinese roots. The vital quality of Chu's prose comes from his ability to appreciate the language spoken around him by a people to whom verbal skill and witty exchanges were valued as a social art. Instead of the "pidgin English" invented for comic effect by Anglo-American writers about the Chinese, Chu translates the idioms and images from Cantonese dialects, presenting them in skillfully crafted dialogues. In these, he gives us a vivid picture of the social relationships and attitudes that governed Chinatown life for many decades.

By deliberately not addressing Anglo American readers, Chu is able to present a non-hegemonic view of his own community within the context of American society—that is, as Milton Murayama says, "setting the record straight . . . with love, with all the warts showing."[25] At the same time, he is able to use the English language in new ways.

Because of differential treatment of Japanese Americans under American laws, American-born, American-educated, English-speaking second generation Japanese *nisei* comprised about half of the Japanese population in the United States by 1930, resulting in the publication of more Japanese American literary work in English earlier than those found in other groups. This work appeared first in ethnic print media. Addressed to fellow *nisei*, it unselfconsciously attempts to appropriate the English language and literary forms for Japanese American use. The essential quality in these writings is a balance made possible by the writers' biculturalism, which gives them two pairs of eyes through which to see both their communities and their American context without distortion or romanticism. By the 1950s, some of this work was published outside the newsprint ghetto.

John Okada's *No-No Boy*[26] was probably rejected by the Japanese American press and community in the 1950s because it depicts both American society and the post-war Seattle Japanese American community in an intensely unflattering light. The characters have little in common with the "model minority" that picks itself up by the bootstraps: incapacitated by self-hatred, their relationships have been distorted by the internment experience. Parents and children, husbands and wives, brothers and friends are pitted against each other in bitter conflicts caused by their collective shame. The protagonist searches desperately for a way to put together the pieces of his own fragmented life. Despite his pain and alienation, he retains his profound faith in the promise of American justice and equality. *No-No Boy* is an indictment of race hatred and a testament to the strength and faith of the oppressed.

Nor is the view of the pre-war Japanese American family and community and its American context a pretty one in Milton Murayama's *All I Asking For Is My Body* (1959).[27] The *nisei* stagger under the combined weight of Japanese family traditions and the uniquely American plantation system of Hawaii. The book challenges unquestioning acceptance of tyranny and hierarchy as impediments to human freedom.

Murayama's dialogues are carefully crafted to express the bicultural realities of the characters in standard and pidgin English and in standard and colloquial Japanese, which is translated into standard and informal English. Murayama decided to print the book himself with the help of a linotype setter from Hawaii because he felt that commercial editors would "correct the English and kill the pidgin."[28]

Gender perspectives in the critique of pre-war Japanese American family and community life on the West Coast are contained in half a dozen remarkable short stories published between 1949 and 1961 by Hisaye Yamamoto.[29] The focus is on the changing roles of women imprisoned with well-meaning but weak and insensitive husbands and on the bleakness and isolation of rural toil. Ultimately, the women are vanquished. The men are never condemned, but they remain in the shadows as guardians of the prison doors, for the most part conventional and colorless in comparison to the women who are the central figures. The women's strength comes from surviving sorrow. They also pass a legacy to their daughters, who as a result may not be subdued in the end. Characteristic of Yamamoto's style is subtle irony and understatement, usually through the juxtaposition of two currents that reflect the quintessential quality of Japanese American life: beneath a placid and respectable surface, there are dark hints of hidden tragedy, tinged with death and violence. Yamamoto accomplishes this by presenting the stories through the eyes of an ingenuous young American-born narrator who understands less about what she is describing than what readers can guess.

Alienation and Loss

The contemporary generation of Japanese American writers, most of whom are of the *sansei* or third generation, grandchildren of the immigrants, is feeling the effects of the internment and dispersal of the Japanese American community Okada and Yamamoto depicted with such familiarity and confidence. Although most returned to California after the U.S. government's largely unsuccessful attempt to scatter them across the United States at the end of the war, they never regained their hold on Pacific Coast agriculture, and the Japantowns that had flourished all along Highway 99, the road that cuts through the fields and past the canneries of Asian America, have disappeared. Nationally, more than half of today's *sansei* marriages are out-marriages. Ronald Tanaka traces the path toward cultural annihilation in a poem about a book of photographs on Japanese American internment:

> the people who put out that book,
> i guess they won a lot of awards.
> it was a very photogenic period
> of california history, especially
> if you were a white photographer
> with compassion for helpless people.
>
> but the book would have been better,
> I think, or more complete, if they
> had put in my picture and yours, with
> our hakujin wives, our long hair and
> the little signs that say, "what? me
> speak japanese?" and "self-determination
> for everyone but us." and then maybe
> on the very last page, a picture of
> our kids. They don't even look like
> japanese[30]

In the decade between 1965 and 1975, playwright Frank Chin and short story writer Jeffery Paul Chan focused their attentions on a search for a viable new identity for Chinese American men, an identity that would link them to the cowboys who settled the American West and the nameless men who built the transcontinental railroad with their bare hands. The identity crises of the young in Chin and Chan's work stems in part from the complicity of older generations of Chinese immigrant men who cling to "mildewed memories" of China and to Chinese American women who cater to tourists' exotic fantasies. The failure of fathers is a favorite theme: in Chin's *Chickencoop Chinaman*,[31] Tam Lum's father is a dishwasher who bathes in his underpants because he fears that little old white ladies might peek at him through a keyhole. Women are represented as insensitive and unsophisticated or else as seekers after white "racist love." The only possible survival is escape from the suffocating environment—escape, ironically, into the culture that invented the fantasy in the first place. After lashing out at the emasculating effects of racial oppression, Chin and Chan accept the oppressors' definition of "masculinity." The result is unresolved tension between contempt and desire to fight for their Asian American characters. Cynicism, sexism, alienation, and preoccupation with death and decay have led not to a new identity but to the conclusion that we are doomed. In 1978, Chin said:

> There is no doubt in my mind that the Asian American is on the doorstep of extinction. There's so much out-marriage now that all that is going to survive are the stereotypes. White culture has not acknowledged Asian American art. Either you're foreign in this country, or you're an honorary white. I hope we can create work that will add to the human estate, but then I think we'll die out.[32]

Reconciliation

Most contemporary Asian American writers do not share Chin's pessimism. By weaving connections between us and our history, our forebears, each other, other people of color in this country and the world, these writers are inventing Asian American identities outside the realm of racial romance and externally imposed definitions.

Much contemporary Asian American literature expresses kinship with other people of color in America, especially blacks and Native Americans, who frequently appear in the works. "Soon the white snow will melt," writes poet Al Robles, and "the brown, black, yellow earth will come to life."[33]

Our self-invention was stimulated by U.S. involvement in Asia, creating links with Asia on our own terms. Because we had been defined historically by race, it was difficult for many of us not to respond to the racial character of the war in Vietnam. Stunned by graphic news coverage of war-torn hamlets, we sometimes saw the faces of our friends and relatives in the visages of Vietnamese peasants. We were susceptible to the argument that U.S. foreign policy in Asia had always been racist and genocidal, that profits had been more important to government policymakers than Asian lives. We perceived the parallels between the war in Vietnam and the conquest of the Philippine resistance during the Spanish American War, in which an estimated one-sixth of the population of Ilocos was exterminated in the name of democracy. We concluded that the use of the atomic bomb on Japanese civilians during World War II evidenced the racist attitudes of military officials and policy makers toward the entire race.

In "The New Anak" (1975), Sam Tagatac writes of a Filipino American soldier in Vietnam who thinks of the land of his birth and his countrymen when he sees the tropical sun and rains, the distant hills, and the peasants with their water buffaloes as they are strafed by American bombers:

> I remember the light of that lagoon, the mythical sound of the flying dragon, spitting fire, one pass, one strafing gun across water for what is water from the sight of the gods, the crosshair splitting in the forming of a real image, so distant the face of . . . your face, my face.[34]

In Maxine Hong Kingston's *China Men*,[35] the Chinese American brother is haunted by nightmares of himself as a soldier in the rescuing army, walking among enemy corpses.

> Laundry tubs drain beneath the bodies. The live women and children on the ironing tables, the last captured, are being dissected. He takes up the sword and hacks into the enemy, slicing them; they come apart in rings and rolls. . . . When he stops, he finds that he has cut up the victims too, who were his own relatives. The faces of the strung-up people are also those of his own family. Chinese faces, Chinese eyes, noses, and cheekbones.[36]

Dedicating her poems to dead heroes of Latin America and Africa like

Orlando Letelier and Steven Biko, *sansei* poet Janice Mirikitani reflects on the connections between the wars waged by the U.S. in the Third World, the bombing of Japan, and the internment of Japanese Americans.

> if you're too dark
> they will kill you
> if you're too swift
> they will buy you
> if you're too beautiful
> they will rape you
>
> watch with eyes open
> speak darkly
> turn your head like the owl
> behind you[37]

Restoring the Foundations

Recognizing our kinship with others who struggle against domination, we must also claim our own identity as Americans. Asian American writers must piece together and sort out the meaning of our past, distorted and omitted by racism, from shreds of stories heard in childhood or from faded photographs that have never been explained. In Wing Tek Lum's "A Picture of My Mother's Family" (1974), the poet searches for the significance of each detail of an old photograph: he must try to make the story of his half-forgotten ancestors relevant to himself. Like many Asian Americans, he does not even know their names, where they were born, or anything about their childhood in a distant land. The photograph is tantalizingly unrevealing.

> It is perhaps morning, the coolness
> captured now in such clear light; they seem
> somehow illuminated by beams from the moon,
> . . . my grandfather . . .
> looks on . . .
> towards his right far away. I imagine a dark rose
> has caught his proud eye, though I do not know
> if such flowers have ever grown there.[38]

Taking up as their task the restoration of the foundations of Asian American history in the U.S., contemporary writers are locating, translating, and publishing work by previously little-known writers in their native languages, literature that illuminates our American roots. *Island: Poetry and History of Chinese Immigrants on Angel Island 1910–1940* (1980) is an anthology of poetry carved in Chinese by unknown immigrants on the walls of the Angel

Island Detention Center barracks. They give voice to the spirit of our forebears:

> How many people ever return from battles?
> . . . . .
> Leaving behind my writing brush and removing my
> sword, I came to America.
> Who was to know two streams of tears would flow upon arriving
> here?
> If there comes a day when I will have attained by ambition and
> become successful
> I will certainly behead the barbarians and spare
> not a single blade of grass.
>
> Don't say that everything within is
> Western styled.
> Even if it is built of jade, it has turned into a cage.[39]

By penetrating and occupying the consciousness of his shadowy forbears,
Lawrence Yep contributes to the effort to repair the foundations of the Asian
American heritage in *Dragonwings*,[40] a historical novel about nineteenth-
century Chinese in America who invented a biplane. Rewriting our history
from an Asian American perspective has brought to light new cultural heroes.
The two characters in David Henry Hwang's play, "The Dance and the
Railroad,"[41] are Chinese railroad workers in the 1867 strike. Many contempo-
rary Japanese American writers focus on the internment. In "Family Album
for Charlotte Davis," Lonnie Kaneko searches for the meaning of the word
"Minidoka" only to discover that the name of that desert camp means water.

> Yesterday Charlotte asked, 'You mean there is still a bitterness?' Something
> wormed its way through my blood. Snake. Water. Earth. 'It is a thirst,' I say.[42]

Sensitive to the foreboding certainty that the elderly and their life experiences will vanish before they can be understood and appreciated, Asian
American writers portray the old with a sense of urgency. Bienvenido N.
Santos, himself a Filipino expatriate who has lived in the United States since
the declaration of martial law in the Philippines, says that his attention
continually returns to the Filipino manongs who are the unsung heroes of
American labor.

> . . . old timers among our countrymen who sat out the evening of their lives
> before television sets in condemned buildings. . . . Then the grin in both story
> and writer kept getting twisted in a grimace of pain close to tears. . . . now I
> realize that perhaps I have also been writing about myself.

The preservation of the oldtimers' tales is important to the young because
through the "transmission of grief from father to son we realize that it is
the son who is singing and leading the dance in the end."[43]

Claiming America requires reconciliation with our fathers and forefathers in this country, Shawn Hsu Wong's short novel *Homebase* opens with a garden book reference to a Chinese tree planted a century ago in California gold country: "Often condemned as a weed tree . . . it must be praised for its ability to create beauty and shade under adverse conditions."[44] The narrator is haunted by the ghosts of the men of his great-grandfather's generation, men who built the railroads over the High Sierras, setting down roots deep in the earth like sharp talons clinging close to the heart of the land. He imagines letters his great-grandfather might have written home to China: "I do not want the seasons to run over my back, letting the days and night, the weather ride me, break me. I will find a piece of land to work where I can remain . . . and watch the seasons ease on that place, root down in this difficult soil, and nurture my land."[45] But the Chinese were "motherless and wifeless . . . in a country that hated (them)." They worked their way from the hinterland to the ocean's edge; Rainsford imagines that they tried to swim home to China and that the desert sands and the white surf are made of their bones, bleached by the sea and sun. Rainsford has been an orphan, living on the fringes of America, speaking Chinese or English like a ventriloquist's dummy through the grimace of clenched teeth. He dreams of traveling across the country with a patronizing, whining, "cheerleader-teaser" white girl who is the "shadow, the white ghost of all my love life . . . the dream of my capture of America . . . she tells me things about me that I am not . . . that I am the product of the richest and oldest culture in the history of the world . . . when in fact I have nothing of my own in America."[46] When Rainsford finally rejects her "love," she becomes irritated and tells him to go back where he came from. Driving on in the dark night, he sees his grandfather in the mountain fog and smells his clothes in the redwood trees as he travels through the canyons and cascades where his forefathers once worked and are buried. An American Indian tells him that he must find out where his people have been and see the town after which he is named, so that he can claim his home, his history, and the legacy of his forefathers. By reaffirming the love that connects his life to the lives of his father and forefathers, and thus his links to Chinese America, he can affirm his American identity: "[I]dentity is a word full of home. Identity is a word that whispers, not whispers, but GETS you to say, 'ever, ever yours. . . .' Dear Father, I say, I write, I sing, I give you my love, this is a letter, whispering those words, 'ever, ever yours.'"

Immigrant fathers and American roots are brought together in Maxine Hong Kingston's *China Men*. Arriving in five different ways, by way of Cuba, Angel Island, or Ellis Island, the father is the "legal" and the "illegal" immigrant, the "father from China" and the "American father." By "banding the nation north and south, east and west" with the transcontinental railroad, these fathers have established their legitimacy as the "binding and building ancestors of this place."[47] Their spirits unbroken by the treatment they face in America, they remain, planting trees that will take years to bear fruit. Each China man claims America in his own way: by bringing his wife, by buying a house here, by insisting that a Chinese explorer discovered America first. The narrator's "American father" has "the power of . . . making places belong to him."[48] He claims America by donning Fred Astaire clothing and admiring himself in hubcap reflections along Fifth Avenue in New York City.

For Kingston's China men, claiming America is an aggressive act; it means refusing to be broken. Although he is worked like an animal on the sugar plantations of Hawaii, Bak Goong seethes with rebellion and a burning desire to break the silence imposed by labor foremen. He camouflages his talk in curses coughed at his oppressors, avenging himself with a sword forged of his words as he sings to his fellow workers:

> "If that demon whips me, I'll catch the whip and yank him off his horse, crack his head like a coconut. In an emergency a human being can do miracles—fly, swim, lift mountains, throw them. Oh, a man is capable of great feats of speed and strength."[49]

Gender Perspectives

Claiming America also means reconciliation between men and women. Racism has created a haunting distance between the sexes in our literature and culture. Certainly the absence of significant female characters in Asian American men's writing reflects the harsh realities of the bachelor life created by exclusion and anti-miscegenation laws. Carlos Bulosan, for example, wrote at a time when Filipino men outnumbered women in some American cities by as many as forty-seven to one. The inscription in American popular culture of Asian men as sexless automatons is complemented by the popular view of Asian women as only sexual beings, which helps explain the phenomenal success of Singapore Airlines, the enormous demand for X-rated films featuring Asian women in bondage, the demand for "oriental" bath house workers in U.S. cities, and the booming business in mail order marriages. There is no doubt that the rift between our men and women caused by racism is reflected in our literature. We can detect, however, an intense yearning for reconciliation. The narrator in Wakako Yamauchi's "That was all" (1980) is haunted by her vision of the slim brown body and mocking eyes of a man she sees only in a fleeting dream as an aging woman.[50] In "The Boatmen on River Toneh" (1976), the narrator is "swept against the smooth brown cheeks of a black-haired youth . . . and into his billowing shirt" only in death.[51] There are no lovers among Kingston's *China Men*. But perhaps a mending of the rift is at hand: the narrator in Shawn Hsu Wong's *Homebase* dreams of the woman he loves: "she is the summit I must return to in the end."[52] In David Henry Hwang's "FOB",[53] it is not only the gap between the immigrant and American-born Chinese that is bridged; the legendary woman warrior Fa Mu Lan teaches Gwan Kung, god of warriors and writers, how to survive in America, and Grace goes off with Steve, the immigrant, at the end of the play. With her, he can claim a new American identity.

Community

Without the reconciliation of the self to the community we cannot invent ourselves. This "community" begins with but extends beyond the boundaries of our families, far beyond Chinatown to wherever resistance to domination is taking place. While the narrator in *The Woman Warrior* has to "get out of hating range"[54] of a community that hates women, that community is the curse and blessing of her life. The escape into the "American-normal" world gives her a new, antiseptic way of seeing things, but it has diminished her. Now when she peeks into the basement window where the villagers say they see a girl dancing like a bottle imp, she no longer sees a spirit in a skirt made of light; instead, concrete pours out of her mouth to cover forests with freeways and sidewalks, replacing the vibrant world she left with plastics, periodical tables, and "TV dinners with vegetables no more complex than peas mixed with diced carrots."[55] It is not the colorless world she seeks refuge in that has taught her who her enemies are, the "stupid racists" and "tyrants who for whatever reason can deny my family food and work." These are easily recognizable, "each boss two feet taller than I am and impossible to meet eye to eye . . . if I took a sword, which my hate must surely have forged out of the air, and gutted [him], I would put color and wrinkles into his shirt."[56] She has temporarily traded the glorious identity of Fa Mu Lan, who could be both woman warrior and model of filial piety, for a "slum grubby" American reality. All she can do in America is get straight As and become a clerk-typist. The question is whether or not her heritage and the tradition of Fa Mu Lan can serve her here. Although she has left the immigrant community, she longs to return:

> The swordswoman and I are not so dissimilar. May my people understand the resemblance so that I can return to them. What we have in common are the words at our backs. . . . And I have so many words—'chink' words and 'gook' words too—that they do not fit on my skin.[57]

If we read Cathy Song's poetry as Asian Americans, we can see that the most effective poems in *Picture Bride*[58] are not the ones replete with images of jade and sour plums or that compare children to dumplings wrapped in wonton skins or describe a girl's cheeks as being like tofu, but the ones that explore the relationship between the persona and her family, from whom she ventures forth and with whom she is eventually reconciled. The volume as a whole traces the strength of kin communion and the ties between the generations. The narrator-character dreams of freedom from the constricted world of her mother, whose vision is limited like that of a seamstress to the piece of cloth she is working on at the moment beneath her fingers. The older woman sleeps in "tight blankets" and catches strands of her daughter's braids in her gold ring. But after the narrator moves across a series of landscapes that carry her ever further away from her family, she comes to rest finally at her mother's feet.

It has taken me all these years
to realize that this is what I must do
to recognize my life.
When I stretch a canvas
to paint the clouds,
it is your spine that declares itself:
arching,
your arms stemming out like tender shoots
to hang sheets in the sky.[59]

This is not an urge to disappear into the ocean of American society. This is a reaffirmation of our invention of ourselves. In *Dangerous Music* (1975), Jessica Tarahata Hagedorn's America is the "loneliest of countries," where the Filipino immigrant can lose her sanity and forget who she is among bottles of foot deodorant, mouthwash, and vaginal spray, where she can die a "natural death" encased in Saran Wrap on the beach. She must "stay crazy all the time"

with songs inside
knifing the air of sorrow
with our dance
a carnival of spirits
shredded blossoms
in the water[60]

However impermeable, Asian American literature is universal. That it is opaque is the source of its strength and vision. What Asian American writers express is the desire to remain as "others" by defining our own "otherness," not as foreigners but as American "others." Our claim on America, then, is part of our resistance to domination.

References

1. "Dear Abby," *San Francisco Chronicle*, 28 April 1986.
2. *New York Tribune*, 22 November 1925.
3. Lady Hosie, "A Voice from Korea," *Saturday Review of Literature*, 4 April 1931, 707.
4. Pardee Lowe, *Father and Glorious Descendant* (Boston: Little, Brown and Co., 1943), book jacket.
5. Jade Snow Wong, *Fifth Chinese Daughter* (New York: Harper and Row, 1950).
6. Jeanne Wakatsuki and James D. Houston, *Farewell to Manzanar* (San Francisco: San Francisco Book Company/Houghton Mifflin, 1973).
7. *Saturday Review World*, 6 November 1973; *Library Journal*, 1 November 1973, 3257.
8. Daniel Okimoto, *American in Disguise* (New York: Walker-Weatherhill, 1971).
9. Phoebe Adams, "Short Reviews: Books," *Atlantic Monthly* 227, no. 4 (April 1971), 104.

10. J. J. Conlin, *Best-Seller* 31, no. 9 (1 April 1971).

11. Okimoto, *American in Disguise*, 206.

12. Maxine Hong Kingston, *The Woman Warrior* (New York: Vintage Books, 1977).

13. *Publisher's Weekly* 212 (September 1976): 72.

14. Kingston, *The Woman Warrior*, 222–23.

15. Jane Kramer, "On Being Chinese in China and America," *New York Times Book Review*, 7 November 1976, 19.

16. Michael Malloy, " 'The Woman Warrior': On Growing Up Chinese, Female, and Bitter," *National Observer*, 9 October 1976, 25.

17. Kingston, *The Woman Warrior*, 35.

18. Lin Yutang, *My Country and My People* (New York: John Day Co., 1937).

19. Chan Wing-Tsit, "Lin Yutang, Critic and Interpreter," *College English* 8, no. 4 (January 1947): 163–64.

20. Younghill Kang, *East Goes West* (New York: Charles Scribner's Sons, 1937).

21. Carlos Bulosan, *America Is in the Heart* (Seattle: Univ. of Washington Press, 1946 and 1973).

22. Ibid., 188–89.

23. Wendy Law-Yone, *The Coffin Tree* (New York: Alfred A. Knopf, 1983).

24. Louis Chu, *Eat a Bowl of Tea* (New York: Lyle Stuart, 1961).

25. Interview, Louis Chu, 7 December 1979.

26. John Okada, *No-No Boy* (Rutland, Vt.: Charles E. Tuttle Co., 1957).

27. Milton Murayama, *All I Asking For Is My Body* (San Francisco: Supa Press, 1959, 1968, 1975).

28. Interview, Milton Murayama, 7 December 1979.

29. "The Legend of Miss Sasagawara," *Kenyon Review* 12, no. 1 (Winter 1950): 99–115; "Yoneko's Earthquake," *Furioso* 6, no. 1 (Winter 1951): 5–16; "Las Vegas Charley," *Arizona Quarterly*, no. 4 (Winter 1961): 303–22; "The Brown House," *Harper's Bazaar*, no. 2879 (October 1951): 166; 283–84 and in *Asian American Authors*, ed. Kai-yu Hsu and Helen Palubinskas (Boston: Houghton Mifflin Co., 1972):114–22; "Seventeen Syllables," *Partisan Review* 16, nos. 7–12 (July–December 1949): 1122–1134 and in *Ethnic American Short Stories*, ed. Katharine D. Newman (New York: Washington Square Press, 1975), 89–103.

30. Ronald Tanaka, "Appendix to Executive Order," *Ayumi: A Japanese American Anthology* (San Francisco: Japanese American Anthology Committee, 1, 1980), 240.

31. Frank Chin, *The Chickencoop Chinaman and the Year of the Dragon* (Seattle: Univ. of Washington Press, 1981).

32. Nikki Bridges, "Conversations and Convergences," Asian American Women Writers' Panel, Occidental College, January 1978, 16.

33. Alfred Robles, Untitled Poem, *Aion* 1, no. 2 (Fall 1971): 81 (Asian American Publications) (ed. Janice Mirikitani).

34. Sam Tagatac, "The New Anak," in *Aiieeeee! An Anthology of Asian-American Writers*, ed. Frank Chin, Jeffery Paul Chan, Lawson Fusao Inada, and Shawn Hsu Wong (Washington D.C.: Howard Univ. Press, 1974), 248.

35. Maxine Hong Kingston, *China Men* (New York: Alfred A. Knopf, 1980).

36. Ibid., 291.

37. Janice Mirikitani, "Japs," *Awake in the River* (San Francisco: Isthmus Press, 1978).

38. Wing Tek Lum, "A Picture of My Mother's Family," *Yardbird Reader*, vol. 3, ed. Frank Chin and Shawn Hsu Wong (Berkeley: Yardbird Publishing Company, 1974), 141.

39. Him Mark Lai, Genny Lim, and Judy Yung, eds., *Island Poetry and History*

of *Chinese Immigrants on Angel Island 1910–1940* (San Francisco: Chinese Culture Center Hoc Doi Project, 1980), 84–85, 134–35.

40. Lawrence Yep, *Dragonwings* (New York: Harper and Row, 1975).

41. David Henry Hwang, *Broken Promises: Four Plays by David Henry Hwang* (New York: Avon Books, 1983).

42. Lonnie Kaneko, "Family Album for Charlotte Davis," *Amerasia Journal* 3, no. 1 (Summer 1975): 135.

43. Bienvenido N. Santos, "Preface," *Scent of Apples* (Seattle: Univ. of Washington Press, 1979), xx; "The Filipino as Exile," *Greenfield Review* 6, nos. 1–2 (Spring 1977): 51.

44. Shawn Hsu Wong, *Homebase* (New York: I. Reed Books, 1979), 1.

45. Ibid., 27.

46. Ibid., 31–32.

47. Kingston, *China Men*, 146.

48. Ibid., 238.

49. Ibid., 101.

50. Wakako Yamauchi, "That Was All," *Amerasia Journal* 7, no. 1 (Spring 1980): 115–120.

51. Wakako Yamauchi, "The Boatmen on Toneh River," *Counterpoint: Critical Perspectives on Asian America*, ed. Emma Gee (Los Angeles: UCLA Asian American Studies Center, 1976), 533.

52. Wong, *Homebase*, 79.

53. David Henry Hwang, "FOB," in *Broken Promises*.

54. Kingston, *The Woman Warrior*, 62.

55. Ibid., 237.

56. Ibid., 58.

57. Ibid., 62–63.

58. Cathy Song, *Picture Bride* (New Haven, Conn.: Yale Univ. Press, 1983).

59. Ibid., 48.

60. Jessica Hagedorn, "Something about You," *Dangerous Music* (San Francisco: Momo's Press, 1975).

[1987]

The Dilemma of the Modern Chicana Artist and Critic

Marcela Christine Lucero-Trujillo

THE LITERARY REBIRTH OF THE CHICANOS IN THE 60S COINCIDED WITH certain simultaneous contemporary historical moments: (1) the passage of the Civil Rights Act of 1964, (2) identification with Cesar Chavez's farmworkers' struggle, (3) the inception of Chicano Studies departments, and (4) the initiation of the socio-economic political national Chicano movement.

Through unification and national mobilization, the Chicanos began to be aware of their history, previously obliterated in U.S. textbooks. The return to Mexican history, the emphasis on Mexican culture and traditions in order to seek self-affirmation and a positive self-identification, was almost in repudiation of this U.S. Anglo-European system which has held us in second-class citizenship status since 1846, denying us the rights and privileges afforded us in the Treaty of Guadalupe Hidalgo and agreed upon by the U.S. government at the close of the Mexican-American war.

As the Chicano movement began its evolution into unification, Chicanos were faced with the problem of diversity. Not all Chicanos were brown; not all were Catholic; not all were Spanish surnamed and not all were Spanish speaking. It therefore became necessary to invent or borrow symbols as common denominators around which all Chicanos could unite.

One of these was the symbol of the mestizaje, the tripartite face of the Indian mother, the Spanish father and their offspring, the mestizo. Another was the concept of a Chicano nation—Aztlan. Linguistically, there was an emergence of pachuquismos and regional dialects in the literature. The pachuco became an ideal Chicano type as the prototype of rebelling against the gringo-racist society at a time when American patriotism was at an all time high: the Second World War.

Like the Latin American, the Chicano also diminished the European psyche by establishing the Chicano Amerindia concept, which emphasized knowledge about the highly developed Aztec and Mayan civilizations as having been equal to, if not superior to, the Greek and Roman civilizations so predominant in all facets of Anglo-American education.

In the beginning, in the early 60s, the Chicanos were repeating the same concerns of the Latin American philosophers and writers of the late nineteenth and twentieth centuries, among them José Martí, José Vasconcelos, Leopoldo Zea, Samuel Ramos, Silva J. Herzog, Iturriaga and Octavio Paz, to name only a few. That dilemma of being an American of this continent, but imbued and dominated by European language, culture and customs called for ethnic self-introspection, which led to a recognition of autochthonous American elements.

Hence the popularity of Mexican writers and historians, especially Octavio Paz's *Labyrinth of Solitude*, which carried a compilation of his predecessors concerning Mexicanism, Mexican philosophy, psyche, thought and all the problematics of achieving economic independence.

Paz's popularity among Chicanos may have stemmed from the fact that he wrote about a Chicano type in his book: the pachuco, and thus, he brought to the present a social phenomenon that Chicanos were familiar with, through oral tradition, or the experience itself.

The questions that Mexicans were asking prior to the 1910 revolution in repudiation of Positivism, the philosophy of Scientism, were repeating themselves in the Chicano movement and the literature. The leitmotif "Yo soy Chicano/a"* predominated in much of the writings; however, as the

---

* I am a Chicano/a.

militancy decreased, the self-affirmation diluted into an anguished question. Was this due to the fact that since the Chicano movement began ten years ago, Chicanos are now realizing that the Mexican identification has not been sufficient to provide us with solutions in order to survive within this capitalist racist oppressive society?

This is more acute for the Chicana than for the Chicano, as evidenced by the statistics that Chicanas place lowest on the financial and educational scale in comparison with any other ethnic group, male or female (Neomi Lorenzo, *De Colores*, p. 11).

The impetus of the woman's movement together with the Chicano movement contributed to the Chicana's latest potential and so she began to focus in on her particular feministic experience through the arts. The Chicanas took the symbols afforded them through the Chicano movement and transformed them according to their feminist perspective. Some Chicanas' poetry is a trajectory of self-examination that terminates with a "cuestionamiento"[†] of all socio-economic and political factors that have taken their toll on their individualism.

Some Chicanas' literature has been a vehicle whereby they could escape into another temporal scene of our folklore, our legends and modus vivendi; of that particular past which seemed a safer and saner world, the world as it ought to be, albeit a very traditional romantic view.

Through the arts there is an attempt at liberation from the Anglo-European culture, that system of government that has conquered and colonized us in the same way it had Cuba and now Puerto Rico, the difference being that Chicanos are peripheral, marginal characters within the Metropolis, whereas the other colonized Latin American countries are controlled by foreign multinational corporations within their midst.

Literature has also provided an outlet for the frustrations of being a woman within the sexist microcosmic Chicano world of machismo, and the alienation of being a Chicano woman in the larger macrocosmic white male club that governs the United States.

In a quest for identity and an affirmation that brown is beautiful, the Chicana has sought refuge in the image of the indigenous mother. Some Chicanas view the Indian mother as Mother Earth; some identify with the bronze reality in religious themes of the Virgin of Guadalupe, the spiritual mother; and still others identify directly with the Mexican Eve, the historical mother, La Malinche. The latter will be explained in more detail.

La Malinche theme:

The fact that some Chicanas view Doña Marina in a sympathetic manner in contrast to the portrayal of Mexican authors may mean that her redefinition may be a Chicana phenomenon.

According to Octavio Paz's aforementioned book, Mexicans view La Malinche as the Mexican Eve, the one who betrayed the country, the one who opened up the country to foreign invaders. This opening up, paving

---

[†] Questioning.

the way for the Conquest, has sexual allusions of opening up her body to procreate the illegitimate sons of a rape called the Conquest. According to Paz, it was her treason, her betrayal, that caused the dual Mexican society of chingones vs. chingados,[†] with Cortés being the prototype of the "chingon," and Malinche being the highest exponent of the "chingado/a." Within this classification of Mexican types, the people who have power are the chingones, but the macho is the "gran chingon."

As the Chingada, according to Paz, Malinche is "the Mother." Not a mother of flesh and blood but a mythical figure. The *Chingada* is one of the Mexican representations of Maternity, like La Llorona or the "long-suffering Mexican mother" who is celebrated on May 10th. The *Chingada* is the mother who has suffered—metaphorically or actually—the corrosive and defaming action implicit in the verb that gives her her name" (Paz, *Labyrinth*, p. 75).

Thus, Paz says, " 'hijos de la chingada'[*] is a true battle cry, charged with a peculiar electricity; it is a challenge and an affirmation, a shot fired against an imaginary enemy, and an explosion in the air." The Mexican denies La Malinche, and the anguish shows when he shouts "Viva Mexico, hijos de la chingada" (Ibid., p. 75).

It is no wonder, then, that the Mexicans wanted to transcend this mythical maternal image to find refuge in a Christian feminine deity, one who could replace the Mexican Eve, and so "La Virgen Morena"—the brown virgin. La Virgen de Guadalupe became the patron saint of Mexico who is often also called "the mother of orphans." She is also called Guadalupe-Tonantzin among some of the Indian population, and this latter concept reflects the Christian-Aztec mingling of religion and culture.

La Virgen de Guadalupe is the Christian virgin, symbolizing, perhaps, the Spanish 16th century concept of honor which considered virginity as the repository of the family honor, a concept deeply rooted in Catholic ideology.

Tonantzin, the Aztec goddess of fertility, is viewed as Mother Nature. In Chicana literature, the technique of pathetic fallacy merges with the symbol of the good mother, Guadalupe or Tonantzin, presenting a harmonious relationship of the universe in fusion with nature.

If Chicanas use the concept of the long-suffering mother, they revert to the identification of La Malinche. Thus, in deciphering the symbols of the historical and spiritual mothers, the word "madre" in Mexican Spanish is at once a prayer or a blasphemy, a word whose antonymical dichotomy is manifested in ambiguities, ambivalence or oscillation in Chicana literature.

In her poem "Chicana Evolution," Sylvia Gonzales sees La Malinche as the feminine Messiah who must return to redeem her forsaken daughters, born out of the violence of the Spanish and Aztec religions and cultures. She moves away from the cosmopolitan ambiance of Greenwich Village in New York to the nativistic world of the Aztecs to encounter Malinche.

[†] Rapists versus the raped, or violators versus the violated.
[*] Sons of the violated one.

In the closing stanza of the aforementioned poem, Sylvia is the collective Chicana, the spiritual sister of the Latin Americans, Mother Nature, mother, daughter, Malinche, the totality of womanhood: "todo seré . . . y hasta bastarda seré, antes de dejar de ser mujer."[†]

Chicanos see themselves as muy mejicanos[‡] in the affinity of the woman and orphanhood concept, illegitimate sons and daughters of La Malinche. This concept, projected within the confines of the U.S. environment, reinforces the feeling of orphanhood, of alienation and marginalization to both U.S. and Mexican societies, in the prismatic view of Indian identity that pervades much of the Chicana's literature.

However, to blame one woman, Doña Marina, for the Conquest, is, in my opinion, a false historical conscience. One woman could not stand in the way of European expansion; one woman could not impede the alliance of native class interests with the foreign invader's economic interests. God, glory and gold, economic, political and religious reasons were one total objective since Church and State were not separated at the time of the Conquest. "Independence" is a misnomer in Latin America as one foreign power after another has influenced and dominated its economic sphere to perpetuate a cycle of dependency and neo-colonial status for its inhabitants.

In the case of the Chicanos, the gringo has replaced the Spaniards as the "gran chingon" by virtue of his having the positions of power. And those in positions of power oppress through racism, which has made Chicanos react and revert to the Indian mother to say, through her, that brown is beautiful. It is this contemporary society which has classified "brown" as inferior in the schematics of relative beauty. Thus, to refute the racism and the stereotypes, Chicanas have emphasized the bronze race which, ironically, in the past, has not appeared in the race classification. Under the present categories, only the black, white, red and yellow races are visible. And, perhaps, for that reason, Chicanos have been called the "Invisible" the "forgotten" or the "Silent Americans."

The Problematics of the Modern Chicana

Sylvia Gonzales in her poetry is first of all a woman, then a Chicana poetess with a mission. Maternal imagery permeates much of her poetry. She writes poetry to her future generations, and she ponders their fate as she weaves in and out of herself, from the first to the third person in the poem that begins "Yo soy la mujer poeta."[*]

"¿Como será la generación; criada con la inquietud de la mujer poeta?"[†] She expresses the anxieties of being a woman poet, not a poetisa, but a

---

[†] I will be everything . . . I will even be illegitimate before forsaking my womanhood.
[‡] Very Mexican.
[*] I am the woman poet.
[†] How will the generation be; fostered by the restlessness of the woman poet?

mujer poeta, who is faced with the sisyphus responsibility of advising and advising well to the future generation of Chicano readers. Her mission is to write, because she has many "consejos"‡ to give.

In her personal Ars Poetica (*De Colores*, p. 15) she gives us her philosophy in declaring that "the artist must be true to her own soul and her own personal experiences, and in so doing, the message will be universal and eternal" (Ibid., p. 15).

Sylvia speaks collectively for the Chicana and for all women when she states that "we are all sisters under the flesh." In her poem, "On an untitled theme," whose principal theme is machismo, she exacerbates the dilemma felt by every intellectual woman who wants to use her head, or who wants to be recognized for her intelligence, and not only for her body. She must convince her macho colleagues that her goal is not their bed. She would reject the finality of the Chicana's life of bearing sons for wars, of being alienated after the children grew up and left home. The choice of bearing sons for wars or as victims of a technological society whose recourse from pressures are drugs is an anxiety that every contemporary mother faces. The Chicana mother whose only life has been her children may have difficulties in her later years. She may seek refuge in the bottle or transform into a nagging wife or a "vieja chismosa."*

The sanctuary of the Chicano home then becomes a replica of the conflictive society. The modern Chicana faces a double conflict. On the one hand, she must overcome Chicano family overprotection, and on the other, she faces contempt from the outside world as she emerges into the professional world, only to find indifference as answers to her questions on reality and life. These are themes that women can relate to in Sylvia's poetry, but amidst these problems, Sylvia affirms her individualism in "Te acuerdas mujer."†

This assertion of intellectualism is indirect in the praises and eulogies to Sra. Juana Ines de la Cruz, the renowned genius of Mexican colonial times. Dorinda Moreno, among other poetesses, identifies with this victim of Catholic machismo who was made to give up her academic life and go out into the world, where she contracted the plague and died a premature death at the age of 45, a martyr to feminine intelligentsia.

The modern Chicana, in her literature, tries to synthesize the material and spiritual conflict of her essence. Her spirit is ingrained in the roots of Mexican culture and traditions, but her body is trying to survive in a hostile capitalistic environment, and she keenly feels the technological battle of scientism vs. humanism. In trying to resolve the two, her literature often shows the contradictions that exist between the two.

Sylvia Gonzales expresses this concern in her article in the following: "There are many Mexican cultural values that we can relate to, but are they

‡ "Advices."
* Shrewish old woman.
† Remember you are a woman.

reliable in our search for an identity within the Anglo American cultural tradition?" The answer, she says, is a link between science and the soul (Gonzales, *De Colores*, pp. 15–18).

An elaboration of that answer can be found in A. Sanchez-Vasquez's book, *Art and Society*. "Creative freedom and capitalist production are hostile to the artist. . . . Art representing denied humanity opposes an inhuman society, and society opposes the artist insofar as he resists reification, insofar as he tries to express his humanity" (A.S.V., p. 116).

The dilemma of the Chicano/a artist is trying to create an art for people's sake, and not for art's sake or for commercialism. He/She is working in a hostile, scientific milieu whose marginalization is twofold: one, because the artist's creation is not scientific, but humanistic, for the enjoyment of humanity, with no utilitarian value, and second, because Chicanos' cultural values are not understood or appreciated by the dominant society. Yet, the Chicano artists and writers must continue to create and to communicate with the grass roots people, and in so doing, will reach the universal masses who identify with their contemporary situation whether in this or other countries, whether in this or another historical moment, for art has its own laws which transcend the artist, his/her time and even the ideology that brought forth his/her art.

Literature is a medium and a praxis whereby we can start to question our oppression, not by escapism into the mythical past in sentimental lyricism reminiscent of other literary ages, but in dealing with the everyday problems. The Chicana can question and confront the society which holds her in double jeopardy, of being a woman and a minority.

Every Chicana's life is a novel, yet we have not read a contemporary Chicana feminist novel. The Chicana has had to be a cultural schizophrenic in trying to please both the Chicano and Anglo publishers, not to mention pleasing the readers, who may neutralize her potential to create within her own framework of ideas.

We must examine closely the published works of Chicanas who have been selected for publication by male editors and publishers. We have to ask ourselves if we have been published because we have dealt with themes that reinforce the male ego. As urban professional Chicanas, we must reinterpret our pantheistic view of the world. Are we really the prototype of the long-suffering indigenous mother? Are we co-opting and neutralizing our emotions by writing what the publishers want to read?

I remind you that "macho" in classical Nahuatl means "image," "reflection of myself." Are we then only a narcissistic reflection, and consequently do we define ourselves as a reflection of the Chicano perspective, as a reaction, rather than action of that definition?

Then it becomes necessary to examine the totality of the Chicana's artistic expression, her motives for writing, the audience for whom it was intended, her biography as a product of all of her past experiences which are projected into her work, and lastly to understand why her particular content is important in this space and time. For in examining a work in this critical vein, we would also be examining ourselves, and could come to a collective conclusion of what direction we are taking within the feministic framework of the Chicano's socioeconomic and political status within the United States.

Therefore, it may be somewhat premature at this time to view the present literature of the Chicanas as a culmination of the Chicana experience. All of the literature has been positive in that it has provided a historical awareness, "una concientización," an inspiration to other Chicanas to affirm their literary talents, and those Chicanas who have been writing and publishing for some time now are progressing steadily on the incline of their own apogee.

[1980]

Playfulness, "World"-Travelling, and Loving Perception

María Lugones

THIS PAPER WEAVES TWO ASPECTS OF LIFE TOGETHER. MY COMING TO consciousness as a daughter and my coming to consciousness as a woman of color have made this weaving possible. The weaving reveals the possibility and complexity of a pluralistic feminism, a feminism that affirms the plurality in each of us and among us as richness and as central to feminist ontology and epistemology.

The paper describes the experience of "outsiders" to the mainstream White/Anglo organization of life in the U.S., and stresses a particular feature of the outsider's existence: the acquired flexibility in shifting from the mainstream construction of life to other constructions of life where she is more or less "at home." This flexibility is necessary for the outsider but it can also be willfully exercised by those who are at ease in the mainstream. I recommend this willful exercise which I call "world"-travelling and I also recommend that the willful exercise be animated by a playful attitude.

As outsiders to the U.S. mainstream, women of color practice "world"-travelling, mostly out of necessity. I affirm this practice as a skillful, creative, rich, enriching and, given certain circumstances, as a loving way of being and living. I recognize that we do much of our travelling, in some sense against our wills, to hostile White/Anglo "worlds." The hostility of these "worlds" and the compulsory nature of the "travelling" have obscured for us the enormous value of this aspect of our living and its connection to loving. Racism has a vested interest in obscuring and devaluing the complex skills involved in this. I recommend that we affirm this travelling across "worlds" as partly constitutive of cross-cultural and cross-racial loving. Thus

I recommend to women of color in the U.S. to learn to love each other by travelling to each other's "worlds."

On the other hand, the paper makes a connection between what Marilyn Frye has named "arrogant perception" and the failure to identify with persons that one views arrogantly or has come to see as the products of arrogant perception. A further connection is made between this failure of identification and a failure to love. Love is not used in the sense Frye has identified as consistent with arrogant perception and as promoting unconditional servitude. "We can be taken in by this equation of servitude with love," Frye says, "because we make two mistakes at once: we think, of both servitude and love that they are selfless or unselfish."[1] Rather, the identification of which I speak is constituted by what I come to characterize as playful "world"-travelling. To the extent that we learn to perceive others arrogantly or come to see them only as products of arrogant perception and continue to perceive them that way, we fail to identify with them—fail to love them—in this particularly deep way.

Identification and Love

As a child, I was taught to perceive arrogantly. I have also been the object of arrogant perception. Though I am not a White/Anglo woman, it is clear to me that I had early training in arrogant perception. I was brought up in Argentina watching men and women of moderate and of considerable means graft the substance[2] of their servants to themselves. I also learned to graft my mother's substance to my own. It was clear to me that both men and women were the victims of arrogant perception and that arrogant perception was systematically organized to break the spirit of all women and of most men. I valued my rural 'gaucho' ancestry because its ethos has always been one of independence in poverty through enormous loneliness, courage and self-reliance. I found inspiration in this ethos and made a commitment not to be broken by arrogant perception. I can say this only because I have learned from Frye's "In and Out of Harm's Way: Arrogance and Love." She has given me a way of understanding and articulating something important in my own life.

Frye is not particularly concerned with women as arrogant perceivers but as the objects of arrogant perception. Her focus is, in part, on enhancing our understanding of women "untouched by phallocratic machinations."[3] She proposes an understanding of what it is to love women inspired by a vision of women unharmed by arrogant perception. To love women is, at least in part, to perceive them with loving eyes. "The loving eye is a contrary of the arrogant eye."[4]

I am concerned with women as arrogant perceivers because I want to explore further what it is to love women. I want to explore two failures of love: my failure to love my mother and White/Anglo women's failure to love women across racial and cultural boundaries in the U.S. As a consequence of exploring these failures I will offer a loving solution to them. My solution modifies Frye's account of loving perception by adding what I call playful "world"-travel.

It is clear to me that at least in the U.S. and Argentina women are taught to perceive many other women arrogantly. Being taught to perceive arrogantly is part of being taught to be a woman of a certain class in both countries. It is part of being taught to be a White/Anglo woman in the U.S. and it is part of being taught to be a woman in both places: to be both the agent and the object of arrogant perception. My love for my mother seemed to me thoroughly imperfect as I was growing up because I was unwilling to become what I had been taught to see my mother as being. I thought that to love her was consistent with my abusing her (using, taking for granted, and demanding her services in a far-reaching way that, since four other people engaged in the same grafting of her substance onto themselves, left her little of herself for herself) and was to be in part constituted by my identifying with her, my seeing myself in her: to love her was supposed to be of a piece with both my abusing her and with my being open to being abused. It is clear to me that I was not supposed to love servants: I could abuse them without identifying with them, without seeing myself in them. When I came to the U.S. I learned that part of racism is the internalization of the propriety of abuse without identification: I learned that I could be seen as a being to be used by White/Anglo men and women without the possibility of identification, i.e. without their act of attempting to graft my substance onto theirs, rubbing off on them at all. They could remain untouched, without any sense of loss.

So, women who are perceived arrogantly can perceive other women arrogantly in their turn. To what extent those women are responsible for their arrogant perceptions of other women is certainly open to question, but I do not have any doubt that many women have been taught to abuse women in this particular way. I am not interested in assigning responsibility. I am interested in understanding the phenomenon so as to find a loving way out of it.

There is something obviously wrong with the way I was taught to love and something right with my failure to love my mother in this way. There is something wrong with my being taught to practice enslavement of my mother and to learn to become a slave through this practice. There is something wrong with my having been taught that love is consistent with abuse, consistent with arrogant perception. But I do not think that what is wrong is my profound desire to identify with her, to see myself in her.

The love I was taught is the love that Frye speaks of when she says "We can be taken in by this equation of servitude with love."[5] Even though I could both abuse and love my mother, I was not supposed to love servants. This is because in the case of servants one is and is supposed to be clear about their servitude and the "equation of servitude with love" is never to be thought clearly in those terms. But I could love my mother because deception is part of this "loving." Servitude is called abnegation and abnegation is not analyzed any further. Abnegation is not instilled in us through an analysis of its nature, but rather through a heralding of it as beautiful and noble. We are coaxed, seduced into abnegation not through analysis but through emotive persuasion. When I say that there is something obviously wrong with the loving that I was taught, I do not mean to say that the connection between loving and abuse is obvious. Rather this connection has to be unveiled. Once it is unveiled, what is obvious is that there is something wrong with the loving.

I did not learn my lessons about loving well. This failure necessitated a separation from my mother: I saw us as beings of quite a different sort. I abandoned my mother while I longed to love her, though, given what I was taught, "love" could not be the right word for what I longed for.

I was disturbed by my not wanting to be what she was. I had a sense of not being quite integrated, my self was missing because I could not identify with her, I could not see myself in her, I could not welcome her world. I saw myself as separate from her, a different sort of being, not quite of the same species. This separation, this lack of love, I saw as a lack in myself, not a fault, but a lack. *Love has to be rethought, made anew.*

There is something similar between my relation to my mother as someone I was not able to love and the relation between women of color in the U.S. and White/Anglo women: there is a failure of love. I want to note here that Frye has helped me understand one of the aspects of this failure, the directly abusive aspect. I think part of the failure of love includes the failure to identify with another woman, the failure to see oneself in other women who are quite different from oneself.

Frye's emphasis on independence in her analysis of loving perception is not particularly helpful in explaining this failure of love. She says that in loving perception, "the object of the seeing is another being whose existence and character are logically independent of the seer and who may be practically or empirically independent in any particular respect at any particular time."[6] But this is not helpful, for example, in allowing me to understand how my failure of love toward my mother (when I ceased to be her parasite) left me not quite whole. It is not helpful since I saw her as logically independent from me. Neither does Frye's emphasis on independence help me understand why the racist or ethnocentric failure of love of White/Anglo women should leave me not quite real among them.

I am not particularly interested in cases of White/Anglo women's parasitism onto women of color but more pointedly in cases where the failure of identification is the central feature of the "relation." I am particularly interested in those cases in which White/Anglo women behave in one or more of the following ways towards women of color: they ignore, ostracize, stereotype, classify us as crazy and render us invisible. This behavior is exhibited *while we are in their midst.* Frye's emphasis on independence as key to loving is unhelpful because the more independent I am, the more independent I am left to be, the more alone I am left to be. Their world and their integrity have no use for me. Yet they rob me of my solidity through indifference, an indifference they can afford and which often seems studied. This points toward separatism in communities where our substance is seen and celebrated; where we become substantive, solid, real through this celebration. But many of us have to work among White/Anglos and our best shot at recognition has seemed to be among White/Anglo women because many of them have expressed a *general* sense of being pained at their failure of love.

Many times White/Anglo women seem to want women of color out of their field of vision. Their lack of concern is a harmful failure of love that leaves me independent from them in the same way that my mother became independent from me once I ceased to be her parasite. But of course, because my mother and I wanted to love each other well, we were not whole in this independence. White/Anglo women are independent from me, I am independent from them, I am independent from my mother, she is independent from me, and we cannot love each other in this independence.

I am incomplete and unreal without other women. I am profoundly dependent on others without having to be their subordinate, their slave, their servant.

Since I am emphasizing here that the failure of love lies in part in the failure to identify, and since I agree with Frye that in perceiving others lovingly one "must consult something other than one's own will and interests and fears and imagination,"[7] I will proceed to explain what I think needs to be consulted. Loving my mother was not possible for me so long as I retained a sense that it was fine to see her through arrogant eyes. Loving my mother also required that I see with her eyes, that I go into my mother's world, that I see both of us as we are constructed in her world, that I witness her own sense of herself from within her world. Only through this travelling to her "world" could I identify with her because only then could I cease to ignore her and to be excluded and separate from her. Only then could I see her as a subject even if one subjected and only then could I see how meaning could arise fully between us. We are fully dependent on each other for the possibility of being understood without which we are not intelligible, we do not make sense, we are not solid, visible, integrated; we are lacking. Travelling to each other's "worlds" enables us to *be* through *loving* each other.

I will lead you to see what I mean by a "world" in the way I proposed the concept to myself: through the kind of ontological confusion that we, women of color, refer to half-jokingly as "schizophrenia" and through my effort to make sense of this ontological confusion.

"Worlds" and "World"-Travelling

Some time ago I was in a state of profound confusion as I experienced myself as both having and not having a character trait: the trait is playfulness. I experienced myself both as a playful person and as a person who is not playful, a person who would be acting out of character if she were to express playfulness. At first I thought that the "multiple personality" problem could be explained away by lack of ease. Maybe my playfulness is very difficult to express or enact in certain worlds. So, it may be that in those worlds I lack the trait. But, of course, I need to explain what "world" means if that explanation is to be serviceable to me in my confusion as to who I am characterwise.

I can explain some of what I mean by a "world." I do not want the fixity of a definition because I think the term is suggestive and I do not want to lose this. A "world" has to be presently inhabited by flesh and blood people. That is why it cannot be a utopia. It may also be inhabited by some imaginary people. It may be inhabited by people who are dead or people that the inhabitants of this "world" met in some other "world" and now have in this "world" in imagination.

A "world" need not be a construction of a whole society. It may be a construction of a tiny portion of a particular society. It may be inhabited by just a few people. Some "worlds" are bigger than others.

A "world" may be incomplete in that things in it may not be altogether constructed or some things may be constructed negatively (they are not what 'they' are in some other "world"). Or the "world" may be incomplete because it may have references to things that do not quite exist in it, references to things like Brazil. Given lesbian feminism, the construction of 'lesbian' in 'lesbian community' (a "world" in my sense) is purposefully and healthily still up in the air, in the process of becoming. To be Hispanic in this country is, in a dominant Anglo construction purposefully incomplete. Thus one cannot really answer questions like "What is a Hispanic?" "Who counts as a Hispanic?" "Are Latinos, Chicanos, Hispanos, black dominicans, white cubans, korean-colombians, italian-argentinians Hispanic?" What it means to be a 'Hispanic' in the varied so-called Hispanic communities in the U.S. is also up in the air. We have not yet decided whether there are any 'Hispanics' in our varied "worlds."

So a "world" may be an incomplete visionary non-utopian construction of life or it may be a traditional construction of life. A traditional Hispano construction of Northern New Mexican life is a "world." Such a traditional construction, in the face of a racist, ethnocentric, money-centered anglo construction of Northern New Mexican life, is highly unstable because Anglos have the means for imperialist destruction of traditional Hispano "worlds."

Some of the inhabitants of a "world" may not understand or accept the way in which they are constructed in it. So, for example, a recent Latin-American immigrant may not understand how she is constructed in White/Anglo "worlds." So, there may be "worlds" that construct me in ways that I do not even understand or I may not accept the construction as an account of myself, a construction of myself. And yet, I may be *animating* such a construction, even though I may not intend my moves, gestures, acts in that way.

One can "travel" between these "worlds" and one can inhabit more than one of these "worlds" at the very same time. I think that most of us who are outside the mainstream U.S. construction or organization of life are "world-travellers" as a matter of necessity and of survival. It seems to me that inhabiting more than one "world" at the same time and "travelling" between "worlds" is part and parcel of our experience and our situation. One can be at the same time in a "world" that constructs one as stereotypically latin, for example, and in a "world" that constructs one as latin. Being stereotypically latin and being simply latin are different simultaneous constructions of persons that are part of different "worlds." One animates one or the other or both at the same time without necessarily confusing them, though simultaneous enactment can be confusing to oneself.

In describing a "world" I mean to be offering a description of experience, something that is true to experience even if it is ontologically problematic. Though I would think that any account of identity that could not be true to this experience of outsiders to the mainstream would be faulty even if ontologically unproblematic. Its ease would constrain, erase, or deem aberrant experience that has within it significant insights into non-imperialistic understanding between people.

Those of us who are "world"-travellers have the distinct experience of being different in different "worlds" and ourselves in them. We can say "That's me there, and I am happy in that 'world.'" The experience is one of having memory of oneself as different without any underlying "I." So, I can say "That's me in there and I am so playful in that 'world.'" I say "That's *me* in that 'world'" *not* because I recognize myself in that person. Rather that person may be very different from myself in this "world" and yet I can say *without inference* "That's me." I may well recognize that that person has abilities that I do not have and yet the having or not having of the abilities is always an "I have . . ." and "I do not have . . . ," i.e., it is always experienced in the first person.

The shift from being one person to being a different person is what I call "travel." This shift may not be willful or even conscious, and one may be completely unaware of being different than one is in a different "world." Even though the shift can be done willfully, it is not a matter of acting. One does not pose as someone else, one does not pretend to be, for example, someone of a different personality or character or someone who uses space or language differently than the other person. Rather one *is* someone who has that personality or character or uses space and language in that particular way.

Being at Ease in a "World"

In investigating what I mean by "being at ease in a 'world,'" I will describe different ways of being at ease. One may be at ease in one or in all of these ways. A maximal way of being at ease, being at ease in all of these ways, is somewhat dangerous because people who are at ease in this way tend not to have any inclination to travel across "worlds" or tend not to have any experience of "world" travelling.

The first way of being at ease in a particular "world" is by being a fluent speaker in that "world." I know all the norms that there are to be followed, I know all the words that there are to be spoken. I know all the moves. I am confident.

Another way of being at ease is by being normatively happy. I agree with all the norms, I could not like any norms better. I am asked to do just what I want to do or what I think I should do. At ease.

Another way of being at ease in a "world" is by being humanly bonded. I am with those I love and they love me too. It should be noticed that I may be with those I love and be at ease because of them in a "world" that is otherwise as hostile to me as "worlds" can get.

Finally one may be at ease because one has a shared history that one sees exemplified by the response to the question "Do you remember poodle skirts?" There you are, with people you do not know at all. The question is posed and then they all begin talking about their poodle skirt stories. I have been in such situations without knowing what poodle skirts, for example, were and I felt so ill at ease because it was not *my* history. The other people did not particularly know each other. It is not that they were humanly bonded. Probably they did not have much politically in common either. But poodle skirts were in their shared history.

Given the clarification of what I mean by a "world," "world"-travel, and being at ease in a "world," we are in a position to return to my problematic attribute, playfulness. It may be that in this "world" in which I am so unplayful I am a different person than in the "world" in which I am playful. Or it may be that the "world" in which I am unplayful is constructed in such a way that I could be playful in it. I could practice, even though that "world" is constructed in such a way that my being playful in it is hard.

My description of what I mean by a "world" favors the first possibility as the one that is truest to the experience of "outsiders" to the mainstream. But that description also makes this possibility problematic because the "I" is identified in some sense as one and in some sense as plural (I am one and many at the same time). I identify myself as myself through memory and retain myself as different in memory. I can be in a particular "world" and have a double image of myself as, for example, playful and unplayful. This is a very familiar and recognizable phenomenon to the outsider to the mainstream in some *central* cases: when in one "world" I animate, for example, that "world's" caricature or stereotype of the person I am in the other "world." I can have both images of myself, and to the extent that I can materialize or animate both images at the same time, I become an ambiguous being. This is very much a part of trickery and foolery. It is worth remembering that the trickster and the fool are significant characters in many non-dominant or outsiders' cultures.

As one sees any particular "world" with these double edges and sees absurdity in them, one animates the person one is in that world differently. Given that latins are constructed in Anglo "worlds" as stereotypically intense and given that many latins, myself included, are genuinely intense, I can say to myself "I am intense" and take a hold of the double meaning. Furthermore, I can be stereotypically intense or be the real thing and, if you are Anglo, you do not know when I am which *because* I am Latin-American. As Latin-American I am an ambiguous being, a two-imaged self: I can see that gringos see me as stereotypically intense because I am, as a Latin-American, constructed that way in their "world." I may or may not *intentionally* animate the stereotype or the real thing knowing that you may not see it in anything other than in the stereotypical construction. This ambiguity is not just funny, it is survival-rich. We can also make a funny picture of those who dominate as precisely because we can see the double edges, we can see *them* doubly constructed, we can see the plurality in us and in them. So we know truths that only the fool can speak and only the trickster can play out without harm. We inhabit "worlds" and travel across them and keep all the memories.

Sometimes the "world"-traveller has a double image of herself and each self includes as important ingredients of itself one or more attributes of the other self: for example being playful and being unplayful. To the extent that an attribute is personality or character central, the "world" in which she has that attribute would have to be changed if she is to cease to have it. For example, the "world" in which I am unplayful would have to be changed for me to be playful in it. It is not as if, if I were to be at ease in that "world," I would be my own playful self. Because the attribute is personality central and there is such a good fit between the "world" in which I am unplayful and my being constructed unplayful in it, I cannot become playful, *I am unplayful* in that "world." To become playful would be for me to become a contradictory being. So, lack of ease cannot be a solution for my problematic case. My problem is not one of lack of ease.

I am suggesting that I can understand my confusion about whether I am or am not playful by saying that I am both and that I am different persons in different "worlds" and can remember myself in both as I am in the other. I am a plurality of selves. This is to understand my confusion because *it is to come to see it as of a piece* with much of the rest of my experience as an outsider in some of the "worlds" that I inhabit and of a piece with significant aspects of the experience of non-dominant people in the "worlds" of their dominators.

So, though I may not be at ease in the "worlds" in which I am not constructed playful, it is not that I am not playful *because* I am not at ease. The two are compatible. But lack of playfulness is not caused by lack of ease but lack of health. I am not a healthy being in the "worlds" that construct me as unplayful.

Playfulness

I had a very personal stake in investigating this topic. Playfulness is not only the attribute that was the source of my confusion and the attitude that I recommend as the loving attitude in travelling across "worlds" but also what

I am scared to do without—ending up a serious human being, someone with no multi-dimensionality, with no fun in life, someone who has had the fun constructed out of her. I am seriously scared of getting stuck in a "world" that constructs me that way. A "world" that I have no escape from and in which I cannot be playful.

I thought about what it is to be playful and what it is to play and I did this thinking in a "world" in which I only remember myself as playful and in which all of those who know me as playful are imaginary beings. A "world" in which I am scared of losing my memories of myself as playful or have them erased from me. Because I live in such a "world," after I formulated my own sense of what it is to be playful and to play I decided that I needed to see what other people had said about play and playfulness. I read two classics on the subject: Johan Huizinga's *Homo Ludens*[8] and Hans-Georg Gadamer's chapter on the concept of play in his *Truth and Method*.[9] I discovered, to my amazement, that what I thought about play and playfulness was in contradiction with their accounts. Though I will not provide the arguments for this interpretation of Gadamer and Huizinga here, I understood that both of them have an agonistic sense of 'play.' Play and playfulness have, ultimately, to do with contest, with winning, losing, battling. The sense of playfulness that I have in mind has nothing to do with those things. So, I tried to elucidate both senses of play and playfulness by contrasting them to each other. The contrast helped me see the attitude that I have in mind as the loving attitude in travelling across "worlds" more clearly.

An agonistic sense of playfulness is one in which *competence* is supreme. You'd better know the rules of the game. In agonistic play, contest, competition, there is risk, there is *uncertainty*, but the uncertainty is about who is going to win and who is going to lose. There are rules that inspire hostility. The attitude of *playfulness is conceived as secondary to or derivative from play*. Since play is agon, contest, then the only conceivable playful attitude is an agonistic, combative, competitive one. One of the paradigmatic ways of playing for both Gadamer and Huizinga is role-playing. In role-playing, the person who is participating in the game has a *fixed conception of him or herself*. I also think that the players are imbued with *self-importance* in agonistic play since they are so keen on winning given their own merits, their very own competence.

When considering the value of "world"-travelling and whether playfulness is the loving attitude to have while travelling, I recognized the agonistic attitude as inimical to travelling across "worlds." The agonistic traveller is a conqueror, an imperialist. Given the agonistic attitude one *cannot* travel across "worlds," though can kill other "worlds" with it. So for people who are interested in crossing racial and ethnic boundaries, an arrogant western man's construction of playfulness is deadly. One needs to give such an attitude up if one wants to travel. Huizinga in his classic book on play, interprets Western civilization as play. That is an interesting thing for Third World people to think about. Western civilization has been interpreted by a white western man as play in the agonistic sense of play: he reviews western law, art, and many other aspects of western culture and sees agon, contest, in all of them.

So then, what is the loving playfulness that I have in mind? Let me begin with one example: We are by the river bank. The river is very, very low. Almost dry. Bits of water here and there. Little pools with a few trout hiding under the rocks. But mostly wet stones, grey on the outside. We walk on the stones for awhile. You pick up a stone and crash it onto the others. As it breaks, it is quite wet inside and it is very colorful, very pretty. I pick up a stone and break it and run toward the pieces to see the colors. They are beautiful. I laugh and bring the pieces back to you and you are doing the same with your pieces. We keep on crashing stones for hours, anxious to see the beautiful new colors. We are playing. The playfulness of our activity does not presuppose that there is something like "crashing stones" that is a particular form of play with its own rules. Rather *the attitude that carries us through the activity, a playful attitude, turns the activity into play.* Our activity has no rules, though it is certainly intentional activity and we both understand what we are doing. The playfulness that gives meaning to our activity includes uncertainty, but in this case the uncertainty is an *openness to surprise.* This is a particular metaphysical attitude that does not expect the world to be neatly packaged, ruly. Rules may fail to explain what we are doing. We are not self-important, we are not fixed in particular constructions of ourselves, which is part of saying that we are *open to self-construction.* We may not have rules, and when we do have rules, *there are no rules that are to us sacred.* We are not worried about competence. We are not wedded to a particular way of doing things. While playful we have not abandoned ourselves to, nor are we stuck in, any particular "world." We are *there creatively.* We are not passive.

Playfulness is, in part, an openness to being a fool, which is a combination of not worrying about competence, not being self-important, not taking norms as sacred and finding ambiguity and double edges a source of wisdom and delight.

So, positively, the playful attitude involves openness to surprise, openness to being a fool, openness to self-construction or reconstruction and to construction or reconstruction of the "worlds" we inhabit playfully. Negatively, playfulness is characterized by uncertainty, lack of self-importance, absence of rules or a not taking rules as sacred, a not worrying about competence and a lack of abandonment or resignation to a particular construction of oneself, others, and one's relation to them. In attempting to take hold of oneself and of one's relation to others in a particular "world," one may study, examine and come to understand oneself. One may then see what the possibilities for play are for the being one is in that "world," one may study, examine and come to understand oneself. One may then see what the possibilities for play are for the being one is in that "world." One may even decide to inhabit that self fully in order to understand it better and find its creative possibilities. All of this is just self-reflection and it is quite different from resigning or abandoning oneself to the particular construction of oneself that one is attempting to take a hold of.

Conclusion

There are "worlds" we enter at our own risk, "worlds" that have agon, conquest, and arrogance as the main ingredients in their ethos. These are "worlds" that we enter out of necessity and which would be foolish to enter playfully.

But there are "worlds" that we can travel to lovingly and travelling to them is part of loving at least some of their inhabitants. The reason why I think that travelling to someone's "world" is a way of identifying with them is because by travelling to their "world" we can understand *what it is to be them and what it is to be ourselves in their eyes.* Only when we have travelled to each other's "worlds" are we fully subjects to each other.*

Knowing other women's "worlds" is part of knowing them and knowing them is part of loving them. The knowing can be done in greater or lesser depth, as can the loving. Travelling to another's "world" is not the same as becoming intimate with them. Intimacy is constituted in part by a very deep knowledge of the other self and "world"-travelling is only part of this knowledge. Some people, in particular those who are outsiders to the mainstream, can be known only to the extent that they are known in several "worlds" and as "world"-travellers.

Without knowing the other's "world," one does not know the other, and without knowing the other one is really alone in the other's presence because the other is only dimly present to one.

Through travelling to other people's "worlds" we discover that there are "worlds" in which those who are the victims of arrogant perception are really subjects, lively beings, resistors, constructors of visions even though in the mainstream construction they are animated only by the arrogant perceiver and are pliable, foldable, file-awayable, classifiable. My mother was apparent to me mostly as a victim of arrogant perception. I was loyal to the arrogant perceiver's construction of her and thus disloyal to her in assuming that she was exhausted by that construction. I was unwilling to be like her and thought that identifying with her, seeing myself in her necessitated that I become like her. I was wrong. I came to realize through travelling to her "world" that she is not foldable and pliable, that she is not exhausted by the mainstream argentinian patriarchal construction of her. I came to realize that there are "worlds" in which she shines as a creative being. Seeing myself in her through travelling in her "world" has meant seeing how different from her I am in her "world." This is the form of identification that I consider incompatible with arrogant perception and constitutive of a new understanding of love.

---

* I agree with Hegel that self-recognition requires other subjects, but I disagree with his claim that it requires tension or hostility.

Notes

1. Marilyn Frye, *The Politics of Reality: Essays in Feminist Theory* (Trumansburg, N.Y.: Crossing Press, 1983), 73.
2. Grafting the substance of another to oneself is partly constitutive of arrogant perception. See Frye, 66.
3. Frye, 53.
4. Frye, 75.
5. Frye, 73.
6. Frye, 77.
7. Frye, 75.
8. Johan Huizinga, *Homo Ludens* (Buenos Aires, Argentina: Emece Editores, 1968).
9. Hans-Georg Gadamer, *Truth and Method* (New York: Seabury Press, 1975).

[1987]

The Politics of Poetics: Or, What Am I, a Critic, Doing in This Text Anyhow?

Tey Diana Rebolledo

IN AN ESSAY "RETRIEVING OUR PAST, DETERMINING OUR FUTURE" POET Pat Mora chose to begin with a pre-Columbian poem:

Also they grow cotton
of many colors:
red, yellow, pink,
purple, green, bluish-green,
blue, light green,
orange, brown, and dark gold.
These were the colors of the cotton itself.
It grew that way from the earth,
no one colored it.
And also they raised these
fowl of rare plumage:
small birds the color of turquoise,
some with green feathers,
with yellow, with flame-colored breasts.

Every kind of fowl
that sang beautifully,
like those that warble in the mountains.[1]

Mora chose this poem because she liked the images of music, color and nature. But then she is a poet. I would like to underscore Mora's choice and begin with some definitions. "*Politics:* intrigue or maneuvering within a group; one's position or attitude on political subjects. *Poetics:* literary criticism dealing with the nature, form and laws of poetry; a study of or treatise on poetry or aesthetics. *Criticism:* the art, skill, or profession of making discriminating judgments, especially of literary or artistic works, detailed investigation of the origin and history of literary documents. *Discourse:* to run about, to speak at length, the process or power of reasoning."[2]

My understanding several months ago was that this symposium "Chicana Creativity and Criticism: Charting New Frontiers in American Literature," would undertake a dialogue between Chicana creative writers and Chicana literary critics with regard to several topics: Are Chicana critics friends or foes to the writers? What function do or can we Chicana critics play in relationship to our literature? And, what the heck are we doing in and to these texts anyway? As Chicanas we are all in this *revoltura* and explosion of literature and poetics together. It is time, perhaps, to take a step back and analyze where we are and where we might be going.

I do not mean the remarks I am about to make to be anti-intellectual, anti-theoretical or anti-aesthetic. Nor do I mean to assume the position of any critic other than myself. Nor am I criticizing the work of any particular literary critic. Nevertheless, I am commenting on what I see as a general phenomenon: one that we need to take stock of and one which affects Chicano male critics as well as the females. Juan Bruce-Novoa, in his recent article "Canonical and Noncanonical Texts," thinks there is now a "body of work" which constitutes Chicano literature and which is recognized as such. He recognizes that previously "any mention of canon was clearly understood as a reference to mainstream literature" and, he adds, "to state we were excluded from the canon was to state the obvious. Moreover, there was an ironic sense of worth associated with being outside the canon, almost a sense of purity, because, beyond the exclusionary ethnocentrism implied by the canon, Chicanos infused the term with a criticism of the very existence of a privileged body of texts."[3]

It seems to me that in spite of the explosion of creative and critical activity on the part of both critics and writers, Chicana writers and critics are still within a framework of marginality among Chicano writing as well as in mainstream writing. Some of this may be attributed to time; that is, time for the maturing of our literature as well as of our criticism. In addition to the creation of new insights and perspectives, we are also at a moment of rupture in which we are just beginning to look back to uncover our traditions, whether they be written or oral, and to talk back—to unsay what had been said and frozen in time and place. We are at the moment of questioning everything, even ourselves. Only when it is accomplished can we, with clear conscience, proceed towards some understanding of critical difference.

At the recent Chicano Studies Conference in Salt Lake City (1987), it became clear that for the past several years social scientists and literary critics alike have been engaged in a desperate search for a theoretical/critical discourse in which to situate what is happening to us. There have been discourses and counter-discourses. We talk about historical/materialist perspectives, transformative perspectives, pluralism (which some called a pre-prostituted dominant discourse) and the word hegemony was used in one session alone thirty-two times. Some of the talks began with a few of the questions to be asked, then discussed the methods used to answer those questions, mostly the methods used. I would say a typical talk could be summarized in the following way: the speaker begins, "This paper will focus on the ideology of cultural practice and its modes of signifying." S/he then spends twenty minutes discussing how the works of whatever theoretical greats s/he selects will define, inform and privilege the work s/he is doing. Such names as Jameson, Said, Williams, Hall, Burke and other contemporary *meros, meros* (mostly male) will be invoked over and over. The speaker is then sent a note by the chair of the panel that there is not time left. And whatever the Chicano/a writing or phenomena that was to be discussed is quickly summarized in two minutes. The talk is over. We have talked so much about theory we never get to our conclusion nor focus on the texts. By appropriating mainstream theoreticians and critics we have become so involved in intellectualizing that we lose our sense of our literature and therefore our vitality. This priority of placing our literature in a theoretical framework to "legitimize" it, if the theory overshadows it, in effect undermines our literature or even places it, once again, in a state of oblivion. Privileging the theoretical discourse de-privileges ourselves.

In puzzling over this scenario, which in fact occurred many times in Salt Lake, one could be left with various insights about what is happening to us:

1. We have internalized the dominant ideology so that only by talking theory (construed as a superior form of logic) can our literature and our cultural practices be intellectually viable, that is, acceptable within the traditional academic canon as "legitimate."
2. We are trying to impress ourselves and others with our ability to manipulate theoretical discourse, to use buzz words such as hegemony, signifying and even the word discourse. Someone once said to me "you are so articulate. You are able to talk in *their* language." I am not sure what this means. On the one hand they may be telling me I am totally assimilated or they may, in reality, be saying that no Chicana can truly be articulate. (I myself often feel that it is only our baroque *conceptismo* that has been transferred into English.)
3. We have entered into the "Age of Criticism" which could be defined as a preoccupation with theoretical structures often not internalized: we feel that theory is power.
4. We have a genuine desire to look beyond the elements (the texts) to the conditions that structured them. We are truly in search of a theoretical frame-

work which yet eludes us or at least some of us (and I count myself among those eludees).

I would like to outline some of the problems that I think we Chicana critics face or that at least I, as a critic in training, think about from time to time. They often as not deal with the question, what am I doing in this text anyhow?

1. First of all I am a reader. But I am not just a reader. My job, as a university professor, is to bring the attention of my students to the text itself. How can I do this if the text is not included in the general course curriculum, in the anthologies or in any way accessible to the student or to the population at large? Perhaps my primary responsibility, therefore, is the promulgation of the works of these writers, to make the writers known. We all know that the material production of Chicana writers is often limited to chapbooks, journals, the few that are accepted by Arte Publico Press and Bilingual Press. It is limited even to the Chicano audience and from one region to the next, from one big city to the next, we may not know what is happening. The work being done by Juan Rodríguez, *Third Woman* and the Centro de Escritores de *Aztlán*, for example, helps but as these texts go out of print, this production becomes more difficult to find. At Salt Lake City a copy of the first printing of Quinto Sol's *El Grito* was proudly held up as the rarity it has become. Of the chapbooks that were and are produced in the 60's, 70's and 80's, many will end up in a rare book room in a library if we are fortunate. Fortunate because it will be preserved as an artifact—the same phenomena which will make the book even more inaccessible.

If this product is inaccessible to those who are its target, in terms of interest, it is virtually unavailable to a larger audience. The role of the Chicana critic then becomes one of facilitator: reproducing and making known the texts of our authors. In itself this may not be an insignificant task since, for example, in a recent struggle with some of my co-authors (not the editors) of a book to be published by Yale University Press, I was told that my method of writing, that is, including entire poems written by Chicanas instead of dissecting them by including between slashes "pertinent" quotes from the text, made my article "hard to read" and "jumpy." While this may be true of my *own* writing, it certainly was not true of those texts of the authors I had included. I was very troubled by the inadequacies of a vision which presumed to have me speak for all Chicanas when they were perfectly able to speak for themselves. My arguments for entire text inclusion were the following: a. These texts were unknown and therefore needed to be reproduced in their entirety; b. These writers were more passionate, forceful and graphic than I; c. I did not want to do to these writers what others have been doing to all of us for centuries, that is, to appropriate their discourse through my discourse. I commented that I had no problem with my strategy and if they were not happy with publishing my chapter as it was, I did not wish it to be included in the volume. Fortunately the article will be published in its jumpy entirety in *The Desert Is No Lady*, title poem by Pat Mora.[4]

2. The second function of a critic may be to analyze the content of the

literary production—stepping back from the product in order to see what may be the dominant concerns and themes. I myself have indulged in this type of descriptive thematic analysis (adding, I hope, some analysis in depth as to cultural context and history). One example is a paper I wrote on Abuelitas, noting the scope and complexity of this recurring figure and offering an explanation as to why this figure was approaching what I considered to be mythic proportions.[5] This article has brought mixed reviews. My secretary, who was typing it, asked to take it home to read to her children, and many others have used it in their classrooms for teaching. Recently a contemporary writer remarked to me about critics writing descriptively about things that "everyone already knew about," such as abuelitas. Yet descriptive thematic analysis serves its purpose too, particularly as it grows in sophistication, and as historical and cultural analysis are linked to it. I hope that since my abuelitas article was published and as I have grown as a scholar that my analysis has too.

3. Another important current function for us as critics is to remember our literary history. While contemporary writers may feel that they are seeing the world anew, those of us who are searching out our literary roots are finding women writers who were raising many of the same concerns women voice today—written in a different tone and style and conforming to a different mode; nevertheless, contemporary writers have not arisen from a complete void. If the written word did not survive in enough texts to be known today, nonetheless the oral forms of women's concerns, of women's images have lived in the tradition from one generation, from one century to another. Thus the critic as literary historian is able to fill in the lacunae and to connect the past and the present.

4. Chicana literary discourse, like most feminist discourse, is a troubled one. It is always searching, questioning and fraught with tensions and contradictions, just as is the creative writing arising from the same creative context. A truly Chicana literary theory would result from the attempt to resolve these things, to mend the rift between doers and thinkers. I think we would all agree that Chicana criticism and theory are still in a state of flux looking for a theoretical, critical framework that is our own, whatever the perspective. I personally find it difficult to have theory (male oriented, French feminist, post structural or whatever is the current fad) be what dictates what we find in our literature. I prefer to have the literature speak for itself and as a critic try to organize and understand it. Perhaps from a more open perspective our own theoretical critical analysis will arise, rather than finding the theory first and imposing it upon the literature.

Recently several Chicana critics have taken up the issue of a theoretical approach to our literature. Norma Cantú in "The Chicana Poet and Her Audience: Notes towards a Chicana Feminist Aesthetic" acknowledges the lack of a methodological approach in our work but feels that it is a sense of place and world as embedded in particular language use that the Chicana poet communicates to her Chicana audience. For Cantú it is the special relationship between writer and listener, the shared cultural referents that make the poems work.[6] Norma Alarcón, in her perceptive study on the image of La Malinche, reevaluates and reconstructs the symbolic and figurative meaning this figure holds for us as Chicana writers and critics, dealing with the significance of language use and silence within our literature.[7] She also sees significant evolution of the Chicana as "speaking subject," one who brings within herself her race, class and gender, expressing this from a self-conscious point of view. Both of these critics, it seems to me, in addition to being theoretically well grounded, look at the literature from within, in an integrative sense.

5. It is very difficult to work on living authors: authors who read what you write and agree or don't agree. But it is just as difficult to work on authors no longer living. In the practice of literary criticism one (or perhaps I speak for myself only) must practice sound and honorable as well as rigorous criticism. That is, facts must be checked, scholarship must be sound. There is always the danger that the critic, immersed in pursuing some essential point, will become over enthusiastic and confuse the authorial voice with that of the narrative or poetic voice. If structuralism has taught us anything at all, it is that the lyric/narrative speaker is just that. As critics we must be careful not to confuse author with speaker.

When dealing with a vigorously living author we must also not be too timid to analyze symbolically what we, as critics, may see in the text—that which the author may not consciously have intended. We know that there are many levels of symbolic discourse that we may not be aware of at any given moment. When the text is published, when the author gives it up to the public domain, it is released and opened up to interpretation by the reader. It exists on its own, separate from the author. The textual interpretation, therefore, is one of integration between the authorial intent, and the text itself, *and* the third (and separate) interpretation or grasping of those two aspects by the reader.

6. We must, as critics, also be careful in our criticism to be honest. I think Chicana critics are often too benign. Our close network between writers and critics makes it difficult to have caustic criticism (which might ruin friendships) but at the same time we may hesitate to be as critical as we should be. One way I know I cope with this, and I imagine others have the same problem, is simply to ignore those texts I don't like, of writers that I do like or to ignore those writers who say nothing to me. This seems to me to be a function of human nature. What is important, however, is that the critic be conscious of her biases. And while we women may be benign to each other, there are still many Chicano critics who refuse to recognize their own biases and misogyny. Raymond Paredes, in a recent review article, is only able to see Chicana literature through a particularly phallocentric focus. If we were to accept his views we would see "if there is one quality that runs consistently through *their* (underlining mine) stories, plays and novels, it is the conviction that men know and care very little about women and that everyone is the worse for it."[8] His review continues with the assumption that men are the focus of Chicana literature, as he assails Beverly Silva,

Cherrie Moraga and Ana Castillo as faulted writers, their work, he says, is more interesting "ideologically" than aesthetically. Back to the old notion of "Are They Any Good?" Those writers whose perspectives Paredes does not agree with he considers superficial, and Denise Chávez, with whom he is more in agreement, is merely "flawed."[9]

7.   Perhaps more dangerous than ignoring texts we dislike is excluding the works of authors whose perspective we do not share or whose perspective we might feel uncomfortable with. Here I mean specifically the perspective of sexual preference. There are some fine Lesbian writers such as Cherrie Moraga, Gloria Anzaldúa, and Veronica Cunningham whose works are often excluded (although less so recently) from our critical thinking. Certainly if critics are serious about historical, cultural and gender context, then all writers need to be included within the general cultural framework. Then too some critics feel more comfortable with socially conscious literature and exclude that coming from the middle class. As the complexities and shades of our literature grows, we must be careful not to canonize a certain few to the exclusion of other equally fine writers.

8.   While some scholars see the need for some resolution of dichotomies, for example of Chicana and feminist, Chicana and poet—as if they were mutually exclusive—others examine the relationship between dominant and ethnic communities. The dominant discourse, if we internalize it, would have us believe that we function under such labels, and to some extent we do. I believe, however, as Bernice Zamora so succinctly expressed it, that our complexities are infinite: that we have grown up and survived along the edges, along the borders of so many languages, worlds, cultures and social systems that we constantly fix and focus on the spaces in between, Nepantla as Sor Juana would have seen it. Categories that try to define and limit this incredibly complex process at once become diminished for their inablity to capture and contain. Those of us who try to categorize these complexities inevitably fail.

Margarita Cota-Cárdenas in her novel *Puppet* examines the way in which this ideology is imposed. She sees this in part as arising from a single vision of what being Chicana should be.

Are you Malinche a malinche? Who are you (who am I mal inche)? Seller or buyer? Sold or bought and at what price? What is it to be what so many should say sold-out malinchi who is who are/are we what? At what price without having been there naming putting label tags what who have bought sold malinchismo what other-ismos invented shouted with hate reacting, striking like vipers like snakes THEIR EYES like snakes what who what.[10]

Her Malinche breaks the silence of centuries and she does not do so quietly:

yes yes I went yelling loud too why why and they said tie her up she's too forward too flighty she thinks she's a princess thinks she's her father's daughter thinks she's hot stuff that's it doesn't know her place a real threat to the tribe take her away haul her off she's a menace to our cause that's it only learned to say crazy things accuse with HER EYES and they didn't want them troublemakers in their country. (86)

These labels, specific here to La Malinche but clearly extended to all Chicanas, are of course the very labels culture uses to restrict and limit women's activity, socially as well as intellectually. Women are so silenced that they are only left to speak with "their eyes." In a country defined as "their" country, one that does not belong to her, Cota-Cárdenas makes the connection between Mexico and the United States:

This country, well I suppose Mexico, Aztlán . . . ? Well, it could have been a little more to the north or a little more to the south, it makes no difference now, what I was telling you was my version, that's it, my version . . . as a woman, that's right, and they can establish the famous dialectic with the other versions that you already know very well. (86)

Cota-Cárdenas thus introduces the complexities, the ambiguities in our lives and, while she does not deny the legitimacy of the other versions (acknowledging them for what they are), overlays another perspective that is hers alone.

These remarks I have made may seem to be arising from some simplistic assumptions. I myself was trained as a structuralist, semiotic critic. But increasingly I have become suspicious and yes, even bored, by a criticism which seems alien to the text about which it purports to talk; by a theoretical basis of patriarchal norms or a theory which does not take the particular concerns of minority writers and culture into account. I am suspicious of criticism which ignores the texts of our writers and which turns the vitality and the passion of those texts of our writers into an empty and meaningless set of letters. This sort of criticism, it seems to me, might as well be analyzing a menu or a telephone directory, and would perhaps be better directed in doing so. As Sor Juana criticized Aristotle—he would have been a better philosopher had he studied cooking,—I believe that our critical discourse should come from within, within our cultural and historical perspective. This is not to say that I am advocating limited, regional, small-minded descriptive literary analysis. But I think we should internalize and revolutionize theoretical discourse that comes from outside ourselves, accepting that which is useful and discarding that which is merely meant to impress. In the search for our own aesthetic, for our own analytical direction, we need to look to each other, to recognize that our literature and our cultural production does not need legitimization from the academy, that it already is legitimate in itself. Above all, we must not forget that the most important aspect of our analysis are the texts themselves. As we ask ourselves where are we, what are we doing, we must never appropriate into our own discourse the discourse of the writer herself. If we are to diffuse, support, promote, analyze and understand the work of our writers, we must let them speak for themselves. As a critic I desire the same as poet Pat Mora, I want to see the cotton of many colors, the small birds the color of turquoise, and hear the birds that warble in the mountains.

References

1. In Miguel León-Portilla, *Pre-Columbian Literature of Mexico* (Norman: University of Oklahoma Press, 1969), 41, cited in Mora, "Tradition and Mythology: Signatures of Landscape in Chicana Literature"; forthcoming in Tey Diana Rebolledo, Ed. *Writing from the Margins.*
2. *Webster's II* (Boston: Houghton Mifflin, 1984).
3. *The Americas Review* 14:3–4 (Fall-Winter, 1986), 119.
4. *The Desert Is No Lady: Southwestern Landscapes in Women's Writing and Art*, Eds. Vera Norwood and Janice Monk (New Haven: Yale University Press, 1987), 96–124.
5. "Abuelitas: Mythology and Integration in Chicana Literature," *Woman of Her Word: Hispanic Women Write*, Ed. Evangelina Vigil, *Revista Chicano-Riqueña* 11:3–4 (1983), 148–58.
6. Rebolledo, Ed. *Writing from the Margins.*
7. "Traddutora, Traditora: A Paradigmatic Figure of Chicana Feminism," in Rebolledo, *Writing.*
8. "Review Essay: Recent Chicano Writing," *Rocky Mountain Review* 41:1–2 (1987), 126.
9. Paredes, 128.
10. *Puppet* (Austin, TX: Relámpago Books Press, 1985), p. 85.

[1988]

The Truth That Never Hurts: Black Lesbians in Fiction in the 1980s

Barbara Smith

IN 1977, WHEN I WROTE *TOWARD A BLACK FEMINIST CRITICISM*, I WANTED to accomplish several goals. The first was simply to point out that Black women writers existed, a fact generally ignored by white male, Black male, and white female readers, teachers, and critics. Another desire was to encourage Black feminist criticism of these writers' work, that is, analyses that acknowledged the reality of sexual oppression in the lives of Black women.

Probably most urgently, I wanted to illuminate the existence of Black Lesbian writers and to show how homophobia insured that we were even more likely to be ignored or attacked than Black women writers generally.

In 1985, Black women writers' situation is considerably different than it was in 1977. Relatively speaking, Black women's literature is much more recognized, even at times by the white, male literary establishment. There are a growing number of Black women critics who rely upon various Black feminist critical approaches to studying the literature. There has been a marked increase in the number of Black women who are willing to acknowledge that they are feminists, including some who write literary criticism. Not surprisingly, Black feminist activism and organizing have greatly expanded, a precondition which I cited in 1977 for the growth of Black feminist criticism. More writing by Black Lesbians is available, and there has even been some positive response to this writing from non-Lesbian Black readers and critics. The general conditions under which Black women critics and writers work have improved. The personal isolation we face and the ignorance and hostility with which our work is met have diminished in some quarters but have by no means disappeared.

One of the most positive changes is that a body of consciously Black feminist writing and writing by other feminists of color actually exists. The publication of a number of anthologies has greatly increased the breadth of writing available by feminists of color. These include *Conditions: Five, The Black Women's Issue* (1979); *This Bridge Called My Back: Writings by Radical Women of Color* (1981); *All the Women Are White, All the Blacks Are Men, But Some of Us Are Brave: Black Women's Studies* (1982); *A Gathering of Spirit: North American Indian Women's Issue* (1983); *Cuentos: Stories by Latinas* (1983); *Home Girls: A Black Feminist Anthology* (1983); *Bearing Witness/Sobreviviendo: An Anthology of Native American/Latina Art and Literature* (1984); and *Gathering Ground: New Writing and Art by Northwest Women of Color* (1984). First books by individual authors have also appeared, such as *Claiming an Identity They Taught Me to Despise* (1980) and *Abeng* (1984) by Michelle Cliff; *Narratives: Poems in the Tradition of Black Women* (1982) by Cheryl Clarke; *For Nights Like This One* (1983) by Becky Birtha; *Loving in the War Years: Lo Que Nunca Pasó por Sus Labios* (1983) by Cherríe Moraga; *The Words of a Woman Who Breathes Fire* (1983) by Kitty Tsui; and *Mohawk Trail* (1985) by Beth Brant (Degonwadonti). Scholarly works provide extremely useful analytical frameworks, for example, *Common Differences: Conflicts in Black and White Feminist Perspectives* by Gloria I. Joseph and Jill Lewis (1981); *Black Women Writers at Work* edited by Claudia Tate (1983); *When and Where I Enter: The Impact of Black Women on Race and Sex in America* by Paula Giddings (1984); and *Black Feminist Criticism: Perspectives on Black Women Writers* by Barbara Christian (1985).

Significantly, however, "small" or independent, primarily women's presses published all but the last four titles cited and almost all the authors and editors of these alternative press books (although not all of the contributors to their anthologies) are Lesbians. In his essay, "The Sexual Mountain and Black Women Writers," critic Calvin Hernton writes:

> The declared and lesbian black feminist writers are pioneering a black feminist criticism. This is not to take away from other writers. All are blazing new trails. But especially the declared feminists and lesbian feminists—Barbara Smith, Ann Shockley, Cheryl Clarke, Wilmette Brown, and the rest—are at the forefront of the critics, scholars, intellectuals, and ideologues of our time.[1]

Yet Hernton points out that these writers are "subpopular," published as they are by nonmainstream presses. In contrast, non-Lesbian Black women writers have been published by trade publishers and are able to reach, as Hernton explains, a "wider popular audience."

In her excellent essay, "No More Buried Lives: The Theme of Lesbianism" in Audre Lorde's *Zami*, Gloria Naylor's *The Women of Brewster Place*, Ntozake Shange's *Sassafras, Cypress and Indigo*, and Alice Walker's *The Color Purple*, critic Barbara Christian makes a similar observation. She writes:

> Lesbian life, characters, language, values are *at present* and *to some extent* becoming respectable in American literature, partly because of the pressure of women-centered communities, partly because publishers are intensely aware of marketing trends. . . . I say, *to some extent*, because despite the fact that Walker received the Pulitzer for *The Color Purple* and Naylor the American Book Award for *The Women of Brewster Place*, I doubt if *Home Girls*, an anthology of black feminist and lesbian writing that was published by Kitchen Table Press, would have been published by a mainstream publishing company.[2]

Significantly, Christian says that "Lesbian life, characters, language, values" are receiving qualified attention and respectability, but Lesbian writers themselves are not. No doubt, this is why she suspects that no trade publisher would publish *Home Girls*, which contains work by women who write openly as Lesbians, and which defines Lesbianism politically as well as literarily.

The fact that there is such a clear-cut difference in publishing options for Black Lesbian writers (who are published solely by independent presses) and for non-Lesbian and closeted Black women writers (who have access to both trade and alternative publishers) indicates what has *not* changed since 1977. It also introduces the focus of this essay.[3] I am concerned with exploring the treatment of Black Lesbian writing and Black Lesbian themes in the context of Black feminist writing and criticism.

Today, not only are more works by and about Black women available, but a body of specifically Black feminist writing exists. Although both the general category of Black women's literature and the specific category of Black feminist literature can be appropriately analyzed from a Black feminist critical perspective, explicitly Black feminist literature has a unique set of characteristics and emphases which distinguishes it from other work. Black feminist writing provides an incisive critical perspective on sexual political issues that affect Black women—for example, the issue of sexual violence. It generally depicts the significance of Black women's relationships with each other as a primary source of support. Black feminist writing may also be classified as such because the author identifies herself as a feminist and has a demonstrated commitment to women's issues and related political concerns. An openness in discussing Lesbian subject matter is perhaps the most obvious earmark of Black feminist writing and not because feminism and Lesbianism are interchangeable, which of course they are not.

For historical, political, and ideological reasons, a writer's consciousness about Lesbianism bears a direct relationship to her consciousness about feminism. It was in the context of the second wave of the contemporary feminist movement, influenced by the simultaneous development of an autonomous gay liberation movement, that the political content of Lesbianism and Lesbian oppression began to be analyzed and defined. The women's liberation movement was the political setting in which anti-Lesbian attitudes and actions were initially challenged in the late 1960s and early 1970s and where, at least in theory, but more often in fact, homophobia was designated unacceptable, at least in the movement's more progressive sectors.

Barbara Christian also makes the connection between feminist consciousness and a willingness to address Lesbian themes in literature. She writes:

> Some of the important contributions that the emergence of the lesbian theme has made to Afro-American Women's literature are: the breaking of stereotypes so that black lesbians are clearly seen as *women*, the exposure of homophobia in the black community, and an exploration of how that homophobia is related to the struggle of all women to be all that they can be—in other words to feminism.
>
> That is not to say that Afro-American women's literature has not always included a feminist perspective. The literature of the seventies, for example, certainly explored the relationship between sexism and racism and has been at the forefront of the development of feminist ideas. One natural outcome of this exploration is the lesbian theme, for society's attack on lesbians is the cutting edge of the anti-feminist definition of women.[4]

Black feminist writers, whether Lesbian or non-Lesbian, have been aware of and influenced by the movement's exploring, struggling over, and organizing around Lesbian identity and issues. They would be much more likely to take Black Lesbian experience seriously and to explore Black Lesbian themes in their writing, in contrast with authors who either have not been involved in the women's movement or who are antifeminist. For example, in her very positive review of *Conditions: Five, The Black Women's Issue*, originally published in *Ms.* magazine in 1980, Alice Walker writes:

> Like black men and women who refused to be the exceptional "pet" Negro for whites, and who instead said they were "niggers" too (the original "crime" of "niggers" and lesbians is that they prefer themselves), perhaps black women writers and nonwriters should say, simply, whenever black lesbians are being put down,

held up, messed over, and generally told their lives should not be encouraged, *We are all lesbians*. For surely it is better to be thought a lesbian, and to say and write your life exactly as you experience it, than to be a token "pet" black woman for those whose contempt for our autonomous existence makes them a menace to human life.[5]

Walker's support of her Lesbian sisters in real life is not unrelated to her ability to write fiction about Black women who are lovers, as in *The Color Purple*. Her feminist consciousness undoubtedly influenced the positiveness of her portrayal. In contrast, an author like Gayl Jones, who has not been associated with or seemingly influenced by the feminist movement, has portrayed Lesbians quite negatively.[6]

Just as surely as a Black woman writer's relationship to feminism affects the themes she might choose to write about, a Black woman critic's relationship to feminism determines the kind of criticism she is willing and able to do. The fact that critics are usually also academics, however, has often affected Black women critics' approach to feminist issues. If a Black woman scholar's only connection to women's issues is via women's studies, as presented by white women academics, most of whom are not activists, her access to movement analyses and practice will be limited or nonexistent. I believe that the most accurate and developed theory, including literary theory, comes from practice, from the experience of activism. This relationship between theory and practice is crucial when inherently political subject matter, such as the condition of women as depicted in a writer's work, is being discussed. I do not believe it is possible to arrive at fully developed and useful Black feminist criticism by merely reading about feminism. Of course every Black woman has her own experiences of sexual political dynamics and oppression to draw upon, and referring to these experiences should be an important resource in shaping her analyses of a literary work. However, studying feminist texts and drawing only upon one's *individual* experiences of sexism are insufficient.

I remember the point in my own experience when I no longer was involved on a regular basis in organizations such as the Boston Committee to End Sterilization Abuse and the Abortion Action Coalition. I was very aware that my lack of involvement affected my thinking and writing *overall*. Certain perceptions were simply unavailable to me because I no longer was doing that particular kind of ongoing work. And I am referring to missing something much deeper than access to specific information about sterilization and reproductive rights. Activism has spurred me to write the kinds of theory and criticism I have written and has provided the experiences and insights that have shaped the perceptions in my work. Many examples of this vital relationship between activism and theory exist in the work of thinkers such as Ida B. Wells-Barnett, W. E. B. Du Bois, Lillian Smith, Lorraine Hansberry, Frantz Fanon, Barbara Deming, Paolo Freire, and Angela Davis.

A critic's involvement or lack of involvement in activism, specifically in the context of the feminist movement, is often signally revealed by the approach she takes to Lesbianism. If a woman has worked in organizations where Lesbian issues have been raised, where homophobia was unacceptable and struggled with, and where she had the opportunity to meet and work with a variety of Lesbians, her relationship to Lesbians and to her own homophobia would undoubtedly be affected. The types of political organizations in which such dialogue occurs are not, of course, exclusively Lesbian and may focus upon a range of issues, such as women in prison, sterilization abuse, reproductive freedom, health care, domestic violence, and sexual assault.

Black feminist critics who are Lesbians can usually be counted upon to approach Black women's and Black Lesbian writing non-homophobically. Non-Lesbian Black feminist critics are not as dependable in this regard. I even question at times designating Black women—critics and noncritics alike—as feminist who are actively homophobic in what they write, say, or do, or who are passively homophobic because they ignore Lesbian existence entirely.[7] Yet such critics are obviously capable of analyzing other sexual and political implications of the literature they scrutinize. Political definitions, particularly of feminism, can be difficult to pin down. The one upon which I generally rely states: "Feminism is the political theory and practice that struggles to free *all* women: women of color, working-class women, poor women, disabled women, lesbians, old women—as well as white, economically privileged, heterosexual women. Anything less than this vision of total freedom is not feminism, but merely female self-aggrandizement."[8]

A Black gay college student recently recounted an incident to me that illustrates the kind of consciousness that is grievously lacking among nonfeminist Black women scholars about Black Lesbian existence. His story indicates why a Black feminist approach to literature, criticism, and research in a variety of disciplines is crucial if one is to recognize and understand Black Lesbian experience. While researching a history project, he contacted the archives at a Black institution that has significant holdings on Black women. He spoke to a Black woman archivist and explained that he was looking for materials on Black Lesbians in the 1940s. Her immediate response was to laugh uproariously and then to say that the collection contained very little on women during that period and nothing at all on Lesbians in any of the periods covered by its holdings.

Not only was her reaction appallingly homophobic, not to mention impolite, but it was also inaccurate. One of the major repositories of archival material on Black women in the country of course contains material by and about Black Lesbians. The material, however, is not identified as such and thus remains invisible. This is a classic case of "invisibility [becoming] an unnatural disaster," as feminist poet Mitsuye Yamada observes.[9]

I suggested a number of possible resources to the student and in the course of our conversation I told him I could not help but think of Cheryl Clarke's classic poem, "Of Althea and Flaxie." It begins:

In 1943 Althea was a welder
very dark
very butch

and very proud
loved to cook, sew, and drive a car
and did not care who knew she kept company with a woman.[10]

The poem depicts a realistic and positive Black Lesbian relationship which survives Flaxie's pregnancy in 1955, Althea's going to jail for writing numbers in 1958, poverty, racism, and, of course, homophobia. If the archivist's vision had not been so blocked by homophobia, she would have been able to direct this student to documents that corroborate the history embodied in Clarke's poem.

Being divorced from the experience of feminist organizing not only makes it more likely that a woman has not been directly challenged to examine her homophobia, but it can also result in erroneous approaches to Black Lesbian literature, if she does decide to talk or write about it. For example, some critics, instead of simply accepting that Black Lesbians and Black Lesbian writers exist, view the depiction of Lesbianism as a dangerous and unacceptable "theme" or "trend" in Black women's writing. Negative discussions of "themes" and "trends," which may in time fade, do not acknowledge that for survival, Black Lesbians, like any oppressed group, need to see our faces reflected in myriad cultural forms, including literature. Some critics go so far as to see the few Black Lesbian books in existence as a kind of conspiracy and bemoan that there is "so much" of this kind of writing available in print; they put forth the supreme untruth that it is actually an advantage to be a Black Lesbian writer.

For each Lesbian of color in print there are undoubtedly five dozen whose work has never been published and may never be. The publication of Lesbians of color is a "new" literary development, made possible by alternative, primarily Lesbian/feminist presses. The political and aesthetic strength of this writing is indicated by its impact having been far greater than its actual availability. At times its content has had revolutionary implications. But the impact of Black Lesbian feminist writing, to which Calvin Hernton refers, should not be confused with easy access to print, to readers, or to the material perks that help a writer survive economically.

Terms like "heterophobia," used to validate the specious notion that "so many" Black women writers are now depicting loving and sexual relationships between women, to the exclusion of focusing on relationships with men, arise in an academic vacuum, uninfluenced by political reality. "Heterophobia" resembles the concept of "reverse racism." Both are thoroughly reactionary and have nothing to do with the actual dominance of a heterosexual white power structure.

Equating Lesbianism with separatism is another error in terminology, which will probably take a number of years to correct. The title of a workshop at a major Black women writers' conference, for example, was "Separatist Voices in the New Canon." The workshop examined the work of Audre Lorde and Alice Walker, neither of whom defines herself as a separatist, either sexually or racially. In his introduction to *Confirmation: An Anthology of African American Women*, co-editor Imamu Baraka is critical of feminists who are separatists, but he does not mention that any such thing as a Lesbian exists. In his ambiguous yet inherently homophobic usage, the term "separatist" is made to seem like a mistaken political tendency, which correct thinking could alter. If "separatist" equals Lesbian, Baraka is suggesting that we should change our minds and eradicate ourselves. In both these instances the fact that Lesbians do not have sexual relationships with men is thought to be the same as ideological Lesbian "separatism." Such an equation does not take into account that the majority of Lesbians of color have interactions with men and that those who are activists are quite likely to be politically committed to coalition work as well.

Inaccuracy and distortion seem to be particularly frequent pitfalls when non-Lesbians address Black Lesbian experience because of generalized homophobia and because the very nature of our oppression may cause us to be hidden or "closeted," voluntarily or involuntarily isolated from other communities, and as a result unseen and unknown. In her essay, "A Cultural Legacy Denied and Discovered: Black Lesbians in Fiction by Women," Jewelle Gomez asserts the necessity for realistic portrayals of Black Lesbians:

> These Black Lesbian writers . . . have seen into the shadows that hide the existence of Black Lesbians and understand they have to create a universe/home that rings true on all levels. . . . The Black Lesbian writer must throw herself into the arms of her culture by acting as student/teacher/participant/observer, absorbing and synthesizing the meanings of our existence as a people. She must do this despite the fact that both our culture and our sexuality have been severely truncated and distorted.
>
> Nature abhors a vacuum and there is a distinct gap in the picture where the Black Lesbian should be. The Black Lesbian writer must recreate our home, unadulterated, unsanitized, specific and not isolated from the generations that have nurtured us.[11]

This is an excellent statement of what usually has been missing from portrayals of Black Lesbians in fiction. The degree of truthfulness and self-revelation that Gomez calls for encompasses the essential qualities of verisimilitude and authenticity that I look for in depictions of Black Lesbians. By verisimilitude I mean how true to life and realistic a work of literature is. By authenticity I mean something even deeper—a characterization which reflects a relationship to self that is genuine, integrated, and whole. For a Lesbian or a gay man, this kind of emotional and psychological authenticity virtually requires the degree of self-acceptance inherent in being out. This is not a dictum, but an observation. It is not a coincidence, however, that the most vital and useful Black Lesbian feminist writing is being written by Black Lesbians who are not caught in the impossible bind of simultaneously hiding identity yet revealing self through their writing.

Positive and realistic portrayals of Black Lesbians are sorely needed, portraits that are, as Gomez states, "unadulterated, unsanitized, specific." By positive I do not mean characters without problems, contradictions, or flaws, mere uplift literature for Lesbians, but instead, writing that is sufficiently sensitive and complex, which places Black Lesbian experience and struggles squarely within the realm of recognizable human experience and concerns.

As African-Americans, our desire for authentic literary images of Black Lesbians has particular cultural and historical resonance, since a desire for authentic images of ourselves as Black people preceded it long ago. After an initial period of racial uplift literature in the nineteenth and early twentieth centuries, Black artists during the Harlem Renaissance of the 1920s began to assert the validity of fully Black portrayals in all art froms including literature. In his pivotal essay of 1926, "The Negro Artist and the Racial Mountain," Langston Hughes asserted:

> We younger Negro artists who create now intend to express our individual dark-skinned selves without fear or shame. If white people are pleased we are glad. If they are not, it doesn't matter. We know we are beautiful. And ugly too. The tom-tom cries and the tom-tom laughs. If colored people are pleased we are glad. If they are not, their displeasure doesn't matter either. We build our temples for tomorrow, strong as we know how, and we stand on top of the mountain, free within ourselves.[12]

Clearly, it was not always popular or safe with either Black or white audiences to depict Black people as we actually are. It still is not. Too many contemporary Blacks seem to have forgotten the universally debased social-political position Black people have occupied during all the centuries we have been here, up until perhaps the Civil Rights Movement of the 1960s. The most racist definition of Black people has been that we were not human.

Undoubtedly every epithet now hurled at Lesbians and gay men—"sinful," "sexually depraved," "criminal," "emotionally maladjusted," "deviant"—has also been applied to Black people. When W. E. B. Du Bois described life "behind the veil," and Paul Laurence Dunbar wrote,

> We wear the mask that grins and lies,
> It hides our cheeks and shades our eyes,—
> This debt we pay to human guile;
> With torn and bleeding hearts we smile,
> And mouth with myriad subtleties.
>
> Why should the world be overwise,
> In counting all our tears and sighs?
> Nay, let them only see us, while
> We wear the mask. . . .[13]

what were they describing but racial closeting? For those who refuse to see the parallels because they view Blackness as irreproachably normal, but persist in defining same-sex love relationships as unnatural, Black Lesbian feminist poet, Audre Lorde, reminds us: "'Oh,' says a voice from the Black community, 'but being Black is NORMAL!' Well, I and many Black people of my age can remember grimly the days when it didn't used to be!"[14] Lorde is not implying that she believes that there was ever anything wrong with being Black, but points out how distorted "majority" consciousness can cruelly affect an oppressed community's actual treatment and sense of self. The history of slavery, segregation, and racism was based upon the assumption by the powers-that-be that Blackness was decidedly neither acceptable nor normal. Unfortunately, despite legal and social change, large numbers of racist whites still believe the same thing to this day.

The existence of Lesbianism and male homosexuality is normal, too, traceable throughout history and across cultures. It is a society's *response* to the ongoing historical fact of homosexuality that determines whether it goes unremarked as nothing out of the ordinary, as it is in some cultures, or if it is instead greeted with violent repression, as it is in ours. At a time when Acquired Immune Deficiency Syndrome (AIDS), a disease associated with an already despised sexual minority, is occasioning mass hysteria among the heterosexual majority (including calls for firings, evictions, quarantining, imprisonment, and even execution), the way in which sexual orientation is viewed is not of mere academic concern. It is mass political organizing that has wrought the most significant changes in the status of Black and other people of color and that has altered society's perceptions about us and our images of ourselves. The Black Lesbian feminist movement simply continues that principled tradition of struggle.

A Black woman author's relationship to the politics of Black Lesbian feminism affects how she portrays Black Lesbian characters in fiction. In 1977, in *Toward a Black Feminist Criticism*, I had to rely upon Toni Morrison's *Sula* (1974), which did not explicitly portray a Lesbian relationship, in order to analyze a Black woman's novel with a woman-identified theme. I sought to demonstrate, however, that because of the emotional primacy of Sula and Nel's love for each other, Sula's fierce independence, and the author's critical portrayal of heterosexuality, the novel could be illuminated by a Lesbian feminist reading. Here I will focus upon three more recent works—*The Women of Brewster Place*, *The Color Purple*, and *Zami: A New Spelling of My Name*—which actually portray Black Lesbians, but which do so with varying degrees of verisimilitude and authenticity, dependent upon the author's relationship to and understanding of the politics of Black Lesbian experience.

Gloria Naylor's *The Women of Brewster Place* (1983) is a novel composed of seven connecting stories. In beautifully resonant language Naylor makes strong sexual political statements about the lives of working poor and working-class Black women and does not hesitate to explore the often problematic nature of their relationships with Black men—lovers, husbands, fathers, sons. Loving and supportive bonds between Black women are central to her characters' survival. However, Naylor's portrayal of a Lesbian relationship in the sixth story, "The Two," runs counter to the positive framework of women bonding she has previously established. In the context of this novel a Lesbian relationship might well embody the culmination of women's capacity to love and be committed to each other. Yet both Lesbian characters are ultimately victims. Although Naylor portrays the community's homophobia toward the lovers as unacceptable, the fate that she designs for the two women is the most brutal and negative of any in the book.

Theresa is a strong-willed individualist, while her lover Lorraine passively yearns for social acceptability. Despite their professional jobs, they have moved to a dead-end slum block because of Lorraine's fears that the residents of their two other middle-class neighborhoods suspected that they were Lesbians. It does not take long for suspicions to arise on Brewster Place, and the two women's differing reactions to the inevitable homophobia they face is a major tension in the work. Theresa accepts the fact that she is an outsider because of her Lesbianism. She does not like being ostracized, but she faces others' opinions with an attitude of defiance. In contrast, Lorraine is obsessed with garnering societal approval and would like nothing more than to blend into the straight world, despite her Lesbianism. Lorraine befriends Ben, the alcoholic building superintendent, because he is the one person on the block who does not reject her. The fact that Ben has lost his daughter and Lorraine has lost her father, because he refused to accept her Lesbianism, cements their friendship. Naylor writes:

". . . When I'm with Ben, I don't feel any different from anybody else in the world."

"Then he's doing you an injustice," Theresa snapped, "because we are different. And the sooner you learn that, the better off you'll be."

"See, there you go again. Tee the teacher and Lorraine the student, who just can't get the lesson right. Lorraine who just wants to be a human being—a lousy human being who's somebody's daughter or somebody's friend or even somebody's enemy. But they make me feel like a freak out there, and you try to make me feel like one in here. That only place I've found some peace, Tee, is in that damp ugly basement, where I'm not different."

"Lorraine." Theresa shook her head slowly. "You're a lesbian—do you understand that word?—a butch, a dyke, a lesbo, all those things that kid was shouting. Yes, I heard him! And you can run in all the basements in the world, and it won't change that, so why don't you accept it?"

"I have accepted it!" Lorraine shouted. "I've accepted it all my life, and it's nothing I'm ashamed of. I lost a father because I refused to be ashamed of it—but it doesn't make me any *different* from anyone else in the world."

"It makes you damned different!"

. . . .

"That's right! There go your precious 'theys' again. They wouldn't understand—not in Detroit, not on Brewster Place, not anywhere! And as long as they own the whole damn world, it's them and us, Sister—them and us. And that spells different!"[15]

Many a Lesbian relationship has been threatened or destroyed because of how very differently lovers may view their Lesbianism, for example, how out or closeted one or the other is willing to be. Naylor's discussion of difference represents a pressing Lesbian concern. As Lorraine and Theresa's argument shows, there are complicated elements of truth in both their positions. Lesbians and gay men are objectively different in our sexual orientations from heterosexuals. The society raises sanctions against our sexuality that range from inconvenient to violent, and that render our social status and life experiences different. On the other hand we would like to be recognized and treated as human, to have the basic rights enjoyed by heterosexuals, and, if the society cannot manage to support how we love, to at least leave us alone.

In "The Two," however, Naylor sets up the women's response to their identity as an either/or dichotomy. Lorraine's desire for acceptance, although completely comprehensible, is based upon assimilation and denial, while Naylor depicts Theresa's healthier defiance as an individual stance. In the clearest statement of resistance in the story, Theresa thinks: "If they practiced that way with each other, then they could turn back to back and beat the hell out of the world for trying to invade their territory. But she had found no such sparring partner in Lorraine, and the strain of fighting alone was beginning to show on her." (p. 136) A mediating position between complete assimilation or alienation might well evolve from some sense of connection to a Lesbian/gay community. Involvement with other Lesbians and gay men could provide a reference point and support that would help diffuse some of the straight world's power. Naylor mentions that Theresa socializes with gay men and perhaps Lesbians at a bar, but her interactions with them occur outside the action of the story. The author's decision not to portray other Lesbians and gay men, but only to allude to them, is a significant one. The reader is never given an opportunity to view Theresa or Lorraine in a context in which they are the norm. Naylor instead presents them as "the two" exceptions in an entirely heterosexual world. Both women are extremely isolated and although their relationship is loving, it also feels claustrophobic. Naylor writes:

> Lorraine wanted to be liked by the people around her. She couldn't live the way Tee did, with her head stuck in a book all the time. Tee didn't seem to need anyone. Lorraine often wondered if she even needed her. . . .
> . . . She never wanted to bother with anyone except those weirdos at the club she went to, and Lorraine hated them. They were coarse and bitter, and made fun of people who weren't like them. Well, she wasn't like them either. Why should she feel different from the people she lived around? Black people were all in the same boat—she'd come to realize this even more since they had moved to Brewster—and if they didn't row together, they would sink together. (p. 142)

Lorraine's rejection of other Lesbians and gay men is excruciating, as is the self-hatred that obviously prompts it. It is painfully ironic that she considers herself in the same boat with Black people in the story, who are heterosexual, most of whom ostracize her, but not with Black people who are Lesbian and gay. The one time that Lorraine actually decides to go to the club by herself, ignoring Theresa's warning that she won't have a good time without her, is the night that she is literally destroyed.

Perhaps the most positive element in "The Two" is how accurately Naylor depicts and subtly condemns Black homophobia. Sophie, a neighbor who lives across the airshaft from Lorraine and Theresa, is the "willing carrier" of the rumor about them, though not necessarily its initiator. Naylor writes:

> Sophie had plenty to report that day. Ben had said it was terrible in there. No, she didn't know exactly what he had seen, but you can imagine—and they did. Confronted with the difference that had been thrust into their predictable world, they reached into their imaginations and, using an ancient pattern, weaved themselves a reason for its existence. Out of necessity they stitched all of their secret fears and lingering childhood nightmares into this existence, because even though it was deceptive enough to try and look as they looked, talk as they talked, and do as they did, it had to have some hidden stain to invalidate it—it was impossible for them both to be right. So they leaned back, supported by the sheer weight of their numbers and comforted by the woven barrier that kept them protected from the yellow mist that enshrouded the two as they came and went on Brewster Place. (p. 132)

The fact of difference can be particularly volatile among people whose options are severely limited by racial, class, and sexual oppression, people who are already outsiders themselves.

A conversation between Mattie Michaels, an older Black woman who functions as the work's ethical and spiritual center, and her life-long friend, Etta, further prods readers to examine their own attitudes about loving women. Etta explains:

> "Yeah, but it's different with them."
> "Different how?"
> "Well . . ." Etta was beginning to feel uncomfortable. "They love each other like you'd love a man or a man would love you—I guess."
> "But I've loved some women deeper than I ever loved any man," Mattie was pondering. "And there been some women who loved me more and did more for me than any man ever did."
> "Yeah." Etta thought for a moment. "I can second that but it's still different, Mattie. I can't exactly put my finger on it, but . . ."
> "Maybe it's not so different," Mattie said, almost to herself. "Maybe that's why some women get so riled up about it, 'cause they know deep down it's not so different after all." She looked at Etta. "It kinda gives you a funny feeling when you think about it that way, though."
> "Yeah, it does," Etta said, unable to meet Mattie's eyes. (pp. 140–141)

Whatever their opinions, it is not the women of the neighborhood who are directly responsible for Lorraine's destruction, but six actively homophobic and woman-hating teenage boys. Earlier that day Lorraine and Kiswana Browne had encountered the toughs who unleashed their sexist and homophobic violence on the two young women. Kiswana verbally bests their leader, C. C. Baker, but he is dissuaded from physically retaliating because one of the other boys reminds him: "'That's Abshu's woman, and that big dude don't mind kickin' ass,'" (p. 163). As a Lesbian, Lorraine does not have any kind of "dude" to stand between her and the violence of other men. Although she is completely silent during the encounter, C. C.'s parting words to her are, "I'm gonna remember this, Butch!" That night when Lorraine returns from the bar alone, she walks into the alley which is the boys' turf. They are waiting for her and gang-rape her in one of the most devastating scenes in literature. Naylor describes the aftermath:

> Lorraine lay pushed up against the wall on the cold ground with her eyes staring straight up into the sky. When the sun began to warm the air and the horizon brightened, she still lay there, her mouth crammed with paper bag, her dress pushed up under her breasts, her bloody pantyhose hanging from her thighs. She would have stayed there forever and have simply died from starvation or exposure if nothing around her had moved. (p. 171)

She glimpses Ben sitting on a garbage can at the other end of the alley sipping wine. In a bizarre twist of an ending Lorraine crawls through the alley and mauls him with a brick she happens to find as she makes her way toward him. Lorraine's supplicating cries of " 'Please. Please.' . . . the only word she was fated to utter again and again for the rest of her life," conclude the story (p. 171, 173).

I began thinking about "The Two" because of a conversation I had with another Black Lesbian who seldom comes in contact with other Lesbians and who has not been active in the feminist movement. Unlike other women with whom I had discussed the work, she was not angry, disappointed, or disturbed by it, but instead thought it was an effective portrayal of Lesbians and homophobia. I was taken aback because I had found Naylor's depiction of our lives so completely demoralizing and not particularly realistic. I thought about another friend who told me she found the story so upsetting she was never able to finish it. And of another who had actually rewritten the ending so that Mattie hears Lorraine's screams before she is raped and saves her. In this "revised version," Theresa is an undercover cop, who also hears her lover's screams, comes into the alley with a gun, and blows the boys away. I was so mystified and intrigued by the first woman's defense of Naylor's perspective that I went back to examine the work.

According to the criteria I have suggested, although the Lesbian characters in "The Two" lack authenticity, the story possesses a certain level of verisimilitude. The generalized homophobia that the women face, which culminates in retaliatory rape and near murderous decimation, is quite true to life. Gay and Lesbian newspapers provide weekly accounts, which sometimes surface in the mainstream media, of the constant violence leveled at members of our communities. What feels disturbing and inauthentic to me is how utterly hopeless Naylor's view of Lesbian existence is. Lorraine and Theresa are classically unhappy homosexuals of the type who populated white literature during a much earlier era, when the only options for the "deviant" were isolation, loneliness, mental illness, suicide, or death.

In her second novel, *Linden Hills* (1985), Naylor indicates that Black gay men's options are equally grim. In a review of the work, Jewelle Gomez writes:

> . . . one character disavows a liaison with his male lover in order to marry the appropriate woman and inherit the coveted Linden Hills home. . . . We receive so little personal information about him that his motivations are obscure. For a middle-class, educated gay man to be blind to alternative lifestyles in 1985 is not inconceivable but it's still hard to accept the melodrama of his arranged marriage without screaming "dump the girl and buy a ticket to Grand Rapids!" Naylor's earlier novel [*The Women of Brewster Place*] presented a similar limitation. While she admirably attempts to portray black gays as integral to the fabric of black life she seems incapable of imagining black gays functioning as healthy, average people. In her fiction, although they are not at fault, gays must still be made to pay. This makes her books sound like a return to the forties, not a chronicle of the eighties.[16]

Gomez's response speaks to the problems that many Lesbian feminists have with Naylor's versions of our lives, her persistent message that survival is hardly possible. I do not think we simply want "happy endings," although some do occur for Lesbians both in literature and in life, but an indication of the spirit of survival and resistance which has made the continuance of Black Lesbian and gay life possible throughout the ages.

In considering the overall impact of "The Two," I realized that because it is critical of homophobia, it is perhaps an effective story for a heterosexual audience. But because its portrayal of Lesbianism is so negative, its message even to heterosexuals is ambiguous. A semi-sympathetic straight reader's response might well be: "It's a shame something like that had to happen, but I guess that's what you get for being queer." The general public does not want to know that it is possible to be a Lesbian of whatever color and not merely survive, but thrive. And neither does a heterosexual publishing industry want to provide them with this information.

The impact of the story upon Lesbian readers is quite another matter. Imagine what might happen if a Black woman who is grappling with defining her sexuality and who has never had the opportunity to read anything else about Lesbians, particularly Black ones, were to read "The Two" as a severely cautionary tale. Justifiably, she might go no further in her exploration, forever denying her feelings. She might eventually have sexual relationships with other women, but remain extremely closeted. Or she might commit suicide. As a Black Lesbian reader, I find Naylor's dire pessimism about our possibilities to be the crux of my problems with "The Two."

Alice Walker's portrayal of a Lesbian relationship in her novel *The Color Purple* (1982) is as optimistic as Naylor's is despairing. Celie and Shug's love, placed at the center of the work and set in a rural southern community between the World Wars, is unique in the history of African-American fiction. The fact that a book with a Black Lesbian theme by a Black woman writer achieved massive critical acclaim, became a bestseller, and was made into a major Hollywood film is unprecedented in the history of the world. It is *The Color Purple* which homophobes and antifeminists undoubtedly refer to when they talk about how "many" books currently have both Black Lesbian subject matter and an unsparing critique of misogyny in the Black community. For Black Lesbians, however, especially writers, the book has been inspirational. Reading it we think it just may be possible to be a Black Lesbian and live to tell about it. It may be possible for us to write it down and actually have somebody read it as well.

When I first read *The Color Purple* in galleys in the spring of 1982, I believed it was a classic. I become more convinced every time I read it. Besides great storytelling, perfect Black language, killingly subtle Black women's humor, and an unequivocal Black feminist stance, it is also a deeply philosophical and spiritual work. It is marvelously gratifying to read discussions of nature, love, beauty, God, good, evil, and the meaning of life in the language of our people. The book is like a jewel. Any way you hold it to the light you will always see something new reflected.

The facet of the novel under consideration here is Walker's approach to Lesbianism, but before going further with that discussion, it is helpful to understand that the work is also a fable. The complex simplicity with which Walker tells her story, the archetypal and timeless Black southern world in which it is set, the clear-cut conflicts between good and evil, the complete transformations undergone by several of the major characters, and the huge capacity of the book to teach are all signs that *The Color Purple* is not merely a novel, but a visionary tale. That it is a fable may account partially for the depiction of a Lesbian relationship unencumbered by homophobia or fear of it and entirely lacking in self-scrutiny about the implications of Lesbian identity.

It may be Walker's conscious decision to deal with her readers' potentially negative reactions by using the disarming strategy of writing as if women falling in love with each other were quite ordinary, an average occurrence which does not even need to be specifically remarked. In the "real world" the complete ease with which Celie and Shug move as lovers through a totally heterosexual milieu would be improbable, not to say amazing. Their total acceptance is one clue that this is indeed an inspiring fable, a picture of what the world could be if only human beings were ready to create it. A friend told me about a discussion of the book in a Black writers' workshop she conducted. An older Black woman in the class asserted: "When that kind of business happens, like happened between Shug and Celie, you know there's going to be talk." The woman was not reacting to *Purple* as a fable or even as fiction, but as a "real" story, applying her knowledge of what would undoubtedly happen in real life where most people just aren't ready to deal with Lesbianism and don't want to be.

Because the novel is so truthful, particularly in its descriptions of sexual oppression and to a lesser extent racism, the reader understandably might question those aspects of the fable which are not as plausible. Even within the story itself, it is conceivable that a creature as mean-spirited as Mr.——— might have something to say about Shug, the love of his life, and Celie, his wife, sleeping together in his own house. For those of us who experience homophobia on a daily basis and who often live in fear of being discovered by the wrong person(s), like the teenage thugs in "The Two," we naturally wonder how Celie and Shug, who do not hide their relationship, get away with it.

Another fabulous aspect of Celie's and Shug's relationship is that there are no references to how they think about themselves as Lesbian lovers in a situation where they are the only ones. Although Celie is clearly depicted as a woman who at the very least is not attracted to men and who is generally repulsed by them, I am somewhat hesitant to designate her as a Lesbian because it is not a term that she would likely apply to herself and neither, obviously, would the people around her. In a conversation with Mr. ——— in the latter part of the book Celie explains how she feels:

> He say, Celie, tell me the truth. You don't like me cause I'm a man?
> I blow my nose. Take off they pants, I say, and men look like frogs to me. No matter how you kiss 'em, as far as I'm concern, frogs is what they stay.
> I see, he say.[17]

Shug, on the other hand, is bisexual, another contemporary term that does not necessarily apply within the cultural and social context Walker has established. There is the implication that this is among her first, if not only sexual relationship with another woman. The first and only time within the novel when Shug and Celie make love, Walker writes:

> She say, I love you, Miss Celie. And then she haul off and kiss me on the mouth.
> Um, she say, like she surprise. I kiss her back, say, um, too. Us kiss and kiss till us can't hardly kiss no more. Then us touch each other.
> I don't know nothing bout it, I say to Shug.
> I don't know much, she say. (p. 109)

Despite her statement of inexperience, Shug is a wonderfully sensual and attractive woman who takes pleasure in all aspects of living from noticing "the color purple in a field" to making love with whomever. When Shug tries to explain to Celie why she has taken up with a nineteen-year-old boy, the two women's differing perspectives and sexual orientations are obvious. Walker writes:

> But Celie, she say. I have to make you understand. Look, she say. I'm gitting old. I'm fat. Nobody think I'm good looking no more, but you. Or so I thought. He's nineteen. A baby. How long can it last?
> He's a man. I write on the paper.
> Yah, she say. He is. And I know how you feel about men. But I don't feel that way. I would never be fool enough to take any of them seriously, she say, but some mens can be a lots of fun.
> Spare me, I write. (p. 220)

Eventually Shug comes back to Celie and Walker implies that they will live out their later years together. The recouplings and reunions that occur in the novel might also indicate that the story is more fantasy than fact. But in Celie and Shug's case, the longevity of their relationship is certainly a validation of love between women.

The day Shug returns, Celie shows her her new bedroom. Walker writes:

> She go right to the little purple frog on my mantelpiece.
>   What this? she ast.
>   Oh, I say, a little something Albert carve for me. (p. 248)

Not only is this wickedly amusing after Celie and Mr. ———'s discussion about "frogs," but Mr. ———'s tolerance at being described as such to the point of his making a joke-gift for Celie seems almost too good to be true. Indeed Mr. ———'s transformation from evil no-count to a sensitive human being is one of the most miraculous one could find anywhere. Those critics and readers who condemn the work because they find the depiction of men so "negative" never seem to focus on how nicely most of them turn out in the end. Perhaps these transformations go unnoticed because in Walker's woman-centered world, in order to change, they must relinquish machismo and violence, the very thought of which would be fundamentally disruptive to the nonfeminist reader's world-view. It is no accident that Walker has Celie, who has become a professional seamstress and designer of pants, teach Mr. ——— to sew, an ideal way to symbolize just how far he has come. In the real world, where former husbands of Lesbian mothers take their children away with the support of the patriarchal legal system, and in some cases beat or even murder their former wives, very few men would say what Mr. ——— says to Celie about Shug: "I'm real sorry she left you, Celie. I remembered how I felt when she left me" (p. 238). But in the world of *The Color Purple* a great deal is possible.

One of the most beautiful and familiar aspects of the novel is the essential and supportive bonds between Black women. The only other person Celie loves before she meets Shug is her long-lost sister, Nettie. Although neither ever gets an answer, the letters they write to each other for decades and Celie's letters to God before she discovers that Nettie is alive, comprise the entire novel. The work joyously culminates when Nettie, accompanied by Celie's children who were taken away from her in infancy, return home.

Early in the novel Celie "sins against" another woman's spirit and painfully bears the consequences. She tells her stepson, Harpo, to beat his wife Sofia if she doesn't mind him. Soon Celie is so upset about what she has done that she is unable to sleep at night. Sofia, one of the most exquisitely defiant characters in Black women's fiction, fights Harpo right back and when she finds out Celie's part in Harpo's changed behavior comes to confront her. When Celie confesses that she advised Harpo to beat Sofia because she was jealous of Sofia's ability to stand up for herself, the weight is lifted from her soul, the women become fast friends, and she "sleeps like a baby."

When Shug decides that Celie needs to leave Mr. ——— and go with her to Memphis, accompanied by Mary Agnes (Squeak), Harpo's lover of many years, they make the announcement at a family dinner. Walker writes:

> You was all rotten children, I say. You made my life a hell on earth. And your daddy here ain't dead horse's shit.
>
> Mr. —— reach over to slap me. I jab my case knife in his hand.
>
> You bitch, he say. What will people say, you running off to Memphis like you don't have a house to look after?
>
> Shug say, Albert. Try to think like you got some sense. Why any woman give a shit what people think is a mystery to me.
>
> Well, say Grady, trying to bring light. A woman can't git a man if peoples talk.
>
> Shug look at me and us giggle. Then us laugh sure nuff. Then Squeak start to laugh. Then Sofia. All us laugh and laugh.
>
> Shug say, Ain't they something? Us say um *hum*, and slap the table, wipe the water from our eyes.
>
> Harpo look at Squeak. Shut up Squeak, he say. It bad luck for women to laugh at men.
>
> She say, Okay. She sit up straight, suck in her breath, try to press her face together.
>
> He look at Sofia. She look at him and laugh in his face. I already had my bad luck, she say. I had enough to keep me laughing the rest of my life. (p. 182)

This marvelously hilarious scene is one of countless examples in the novel of Black women's staunch solidarity. As in *The Women of Brewster Place*, women's caring for each other makes life possible; but in *The Color Purple* Celie and Shug's relationship is accepted as an integral part of the continuum of women loving each other, while in the more realistic work, Lorraine and Theresa are portrayed as social pariahs.

If one accepts that *The Color Purple* is a fable or at the very least has fablelike elements, judgments of verisimilitude and authenticity are necessarily affected. Celie and Shug are undeniably authentic as Black women characters—complex, solid, and whole—but they are not necessarily authentic as Lesbians. Their lack of self-consciousness as Lesbians, the lack of scrutiny their relationship receives from the outside world, and their isolation from other Lesbians make *The Color Purple's* categorization as a Lesbian novel problematic. It does not appear that it was Walker's intent to create a work that could be definitively or solely categorized as such.

The question of categorization becomes even more interesting when one examines critical responses to the work, particularly in the popular media. Reviews seldom mention that Celie and Shug are lovers. Some critics even go so far as to describe them erroneously as good friends. The fact that their relationship is simply "there" in the novel and not explicitly called attention to as Lesbian might also account for a mass heterosexual audience's capacity to accept the work, although the novel has of course also been homophobically attacked.[18] As a Black Lesbian feminist reader, I have questions about how accurate it is to identify Walker's characters as Lesbians at the same time that I am moved by the vision of a world, unlike this one, where Black women are not forced to lose their families, their community, or their lives, because of whom they love.

A realistic depiction of African American Lesbian experience would neither be a complete idyll nor a total nightmare. Audre Lorde terms *Zami: A New Spelling of My Name* (1982) a "biomythography," a combination of autobiography, history, and myth. I have chosen to discuss it here, because it is the one extended prose work of which I am aware that approaches Black Lesbian experience with *both* verisimilitude and authenticity. *Zami* is an essentially autobiographical work, but the poet's eye, ear, and tongue give the work stylistic richness often associated with well-crafted fiction. At least two other Black women critics, Barbara Christian and Jewelle Gomez, have included *Zami* in their analyses of Black Lesbians in fiction.[19] Because *Zami* spans genres and carves out a unique place in African-American literature as the first full-length autobiographical work by an established Black Lesbian writer, it will undoubtedly continue to be grouped with other creative prose about Black Lesbians.

The fact that *Zami* is autobiographical might be assumed to guarantee its realism. But even when writing autobiographically, an author can pick and choose details, can create a persona that has little or nothing to do with her own particular reality, or she might fabricate an artificial persona with whom the reader cannot possibly identify. A blatant example of this kind of deceptive strategy might be an autobiographical work by a Lesbian that fails to mention that this is indeed who she is; of course there are other less extreme omissions and distortions. Undoubtedly, Lorde has selected the material she includes in the work, and the selectivity of memory is also operative. Yet this work is honest, fully rounded, and authentic. It is not coincidental that of the three works considered here, *Zami* has the most to tell the reader about the texture of Black Lesbian experience and that it is written by an out Black Lesbian feminist. The candor and specificity with which Lorde approaches her life are qualities that would enhance Black Lesbian writing in the future.

Zami is a Carriacou word "for women who work together as friends and lovers."[20] Just as the title implies, *Zami* is woman-identified from the outset and thoroughly suffused with an eroticism focusing on women. Lorde connects her Lesbianism to the model her mother, Linda, provided—her pervasive, often intimidating, strength; her fleeting sensuality when her harsh veneer was lifted—and also to her place of origin, the Grenadian island of Carriacou, where a word already existed to describe who Linda's daughter would become. As in the two novels *The Color Purple* and *The Women of Brewster Place*, in *Zami* relationships between women are at the center of the work. Here they are complex, turbulent, painful, passionate, and essential to the author's survival.

Although Lorde continuously explores the implications of being a Black Lesbian and she has an overt consciousness about her Lesbianism which is missing from Naylor's and Walker's works, she does not define Lesbianism as a problem in and of itself. Despite homophobia, particularly in the left of the McCarthy era; despite isolation from other Black women because she is gay; and despite primal loneliness because of her many levels of difference, Lorde assumes that her Lesbianism, like her Blackness, is a given, a fact of life which she has neither to justify nor explain. This is an extremely strong and open-ended stance from which to write about Black Lesbian experience, since it enables the writer to deal with the complexity of Lesbianism and what being a Black Lesbian means in a specific time and place. Lorde's position allows Black Lesbian experience to be revealed from the inside out. The absence of agonized doubts about her sexual orientation and the revelation of the actual joys of being a Lesbian, including lush and recognizable descriptions of physical passion between women, make *Zami* seem consciously written for a Lesbian reader. This is a significant point because so little is ever written with us in mind, and also because who an author considers her audience to be definitely affects her voice and the levels of authenticity she may be able to achieve. Writing from an avowedly Black Lesbian perspective with Black Lesbian readers in mind does not mean that a work will be inaccessible or inapplicable to non-Black and non-Lesbian readers. Works like *Zami*, which are based in the experiences of writers outside the "mainstream," provide a vitally different perspective on human experience and may even reveal new ways of thinking about supposedly settled questions. Or, as Celie puts it in *The Color Purple*: "If he [God] ever listened to poor colored women the world would be a different place, I can tell you" (p. 175). It would be more different still if "he" also listened to Lesbians.

The fact that *Zami* is written from an unequivocally Black Lesbian and feminist perspective undoubtedly explains why it is the one book of the three under discussion that is published by an alternative press, why it was turned down by at least a dozen trade publishers, including one that specializes in gay titles. The white male editor at that supposedly sympathetic house returned the manuscript saying, "If only you were just one," Black or Lesbian. The combination is obviously too much for the trade publishing establishment to handle. We bring news that others do not want to hear. It is unfortunate that the vast majority of the readers of *The Women of Brewster Place* and *The Color Purple* will never have the opportunity to read *Zami*.

Lorde's description of Black "gay-girl" life in the Greenwich Village of the 1950s is fascinating, if for no other reason than that it reveals a piece of our cultural history. What is even more intriguing is her political activist's sense of how the struggles of women during that era helped shape our contemporary movement and how many of our current issues, especially the desire to build a Black Lesbian community, were very much a concern at that time. The author's search for other Black Lesbians and her lovingly detailed descriptions of the fragments of community she finds give this work an atmosphere of reality missing in "The Two" and *The Color Purple*. Unlike Lorraine and Theresa and Celie and Shug, Lorde is achingly aware of her need for peers. She writes:

> I remember how being young and Black and gay and lonely felt. A lot of it was fine, feeling I had the truth and the light and the key, but a lot of it was purely hell.

There were no mothers, no sisters, no heroes. We had to do it alone, like our sister Amazons, the riders on the loneliest outposts of the kingdom of Dahomey. . . . There were not enough of us. But we surely tried. (pp. 176–177)

Every Black woman I ever met in the Village in those years had some part in my survival, large or small, if only as a figure in the head-count at the Bag on a Friday night.

Black lesbians in the Bagatelle faced a world only slightly less hostile than the outer world which we had to deal with every day on the outside—that world which defined us as doubly nothing because we were Black and because we were Woman—that world which raised our blood pressures and shaped our furies and our nightmares. . . . All of us who survived those common years have to be a little proud. A lot proud. Keeping ourselves together and on our own tracks, however wobbly, was like trying to play the Dinizulu War Chant or a Beethoven sonata on a tin dog-whistle. (p. 225)

The humor, tenacity, and vulnerability which Lorde brings to her version of being in "the life" are very precious. Here is something to grab hold of, a place to see one's face reflected. Despite the daily grind of racism, homophobia, sexual, and class oppression, compounded by the nonsolutions of alcohol, drugs, suicide, and death at an early age, some women did indeed make it.

Lorde also describes the much more frequent interactions and support available from white Lesbians who were in the numerical majority. Just as they are now, relationships between Black and white women in the 1950s were often undermined by racism, but Lorde documents that some women were at least attempting to deal with their differences. She writes:

However imperfectly, we tried to build a community of sorts where we could, at the very least, survive within a world we correctly perceived to be hostile to us; we talked endlessly about how best to create that mutual support which twenty years later was being discussed in the women's movement as a brand new concept. Lesbians were probably the only Black and white women in New York City in the fifties who were making any real attempt to communicate with each other; we learned lessons from each other, the values of which were not lessened by what we did not learn. (p. 179)

Lorde approaches the meaning of difference from numerous vantage points in *Zami*. In much of her work prior to *Zami* she has articulated and developed the concept of difference which has gained usage in the women's movement as a whole and in the writing of women of color specifically. From her early childhood, long before she recognizes herself as a Lesbian, the question of difference is *Zami*'s subtext, its ever-present theme. Lorde writes: "*It was in high school that I came to believe that I was different from my white classmates, not because I was Black, but because I was me*" (p. 82). Although Lorde comes of age in an era when little if any tolerance existed for those who did not conform to white male hegemony, her stance and that of her friends is one of rebellion and creative resistance, including political activism, as opposed to conformity and victimization. *Zami* mediates the versions of Lesbianism presented in *The Women of Brewster Place* and *The Color Purple*. It is not a horror story, although it reveals the difficulties of Black Lesbian experience. It is not a fable, although it reveals the joys of a life committed to women.

Since much of her quest in *Zami* is to connect with women who recognize and share her differences, particularly other Black Lesbians, it seems fitting that the work closes with her account of a loving relationship with another Black woman, Afrekete. Several years before the two women become lovers, Lorde meets Kitty at a Black Lesbian house party in Queens. Lorde writes:

> One of the women I had met at one of these parties was Kitty.
> When I saw Kitty again one night years later in the Swing Rendezvous or the Pony Stable or the Page Three—that tour of second-string gay-girl bars that I had taken to making alone that sad lonely spring of 1957—it was easy to recall the St. Alban's smell of green Queens summer-night and plastic couch-covers and liquor and hair oil and women's bodies at the party where we had first met.
> In that brick-faced frame house in Queens, the downstairs, pine-paneled recreation room was alive and pulsing with loud music, good food, and beautiful Black women in all different combinations of dress. (p. 241)

The women wear fifties dyke-chic, ranging from "skinny straight skirts" to Bermuda and Jamaica shorts. Just as the clothes, the smells, the song lyrics, and food linger in the author's mind, her fully rendered details of Black Lesbian culture resonate within the reader. I recalled this party scene while atending a dinner party at the home of two Black Lesbians in the deep South earlier this year. One of the hostesses arrived dressed impeccably in white Bermuda shorts, black knee-socks, and loafers. Her hair straightened, 1980s style much like that of the 1950s, completed my sense of déjà vu. Contemporary Black Lesbians are a part of a cultural tradition which we are just beginning to discover through interviews with older women such as Mabel Hampton and the writing of authors like Ann Allen Shockley, Anita Cornwell, Pat Parker, and Lorde.

When she meets Afrekete again, their relationship helps to counteract Lorde's loneliness following the break-up of a long-term relationship with a white woman. The bond between the women is stunningly erotic, enriched by the bond they share as Black women. Lorde writes:

> By the beginning of summer the walls of Afrekete's apartment were always warm to the touch from the heat beating down on the roof, and chance breezes through her windows rustled her plants in the window and brushed over our sweat-smooth bodies, at rest after loving.
> We talked sometimes about what it meant to love women, and what a relief it was in the eye of the storm, no matter how often we had to bite our tongues and stay silent. . . .
> Once we talked about how Black women had been committed without choice to waging our campaigns in the enemies' strongholds, too much and too often,

and how our psychic landscapes had been plundered and wearied by those repeated battles and campaigns.

"And don't I have the scars to prove it," she sighed. "Makes you tough though, babe, if you don't go under. And that's what I like about you; you're like me. We're both going to make it because we're both too tough and crazy not to!" And we held each other and laughed and cried about what we had paid for that toughness, and how hard it was to explain to anyone who didn't already know it that soft and tough had to be one and the same for either to work at all, like our joy and the tears mingling on the one pillow beneath our heads. (p. 250)

The fact that this conversation occurs in 1957 is both amazing and unremarkable. Black Lesbians have a heritage far older than a few decades, a past that dates back to Africa, as Lorde herself documents in the essay, "Scratching the Surface: Some Notes on Barriers to Women and Loving."[21] Lorde's authentic portrayal of one segment of that history in *Zami* enables us to see both our pasts and futures more clearly. Her work provides a vision of possibility for Black Lesbians surviving whole, despite all, which is the very least we can demand from our literature, our activism, and our lives.

Despite the homophobic exclusion and silencing of Black Lesbian writers, the creation of complex, accurate, and artistically compelling depictions of Black Lesbians in literature has been and will continue to be essential to the development of African-American women's literature as a whole. The assertion of Black women's right to autonomy and freedom, which is inherent in the lives of Black Lesbians and which is made politically explicit in Black Lesbian feminist theory and practice, has crucial implications for all women's potential liberation. Ultimately, the truth that never hurts is that Black Lesbians and specifically Black Lesbian writers are here to stay. In spite of every effort to erase us, we are committed to living visibly with integrity and courage and to telling our Black women's stories for centuries to come.

Notes

1. Calvin Hernton, "The Sexual Mountain and Black Women Writers," *The Black Scholar* 16, no. 4 (July/August 1985). 7. . . .

2. Barbara Christian, *Black Feminist Criticism: Perspectives on Black Women Writers* (New York: Pergamon, 1986), p. 188.

3. Audre Lorde and Ann Allen Shockley are two exceptions. They have published with both commercial and independent publishers. It should be noted that Lorde's poetry is currently published by a commercial publisher, but that all of her works of prose have been published by independent women's presses. In conversation with Lorde, I have learned that *Zami: A New Spelling of My Name* was rejected by at least a dozen commercial publishers.

4. Christian, *Black Feminist Criticism*, pp. 199–200.

5. Alice Walker, "Breaking Chains and Encouraging Life," in *In Search of Our*

Mothers' Gardens: Womanist Prose (New York: Harcourt Brace Jovanovich, 1984), pp. 288–289.

6. In her essay, "The Black Lesbian in American Literature: An Overview," Ann Allen Shockley summarizes Jones's negative or inadequate treatment of Lesbian themes in her novels *Corregidora* and *Eva's Man* and in two of her short stories. Ann Allen Shockley, "The Black Lesbian in American Literature: An Overview," in *Home Girls: A Black Feminist Anthology,* ed. Barbara Smith (Latham, N.Y.: Kitchen Table Press, 1982), p. 89.

7. In her essay "The Failure to Transform: Homophobia in the Black Community," Cheryl Clarke comments: "The black lesbian is not only absent from the pages of black political analysis, her image as a character in literature and her role as a writer are blotted out from or trivialized in literary criticism written by black women." Clarke also cites examples of such omissions. In *Home Girls,* ed. Smith, pp. 204–205.

8. Barbara Smith, "Racism and Women's Studies," in *All the Women Are White, All the Blacks Are Men, But Some of Us Are Brave: Black Women's Studies,* ed. Gloria Hull, Patricia Bell Scott, and Barbara Smith (New York: Feminist Press, 1981), p. 49.

9. Mitsuye Yamada, "Invisibility Is an Unnatural Disaster: Reflections of an Asian American Woman," in *This Bridge Called My Back: Writings by Radical Women of Color,* ed. Cherríe Moraga and Gloria Anzaldúa (Latham, N.Y.: Kitchen Table Press, 1984), pp. 35–40.

10. Cheryl Clarke, *Narratives: Poems in the Tradition of Black Women* (Latham, N.Y.: Kitchen Table, 1983), p. 15.

11. Jewelle Gomez, in *Home Girls,* ed. Smith, p. 122.

12. Langston Hughes, "The Negro Artist and the Racial Mountain," in *Voices from the Harlem Renaissance,* ed. Nathan Huggins (New York: Oxford, 1976), p. 309. It is interesting to note that recent research has revealed that Hughes and a number of other major figures of the Harlem Renaissance were gay. See Charles Michael Smith, "Bruce Nugent: Bohemian of the Harlem Renaissance," in *In the Life: A Black Gay Anthology,* ed. Joseph F. Beam (Boston: Alyson, 1986), pp. 213–214 and selections by Langston Hughes in *Gay and Lesbian Poetry in Our Time: An Anthology,* ed. Carl Morse and Joan Larkin (New York: St. Martin's, 1988), pp. 204–206.

13. Paul Dunbar, "We Wear the Mask," in *The Life and Works of Paul Laurence Dunbar,* ed. Wiggins (New York: Kraus, 1971), p. 184.

14. Audre Lorde, "There is No Hierarchy of Oppressions," in *The Council on Interracial Books for Children Bulletin, Homophobia and Education: How to Deal with Name-Calling,* ed. Leonore Gordon, Vol. 14, nos. 3 & 4 (1983), 9.

15. Gloria Naylor, *The Women of Brewster Place* (New York: Penguin, 1983), pp. 165–166. All subsequent references to this work will be cited in the text.

16. Jewelle Gomez, "Naylor's Inferno," *The Women's Review of Books* 2, no. 11 (August 1985), 8.

17. Alice Walker, *The Color Purple* (New York: Washington Square, 1982), p. 224. All subsequent references to this work will be cited in the text.

18. In his essay, "Who's Afraid of Alice Walker?" Calvin Hernton describes the "hordes of . . . black men (and some women)" who condemned both the novel and the film of *The Color Purple* all over the country. He singles out journalist Tony Brown as a highly visible leader of these attacks. Brown both broadcast television shows and wrote columns about a book and movie he admitted neither to have read nor seen. Hernton raises the question, "Can it be that the homophobic, nitpicking screams of denial against *The Color Purple* are motivated out of envy, jealousy and

guilt, rather than out of any genuine concern for the well-being of black people?" Calvin Hernton, *The Sexual Mountain and Black Women Writers* (New York: Anchor, 1987), pp. 30–36.

19. Christian, *Black Feminist Criticism*, pp. 187–210. Gomez, in *Home Girls*, ed. Smith, pp. 118–119.

20. Audre Lorde, *Zami: A New Spelling of My Name* (Freedom, Calif.: Crossing, 1983), p. 255. All subsequent references to this work will be cited in the text.

21. Audre Lorde, *Sister Outsider* (Freedom, Calif.: Crossing, 1984), pp. 45–52.

[1990]

Black Feminist Theory and the Representation of the "Other"

Valerie Smith

IN HER NOW CLASSIC REVIEW ESSAY "CRITICAL CROSS-DRESSING: MALE Feminists and the Woman of the Year," Elaine Showalter considers the ways in which a number of prominent English and American male theorists—among them Wayne Booth, Robert Scholes, Jonathan Culler, and Terry Eagleton—have employed feminist criticism within their own critical positions. Although Showalter praises Culler's ability to read as a feminist and confront "what might be implied by reading as a man and questioning or [surrendering] paternal privileges," she suggests that often male theorists, specifically Eagleton, borrow the language of feminism to compete with women instead of examining "the masculinist bias of their own reading system."[1] This general direction by male theorists, she argues, resembles a parallel phenomenon in popular culture—the rise of the male heroine. Her discussion of *Tootsie* indicates that Dorothy Michaels, the woman character Dustin Hoffman impersonates in the movie, derives her power not in response to the oppression of women but from an instinctive male reaction to being treated like a woman. For a man to act/write like/as a woman is thus not necessarily a tribute to women, but more likely a suggestion that women must be taught by men how to assert themselves.

In her essay Showalter problematizes the function of feminist criticism in response to a growing tendency among Western white male theorists to incorporate feminism in their critical positions. Because the black feminist as writer of both critical and imaginative texts appears with increasing frequency in the work of male Afro-Americanists and Anglo-American feminists, I consider here the place of the black feminist in these apposite modes of inquiry. I begin by defining various stages of the black feminist enterprise within the context of changes in these other theoretical positions, and I suggest how the black feminist has been employed in relation to them. I then offer a reading of *Sarah Phillips* (1984) by Andrea Lee, a fictional text about an upper-middle-class young black woman that thematizes this issue of the status of the "other" in a text by and about someone simultaneously marginal and privileged.

It is not my intention to reclaim the black feminist project from those who are not black women; to do so would be to define the field too narrowly, emphasizing unduly the implications of a shared experience between "black women as critics and black women as writers who represent black women's reality."[2] Indeed, as the following remarks indicate, I understand the phrase *black feminist theory* to refer not only to theory written (or practiced) by black feminists, but also to a way of reading inscriptions of race (particularly but not exclusively blackness), gender (particularly but not exclusively womanhood), and class in modes of cultural expression. Rather, I examine black feminism in the context of these related theoretical positions in order to raise questions about the way the "other" is represented in oppositional discourse. This sort of question seems especially important now that modes of inquiry once considered radical are becoming increasingly institutionalized.

Feminist literary theory and Afro-Americanist literary theory have developed along parallel lines. Both arose out of reactive, polemical modes of criticism. Recognizing that the term *literature* as it was commonly understood in the academy referred to a body of texts written by and in the interest of a white male elite, feminist critics (mostly white) and Afro-Americanist critics (mostly male) undertook the archaeological work of locating and/or reinterpreting overlooked and misread women and black writers.

Black feminist criticism originated from a similar impulse. In reaction to critical acts of omission and condescension, the earliest practitioners identified ways in which white male, Anglo-American feminist, and male Afro-Americanist scholars and reviewers had ignored and condescended to the work of black women and undertook editorial projects to recover their writings. To mention but a few examples: Mary Helen Washington called attention to the ways in which the androcentric Afro-American literary tradition and establishment privileged the solitary, literate adventurers found in texts by male authors such as Frederick Douglass and Richard Wright and ignored the more muted achievements of the female protagonists featured in the work of women writers such as Harriet Jacobs, Zora Neale Hurston, and Gwendolyn Brooks.[3] Barbara Smith notes the ways in which not only Elaine Showalter, Ellen Moers, and Patricia Meyer Spacks, but also Robert Bone and Darwin Turner dismiss the writings of black women. And Deborah E. McDowell cites the omissions of Spacks, Bone, David Littlejohn, and Robert Stepto.[4] The legacy of oversights and condescension occasioned a number of editorial projects that recovered black women's writings; these much-needed projects continue to be undertaken.[5]

From the reactive impulse of these first-stage archaeological projects developed work of greater theoretical sophistication. More recent studies are less concerned with oversights in the work of others, involved instead with constructing alternative literary histories and traditions and exploring changes in assumptions about the nature of critical activity as assumptions about the nature of literature are transformed. As the kinds of questions Anglo-American feminists and male Afro-Americanists pose became increasingly self-referential—for instance, revealing the critics' own complicities and conceptualizing the links between various instances of practical criticism—they have each been drawn inevitably toward a third oppositional discourse: the discourse of deconstruction.

It should not surprise us that a number of Anglo-American feminists and Afro-Americanists have found contemporary theory compatible with the goals of their broader critical enterprise. The techniques and assumptions of deconstructive criticism destabilize the narrative relations that enshrine configurations according to genre, gender, culture, or models of behavior and personality. However, the alliances between contemporary theory on the one hand, and Anglo-American feminists or Afro-Americanists on the other, have raised inevitable questions about the institutionalization of each of these putatively marginal modes of inquiry. Anglo-American feminists as well as male Afro-Americanists are being asked to consider the extent to which their own adherence to a deconstructive practice, which by now has been adopted into the academy, undermines the fundamental assumptions of their broader, more profoundly oppositional enterprise.

The question of the place of feminist critical practice in the institution, for instance, prompted the 1982 dialogue in *Diacritics* between Peggy Kamuf and Nancy K. Miller. Kamuf argues that as long as mainstream feminists install writing by and about women at the center of their modes of inquiry and attempt to locate knowledge about women within an institutionalized humanistic discourse, they sustain the very ways of knowing that have historically excluded women's work:

> If feminist theory lets itself be guided by questions such as what is women's language, literature, style or experience, from where does it get its faith in the form of these questions to get at truth, if not from the central store that supplies humanism with its faith in the universal truth of man?[6]

In turn, Miller addresses what she perceives to be Kamuf's over-investment in deconstructive operations. Reasserting the significance of women as historical and material subjects, she suggests that the destabilization of all categories of identity, including the category "woman," may well serve the interests of a male hegemony whose own power is under siege. As she argues,

> What bothers me about the metalogically "correct" position is what I take to be its necessary implications for practice: that by glossing "woman" as an archaic signifier, it glosses over the *referential* suffering of women. . . . It may also be the case that having been killed off with "man," the author can now be rethought beyond traditional notions of biography, now that through feminist rewritings of literary history the security of a masculine identity, the hegemony of homogeneity, has been radically problematized.[7]

Some of the most provocative and progressive work in Anglo-American feminist theory seeks to mediate these two positions. In *Crossing the Double-Cross: The Practice of Feminist Criticism*, Elizabeth A. Meese explores the possibilities of an interactive relation between feminist literary criticism and deconstruction. She argues for and illustrates a mode of feminist inquiry that employs the power of deconstruction's critique of difference even as it seeks to challenge and politicize the enterprise of critical theory.[8] Likewise, Teresa de Lauretis situates her collection of essays entitled *Feminist Studies/ Critical Studies* as a juncture in which "feminism is being both integrated and quietly suffocated within the institutions."[9] She urges a feminist model of identity that is "multiple, shifting, and often self-contradictory . . . an identity made up of heterogeneous and heteronomous representations of gender, race, and class, and often indeed across languages and cultures":[10]

> Here is where . . . feminism differs from other contemporary modes of radical, critical or creative thinking, such as postmodernism and philosophical antihumanism: feminism defines itself as a political instance, not merely a sexual politics but a politics of experience, of everyday life, which later then in turn enters the public sphere of expression and creative practice, displacing aesthetic hierarchies and generic categories, and which thus establishes the semiotic ground for a different production of reference and meaning.[11]

Recent work in Afro-American literary theory has occasioned a similar anxiety about institutionalization. Robert B. Stepto, Henry Louis Gates, and Houston A. Baker have been accused of dismantling the black subject when they bring contemporary theory to bear on their readings of black texts. In his 1984 study, *Blues, Ideology, and Afro-American Literature: A Vernacular Theory*, Baker himself argues that the presence of Afro-American critics in historically white academic institutions of higher learning has spawned a generation of scholars whose work is overly dependent on their white colleagues' assumptions and rhetoric.[12] To his mind, Stepto and Gates, two self-styled Reconstructionists, fall victim to this kind of co-optation in their early work. Both Stepto's "Teaching Afro-American Literature: Survey or Tradition: The Reconstruction of Instruction" and Gates's "Preface to Blackness: Text and Pretext" seek to explore the figurative power and complexity not only of Afro-American written art, but indeed of Afro-American cultural life more broadly defined.[13] Stepto's essay, like his book, *From Behind the Veil: A Study of Afro-American Narrative*, argues for the primacy of a pregeneric myth, the quest for freedom and literacy, in the Afro-American literary tradition.[14] But as Baker argues, Stepto's articulation of this myth underscores its apparent "agentlessness." According to Stepto, the pregeneric myth is simply "set in motion." Writes Baker, "the efficacy of motion suggested here seems to have no historically based community or agency or agencies for its origination or perpetuation."[15]

Gate's "Preface to Blackness" explores the extent to which social institutions and extraliterary considerations have intruded into the critical discourse about Afro-American literature. In order to reaffirm the textuality of instances of black written art, he argues for a semiotic understanding of literature as a system of signs that stand in an arbitrary relation to social reality. For Baker, such a theory of language, literature, and culture suggests that "'literary' meanings are conceived in a nonsocial, noninstitutional manner by the 'point of consciousness' of a language and maintained and transmitted, without an agent, within a closed circle of 'intertextuality,'"[16] Baker's position indicates his concern that in their efforts to align the aims of Afro-American critical activity with the goals and assumptions of prevailing theoretical discourses, both Stepto and Gates extract black writers from their relationship to their audience and from the circumstances in which they wrote and were read.

Interestingly, Baker's critique of Stepto and Gates appears in revised form within the same work in which he develops his own considerations about ways in which contemporary theory may be used to explore the workings of the vernacular in black expressive culture. Whether he succeeds in his effort to adjust the terms of poststructuralist theory to accommodate the nuances of black vernacular culture remains debatable. For Joyce Ann Joyce, however, Gates, Stepto, and Baker have all adopted a critical "linguistic system" that reflects their connection to an elite academic community of theoreticians and denies the significance of race for critic and writer alike. The intensity of this debate among Afro-Americanists is underscored by the fact that Joyce's essay occasions strikingly acrimonious responses from both Gates and Baker.

At these analogous points of self-scrutiny, then, feminists and Afro-Americanists alike have considered the extent to which they may betray the origins of their respective modes of inquiry when they seek to employ the discourse of contemporary theory. When Anglo-American feminists have argued for the inclusion of Anne Bradstreet or Kate Chopin within the literary canon, and when male Afro-Americanists have insisted on the significance of Charles Chesnutt or Jean Toomer, what they have argued is a recognition of the literary activity of those who have written despite political, cultural, economic, and social marginalization and oppression. They argue, in other words, that to exclude the work of blacks and women is to deny the historical existence of these "others" as producers of literature. If feminists and Afro-Americanists now relinquish too easily the material conditions of the lives of blacks and women, they may well relinquish the very grounds on which their respective disciplines were established.

These debates from within feminist and Afro-Americanist discourse coincided with black feminist charges that the cultural productions of black women were excluded from both modes of inquiry. Audre Lorde, bell hooks (Gloria Watkins), Angela Davis, Barbara Smith, Mary Helen Washington, and Deborah McDowell, to name but a few, have all argued that the experiences of women of color needed to be represented if these oppositional discourses were to remain radical. The eruptions of these critical voices into feminist and Afro-Americanist literary theory, like their self-contained critical and theoretical utterances, question the totalizing tendencies of mainstream as well as reactive critical practice and caution that the hope of oppositional discourse rests on its awareness of its own complicities.

These twin challenges have resulted in an impulse among Anglo-American feminists and Afro-Americanists to rematerialize the subject of their theoretical positions. Meese, as I suggested earlier, examines the contributions deconstructive method can make to feminist critical practice, but only insofar as feminist assumptions repoliticize her use of theory. De Lauretis affirms the basis of feminism in "a politics of everyday life." And similarly, in his more recent work, for instance "The Blackness of Blackness: A Critique of the Sign of the Signifying Monkey," Gates argues for a material basis of his theoretical explorations by translating them into the black idiom, renaming principles of criticism where appropriate, and naming indigenous principles of criticism.

The black woman as critic, and more broadly as the locus where gender-, class-, and race-based oppression intersect, is often invoked when Anglo-American feminists and male Afro-Americanists begin to rematerialize their discourse. This may be the case because the move away from historical specificity associated with deconstruction resembles all too closely the totalizing tendency commonly associated with androcentric criticism. In other words, when historical specificity is denied or remains implicit, all the women are presumed white, all the blacks male. The move to include black women as historical presences and as speaking subjects in critical discourse may well then be used as a defense against charges of racial hegemony on the part of white women and sexist hegemony on the part of black males.

Meese ensures that the discourse of feminism grounds her explorations into deconstructive practice by unifying her chapters around the problems of race, class, and sexual preference. She thus offers readings not only of works by Mary Wilkins Freeman, Marilynne Robinson, Tillie Olsen and Virginia Woolf, but also of the fiction of Alice Walker and Zora Neale Hurston. The politics of de Lauretis's introduction are likewise undergirded in the material conditions of working women's lives. She buttresses, for instance, her observations about the conflicting claims of different feminisms with evidence drawn from a speech by the black feminist activist, writer, and attorney Flo Kennedy. And in her critique of the (white) feminist discourse in sexuality, she cites Hortense Spillers's work on the absence of feminist perspectives on black women's sexuality. Zora Neale Hurston, Phillis Wheatley, Alice Walker, and Rebecca Cox Jackson, the black Shaker visionary, ground Gates's essay "Writing 'Race' and the Difference It Makes," just as discussions of writings by Hurston and Linda Brent are central to Baker's consideration of the economics of a new American literary history.

That the black woman appears in all of these texts as a historicizing presence testifies to the power of the insistent voices of black feminist literary and cultural critics. Yet it is striking that at precisely the moment when Anglo-American feminists and male Afro-Americanists begin to reconsider the material ground of their enterprise, they demonstrate their return to earth, as it were, by invoking the specific experiences of black women and the writings of black women. This association of black women with reembodiment resembles rather closely the association, in classic Western philosophy and in nineteenth-century cultural constructions of womanhood, of women of color with the body and therefore with animal passions and slave labor. Although in these theoretical contexts the impulse to rehistoricize produces insightful readings and illuminating theories, and is politically progressive and long overdue, nevertheless the link between black women's experiences and "the material" seems conceptually problematic.

If *Tootsie* can help us understand the white male theorists' use of feminism, I suggest that Amy Jones's 1987 film *Maid to Order* might offer a perspective on the use of the black woman or the black feminist in Anglo-American feminist or Afro-Americanist discourse. *Maid to Order* is a comic fantasy about a spoiled, rich white young woman from Beverly Hills (played by Ally Sheedy) who is sent by her fairy godmother (played by Beverly D'Angelo) to work as a maid in the home of a ludicrously *nouveau riche* agent and his wife in Malibu. She shares responsibilities with two other maids—one black, played by Merry Clayton, and one Latina, played by Begona Plaza. From the experience of deprivation and from her friendship with the black maid, she learns the value of love and labor; she is transformed, in other words, into a better person.

With its subtle critique of the racist policies for hiring domestic help in Southern California, *Maid to Order* seems rather progressive for a popular fantasy film. Yet even within this context, the figure of the black woman is commodified in ways that are familiar from classic cinematic narratives. From movies such as John Stahl's 1934 version of *Imitation of Life* (or Douglas Sirk's 1959 remake) and Fred Zinnemann's 1952 *Member of the Wedding* to a contemporary film such as *Maid to Order*, black women are employed, if not sacrificed, to humanize their white superordinates, to teach them something about the content of their own subject positions. When black women operate in oppositional discourse as a sign for the author's awareness of materialist concerns, then they seem to be fetishized in much the same way as they are in mass culture.

If Anglo-American feminists and male Afro-Americanists are currently in the process of rematerializing their theoretical discourse, black feminists might be said to be emerging into a theoretical phase. The early, archaeological work gave way among black feminists as well to a period in which they offered textual analyses of individual works or clusters of works. Recent, third-stage black feminist work is concerned much less with the silences in other critical traditions; rather, the writings of Susan Willis, Hazel V. Carby, Mary Helen Washington, Dianne F. Sadoff, Deborah E. McDowell, Hortense Spillers, and others have become increasingly self-conscious and self-reflexive, examining ways in which literary study—the ways in which, for instance, we understand the meaning of influence, the meaning of a tradition, the meaning of literary periods, the meaning of literature itself—changes once questions of race, class, and gender become central to the process of literary analysis. In this third stage, then, black feminist theorists might be said to challenge the conceptualizations of literary study and to concern themselves increasingly with the effect of race, class, and gender on the practice of literary criticism.

Black feminist literary theory proceeds from the assumption that black women experience a unique form of oppression in discursive and nondiscursive practices alike because they are victims at once of sexism, racism, and by extension classism. However, as Elizabeth V. Spelman and Barbara Smith demonstrate separately, one oversimplifies by saying merely that black women experience sexism and racism. "For to say merely *that*, suggests that black women experience one form of oppression, as blacks—the same thing black men experience—and that they experience another form of oppression, as women—the same thing white women experience."[17] Such a formulation erases the specificity of the black woman's experience, constituting her as the point of intersection between black men's and white women's experience.

As an alternative to this position, what Smith calls the additive analysis, black feminist theorists argue that the meaning of blackness in this country shapes profoundly the experience of gender, just as the conditions of womanhood affect ineluctably the experience of race. Precisely because the conditions of the black woman's oppression are thus specific and complex, black feminist literary theorists seek particularized methodologies that might reveal the ways in which that oppression is represented in literary texts. These methods are necessarily flexible, holding in balance the three variables of race, gender, and class and destabilizing the centrality of any one. More generally, they call into question a variety of standards of valuation that mainstream feminist and androcentric Afro-Americanist theory might naturalize.

Proceeding from a point related to but different from the centers of these other modes of inquiry, black feminist critics demonstrate that the meaning of political action, work, family, and sexuality, indeed any feature of the experience of culture, varies depending on the material circumstances that surround and define one's point of reference. And as gender and race taken separately determine the conditions not only of oppression but also of liberation, so too does the interplay between these categories give rise to its own conception of liberation.

I want to resist the temptation to define or overspecify the particular questions that a black feminist theoretical approach might pose of a text. But I would characterize black feminist literary theory more broadly by arguing that it seeks to explore representations of black women's lives through techniques of analysis which suspend the variables of race, class, and gender in mutually interrogative relation.

The fiction of tradition represents one theoretical conception to which a number of black feminist theorists return. In a persuasively argued recent essay, Deborah McDowell examines the relationship between novels of racial uplift in the 1920s and recent black fiction.[18] Although Hazel V. Carby asserts in her book, *Reconstructing Womanhood*, that she is not engaged in the process of constructing the contours of a black female literary tradition, yet she establishes a lineage of black women intellectuals engaged in the ideological debates of their time. Mary Helen Washington and Dianne Sadoff likewise consider how race, class, and gender affect, respectively, the meaning of literary influence and the politics of literary reception. I focus here for a moment on the ways in which Washington's "'Taming All That Anger Down': Rage and Silence in Gwendolyn Brooks's Maud Martha"[19] and Sadoff's "Black Matrilineage: The Case of Alice Walker and Zora Neale Hurston"[20] make use of these three variables in their reformulation of the fiction of literary tradition.

In this essay, as in much of her recent writing, Washington argues that the material circumstances of black woman's lives require one to develop revisionist strategies for evaluating and reading their work. She demonstrates here that precisely because the early reviewers and critics failed to comprehend the significance of race and gender for both a black woman writer and a young black urban girl, they trivialized Brooks and her only novel, a text made up of vignettes which are themselves comprised of short, declarative sentences.

Contemporary reviewers likened Brooks's style "to the exquisite delicacy of a lyric poem," Washington writes. They gave it "the kind of ladylike treatment that assured its dismissal."[21] But by examining the subtext of color prejudice, racial self-hatred, sexual insecurity, and powerlessness that underlies virtually every chapter, Washington demonstrates that the structure and grammar of the novel enact not what one reviewer called the protagonist's "spunk," but rather her repressed anger. In her discussion of the historical conditions that circumscribe the lives of black women in the 1940s and 1950s, Washington suggests ways in which Maud's oppression recalls Brooks's own marginal position within the publishing industry. Brooks inscribes not only Maud Martha's frustration, then, but also her own.

Washington's discussion here considers as well Brooks's reluctance to represent black women as heroic figures as a further sign of her oppression by a racist and sexist literary establishment. She thus prompts not only new readings of the text, but also of the relation between author and character. Indeed, Washington's discussion, turning as it does on the representation of the circumstances of Maud's life, enables a redefinition of the way a range of texts in the Afro-American canon are read. In her words, "if Maud Martha is considered an integral part of the Afro-American canon, we will have to revise our conception of power and powerlessness, of heroism, of symbolic landscapes and ritual grounds."[22]

In her article, Dianne Sadoff argues that black women writers share neither the anxiety of influence Harold Bloom attributes to male writers nor the primary anxiety of authority Sandra Gilbert and Susan Gubar attribute to white women writers. Rather, she demonstrates that "race and class oppression intensify the black woman writer's need to discover an untroubled matrilineal heritage. In celebrating her literary foremothers, the contemporary black woman writer covers over more profoundly than does the white writer her ambivalence about matrilineage, her own misreading of precursors, and her link to an oral as well as a written tradition."[23]

Sadoff's examination of the relationship between Zora Neale Hurston and Alice Walker reveals a compelling tension between the explicit subjects of each author's work and the subversive material that underlies those surfaces. An ancestor claimed as significant by most recent black women writers, Zora Neale Hurston misrepresents herself within her fiction, Sadoff argues. *Their Eyes Were Watching God* may announce itself, for instance, as a celebration of heterosexual love, but Hurston manipulates narrative strategies to ensure that the male is eliminated and the female liberated. Sadoff goes on to show that Walker affirms her tie to Hurston by inscribing a similar double agenda throughout her work, problematizing the status of heterosexual love in similar ways. Moreover, while her essays document her enthusiastic pursuit of Hurston as a literary foremother, her novels display a profound anxiety about biological motherhood. Sadoff's readings demonstrate, then, that the peril of uniqueness compels an intense need on the part of black women writers to identify a literary matrilineage even as their historical circumstances occasion their ambivalence about the fact and process of mothering.

These two essays thus show that the black feminist enterprise, at this stage necessarily materialist, calls for a reconception of the politics of literary reception, the meaning of literary influence, and the content of literary tradition.

At this point in its evolution, black feminist literary theory does not yet appear to replicate the totalizing tendency I attributed to Anglo-American feminism and male Afro-Americanism earlier. No doubt because it has remained marginal, what has been primarily a heterosexual, Afro-American-centered feminist discourse has been concerned with refining its own mode of inquiry, perhaps at the expense of annexing to itself the experiences of "others" such as lesbians and other women of color.

Fiction by black women has, however, achieved significant visibility operating simultaneously as a body of texts both marginal and mainstream. Andrea Lee's *Sarah Phillips* thematizes this very issue and suggests that the very activity of conceptualizing the self as insider may occasion a fetishization of the "other."

The stories that make up Andrea Lee's *Sarah Phillips* appeared separately in *The New Yorker* magazine before they were collected and published together in 1984. This fact about the publishing history alone suggests that in at least one way this is a text of privilege; the content of the stories themselves also foregrounds the issue of class position. Each story is a vignette taken from the life of the title character, the daughter of a prosperous Baptist minister and his schoolteacher wife. With the exception of the first, entitled "In France," the stories are arranged chronologically to sketch Sarah Phillips's girlhood and adolescence in private schools and progressive summer camps in and around Philadelphia, undergraduate years at Harvard, and obligatory expatriation to Europe after graduation.

In addition to their common subject, the majority of the stories share a common structure. Most of the stories establish a community of insiders, disparate voices brought into unison, poised in a continuous present. In each instance, the stasis achieved by the choice of verb tenses, imagery, and patterns of allusion is interrupted by the presence of an outsider, some-one who is constituted as the "other" according to the characteristics and assumptions of the narrative community. In virtually every instance, the presence of this "other" serves to historicize a vignette that had existed for the narrator as a moment out of time. The stories thus enact a tension between the narrative of the community of privilege, posited as ahistorical, and a destabilizing eruption, posited as inescapably historical.

Contemporary reviews identified two problematic areas of the text—the significance of Sarah's class position and the ambiguous relation between narrator and protagonist. Mary Helen Washington places it in a tradition with William Wells Brown's *Clotel*, Frances E. W. Harper's *Iola Leroy*, and James Weldon Johnson's *Autobiography of an Ex-Colored Man*, all works about a privileged black narrator tenuously connected to his or her blackness who needs to escape the problematic meanings of that identity. Washington argues that in these other novels, in varying degrees the narrators recognize the complex interplay between issues of class and race. The narrator of *Sarah Phillips*, in contrast, participates in the character's capitulation to her own position. Washington writes: "By the fourth or fifth story, I felt that the privileged kid had become the privileged narrator, no longer willing to struggle over issues of race and class, unable to bear the 'alarming knowledge' that these issues must reveal."[24]

Sherley Anne Williams compares the text to Richard Wright's *Black Boy*, arguing that both works "literally and figuratively [renounce] oral culture and black traditions for personal autonomy." She remarks that *Sarah Phillips* holds up to mockery "not the pretensions of her upper middle class heroine, but the 'outworn rituals' of black community."[25]

Both reviews suggest a point of contrast between Lee on the one hand and other contemporary black women writers who construct fictional com-munities of privilege. Toni Morrison, like Paule Marshall, Gloria Naylor, and Ntozake Shange, to name but a few, occasionally centers her novels on middle-class black characters. But as Susan Willis has written, in Morrison's novels, black middle-class life is generally characterized by a measure of alienation from the cultural heritage of the black rural South. Her characters are saved from "the upper reaches of bourgeois reification" by "eruptions of 'funk'"—characters or experiences that invoke the characters' cultural past and repressed emotional lives.[26] The energy of the text is thus in every case with the characters who represent "funk": Sula, Pilate, Son, even Cholly Breedlove; Morrison consistently problematizes what it means to be black and privileged.

Lee's narrator, on the other hand, seems as alienated from outsiders as the protagonist does. The text is sufficiently invested in its own construction of what it means to be privileged that it marginalizes those different from the protagonist herself. Rather than disparage *Sarah Phillips* on the basis of its politics, however, I should like to consider ways in which the "other" is figured here. For it seems to me that like the examples drawn earlier from feminist and Afro-Americanist discourse, this text also equates that "other" with the historical or the material.

My argument focuses primarily on a story entitled "Gypsies," in which a family of itinerants disrupt the orderliness of Sarah's suburban girlhood and force at least a symbolic acknowledgment of her place in a broader historical reality. But I begin with a reading of "In France," the story with which the volume begins, for it establishes a perspective by means of which the other stories may be read.

"In France" violates the chronological arrangement of stories, since it recounts the most recent events in the protagonist's life. The story breaks the pattern of the other stories in the volume in yet another way, for it is the only one to situate Sarah as an alien in her environment. The reader learns at once that Sarah is an American in Paris, but her story is filtered through the account of another American living there, a girl named Kate who seems to be missing. Rumors circulate that Kate is being held hostage by her present lover and ex-boyfriend lover who were "collecting her allowance and had bought a luxurious Fiat—the same model the Pope drove—with the profits."[27]

As it is recounted here, Kate's story invokes an absent double, underscoring Sarah's isolation. Moreover, the rumor of her mistreatment at the hands of her male friends presages the abuse Sarah's lover Henri and his friends inflict on her later in the story. We learn that after the death of her father and her graduation from Harvard, Sarah "cast off kin and convention in a foreign tongue" (4) and went to study French in Switzerland. Upon meeting Henri she leaves school and moves into the Paris apartment he shares with his friends Alain and Roger. Together they spend their time in cafés, museums, their apartment, and on occasional weekend expeditions into the country. The story turns on one such trip to the island of Jersey, when ostensibly harmless banter among the four of them suddenly turns nasty.

In this exchange Henri verbally assaults Sarah with racial insults, saying:

Did you ever wonder . . . why our beautiful Sarah is such a mixture of races? . . . It's a very American tale. This *Irlandaise* was part redskin, and not only that but part Jew as well—some Americans are part Jew, aren't they? And one day this *Irlandaise* was walking through the jungle near New Orleans, when she was raped by a jazz musician as big and black as King Kong, with sexual equipment to match. And from this agreeable encounter was born our little Sarah, *notre Negresse pasteurisée.* (11)

Sarah responds in two ways. In the shock of the moment she recognizes that she cannot ignore this parody of miscegenation. Her class position notwithstanding, she plays some role in the drama of race relations from which such stereotypes derive. Several hours later, the meaning of the insult strikes her again, this time in a dream—one that impels her to return home: "I awoke with a start from a horrid dream in which I was conducting a monotonous struggle with an old woman with a dreadful spidery strength in her arms; her skin was dark and leathery, and she smelled like one of the old Philadelphia churchwomen who used to babysit with me" (14).

The dream prompts her to reflect more calmly on the fact that she will never be able to escape the call of her personal history. She remarks:

> I had hoped to join the ranks of dreaming expatriates for whom Paris can become a self-sufficient universe, but my life there had been no more than a slight hysteria, filled with the experimental naughtiness of children reacting against their training. It was clear, much as I did not want to know it, that my days in France had a number, that for me the bright, frank, endlessly beckoning horizon of the runaway had been, at some point, transformed into a complicated return. (15)

The story thus suggests that the past is inescapable. It anticipates Sarah's return home even though that return remains undramatized. I would argue that the subsequent stories, all of which center on events from Sarah's earlier life, function symbolically as that return home. The recurrent patterns that run through these other vignettes recapitulate the tension within the first story between escape and return. They indicate that the past may elude integration into the present, but it can also never be avoided.

In "Gypsies," the narrator attributes to Franklin Place, the street on which Sarah grows up, the ubiquity of a symbol. The opening description works against historical or geographical specificity, and instead represents the neighborhood in terms of the icons of upper-middle-class suburban culture. That is to say, in the opening paragraph the narrator locates the street in her dreams and nightmares, in her patterns of associations, before she locates it in a Philadelphia suburb. In this description, the suburb is represented as an abstraction, the fulfillment of a fantasy, distinct from the conditions of the world outside its boundaries:

> Franklin Place, the street that ran like a vein through most of my dreams and nightmares, the stretch of territory I automatically envisioned when someone said "neighborhood," lay in a Philadelphia suburb. The town was green and pretty, but had the constrained, slightly unreal atmosphere of a colony or a foreign enclave, that was because the people who owned the rambling houses behind the shrubbery were black. For them—doctors, ministers, teachers who had grown up in Philadelphia row houses—the lawns and tree-lined streets represented the fulfillment of a fantasy long deferred, and acted as a barrier against the predictable cruelty of the world. (39)

If this opening paragraph bestows a quality of unreality on the landscape against which this and several of the other stories take place, subsequent paragraphs render the world beyond the neighborhood even more ephemeral. From the narrator's perspective, historical events and political struggle represent levels of experience with which one may engage, but only imaginatively, the songs of cicadas providing a musical transition from Franklin Place to the world of those less privileged. As the narrator remarks:

> For as long as I could remember, the civil rights movement had been unrolling like a dim frieze behind the small pleasures and defeats of my childhood; it seemed

dull, a necessary burden on my conscience, like good grades or hungry people in India. My occasional hair-raising reveries of venturing into the netherworld of Mississippi or Alabama only added a voluptuous edge to the pleasure of eating an ice-cream cone while seated on a shady curb of Franklin Place. (39–40)

The image of the civil rights movement as a frieze fixes and aestheticizes the process of historical change, as if the inertia of Sarah's life had afflicted the world beyond the parameters of her neighborhood.

The illusion of timelessness and unassailability is sustained additionally by the narrator's tendency to cast the particular in terms of the habitual or familiar through her use of the second-person pronoun and the English equivalent of the French imperfect tense. For even as she narrows the focus of the story to the time of her encounter with the gypsies, the narrator describes that particular day in terms that homogenize or encompass, terms that, in other words, move away from particularity. Indeed, the impulse toward generalization and away from particularity is rendered nowhere more clearly than in the description of Sarah in which she is described as if she were a twin of her best friend Lyn Yancey.

On the day in question, a battered red pickup truck bearing its load of log furniture and a family of gypsies disturbs the peace of Franklin Place, a neighborhood of sedans, station wagons, and sports cars. Neither black nor white, the gypsies defy the categories available to Sarah and Lyn: the wife's breasts swaying back and forth in a way in which "the well-contained bosoms of [their] mothers never do" (43). Despite their marginal status, the gypsies articulate the assumptions about race and class shared by the majority culture. "It's a real crime for colored to live like this," says the wife. "You are very lucky little girls, very lucky, do you understand? When my son was your age he never got to play like you girls" (43).

At dinner that evening, Sarah repeats for her family her conversation with the gypsies. The exchange that ensues disrupts the veneer of family harmony, introducing social reality into the magic of the private sphere. Her father, ordinarily a man of great restraint, loses his sense of decorum. "Most of the world despises gypsies, but a gypsy can always look down on a Negro! Heck, that fellow was right to spit! You can dress it up with trees and big houses and people who don't stink too bad, but a nigger neighborhood is still a nigger neighborhood" (44).

Sarah and Lyn later meet at the swim club. The narrator's description of the pool at night betrays if not the young girls' yearnings, then her own nostalgia for the familiar tranquility. The language thus shifts dramatically from the father's clipped vernacular speech. Their rediscovered contentment lasts only until the return home, however, for on the street they confront the gypsies again, an insistent presence that cannot be ignored. The final paragraph of the story suggests that the protagonist's life has been altered profoundly. The narrator remarks, "nothing looked different, yet everything was, and for the first time Franklin Place seemed genuinely connected to a world that was neither insulated nor serene. Throughout the rest of the summer, on the rare occasions when a truck appeared in our neighborhood,

Lyn and I would dash to see it, our hearts pounding with perverse excitement and a fresh desire for knowledge" (46). This final formulation resonates with a certain falseness; the narrator allows Sarah and Lyn the freedom to be entertained by historical events, as if the dim frieze of the civil rights movement might somehow amuse or stimulate them. Indeed, throughout the collection, stories conclude with similar ambivalence; Lee leaves unresolved the issue as to whether the insiders' acknowledgment of the other is symbolic or transformative.

The story thus constitutes a community of insiders rendered ahistorical and homogeneous by the allusions, descriptions, and grammar of the narrator. The presence of someone from outside of that community reminds the residents of Franklin Place of the contingencies on which their apparently stable lives are founded. Simultaneously, the outsider reminds the privileged community of the circumstances of their history. The exchange destabilizes the narrator's ability to totalize the experience the story describes.

Lee's persistent interest in eruptions into communities of privilege causes these stories to be useful texts within which to observe the relation between the presence of the "other" in theoretical discourse. The black woman protagonist in these stories locates herself within, rather than outside of, the normative community, be it an integrated camp for middle-class children, her neighborhood, or her family. Her very presence within these exclusionary communities suggests that the circumstances of race and gender alone protect no one from the seductions of reading her own experience as normative and fetishizing the experience of the other.

This essay offers three perspectives on the contemporary black feminist enterprise. It shows how black feminism is invoked in mainstream feminist and Afro-Americanist discourse, it presents in broad outlines the space black feminist theory occupies independently, and it suggests how one contemporary black woman novelist thematizes the relationship between those who occupy privileged discursive spaces and the "other."

I have approached the subject from three perspectives in part because of my own evident suspicion of totalizing formulations. But my approach reflects as well the black feminist skepticism about the reification of boundaries that historically have excluded the writing of black women from serious consideration within the academic and literary establishments. Since, to my mind, some of the most compelling and representative black feminist writing treads the boundary between anthology and criticism, or between cultural theory and literary theory, it seems appropriate that a consideration of this critical perspective would approach it from a variety of points of view.

Notes

1. Elaine Showalter, "Critical Cross-Dressing: Male Feminists and the Woman of the Year," in Alice Jardine and Paul Smith, eds., *Men in Feminism* (New York: Methuen, 1987), 127.

2. Hazel V. Carby, *Reconstructing Womanhood: The Emergence of the Afro-American Woman Novelist* (New York: Oxford University Press, 1987), 9.

3. Mary Helen Washington, "Introduction," in Mary Helen Washington, ed., *Black-Eyed Susans: Classic Stories by and about Black Women* (Garden City, N.Y.: Anchor Books, 1975), x–xxxii.

4. See Barbara Smith, "Toward a Black Feminist Criticism," *Conditions Two* I (October 1977), and Deborah E. McDowell, "New Directions for Black Feminist Criticism," *Black American Literature Forum* 14. Both were reprinted in Elaine Showalter, ed., *The New Feminist Criticism: Essays on Women, Literature and Theory* (New York: Pantheon, 1985), 168–185 and 186–199, respectively.

5. See, for instance, the reprint series that McDowell edits for Beacon Press and her Rutgers University Press reprint of Nella Larsen's *Quicksand* and *Passing*; Washington's three anthologies, *Black-Eyed Susans, Midnight Birds*, and *Invented Lives* and her Feminist Press edition of Paule Marshall's *Brown Girl, Brownstones*; Nellie McKay's edition of Louise Meriwether's *Daddy Was a Number Runner*; and Gloria T. Hull's edition of Alice Dunbar-Nelson's diary, *Give Us Each Day*, to name but a few. Black women are not exclusively responsible for these kinds of editorial projects. See also William Andrews, *Sisters of the Spirit: Three Black Women's Autobiographies of the Nineteenth Century*; Henry Louis Gates's edition of Harriet E. Wilson's *Our Nig* and his Oxford University Press reprint series; and Jean Fagan Yellin's edition of Harriet Jacobs's *Incidents in the Life of a Slave Girl*.

6. Peggy Kamuf, "Replacing Feminist Criticism," *Diacritics* 12 (Summer 1982): 44.

7. Nancy K. Miller, "The Text's Heroine: A Feminist Critic and Her Fictions," *Diacritics* 12 (Summer 1982): 49–50.

8. Elizabeth A. Meese, *Crossing the Double-Cross: The Practice of Feminist Criticism* (Chapel Hill: University of North Carolina Press, 1986).

9. Teresa de Lauretis, "Feminist Studies/Critical Studies: Issues, Terms, and Contexts," in Teresa de Lauretis, ed., *Feminist Studies/Critical Studies* (Bloomington: Indiana University Press, 1986), 2.

10. Ibid., 9.

11. Ibid., 10.

12. Houston A. Baker, Jr., *Blues, Ideology, and Afro-American Literature* (Chicago: University of Chicago Press, 1984).

13. See Robert B. Stepto, "Teaching Afro-American Literature: Survey or Tradition: The Reconstruction of Instruction," and Henry Louis Gates, Jr., "Preface to Blackness: Text and Pretext," both in Dexter Fisher and Robert B. Stepto, eds., *Afro-American Literature: The Reconstruction of Instruction* (New York: Modern Language Association of America, 1979), 8–24 and 44–69, respectively.

14. Robert B. Stepto, *From Behind the Veil: A Study of Afro-American Narrative* (Urbana: University of Illinois Press, 1979).

15. Baker, *Blues*, 94.

16. Ibid., 101.

17. Elizabeth V. Spelman, "Theories of Race and Gender: The Erasure of Black Women," *Quest* 5 (1979): 42.

18. Deborah E. McDowell, " 'The Changing Same': Generational Connections and Black Women Novelists," *New Literary History* 18 (Winter 1987).

19. Mary Helen Washington, " 'Taming All That Anger Down': Rage and Silence in Gwendolyn Brooks's *Maud Martha*," in Henry Louis Gates, Jr., ed., *Black Literature and Literary Theory* (New York: Methuen, 1984), 249–262.

20. Dianne F. Sadoff, "Black Matrilineage: The Case of Alice Walker and Zora Neale Hurston," *Signs* 11 (Autumn 1985): 4–26.

21. Washington, "Taming," 249.

22. Ibid., 260.

23. Sadoff, "Black Matrilineage," 5.

24. Mary Helen Washington, "Young, Gifted and Black," *Women's Review of Books* 2 (March 1985): 3.

25. Sherley Anne Williams, "Roots of Privilege: New Black Fiction," *Ms.* 13 (June 1985): 71.

26. See Susan Willis, "Eruptions of Funk: Historicizing Toni Morrison," in *Specifying: Black Women Writing the American Experience* (Madison: University of Wisconsin Press, 1987), 83–109.

27. Andrea Lee, *Sarah Phillips* (New York: Penguin Books, 1984), 3. Subsequent references to this edition are noted in the text by page number.

[1989]

Biography

ETEL ADNAN (b. 1925) is the author of the novel *Sitt Marie Rose*, which has been translated into several languages, as well as several volumes of poetry. In 1972, she returned to Lebanon, where she worked for several years before moving to France. She has produced two documentaries on Lebanon at war.

AI (PELORHANKHE OGAWA) (b. 1947) is the daughter of a Japanese father and an African American, Choctaw Indian, and Irish mother. Her poetry collections include *Cruelty, Killing Floor*, which was the 1978 Lamont Poetry Selection, and *Sin*, which won the Before Columbus Foundation American Book Award in 1986. She has received fellowships from the National Endowment for the Arts and the Guggenheim Foundation. Her poems have appeared in *Antaeus, Choice, American Poetry Review*, and the *American Poetry Anthology*. Ai is writer-in-residence at the College of the Holy Cross.

PAULA GUNN ALLEN (b. 1939) is of Laguna/Lakota and Lebanese-Jewish descent. In 1986, she published *The Sacred Hoop: Recovering the Feminine in American Indian Traditions*, now in its second edition. She is also the author of *Indian Perspectives, Grandmothers of the Light: A Medicine Woman's Sourcebook*, five books of poetry, and a novel.

MAYA ANGELOU (b. 1928) is an African American poet, screenwriter, actor, activist, producer, and storyteller. She has also been a Creole cook, a streetcar conductor, a waiter, a dancer, a madam, an unwed mother, a singer, a playwright, an editor for an English-language magazine in Egypt, a lecturer, and a civil rights activist. Her works include a five-part autobiographical series: *I Know Why the Caged Bird Sings*, which won the National Book Award, *Gather Together in My Name, Singin' and Swingin' and Gettin' Merry Like Christmas, The Heart of a Woman*, and *All God's Children Need Traveling Shoes*. She also has written four collections of poetry, including *Shaker, Why Don't You Sing?* and *And Still I Rise*. She is the Z. Smith Reynolds Professor of American Studies at Wake Forest University. Angelou composed and read the poem "A Rock, a River, a Tree" for President Bill Clinton's inauguration in 1993.

GLORIA ANZALDÚA (b. 1942) is a Chicana lesbian who has taught Chicano studies, feminist studies, and creative writing. She is the editor of *Making Face, Making Soul: Haciendo Caras* and the author of *Borderlands/La Front-*

era: The New Mestiza. She coedited *This Bridge Called My Back* with Cherríe Moraga, which won the 1986 Before Columbus Foundation American Book Award. Her work has also appeared in journals such as *Bilingual Review* and *Conditions.*

TONI CADE BAMBARA (b. 1939) is a free-lance writer and lecturer. She is a well-known and respected civil rights activist and the editor of three anthologies of African American literature: *The Black Woman, Tales and Stories for Black Folks,* and *Southern Black Utterances Today.* Her other works include the novels *If Blessing Comes* and *The Salt Eaters,* which won the 1981 American Book Award, the short-story collection *Gorilla, My Love,* and many screenplays. She took the name Bambara from a signature she found in her great-grandmother's trunk.

S. BRANDI BARNES is an African American poet and journalist. She has been the recipient of the Gwendolyn Brooks Poet Laureate Award, the Literary Excellence Award from Columbia College, and a Robert McCormick Fellowship. She has contributed to numerous literary magazines, anthologies, and newspapers, and she has published a collection of poetry, *BlackBerries in the ChinaCabinet.*

ESMERALDA BERNAL has studied in the history of consciousness program at the University of California, Santa Cruz. Her research centers on indigenous women and the social construction of gender under colonialism.

MEI-MEI BERSSENBRUGGE (b. 1947) has been the recipient of two grants from the National Endowment for the Arts and a Before Columbus Foundation American Book Award. A Chinese American playwright and poet, she has served as a member of the board of Tooth of Time Press. Her collection of poetry, *Empathy,* was published in 1987, and she has staged her play *One, Two Cups* in New York City and Seattle. Her most recent works are *Mizu* and *Sphericity.*

SUJATA BHATT (b. 1956), who was born in India and came to the United States in 1968, has a M.F.A. from the Writer's Workshop of Iowa State University. Since her first book, *Brunizem* (1988), she has contributed to numerous journals, including *Painted Bird Quarterly, Calyx, Iowa Journal of Literary Studies,* and *Yellow Silk.* Her poetry has been published in the United States, Ireland, and England.

NORA BROOKS BLAKELY has been around the arts all her life, as the daughter of two writers, Gwendolyn Brooks and Henry Blakely. A former teacher in the Chicago Public Schools, she has also been a member of several Chicago arts organizations, including Kuumba Theatre, Muntu Dance Theatre, and the Organization of Black American Culture Writers Workshop. In addition to her poetry, Blakely writes articles, plays, and stories for children and young adults. She is the founder and director of Chocolate Chips Theatre Company, an adult company that presents plays for young people.

BETH BRANT (b. 1941) is a Bay of Quinte Mohawk from Tyendinage Mohawk who belongs to the Turtle clan. She is a lesbian mother and grandmother. She is editor of *A Gathering of Spirit: A Collection by North American Indian Women* and author of *Foods and Spirits* and *Mohawk Trail*.

GWENDOLYN BROOKS (b. 1917) has received many awards and honors; notably, she was the first African American to win the Pulitzer Prize for Poetry (in 1950 for *Annie Allen*). Her works, which include the poetry collections *Black Love, To Disembark, The Near Johannesburg Bay, and Other Poems,* and *Winnie* and the novel *Maud Martha,* are concerned with the tragic and comic instances of the black person's experience in a world where race is important. She has also written several children's books, which include *Bronzeville Boys and Girls* and *The Tiger Who Wore White Gloves,* and an autobiography, *Report from Part One.*

LORNA DEE CERVANTES (b. 1954) explores themes of identity, domestic violence, and social oppression from a feminist viewpoint in her first book, *Emplumada* (1981), which won the Before Columbus Foundation American Book Award. She has contributed poems to *Samisdat, London Meadow Quarterly,* and *Revista Chicano-Rigueña,* among other journals. Her honors include a National Endowment for the Arts Fellowship in 1979 and the London Meadow Fellowship. Cervantes teaches at the University of Colorado.

SUCHENG CHAN is a professor of history and the director of Asian-American Studies of the University of California, Santa Barbara. She held a Guggenheim Fellowship in 1988–89. Her book *This Bittersweet Soil: The Chinese in California Agriculture, 1860–1910* won the 1988 Association for Asian American Studies Book Award, the 1987 American Historical Association Pacific Coast Branch Book Award, and the 1986 Theodore Saloutos Award in Agricultural History.

DIANA CHANG (b. 1934) was born in New York City but spent much of her early life in China. A writer and a painter, she has written two collections of poetry, including *What Matisse Is After* and *Saying Yes,* and six novels, among them *The Frontiers of Love* and *A Woman of Thirty.* She has also been an editor in various publishing houses and a contributor in solo and group art exhibitions.

DENISE CHÁVEZ (b. 1948) has written numerous plays and stories that have been produced and published throughout the Southwest. The title work of her short-story collection *The Last of the Menu Girls* won the 1986 Steele Jones Fiction Award. She has been the recipient of several honors, including a National Endowment for the Arts InterArts grant to produce her play *Hecho en Mexico* and a Rockefeller Playwright grant.

EILEEN CHERRY was born in Toledo, Ohio, and began writing at fourteen. Her poetry and fiction has appeared in *Black World, Nommo, Spoon River Quarterly,* and *Callaloo,* among others. She received an Illinois Arts Council

Creative Fellowship and the Gwendolyn Brooks Poet Laureate Award. She lives in Chicago.

MARILYN (MEI LING) CHIN (b. 1955) is professor of creative writing at San Diego State University. Much of her work involves translating the work of contemporary Chinese poets. Her poetry collections include *Dwarf Bamboo* and *The Phoenix Gone, The Terrace Empty*.

BARBARA CHRISTIAN (b. 1943) is an African-American writer and professor of Afro-American Studies at the University of California, Berkeley. She is currently working on a collection of contemporary African-American feminist essays. She has been a contributor to *Black Scholar* and *Journal of Ethnic Studies*. Her works include *Teaching Guide to Black Foremothers*, *Black Feminist Criticism: Perspectives on Black Women Writers*, and *Black Women Novelists: Development of a Tradition, 1892–1976*.

CHRYSTOS (b. 1946) is a lesbian Native American, Menominee tribe, Indigenous Land and Treaty Rights activist. She is also a self-educated speaker, artist, and writer. Her works include *Not Vanishing* and *Dream On*. She received a National Endowment for the Arts Fellowship in 1990.

SANDRA CISNEROS (b. 1954) is the daughter of a Mexican father and Chicana mother. Her collections of stories include *My Wicked, Wicked Ways* and *Woman Hollering Creek*. Her young-adult book *The House on Mango Street* won the 1985 Before Columbus Foundation American Book Award. She has taught at several universities and is associate editor for *Third Woman* literary journal. She has also been the recipient of two National Endowment for the Arts Fellowships, one in poetry and one in fiction.

PEARL CLEAGE (b. 1948) is an Atlanta-based African American playwright and poet who serves as artistic director of the Just Us Theater Company and the editor of *Catalyst* magazine. Her works include *Mad at Miles* and the chapbook *One for the Brothers*. Her many plays include *Essentials* and *Good News*. She has received five Audelco Recognition Awards for a member of a black theater—one in 1983 for *Hospice*—and a Seed Grant in 1987 from the Coordinating Council of Literary Magazines for *Catalyst*. Her works also have appeared in *Readers and Writers*, *New York Times Book Review*, and *Southern Voices*.

LUCILLE CLIFTON (b. 1936) lives in Maryland and California, where she teaches at the University of Santa Cruz, and is the author of several books of poetry, including *Good Times: Poems*, *An Ordinary Woman*, and *Two-Headed Woman*. She is also the author of several children's books, including *Sonora Beautiful*, *My Friend Jacob*, *The Lucky Stone*, *Amifika*, and the *Everett Anderson* series. She was poet laureate of Maryland.

JUDITH ORTIZ COFER (b. 1952), who was born in Puerto Rico and now lives in Georgia, conducts poetry workshops and gives poetry readings. Most of her poetry centers around her family. Her works include the novel *Line of the Sun*, which was nominated for a Pulitzer Prize, the chapbook *Peregrina*, and her 1990 book *Silent Dancing: A Partial Remembrance of a Puerto Rican Childhood*. She received a National Endowment for the Arts Fellowship in 1989.

PATRICIA HILL COLLINS (b. 1948) is a professor of Afro-American studies and sociology at the University of Cincinnati. Her works include *Black Feminist Thought: Knowledge, Consciousness, and the Politics of Empowerment*.

ELIZABETH COOK-LYNN (b. 1930) is a member of the Crow Creek Sioux tribe. She is associate professor emeritus at Eastern Washington University and is the author of *Then Badger Said This*, a book of poetry, and *The Power of Horses and Other Stories*. Her literary criticism has appeared in the CCCC *Journal* and *Indian Historian*, and her poetry has been published in *South Dakota Review* and *Prairie Schooner*.

LUCHA CORPI (b. 1945), who was born in Mexico and then emigrated to the United States, is the author of the poetry collection *Palabras de mediodía: Noon Words* and the novel *Delia's Song*. She was awarded a National Endowment for the Arts Fellowship in 1979 and won first prize in the *Palabra nueva* literary contest in 1983. Corpi writes predominantly in Spanish.

JAYNE CORTEZ was born in Arizona, grew up in California, and lives in New York City. She is author of eight books and producer of five recordings of poetry. Her most recent book is *Poetic Magnetic* and her latest recording is "Everywhere Drums." Her work has been published in journals, magazines, and anthologies such as *Women on War*, *Early Ripening*, *Powers of Desire*, *The Poetry of Black America*, *Free Spirits*, *Black Scholar*, and *UNESCO Courier*. She is the recipient of several awards: the National Endowment for the Arts, American Book Award and the New York Artists Foundation Award for poetry. Her work has been translated into many languages. She has lectured and read her poetry with and without music throughout the United States, Africa, Europe, Latin America, and the Caribbean.

THADIOUS M. DAVIS (b. 1944) is professor of English at Brown University, where she teaches courses in African American, Southern, and women's literature. She has been publishing poetry since the 1960s and continues to write poems in love and hope.

ANGELA DE HOYOS (b. 1940) is a Mexican-born painter and poet. Her works, which have been published in the United States and abroad, have appeared in, among others, *Caracol*, *Tejidos*, *Fuego de Aztlan*, and *Revista Chicano-Requeña*. Her books include *Selected Poems–Selecciones* and *Woman, Woman*. Her many art and literary awards include second prize for poetry in the CSSI International Competition, Italy.

RITA DOVE (b. 1952) is associate editor of *Callaloo*, a journal of African American and African arts and letters, and she teaches creative writing at the University of Virginia. Her poetry collections include *Grace Notes* and *Thomas and Beulah*, which won the 1987 Pulitzer Prize. Her collection of short stories, *Fifth Sunday*, was the inaugural volume in the Callaloo Fiction Series. In 1993, Dove was named poet laureate of the United States.

Sue Kunitomi Embrey (b. 1923) has published short stories and articles and is the coeditor of *Contacts and Conflicts—The Asian Immigration Experience*. She has served as the managing editor of the *Manzanar Free Press* in California and on the Los Angeles City Commission on the Status of Women.

Louise Erdrich (b. 1954) is a Turtle Mountain Chippewa. She achieved critical and popular success with her novel *Love Medicine*, which won the 1984 National Book Critics Circle Award for fiction. Previously, she had served as editor of the Boston Indian Council newspaper, *The Circle*. Her works include *Baptism of Desire: Poems* and the novel *The Beet Queen*. Her latest work is *The Crown of Columbus*, which she coauthored with Michael Dorris, her husband. She has also contributed to *Chicago, North American Review, Frontiers*, and the *Atlantic*.

Mari Evans is the author of poems, children's books, stories, plays, and articles. Her poetry, which has been widely anthologized, includes the collections *Night Star: 1973–78, I Am a Black Woman*, and *Where Is All the Music?* Her children's books include *J.D., I Look at Me*, and *Rap Stories*. From 1968 to 1973, Evans wrote, directed, and produced *The Black Experience* for WTTV in Indianapolis.

Guadalupe Valdés Fallis (b. 1941) was born in El Paso but lived in Chihuahua, Mexico, for the first twenty years of her life. She has written about Spanish for Spanish speakers and has been an editor of a Spanish newsletter. She also has taught Spanish at New Mexico State University.

Nikki Giovanni (b. 1943), one of the best known African American poets, has published many books, including the poetry collections *The Women and the Men* and *My House* and the essay collection *Sacred Cows . . . and Other Edibles*. She is a professor at Virginia Polytechnic and State University.

Rebecca Gonzales is the author of the 1985 book *Slow Work to the Rhythm of Cicadas*. Her poems have also appeared in journals such as the *New Mexico Humanities Review* and *Cedar Rock*.

Rayna Green (b. 1942), a Cherokee, is director of the American Indian Program at the National Museum of American History at the Smithsonian Institution. She is the editor of *That's What She Said: Contemporary Fiction and Poetry by American Indian Women*.

Jessica Hagedorn (b. 1949), who was born in the Philippines, is a performance artist, poet, and playwright who commentates *Crossroads* on public radio. Her interest is in postwar popular culture. Her books include *Dangerous Music, Pet Food & Tropical Apparitions*, and *Dogeaters*, which was nominated for a National Book Award. She has had theatrical pieces produced extensively, including at the New York Public Theater.

ELAINE HALL is a member of the Creek tribe and a lesbian who writes poems and stories. She was born in Alabama but now lives in Los Angeles.

JOY HARJO (b. 1951) is a member of the Creek (Muscogee) tribe who edits, writes for the screen, and plays tenor sax. She has published four books of poetry, including *In Mad Love and War* and *She Had Some Horses*, and has made recordings of her poetry. She has also served on the board of directors of the Native American Public Broadcasting Consortium and is professor of creative writing at the University of New Mexico.

LINDA HOGAN (b. 1947) is a member of the Chickasaw tribe interested in rehabilitating wildlife and trying to create world survival techniques. Her works include the novels *Mean Spirit* and *The Failures of Love*, a book of poems, *Hands*, and a collection of short fiction, *The Stories We Hold Secret*, which she coedited. Hogan teaches at the University of Colorado.

BELL HOOKS is the pseudonym of Gloria Watkins (b. 1952). She is a feminist writer and cultural critic. She teaches English and women's studies at Oberlin College. Her books include *Yearning: Race, Gender and Cultural Politics*, *A Woman's Mourning Song*, *Black Looks: Race and Representation*, *Breaking Bread: Insurgent Black Intellectual Life*, and *Ain't I a Woman: Black Women and Feminism*.

ANGELA JACKSON (b. 1951) is a playwright and poet whose works include *Solo in the Boxcar Third Floor E*, *Dark Legs and Silk Kisses: The Beatitudes of the Spinners*, and *And All These Roads Be Luminous*. *When the Wind Blows*, which appeared in Chicago in 1984, is only one of several of her plays that have been produced. Since 1976, she has been the chair of Chicago's Organization of Black American Culture Writers Workshop. In 1977, she was selected to represent the United States at the Second World Festival of Black and African Arts and Culture in Lagos, Nigeria. She received the Pushcart Prize for poetry in 1989.

SANDRA JACKSON-OPOKU is a poet, freelance journalist, and television script writer. Her works have been published in *Black World*, *First World*, *African Woman*, *Essence*, *Open Places*, *Heresies*, and *Black Enterprise*. She is the recipient of a National Endowment for the Arts Fellowship, the New York International Film and TV Silver Medal Award, the General Electric Foundation Award for younger writers, and the DuSable Museum Writers' Conference Hoyt W. Fuller Award.

PATRICIA JONES (b. 1951) has written criticism for *Essence*, *The Village Voice*, and *Live!* Her works include *I Can't Let Go* and *Mythologizing Always: Seven Sonnets*. She also has collaborated on a performance piece, *Women in Research*.

JUNE JORDAN (b. 1936) is a lesbian poet, essayist, and political activist whose poetry and prose have been published in six languages. She is professor of

Afro-American studies and women's studies at the University of California, Berkeley, and has published nineteen books, including *Naming Our Destiny: New and Selected Poems* and *Technical Difficulties: African American Notes on the State of the Union.* In 1991, she published a children's book, *Kimako's Story.*

ALISON KIM is a Chinese Korean born in Hawaii and raised in California. She is a lesbian activist, writer, and artist.

ELAINE H. KIM (b. 1942), professor of Asian American studies at the University of California, Berkeley, has been a member of various university and community organizations, including Asian Women United of California, which promotes social and economic welfare for Asian American women. She was the Asian Women United project director for *With Silk Wings: Asian American Women at Work* and is the author of *Asian American Literature: An Introduction to the Writings and Their Social Context.*

MYUNG MI KIM has taught English as a second language, translated, and tutored. She is the director of Student Support Services at Luther College. She is the author of *Under Flag,* and her poetry has been published in *Ironweed, Antioch Review, Pavement,* and other journals.

JAMAICA KINCAID (b. 1949) is originally from the West Indian island of Antigua. Her works include *Annie John,* an autobiographical novel *A Small Place,* and *Lucy.* In 1983, she received the Morton Dauwen Zabel Award from the American Academy and Institute of Arts and Letters for *At the Bottom of the River,* a collection of short stories. She is also a frequent contributor to the *New Yorker, Rolling Stone,* and *Paris Review.*

GERALDINE KUDAKA (b. 1951) is the daughter of a plantation hand and a maid from Okinawa. She has worked as a free-lance photographer, a writer, a poet-teacher for Poetry in the Schools, and an editor of *Beyond Rice.* Her works have appeared in the anthologies *Third World Women* and *Time to Greez,* and the journals *Greenfield Review* and *Yardbird Reader.*

GENNY LIM (b. 1946) has written poetry and plays, as well as edited a collection of papers on the Chinese American experience and coauthored *Island: Poetry and History of Chinese Immigrants on Angel Island 1910–1940,* which won a Before Columbus Foundation American Book Award in 1982. Her play *Paper Angels* won the 1982 Downtown Villager Award in New York and was adapted for the public television series *American Playhouse* in 1985. She has also published a book of poetry, *Winter Place.*

ABBEY LINCOLN (AMINATA MOSEKA) (b. 1930) is a singer, composer, actor, and poet. She began her career as a singer in California and Hawaii, but went on to motion pictures, appearing in four, including *The Girl Can't Help It* (1957) and *A Short Walk to Daylight* (1972). She has also written two plays, *A Pig in a Poke* and *A Steak O'Lean.*

CLARICE LISPECTOR (1925–1977), who was born in the Ukraine, was raised in Recife and Rio de Janeiro in Brazil. She spent a number of years in the

United States and Europe before settling in Rio de Janeiro. Having first published when she was nineteen, she was the author of several short-story collections and six novels, including *The Apple in the Dark*. She remains one of the most prolific writers in Portuguese. Her work has been translated into French, German, Spanish, English, and Czech.

AUDRE LORDE (1934–1992) was the daughter of Grenadian parents and was a black lesbian feminist poet and essayist. She wrote about lesbian love, racism in the women's movement, and sexism in black communities. Her many volumes of poetry include *The First Cities, Undersong: Chosen Poems Old and New*, and *Our Dead Behind Us: Poems*. In 1974, she was nominated for a National Book Award for *From a Land Where Other People Live*. Her works include the essay collections *Sister Outsider* and the autobiographical novel *Zami: A New Spelling of My Name*. Lorde died of breast cancer.

MARCELA CHRISTINE LUCERO-TRUJILLO (1931–1984) was a Chicana American poet. Her poetry has appeared in anthologies, including *The Third Woman*, and other publications, including *La Luz*.

MARÍA LUGONES (b. 1944), a feminist philosopher and grass-roots political educator and organizer, was born in Buenos Aires, Argentina, but emigrated to the United States in 1967. She has taught at Carleton College and La Escuela Popular Norteña, the New Mexican folk school devoted to radical thinking.

NAOMI LONG MADGETT (b. 1923) is the author of several collections of poetry, including *Octavia and Other Poems*, which won the College Language Association Creative Achievement Award. She is professor emeritus at Eastern Michigan University and an editor at Lotus Press in Detroit.

VALERIE MATSUMOTO is assistant professor of Asian American history and U.S. women's history at University of California, Los Angeles. Her dissertation was a study of three generations of a Japanese American farming community in central California. She is currently researching Nisei women's writings in the 1930s.

TRINH T. MINH-HA (b. 1952) is a writer, filmmaker, and composer. She has published a volume of poetry, *En miniscules*. Her films include *Reassemblage, Naked Spaces—Living Is Round*, and *Surname Viet Given Name Nam*. She is also the author of *When the Moon Waxes Red: Representation, Gender and Cultural Politics*, and *Woman, Native, Other: Writing Postcoloniality and Feminism*.

JANICE MIRIKITANI (b. 1942) is the program director and president of the Corporation at Glide Church/Urban Center in San Francisco. She is the author of *Shedding Silence: Poetry and Prose* and *Awake in the River*. She has edited several books, including *Time to Greez: Incantations from the Third World*.

CHERRÍE MORAGA (b. 1952) is a Chicana feminist lesbian, and her writings reflect her exploration of this identity. She has written poetry, plays, and essays; coedited two collections; and helped found Kitchen Table/Women of Color Press. Her works include the plays *Giving Up the Ghost: Teatro in Two Acts* and *Shadow of a Man*, the volume of poems *Dreaming of Other Planets*, and the anthology *This Bridge Called My Back*, which she coedited with Gloria Anzaldúa and which won the 1986 Before Columbus Foundation American Book Award.

TONI MORRISON (b. 1931) has won many awards, including the 1988 Pulitzer Prize for her novel *Beloved*. Her other novels include *The Bluest Eye, Sula, Song of Solomon, Tar Baby*, and *Jazz*. She also edited *Race-ing Justice, Engendering Power: Essays on Anita Hill, Clarence Thomas, and the Construction of Social Reality*. As a senior editor at Random House, she helps bring into print the works of African American writers. Morrison is also Robert F. Goheen Professor of Humanities at Princeton University.

BHARATI MUKHERJEE (b. 1940) was born in Calcutta and came to the United States in 1961. She has written three novels, including *Wife* and *The Tiger's Daughter*, two books of nonfiction, and two collections of short stories. *The Middleman and Other Stories* won the 1988 National Book Critics Circle Award for fiction.

TAHIRA NAQVI was born in Pakistan and now lives in Connecticut. She has published two anthologies of translations of Urdu short fiction and a collection of her own stories, *Journeys*.

NAOMI SHIHAB NYE (b. 1952) was born in St. Louis to an American mother and a Palestinian father. She published the poetry collection *Different Ways to Pray*, and her poetry has appeared in several anthologies. Her most recent work is an anthology she edited, *This Same Sky: A Collection of Poems from around the World*. Nye lives in San Antonio, Texas.

PAT PARKER (1944–1989) was a poet, activist, mother of two daughters, and a medical administrator. She wrote five volumes of poetry about being African American, female, and gay, including *Movement in Black*. Parker died of breast cancer at the age of forty-five.

ESTELA PORTILLO (b. 1936) is a Chicana playwright, poet, and fiction writer. Her works include *Impressions*, a collection of poetry, *Morality Play*, a musical comedy, and *Sun Images*, a drama. Her writing reflects the quest for self-determination of women and Chicanos, who have been assigned to subservient roles in society.

CARMEN M. PURSIFULL (b. 1930) is a poet whose works include *Carmen by Midnight* and *The Ling Migration to Illinois*. In 1986, she won the University of Illinois La Casa Cultural Latina Award.

TEY DIANA REBOLLEDO has served as director of the women's studies program and has been an associate professor of Spanish at the University of New Mexico. She is editor of *Writing from the Margins* and coauthor of *Infinite Divisions: An Anthology of Chicana Literature*.

DIANA RIVERA has published poems in several journals, including *Seattle Review* and *Bilingual Review* and has had her short fiction appear in *Hispanics in the United States: An Anthology of Creative Literature* and *Sealed Lips*. She is also a painter.

MARINA RIVERA (b. 1942) has written two chapbooks of poetry: *Sobra* and *Mestiza*. Her poetry also was included in *The Face of Poetry* and *Southwest: A Contemporary Anthology*. She donates the profits from her poetry to a group that grants scholarships to talented Chicano youth who otherwise would not have funds to continue in school.

CAROLYN M. RODGERS (b. 1945) is an African American poet whose several books include *Finite Forms: Poems, Morning Glory,* and *Adobe*. Her works also include the novels *A Little Lower Than the Angels* and *Arise* and a collection of short stories, *Rain*. She was a recipient of the Carnegie Award in 1979 and a National Endowment for the Arts grant in 1970. In 1976, *how i got ovah: New and Selected Poems* was nominated for a National Book Award.

WENDY ROSE (b. 1948), the daughter of a Hopi father and a Miwok mixed-blood mother, is active in various Native American organizations and is a former editor of the *American Indian Quarterly*. She is a poet and a painter. In 1985, she published *The Halfbreed Chronicles and Other Poems*. Her earlier works include *What Happened When the Hopi Hit New York, Lost Copper,* and *Builder Kachina: A Home-Going Cycle*. She has contributed to the anthologies *The Fire of Finding: Women Poets of the World, Anthology of Magazine Verse,* and *This Song Remembers* and numerous journals.

GEORGIANA VALOYCE SANCHEZ is from the Pima/Papago and Chumash tribes. She is a high-school dropout who returned to school and eventually received her master's in English literature because she wanted to write about her experience as an American Indian. She believes that real wisdom comes from faith in God and in the old stories of her people.

SONIA SANCHEZ (b. 1934), an African American poet, holds the Laura Cornell Chair in English at Temple University. Since her first book of poetry, *Homecoming* (1969), Sanchez has written more than fifteen books of poetry and juvenile fiction and five plays. She also has been the recipient of many awards. Her poetry collection *homegirls & handgrenades* won the 1985 Before Columbus Foundation American Book Award. In 1988, she received the Peace and Freedom Award from the Women's International League for Peace and Freedom.

YVONNE SAPIA (b. 1946) gives poetry readings, and her poetry has appeared in anthologies. Her writing reconstructs memories, dreams, and reflections to explore relationships. Her books include *The Fertile Crescent* and *Valentino's Hair: Poems*.

NTOZAKE SHANGE (b. 1948) writes dramatic poetry and prose to express her dissatisfaction with the role of black women in society. Her most famous work is *For Colored Girls Who Have Considered Suicide/When the Rainbow Is Enuf: A Choreopoem*, which won a 1977 Obie Award. Her works also include the plays *The Love Space Demands: A Continuing Saga* and *Spell #7*, the poetry collection *Nappy Edges*, and the novels *Sassafras, Cypress & Indigo*, and *Betsey Brown*.

LESLIE MARMON SILKO (b. 1948) is a Laguna who has earned acclaim for her writing about Native Americans. After her novel *Ceremony* became popular, she received greater recognition for her earlier short stories. Her works include the volume of poetry *Laguna Woman*, the short-story collection *The Storyteller*, and most recently, the novel *Almanac of the Dead*.

BARBARA SMITH is a cofounder of Kitchen Table/Women of Color Press, and she has coedited three major collections of writing by African American women. *Conditions V: The Black Women's Issue, All the Women Are White, All the Blacks Are Men, But Some of Us Are Brave: Black Women's Studies*, and *Home Girls: A Black Feminist Anthology*. She is a coauthor with Elly Bulkin and Minne Bruce Pratt of *Yours in Struggle: Three Feminist Perspectives on Anti-Semitism and Racism*. Smith is currently completing a collection of short stories.

VALERIE SMITH (b. 1956) is an executive committee member of the MLA Division of Black American Literature and Culture and teaches at the University of California, Los Angeles. Her most recent book is *Self-Discovery and Authority in Afro-American Narrative*.

CAROL P. SNOW is a native of the Allegany Indian Reservation in New York state. Her tribal affiliation is Seneca. She has two degrees in zoology, and she has written and illustrated numerous reports on endangered and rare species for the United States Bureau of Land Management.

DEBRA SWALLOW (b. 1954) is of the Oglala tribe. She attended Oglala Community College and now lives in South Dakota.

TAHNAHGA is a Mohawk woman with a degree in rehabilitation counseling with an emphasis on chemical dependency and traditional healing methods for Native American people. She has given several poetry readings throughout the Milwaukee area and has been a guest writer/speaker with the Milwaukee ArtReach Board.

MARY TALLMOUNTAIN (b. 1918) is an Athabaskan who has contributed to anthologies of writing by Native Americans. Her fiction and poetry are devoted to social justice and societal problems. Her books include *The Light on the Tent Wall* and *There Is No Word for Goodbye*, which won the Pushcart Prize in 1981.

AMY TAN (b. 1952) is a Chinese American writer whose first book, *The Joy Luck Club*, was a great success. She has also published *The Kitchen God's Wife* and contributed to the *Atlantic* and *Grand Street*.

Gina Valdés (b. 1943), a poet and prose writer, is the author of *There Are No Madmen Here Tonight*. She is concerned with female workers on both sides of the Mexican–United States border.

Sherezada (Chiqui) Vicioso is a poet, literary critic, and educator from the Dominican Republic. She has published two books of poetry: *Viajes desde el agua* and *Un extraño ulular traía el viento*. She has also edited a book on Julia de Burgos entitled *Julia, la nuestra*. Vicioso lived in New York for seventeen years where she attended Brooklyn College and Columbia University. She now lives in Santo Domingo.

Helena María Viramontes (b. 1954) teaches at the University of California, Irvine, and has been coordinator of the Los Angeles Latino Writers Association, literary editor of *Xhisme Arte* magazine, and has received the University of California, Irvine, Chicano Literary Award. In 1988, she published a collection of short stories, *The Moths and Other Stories*.

Alice Walker (b. 1944) is an African American author perhaps best known for her book *The Color Purple*, which won the Pulitzer Prize and the American Book Award in 1983. Even though most of her central characters are African American women and her themes are sexism and racism, her work knows no racial or sexual boundaries. Her novels include *Meridian*, *The Temple of My Familiar*, and *Possessing the Secret of Joy*. Her other works of fiction include *To Hell with Dying*, *You Can't Keep a Good Woman Down*, and *In Love and Trouble: Stories of Black Women*. She has published several books of poems, including *Horses Make a Landscape Look More Beautiful*, and several essay collections, including *In Search of Our Mothers' Gardens: Womanist Prose*. She is also the editor of *I Love Myself When I'm Laughing . . . and Then Again When I Am Looking Mean and Impressive: A Zora Neale Hurston Reader*.

Roberta Hill Whiteman (b. 1947), a member of the Oneida tribe, has taught courses in creative writing and American Indian literature. Her first collection of poetry, *Star Quilt*, won the 1985 Wisconsin Writers' Award. Her poems also have appeared in the *Nation*, *North American Review*, and the anthologies *A Book of Women Poets from Antiquity to Now* and *Carriers of the Dream Wheel*. She is the recipient of a National Endowment for the Arts Fellowship.

Patricia J. Williams is a lawyer and professor of commercial law at the University of Wisconsin. Her book *The Alchemy of Race and Rights: Diary of a Law Professor* is an autobiographical work using critical literary and legal theory to illuminate the intersections of race, gender, and class.

Sherley Anne Williams (b. 1944) is professor of Afro-American literature at the University of San Diego. Her first collection of poems, *The Peacock Poems*, was nominated for the 1976 National Book Award in poetry. *Give Birth to Brightness* contains groundbreaking literary criticism of African-American literature. A former Fulbright lecturer at the University of Ghana, in 1992 she published a children's story, *Working Cotton*, and she is currently working on a new novel, tentatively titled *Licensed to Dream*.

NELLIE WONG (b. 1934) describes herself as a socialist feminist poet, writer, and activist. Her poetry collections include *The Death of Long Steam Lady* and *Dreams in Harrison Railroad Park*. She is cofeatured with Mitsuye Yamada in the documentary *Mitsuye and Nellie, Asian American Poets*.

MERLE WOO is a socialist feminist lesbian and unionist who fights for these causes through her teaching, her activism, and her poetry. Her essays, stories, and poems have been published in magazines and anthologies, and a collection of her poems, *Yellow Woman Speaks*, appeared in 1986. Woo teaches women's studies at San Francisco State University.

MITSUYE YAMADA (b. 1923) is a Japanese American poet who was interned with her family in a relocation camp in Idaho during World War II. She is a founder of the Multi-Cultural Women Writers of Orange County and was elected to the board of directors of Amnesty International in 1988. Her works include *Camp Notes and Other Poems* and *Desert Run: Poems and Stories*. She is also coeditor of *Sowing Ti Leaves: Writings by Multicultural Women*.

HISAYE YAMAMOTO (b. 1921) was interned in a relocation camp in Poston, Arizona, from 1942 to 1945. Her stories explore the complexities of cross-cultural experiences and family relationships. Her work was first published in 1948, and in 1986 she received the Before Columbus Foundation American Book Award for Lifetime Achievement. In 1988, she published a collection of short stories, *Seventeen Syllables and Other Stories*.

WAKAKO YAMAUCHI (b. 1924) is a free-lance writer. Her stories have appeared in *Aiiieeeee!: An Anthology of Asian American Writers* and *Ayumi: The Japanese American Anthology* and in journals such as *Yardbird Reader* and *Amerasia Journal*. She adapted her story "And the Soul Shall Dance" into a play that appeared on public television. She has also written the plays *The Music Lessons* and *Memento*.

MARIAN YEE is a Chinese American whose poetry has been published in several anthologies. She has studied at Rutgers University.

Acknowledgments (continued from copyright page)

Adnan, Etel, "The Beirut-Hell Express." Reprinted by permission of the author who holds the copyright.

Ai, "The Prisoner," from *Sin* by Ai. Copyright © 1986 by Ai. Reprinted by permission of Houghton Mifflin Co. All rights reserved.

Allen, Paula Gunn, "Deep Purple." From *Spider Woman's Granddaughters* by Paula Gunn Allen. Copyright © 1986 by Paula Gunn Allen. Reprinted by permission of Beacon Press.

Allen, Paula Gunn, "Something Sacred Going On out There: Myth and Vision in American Indian Literature." From *The Sacred Hoop* by Paula Gunn Allen. Copyright © 1986, 1992 by Paula Gunn Allen. Reprinted by permission of Beacon Press.

Allen, Paula Gunn, "Suicid/ing(ed) Indian Women" from *A Cannon between My Knees,* © copyright by Paula Gunn Allen 1981. Reprinted by permission of Strawberry Press.

Angelou, Maya, "Our Grandmothers." From *I Shall Not Be Moved* by Maya Angelou. Copyright © 1990 by Maya Angelou. Reprinted by permission of Random House, Inc.

Anzaldúa, Gloria, "La conciencia de la mestiza: Towards a New Consciousness" from *Borderlands/La Frontera: The New Mestiza.* Copyright © 1987 by Gloria Anzaldúa. Reprinted by permission of Aunt Lute Books (415) 558-8116.

Bambara, Toni Cade, "A Girl's Story." From *The Sea Birds Are Still Alive* by Toni Cade Bambara. Copyright © 1974, 1976, 1977 by Toni Cade Bambara. Reprinted by permission of Random House, Inc.

Barnes, S. Brandi, "I Want to Renegade." Reprinted by permission of the author.

Bernal, Esmeralda, "My Womb" in *The Americas Review* 14 (2), 49. Copyright © 1986 Esmeralda Bernal. Reprinted by permission of the publisher.

Berssenbrugge, Mei-Mei, "Farolita" as appeared in *Breaking Silence*, The Greenfield Review Press, 1989. Reprinted by permission of the author.

Bhatt, Sujata, "Muliebrity" was first published in *The Forbidden Stitch: An Asian American Women's Anthology*, edited by Shirley Geok-lin Lim, Mayumi Tsutakawa, & M. Donnelly, © 1989, CALYX Books. Reprinted by permission of the publisher.

Blakely, Nora Brooks, "For Mama (and her mamas, too)." Copyright © 1979 by Nora Brooks Blakely. Reprinted by permission of the author.

Blakely, Nora Brooks, "To Grandmother's House We Go." Copyright © 1984 by Nora Brooks Blakely. Reprinted by permission of the author.

Brant, Beth, "for all my Grandmothers" from *Mohawk Trail* by Beth Brant. Copyright © 1985 by Beth Brant. Reprinted by permission of Firebrand Books, Ithaca, New York.

Brooks, Gwendolyn, "The Lovers of the Poor." From *Selected Poems by Gwendolyn Brooks*, Harper & Row Publishers, New York, 1944. Reprinted by permission of the author.

Castillo, Ana, "The Antihero" from *Women Are Not Roses.* Copyright © 1984 by Ana Castillo. First published by Arte Publico Press, Houston. Reprinted by permission of Susan Bergholz Literary Services, New York.

Cervantes, Lorna Dee, "Poem For The Young White Man Who Asked Me How I, An Intelligent, Well-Read Person, Could Believe In The War Between Races." Reprinted from *Emplumada*, by Lorna Dee Cervantes, by permission of the University of Pittsburgh Press. © 1981 by Lorna Cervantes.

Chan, Sucheng, "You're Short, Besides!" From *Making Waves* by Asian Women United of California. Copyright © 1989 by Asian Women United of California. Reprinted by permission of Beacon Press.

Chang, Diana, "Second Nature" as appeared in *Breaking Silence*, The Greenfield Review Press, 1983. Reprinted by permission of the author.

Chávez, Denise, "Novena Narrativas." Copyright © 1987 by Denise Chávez. First published in *Chicana Creativity and Criticism: Charting New Frontiers in American Literature, Americas Review* 15(3–4), Arte Publico Press, Houston. Reprinted by permission of Susan Bergholz Literary Services, New York.

Cherry, Eileen, "africans sleeping in the park at night." Nommo: A Literary Legacy in Black Chicago, Chicago, IL, OBAC Writer's Workshop. Reprinted by permission of the author.

Chin, Marilyn (Mei Ling), "We Are Americans Now, We Live in the Tundra" was first published in *The Forbidden Stitch: An Asian American Women's Anthology* edited by Shirley Geok-lin Lim, Mayumi Tsutakawa, & M. Donnelly, Copyright © 1989, CALYX Books. Reprinted by permission of the publisher.

Christian, Barbara, "The Highs and the Lows of Black Feminist Criticism." Reprinted by permission of the author.

Chrystos, "I Make the Fire." From *Dream On*, copyright © 1991 (Press Gang Publishers, Vancouver). Reprinted by permission of the publisher.

Chrystos, "Those Tears." From *Dream On*, copyright © 1991 (Press Gang Publishers, Vancouver). Reprinted by permission of the publisher.

Cisneros, Sandra, "Never Marry a Mexican" from *Woman Hollering Creek*. Copyright © 1991 by Sandra Cisneros. Published in the United States by Vintage Books, a division of Random House, Inc., New York, and simultaneously in Canada by Random House of Canada Limited, Toronto. Originally published in hardcover by Random House, Inc., New York, in 1991. Reprinted by permission of Susan Bergholz Literary Services, New York.

Cleage, Pearl, "Hospice." Reprinted by permission of the author.

Clifton, Lucille, "what the mirror said" from *two-headed woman*. Copyright © 1980 by Lucille Clifton. Reprinted by permission of Curtis Brown, Ltd.

Cofer, Judith Ortiz, "Una Mujer Loca" in *The Americas Review* 14(2), 41. Copyright © 1986 by Judith Cofer. Reprinted by permission of the publisher.

Cofer, Judith Ortiz, "What the Gypsy Said to Her Children." From *Triple Crown* by Judith Ortiz Cofer. Copyright © 1987 Bilingual Press/Editorial Bilingue. Reprinted by permission.

Collins, Patricia Hill, "Defining Black Feminist Thought" from *Black Feminist Thought* by Patricia Hill Collins. Copyright © 1991 by Routledge, Chapman and Hall, Inc. Reprinted by permission.

Cook-Lynn, Elizabeth, "You May Consider Speaking About Your Art." Reprinted from *I Tell You Now: Autobiographical Essays by Native American Writers*, edited by Brian Swann and Arnold Krupat, by permission of the University of Nebraska Press. Copyright © 1987 the University of Nebraska Press.

Corpi, Lucha, translated from the original Spanish by Catherine Rodriguez-Nieto, "Dark Romance" from *San Jose Studies*, IV:1, 1978. Reprinted by permission of the author and the translator, who each own copyright in their version of the poem.

Corpi, Lucha, translated from the original Spanish by Catherine Rodriguez-Nieto, "Marina" (Fireflight: Three Latin American Poets, Berkeley: Oyez, 1976). Reprinted by permission of the author and the translator, who each own copyright in their version of the poem.

Cortez, Jayne, "In the Morning" in *Mouth on Paper* by Jayne Cortez. Copyright © 1993 by Jayne Cortez. Reprinted by permission of the author.

Davis, Thadious M., "Reunion." Reprinted by permission of the author.

de Hoyos, Angela, "Hermano," from *Chicano Poems: For the Barrio*, Backstage Books, Bloomington, Indiana, 1975. Copyright © 1975 by Angela de Hoyos. Reprinted by permission of the author.

Dove, Rita, "Adolescence I, II, III." Reprinted from *The Yellow House on the Corner* by Rita Dove. Copyright © 1980 by Rita Dove, © 1989 (Second Edition) Carnegie Mellon University Press. By permission of Carnegie Mellon University Press.

Embrey, Sue Kunitomi, "Some Lines for a Younger Brother . . ." Originally published in *Gidra*, Vol. II, No. 5, May 1970. Copyright © 1970 by Sue Kunitomi Embrey. Reprinted by permission of the author.

Erdrich, Louise, "American Horse." From *Spider Woman's Granddaughters* by Paula Gunn Allen. Copyright © Introduction Notes © 1986 by Paula Gunn Allen. Reprinted by permission of Beacon Press.

Erdrich, Louise, "Dear John Wayne." From *Jacklight* by Louise Erdrich. Copyright © 1984 by Louise Erdrich. Reprinted by permission of Henry Holt and Company, Inc.

Evans, Mari, "I Am a Black Woman." From *I Am a Black Woman* by Mari Evans, published by William Morrow & Company, 1970. Reprinted by permission of the author.

Fallis, Guadalupe Valdés, "Recuerdo" was first published in *De Colores Journal*, 2, No. 3 (1976). Copyright © 1976 by De Colores. Reprinted by permission of De Colores.

Giovanni, Nikki, "Adulthood." Text of "Adulthood" from *Black Feeling, Black Talk, Black Judgment* by Nikki Giovanni. Copyright © 1968, 1970 by Nikki Giovanni. By permission of William Morrow & Company, Inc.

Gonzales, Rebecca, "The Second Time" in Revista Chicano-Riquena, 9(1), 13. Copyright © 1981 Rebecca Gonzales. Reprinted by permission of the publisher.

Green, Rayna, "When I Cut My Hair." Reprinted by permission from *The Massachusetts Review*, Vol. 24, No. 1, Spring 1983. Copyright © 1983 The Massachusetts Review, Inc.

Hagedorn, Jessica, "Motown/Smokey Robinson." Reprinted from *Pet Food & Tropical Apparitions* by Jessica Hagedorn (Momo's Press, 1981) and *Danger and Beauty* by Jessica Hagedorn (Penguin, 1993). Copyright © 1981, 1993 by Jessica Hagedorn. Reprinted by permission of the author and the author's agent, Harold Schmidt Literary Agency.

Hagedorn, Jessica, "Something About You." From "Something About You" in *Danger and Beauty* by Jessica Hagedorn. Copyright © 1993 Jessica Hagedorn. Reprinted by permission of Viking Penguin, a division of Penguin Books USA Inc.

Hall, Elaine, "Spider Dream" from *A Gathering of Spirit*, edited by Beth Brant. Copyright © 1984 by Elaine Hall. Reprinted by permission of Firebrand Books, Ithaca, New York.

Harjo, Joy, "Fire." Reprinted by permission of the author.

Harjo, Joy, "I Give You Back." From the book, *She Had Some Horses* by Joy Harjo. Copyright © 1983 by Thunder's Mouth Press. Used by permission of the publisher, Thunder's Mouth Press.

Hogan, Linda, "The History of Fire" and "The Lost Girls" first appeared in *Savings* by Linda Hogan, Coffee House Press, 1988. Reprinted by permission of the publisher. Copyright © 1988 by Linda Hogan.

Hogan, Linda, "Making Do." From *Spider Woman's Granddaughters* by Paula Gunn Allen. Copyright © 1986 by Paula Gunn Allen. Reprinted by permission of Beacon Press.

hooks, bell, "Homeplace: A Site of Resistance." Reprinted from *Yearning: Race, Gender, and Cultural Politics* by bell hooks with permission from the publisher, South End Press, 116 Saint Botolph St., Boston, MA 02115.

hooks, bell, from "Black is a Woman's Color" in *Callaloo*, Vol. 12, No. 2, Spring 1989, pp. 382-388. Reprinted by permission of The Johns Hopkins University Press.

Jackson, Angela, "In Her Solitude: The Inca Divining Spider (Ana)." Reprinted by permission of the author.

Jackson, Angela, "Shango Diaspora: An African-American Myth of Womanhood and Love." Reprinted by permission of the author.

Jackson, Angela, "What I Said as a Child." Nommo: A Literary Legacy in Black Chicago, Chicago, IL, OBAC Writer's Workshop. Reprinted by permission of the author.

Jackson-Opoku, Sandra, "Ancestors: In Praise of the Imperishable." Nommo: A Literary Legacy in Black Chicago, Chicago, IL, OBAC Writer's Workshop, Reprinted by permission of the author.

Jones, Patricia Spears, "I Done Got So Thirsty That My Mouth Waters at the Thought of Rain." Reprinted by permission of the author.

Jordan, June, "War and Memory." From the book, *Naming Our Destiny* by June Jordan. Copyright © 1989 by June Jordan. Used by permission of the publisher, Thunder's Mouth Press.

Kim, Alison, "Sewing Woman" was first published in *The Forbidden Stitch: An Asian American Women's Anthology* edited by Shirley Geok-lin Lim, Mayumi Tsutakawa, & M. Donnelly, © 1989. CALYX Books. Reprinted by permission of the publisher.

Kim, Elaine H., "Defining Asian American Realities through Literature" in *Cultural Critique*, Spring 1987, (#6), pp. 87–112. Copyright © 1987, *Cultural Critique*, Oxford University Press. Used with permission.

Kim, Myung Mi, "Into Such Assembly" was first published in *The Forbidden Stitch: An*

Asian American Women's Anthology edited by Shirley Geok-lin Lim, Mayumi Tsutakawa, & M. Donnelly, © 1989, CALYX Books. Reprinted by permission of the publisher.

Kincaid, Jamaica, "At the Bottom of the River" from *At the Bottom of the River* by Jamaica Kincaid. Copyright © 1983 by Jamaica Kincaid. Reprinted by permission of Farrar, Straus and Giroux, Inc.

Kudaka, Geraldine, "On Writing Asian-American Poetry." Copyright © 1977 by Geraldine Kudaka. Reprinted by permission of the author.

León-Portilla, Miguel. From *Pre-Columbian Literatures of Mexico*, by Miguel León-Portilla. Copyright © 1969 by the University of Oklahoma Press. Reprinted by permission.

Lim, Genny, "Children Are Color-blind" was first published in *The Forbidden Stitch: An Asian American Women's Anthology* edited by Shirley Geok-lin Lim, Mayumi Tsutakawa, & M. Donnelly, © 1989, CALYX Books. Reprinted by permission of the publisher.

Lim, Genny, "Wonder Woman" from *This Bridge Called My Back: Writings by Radical Women of Color.* Copyright © 1983 by Cherríe Moraga and Gloria Anzaldúa. Used with permission of the author and Kitchen Table: Women of Color Press, P.O. Box 908 Latham, NY 12110.

Lincoln, Abbey (Aminata Moseka), "I Am the Weaver." Copyright © 1972 Abbey Lincoln. Reprinted by permission of the author.

Lispector, Clarice, "Preciousness." Reprinted from *Family Ties* by Clarice Lispector, translated by Giovanni Pontiero, Copyright © 1972. By permission of the University of Texas Press.

Lorde, Audre, "Learning from the 60s" from *Sister/Outsider*, The Crossing Press, Freedom, CA. Copyright © 1984 by Audre Lorde. Reprinted by permission of the Charlotte Sheedy Literary Agency, Inc.

Lorde, Audre, "The Woman Thing" is reprinted from *Undersong: Chosen Poems Old and New*, Revised Edition, by Audre Lorde, by permission of W. W. Norton & Company, Inc. Copyright © 1992, 1982, 1976, 1974, 1973, 1970, 1968 by Audre Lorde.

Lucero-Trujillo, Marcela Christine, "The Dilemma of the Modern Chicana Artist and Critic" was first published in *De Colores Journal*, 3, No. 3 (1977). Copyright © 1977 by De Colores. Reprinted by permission of De Colores.

Lugones, María, "Playfulness, 'World'- Travelling, and Loving Perception." Reprinted by permission of the author.

Lum, Wing Tek, from "A Picture of My Mother's Family." Copyright © 1973 by Wing Tek Lum. Reprinted by permission of the author.

Madgett, Naomi Long, "Offspring." From *Pink Ladies in the Afternoon* by Naomi Long Madgett. (Detroit: Lotus Press, 1972, 1990). By permission of the author.

Matsumoto, Valerie, "Two Deserts" was first published in *The Forbidden Stitch: An Asian American Women's Anthology*, edited by Shirley Geok-lin Lim, Mayumi Tsutakawa, and M. Donnelly, © 1989, CALYX Books. Reprinted by permission of the publisher.

Minh-ha, Trinh T., "Grandma's Story" from *Woman, Native, Other* by Trinh T. Minh-ha. Copyright © 1989 by Trinh T. Minh-ha. Reprinted by permission of Indiana University Press and the author.

Mirikitani, Janice, "Generations of Women" excerpted from *Shedding Silence* by Janice Mirikitani. Copyright © 1987 by Janice Mirikitani. Reprinted by permission of Celestial Arts, P.O. Box 7327, Berkeley, CA 94707.

Mirikitani, Janice, "Japs." Reprinted from *Awake in the River*, by Janice Mirikitani, © copyright by Janice Mirikitani 1978, San Francisco, CA.

Mirikitani, Janice, "Loving from Vietnam to Zimbabwe" reprinted from *Awake in the River*, Poetry & Prose by Janice Mirikitani. © copyright, Janice Mirikitani, 1978. Published in *Ayumi* with permission by the author.

Moraga, Cherríe, "La Güera" from *This Bridge Called My Back: Writings by Radical Women of Color.* Copyright © 1983 by Cherríe Moraga and Gloria Anzaldúa. Used with permission of the author and Kitchen Table: Women of Color Press, P.O. Box 908 Latham, NY 12110.

Moraga, Cherríe, "The Welder" from *This Bridge Called My Back: Writings by Radical Women of Color.* Copyright © 1983 by Cherríe Moraga and Gloria Anzaldúa. Used with permission of the author and Kitchen Table: Women of Color Press, P.O. Box 908 Latham, NY 12110.

Morrison, Toni, "Rootedness: The Ancestor as Foundation", from *Black Women Writers* (1950–1980), edited by Mari Evans. Copyright © 1983 by Mari Evans. Used by permission of Doubleday, a division of Bantam Doubleday Dell Publishing Group, Inc.

Mukherjee, Bharati, "A Wife's Story" from The Middleman and Other Stories by Bharati Mukherjee. Copyright © 1988 by Bharati Mukherjee. Reprinted by permission of Grove Press, Inc. and Bharati Mukherjee.

Naqvi, Tahira, "Paths upon Water" was first published in *The Forbidden Stitch: An Asian American Women's Anthology*, edited by Shirley Geok-lin Lim, Mayumi Tsutakawa, and M. Donnelly, © 1989, CALYX Books. Reprinted by permission of the publisher.

Nye, Naomi Shihab, "My Father and the Figtree." Reprinted by permission of the author.

Parker, Pat, "Where Will You Be?" from *Movement in Black* by Pat Parker. Copyright © 1978 by Pat Parker. Reprinted by permission of Firebrand Books, Ithaca, New York.

Pursifull, Carmen M., "First Stop/City of Senses" in *The Americas Review* 14(2), 49–51. Copyright © 1986 Carmen Pursifull. Reprinted by permission of the publisher.

Rebolledo, Tey Diana, "The Politics of Poetics: Or, What Am I, a Critic, Doing in This Text Anyhow?" from *The Americas Review*, 16. Copyright © 1988 Tey Diana Rebolledo. Reprinted by permission of the author.

Rivera, Diana, "Good-bye, My Loved One" in *The Americas Review* 17(1), 59–61. Copyright © 1989 Diana Rivera. Reprinted by permission of the publisher.

Rivera, Marina, "Our Side of It" was first published in *De Colores Journal*, 1976. Copyright © 1976 by De Colores. Reprinted by permission of De Colores.

Rodgers, Carolyn M., "Poem for Some Black Women", copyright © 1971 by Carolyn Rodgers. From *How I Got Ovah* by Carolyn M. Rodgers. Used by permission of Doubleday, a division of Bantam Doubleday Dell Publishing Group, Inc.

Rose, Wendy, "Julia" and "Sipapu" from *The Halfbreed Chronicles*, published by West End Press. Reprinted by permission.

Sanchez, Georgiana Valoyce, "The Heart of the Flower" as appeared in *The Stories We Held Secret*, The Greenfield Review Press, 1986. Reprinted by permission of the author.

Sanchez, Sonia. "Past/Woman/Earth Mother/young black girl" in *I've Been a Woman.* Chicago, IL: Third World Press, pp. 55–61. Reprinted by permission of Third World Press.

Sapia, Yvonne, "Defining the Grateful Gesture" in *The Americas Review* 14(3–4). Copyright © 1987 by Yvonne Sapia. Reprinted by permission of the publisher.

Shange, Ntozake, "five" from the book *Nappy Edges* by Ntozake Shange. Copyright © 1972, 1974, 1975, 1976, 1977, 1978. Reprinted by permission of St. Martin's Press, Inc., New York, NY.

Silko, Leslie Marmon, "Landscape, History, and the Pueblo Imagination from a High Arid Plateau in New Mexico." Reprinted by permission of Wylie, Aitken & Stone, Inc.

Silko, Leslie Marmon, "Storyteller" first appeared in *Puerto del Sol*, Fall 1975. Copyright © 1975 by Leslie Marmon Silko. Reprinted by permission of Wylie, Aitken & Stone, Inc.

Smith, Barbara, "The Truth That Never Hurts: Black Lesbians in Fiction in the 1980s" in *Wild Women in the Whirlwind: Afra-American Culture and the Contemporary Literary Renaissance* by Joanne M. Braxton and Andree Nicola McLaughlin, editors. Copyright © 1990 by Rutgers, The State University.

Smith, Valerie, "Black Feminist Theory and the Representation of the 'Other' " in *Changing Our Own Words: Essays on Criticism, Theory, and Writing by Black Women* edited by C.A. Wall. Copyright © 1989 by Rutgers, The State University.

Snow, Carol P., "Metamorphosis" as appeared in *New Voices from the Longhouse: An Anthology of Contemporary Iroquois Writing*, The Greenfield Review Press, 1989. Copyright © Carol Snow. All rights reserved. Reprinted by permission of the author.

Song, Cathy, from "Blue and White Lines after O'Keeffe" from *Picture Bride*. Copyright © 1983 by Yale University Press. Reprinted by permission.

Swallow, Debra, "Keep a Dime" from *A Gathering of Spirit*, edited by Beth Brant. Copyright © 1984 by Debra Swallow. Reprinted by permission of Firebrand Books, Ithaca, New York.

Tahnahga, "Giving Back" and "Suburban Indian Pride" as appeared in *New Voices from the Longhouse: An Anthology of Contemporary Iroquois Writing,* The Greenfield Review Press, 1989. All rights reserved. Reprinted by permission of the author.

Tallmountain, Mary, "Matmiya" from *There Is No Word for Goodbye: Poems by Mary Tallmountain,* Open Heart Press, 1988. Copyright © 1988 by Mary Tallmountain. Reprinted by permission.

Tan, Amy, "Two Kinds." Reprinted by permission of The Putnam Publishing Group from *The Joy Luck Club* by Amy Tan. Copyright © 1989 by Amy Tan.

Trambley, Estela Portillo, "The Day of the Swallows." Reprinted by permission of the author.

Valdés, Gina, "My Mother Sews Blouses" in *Comiendo Lumbre/Eating Fire,* 1986. Reprinted by permission of Maize Press.

Van Buren, Abigail. As seen in a *Dear Abby* column by Abigail Van Buren. Copyright 1986 Universal Press Syndicate. Reprinted with permission. All rights reserved.

Vicioso, Sherezada (Chiqui), "An Oral History." Reprinted from *Breaking Boundaries: Latina Writing and Critical Readings,* Asuncion Horno-Delgado, Eliana Ortega, Nina M. Scott, and Nancy Saporta Sternbach, eds. (Amherst: The University of Massachusetts Press, 1989), copyright © 1989 by The University of Massachusetts Press.

Viramontes, Helena María, "Miss Clairol." Copyright © 1992 by Helena María Viramontes. Reprinted by permission of Marie Brown Associates.

Walker, Alice, "In Search of Our Mothers' Gardens" from *In Search of Our Mothers' Gardens: Womanist Prose,* copyright © 1974 by Alice Walker, reprinted by permission of Harcourt Brace & Company.

Whiteman, Roberta Hill, "In the Summer after 'Issue Year' Winter (1873)" and "Star Quilt." Reprinted by permission from *Star Quilt* by Roberta Hill Whiteman. Copyright © 1984 by Roberta Hill Whiteman.

Williams, Patricia, "Fire and Ice." *For permission to photocopy this selection, please contact Harvard University Press. Reprinted by permission of the publishers from *The Alchemy of Race and Rights: Diary of a Law Professor* by Patricia Williams, Cambridge, Mass.: Harvard University Press, Copyright © 1991 by the President and Fellows of Harvard College.

Williams, Sherley Anne, "The Iconography of Childhood." Reprinted by permission of the Sandra Dijkstra Literary Agency.

Wong, Nellie, "When I Was Growing Up" from *This Bridge Called My Back: Writings by Radical Women of Color.* Copyright © 1983 by Cherrie Moraga and Gloria Anzaldúa. Used with permission of the author and Kitchen Table: Women of Color Press, P.O. Box 908 Latham, NY 12110.

Wong, Nellie, "For an Asian Woman Who Says My Poetry Gives Her a Stomachache" was first published in *The Forbidden Stitch: An Asian American Women's Anthology* edited by Shirley Geok-lin Lim, Mayumi Tsutakawa, & M. Donnelly, © 1989, CALYX Books. Reprinted by permission of the publisher.

Woo, Merle, "Letter to Ma" from *This Bridge Called My Back: Writings by Radical Women of Color,* edited by Cherríe Moraga and Gloria Anzaldúa. Copyright © 1983 by Merle Woo. Used with permission of the author and Kitchen Table: Women of Color Press, P.O. Box 908 Latham, NY 12110.

Yamada, Mitsuye, "Invisibility Is an Unnatural Disaster: Reflections of an Asian American Woman" from *This Bridge Called My Back: Writings by Radical Women of Color.* Copyright © 1983 by Cherríe Moraga and Gloria Anzaldúa. Used with permission of the author and Kitchen Table: Women of Color Press, P.O. Box 908 Latham, NY 12110.

Yamamoto, Hisaye, "Wilshire Bus" from *Pacific Citizen,* Dec. 23, 1950. Copyright Hisaye Yamamoto DeSoto, *Seventeen Syllables and Other Stories,* 1988, Kitchen Table: Women of Color Press, P.O. Box 908 Latham, NY 12110.

Yamauchi, Wakako, "And the Soul Shall Dance." Reprinted by permission of Darhansoff & Verrill Literary Agency.

Yee, Marian, "The Handbook of Sex of the Plain Girl" was first published in *The Forbidden Stitch: An Asian American Women's Anthology* edited by Shirley Geok-lin Lim, Mayumi Tsutakawa, & M. Donnelly, © 1989, CALYX Books. Reprinted by permission of the publisher.